Nelson-Jones'
Theory and Practice of
Counselling and
Psychotherapy

Nelson-Jones'
Theory and Practice of
Counselling and
Psychotherapy

Sixth Edition

Richard Nelson-Jones

Los Angeles | London | New Delhi
Singapore | Washington DC

Los Angeles | London | New Delhi
Singapore | Washington DC

SAGE Publications Ltd
1 Oliver's Yard
55 City Road
London EC1Y 1SP

SAGE Publications Inc.
2455 Teller Road
Thousand Oaks, California 91320

SAGE Publications India Pvt Ltd
B 1/I 1 Mohan Cooperative Industrial Area
Mathura Road
New Delhi 110 044

SAGE Publications Asia-Pacific Pte Ltd
3 Church Street
#10-04 Samsung Hub
Singapore 049483

Editor: Susannah Trefgarne
Assistant editor: Laura Walmsley
Production editor: Rachel Burrows
Copyeditor: Fabienne Pedroletti-Gray
Proofreader: Fabienne Pedroletti-Gray
Marketing manager: Camille Richmond
Cover design: Lisa Harper-Wells
Typeset by: C&M Digitals (P) Ltd, Chennai, India
Printed in Great Britain by Henry Ling Limited at
The Dorset Press, Dorchester, DT1 1HD

First edition published by Holt, Rinehart and Winstone Ltd
Second edition published by Cassell
Third edition published 2001 by Cassell, reprinted by SAGE
Publications 2003, 2004
Fourth edition published 2006 by SAGE Publications, reprinted
2008, 2009
Fifth edition published 2011, reprinted 2013
This sixth edition published 2015

Library of Congress Control Number: 2014936859

British Library Cataloguing in Publication data

A catalogue record for this book is available from
the British Library

ISBN 978-1-4462-9555-7
ISBN 978-1-4462-9556-4 (pbk)

MIX
Paper from
responsible sources
FSC
www.fsc.org   FSC™ C013985

At SAGE we take sustainability seriously. Most of our products are printed in the UK using FSC papers and boards.
When we print overseas we ensure sustainable papers are used as measured by the Egmont grading system.
We undertake an annual audit to monitor our sustainability.

CONTENTS

ABOUT THE AUTHOR

Richard Nelson-Jones was born in London in 1936. Having spent five years in California as a Second World War refugee, he returned in the 1960s to obtain a Masters and PhD from Stanford University. In 1970, he was appointed a lecturer in the Department of Education at the University of Aston to establish a Diploma in Counselling in Educational Settings, which started enrolling students in 1971. During the 1970s, he was helped by having three Fulbright Professors from the United States, each for a year, who both taught students and improved his skills. During this period he broadened out from a predominantly client-centred orientation to becoming much more cognitive-behavioural. He also wrote numerous articles and the first edition of what is now *Nelson-Jones' Theory and Practice of Counselling and Psychotherapy*, which was published in 1982. In addition, he chaired the British Psychological Society's Working Party on Counselling and, in 1982, became the first chairperson of the BPS Counselling Psychology Section.

In 1984, Richard took up a position as a counselling and later counselling psychology trainer at the Royal Melbourne Institute of Technology, where he became an Associate Professor. He continued writing research articles, articles on professional issues and books, which were published in London and Sydney. As when he worked at Aston University, he also counselled clients to keep up his skills. In 1997, he retired from RMIT and moved to Chiang Mai in Thailand. There, as well as doing some counselling and teaching, he has continued as an author of counselling and counselling psychology textbooks. A British and Australian citizen, he now divides his time between Chiang Mai and London and regularly spends time in Australia.

Welcome to the sixth edition of *Nelson-Jones' Theory and Practice of Counselling and Psychotherapy*. In this introductory textbook I aim to provide you with clear, concise, easily accessible presentations of the major concepts and practices of many of the main therapeutic approaches used in the helping professions. The focus of this book is on individual therapy. Its purpose is to help you become more aware of both *how* you might counsel or conduct therapy and also of the underlying reasons *why* you might choose to work that way. Furthermore, the relevance of the theoretical positions extends beyond assisting clients in therapy to become happier and more fulfilled to the personal agenda of helping you as well.

INTENDED READERSHIP

This is a basic introductory textbook for undergraduate and postgraduate counselling and psychotherapy courses in counsellor education, psychology, social work, nursing, personnel and human resources management, career development, pastoral care, welfare, teacher training and other areas of helping professions education. Another important readership consists of participants in counselling and therapy courses run by voluntary agencies. In addition, this book can be used as a user-friendly introduction to the theory and practice of counselling and therapy for undergraduate students in the behavioural and social sciences.

CONTENTS

The book is divided into seven parts. Part one, Introduction, contains the first chapter which discusses the structure and functions of theoretical statements, explores the creation of therapeutic approaches, and then looks at how you can develop your own ideas. In Parts Two to Four I review therapeutic approaches selected from each of the three main schools influencing contemporary therapy practice. From the psychodynamic school, I present Freud's psychoanalysis and Jung's analytical therapy. From the humanistic-existential school, I present person-centred therapy, gestalt therapy, transactional analysis, and existential therapy. From the cognitive behaviour school, I present behaviour therapy, rational emotive behaviour therapy, cognitive therapy and multimodal therapy.

In instances where the originators have died – for instance, Freud, Jung, Perls, and Rogers – the chapters focus mainly on their presentation of their positions, though mention is also made of further developments since their death. A major reason for this focus is that I think students should start knowing about the original positions and then learn about variations to them.

In Part Five, Recent therapies, I include four newer approaches, namely de Shazer and Berg's solution-focused therapy, White and Epston's narrative therapy, Seligman's positive therapy, and mindfulness in therapy. In Part Six, Culture and gender therapies, I review multicultural therapy and gender therapy, areas which are becoming increasingly prominent in the therapeutic literature both on their own and as parts of other approaches. In Part Seven, Concluding comments, the book's final chapter reviews issues in assessing the quality of the different therapeutic approaches as well as the topics of eclecticism and integration. In addition to the book's seven parts, I provide a glossary.

For those familiar with the fifth edition of this text, the main changes in the sixth edition are new chapters on positive therapy and mindfulness in therapy. In addition I have revised and updated all existing chapters, including the further developments section, to indicate some contemporary approaches to the positions.

FEATURES

I draw your attention to the following features of the book, which I hope will make it attractive for you.

- *Authoritative* This book, which is written from primary sources, provides accurate presentations of the foundations of each counselling and therapy approach. In addition, I gave either the theorists themselves or prominent adherents of the approach the opportunity to preview chapters and to suggest alterations.
- *Thorough and clear presentation* Each of the therapeutic approaches is in a standard chapter format that helps to ensure that the approach is thoroughly and clearly presented. Though you may not understand the meaning some of the following headings now, once you start working with the book you should experience no difficulty in so doing.

  (a) Introduction
  (b) Originator's biography
  (c) Theory

      Basic concepts
      Acquisition
      Maintenance

  (d) Therapy

      Therapeutic goals
      Process of therapy
      The therapeutic relationship
      Therapeutic interventions

    (e)   Case material
    (f)   Further developments
    (g)   Review and personal questions
    (h)   Annotated bibliography
    (i)   References and further reading

- *Focus on fundamentals* The chapters emphasize presenting the theory and practice of the originator of each approach. Some contributions by other adherents of the approach are mentioned in the 'Further developments' section of chapters. However, the chapters emphasize the basic or classical version of each approach. Getting down to basics is important, since introducing developments from the original approach too soon can be confusing. In all of the chapters I review the originator's case material and in most chapters I give directions about accessing audiovisual resources. If available and where budgets permit, I encourage lecturers to use relevant audio- and video-recordings as an accompaniment to using this book.
- *Personal focus* Originating counselling and psychotherapy approaches is a personal journey. A distinctive feature of this book is the degree to which the lives of the originators are seen as important in understanding the development of their therapeutic approaches. Learning about counselling and psychotherapy approaches is also a personal journey. Each chapter ends not only with review questions, but with personal questions as well that encourage you to relate the material to your own life.
- *Aids to comprehension and revision* Boxes are used throughout the book to highlight concepts and provide examples of specific interventions. Towards the end of each chapter, I provide a summary and review questions designed to help you learn and revise material for assignments and course requirements.
- *Help with further reading* I encourage you to use the chapters in this book as stepping-stones to reading primary sources. Each chapter ends with an annotated bibliography and with a list of references. I also encourage you to read further about recent developments in those theoretical positions that interest you.
- *Simple English* I have tried to use simple, accessible English, while remaining sensitive to the distinctive therapeutic languages used by the different theorists.

ACKNOWLEDGMENTS

I acknowledge with gratitude the distinctive contributions of all the originators of counselling and therapy approaches presented in this book. I also thank my editors, Susannah Trefgarne and Laura Walmsley, for their helpful contributions, and, last but not least, the production staff at Sage for their good work in bringing this book to life.

Since each of the approaches is presented as a self-contained unit, lecturers and readers can chose which parts to study in the order that best suits your purposes. I hope that you enjoy reading and interacting with this book and share my enthusiasm for studying and learning more about counselling and therapy approaches.

Richard Nelson-Jones

INTRODUCTION

Chapter 1, Creating counselling and psychotherapy approaches, starts by examining counselling and psychotherapy and then defines how terms are used in the book. The four approaches – psychodynamic, humanistic-existential, cognitive behaviour, and more recent therapies – covered in this book are introduced. There follows a discussion of what is a counselling and psycho-therapy theory. The functions of theories include being concep-tual frameworks, languages and research hypotheses. Limitations of theories are also examined.

Origins of counselling and psychotherapy approaches are explored including their historical and cultural contexts, the fact that many theorists were psychologically wounded, their exceptional interest in writing and communicating ideas, their professional experiences and frustrations, among other reasons. The chapter ends with exploring numerous ways in which you can create your own theoretical approach.

CREATING COUNSELLING AND PSYCHOTHERAPY APPROACHES

1

Theoretical approaches to counselling and psychotherapy do not spring fully formed out of the heads of their originators. Rather their creation is a process in which many personal, academic and professional factors interact. Furthermore, the theorists covered in this book tended to refine and rework their ideas. In addition other people have contributed to the development of their theoretical positions. Thus theory creation and development is an intensely human and ongoing process combining both subjective experiencing and objective information.

As a counselling and psychotherapy trainee, you too are engaging in a process of trying to make sense of numerous personal, academic and professional factors to create and develop a way of seeing the therapeutic world that has validity for you and gets results for your clients. Just like the major theorists, you are likely to find yourself continually refining and reworking your ideas. Working with a theoretical approaches text, such as this one, is an early step in the exciting and life-long endeavour of creating, developing and refining your theory and practice.

COUNSELLING AND PSYCHOTHERAPY

The word therapy is derived from the Greek word 'therapeia' meaning healing. Literally psychotherapy means healing the mind or the soul. Nowadays, most commonly the meaning of psychotherapy is broadened to become healing the mind by psychological methods that are applied by suitably trained and qualified practitioners. However, as illustrated in this book, there are different approaches to psychotherapy and, consequently, it is more accurate to speak of the psychotherapies rather than a uniform method of psychotherapy. Moreover, there are different goals for psychotherapy including dealing with severe mental disorder, addressing specific anxieties and phobias, and helping people find meaning and purpose in their lives. Each of the different therapeutic approaches may be more suitable for attaining some goals than others.

Does counselling differ from psychotherapy? Attempts to differentiate between counselling and psychotherapy are never wholly successful. Both counselling and psychotherapy represent diverse rather than uniform knowledge and activities and both use the same theoretical models. In 2000, the British Association for Counselling acknowledged the similarity between counselling and psychotherapy by becoming the British Association for Counselling and Psychotherapy. In 1998, the Psychotherapy & Counselling Federation of Australia was established.

Nevertheless, some people such as Corsini (2008) try to distinguish counselling from psychotherapy. For instance, psychotherapists may be more thoroughly trained; psychotherapy may focus more deeply on uncovering unconscious influences and be longer term; and psychotherapy may be more a medical term that characterizes the work of psychiatrists and clinical psychiatrists, whereas counselling relates more to activities in non-medical settings: for example, college counselling centres. All of these distinctions can be refuted: for example, there are psychodynamic counsellors; both counselling and psychotherapy can be either brief, medium-term or long-term; and much counselling is performed both by medically and non-medically qualified people inside and outside of medical settings.

Though some perceive different shadings of meaning between counselling and psychotherapy, when it comes to the offering of professional as contrasted with voluntary services, similarities outweigh differences. Frequently the terms are used interchangeably and most theorists view their work as applicable to both counselling and psychotherapy, Carl Rogers and Albert Ellis being prime examples.

Counselling and psychotherapy also overlap with coaching. Life coaching involves coaches using their skills to help generally adequately functioning people improve and maintain how they perform and live in different aspects of their lives – personal, relationships, business and sports. Though a relatively recent phenomenon, coaching is undoubtedly here to stay. In varying degrees, much of this book is relevant to coaching as well as to counselling and psychotherapy.

DEFINING TERMS

Throughout this book, for the sake of consistency, for the most part I use the terms psychotherapy or therapy, therapist and client. Psychotherapy refers both to the theoretical approach and to the process of helping clients. It is notable that the originators of most psychotherapeutic approaches include the word therapy in their approach's title: for instance, person-centred therapy, gestalt therapy, rational emotive behaviour therapy and cognitive therapy. Therapist refers to the providers of therapy services to clients, be they psychoanalysts, psychiatrists, clinical psychologists, counselling psychologists, counsellors, psychotherapists, social workers or other suitably trained and qualified persons. Client refers to the recipient of therapeutic services whether inside or outside of medical settings.

OVERVIEW OF COUNSELLING AND PSYCHOTHERAPY APPROACHES

A useful distinction exists between *schools* of counselling and psychotherapy and *theoretical approaches* to counselling and psychotherapy. A theoretical approach presents a single position regarding the theory and practice of counselling and psychotherapy. A school of counselling and psychotherapy is a grouping of different theoretical approaches that are similar to one another in terms of certain important characteristics that distinguish them from theoretical approaches in other counselling and psychotherapy schools

Probably the three main schools that have influenced contemporary individual counselling and psychotherapy practice are the psychodynamic school, the humanistic school, and the cognitive behaviour school. Sometimes the humanistic school incorporates existential therapeutic approaches and then can get the broader title of the humanistic-existential school. A fourth school, the postmodern school, comprises some more recent approaches. In addition, there are other recent theoretical approaches that do not fit neatly into this school heading, for instance positive therapy. Be careful not to exaggerate the differences between counselling and psychotherapy schools, since there are similarities as well differences among them. Box 1.1 briefly describes some distinguishing features of the psychodynamic, humanistic-existential, cognitive behaviour and postmodern schools.

BOX 1.1   FOUR COUNSELLING AND PSYCHOTHERAPY SCHOOLS

THE PSYCHODYNAMIC SCHOOL

The term psychodynamic refers to the transfer of **psychic or mental energy** between the different structures and levels of consciousness within people's minds. Psychodynamic approaches emphasize the importance of **unconscious influences** on how people function. Therapy aims to increase clients' abilities to exercise **greater conscious control** over their lives. **Analysis or interpretation of dreams** can be a central part of psychotherapy.

THE HUMANISTIC-EXISTENTIAL SCHOOL

The humanistic school is based on humanism, a system of values and beliefs that emphasizes the better qualities of humankind and people's abilities to develop their **human potential**. Humanistic therapists emphasize enhancing clients' abilities to **experience their feelings** and think and act in harmony with their underlying tendencies to **actualize themselves** as unique individuals. Existential approaches to psychotherapy stress people's capacity to **choose** how they create their existences.

THE COGNITIVE BEHAVIOUR SCHOOL

Traditional behaviour therapy focuses mainly on changing **observable behaviours** by means of providing different or rewarding consequences. The cognitive behaviour school broadens behaviour therapy to incorporate the contribution of **how people**

(Continued)

(Continued)

think to creating, sustaining and changing their problems. In cognitive behaviour approaches, therapists **assess** clients and then **intervene** to help them to **change specific ways of thinking and behaving** that sustain their problems.

THE POSTMODERN SCHOOL

The postmodern therapies adopt a **social constructionist** viewpoint, assuming that how people process and construct information about themselves and their world is central to their existence. Rather than conceptualizing progress as a departure from and rejection of the past, postmodernism **draws on the past to serve the present.** People's experience of emotions depends on the names that they give to these emotions. People's beliefs about their relationships affect how they interpret the reactions of others and how they respond to them. **Personal behaviour results from** these cognitive processes and is therefore open to change.

Box 1.2 introduces the theoretical approaches, grouped as closely as feasible according to counselling and psychotherapy school, included in this book. The postmodern school therapies have been listed under more recent therapies. So that readers can obtain a sense of the history of the development of ideas within counselling and psychotherapy, I have included the dates of the originators of each approach. The descriptions provided in Box 1.2 reflect the position of the originators of the different positions, rather than developments within a theoretical approach stimulated by others.

BOX 1.2 OVERVIEW OF COUNSELLING AND PSYCHOTHERAPY APPROACHES

PSYCHODYNAMIC SCHOOL

Classical psychoanalysis *Originator: Sigmund Freud (1856–1939)*

Pays great attention to unconscious factors related to infantile sexuality in the development of neurosis. Psychoanalysis, which may last for many years, emphasizes working through the transference, in which clients perceive their therapists as reincarnations of important figures from their childhoods, and the interpretation of dreams.

Analytical therapy *Originator: Carl Jung (1875–1961)*

Divides the unconscious into the personal unconscious and the collective unconscious, the latter being a storehouse of universal archetypes and primordial images. Psychotherapy includes analysis of the transference, active imagination and dream analysis. Jung was particularly interested in working with clients in the second half of life.

HUMANISTIC-EXISTENTIAL SCHOOL

Person-centred therapy *Originator: Carl Rogers (1902–87)*

Lays great stress on the primacy of subjective experience and how clients can become out of touch with their organismic experiencing through introjecting others' evaluations and treating them as if their own. Psychotherapy emphasizes a relationship characterized by accurate empathy, respect and non-possessive warmth.

Gestalt therapy *Originator: Fritz Perls (1893–1970)*

Individuals become neurotic by losing touch with their senses and interfering with their capacity to make strong contact with their environments. Psychotherapy emphasizes increasing clients' awareness and vitality through awareness techniques, experiments, sympathy and frustration, and dream work.

Transactional analysis *Originator: Eric Berne (1910–70)*

Transactions between people take place between their Parent, Adult and Child ego states. Psychotherapy includes structural analysis of ego states, analysis of specific transactions, analysis of games – series of transactions having ulterior motivations, and analysis of clients' life scripts.

Existential therapy *Originators: Irvin Yalom (1931–) and Rollo May (1909–94)*

Draws on the work of existential philosophers and focuses on helping clients deal with anxieties connected with four main ultimate concerns of human existence: death, freedom, isolation and meaninglessness. Psychotherapy focuses on clients' current situations, with different interventions used according to the nature of clients' enveloping fears.

COGNITIVE BEHAVIOUR SCHOOL

Behaviour therapy *Important figures: theory, Ivan Pavlov (1849–1936) and B. F. Skinner (1904–90); practice, Joseph Wolpe (1915–97)*

Emphasizes the learning of behaviour through classical conditioning, operant conditioning and modelling. Psychotherapy consists of learning adaptive behaviours by methods such as systematic desensitization, reinforcement programmes and behaviour rehearsal.

Rational emotive behaviour therapy *Originator: Albert Ellis (1913–2007)*

Emphasizes clients re-indoctrinating themselves with irrational beliefs that contribute to unwanted feelings and self-defeating actions. Psychotherapy involves disputing clients' irrational beliefs and replacing them with more rational beliefs. Elegant or profound psychotherapy entails changing clients' philosophies of life.

(Continued)

(Continued)

Cognitive therapy *Originator: Aaron Beck (1921–)*

Clients become distressed because they are faulty processors of information with a tendency to jump to unwarranted conclusions. Psychotherapy consists of educating clients in how to test the reality of their thinking by interventions such as Socratic questioning and conducting real-life experiments.

Multimodal therapy *Originator: Arnold Lazarus (1932–2013)*

Clients respond to situations according to their predominant modalities: behaviour, affect, sensation, imagery, cognition, interpersonal and drugs/biology. Based on a multimodal assessment, therapists are technically eclectic, using a range of techniques selected on the basis of empirical evidence and client need.

RECENT THERAPIES

Solution-focused therapy *Originators: Steve de Shazer (1940–2005) and Insoo Kim Berg (1934–2007)*

Theories of causation are irrelevant to the process of achieving goals and resolving problems. The therapist is responsible for directing the conversation towards the client's goals and acknowledging their difficulties. Specific uses of language and styles of questioning are used to encourage creativity and flexible thinking around the relevant issues.

Narrative therapy *Originators: Michael White (1948–2008) and David Epston (1944–)*

Images and concepts of past and present by which people define and give meaning to their lives derive from selective memory strongly influenced by their social, cultural and historical contexts. Psychotherapy principally consists of assisting persons to escape the dominance of 'problem-saturated' self-stories by encouraging them to narrate and discuss the meaning of 'thicker' or 'richer' self-stories more fully representing their concrete experience.

Positive therapy *Originator: Martin Seligmann (1942–)*

As well as leading directly to suffering, emotional distress constrains people's lives, cutting them off from many of the personal and social resources that would help to alleviate their symptoms and to enable them to maintain a good quality of life. Positive therapy focuses on promoting wellbeing, resilience and personal strengths, thus weakening the negative factors that maintain symptoms and distress.

Mindfulness in therapy *Originating with the Buddha (around 2500 BC)*

An integrative approach to therapy with a theoretical background drawn from Buddhist psychology. Mindfulness meditation supports the therapist in bringing an embodied, attuned presence to the therapeutic relationship and short meditation practices may be brought into therapy. There is an emphasis on cultivating moment-to-moment awareness of experience as it arises and on bringing a reflective enquiry process to experience.

So far I have presented the different schools and theoretical approaches as though they are separate. In reality, many counsellors and therapists regard themselves as working in either eclectic or integrative ways. Though addressed in the final chapter, a detailed discussion of eclecticism and integration is beyond the scope of this book. Suffice it for now to say that eclecticism is the practice of drawing from different counselling and psychotherapy schools in formulating client problems and implementing treatment interventions. Integration refers to attempting to blend together theoretical concepts and/or practical interventions drawn from different counselling and psychotherapy approaches into coherent and integrated wholes.

WHAT IS A COUNSELLING AND PSYCHOTHERAPY THEORY?

A theory is a formulation of the underlying principles of certain observed phenomena that have been verified to some extent. A criterion of the power of a theory is the extent to which it generates predictions that are confirmed when relevant empirical data are collected. The more a theory receives confirmation or verification, the more accurate it is. Facts strengthen rather than replace theories.

FUNCTIONS OF COUNSELLING AND PSYCHOTHERAPY THEORIES

What do counselling and psychotherapy theories do? Why are they useful? Therapists cannot avoid being counselling and psychotherapy theorists. All make assumptions about how clients become and stay the way they are and about change. Three of the main functions of counselling and psychotherapy theories are: providing conceptual frameworks, providing languages, and generating research.

THEORIES AS CONCEPTUAL FRAMEWORKS

Therapists are decision makers. They continually make choices about how to think about clients' behaviour, how to treat them, and how to respond on a moment-by-moment basis during therapy sessions. Theories provide therapists with concepts that allow them to think systematically about human development and the therapeutic process.

Counselling and psychotherapy theoretical approaches may be viewed as possessing four main dimensions if they are to be stated adequately. In this context behaviour incorporates both observable behaviour and internal behaviour or thinking. The dimensions are:

1. a statement of the *basic concepts* or assumptions underlying the theory;
2. an explanation of the *acquisition* of helpful and unhelpful behaviour;
3. an explanation of the *maintenance* of helpful and unhelpful behaviour; and
4. an explanation of how to help clients *change* their behaviour and *consolidate* their gains when therapy ends.

When reading about the different counselling and psychotherapy approaches, you may observe that many if not most have significant gaps in their conceptual frameworks. They are partial rather than complete or comprehensive theoretical statements. Arguably, some of the missing concepts in the theories are implicit rather than explicit. Theorists select for more thorough treatment those dimensions of a theory that they consider important. For instance, Ellis' rational emotive behaviour theory has a wider variety of explanatory concepts concerning how behaviour is maintained than how it is initially acquired.

THEORIES AS LANGUAGES

Swiss psychiatrist Carl Jung used to stress that, since all clients are different individuals, therapists require a different language for each client (Jung, 1961). Another function of theories is similar to that provided by languages. Languages are vocabularies and linguistic symbols that allow communication about phenomena. Like the major spoken languages of English, Spanish and Mandarin Chinese, the different theorists develop languages for the phenomena they wish to describe: for instance, cognitive, psychoanalytic or person-centred languages. Language can both unite and divide. It can encourage communication between people who speak the same language, but discourage communication if they do not. Each theoretical position has concepts described in unique language. However, the uniqueness of the language may mask common elements among theories: for example, the meaning of conditions of worth in person-centred therapy overlaps with that of super-ego in Freud's psychoanalytic therapy, though you would not know this from the language!

The psychotherapy process is a series of conversations requiring languages. In any therapeutic relationship there are at least four kinds of conversations going on: namely, therapist and client inner and outer speech. All therapists who operate out of explicit theoretical frameworks are likely to talk to themselves about clients in the language of that framework. In varying degrees their therapeutic practice will match their language. Therapists do not always act according to how they think. Furthermore, in varying degrees therapists share their theoretical language with clients. For example, unlike in rational emotive behaviour therapy, the language in which person-centred theory is expressed tends not to be shared with clients. Instead, person-centred therapists try more to reflect and match clients' outer speech.

Clients are also theorists, though usually without the sophistication of their therapists. Approaches like rational emotive behaviour therapy and cognitive therapy actively try to influence the language in which clients talk to themselves so that it becomes helpful rather than harmful. In a sense the therapist's language is being exported to and imported by clients so that they can better assist themselves once therapy ends.

THEORIES AS SETS OF RESEARCH HYPOTHESES

Theories can be both based on research and stimulate research. For example, cognitive behaviour therapy is based on research into how people think and into how both people and animals behave. Furthermore, cognitive behaviour approaches, such as rational emotive behaviour therapy and cognitive therapy, have stimulated research into their processes and outcomes.

Theories also provide therapists with frameworks within which to make predictive hypotheses during their practice of psychotherapy. Whether acknowledging it or not, all therapists are practitioner-researchers. Therapists make hypotheses every time they decide how to work with specific clients and how to respond to single or series of client utterances.

Clients are also practitioner-researchers who make predictions about how best to lead their lives. If valid theories of counselling and psychotherapy are transmitted to clients, they may increase the accuracy with which clients can predict the consequences of their behaviours and, hence, gain more control over their lives.

LIMITATIONS OF COUNSELLING AND PSYCHOTHERAPY THEORIES

All counselling and psychotherapy theories should carry the psychological equivalent of health warnings. They can be used for ill as well as for good. A criticism of many theories is that they present partial truths as whole truths. For instance, Rogers posits a unitary diagnosis of all clients' problems, namely that there is incongruence between self-structure and experience, and sees six relationship conditions as necessary and sufficient in all instances (Rogers, 1951, 1959). Ellis focuses on irrational beliefs at risk of paying insufficient attention to other aspects of thinking, for instance perceiving accurately or using coping self-talk. Freud emphasizes uncovering unconscious material through the analysis of dreams, but says little about developing specific effective behaviours to deal with everyday problems.

Some theories may lead to focusing more on what is wrong rather than on what is right with clients, a criticism which positive therapy specifically addresses. They can make clients' problems out to be more severe than they are. For instance, psychoanalysts can view aspects of learned ineffective behaviour as symptomatic of deeper underlying conflicts.

The different languages of theoretical approaches can disguise similarities between them. Theoretical rigidity is also fostered when language differences lead therapists mainly to talk with those speaking the same language rather than to a broader sharing of knowledge and experience. The language of theories can also create a power imbalance between therapists and clients. Therapists who think in a special theoretical language that they do not share can put themselves in superior–inferior relationships with clients. Furthermore, the language of some theories does little to empower clients once they end therapy.

Ideally, the language of therapy is that of self-helping. Clients unable to articulate what to think and do when faced with problems after therapy are less likely to maintain gains than clients who can instruct themselves appropriately.

Possibly all the theorists in this book insufficiently take into account cultural differences. In addition, theorists can either ignore or underestimate how socio-environmental conditions like poverty, poor housing and racial discrimination may contribute to explaining ineffective behaviour. Though feminist and gender-aware theorizing is attempting to redress the balance, most theorists insufficiently take into account the influence of sex-role conditioning. In addition, theorists tend to assume heterosexuality and often insufficiently take into account the needs of gay, lesbian and bisexual clients.

ORIGINS OF COUNSELLING AND PSYCHOTHERAPY APPROACHES

Theoretical approaches to counselling and psychotherapy are created by human beings. To a large extent these theories reflect the historical context and personal and intellectual life histories of their founders. All theorists are influenced by their families of origin and by previous writers and thinkers. The following section suggests some important factors that have influenced the creation and development of counselling and psychotherapy theory and practice.

HISTORICAL AND CULTURAL CONTEXTS

Theoretical approaches do not incubate and emerge in vacuums. Theorists are influenced by the historical and cultural contexts in which they live. For example, the prevalence of sexual repression in turn-of-the-century Austria influenced Freud to develop a theoretical position in which unacknowledged sexuality plays a large part. Another example is that, during the first half of the twentieth century, parents tended to dominate their families more than they do now. Carl Rogers was brought up in the first quarter of the century. His person-centred therapy reflects the need for individuals to have nurturing and accepting relationships within which to work through the effects of judgemental family upbringings so that they can 'become persons' (Rogers, 1961, 1980). Whereas Rogers reacted against certainty, the popularity of existential therapy partly represents a reaction to the lack of structure of much of modern society (Yalom, 1980). Old certainties provided by institutions like family and church no longer exist to the same extent and many people are faced with a more obvious need to create their own meaning.

Culture also influences how theoretical approaches develop. For example, ideas of desirable behaviour differ greatly between Western and Eastern cultures. Western psychotherapies attach a high value to individualism that people from Eastern cultures, with their greater emphasis on group harmony, may find uncongenial (Laungani, 1999). Distance from Europe and the USA combined with the authority-suspecting 'bloody-mindedness' of white Australian and New Zealand cultures emboldened White and Epston in their narrative therapy to draw from disciplines outside the mainstream of traditional psychiatry and also to incorporate concepts from indigenous sources. Seligmann may have been partly motivated to develop positive therapy because of the American cultural context of getting ahead and making the most out of life.

The topic of cultural considerations in psychotherapy theory and practice is developed in greater detail later in this book.

WOUNDED THEORISTS

The origins of behaviour therapy are more in the animal laboratory than in the personal experiences of behavioural theorists. However, many of the other theorists whose work is described in this book encountered periods of significant psychological suffering in their lives. Box 1.3 illustrates this point. Jung's observation that 'Only the wounded physician heals' might be amended to become: 'Only the wounded healer creates a counselling and psychotherapy approach'.

BOX 1.3　WOUNDED THEORISTS

Sigmund Freud *(Psychoanalysis)* suffered for many years from periodic depressions, mood variations and anxiety attacks. Freud also had occasional attacks of dread of dying, some psychologically induced fainting spells, and became very frightened about train travel.

Carl Jung *(Analytical therapy)* was a solitary child who, at one stage, used fainting spells to get out of going to secondary school. In his late thirties and early forties Jung experienced schizophrenic-like symptoms.

Carl Rogers *(Person-centred therapy)* was an extremely shy and solitary child who grew up considering his parents as masters of subtle emotional manipulation. Rogers felt it unsafe to share much of his personal feelings at home for fear of being judged negatively.

Fritz Perls *(Gestalt therapy)* grew up in a distressed family where his parents had many bitter verbal and physical fights. Perls' mother beat him with carpet-beating rods. He hated his father's pompous righteousness.

Eric Berne *(Transactional analysis),* when eleven, experienced the death from tuberculosis of his beloved physician father, leaving his mother to support him and his sister.

(Continued)

(Continued)

Irvin Yalom and Rollo May *(Existential therapy)* Yalom grew up spending many hours hating his mother's vicious tongue. May grew up in a discordant and unhappy family atmosphere. He described his mother as a 'bitch-kitty on wheels.'

Albert Ellis *(Rational emotive behaviour therapy)* was a sickly child who was unusually shy and introverted during his childhood and adolescence. Ellis' mother was self-involved and neglectful and his father was often physically absent. Aged 12, Ellis discovered his parents had divorced.

Aaron Beck's *(Cognitive therapy)* mother was deeply depressed. She could also be moody, inconsistent and excitable. While growing up Beck developed many anxieties, including fears related to abandonment, surgery, suffocation, public speaking and heights.

Arnold Lazarus *(Multimodal therapy)* was the youngest of four children and grew up feeling ignored and unimportant at home, which contributed to his feeling shy, inadequate and hypersensitive. Lazarus was also a skinny kid who was bullied a lot.

If one accepts that many originators of counselling and psychotherapy theories experienced more than their fair share of psychological suffering, the question still remains how this affected their theorizing. For some leading theorists, shyness with people may have stimulated a desire to communicate through words. In addition, early feelings of inferiority may have fuelled their ambition to make their mark. Furthermore, having suffered themselves, theorists may be motivated to develop theories that can alleviate the suffering of others.

Some theorists seem to have been motivated to develop theoretical positions that would help not just clients, but themselves. Freud's self-analysis helped him address his personal suffering at the same time as providing important insights for his main work, *The Interpretation of Dreams* (Freud, 1976; Jones, 1963). Jung's confrontation with his own unconscious archetypes and primordial images provided a rich source of ideas for helping both himself and others (Jung, 1961). Rogers' person-centred therapist has the attributes of empathy, respect and non-possessive warmth that Rogers found missing in his parents and required for his own growth.

Albert Ellis, in his late teens, regularly went to the Bronx Botanic Gardens in New York and forced himself to sit next to women on park benches and strike up conversations with them so that he could learn to control his shyness and build his relating skills. Here, early in life, Ellis was trying to think and behave more rationally in one of his problem areas.

A final word is that Michael White (narrative therapy) suggested that seeing therapists as 'wounded healers' might be less helpful for understanding the development of theories than honouring their consciously achieved values, beliefs and commitments.

INTEREST IN WRITING AND COMMUNICATING IDEAS

As well as a talent for theorizing, theorists need the ability to write passably well in order to get published. When researching the theorists' biographical sketches for this book, I was struck by how many early in life showed an interest in writing. Furthermore, some theorists, for instance Jung and Yalom, were avid readers right from their early years.

In his teens, Lazarus helped edit a bodybuilding magazine and then entered university with a view to becoming a journalist and a writer. Beck was editor of his high school newspaper and an undergraduate English major. Skinner majored in English and planned to become a writer. Ellis too envisaged a writing career and wrote reams in his quest to become the Great American Novelist. May's main interest at college was English literature. Berne studied English along with psychology and pre-medicine as an undergraduate and his mother was a journalist. Later in life at least two theorists, Skinner and Yalom, branched out to write novels (for example, Skinner, 1948; Yalom, 1992; 1996, 2005; 2012).

An ambition to communicate distinctive ideas, become known and, possibly, reap the financial rewards of successful authorship may also fuel theorists' productivity. However, readers should be circumspect about attributing commercial motives to theorists. For example, for over forty-five years, Ellis donated all his royalty, client and workshop income to the Albert Ellis Institute. Furthermore, when theorists start writing books they have no guarantee that their time and effort with be remunerative.

All theorists think they have something of value to offer and want to share it. For instance, throughout his professional life Rogers was very concerned with making an impact on others. Though motivation is complex, probably altruism, social interest and enjoyment are among the primary factors shaping theorists' willingness to generate and share ideas.

PROFESSIONAL EXPERIENCES AND FRUSTRATIONS

Though behaviour therapy owes much to experimental psychology, for the most part major counselling and psychotherapy theories emanate from people who were practitioners as well as scholars. Frustration, creative insights, clinical experimentation and careful observation can each contribute to developing a theory. Beck, Berne, Ellis, and Perls were trained in psychoanalysis. Their negative experiences practising psychoanalysis challenged them develop their own positions. Each used their work with clients to develop and experiment with different ways of helping them.

Lazarus was stimulated to develop his multimodal therapy approach as a reaction to the restrictiveness of traditional behaviour therapy. Rogers developed his person-centred approach from discovering the limitations of existing ways of working. He recalls that, when in the 1930s he worked at the Rochester Child Study Department (later renamed the Child Guidance Center), he obtained far better results with clients from listening to them than from diagnostic under-standing and advice (Rogers, 1980). Michael White and David Epston developed narrative therapy partly as a reaction to the hierarchical and dehumanizing ways they perceived people were treated in psychiatric hospitals.

RESEARCH FINDINGS

Research can both influence the initial development of theory and test its use-fulness. Behaviour therapy theory is based on the findings of experimental research: for instance, Pavlov's classical conditioning is based on experiments with dogs; Skinner's operant conditioning on experiments with pigeons and rats; and Wolpe's counter-conditioning by reciprocal inhibition on experi-ments with cats.

Theory can also be developed and validated from researching the processes and outcomes of psychotherapy. Theorists are practitioner-researchers generating and testing hypotheses in their psychotherapy practice. Thus pro-fessional experience can act as informal psychotherapy process and outcome research. Theorists and their adherents differ in the extent to which they either engage in or generate more formal psychotherapy research. On the one hand, the processes and outcomes of approaches like cognitive therapy, rational emo-tive behaviour therapy, person-centred therapy and behaviour therapy are heavily researched. On the other hand, there is a paucity of research into approaches like transactional analysis, gestalt therapy and existential therapy.

PROFESSIONAL AFFILIATION

A group of theorists whose work is presented in this book were or are psychia-trists: for example, Beck, Berne, Freud, Jung and Yalom. Many of the remainder trained as clinical psychologists: for instance, Ellis, Lazarus, May, Rogers and Seligmann. Of the clinical psychologists, only Lazarus and Seligmann were affiliated in academic psychology. De Shazer, Berg, White and Epston were social workers and counsellors.

SEX AND SEXUAL ORIENTATION

Probably most readers have noticed that, with the exception of Insoo Kim Berg, all of the major theorists presented in this book are men. However, women have been prominent in psychodynamic approaches to therapy: for instance, Anna Freud, Karen Horney and Melanie Klein. In addition, Perls' wife Laura is considered by some to be the co-founder of gestalt therapy (Yontef and Jacobs, 2014). Furthermore, women have contributed to the development of other approaches presented in this book as well as being the driving force behind feminist therapy. All the major theorists appear to have been heterosexual, at least as far as their public personas.

COUNTRY OF ORIGIN AND RACE

The countries of birth of the theorists are as follows: America – Beck, de Shazer, Ellis, May, Rogers, Seligmann and Yalom; Austria – Freud; South Africa – Lazarus and Wolpe; Canada – Berne and Epston; Switzerland – Jung; Germany – Perls; Korea – Berg; and Australia – White. Of the non-American born theorists, Berg, Berne, Lazarus, Perls and Wolpe spent the bulk of their professional lives in the United States. A proportion of the theorists in this book are Jewish: for example, Beck, Berne, Freud and Yalom. In addition, Ellis had a Jewish mother.

LONGEVITY

If you are going to be a major counselling and psychotherapy theorist, it helps to have good genes. Longevity helps major theorists to develop, refine, proselytize and defend their work. Ellis lived into his nineties, Freud, Jung, May, Rogers and Lazarus lived into their eighties, and Perls lived to over seventy-five. Probably Berne's premature death at aged sixty robbed transactional analysis of many useful developments and insights. Of the living theorists Beck (b. 1921) is over ninety, Yalom (b. 1931) is over eighty, and Epston (b. 1944) and Seligmann (b. 1942) are over seventy. Another aspect of longevity is that many, if not most, major theorists did not publish original work until they were over forty.

CREATING YOUR OWN THEORETICAL APPROACH

Each of you reading this book is engaging in the process of creating your own theoretical approach. Theory creation is both a subjective process of making sense of material as well as an external process of reading, learning, researching and practising psychotherapeutic skills. How can you make yourself a better theorist and hence a more effective therapist? The following are some suggestions.

WORK WITH THIS BOOK

Though largely based on the writings of the original theorists, this book is a secondary source. Nevertheless, it should provide you with a faithful overview of some of the main counselling and psychotherapy theories. To understand any theory you need to master its basic concepts. It is insufficient just to read about them. You will need actively to work on understanding and memorizing them. At the end of each theory chapter I, and other authors, provide review questions that test your knowledge of basic concepts.

GET PERSONAL

Jung observed: 'My life is a story of the realization of the unconscious' (Jung, 1961, p. 17). What about your life's story and what are you trying to realize through your interest in counselling and psychotherapy? Applying the different theories to your own life is one way to make learning more personal, involving and interesting. What do the theories say that seems applicable to you and why? Another way to understand the theories is to think how applicable they are to past, present or future clients. What in different theories might prove useful in your practical work and why? You can also compare and contrast different theories in an attempt to critically evaluate their strengths and weaknesses for you as a person and as a therapist. At the end of each chapter I, and other authors, provide personal questions so that you may apply your learning and insights to yourself.

Another way to learn about the theories is to try to develop a theoretical approach of your own. For over twenty-five years I asked counselling and counselling psychology trainees taking my theories classes to write a paper presenting their current theoretical approach.

READ PRIMARY SOURCES

Primary sources are books and articles written by the theorists themselves. Ultimately, there is no substitute for reading primary sources. You will get a much broader and deeper impression of the different theories if you read widely the works of their originators. You can also learn about how the originators applied their counselling and psychotherapy theories by reading case studies of their work. A section on case material is provided towards the end of each chapter on the different therapies. In addition, after describing the work of each theorist, there is a brief annotated bibliography plus other primary source references.

READ SECONDARY SOURCES

You can read secondary sources other than this book. Some secondary sources are counselling and psychotherapy textbooks and here you should always look out for the most recent editions. *Current Psychotherapies* is a widely respected edited therapy textbook containing a mixture of primary and secondary sources (Wedding and Corsini, 2014). All major therapy approaches beget many secondary source books: for instance, Mearns and Thorne's *Person-Centred Counselling in Action* (2013) and Clarkson with Cavecchia's *Gestalt Counselling in Action* (2013).

Here is a warning about reading secondary sources. Choose carefully because some secondary source writers do not really understand the theoretical positions they present. Following are three more traps into which secondary source textbook writers can fall. One trap is to mix the writings of the original theorist together with recent developments in theory, so the student has difficulty in knowing which is which. A second trap is to merge the writings of different theorists into the same chapter: for example, to have a chapter combining either psychodynamic theories or humanistic theories. A problem with this approach is that no theory gets presented thoroughly. If you doubt this point, look at the next two chapters on Freudian psychoanalysis and Jung's analytical therapy and see how well nigh impossible it would be to combine them so that readers obtain a good introduction to both Freudian and Jungian theory and practice, let alone of recent developments in each approach. A third trap is for the secondary source writer only to present case examples of their own work. A risk here is that this secondary source case material does not truly reflect how the originator practised or practises therapy.

WATCH AND LISTEN TO AUDIO-VISUAL MATERIAL

You can obtain a further insight into the different theorists by watching films, CDs and video and also listening to audio-recordings of them discussing their theories and working with clients. For instance, audio-visual material is available for theorists like Beck, Ellis, Perls and Rogers.

ATTEND TRAINING COURSES AND WORKSHOPS

You may expand your knowledge and skills in the different theories by attending training courses and workshops run by competent adherents of the different approaches. Introductory theories of counselling and psychotherapy courses are likely to be limited in presenting different approaches both by time constraints and by lecturer preferences. You may get a much more thorough introduction to any single approach if you attend workshops and courses run by specialists in it. However, when considering training courses and workshops, be careful about spreading yourself too thinly.

UNDERGO SUPERVISION

A good way to learn about the theory and practice of a psychotherapy approach is to be supervised by a practitioner skilled in it. For instance, you can learn the theory and practice of one psychotherapeutic approach more thoroughly by being supervised by someone knowledgeable and competent in that approach. Then you can broaden how you work by obtaining supervision from practitioners of one or more different approaches. Many consider that supervision for those practising counselling and psychotherapy is essential throughout their careers.

UNDERGO PERSONAL PSYCHOTHERAPY

If a counselling and psychotherapy approach particularly appeals to you, one way to learn about its theory and practice is to become a client of a skilled practitioner in the approach. For some approaches, for example psychoanalysis and analytical therapy, a training analysis is an integral part of learning the approach. Where personal psychotherapy is not a requirement of a particular approach, the need to develop self-awareness and reflective skills about your practice is important.

EVALUATE THEORETICAL APPROACHES

In creating your own theoretical approach you will undoubtedly undergo a process of evaluating the existing theoretical approaches. Many considerations go into evaluating theoretical approaches: for instance, how well you understand the theoretical approaches you are trying to evaluate, how thoroughly each approach is researched, and how their goals differ. I leave a more detailed discussion about evaluating counselling and psychotherapy approaches to this book's final chapter.

REVIEW AND PERSONAL QUESTIONS

REVIEW QUESTIONS

1. How would you define the terms counselling and psychotherapy?
2. To what extent do you consider the terms counselling and psychotherapy describe different activities and why?
3. What is a theory?
4. What are the functions of counselling and psychotherapy theories?
5. What are some potential limitations or disadvantages of counselling and psychotherapy theories?
6. What factors are influential in creating counselling and psychotherapy theoretical approaches?

PERSONAL QUESTIONS

1. Do you consider yourself a prospective counsellor and/or a prospective therapist and why?
2. Describe your present preferences regarding counselling and psychotherapy theoretical approaches?
3. How can you best learn about counselling and psychotherapy approaches?
4. How can you best develop a theoretical position to guide your counselling and psychotherapy practice?

ANNOTATED BIBLIOGRAPHY

Wedding, D. and Corsini R. J. (eds) (2014) *Current Psychotherapies* (10th ed.). Belmont, CA: Brooks/Cole.

This book is a mixture of primary and secondary sources. For instance, chapters on cognitive, existential, person-centred and rational emotive behaviour psychotherapies are written by their originators, sometimes with co-authors. Secondary source chapters include those on psychoanalytic, Adlerian, behaviour, gestalt, family, contemplative and integrative psychotherapies.

REFERENCES AND FURTHER READING

Clarkson, P. with Cavecchia, S. (2013) *Gestalt Counselling in Action* (4th ed.). London: Sage.

Corsini, R. J. (2008) Introduction. In R. Corsini and D. Wedding (eds) *Current Psychotherapies* (8th ed., pp. 1–14). Belmont, CA: Thomson Brooks/Cole.

Freud, S. (1976) *The Interpretation of Dreams*. Harmondsworth, Middlesex: Penguin Books. Original edition, 1900.

Jones, E. (1963) *The Life and Work of Sigmund Freud*. New York: Anchor Books.

Jung, C. G. (1961) *Memories, Dreams, Reflections*. London: Fontana Press.

Laungani, P. (1999) Culture and identity: Implications for counselling. In S. Palmer and P. Laungani (eds), *Counselling in a Multicultural Society* (pp. 35–70). London: Sage.

Mearns, D. and Thorne, B. with McLeod, J. (2013) *Person-Centred Counselling in Action* (4th ed.). London: Sage.

Rogers, C. R. (1951) *Client-Centered Therapy*. Boston: Houghton Mifflin.

Rogers, C. R. (1959) A theory of therapy, personality, and interpersonal relationships, as developed in the client-centered framework. In S. Koch (ed.), *Psychology: A Study of Science* (Study 1, Volume 3, pp. 184–256). New York: McGraw-Hill.

Rogers, C. R. (1961) *On Becoming a Person*. Boston, MA: Houghton Miflin.

Rogers, C. R. (1980) *A Way of Being*. Boston, MA: Houghton Miflin.

Skinner, B. F. (1948) *Walden Two*. New York: MacMillan.

Wedding, D. and Corsini R. J. (eds) (2014) *Current Psychotherapies* (10th ed.). Belmont, CA: Brooks/Cole.

Yalom. I. D. (1980) *Existential Psychotherapy*. New York: Basic Books.

Yalom, I. D. (1992) *When Nietzsche Wept*. New York: Basic Books.

Yalom, I. D. (1996) *Lying on the Couch*. New York: Harper Perennial.

Yalom, I. D. (2005) *The Schopenhauer Cure: A Novel*. New York: HarperCollins.

Yalom, I. D. (2012) *The Spinoza Problem*. New York: Basic Books.

Yontef, G. and Jacobs, L. (2014) Gestalt therapy. In D. Wedding and R. J. Corsini (eds). *Current Psychotherapies* (10th ed., pp. 299–338). Belmont, CA: Thomson Brooks/Cole.

Sigmund Freud, the originator of psychoanalysis, is possibly still the best known of the theorists whose work is described in this book. Freud lived in a time of conflict, a major theme of his work. One area of conflict was that between the straight-laced 'Victorian' public morality of late nineteenth century Austria and human sexuality. To a large extent public acknowledgment of sexuality was frowned upon which fostered widespread ignorance of healthy sexual functioning. Another area of conflict was that caused by human aggression. The nineteenth century had started with the Napoleonic wars, in the second half of the century the Franco-Prussian war took place, and, in the second decade of the twentieth century, matters were to get worse with the horrors of the First World War. Though Freud died within a month of the start of the Second World War, he was very conscious of the factors leading up to it, not least because all his professional life, as a Jew, he had been acutely aware of the anti-Semitism in his home land, and he was to die in exile in Britain, a refugee from Nazism.

Sigmund Freud and Carl Jung's lives overlapped, for a time they were close associates, and what Jung called his 'analytical psychology' has some of its roots in Freudian psychoanalysis. Nevertheless, Jung developed a very different psychodynamic theory and practice to that of Freud. In particular, Jung and Freud diverged in their views of the unconscious. While Freud emphasized sexual repression, Jung considered that, at its deepest level, the unconscious consisted of archetypes, or inborn possibilities for psychological apprehension and representation, which may then be expressed in universal myths and symbols.

In 1906, Jung and Freud became friends and intellectual companions. Freud admired Jung's brilliance and regarded him as his crown prince and heir. In addition, Freud thought that, by having Jung prominent in the movement, he might avoid the risk of psychoanalysis being viewed as a mainly Jewish activity. Jung had gone through a troubled relationship with his own father and was fiercely intellectually independent. It was an error of judgement on both men's part to think that any 'father–son' relationship could be maintained. In 1913, Jung and Freud split bitterly never to meet again in the remaining twenty-six years of Freud's life.

FREUD'S PSYCHOANALYSIS 2

INTRODUCTION

The main part of this chapter describes Freud's psychoanalysis. However, this way of working has 'evolved over the last century, so that classical and modern psychoanalytic approaches now exist' (Luborsky, O'Reilly-Landry and Arlow, 2008, p. 15). Consequently, there is a section on contemporary psychoanalysis towards the end of the chapter.

SIGMUND FREUD (1856–1939)

Sigmund Freud was born at Freiberg, a small town in what is now the Czech Republic. He was the eldest son of his father's second wife, who subsequently bore five daughters and two other sons. Jones (1963) writes of Freud's mother's pride in and love for her first-born and also mentions that between the ages of two and two and a half Freud's libido had been aroused towards his mother on seeing her naked. Freud writes: 'My parents were Jews, and I have remained a Jew myself' (Freud, 1935, p. 12). His father, Jakob, was a wool merchant who, when Freud was four, moved his family to Vienna. Freud's early years in Vienna were hard and, throughout his upbringing, his family appears to have been short of money.

When he was nine Freud went to high school (Sperl Gymnasium), where he was at the top of his class for seven years, enjoyed special privileges, and was required to pass few examinations. Freud was a hard worker who enjoyed reading and studying. On leaving school with distinction at 17 he faced the choice of a career, which for a Viennese Jew had to be in industry, business, law or medicine. He recalls not feeling any particular predilection for medicine, since his interests were directed more towards human concerns than natural objects. Freud writes '… and it was hearing Goethe's beautiful essay on Nature read aloud by Professor Carl Bruhl just before I left school that decided me to become a medical student' (Freud, 1935, p. 14).

In 1873 Freud enrolled at the University of Vienna to study medicine, though when he was there his academic interests were more wide-ranging. In 1876 he began the first of his researches, a study of the gonadic structure of eels. Soon afterwards he entered Ernst Brucke's physiological laboratory, where he worked, with short interruptions, from 1876 to 1882. During this period

Freud focused chiefly on work connected with the histology of nerve cells. He found 'rest and satisfaction' in Brucke's laboratory as well as scientists 'whom I could respect and take as my models' (Freud, 1935, p. 15). He thought especially highly of Brucke himself. Freud recalls being decidedly negligent in pursuing his medical studies. Nevertheless, in 1881 he passed his final examinations to become a Doctor of Medicine with the grade of 'excellent'.

In 1882 Freud left Brucke's laboratory, where the year before he had been appointed a demonstrator. For financial reasons, probably influenced by falling in love, Freud decided to earn his living as a physician. He entered the General Hospital of Vienna, where he gained experience in various departments and became an active researcher in the Institute of Cerebral Anatomy. During this period 'with an eye to material considerations, I began to study nervous diseases' (Freud, 1935, p. 18). Because of inadequate opportunities for learning this subject, Freud was forced to be his own teacher. He published a number of clinical observations on organic diseases of the nervous systems and, in 1885, was appointed lecturer in neuropathology. Around this period Freud both took cocaine and conducted research into its use. Jones (1963) observes: 'For many years he suffered from periodic depressions and fatigue or apathy, neurotic symptoms which later took the form of anxiety attacks before being dispelled by his own analysis' (pp. 54–5). Cocaine apparently calmed the agitation and eased the depression. Jones also mentions that all his life Freud was subject to severe bouts of migraine that were refractory to any treatment.

On the award of a travelling fellowship Freud went to Paris where, from October 1885 to February 1886, he studied at the Salpetriere (hospital for nervous diseases) under Charcot. He was very impressed with Charcot's investigations into hysteria, confirming the genuineness of hysterical phenomena, including hysterical paralyses and contractures by hypnotic suggestion. In 1886 Freud returned to Vienna to marry Martha Bernays and to set up a private practice as a specialist in nervous diseases. His 'therapeutic arsenal contained only two weapons, electrotherapy and hypnotism ...' (Freud, 1935, p. 26). He soon dropped electrotherapy and increasingly realized the limitations of hypnotic suggestion. During the period 1886 to 1891 he did little scientific work, though in 1891 he jointly published the first of his studies on the cerebral paralyses of children.

In the early 1880s Freud had developed a close friendship with Joseph Breuer, a prominent Viennese physician, who told him how, between 1880 and 1882, he had successfully treated a young girl with hysterical symptoms. His method was to hypnotize her deeply and then encourage her to express in words her memories of earlier emotional situations that were oppressing her. In the late 1880s Freud began repeating Breuer's technique with his own patients, being aware 'of the possibility that there could be powerful mental processes which nevertheless remained hidden from the consciousness of man' (Freud, 1935, p. 29). In 1893 Freud and Breuer wrote a preliminary paper on the cathartic method and, in 1895, published their book *Studies on Hysteria*.

During the 1890s the transition from catharsis to psychoanalysis proper took place. Jones writes: 'there is ample evidence that for ten years or so – roughly comprising the nineties – he suffered from a very considerable psychoneurosis ... yet it was just in the years when the neurosis was at its height, 1897–1900, that Freud did his most original work' (Jones, 1963, p. 194). Although he showed no conversion symptoms, he had extreme alterations of mood between elation and self-confidence, and depression and inhibition. In the latter moods Freud could neither write nor concentrate, apart from his professional work. Additionally, he had occasional attacks of dread of dying and also became very anxious about travelling by rail.

During the period 1887 to 1900 Freud had an intense friendship with Wilhelm Fleiss, a nose and throat specialist two years younger than him. Fleiss saw sexual problems as central to his own work, encouraged Freud and gave him permission to develop his theories. Jones notes Freud's dependency on Fleiss' good opinion and calls him Freud's 'sole public' during this period. Jones rated Fleiss as intellectually far inferior to Freud.

Against this background, Freud started developing his ideas on the sexual bases of neuroses, abandoned hypnotism yet retained his practice of requiring the patient to lie on a sofa while he sat behind. During 1897 to 1899, he wrote his major work, *The Interpretation of Dreams*. In the summer of 1897 Freud undertook a psychoanalysis of his own unconscious, and this self-analysis generated material for the book. Freud discovered his childhood passion for his mother and his intense hatred and jealousy of his father, which he considered a pervasive human characteristic that he termed the Oedipus complex. It took eight years to sell the first edition of 600 copies of *The Interpretation of Dreams*. Jones observes of Freud's self-analysis: 'The end of all that labor and suffering was the last and final phase in the evolution of Freud's personality. There emerged the serene and benign Freud, henceforth free to pursue his work in imperturbable composure' (Jones, 1963, p. 205). Fromm's (1959) biography is less kind, suggesting that Freud continued to exhibit some insecurity and egotism in areas of both his professional and his personal life. In 1905 Freud published what is perhaps his other major work, *Three Contributions to the Theory of Sex*, which traces the development of sexuality from its earliest childhood beginnings.

In his autobiographical study Freud observed that, after the preliminary cathartic period, the history of psychoanalysis falls into two phases. From around 1895 until 1906 or 1907 he worked in isolation, but thereafter the contributions of his pupils and collaborators increasingly grew in importance. The historical development of Freud's ideas will be left at this stage. Suffice it to say that for the remainder of his life he published numerous books and articles not only on psychoanalysis as a method of treating the disturbed, but also on the relevance of his theories to everyday life. In 1910, at a congress held at Nuremberg, the analysts formed themselves into an International Psychoanalytical Association divided into a number of local societies, but under a common president. By 1935 the number of the Association's supporters had increased considerably. The growth of psychoanalysis, however, was not smooth and aroused considerable antipathy.

Freud was in the habit of smoking an average of 20 cigars a day and, in 1923, learned that he had cancer of the jaw. He lived the last 16 years of his life in pain that was often extreme, and a total of 33 operations were performed on his jaw. In 1938 Nazism caused Freud to leave Austria with his family and settle in his admired England, which he had first visited when he was nineteen. He died in London a year later.

Freud had observed that he was by temperament a conquistador or adventurer, with the accompanying traits of curiosity, boldness and tenacity. A modern term for Freud might be an 'ideas person'.

THEORY

BASIC CONCEPTS

Although many of Freud's basic concepts are to be found in *The Interpretation of Dreams* (1900/1976), he was developing and refining his ideas continuously. Thus the same concept may appear in different sources, only some of which will be mentioned here. In general, this chapter represents Freud's later presentation of his work.

THE PLEASURE PRINCIPLE

Originally presented as the unpleasure principle, the pleasure principle follows from the constancy hypothesis that 'the mental apparatus endeavours to keep the quantity of excitation in it as low as possible or at least to keep it constant' (Freud, 1920/1961, p. 3). Thus everything that increases the quantity of excitation will be felt as unpleasurable and anything which diminishes it will be experienced as pleasurable. Freud qualified the idea of the dominance of the pleasure principle by observing that, although in the mind there exists a strong tendency towards the pleasure principle, there are also other forces opposing it, with the final outcome not always fulfilling the tendency towards pleasure.

THE INSTINCTS

Instincts represent somatic or biological demands upon the mind. While acknowledging the possibility of distinguishing many instincts, Freud assumed that these could be grouped into two basic instincts, *Eros* and the *destructive instinct*. The erotic instincts 'seek to combine more and more living substance into even greater unities', while the death instincts 'oppose this effort and lead what is living back to an inorganic state' (Freud, 1932/1973, p. 140). Eros includes the instincts of self-preservation, the preservation of the species, ego-love and object-love, and its energy is called *libido*. Throughout life the basic instincts may either work together (for instance the sexual act is also an act of aggression) or oppose each other.

Freud saw instincts as historically acquired and conservative and stated: 'It seems, then, that an instinct is an urge inherent in life to restore an earlier state of things' (Freud, 1920/1961, p. 30). Given the assumption that living things appeared later than inanimate ones and arose out of them, the death instinct may be viewed as a compulsion to repeat this earlier inorganic state. Consequently, the aim of all life is death. Eros, however, does not follow the same formula. Freud considered that sexual instincts were the single exception among the instincts in not seeking to restore an earlier state of things.

Freud viewed the inclination to aggression as an original instinctual disposition in humans. He quoted Plautus: *'Homo homini lupus'*, a translation of which is 'Man is a wolf to man'. The aggressive instinct is the derivative and main representative of the death instinct. The evolution of civilization represents the struggle between the life and death instincts in the human species. The fateful question that Freud posed at the end of *Civilization and its Discontents* was whether Eros would assert itself, 'But who can foresee with what success and what results?' (Freud, 1930/1962, p. 92).

THE UNCONSCIOUS AND CONSCIOUSNESS

Heavily influenced by his study of dreams, Freud made a distinction between the unconscious and consciousness. From the very beginning, he stated that there were two kinds of unconscious and three levels of consciousness.

- *The unconscious:* The unconscious (Ucs), or unconscious proper, is material that is inadmissible to consciousness through repression. In other words, with the unconscious the censorship on material coming into awareness is very strong indeed. The object of psychoanalysis is to help make some of this material accessible to awareness, though during the process strong resistances may be aroused, not least because of the forbidden sexual connotations of much of what is being repressed.
- *The preconscious:* The preconscious (Pcs) consists of everything that can easily exchange the unconscious state for the conscious one. Thus the preconscious is latent and capable of becoming conscious, while the unconscious is repressed and is unlikely to become conscious without great difficulty. Material may remain in the preconscious, though usually it finds its way into consciousness without any need for psychoanalytic intervention. The preconscious may be viewed as a screen between the unconscious and consciousness, with, as in the case of dreams, modifications being made in unconscious material through censorship.
- *Consciousness:* Consciousness (Cs or Pcpt Cs) has the function of a sense organ for the perception of psychical qualities. Unlike the two kinds of unconscious, consciousness has no memory and a state of consciousness is usually very transitory. Material becomes conscious, or flows into the consciousness sense organ, from two directions: the external world and inner excitations. Furthermore, the function of speech enables internal events such as sequences of ideas and intellectual processes to become conscious.

STRUCTURE OF THE MENTAL APPARATUS

Freud structured the mental apparatus into three systems or agencies: the id, the ego and the super-ego. Psychological wellbeing depends on whether these

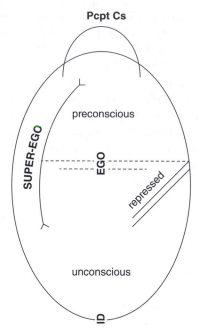

Figure 2.1   Structural relations of the mental apparatus

three systems are interrelating effectively. Figure 2.1 shows Freud's own sketch of the structural relations of the mental apparatus, though he acknowledges that the space occupied by the unconscious id ought to have been much greater (Freud, 1932/1973, p. 111).

THE ID

The id or 'it' is the oldest of these systems and contains everything that is inherited and fixed in the constitution. The instincts, which originate in the somatic organization, find their mental expression in the id. The id, filled with energy from the instincts, strives to bring about the satisfaction of instinctual needs on the basis of the pleasure principle. Thus the activity of the id is directed towards securing the free discharge of quantities of excitation. The psychical processes of the id are known as primary processes because they are present in the mental apparatus from the first. Furthermore, no alteration in the id's mental processes is produced by the passage of time. Freud viewed the id as 'a chaos, a cauldron full of seething emotions', which 'knows no judgments of values: no good and evil, no morality' (Freud, 1932/1973, pp. 106–7). The id consists of wishful impulses. It is not governed by logic, and this applies especially to the law of contradiction, since it contains contrary impulses side by side. In short, the id is the individual's primary subjective reality at the unconscious level.

THE EGO

The ego or 'I' is first and foremost a bodily ego ultimately derived from bodily sensations, in particular those coming from its surface. The ego is a portion of the id that has undergone a special development or modification through the influence of the external world. The ego acts as an intermediary between the id and the external world and ideally represents reason and common sense, whereas the id contains instinctual passions and would destroy itself without the intervention of the ego. The ego strives to bring the reality principle to bear upon the id in substitution for the pleasure principle. The processes of the ego, which include perception, problem solving and repression, are later developments or secondary processes, in contrast to the original or primary processes of the id. Nevertheless, the ego seeks pleasure and the avoidance of unpleasure, differing from the id only in the means of attaining common ends. A foreseen increase in unpleasure is met by a signal of anxiety. As Figure 2.1 shows, the perceptual-conscious system is the outer layer of the ego, which also includes much preconscious and unconscious material.

The ego is in control of voluntary movement, but interposes thought between experiencing a need and acting on it. The ego deals with external events through perception, memory, avoiding excessive stimuli, adapting to moderate stimuli, and engaging in activities designed to modify the external world to its advantage. Regarding internal events in relation to the id, the ego attempts to control instinctual demands by deciding the timing and manner of their gratification or by suppressing their excitations. Freud makes the analogy of the id being the horse, while the ego is the rider. He observes that often, however, the ego is weak in relation to the id and so is in the habit of transforming the id's will into action as if it were its own.

THE SUPER-EGO

The super-ego is a residue formed within the ego in which parental influence is prolonged. Parental influence may be defined broadly as including cultural, racial and family influences. As the person grows up, the nature of the 'parental' influence may vary, partly because parents may behave differently. Teachers, admired figures in public life and many others may also contribute to the development of an individual's super-ego, which normally departs more and more from original parental influences.

The function of the super-ego, which engages in self-observation, is to contain the demands of the id through moral influence on the ego. Originally the child engages in instinctual renunciation through fear of loss of love or through fear of aggression from an *external* or parental authority. Subsequently a secondary situation develops in which the external restraint is internalized and thus instinctual renunciation comes about through fear of an *internal* authority, or super-ego.

A characteristic of the super-ego is the ego-ideal, based on the admiration which the child felt for the perfection it saw in its parents and which it strives to emulate. In fact the terms 'super-ego' and 'ego-ideal' are virtually synonymous. The ego-ideal consists of both precepts – 'You ought to be like this' – and prohibitions – 'You ought not to be like that'. These precepts and prohibitions are based in part on the identifications and repressions resulting from the resolution of the Oedipus complex. They represent the individual's conscience, transgressions of which are likely to result in a sense of inferiority and guilt and also possibly in a need for punishment. Freud observed: 'The super-ego is the representative for us of every moral restriction, the advocate of a striving towards perfection – it is, in short, as much as we have been able to grasp psychologically of what is described as the higher side of human life' (Freud, 1932/1973, p. 98).

In addition to the demands of the instincts and of the external world, the ego has to take into account the demands of the super-ego. Individuals vary in the severity of their super-egos, which may be benign or punitively harsh and restricting. Conflicts can arise between ego and super-ego, with large portions of both agencies remaining unconscious.

ANXIETY

Freud defined anxiety as a specific state of unpleasure accompanied by motor discharge along definite pathways. He saw anxiety as the universal reaction to the situation of danger and the ego as the sole seat of anxiety. In later life, a source of anxiety that is involuntary occurs whenever a dangerous situation arises. Another source is anxiety generated by the ego when danger is merely threatened and the ego feels weak in relation to it. Hence there are three kinds of anxiety, one for each of the ego's three 'taskmasters':

- *realistic* anxiety regarding the dangers of the external world,
- *moral* anxiety regarding conflict with the super-ego, and
- *neurotic* anxiety regarding conflict with the strength of the id's instinctual impulses.

Thus anxiety is either a reaction to actual danger or a signal involving the perception of impending danger.

PSYCHICAL ENERGY, CATHEXIS AND ANTI-CATHEXIS

Psychoanalysis is often referred to as having a dynamic view of psychology. What this means is that the concept of psychical or mental energy and its distribution among the id, ego and super-ego is central to psychoanalysis. The id is the source of this somatically based psychical energy, being filled with energy reaching it from the instincts. Sexual excitation is an example of instinctual psychical energy. As the ego and the super-ego are formed they also become charged with energy.

The words 'cathexis' and to 'cathect' describe the idea of psychical energy being drawn to mental agencies and processes, somewhat analogous to an electric charge. Cathexes are the charges of instinctual energy seeking discharge, whereas anti-cathexes are charges of energy that block and inhibit such discharge. The id has only primary-process instinctual cathexes seeking discharge. However, the ego and the super-ego have both urging cathexes and restraining anti-cathexes. Throughout life the ego is the avenue by which libidinal cathexes are transferred to objects and into which they may also be withdrawn again. Two characteristics of libidinal cathexes are mobility, the ease with which they pass from one object to another, and, in contrast, fixation, or being bound to particular objects.

BISEXUALITY

Freud observed that it was a long-known anatomical fact that in every normally formed male or female there are traces of the apparatus of the other sex, though in atrophied form. Anatomically there may have been an original predisposition to bisexuality, which in the course of the development of the human species has largely been altered to monosexuality.

Psychologically Freud considered that the sexual impulse is probably entirely independent of its object and therefore is not originated by chemical attraction. Another way of stating this is that there is only one libido and it cannot be assigned a sex. Therefore the direction of both heterosexual and homosexual object selection requires further explanation. By studying covert sexual excitations, psychoanalytic research discovered that all men are capable of homosexual object selection and actually accomplish this in the unconscious. Furthermore, homosexual libidinous feelings 'play no small role as factors in normal psychic life' and an even greater role as 'causative factors of disease' (Freud, 1905/1962, p. 10).

Freud considered that the same free attachment to male and female objects as observed in childhood and primitive and prehistoric states forms the basis on which both normal and homosexual or inverted sexual development takes place. A degree of homosexuality is congenital in everyone, with the final determination of sexual behaviour being the result of the intensity of constitutional predisposition as well as of life experiences and restrictions in one or the other direction. Both the woman and the man develop out of a child with a bisexual disposition.

ACQUISITION

INFANTILE SEXUALITY AND AMNESIA

Freud distinguished between the sexual impulse, the sexual object, and the sexual aim. The sexual impulse is the sexual aspect of libido, the sexual object is the person in whom sexual attraction is lodged, and the sexual aim refers to the action, such as touch or intercourse, towards which the sexual impulse strives. Freud further made a sharp distinction between 'sexual' and 'genital', considering that sexual life consists of gaining pleasure from zones of the body sensitive to sexual stimulation and that this is not necessarily in the service of reproduction. Additionally, sexual life includes affectionate and friendly impulses often called 'love'. In a sense, all adult sexual behaviour whose goal is not reproduction, a heterosexual object and intercourse may be considered perverse. Adult sexual behaviour does not suddenly emerge at puberty but develops out of prior sexual dispositions and experiences.

Sexual life starts soon after birth. Infantile sexuality, in the absence of genital maturation and of ego and super-ego development, lacks a central coordinating focus. Instead the component sexual instincts seek their own pleasure. Infantile sexuality is fundamentally auto-erotic in that the infant finds pleasure in the object of its own body. Freud considered that the infantile sexual disposition contained great tendencies to perversion and that normal sexual behaviour develops partly in response to organic changes and partly as a result of psychic inhibitions and repressions.

The years of childhood are when the individual is most impressionable. Nevertheless, people are largely unaware of the beginnings of their sexual life and tend to view their childhood as if it were a prehistoric time. However, infantile and childhood sexual experiences leave deep traces in the individual's psychical life, acting as significant determinants for future development. Freud used the term 'infantile amnesia' to refer to the phenomenon by which a veil is drawn over early sexual experiences.

SEXUAL DEVELOPMENT

The onset of sexual life takes place in two stages. The first or pre-genital stage of sexual development is a steady process that reaches a climax towards the end of a child's fifth year. After this there is a lull or period of latency. The second or genital stage starts with the re-emergence of the sexual impulse at menarche or puberty. The pre-genital and genital stages of sexual organization are distinguished by whether or not the genital zones have assumed a dominating role.

• THE PRE-GENITAL STAGE (BIRTH TO ABOUT AGE 6)

The pre-genital stage itself consists of three separate phases of sexual organization through which individuals normally pass smoothly, though fixations or arrested development may occur at each phase. Both sexes seem to pass through the early stages of sexual development in the same manner.

(a) Oral phase (first eighteen months)

The first organ to be an erogenous zone is the mouth, and hence sexual development starts with the *oral* phase. The infant's act of sucking goes beyond that needed for the taking of nourishment to what may be viewed as the seeking of sexual organ-pleasure independent of nourishment. The oral phase can be further subdivided. The first sub-stage is where there is a focus only on oral incorporation, whereas the second sub-stage is 'oral-sadistic', with the emergence of biting activity. These two sub-stages of the oral phase are the first manifestation of the phenomenon of ambivalence.

(b)   Anal phase (18 months to 3 years of age)

The second organ to become an erogenous zone is the anus, and normal sexual development proceeds from the oral to the *sadistic-anal* phase. The active aspect of this phase is
the impulse for mastery (sadism), with the strengthening of the musculature of the body
and control of sphincter functions. The erogenous mucous membrane of the anus also
manifests itself as an organ with a passive sexual aim. Character traits associated with this
phase are orderliness, parsimony and obstinacy, which together define the so-called 'anal
character'.

(c)   Phallic phase (from about age 3 to 5 or 6)

The third organ to become an erogenous zone is the genital apparatus. The period of sexual
development in which the male sexual organ (the phallus) and the female clitoris become important is known as the *phallic* phase, which starts in about the child's third year. Here pleasure is
obtained from masturbation. During the phallic phase the sexuality of early childhood reaches its
greatest intensity and it is during this phase that male and female sexual development become
different. The *Oedipus* phase is part of the phallic phase for both sexes (see Box 2.1).

BOX 2.1   THE OEDIPUS COMPLEX

FOR BOYS

At an early age the little boy develops an object-cathexis for his mother and identifies
with his father. During the phallic phase the body's libidinal object-cathexis of his mother
intensifies and he wishes to get rid of his father and to take his father's place with his
mother. The threat of castration causes the boy to abandon and repress his incestuous
wishes. The resolution of the boy's Oedipus complex involves renouncing his object-
cathexis of his mother, which may lead to an identification with his mother or, more
normally, to an intensification of his identification with his father, consolidating the masculinity in his character. The Oedipus situation is often more complex because of the
child's bisexual disposition. Thus, instead of affection for his mother and ambivalence
towards his father, he may have a mixture of affection for and ambivalence towards each
parent. Freud observes that 'in both sexes the relative strength of the masculine and
feminine sexual dispositions is what determines whether the outcome of the Oedipus
situation shall be an identification with the father or with the mother' (Freud, 1923/1962,
p. 23). Perhaps it is more accurate to consider the outcome as a predominant rather than
an exclusive identification with one or the other parent. Freud further asserts that, especially with neurotics, a bisexual Oedipus complex should be assumed.

FOR GIRLS

As with the boy, the girl's mother is the first object of her love. During the phallic
phase the clitoris is her predominant erogenous zone. Freud considered that during

(Continued)

(Continued)

the girl's development to femininity she should change both her predominant erogenous zone (to the vagina) and also the sex of her love object. The powerful attachment of the girl to her mother is ended when the girl, discovering the inferiority of
her clitoris and the fact that she does not have a penis, holds her mother responsible.
Penis envy or the wish for a penis is a very important feminine trait. The wish for a
penis-baby from the father replaces the wish for a penis, and it is at this stage that
the girl has entered her Oedipus situation, desiring her father and wishing to be rid
of her mother. Again the situation may be complicated by her bisexual disposition.
Girls remain in their Oedipus situation for an indeterminate length of time and
resolve it late and often incompletely. Whereas the boy is encouraged to surmount
the Oedipus complex through fear of castration, the girl has no such motivation. As
time goes by the female Oedipus complex weakens, partly as a result of inevitable
disappointments from her father.

- ## THE LATENCY PERIOD (ABOUT AGE 6 TO 12)

The period from around the beginning of the child's sixth year, probably later for girls, to
menarche and puberty constitutes the sexual latency period. Latency may be total or partial
and, during this period, sexual inhibitions develop. One of the mechanisms by which sexual
energy is diverted is called sublimation or the displacement of libido to new aims and cultural
pursuits. Furthermore, as the individual develops, libidinous impulses may call forth contrary
anti-cathexes or reactions (reaction formations) such as disgust, shame and morality.

- ## THE GENITAL STAGE (ABOUT AGE 12 AND THEN ONWARDS)

The *genital* stage, which starts at menarche or puberty, involves the subordination of all
sources of sexual feeling to the primacy of the genital zones. Earlier libidinal cathexes may be
retained, included in sexual activity or preliminary or auxiliary acts, or in some way repressed
or diverted. Puberty brings a greater increase of libido in boys, but in girls there is an increase
in repression, especially regarding clitoral sexuality. At menarche and puberty, along with the
overcoming of incestuous object-choices, comes the breaking away from parental authority. Given a reasonably adequate prior sexual development, the individual is now ready to
engage in a heterosexual genital relationship.

IDENTIFICATION

Identification is an important concept for understanding ego and super-ego
development. Identification may be viewed in three ways:

1. as the original form of emotional tie with an object,
2. as a regressive substitute for a libidinal object-tie by means of introjection of the object
   with the ego, so that the ego assumes the characteristics of the object (e.g. a female
   patient imitating her father's cough), and

3. as a feeling generated by the perception of a common quality with another person who is not libidinally cathected.

The development of the super-ego may be seen in terms of identification with the parental agency, by which young people, wishing to be like their parents, mould their egos after the fashion of those taken as their models. Identification is part of the normal process of development. However, the ego may be restricted, as well as enhanced, depending on the nature of the identification.

DEFENCE MECHANISMS

During the child's early years its ego is relatively feeble, yet it has to deal with strong instinctual sexual impulses. At this stage anxiety may be generated by loss of an object or loss of love, which may persist into later life. Later sources of anxiety include fear of castration during the phallic phase, and fear of the super-ego during and after the latency period.

In order to cope with the sources of anxiety the ego uses defence mechanisms. Freud doubted that the ego could do without them during normal development. In many instances, however, the ego pays a high price for employing these mechanisms, since they restrict its functioning, also using in their anti-cathexes psychical energy which might better be expended elsewhere. Defence mechanisms are infantilisms that operate unconsciously and may impede realistic behaviour long after they have outlived their usefulness. Individuals do not make use of all the possible mechanisms of defence, but selects some, which become fixated in their egos. The establishment of defensive mechanisms is largely a feature of the child's struggle against its sexuality during the first five years of life. Box 2.2 describes the five main defensive ways in which the ego strives to contain the threatening instinctual cathexis when the ego observes that an emerging instinctual demand may place it in danger.

BOX 2.2   THE EGO'S MAIN MECHANISMS OF DEFENCE

Repression: Purposely forgetting something and remaining unaware of having done this. The process of repression is of two kinds:

1. material which is in the preconscious and hence admissible to consciousness is pushed back into the unconscious, and
2. unconscious material may be forbidden by censorship to enter the preconscious and hence has to remain unconscious.

(Continued)

(Continued)

For example, either kind of repression might apply to an individual's latent sexually perverted impulses. Repression is the central underlying defensive mechanism of the ego, the basis of all other defences.

Reaction-formation: Adopting thoughts, feelings and behaviours that are the opposite to one's true thoughts and feelings. The ego acknowledges impulses contrary to the ones by which it is threatened. For instance, sexual impulses may be warded off by excessive shame, disgust and loathing of sexuality.

Projection: The ego deals with the threat of an unacceptable instinctual impulse by externalizing it. Thus individuals, instead of acknowledging the extent of their own libidinal and aggressive impulses, may become very aware of such characteristics in others and actually attribute them incorrectly.

Fixation: Where people get highly anxious about moving on to the next phase of their sexual development, they may lag behind or become fixated in varying degrees to an earlier stage in terms of satisfaction of their instincts. For instance, children may cling dependently to their mothers' love rather than make new object-cathexes.

Regression: Resuming behaviours appropriate to an earlier stage of sexual development. Under threat, an individual returns to an earlier phase at which she or he may previously have been fixated. In fact, regressions may be of two kinds: a return to the incestuous objects first cathected by the libido and a return of the sexual organization as a whole to an earlier phase.

NORMAL DEVELOPMENT

To summarize, the Freudian view of the normal development of personality may be seen in terms of three interrelated strands.

1. The individual's libidinal development, which starts with a mixture of constitutional and infantile predispositions which mature into genital sexuality in successive but overlapping phases, interrupted by the latency period.
2. The development of both the ego, as it gains in ability to mediate between instinctual demands and the reality of the external world, and the super-ego, based on identifications with parental influences.
3. The establishment of favoured defensive mechanisms on the part of the ego to ward off the anxiety caused by the strength and persistence of the id's libidinal impulses.

Thus normal development may be viewed as passing through successive stages of sexual maturation without major fixations and regressions, developing an ego which copes reasonably effectively with the external world, developing a super-ego based on identifications which are constructive and not punitively moralistic, and evolving defensive mechanisms which drain off some of the energy of the id without serious restriction of ego functioning. Normal development is a dynamic process entailing a continuing distribution and redistribution of psychical energy among id, ego and super-ego, the three systems of the mental apparatus.

DEVELOPMENT AND ACTIVATION OF NEUROSIS

Freud saw biological, phylogenetic and psychological factors as each contributing to neurosis.

The *biological factor* is that the human animal is born relatively unfinished and thus has to undergo a protracted period of helplessness and dependence. This helplessness creates the initial situation of danger regarding fear of object loss, which in turn creates the human's need to be loved, which it never renounces.

The *phylogenetic factor* is inferred from the interruption in human sexual development of the latency period, whereas the sexual maturation of related animals proceeds uninterrupted. Freud believed that something momentous must have taken place in the history of the human species to bring about this situation and that its pathogenic importance is that most of the instinctual demands of infantile sexuality are treated as dangers to be guarded against by the ego. Furthermore, there is the danger that the sexual impulses of puberty will follow their infantile prototypes into repression.

The *psychological factor* involves three elements that together make for a pathogenic neurotic conflict.

1. *Frustration of sexual impulses* or the damming up of the sexual instinct by the ego. Repressions are especially likely to take place in infancy and early childhood, when the ego is underdeveloped and feeble in relation to the strength of the sexual impulses. Freud observed: 'We recognize the essential precondition of neuroses in this lagging of ego development behind libidinal development' (Freud, 1949, p. 113). The process of repression takes place under the influence of anxiety, in that the ego anticipates that satisfaction of the emerging sexual cathexis will lead to danger. In fact the ego allows an initial reproduction of the feared unpleasure. This feeling of anxiety brings the unpleasure-pleasure mechanism into operation and so causes the ego to repress the dangerous instinctual impulse. By the act of repression, however, the ego has renounced a portion of its organization and the repressed instinctual impulse remains inaccessible to its influence.

2. *Transformation of frustrated sexual impulses into neurotic symptoms.* Frustrated sexual impulses may not disappear, instead getting transformed into neurotic symptoms. Freud saw symptoms such as hysterical or conversion symptoms as the substitute satisfactions for the frustrated sexual instincts. Repression, however, does not always result in symptom formation. For instance, in a successful dissolution of the Oedipus complex the repressed sexual impulses may be destroyed, with their libido being put permanently to other uses.

3. *Inadequacy of previously used repressions.* While repressions may be effective during early childhood and the latency period, they may turn out to be inadequate with the re-awakening

and intensification of the sexual instincts at menarche and puberty. When this occurs the individual may experience an intense neurotic conflict with all its suffering. Without assistance in undoing its repressions, the ego will have little or no influence over the transformed instincts of the repressed id. Furthermore, the conflict is often heightened through an alliance of the id and super-ego against the ego.

BOX 2.3   EXAMPLES OF NORMAL AND NEUROTIC DEVELOPMENT

Freud (1932/1973) gives as an example of normal and neurotic development the story of the caretaker's and the landlord's little daughters. When young, the two girls played games that took on a sexual character, including exciting each other's genitals. These experiences awakened sexual impulses that afterwards found expression in masturbation.

NORMAL DEVELOPMENT

The caretaker's daughter, unscarred by her early sexual activity which she regarded as natural and harmless, took a lover and became a mother.

NEUROTIC DEVELOPMENT

While still a child the landlord's daughter, as a result of education, got the idea that she had done something wrong. She turned into an intelligent and high-minded girl who renounced her sexuality and whose subsequent neurosis precluded her from marrying. While consciously unaware of her sexual impulses, unconsciously these impulses were still attached to her experiences with the caretaker's daughter. Freud observes that, owing to the higher moral and intellectual development of her ego, she came into conflict with the demands of her sexuality.

MAINTENANCE

Freud considered that neuroses are acquired only during early childhood, up to the age of six, even though the symptoms of the neurotic conflict may not appear until much later. He acknowledged the truth of the common assertion that the child is psychologically father of the man or woman. Neurotic people, despite their suffering, are unable to heal their disordered egos and thus their misery is maintained. The reason for this is that, by definition, the significant repressions made by their weak childhood egos are unconscious. Thus their egos pay the price of their defensive operations by not having conscious access to the material through which the neurotic conflict might be resolved. Neurotic people's egos are weakened by their repressions and their personality functioning is impaired by psychical energy being used in harmful defensive anti-cathexes. As long as the repressions continue, so do the conditions for the formation of neurotic symptoms through the rechannelling of frustrated libidinous impulses.

Freud (1936) also saw neurotic disturbances as being perpetuated by the primary and secondary gains that they provide. Primary gain is intrapsychic and is the main means of reinforcing or perpetuating psychological symptoms. Acknowledging the anxiety and distress caused by the symptom is more bearable than recognizing one's own forbidden wishes. Secondary gain refers to gaining the advantages of having an established symptom, for instance getting extra attention because of it.

In a broader sense, maintenance of neurosis results from the unsatisfactory way in which society tries to regulate sexual matters. Freud considered that what is described as morality, or the group super-ego, requires a bigger sacrifice of libidinal impulses than is necessary or desirable. He found it impossible to side with conventional sexual morality and considered that anyone with real self-knowledge would be protected against the dangers of morality, while possibly adopting a lifestyle different from the conventions of their society.

THERAPY

THERAPEUTIC GOALS

The goals of psychoanalysis are threefold:

1. *a less constricted id* – the freeing of impulse,
2. *a stronger ego* – the strengthening of reality-based ego functioning, including widening its perceptions so that it appropriates more of the id, and
3. *a more humane super-ego* – the alteration of the contents of the super-ego so that it represents humane rather than punitive moral standards.

A definition of a neurotic is someone who is incapable of enjoyment and efficiency. To be capable of enjoyment neurotics require the ability to deploy their libido onto real objects instead of transforming it into symptoms. To live efficiently the ego needs to have the energy of the libido at its disposal rather than wasting energy in warding off libidinous impulses through repression. Furthermore, people's super-egos need to be such as to allow them libidinal expression and the efficient use of their egos.

Freud considered psychoanalytic treatment effective for a number of nervous diseases, such as hysteria, anxiety states and obsessional neurosis. Since the alliance between the analyst and the client's ego is a mutual one, the client's ego needs to have retained a minimum degree of coherence or reality orientation. This is not to be expected with psychotics, with whom, therefore, psychoanalysis is contra-indicated.

PROCESS OF THERAPY

Freud saw the practice of psychoanalysis as having three main parts:

1. Inducing clients' weakened egos to participate in the intellectual work of interpretation to fill in the gaps of their mental resources and transfer to their analysts the authority of their super-egos,
2. Stimulating clients' egos to struggle against each of the id's demands and to defeat the resistances arising in connection with them, and
3. Restoring order to clients' egos 'by detecting material and impulses which have forced their way in from the unconscious' (Freud, 1949, p. 77). Such material is both traced back to its origin and exposed to criticism.

Psychoanalysis is a process of re-educating the ego. Repressions were instituted when clients' egos were weak. However, now not only have clients' egos grown stronger, but they possess allies in analysts. Methods by which analysts help weakened egos to lift their repressions, gain insight and make realistic decisions are discussed below. The pathogenic conflicts of neurotics are different from normal mental conflicts because of the ego's weakness relative to the other mental agencies.

Classical psychoanalytic therapy often involves at least four sessions a week with each session lasting for a minimum of 45 minutes. A course of psychoanalytic therapy may last for several years. Freud considered that ultimately the success of psychoanalysis depended upon the quantitative relationship between the amount of energy analysts can mobilize in clients to their advantage in comparison with the amount of energy of the forces working against them.

THE THERAPEUTIC RELATIONSHIP

As I write this section, I am looking at pictures of Freud's consulting rooms in Vienna and Hampstead. In each, there is a couch that has no back, but one end is raised so that the client's head may comfortably rest there. Cushions are placed at back of the couch against the wall. A middle-Eastern rug hangs on the wall just above the couch, which itself has a thick middle-Eastern cover. Freud's tub chair facing into the room is placed against the wall behind the raised part of the couch. The nature and positioning of the furniture in psychoanalysis indicates that this is going to be a relationship far removed from normal social interaction: for example, the client cannot see the therapist who, in turn, cannot directly see the client's face.

Seated behind the couch and thus physically keeping out of the way, the analyst encourages the client to say whatever comes into her or his mind without censorship. A major feature of the therapeutic relationship is the development of transference, which is discussed later.

As well as the positioning of client and therapist, a number of other features of the therapist–client relationship aim to encourage clients to reveal the intimate secrets of their minds. Therapists remain anonymous in terms of their own personal life and views. Furthermore, any form of immature personal gratification from the therapeutic relationship is forbidden; for instance, meeting the therapist's own needs for friendship and affection. In addition, confidentiality is strictly observed.

Analysts keep their relationships with clients formal. At the same time they are intensely involved with helping clients gain insight, compassionate, yet emotionally detached. As they spend long periods quietly listening, they attempt to ensure that the patient's thoughts and associations do not represent responses to external stimulation or manipulation. Much power resides with analysts who, like Freud, decide which interpretations are valid and when and how their clients are resisting the therapeutic process.

The practical aspects of the therapeutic contract are strictly regulated. For example, clients are expected to adhere to a fixed schedule of appointments and fees. However, even Freud had problems with bad debts, one of which contributed to the following slip of the tongue and possibly reveals the unconscious fulfillment of a wish. Freud reported repeatedly addressing a patient Mrs James, who was refusing to pay for her treatment, as Mrs Smith, who paid her fees promptly (Freud, 1901/1960).

THERAPEUTIC INTERVENTIONS

FREE ASSOCIATION

A basic pact lies at the heart of analytic relationships. Freud stated: 'The patient's sick ego promises us the most complete candor, … we, on the other hand, assure him of the strictest discretion and put at his service our experience in interpreting material that has been influenced by the unconscious' (1949, p. 63). The fundamental rule for clients is that of free association. Clients must tell their analysts everything that occurs to them, even if it is disagreeable or if it seems meaningless. As far as possible, clients are encouraged to put their self-criticism out of action and share all their thoughts, feelings, ideas, memories and their associations. The object of free association is to help lift repressions by making unconscious material conscious.

RESISTANCE

Free association is not really free, in that clients associate within the context of the analytic situation. Thus everything that occurs to them has some reference to that situation and they are likely to resist reproducing the repressed material. At its simplest level, resistance involves intentionally not adhering to the fundamental rule. Even if this level of resistance is overcome, resistance will find less obvious means of expression. The client's ego is fearful of potential unpleasure caused by exploring material that it has repressed in the unconscious. The ego protects itself from the repressed id by means of anti-cathexes. The more threatening the repressed material is, the more tenaciously the ego clings to its anti-cathexes, and the more remote are clients' associations from the unconscious material that their analysts seek.

Freud described all the forces that oppose the work of recovery as clients' resistances. He outlined five kinds of resistance.

1. The repression resistance described above.
2. The transference resistance mentioned next.
3. The resistance to foregoing the gain from illness.
4. The resistance of the id, which may resist a change in the direction of its satisfaction and need to 'work through' to a new mode of satisfaction.
5. The resistance, emanating from the super-ego, of the unconscious sense of guilt or need for punishment which resists any success through analysis. Clients must remain ill for they deserve no better. This is the most powerful kind of resistance and the one analysts most dread.

The struggle to overcome resistances is the main work of psychoanalysis and this part of analytic treatment cannot easily be hurried. Forces helping analysts to overcome resistances are clients' needs for recovery, any intellectual interest they may have in the analytic process and, most important, their positive transferences with their analysts.

TRANSFERENCE

From early in his career Freud attached great importance to his relationships with clients. He discovered that clients perceive their analysts as reincarnations of important figures from their childhoods and transfer onto them moderate to intense feelings and emotions appropriate to these earlier models. Freud speaks of transference-love and observes that this love is ambivalent, being a mixture of affection with a reverse side of hostility, exclusiveness and jealousy. The transference represents a development of the original neurosis into a transference neurosis in relation to the analyst.

The transference has at least three advantages.

1. It may start by being positive, which helps analysts, since their clients work to please them. The weak ego can become stronger and the client achieves gains out of love for the analyst.
2. When clients put analysts in the places of their fathers or mothers, they give them access to the power their super-egos have over their egos. Analysts as new super-egos can use their power for 'a sort of *after-education* of the neurotic' (Freud, 1949, p. 67). They can remedy earlier errors in parental education. However, analysts need always respect their clients' need for independence.
3. In the transference clients reproduce, rather than just remember, important parts of their life history. They act out, in front of their analysts, mental attitudes and defensive reactions connected with their neuroses.

Almost invariably the transference becomes negative and hostile, thus turning into a resistance. The onset of the negative transference is connected with analysts frustrating their clients by being unwilling to satisfy their erotic demands towards them. The revival of pathogenic conflicts gives analysts access to much repressed material, insight into which helps to strengthen their clients' egos. Analysis of the transference has to be continued many times and in many different ways. Working through is a process that consists of repetition, elaboration and amplification. Often the experience of successful analysis of transference stimulates recall of some important event or fantasy that in turn illuminates the nature of the transference.

Handling the transference is a critical skill of analysts, who must again and again show clients the prototype of their feelings in their childhoods. Analysts need to take care that transferences do not get out of hand. They can forewarn clients of this possibility and be alert to early signs of this happening. They can encourage clients not to act out their transferences outside of the analytic setting.

INTERPRETATION

Interpretations are constructions or explanations. They can focus both on what has happened to clients and been forgotten and on what is now happening to clients without their understanding it. Interpretation is the means by which material that is repressed and unconscious is transformed into preconscious material and consciousness.

Analysts employ interpretation not only to understand the impulses of the id, but also to help clients to gain insight into the defensive mechanisms and resistances that their egos use both to cope with the repressed material and to thwart the analytic endeavour. Part of the work of interpretation consists of filling in memory gaps. Analysts interpret the impulses that have become subject to repression and the objects to which they have become attached with the aim of helping clients to replace these repressions by acts of judgement appropriate to their present-day rather than to their childhood situations. The analyst works with the client's ego, encouraging it to overcome resistances and to take control of hitherto repressed libidinal energy. Unconscious impulses are exposed to criticism by being traced back to their origin.

The material for interpretation is obtained from a number of sources. These include the clients' free associations, parapraxes or slips of the tongue, dreams, and their transference relationships with their analysts. Analysts need to clearly distinguish between their own and their clients' knowledge. Appropriate timing of interpretations is very important, since if attempted at the wrong time, they meet with resistance. Therefore clients need to be very near to the moment of insight before analysts make interpretations. The closer interpretations are to the details of what has been forgotten, the easier it is for clients to accept them. The later stages of psychoanalysis involve a working through by repeated interpretations, and this is often the most difficult and frequently an incomplete part of analysis.

INTERPRETATION OF DREAMS

Interpreting dreams represents an important – sometimes the most important – part of the analyst's work. When Freud's clients were told to communicate to him every idea or thought that occurred in relation to a particular topic, among other things they told him their dreams. This taught Freud that 'a dream can be inserted into the psychical chain that has to be traced backwards in the memory from a pathological idea' (Freud, 1900/1976, p. 175). During sleep the ego reduces its repression and thus unconscious material becomes conscious in the shape of dreams. Freud saw dreams as wish-fulfillments, the disguised fulfillment of repressed wishes. However, even in sleep the ego still retains some censorship over repressed material and the latent dream thoughts are distorted so as to make the manifest dream content less threatening. Dreams, in fact, are compromises between repressed id impulses and the defensive operation of the ego.

The interpretation of a dream involves understanding the latent dream thoughts that are disguised by the process of dream work. Elements of dream work involve condensing the latent dream thoughts into much smaller dream content, displacing the psychical intensity between elements, and using symbolism. Frequently, symbols in dreams represent sexual material. For instance, all elongated objects, such as sticks, tree trunks, knives, daggers and umbrellas may stand for the penis. The opening of an umbrella may symbolize an erection. Boxes, cases, chests, cupboards and ovens represent the uterus. A dream of going through a suite of rooms is a brothel or harem dream. Not all dream symbols are sexual: for instance, emperors or empresses may represent parents.

Freud prepared clients in two ways for working with their dreams. First, he asked them to increase the attention that they paid to their psychical perceptions. To enhance this, it was advantageous that they 'lie in a restful attitude' (Freud, 1900/1976, p. 175). However, he soon abandoned also stressing that they needed to shut their eyes. Second, he explicitly insisted that clients abandon all criticism of the thoughts that they perceived (a feature of free association). Clients differed in the ease with which they could adopt the required mental attitude and abandon their critical functions.

Box 2.4 provides a brief illustration, taken from *The Interpretation of Dreams,* of Freud interpreting one of his own dreams (Freud, 1900/1976, pp. 180–99). Dream interpretation can be a complex, multi-layered and lengthy process. For example, Freud took about twenty pages to describe the interpretation of the dream illustrated in Box 2.4. Also, in his famous study of Dora, a case of hysteria, Freud's (1905/1963) descriptions of his interpretations of her first and second dreams take up about thirty and twenty pages respectively.

BOX 2.4   AN EXAMPLE OF DREAM INTERPRETATION

THE CONTEXT

Freud had been giving psychoanalytic treatment to Irma, a good friend of his and his family's. The treatment was partially successful in that Irma was relieved of her hysterical anxiety, but without losing all somatic symptoms. One day Freud received a visit from a junior colleague called Otto, who had been staying with Irma and her family at a country resort. Otto answered Freud's enquiry about Irma with: 'She's better, but not quite well.' Freud was annoyed with Otto's words, detecting reproof in them. That evening he wrote out Irma's case history with the idea of giving it to Dr M, a common friend.

THE DREAM

The following night or morning, Freud had a dream, which he noted down as soon as he awoke. The dream involved Irma, Otto, Dr M, and a friend called Leopold. Without going into great detail, in the dream Otto was implicated in infecting Irma by giving her an injection with a syringe that was probably unclean.

THE INTERPRETATION OF THE DREAM

The conclusion of Freud's interpretation of his dream was that, in it, he was not responsible for the persistence of Irma's present pains, rather Otto was. Freud observed of his dream: '*Thus its content was the fulfillment of a wish and its motive was a wish*' (Freud, 1900/1976, p. 196).

CASE MATERIAL

Accounts of analyses by other therapists lose the flavour of how Freud actually worked. Freud published few case studies, possibly because he feared breaking confidentiality. Those wishing to become familiar with how Freud worked are encouraged to read one of more of the following case studies.

- *Dora* was an 18-year-old woman. Freud's analysis revealed her hysterical symptoms as manifestations of repressed sexual impulses that included her homosexual love for an older admirer's wife (Freud, 1905/1963).
- *Little Hans,* five years old, feared a horse would bite him if he went out into the street. Freud helped Hans' doctor father treat him and his analysis demonstrated that Hans' fear expressed phallic phase dynamics, including the Oedipus complex and castration anxiety (Freud, 1909/1955).
- *Schreber* was an appeals court judge who wrote an account of his illness that was diagnosed as paranoia. Based only on Schreber's written account, Freud's analysis demonstrated how Schreber's paranoid delusions were related to his latent homosexuality (Freud, 1911/1958).
- *Wolf Man*, in his twenties, had contracted gonorrhoea, which in turn triggered castration anxiety. Freud analysis established the relationship between the castration anxiety and a frightening childhood dream involving wolves that followed real or imagined observation of parental sexual intercourse (Freud, 1918/1955).

FURTHER DEVELOPMENTS

CONTEMPORARY PSYCHOANALYSIS

In 1913, the British Psychoanalytic Society was founded under the leadership of Ernest Jones. The Society had three distinct groups – the Contemporary Freudians, the Kleinians and the Independents, but now the three groups are no longer formally represented within the structure of the society (Yakeley, 2014). The term contemporary Freudians was adopted some 30 years ago to reflect developments in psychoanalysis that have transpired since Freud's death. There are, however, still some psychoanalysts who practise in a more traditional Freudian style.

Within psychoanalysis as a whole, there has been the development of less intensive therapies. Many contemporary Freudians practise psychodynamic psychotherapy which 'utilizes similar techniques to psychoanalysis but sessions are less frequent, provided once or twice a week over a shorter time span, and "face to face", with the patient sitting up rather than lying on the couch, as in psychoanalysis' (Yakeley, 2014, p. 22).

What are some other features of a contemporary approach based on Freud? Freud's approach to how the mind works was deterministic in that all events were determined by a sequence of cause, nothing was accidental and links could be traced to early experiences. Contemporary Freudians, such as the Sandlers (1984), distinguish between the past unconscious, which stores non-conscious knowledge of formative interpersonal relationships and is not directly accessible in the form of autobiographical memories, and the present unconscious. The present unconscious refers to here-and-now unconscious strivings and responses and, though they are frequently subject to censorship before becoming conscious, its contents may become so. The actual experiences that contribute to the templates of our behaviour were set down very early in our lives and thought to be irretrievable.

Freud emphasized psychic determinism, a 'one-person psychology' that stressed that clients' functioning was exclusively based on intra-psychic factors contributed to by early childhood experiences. Contemporary Freudians regard a client's functioning as not completely determined by early experiences. They regard it as difficult to be very specific about the long-term consequences of childhood events. Instead, they espouse what is termed a 'two-person psychology' that reflects the importance of the attachments developed throughout life and how these contribute to changes in how clients relate based on initial family experiences.

Freud's idea of transference was that clients transfer onto the analyst feelings and attitudes that represent a repetition and displacement of feelings and reactions that related to significant figures in early childhood. Thus the transference is a repetition of earlier relationships. Contemporary Freudians acknowledge that the intensity of the therapist–client relationship arouses latent emotional experiences. However, what transpires between clients and their therapists is regarded as a new experience that has been influenced by the past rather than just a repetition of old experience. Contemporary Freudians may wait longer before interpreting the transference, waiting until the client is aware of her/his feelings towards the analyst (Yakeley, 2014).

There has also been a shift in the way counter-transference, involving the therapists' feelings about and reactions to the client, is regarded. Instead of the Freudian view that counter-transference is something that interferes with analysis, counter-transference feelings and responses by therapists can be constructively used to understand a client's unconscious communications. Thus, they can act as direct guides for analytic interpretations of current material (Lemma, 2007).

Freud viewed dream interpretation as the royal road to the unconscious (Freud, 1905/1962). Yakeley (2014) observes that dream interpretation no longer holds a central place within psychoanalytic technique today. Nevertheless contemporary Freudians still view dreams as an important way of discovering about a client's unconscious life. When working with dreams, psychoanalysts ask clients to associate hidden or latent elements of dreams so that their latent meaning can be accessed. Interpretations of dreams are based on an understanding of the meaning of clients' personal associations to them.

Contemporary Freudians believe that understanding how clients construe their early experiences, the meaning they attach to them, is more important than finding out what actually happened in the past. This is in line with contemporary research suggesting that autobiographical memory is unreliable. Thus change no longer stems from accessing repressed memories. Lemma writes: 'Rather change occurs through understanding the vicissitudes of the new relationship created between the patient and the therapist, which is informed by the past and thus gives some clues as to the model that the patient operates from' (Lemma, 2007, p. 49). Especially important in the practice of contemporary Freudian psychoanalysis is the interpretation of transference. Though there is some variation in emphasis, contemporary Freudians tend to view therapy's outcome as being related to the successful re-evaluation of patterns of relating which become accessible through the analysis and interpretation of transference phenomena.

Yakeley summarizes contemporary psychoanalysis as follows:

'Psychoanalysts today are more interested in how patients construe and ascribe meaning to their historical experiences rather then trying to reconstruct historical facts accurately. Change occurs through identifying and making explicit the patient's implicitly coded templates via understanding the new relationship formed with the analyst. … However, it is important not to neglect classical psychoanalytic techniques of reconstruction, free association and dream intrerpretation that may also contribute to change' (Yakeley, 2014, p. 38).

FREUD AS A STIMULUS TO OTHERS

It is almost impossible to grasp the extent to which psychoanalysis has changed since Freud's death in 1939 (Arlow, 2005). Even within Freud's lifetime, Jung had broken away from psychoanalysis to develop analytical therapy and Adler was developing a form of analysis based on his individual psychology. The Austrian-born Melanie Klein, who was to spend most of her professional life in Britain, developed the so-called English school of psychoanalysis. Klein's position emphasized the importance of primitive fantasies of loss (the depressive position) and persecution (the paranoid position) in the pathogenesis of mental illness (Klein, 1932, 1960). Anna Freud conducted long-term studies of childhood development and wrote *The Ego and the Mechanisms of Defence* (1936), an outstanding contribution to the psychoanalytic literature.

British psychiatrists Winnicott (1953) and Bowlby (1958) also made significant contributions underlining the importance of the child's early attachment to the mother and the emergence of a sense of self. Winnicott emphasized the continuing influence of the psychological experience of the young child at the stage where the distinction between self and object is not clearly defined and where representations of the external world for a period constitute a stage that he termed the stage of the *transitional object*. Winnicott stressed how subsequent psychological experience demonstrated the role of the transitional object.

Other psychoanalytic approaches influenced by and, in some ways stemming from Freud's work, include Sullivan's interpersonal theory of psychiatry (1953) and Fromm's socially oriented work on both psychoanalysis and on understanding society (Fromm, 1955, 1995; Funk, 2000). More recently, a separate school of analysis known as *self psychology* owes much to the work of Kohut (1971) and Goldberg (1998). The above are just some of the many people who have developed psychoanalysis.

In varying degrees Freud has influenced humanistic and existential psychologists and psychiatrists. For example, points of contact with transactional analysis include the tripartite structure of personality and the importance of early experience. Furthermore, Rogers' concept of levels of awareness resembles Freud's idea of levels of consciousness. In addition, May and Yalom's version of existential dynamics, motivated by underlying death anxiety, also originates in psychoanalysis.

Psychoanalysis, based on the Freudian model, continues to develop and evolve. One stimulus for change is that problems tend to alter with the times: for instance, hysteria and conversion symptoms are less frequent now, but there is an increase in clients suffering from masochistic character disorders and from narcissistic neuroses (Arlow, 2005). Often clients complain of inner emptiness, lack of goals, and of inability to make lasting love relationships.

More analysts are developing forms of brief psychoanalytic therapy. Reasons for brief psychoanalysis include hoped for cost-effectiveness; the fact that governments, health insurers and most private individuals cannot afford long-term therapy; and to meet the pressing need to treat more people. However, brief psychoanalytic therapy is essentially different from Freud's version of psychoanalysis described in this chapter. Group psychoanalytic therapy is also offered. However, group psychoanalysis also does not strictly follow from Freud's approach, but reflects an integration of different strands of psychoanalytic thought.

Those readers wanting contemporary information are referred to the British Psychoanalytic Society's *International Journal of Psycho-Analysis*, the *American Journal of Psychoanalysis*, the British published *Psychodynamic Counselling* and the American published *Psychoanalytic Quarterly*.

To conclude this chapter, I quote Safran and Kris' observation.

Psychoanalysis originated more than 100 years ago, and it has evolved dramatically since then. It has become more flexible, less authoritarian, more practical, and more responsive to the needs of a wider range of clients from diverse racial, cultural, and social class backgrounds. (2014, p. 50)

REVIEW AND PERSONAL QUESTIONS

REVIEW QUESTIONS

1. How did Freud view the instincts
2. Describe each of Freud's three levels of consciousness.
3. How did Freud describe the id, the ego and the super-ego and their functions?
4. Why is psychoanalysis often referred to as presenting a dynamic view of psychology?
5. Describe each stage and phase of a person's sexual development.
6. What is the function of defence mechanisms? Illustrate with specific examples.
7. Describe Freud's views on the development and maintenance of neurosis.
8. What is meant by the term resistance in psychoanalysis and why is it so important?
9. What is meant by the term transference in psychoanalysis and why is it so important?
10. Describe as best you can how Freud approached the interpretation of a dream.
11. What are some developments in psychoanalysis since Freud's death that go under the heading of contemporary psychoanalysis?

PERSONAL QUESTIONS

1. Can you think of material or events in your life that you might view as evidence for unconscious mental processes? If so, provide examples (e.g. dreams).
2. What are some of the significant influences that contributed to the formation of your super-ego? With what moral guidelines, if any, do you consider that your super-ego restricts you from the realistic pursuit of pleasure?
3. Are you aware that your ego uses defence mechanisms to ward off anxiety? If so, what are they? Do you consider that your use of defence mechanisms is normal or neurotic?
4. What do you consider the relevance of Freud's ideas on the interpretation of dreams to interpreting your own dreams?
5. What is the relevance of Freud's and the contemporary Freudians' work to understanding your life?
6. How have Freud and the contemporary Freudians influenced the way you think about and practise counselling and therapy?

ANNOTATED BIBLIOGRAPHY

Freud, S. (1900/1976) *The Interpretation of Dreams*. Harmondsworth, Middlesex: Penguin Books.
This book is Freud's major work. In it he reviews the scientific literature about dreams, demonstrates his method of interpreting dreams, and discusses dreams

as fulfillments of wishes, distortion in dreams, the material and sources of dreams, dream-work, and the psychology of the dream process. The present translation is based on the reprint of the eighth edition (1930), the last published during Freud's life.

Freud, S. (1905/1962) *Three Contributions to the Theory of Sex*. New York: E. P. Dutton.
This book is Freud's major statement on the nature and development of human sexuality. The three contributions are entitled: the sexual aberrations, infantile sexuality, and the transformations of puberty. Apart from *The Interpretation of Dreams*, this was the only other book that Freud kept more or less systematically up to date.

Freud, S. (1949) *An Outline of Psychoanalysis*. New York: W. W. Norton. Originally published posthumously in 1940.
Written just before Freud's death, this book provides an excellent concise introduction to psychoanalysis. The book consists of three parts: the mind and its workings, the practical task, and the theoretical yield.

Jones, E. (1963) *The Life and Work of Sigmund Freud*. Edited and abridged in one volume by Lionel Trilling and Steven Marcus. New York: Anchor Books. Also available in a Penguin edition.
Written in three volumes by a close associate, this book is the definitive biography of Freud. It records the main facts of Freud's life and relates his personality and life experiences to the development of his ideas. In addition, the book traces the history of the psychoanalytic movement during Freud's lifetime.

Yakeley, J. (2014) Psychodynamic therapy: Contemporary Freudian approach. In W. Dryden and A. Reeves (eds) *The Handbook of Individual Therapy* (6th ed.). London: Sage, pp. 21–47.
An introduction to more recent developments in Freudian psychoanalysis.

REFERENCES AND FURTHER READING

Arlow, J. A. (2005) Psychoanalysis. In R. J. Corsini and D. Wedding (eds) *Current Psychotherapies* (7th ed.). Belmont, CA: Thomson Brooks/Cole, pp. 15–51.
Bowlby, J. (1958) The nature of the child's ties to the mother. *International Journal of Psychoanalysis*. 52, 137–44.
Freud, A. (1936) *The Ego and the Mechanisms of Defence*. London: Karnac.
Freud, S. (1900/1976) *The Interpretation of Dreams*. Harmondsworth, Middlesex: Penguin Books.
Freud, S. (1901/1960) *Psychopathology of Everyday Life*. London: Hogarth Press.
Freud, S. (1905/1962) *Three Contributions to the Theory of Sex*. New York: E. P. Dutton.

Freud, S. (1905/1963) *Dora: An Analysis of a Case of Hysteria*. New York: Collier Books.

Freud, S. (1909/1955) 'Analysis of a phobia in a five-year-old boy', in S. Freud, *Standard Edition of the Complete Works of Sigmund Freud* (Vol. 10). London: Hogarth Press.

Freud, S. (1911/1958) 'Psycho-analytic notes on an autobiographical account of a case of paranoia (dementia paranoides)', in S. Freud, *Standard Edition of the Complete Works of Sigmund Freud* (Vol. 12). London: Hogarth Press.

Freud, S. (1918/1955) 'From the history of an infantile neurosis', in S. Freud, *Standard Edition of the Complete Works of Sigmund Freud* (Vol. 17). London: Hogarth Press.

Freud, S. (1920/1961) *Beyond the Pleasure Principle*. London: Hogarth Press

Freud, S. (1921/1959) *Group Psychology and the Analysis of the Ego*. London: Hogarth Press.

Freud, S. (1923/1962) *The Ego and the Id*. London: Hogarth Press.

Freud, S. (1926/1964) *The Question of Lay Analysis*. New York: Anchor Books.

Freud, S. (1930/1962) *Civilization and its Discontents*. New York: W. W. Norton.

Freud, S. (1932/1973) *New Introductory Lectures on Psychoanalysis*. Harmondsworth, Middlesex: Penguin Books.

Freud, S. (1935) *An Autobiographical Study*. London: Hogarth Press.

Freud, S. (1936) *The Problem of Anxiety*. New York: W. W. Norton. Originally published in 1926 under the title *Inhibitions, Symptoms and Anxiety*.

Freud, S. (1937/1950) 'Analysis terminable and interminable', in S. Freud, *Collected Papers* (Vol. 5). London: Hogarth Press.

Freud, S. (1949) *An Outline of Psychoanalysis*. New York: W. W. Norton. Originally published posthumously in 1940.

Freud, S (1953–73) *Standard Edition of the Complete Works of Sigmund Freud*. London: Hogarth Press.

Freud, S. and Breuer, J. (1895/1956) *Studies on Hysteria*. London: Hogarth Press.

Fromm, E. (1955) *The Sane Society*. New York: Holt Rinehart and Winston.

Fromm, E. (1959) *Sigmund Freud's Mission*. London: George Allen and Unwin.

Fromm, E. (1995) *The Essential Fromm: Life Between Having and Being*. London: Constable.

Funk, R. (2000) *Erich Fromm: His Life and Ideas*. London: Continuum.

Goldberg, A. (1998) Self-psychology since Kohut. *Psychoanalytic Quarterly, 67,* 240–55.

Jones, E. (1963) *The Life and Work of Sigmund Freud*. Edited and abridged in one volume by Lionel Trilling and Steven Marcus. New York: Anchor Books. Also available in a Penguin edition.

Klein, M. (1932) *The Psychoanalysis of Children*. London: Hogarth Press.

Klein, M. (1960) *Our Adult World and Its Roots in Infancy*. London: Tavistock.

Kohut, H. (1971) *The Analysis of the Self. Monograph Series of the Psychoanalytic Study of the Child (No. 4)*. New York: International Universities Press.

Lemma, A. (2007) Psychodynamic therapy: The Freudian approach. In W. Dryden (ed.), *Dryden's Handbook of Individual Therapy* (5th ed.). London: Sage, pp. 27–55.

Luborsky, E. B., O'Reilly-Landry, M. and Arlow, J. A. (2008) Psychoanalysis. In R. J. Corsini and D. Wedding (eds) *Current Psychotherapies* (8th ed.). Belmont, CA: Thomson Brooks/Cole, pp. 15–62.

Safran, J. D. and Kris, A. (2014) Psychoanalytic psychotherapies. In D. Wedding and R. J. Corsini (eds) *Current Psychotherapies* (10th ed.). Belmont, CA: Brooks/Cole, pp. 19–54.

Sandler, J. and Sandler, A. M. (1984) The past unconscious, the present unconscious: An interpretation of the transference. *Psychonalytic Enquiry, 4,* 367–99.

Sullivan, H. S. (1953) *The Interpersonal Theory of Psychiatry.* New York: W. W. Norton.

Winnicott, D. W. (1953) Transitional objects and transitional phenomena: A study of the first not–me possession. *International Journal of Psychoanalysis, 34,* 89–97.

Yakeley, J. (2014) Psychodynamic therapy: Contemporary Freudian approach. In W. Dryden and A. Reeves (eds), *The Handbook of Individual Therapy* (6th ed.). London: Sage, pp. 21–47.

JUNG'S ANALYTICAL THERAPY 3

INTRODUCTION

The main part of this chapter is devoted to describing Jung's analytical therapy. However the chapter concludes by discussing further developments in treatment, including different ways of working such as group therapy.

CARL GUSTAV JUNG (1875–1961)

In July 1875, Carl Gustav Jung was born in Kesswil, a small village by Lake Constance in northeast Switzerland, the only surviving son of his parents who had lost two previous boys in infancy. Jung was named after his paternal grandfather who, in 1822, had moved from Germany to become professor of surgery at the University of Basel. Jung's father was a Swiss Reform Church pastor and his mother was the daughter of a well-established Basel family. When Jung was nine, the family was completed by the birth of his sister.

Jung was an introverted, sensitive, solitary and lonely child. His parents, Paul and Emilie had a troubled marriage and, in 1878, they separated temporarily and his mother spent some time in a mental hospital. During his childhood Jung suffered from his mother's depressive invalidism and critical tongue. However, he also admired his mother and could enjoy her companionship and cooking. Jung had to contend with his father's irritability, partly connected with his agonizing over his religious faith. Nevertheless in the autobiography compiled at the end of his life Jung refers to his 'dear and generous father', who never tyrannized over him (Jung, 1961).

The earliest dream Jung remembered was when he was between three and four. He had a rich inner life of dreams, fantasies and thoughts about the world. Aged ten, at the end of a ruler Jung carved a manikin about two inches long with frock coat, top hat, and shiny black boots. He placed the manikin and an oblong blackish stone from the Rhine in a case and took it to the attic. Whenever Jung felt hurt or stressed he would think of the manikin and, from time to time, visit it in the forbidden attic. Jung regarded this manikin episode, which lasted about a year, as the conclusion of his childhood.

In 1879, the Jungs had moved to Klein Hunigen, near Basel. Age six Jung went to the local school and, at age eleven, he was uprooted from his rustic schoolmates and sent to the Gymnasium at Basel. Jung hated mathematics, was exempted from drawing on the grounds of incapacity, and also loathed gymnastics. Regarding mathematics he writes: 'But my fear of failure and sense of smallness in face of the vast world around me created in me not only a dislike, but a kind of silent despair which completely ruined school for me' (Jung, 1961, p. 45). For a time Jung suffered from fainting spells connected with school. He also saw himself as being two persons: a schoolboy who was less intelligent, hard-working and decent than many other boys and an old man mistrustful of humans but close to nature, to dreams and to whatever God worked through him.

In reality, Jung was a highly intelligent student who, in 1895 passed his final examinations at the Gymnasium and entered the University of Basel Medical School. During medical school Jung suffered from financial worries, partly stemming from the death of his father in 1896. In 1900, he graduated equal first in his medical school class. His medical school thesis was on the psychological foundations of the occult. Jung chose to specialize in psychiatry, which provided a bridge between his scientific, humanities and psychological interests.

Shortly after graduation, he accepted a post at the Burgholzli Mental Hospital in Zurich. The Burgholzli's director was Eugen Bleuler, an expert on schizophrenia, whose influence Jung valued. In 1902, he spent several months studying at the Salpetriere Hospital in Paris with the famous psychiatrist, Pierre Janet. In 1905, in addition to his work at the Burgholzli, he became lecturer in psychiatry at the University of Zurich and senior physician at the psychiatric clinic. He continued to lecture there until 1913. At the Burgholzli, as well as working with patients, Jung conducted research on word associations and the underlying psychological complexes indicated by how people responded. He also had a private practice that became so successful that, in 1909, he resigned from the Burgholzli. As mentioned, Jung also developed a relationship with Freud and became prominent in the psychoanalytic movement.

In 1907, Jung had travelled to Vienna to meet with Freud. Though initially the two seemed to have much in common, by 1912 the strains between them became insurmountable and the relationship came to a mutually painful and bitter end (Safran and Kris, 2014).

After his break with Freud, Jung went through a profound mid-life crisis which lasted from 1913 to 1918, and which took him to the edge of insanity. During much of this period of inner uncertainty and disorientation, he continued seeing patients, lived a normal family life, and did his Swiss military service. He developed his ideas of the collective unconscious during this period of confrontation with his own unconscious. He writes:

> The years when I was pursuing my inner images were the most important in my life – in them everything essential was decided. It all began then; the later details are only supplements and clarifications of the material that burst forth from the unconscious, and at first swamped me. It was the *prima materia* for a lifetime's work.' (Jung, 1961, p. 225)

Jung was fond of women, who played a crucial role throughout his life. In 1903 he had married the extremely wealthy Emma Rauschenbach. Under Swiss law at the time Emma married Jung, husbands had complete access to their wive's money and could spend it as they wished without consent. In short, though Jung was always a hard worker, he was financially set up for life independent of his own endeavours.

Despite his wife's disapproval of his behaviour and his growing family, Jung was sexually attracted to other women, allegedly extending to intimate relationships with one or more of his patients, for example Sabina Spielrein, though this has never been evidentially corroborated. An ex-patient, Toni Wolff, was able to be of special comfort to him during his near psychotic period so much so that, in 1916, Jung persuaded Emma to accept her as part of a permanent domestic threesome. Probably Jung abandoned his philandering at this stage. He encouraged Emma to become a Jungian therapist and, eventually, Toni became one too.

After Jung returned to feeling more normal, there were a number of ongoing and interweaving strands in his life. At his beautiful home by Lake Zurich, though not the warmest and most present of fathers, Jung engaged in family activities with his wife, four daughters and a son. In 1922, he bought some land at Bollingen, at the upper end of Lake Zurich and, over the next thirty or so years, developed the 'Tower', a house he built for himself as a retreat from his family. While the family home was the territory of his wife, the only person Jung allowed to stay at Bollingen was Toni Wolff and, in later years, a companion-housekeeper.

Jung continued his large private practice, which he regarded as a valuable source of information for understanding the psyche. Most of Jung's clients were women, almost all were reasonably well off, and a minority were fabulously wealthy Americans, for instance one of John D. Rockefeller's daughters and a member of the Mellon banking family. Jung also continued his own inner journey, analysing his dreams, fantasies and visions.

Jung engaged in wide-ranging scholarly activities. His *The Red Book* (Shamdasani, 2009), produced over a period of sixteen years from 1914 to 1930, is where he developed his concepts of individuation and the self. In 1921, Jung published a large work on psychological types. As well as reading widely in philosophy, world literature, mythology, and astrology, he became increasingly interested in alchemy. He also conducted what might be called fieldwork, by visiting North Africa, Kenya and Uganda, the Pueblo Indians in North America, and India. Jung was immensely interested in the presence and universality of myths and symbols across cultures and in primitive as well as civilized cultures. Based on his scholarly researches, field trips, wide reading and professional and personal experiences, right up to his death Jung was a prolific author across a range of subjects including psychiatry and psychology, parapsychology, alchemy and religion.

Jung lectured extensively not only in the Germanic, but in the English-speaking world. In 1909 he had gone with Freud to Clark University in Massachusetts, where both men received honorary doctorates, and he was to return to America repeatedly in the following thirty years. Jung was also an Anglophile and visited England many times, for example giving a notable series of lectures at the Tavistock Clinic in 1935. His honorary doctorates included those from Harvard and Oxford Universities. In addition, from the early 1930s, Jung regularly attended the annual Eranos conferences on Jungian studies. At these conferences, held on the estate at the northern end of Lake Maggiore, Italy, of a wealthy woman who had built a conference hall especially for them, Jung tended to be lionized by the mostly female participants.

Intimations of Jung's mortality included a severe heart attack in 1944, the death of Toni Wolff in 1953, and his wife's death in 1955. Jung's companion-housekeeper during his final years was Ruth Bailey, an Englishwoman. On June 6, 1961, Jung died after a brief illness.

It is tempting when looking at pictures of Jung to view him as a gentle, spiritual, scholarly sage full of the milk of human kindness. Undoubtedly, Jung had many attractive features as well as a charismatic personality, especially for women. However, he was not without his shadow aspects. For various reasons, he strongly favoured the death penalty. Possibly somewhat anti-Semitic, Jung has been criticized for not speaking out loudly enough against the rise of Nazism. He could be domineering and hectoring at professional meetings and a domestic tyrant at home. He could also be a bile-laden person and his relationship with Freud became particularly bitter. In addition, he had been a philandering husband, conceivably including some clients among his lovers, though there is no real proof of this.

Like Freud, Jung was an ideas man with an amazing breadth of vision. Some of his ideas have stood the test of time in terms of becoming part of Western psychological consciousness, for example the concepts of the collective unconscious and extraversion/introversion. In addition, Jung was the founder of an analytical approach to therapy that still claims many adherents.

THEORY

BASIC CONCEPTS

Psychology is first the science of consciousness and then the science of the products of the unconscious psyche. Jung used the term psyche to refer to the mind or soul. He distinguished between three psychic levels of consciousness. In addition, his was a dynamic psychology that paid attention to the distribution of psychic energy between the different psychic levels. Furthermore, Jung presented a typology of different personality types.

STRUCTURE OF THE PSYCHE

Jung goes beyond distinguishing consciousness from unconsciousness to divide the latter into its personal and collective elements. Thus, the psyche's three levels are:

(1) consciousness, (2) the personal unconscious, and (3) the collective unconscious. Though Jung did not wish to push the analogy too far, he saw consciousness like an island arising out of a vast sea of unconsciousness.

CONSCIOUSNESS

Jung observes: '... the child develops out of an originally unconscious, animal condition into consciousness, primitive at first, and then slowly becoming more civilized' (Jung, 1981, p. 53). Consciousness is an intermittent phenomenon since people enter the unconscious every time they go to sleep. The conscious mind is narrow since it can only hold a few simultaneous contents at a given moment. Furthermore, consciousness is transitory and people can only get an awareness of the external world through a succession of conscious moments.

The *ego* is the indispensable centre of a person's consciousness. Sometimes Jung refers to it as the ego-complex. The ego gives a person a sense of identity and continuity and it has both external and internal tasks. Its external task is to provide a system of relationship between consciousness and the facts and data coming from the environment. Sensation, thinking, feeling and intuition are four functions by means of which it performs its ecto-psychic task. The ego's internal task is to provide a system of relationship between the contents of consciousness and the processes of the unconscious. Jung states: 'The ego is only a bit of consciousness that floats on an ocean of dark things. The dark things are the inner things' (1968, p. 21).

THE PERSONAL UNCONSCIOUS

The contents of the personal unconscious are definitely of a personal origin. These contents fall into two main categories. First, there is material that lost its intensity because it was either forgotten or repressed. Second, there is material that never possessed sufficient intensity to reach consciousness but has some-how entered the psyche: for instance, some sense-impressions. There is nothing peculiar about the contents of the personal unconscious and its contents might just as well be conscious. People differ in regard to the contents of their personal unconscious – some are conscious of things that others are not.

Complexes are an important feature of the personal unconscious. Jung discovered the complex through his research on word associations, finding that complexes disturbed memory and produced blockages in the flow of associations. Complexes are accumulations of associations, sometimes of a traumatic nature, that possess strong emotional content. They are energy-filled constellations of psychic elements that have an archetypal core and erupt into consciousness, often in an autonomous way (Douglas, 2008).

The mother complex is an example of a complex. Jung considered that 'the mother always plays an active part in the origin of the disturbance, especially in infantile neuroses or in neuroses whose aetiology undoubtedly dates back to early childhood' (Jung, 1982, p. 113). Typical effects of the mother complex on the son are homosexuality, Don Juanism and, sometimes, impotence. In daughters the mother complex can lead to an exaggeration of the feminine side of personality or its neglect. Other examples of complexes include those connected with inferiority, sex, aesthetic beauty and money.

THE COLLECTIVE UNCONSCIOUS

Unlike Freud, who saw the unconscious as a receptacle for things that were repressed, Jung considered the deeper layers of the unconscious lose their uniqueness as they retreat further and further from consciousness. At its deepest levels the unconscious is a vast collective and universal historical storehouse whose contents belong to mankind in general. While the contents of the personal unconscious owe their existence to personal experience, the contents of the collective unconscious have never been in consciousness, but owe their existence to heredity.

Archetypes are inborn possibilities or patterns for representation. Jung borrowed the term archetype from St Augustine. He observes: 'Whereas the personal unconscious consists for the most part of *complexes*, the content of the collective unconscious is made up essentially of *archetypes*' (Jung, 1976a, p. 60). Similar to instinctive patterns for action, archetypes provide instinctive patterns for mental activity. Archetypes are 'primordial images' and 'primordial thoughts' rather than the representations of the images or thoughts themselves. For example, well known motifs appear in myths, fairy tales, legends and folklore across a range of cultures and historical periods. Such motifs include the hero, the redeemer, the dragon, the mother, the wise old man and the descent into the cave. Archetypes are evolutionary predispositions or potentials for such motifs rather than the forms in which the contents become expressed.

Symbols are the images by means of which archetypes are expressed. Jung distinguished between a sign and a symbol. If the image denotes a known thing it is a sign. A symbol is an intuitive way of knowing the not fully knowable. Symbolic images express the best possible formulation of a relatively unknown thing, which for that reason cannot be more clearly or characteristically represented. For example, a triangle with a bare eye enclosed in it is so meaningless that it conjures up a symbolic interpretation.

Archetypes important in shaping the development of personality include the persona, the anima and animus, the shadow and the self.

The persona The persona is a concept derived from the mask worn by actors in antiquity. At one level, the persona is the individual's system of adaptation or way of coping with the world. At a different level, the persona is not just an individual mask, but a mask of the collective psyche, 'a mask that *feigns individuality*, making others and oneself believe that one is an individual, whereas one is simply acting out a role through which the collective psyche speaks' (Jung, 1976b, p. 105).

The persona exists for reasons of personal convenience, but should not be confused with genuine individuality. The persona is exclusively concerned with relation to outer objects, an outer attitude. This outer attitude must be distinguished from an inner attitude, which is the relation to the subject or 'inner object' that is the unconscious.

In reality, individuals may have more than one persona, for example wearing different masks at work and home. Furthermore, each profession has its own characteristic persona. However, there is a danger that people become identified with their personas, for instance the professor with his textbook. Too rigid adherence to a persona can lead people to become alienated from the 'subject', the stirrings, feelings, thoughts and sensations that well up from their unconscious. Identifications with social roles are often fruitful sources of neuroses. Jung regarded it as essential for individuals to be able to distinguish themselves from their personas.

The anima and the animus People are psychologically bisexual. In individuals, the smaller number of opposite sex genes appears to produce a corresponding opposite sex character, which usually remains unconscious. The anima is the personification of the feminine nature in a man's unconscious, whereas the animus is the personification of the masculine nature in a woman's unconscious. Every man or woman carries within themselves an imprint or archetype of all the ancestral experiences of the opposite sex.

Jung thought that in its primary form the animus is composed of spontaneous, unpremeditated opinions that exercise a powerful influence on the woman's emotional life. Similarly, the anima is composed of feelings that thereafter distort and influence a man's understanding. He wrote: 'as the anima produces *moods*, so the animus produces *opinions*; and as the moods of a man issue from a shadowy background, so the opinions of a woman rest on equally unconscious prior assumptions' (Jung, 1982, pp. 95–6). Jung stressed the importance of people acknowledging their distinction, not only from their persona but from their anima or animus as well. The animus and anima should function as a bridge leading to the images of the collective unconscious. Both men and women should learn to acknowledge and appropriately express the opposite sex characteristics of their personalities and avoid falsely projecting them onto others.

The shadow The shadow archetype reflects the realm of humankind's animal ancestors and, as such, comprises the whole historical aspect of the unconscious. For the most part, the shadow consists of inferior traits of personality that individuals refuse to acknowledge. Though Jung emphasized the darker aspects of the shadow, he acknowledged that it also displayed some good qualities, such as normal instincts, appropriate reactions, realistic insights and creative impulses. The shadow is compensatory to consciousness and its effects can be positive as well as negative.

In general people do not like looking at the shadow-side of themselves. However, with insight and goodwill, much of the shadow can be assimilated into the conscious personality without too much difficulty. Nevertheless, there are some unconscious projections from the shadow whose recognition meets the most obstinate resistance and thus prove almost impossible to influence. As a result, the shadow is not, with time, fully assimilated.

The self The self is the central archetype, the archetype of order. The self, expressing the unity of personality as a whole, encompasses both conscious and unconscious components. The self is a super-ordinate construct to the ego that is restricted to being the focal point of the conscious mind. The ego is related to the self like a part to the whole. Jung considered that there was little hope of ever being able to reach even approximate consciousness of the self, given the huge and indeterminate amount of unconscious material that belongs to it.

The main symbol for the unity of the self archetype is the mandala. The word mandala (Sanskrit for 'circle') is a circular form that often contains a quaternity, symmetrical arrangements of the number four and its multiples. The self also appears in dreams, myths and fairytales in the figure of a super-ordinate personality, such as a king, hero, prophet or saviour.

DYNAMICS OF THE PSYCHE

Psychodynamics refers to the activity and interrelation of the various parts of an individual's personality or psyche. More specifically, psychodynamics entail the generation and transfer of energy within the structure of the psyche. Jung's ideas on psychodynamics were influenced by his interest in and knowledge of physics, the branch of science dealing with the properties and interactions of matter and energy.

PSYCHIC ENERGY

Jung emphasized the concept of psychic energy, sometimes referred to as libido, as the psychic analogue of physical energy. All the instincts, including hunger, sex and aggression, are expressions of psychic energy. In physics there are different manifestations of energy, such as electricity, heat and light. The same situation occurs in psychology where energy can appear in various guises. Psychic energy is also provided from the external environment by way of one's senses and feelings. The psyche is a relatively closed energy system. Psychic energy derived from both internal and external sources is continually being shifted and redistributed among the structures of the psyche.

A psychic value is the amount of energy invested in a particular psychic element. When a person places a high value on something, such as an idea or feeling, this means that the idea or feeling exerts a particularly strong influence on them. Complexes, which by definition are strongly emotionally toned, are examples of mental elements with high psychic value.

OPPOSITION

Jung (1961) observed: 'Among other things, the psyche appears as a dynamic process which rests on a foundation of antithesis, on a flow of energy between two poles' (p. 383). Just as in physics all energy proceeds from opposition, so the psyche possesses an inner polarity that is an essential prerequisite for its aliveness. Tension and conflict arising from the clash of opposites are central to Jungian personality dynamics. Consciousness opposes unconsciousness, feminine opposes masculine, ego opposes shadow, and positive aspects of archetypal images oppose their negative elements.

COMPENSATION

The function of compensation is to balance or adjust the energy distributed throughout the psyche. Compensation, for the most part, is an unconscious process that entails an inherent self-regulation of the psychic apparatus. The activity of the unconscious balances the one-sidedness produced by consciousness. Consciousness, because of its selectiveness and need for focus, is bound to become one-sided. As consciousness becomes more and more one-sided, the more antagonistic are the contents arising from the unconscious, so that there is a real opposition between the two. For the most part, unconscious compensation balances rather than opposes consciousness. For example, in dreams the unconscious supplies 'all those contents that are constellated by the conscious situation but are inhibited by conscious selection, although a knowledge of them would be indispensable for complete adaptation' (Jung, 1971, p. 420).

BREAKTHROUGH OF UNCONSCIOUS CONTENT

The energy of all unconscious contents, once they are activated, is normally insufficient to propel their content into consciousness. A lowering of energy in the conscious mind that allows unconscious material to break through into consciousness may come about in two ways. First, there may be a malfunctioning of the conscious mind. Just as 'primitive' people can suffer from loss of soul, so can 'civilized' people suffer from loss of initiative for no apparent reason. Carelessness, neglected duties, willful outbursts of defiance can dam up energy so that certain quanta of it, no longer finding a conscious outlet, stream off into the unconscious. Here they activate other compensating contents, which can in turn start exerting a compulsive influence on the conscious mind. Jung (1966) illustrates this point with the common example of extreme neglect of duty combined with a compulsion neurosis.

   The second way in which a loss of energy to the conscious mind may come about is through a 'spontaneous' activation of unconscious contents, which then react upon consciousness. During the incubation period of changes in personality, the new development draws off the loss of energy it needs from consciousness. For example, lowering of energy from the conscious mind takes place before the onset of psychosis and a fallow and quiet period precedes creative work. Jung (1966) observed: 'The remarkable potency of unconscious contents, therefore, always indicates a corresponding weakness in the conscious mind and its functions' (p. 181). In the near psychotic period of his life,

Jung himself had to struggle with the heightened energy of his unconscious contents in relation to his conscious ego.

THE TRANSCENDENT FUNCTION

The transcendent function is a psychological function similar to a mathematical function of the same name, which is a function of real and imaginary numbers. In face of the disturbing energy of the unconscious, Jung postulates a synthesizing process, the transcendent function, which can get rid of some of the separation between consciousness and unconsciousness.

The transcendent function is both a process and a method. Jung postulated that there are certain spontaneous *processes* in the unconscious that, by virtue of their symbolism, can compensate the defects in the conscious mind. In turn these reactions, usually manifested in dreams, are brought to conscious realization through the analytical *method* (Jung, 1971).

The confrontation of two opposed positions can generate a tension charged with energy which creates a living, third thing. Jung talked about the transcendent function manifesting itself as 'a movement out of the suspension between opposites, a living birth that leads to a new level of being, a new situation. The transcendent function manifests itself as a quality of conjoined opposites' (1976c, p. 298). By means of the transcendent function, consciousness is widened through the confrontation with previously unconscious contents.

The transcendent function is the means by which progress is made toward realizing the unfolding of the individual's original potential for wholeness. However, attaining integration at a new level of consciousness by means of the transcendent function does not always take place. Apart from insufficient skills on the part of therapists, there are many reasons why the synthesizing of opposites to create a new way of being may not take place. These reasons include people having insufficient intelligence to understand the procedure, lacking self-confidence, and being mentally and morally too lazy.

PSYCHOLOGICAL TYPES

In 1921, Jung published his famous work entitled *Psychological Types*. Here he distinguished between attitude-types, based on the habitual direction of an individual's interests, and function-types, based on the individual's most differentiated function of psychological adaptation. For simplicity, here these are called attitudes and functions.

ATTITUDES: INTROVERSION AND EXTRAVERSION

The *introvert's* predominant, but not exclusive, conscious attitude is one in which the main interest is the withdrawal of psychic energy from the object as though to prevent the object from gaining power over her or him. The introvert thinks, feels and acts as though the subjective is what is most important and the object is of secondary importance. The introverted attitude type is characterized by an orientation in life that particularly values subjective psychic contents. Introverts tend to be reserved, inscrutable and rather shy people.

The *extravert's* predominant, but not exclusive, conscious attitude is characterized by concentration of interest on the external object. The extravert thinks, feels and acts as though the object were of most importance. This is done so directly and clearly that no doubt can remain about his or her dependence on the object. Extraverts tend to be open, friendly and sociable or they may quarrel with everybody. Nevertheless extraverts always relate to people in some way and in turn are affected by them.

In sum, introversion is characterized by interest in one's internal world and extraversion is characterized by interest in the external world. However matters are not that simple, since a conscious extraverted attitude is compensated by an unconscious introverted attitude and a conscious introverted attitude is compensated by an extraverted unconscious attitude.

FUNCTIONS: THINKING, FEELING, SENSATION AND INTUITION

The four psychological functions are thinking, feeling, sensation and intuition. As a rule one function predominates.

The *thinking* individual is mainly governed by reflective thinking so that important actions proceed, or are intended to proceed, from intellectually considered motives. The *feeling* individual is mainly governed by values placed on things arising from feelings. Here Jung is regarding feeling as an evaluative function. Thinking and feeling individuals are *rational* types because they are characterized by the primacy of the reasoning and judging functions.

The *sensation* individual is mainly governed by their awareness of external facts provided through the function of the senses: seeing, hearing, touching, tasting and smelling. The *intuition* individual is mainly governed by hunches and insights. Intuition is a predominantly unconscious process. The conscious aspect of intuition is to transmit images or perceptions of relations between things that could not be transmitted by the other functions. Sensation and intuition individuals are *irrational* types because their actions are based on the sheer intensity of perception rather than on any rational judgement.

COMBINING ATTITUDES AND FUNCTIONS TO FORM PSYCHOLOGICAL TYPES

Jung combined attitudes and functions to provide eight main psychological types (see Box 3.1). Though one main attitude and one main function combine in each individual, people categorized within the eight psychological types vary. Furthermore, the other attitudes and functions are always part of someone's personality.

BOX 3.1   JUNG'S PSYCHOLOGICAL TYPES

Following are brief descriptions of each of the eight main psychological types.

- *Extraverted-thinking type:* This type makes all activities dependent on intellectual functioning oriented to objective data in the form of external facts or generally accepted ideas. Jung cites the scientist Charles Darwin as an example.
- *Introverted-thinking type:* This type makes all activities dependent on intellectual functioning oriented to subjective data. Jung cites the philosopher Immanuel Kant as an example.
- *Extraverted-feeling type:* This type consists almost exclusively of women who are guided by feelings that appear adjusted to harmonize with objective situations and general values: for instance, the love choice of a 'suitable' man
- *Introverted-feeling type:* This type is predominantly guided by subjective feelings and their true motives generally remain hidden. This type mainly consists of women of whom it may be said 'still waters run deep'.
- *Extraverted-sensation type:* This type consists mainly of men for whom anything new that comes within their range of interest is acquired by way of sensations received from the outside. Guided by the intensity of objective influences, this type encompasses the grossly sensual and those whose sensations are aesthetically highly developed.
- *Introverted-sensation type:* This type is guided by the intensity of the subjective sensation. No proportional relationship exists between object and sensation, but one that is unpredictable and arbitrary.
- *Extraverted-intuition type:* For this type intuition as the function of unconscious perception is directed wholly to external objects. This type uses intuition to apprehend the widest range of possibilities in objective situations and to discover what they hold in store.
- *Introverted-intuition type:* The peculiar intuition of this type produces mystical dreamers, seers, artists and cranks. The intensification of intuition may lead this type to be out of touch with tangible reality and to experience difficulty in communicating to others.

ACQUISITION

Jung never developed a rigorous elaboration of the development of the psyche and of human behaviour. A possible reason for this is that he was more interested in researching and understanding the collective unconscious, which he perceived as the inherited foundation of psychological life.

STAGES OF LIFE

To Jung the arc of life has four stages: childhood, youth, middle age and extreme old age (Jung, 1989). He was particularly interested in the problems of middle age.

CHILDHOOD (BIRTH TO PUBERTY)

Jung likened children, during the first two or three years of life when they are unconscious of themselves, to being in an animal state. In early infancy the psyche is to a large extent the maternal psyche and soon comprises the paternal psyche as well. Gradually the ego develops as the organizing centre for the child's psychic processes and only when children begin to say 'I' is there any perceptible continuity of consciousness. The conscious mind progressively arises out of the unconscious as fragments of the unconscious are added to consciousness and separated from their previous source in the unconscious (Jung, 1981).

Jung saw the origins of childhood neuroses mainly as symptoms of the mental conditions of parents. He wrote:

> The child is hopelessly exposed to the psychic influence of the parents and is bound to copy their self-deception, their insincerity, their hypocrisy, cowardice, self-righteousness, and selfish regard for their own comfort, just as wax takes up the imprint of the seal. (Jung 1981, p. 79)

Jung did not expect parents to commit no faults, but to recognize them for what they were, thus creating a more honest psychological atmosphere for their children.

YOUTH (PUBERTY TO 35–40 YEARS)

The human mind's growth keeps pace with a widening range of consciousness and each step forward can be an extremely painful and laborious achievement. During youth the demands of life put an end to childhood, for example the transitions to marriage and a career. In addition, young people may experience inner psychic difficulties concerned with the sexual instinct or feelings of inferiority. The essential feature of the problems of youth is a clinging to the childhood level of consciousness. Achievement, usefulness and getting established are ways of proceeding out from the problems of the period of youth. People can adapt what they have been given from the past to the possibilities and demands of the future.

MIDDLE AGE (35–40 TO EXTREME OLD AGE)

Jung used the analogy of the sun that rises to a peak in the first part of the day and then descends and in the process illuminates itself. Likewise human life does not inexorably expand, but there is an inexorable and deep-seated shift in the psyche towards contraction with the possibility of self-illumination. While the tasks of the first half of life concern the individual's development and entrenchment in the outer world, the tasks of the second half of life are for people to devote serious attention to understanding and developing themselves more fully. Just as neurotic problems in youth sprung from people not escaping from their childhood, so neurotic problems in middle age can spring from people not escaping from their youth. Jung did not regard this psychological shrinking from approaching old age to be caused by fear of death, rather than from a basic change in the human psyche that takes place around that time. Middle age is a time for contemplation, self-realization and learning to live more in harmony with primordial images and symbols.

EXTREME OLD AGE

Though childhood and extreme old age are utterly different, Jung regarded them as having one thing in common: submersion into unconscious psychic happenings. The child's mind and ego grow out of unconsciousness. The very old person sinks again into unconsciousness and progressively vanishes within it. Jung viewed childhood and extreme old age as being stages of life without any conscious problems and, hence, they were not his major focus.

PROGRESSION AND REGRESSION

Life requires an ongoing process of psychological adaptation to the reality of the environment. Progression and regression are two important uses of psychic energy. *Progression* is 'the daily advance of the process of psychological adaptation ... a continual satisfaction of the demands of environmental conditions' (Jung, 1983, p. 59). In progression, the psychic value of conscious and unconscious opposites become balanced through regular interaction and mutual influence.

Regression is the backward movement of psychic energy when a frustrating situation dams the energy of the libido: for instance, a thinking-attitude may attempt to deal with a situation that can only be solved by feeling. Regression confronts the individual with the problem of the inner psyche as contrasted with outward adaptation to reality. The struggle between opposites would persist, but for regression which raises the psychic value of material of which the individual was only dimly conscious or totally unconscious. Regression can be positive as well as negative with its unconscious contents containing not only psychological slime, but the seeds of new possibilities. For example, if thinking fails as the adapted function, the unconscious material activated by regression will contain the missing feeling function, although still in embryonic, archaic and undeveloped form. Regression occurs regularly in dreams that can reveal important unconscious material.

INDIVIDUATION

A central concept of Jung's psychology is the process of individuation. Individuation is the process by which the person becomes differentiated as a separate psychological individual, a separate whole as distinct from the collective psychology. However, the process of individuation also raises a person's consciousness of the human community since it makes people aware of the unconscious, which unites all humankind.

The goal of psychic development is the self, which as shown previously differs from the ego. Individuation may be viewed as coming to self-hood or self-realization. The transcendent function is the means by which individuals are able to bridge some of the gap between consciousness and unconsciousness and live more in harmony with their unconscious processes.

Individuation involves a process of assimilating unconscious content into consciousness. There is a shift of the centre of personality from the ego, which is the centre of consciousness, to the self that moves from being located in the centre of unconsciousness to being at the central point between consciousness and unconsciousness. Creating this new balance between consciousness and unconscious allows the personality to rest on a new and more solid foundation.

Although the self-archetype is present from birth, its influence does not become significant until middle age. Individuation proceeds in life's morning though education and appropriate life experiences. However, a major emphasis on realizing the self through the process of individuation might be viewed more as a task of the afternoon of human life.

MAINTENANCE

Jung never systematically identified the factors that contribute to individuals maintaining lower levels of psychic development and individuation than desirable. He differentiated between the tasks of the first part of life, which entailed practical adaptations concerning such matters as relationships and occupation, and the second part of life, which concerned realizing the underlying self. The concept of maintenance should ideally take into account the different factors contributing to problems connected to addressing the tasks of each life stage. To avoid repetition and for the sake of simplicity, the following discussion is restricted to some central, sometimes overlapping, factors.

- *Rigid persona*: People who develop rigid personas develop in a very one-sided fashion and become out of touch with the subjective and unconscious side of themselves. This one-sidedness seeks social adaptation at the expense of inner alienation.
- *Mass collective consciousness*: The collective consciousness in a group, for instance the Swiss nation, may be one that encourages people to avoid examining themselves and dealing more deeply with problems in life. Allied to this, the collective consciousness may be conducive to people reinforcing one another's rigid personas.
- *Complexes*: Complexes, such as the mother complex, form part of the personal unconscious. Individuals who remain unaware of their complexes are likely to maintain them.
- *Fear of the shadow*: Individuals tend not to like examining what they perceive as undesirable and inferior traits in themselves. People who possess rigid personas may be particularly prone to avoid looking at their shadow sides.

- *Fear of the contents of the unconscious*: Fear of the shadow is just one aspect of fear of the unconscious. At varying levels of awareness, individuals may fear that their conscious functioning may be overwhelmed by the strength of their unconscious, with its archetypes and symbolic messages. People may possess insufficient courage to face their inner selves. For example, men and women may be reluctant to admit and explore their feminine (anima) and masculine (animus) aspects, respectively.
- *Projection*: Projection means the expulsion of a subjective content into an object. By means of projections, which are unintentional and purely automatic occurrences, individuals get rid of incompatible aspects of themselves by projecting them onto others. Most often these subjective contents are painful, for instance aspects of one's shadow. However, sometimes projections are positive, but for reasons of self-depreciation are inaccessible to individuals.
- *Regression*: Earlier, it was mentioned that regression involves the backward flow of psychic energy. Regression only becomes negative, when the individual becomes stuck in the unconscious activity and material generated by it, rather than being able to use it for regeneration.
- *Inability to understand the language of dreams*: The issue of understanding dreams is covered in the following section on therapy. Suffice it for now to say that inability to attend to dreams and understand their language and meaning is likely to contribute to maintaining pathology. The corollary of this is that heeding and understanding the language of dreams can foster the process of individuation.
- *Problems using the transcendent function*: The transcendent function is the synthesizing or integrating process whereby unconscious material opposes conscious material to provide a third living thing resembling the conjunction of opposites. Reasons why this synthesizing of opposites to create something new may not take place include ignorance, laziness, and insufficient intelligence and courage.

THERAPY

THERAPEUTIC GOALS

In his paper entitled 'The aims of psychotherapy', Jung (1966) talks about the psychology of life's morning and the psychology of its afternoon. The main therapeutic goal for youth is normal adaptation to overcome neuroses connected with shrinking back from the concrete life tasks. Therapy is mainly focused on attaining specific goals, dealing with complexes, and strengthening consciousness and ego functioning. Jung emphasized the importance for young people, who were still un-adapted and yet to achieve anything, to educate their conscious will.

People in the second half of life no longer need to educate their conscious will but to understand their own inner being and the meaning of their lives. Two thirds of Jung's clients were in the second half of life and about one third of his clients were not suffering from any clinically definable neuroses, but from the senselessness and aimlessness of their lives. Most of these patients were socially well-adapted individuals to whom normalization meant nothing. For such people, the major therapeutic goal was self-realization involving a deeper comprehension of their psyche and incorporating more unconscious material so that a new balance was created between consciousness and unconsciousness.

Jung did not believe in the concept of cure, rather in being better able to engage in the processes of attaining life's tasks and of synthesizing conscious and unconscious material. Until his death, Jung continued his quest for individuation and self-realization by understanding the meaning of the dreams and symbols from his own unconscious.

PROCESS OF THERAPY

Jungian analysis definitely does not follow the medical model of diagnosis, prognosis and treatment. Jung thought that clinical diagnosis was all but meaningless and that the true nature of a neurosis only reveals itself during the course of therapy.

Jung postulated four stages in analytic psychotherapy: confession, elucidation, education, and transformation (see Box 3.2). Though each of the stages has a curious sense of finality about it, normal adaptation will usually only be achieved by proceeding through the first three stages. The fourth stage, transformation, fulfils a further need beyond the scope of the other stages, but is not a final truth.

Jungian analysis is very much tailored to each individual. The process of therapy varies depending on such factors as: the client's stage of life, their personality characteristics, and the nature of their problems. The four stages of therapy are indicative rather than prescriptive. For instance, clients vary in how much work is required in dealing with the transference and its projections. Furthermore, the fourth stage of transformation is more appropriate to those facing problems of self-realization in the afternoon of their lives.

BOX 3.2 THE FOUR STAGES OF ANALYTICAL THERAPY

STAGE ONE: CONFESSION

The prototype of analytical therapy is confession. The first step in the therapeutic process is to share secrets and reveal inhibited emotions. Cathartic confession restores to the ego contents which should normally be part of it and which are capable of becoming conscious. However, confession should not be regarded as a panacea.

STAGE TWO: ELUCIDATION

Elucidation is a process of throwing light upon and clearing up the contents elicited by the transference. Partly by analysing clients' dreams, therapists interpret and explain

(Continued)

(Continued)

what clients project on to them. The effects of elucidation are that clients gain insight into their personal unconscious and the infantile origins of their projections and, thus, become more accepting of their shortcomings.

STAGE THREE: EDUCATION

Elucidation can leave clients intelligent, but still incapable children. Education entails helping clients draw out new and adaptive habits to replace the self-defeating habits of their neurosis. In this stage, therapy moves beyond insight to training clients in responsible actions.

STAGE 4: TRANSFORMATION

For many people completion of the first three stages may be sufficient. However, some people wish to move beyond being normal and adapted persons because their deepest needs are to be healthy in leading 'abnormal' lives. In the transformation stage with such clients, the therapist as well as the client is 'in the analysis'. In the personal relationship between them there are imponderable factors that bring about a mutual transformation, with the stronger and more stable personality deciding the final issue. The personality of the therapist is the curative or harmful factor and the educator must now become the self-educator going through the stages of confession, elucidation and education so that her or his personality does not react unfavourably on the client.

With difficult cases, Jung would start with three or four sessions a week. He would commence seeing most clients twice weekly, but once analytic therapy was under way, sessions would be reduced to once a week. Jung would also encourage clients to perform between-session activities, for instance recording dreams and painting, which would enable them to make a contribution to their common work. Approximately once every ten weeks Jung would break off treatment both to stop clients from becoming too dependent and to allow time to be a healing factor. A thorough course of analytic therapy could last for some years. Jung thought that, in most instances, very frequent sessions did not shorten the length of treatment. With clients of limited means, Jung would space sessions out and get clients to work on their own in the interim.

THE THERAPEUTIC RELATIONSHIP

Jung (1961) wrote: 'Analysis is a dialogue involving two partners. Analyst and patient sit facing one another, eye to eye; the doctor has something to say, but so does the patient' (p. 153). Therapy is different in every case with each client requiring individual understanding. Furthermore, clients needed to reach their own view of things without therapist compulsion or attempts at conversion.

Jung was very aware that, within and between therapists and clients, relationships take place on conscious and unconscious levels. Since treatment is a dialectical process in which the therapist participates just as much as the client, the personalities of therapists and clients may be more important to treatment outcomes than what the therapist says or does. Therapists should not hide behind professional facades, but be human enough to allow themselves to be influenced by their clients. Nevertheless, boundaries must be observed, including therapists monitoring themselves and questioning how their unconscious experiences situations.

As an example of unconscious contamination, the transference can evoke a counter-transference. Just as patients project unconscious material on to therapists, the reverse might be the case to the detriment of therapeutic outcomes. Jung strongly favoured training analyses so that therapists would be better able to protect clients from their own infections as well as to resist being infected by their clients' problems. Furthermore, Jung favoured ongoing contact with a third person, who could monitor the therapists' functioning, and observed that even the Pope had a confessor.

The relationship in analytic therapy differs according to the stage of therapy. For example, the relationship established during the confession stage can lay the foundation for the development of a transference relationship. Furthermore, the deeper levels of therapists' personalities are likely to be more involved in the transformation stage than in the earlier stages, which is why Jung stressed the self-education aspects of this stage.

The therapeutic relationship takes place not only face-to-face, but also in both therapist and client dreams and fantasies. Therapists need be sensitive to the meaning of any dreams involving their clients. Once when analysing his dreams, Jung understood the message that he was putting a woman, whom he recognized to be a patient, so high that his neck hurt to see her as a compensation for the fact that he was looking down on her in therapy. After disclosing the dream and sharing his analysis of it with her, treatment proceeded much better (Jung, 1968).

Jung could also confront clients if he thought it necessary. When one imperious aristocratic lady client threatened to slap him after he had to say something unpleasant to her, Jung jumped up and said to her 'Very well, you are the lady. You hit first – ladies first! But then I hit back!' (Jung, 1961, p. 165). The client then slumped back into her chair, observed that no one had ever talked to her like that before, and proceeded to work better in therapy.

THERAPEUTIC INTERVENTIONS

Jung advocated flexibility in adapting the therapy to the client. With people in the morning of life, Jung (1966) generally went along with Freudian and Adlerian approaches since these seemed to bring clients to appropriate levels of adaptation without leaving disturbing after-effects. He also observed: 'We need a different language for every patient. In one analysis I can be heard talking the Adlerian dialect, in another the Freudian' (Jung, 1961, p. 153). Jungian language and dialect appears most appropriate for those in the second half of life.

ANALYSIS OF THE TRANSFERENCE

Transferences are emotionally toned unconscious projections that occur from client to therapist. Projections take place because an activated unconscious content seeks expression. The intensity of the transference is related to the importance of the emotional content to the client. Because they are emotionally toned, transference projections arouse emotions in therapists. Counter-transference takes place when the unconscious contents of a client's projections are identical with the therapist's own unconscious processes. If therapist and client are bound together by mutual unconsciousness, the result can be highly counterproductive for analytical therapy.

Any highly emotional contents of the unconscious can be a matter for projection, including erotic material and activated archetypes. Thus transference projections can come from the personal and the collective unconscious. Though transference can be a spontaneous reaction, usually it occurs during analysis. Very often transference compensates for lack of genuine rapport between therapist and client. Therapists should not actively seek to promote transference projections. Transferences are not necessary for effective analysis, because therapists can obtain all the material they need from dreams anyway.

Transferences take up clients' psychic energy. Once the transference projections are extracted and consciously understood, a corresponding amount of energy will fall back into the client's possession, instead of being wasted.

Jung (1968) described four stages of analysis or therapy of the transference. However, it is possible to condense these four stages into two main stages: handling transference projections from the personal unconscious and handling transference projections from the collective unconscious.

The first main stage involves working through transference projections that are repetitions based on clients' former personal experiences with authority figures. There are basically two tasks. The first task is for clients to realize that they are projecting past negative and positive experiences, with their associated emotions, on to their therapists. The second task is for clients to withdraw the projections from their therapists and assimilate them into their own personalities. Clients need to learn how to assume responsibility for being whole persons, including their good and bad sides. For example, clients who project negative qualities can realize that these qualities represent their shadow side that they find difficulty in acknowledging because they would rather possess a more positive image of themselves. Clients who project positive qualities can realize that perhaps they should develop these qualities in themselves.

The second main stage of transference analysis comes after the projection of personal images has been worked through and dissolved through conscious realization. A transference may still remain based on impersonal and collective rather than on personal unconscious contents. Clients need to learn to discriminate between the personal and the impersonal contents that they project on to their therapists. Jung advocated great sensitivity in handling impersonal projections and taking them seriously rather than trying to dissolve their contents. He provides the example of it being a great mistake to say to a client: 'You see, you simply project the saviour image into me. What nonsense to expect a saviour and to make me responsible' (Jung 1968, pp. 180–1). The saviour archetypal image is everywhere and clients need to keep in touch with their impersonal images.

As part of the second stage of transference analysis, clients can learn to differentiate their personal relationship to the therapist from impersonal archetypal images. Clients can have normal human reactions to their therapists for helping them, but such reactions are human and decent only when not sullied by impersonal factors. Clients need also to realize the importance of their archetypal images, many of which have a religious nature. For some clients, the recognition of impersonal values may mean that they join a church or religious creed.

Therapy of the transference is complete when clients learn to objectify their impersonal images. Detaching consciousness from the object, a major aim of Eastern religious practices, is an essential part of the process of individuation. Clients learn to assume responsibility for their lives and no longer place the guarantees of their happiness on factors outside of themselves. They attain a condition of detachment in which their centre of gravity becomes themselves rather than external objects on which they depend.

ACTIVE IMAGINATION

Active imagination is a technique devised by Jung to help people get in touch with unconscious material. Clients begin by concentrating on a starting point. Then they allow their unconscious to produce a series of images, which may make a complete story. Box 3.3 provides two examples of active imagination, the second in abbreviated form (Jung, 1968, pp. 190–3).

Though not the only starting point, clients can use a dream as a stimulus for active imagination. If clients do not allow conscious reason to interfere, the images can have a life of their own, which is the origin of the term active imagination. After the active imagination process stops, some clients proceed to develop their unconscious images through painting, drawing, sculpting, weaving, dancing or writing.

Jung stressed that active imagination is not a panacea and that he only used it with some clients. He advised against forcing active imagination upon clients. Sometimes Jung found using active imagination particularly valuable in the later stages of therapy.

BOX 3.3   EXAMPLES OF ACTIVE IMAGINATION

EXAMPLE 1: JUNG AS A CHILD

As a little boy, Jung would go to a spinster aunt's house. The house was full of beautiful old coloured engravings. One of these was a picture of his grandfather on his mother's side, a sort of bishop represented as coming out of the house and standing at the top of a little terrace. There were some stairs coming down from the terrace and a footpath leading to the cathedral. Jung would kneel and look at the picture until he 'actively imagined' his grandfather coming down the steps.

EXAMPLE 2: THE YOUNG ARTIST

A young artist client of Jung's looked at a railway station poster about a place in the Bernese Alps and imagined himself in the poster. He walked up the hill and among the cows depicted in the poster and then imagined himself coming to the top and looking down the other side. He walked down the meadow on the other side, over a stile, and then down a footpath that ran round a ravine, and a rock, and then he came to a small chapel with the door ajar. He pushed open the door and saw an altar with flowers and a wooden Mother of God. At the exact moment he looked up at her face, something with pointed ears disappeared behind the altar.

DREAM ANALYSIS

Dreams are utterances or statements from the unconscious. They are the doors to the innermost secrets of the psyche. Jung thought that the idea that dreams were merely wish fulfillments as hopelessly out of date. As well as wishes and fears, dreams 'may contain ineluctable truths, philosophical pronouncements, illusions, wild fantasies, memories, plans, anticipations, irrational experiences, even telepathic visions, and heaven knows what else besides' (Jung, 1968, p. 147). Dreams may also point to solutions to issues and problems and be prescient about future events.

Jung regarded dreams as containing their whole meaning and not having false fronts. Dreams are comparable to texts that appear unintelligible, but the therapist has to discover how to read them. Dreams do not conceal, rather therapists need to discover their language. An understanding of myths and symbols is central to being able to read the language of dreams.

Jung distinguished between various kinds of dreams. Initial dreams are those that occur at the start of analysis and may deal with the client's attitude towards the therapist. For instance, a client predicted a brief and unsuccessful therapeutic contact with the dream *'I have to cross the frontier into another country, but cannot find the frontier and nobody can tell me where it is'* (Jung, 1968, p. 144). Another distinction is between little dreams, which are concerned with relatively unimportant matters, and big dreams. Big dreams are numinous, a favourite Jung term for inexpressible, mysterious, terrifying and intensely mysterious experiences. Big dreams are of particular importance. Another distinction is that between single dreams and a series of dreams, with Jung's strong preference being to work with series of dreams.

TASKS OF DREAM ANALYSIS

The first task in analysing a dream is to establish its context. Here Jung used a technique he called amplification. Amplification involves the elaboration and clarification of dream images by way of directed association. Rather than encourage free association, therapists must encourage clients' associations that stick as close as possible to the dream images. For example, the dream image of a simple peasant's house may mean different things to different clients. To establish the context of the simple peasant's house, Jung would ask: 'So how does that appear to you?' or 'What are your associations to a simple peasant's house?' In this instance, the client replied: 'It is the lazar-house of St Jacob near Basel' (Jung, 1968, p. 97). From this association, Jung was able to make many connections: for example, the client feeling himself an outcast and being in great danger.

Another example of clarifying context is that of a client, whose writing desk is different, dreaming of 'deal table'. Jung would keep returning to the image and say: 'Suppose I had no idea what the words "deal table" mean, describe this object and give me its history in such a way that I cannot fail to understand what sort of thing it is.' (Jung, 1966, pp. 149–50). Therapist and client need to work on establishing the context for all the images in the dream.

Interpretation is the second task of dream analysis. Since basic ideas and themes can be much more clearly recognized in a dream series than in single dreams, clients should keep a careful record of their dreams and of the inter-pretations made. Jung would also train clients in how to work on their dreams between sessions so that they could come prepared to the next consultation with the dream and its context written out. When interpreting dreams, a basic question for the therapist to address is 'What conscious attitude does it compensate?'

Related to the interpretation of dreams is the third task of dream analysis, assimilation. Jung valued unconscious contents and sought to bring about change in and through the unconscious as well. Assimilation 'means mutual penetration of conscious and unconscious, and not – as is commonly thought and practised – a one-sided evaluation, interpretation, and deformation of unconscious contents by the conscious mind' (Jung, 1966, p.152). Unconscious contents lose their danger the moment clients begin to assimilate contents that were previously repressed.

Assimilation requires the assent of the client to the therapist's interpreta-tions. The values of the client's conscious personality must be respected and left intact, because unconscious compensation requires co-operation with an 'inte-gral consciousness'. Box 3.4 provides an abbreviated version of Jung's analysis of a young man's dream (Jung, 1966, pp. 154–5).

BOX 3.4   EXAMPLE OF DREAM ANALYSIS

THE YOUNG MAN'S DREAM

My father is driving away from the house in his new car. He drives very clumsily, and I get very annoyed over his apparent stupidity. He goes this way and that, forwards and back-wards, and manoeuvres the car into a dangerous position. Finally he runs into a wall and damages the car badly. I shout out at him in a perfect fury that he ought to behave himself. My father only laughs and then I see that he is dead drunk.

CONTEXT OF THE DREAM

The young man has a genuinely positive and admiring relationship with an unusually successful father. There was nothing neurotically ambivalent about the relationship.

JUNG'S INTERPRETATION OF THE DREAM

The client's relationship to his father is too good and his father is still doing too much for him, so that the client's unconscious is compensating by trying to take the father down a peg. The son's danger is that he cannot see his own reality. The dream forces the son to contrast himself with his father and so that he can become conscious of himself.

THE CLIENT'S ASSIMILATION OF THE DREAM

Jung's interpretation struck home with the client and received his immediate assent. Jung points out that the interpretation damaged no real conscious values for either father or son.

Dream symbols are expressions of content not yet consciously recognized or consciously formulated. Box 3.5 illustrates Jung's interpretation of the symbol in one of the dreams of a 17-year-old female client (Jung, 1966, p. 158–60). This dream was taken from long-term analytical therapy where the goal is the client's progressive individuation. In such therapy, over a period of months and years there are successive assimilations of unconscious dream material. This process realizes more of the client's self in the interests becoming a whole human being.

BOX 3.5   EXAMPLE OF INTERPRETING A DREAM SYMBOL

THE YOUNG WOMAN'S DREAM

I am coming home at night. Everything is quiet as death. The door to the living room is half open, and I see my mother hanging from the chandelier, swinging to and fro in the cold wind that blows through the open windows.

PART OF THE DREAM'S CONTEXT

Jung was called in after two specialists had made contrary diagnoses of this 17-year-old young woman. One specialist thought she might be in the first stages of progressive muscular atrophy. The other specialist thought that she was a case of hysteria.

JUNG'S INTERPRETATION OF THE DREAM

The mother symbol refers to the archetype of the place of origin, to nature. The symbol also stands for the instinctive and unconscious life and the body. Jung's interpretation was that the unconscious life is destroying itself or that the dream pointed to a grave organic disease that would have a fatal outcome. This prognosis was soon confirmed.

CASE MATERIAL

Perhaps some indication of Jung's attitude to case material can be gleaned from the following quotation: 'Each individual analysis by itself shows only one part of one aspect of the deeper process, and for this reason nothing but hopeless confusion can result from comparative case histories' (Jung, 1966, p. 161). Case material that illustrates analytic therapy comes from both primary and secondary sources. In his autobiographical *Memories, Dreams, Reflections*, Jung (1961) provides case material, including many dreams, from his own explorations and confrontations with his unconscious. In his 1935 Tavistock Lectures, published as *Analytical Psychology* (1968), Jung provides case examples illustrating active imagination and dream analysis. Numerous further examples of how Jung worked are to be found in the various papers that comprise *The Practice of Psychotherapy* (Jung, 1966). In addition, *Symbols of Transformation* (Jung, 1967) provides lengthy analyses of symbolic material contained in the fantasies of a young American lady, Miss Miller.

Jung was a very original and individualistic therapist with a vast range of scholarship to draw upon. Secondary source case material, such as that provided by Douglas (2008) and Casement (2014) towards the end of their textbook chapters, can only go part way to catching the real essence of how Jung himself worked

FURTHER DEVELOPMENTS

IN TREATMENT

Samuels (1985) divided the development of analytical psychology into three schools: classical, developmental and archetypal. The classical school is that most closely based on Jung's original theory and practice, the topic of this chapter. Douglas (2008) observes that there is a backlash among conservative

Jungians who consider that Jung's original words, however socio-culturally suspect they may be by today's standards, should be taught as Jung originally presented them. The developmental school incorporates psychoanalytic ways of thinking and working. The archetypal school focuses on the development of symbols and images in the psyche.

The rise of feminism is leading to a reappraisal of Jung's ideas about masculine and feminine characteristics and influences how analysts work with members of each sex. Not surprisingly, Jung's views on women and on his anima–animus concepts have been open to discussion and revision. Douglas observes that since so much about gender and gender roles is in flux today, current images no longer match those of Jung's time and are changing as culture and experience change. She also considers that contemporary re-evaluation of these concepts holds much promise for the possibility of reappraising homosexuality as a natural occurrence (Douglas, 2008).

Michael Fordham, who tirelessly tried to repair the split between the work of Jung and Freud, is prominent in the developmental school. Fordham extended Jungian theory by stating that a 'primary self' operates in infants from the beginning. Based on his work with infants and children, Fordham considered that this primary self 'de-integrates' from a state of inner wholeness to bring the infant into relation with the environment. In this way the infant's expectation of feeding evokes the appropriate response from the mother's breast in the external world. By postulating that a primary self exists from the beginning of life, Fordham fills a gap in classical psychoanalytic and analytic psychology theory. While deintegration represents energy going out to objects in the environment, reintegration is the term Fordham used for energy returning to the self (Casement, 2014; Fordham, 1993).

Fordham's view is that individuation does not have to wait until middle age. Jung thought that individuation was equated with achieving consciousness through differentiation of subject from object. Fordham showed that the child's gradual separation from the mother during it first two years of life is also a process of individuation. He demonstrates how, after birth, the infant's primary self de-integrates and, through increasing identification with the mother, begins to move toward early object-relating. There are other early developments, not mentioned here, which are pre-requisites for the goal of individuation, which is a natural part of maturing (Fordham, 1976).

Jung was more flexible than Freud about positive as well as negative effects of counter-transference. Fordham (1957) developed a position in which there are two kinds of counter-transference: syntonic and illusory. Syntonic counter-transference occurs when analysts may be so in tune with clients' inner worlds that they feel or behave in ways that they come to realize show that there are aspects of their clients' inner worlds projected into them. Thus clients receive the benefit of parts of their analysts that are spontaneously responding to them in ways that are needed.

Illusory counter-transference is when situations from analysts' pasts replace or interfere with their relationships to their patients. Fordham listened to a recording he made of an analytic session he conducted with an 11 year-old boy who had problems with aggression. He discovered that his own aggression had been present, which was due to reactivating a past event from his own childhood. During this time, analysis of his client was impossible (Casement, 2007).

Another development in the work of Jungians is to question the value of verbal interpretation as the main mode of analysis. Instead, clients' affect, feelings and body awareness are emphasized, and analysts are more likely to use the traditionally feminine realm of subjective and shared experience (Douglas, 2008).

DIFFERENT WAYS OF WORKING

Individual therapy is the main way of conducting analytical therapy. In the United States, the impact of managed care has led to some analysts experimenting with brief therapy (Douglas, 2008). Casement (2014) also mentions brief therapy, giving an example of work with a client done over ten sessions.

Douglas (2008) writes about developments in Jung's work extending into many different areas only some of which are mentioned here.

GROUP THERAPY

Groups, which are of approximately 6 to 10 members, are often an adjunct to individual therapy and participants are usually clients of the analyst, though some analysts accept referrals. Meetings tend to be weekly and run for about ninety minutes. Douglas sees group therapy as particularly suitable for introverts, who have been drawn to Jungian psychology. In group therapy, members tend to project their shadow on to the group and the group inevitably picks up on parts of the personality that an individual conceals. Resistances are more obvious and can be dealt with more easily than in individual therapy.

FAMILY AND MARITAL THERAPY

Contemporary Jungian analysts also often use or refer their patients to analytical marital or family therapy. Analysts often administer a typology test to the couple or family members and differences can often be worked with more easily when they are interpreted as a clash of typologies. People often choose partners whose typology is the opposite to their own. Analysts working with families and couples also emphasize family dynamics caused by members' shadow and anima–animus projections onto other family members.

BODY/MOVEMENT THERAPY

Jung would have his clients engage in active imagination through body movement and dance. He believed that the body stores, experiences and communicates emotional experience as much, if not more than words.

ART THERAPY

Jung felt that drawing an image from a dream or from active imagination was especially valuable for people out of touch with their feelings and who try to deal with their experience solely through logic. Art therapy is a conscious way to express elements of the unconscious. It is not the quality of the finished product that is valuable, but the fact that art therapy allows an active dialogue with the unconscious.

SAND TRAY THERAPY

Jung constructed stone 'villages' during his self-analysis. Dora Kalff developed Jung's ideas by filling a rectangular box approximately 30 x 20 x 3 inches with sand to become a miniature world that can be shaped by arranging any of the hundreds of figurines provided by the analyst. Use of the sand tray, like other forms of active imagination, provides a bridge to the unconscious.

CHILD ANALYSIS

Analysts not only treat the child, but also intervene when needed to improve the child's family and life situation. Child analysis is similar to adult analysis, but uses a wide variety of touch and non-verbal methods more. Children are encouraged to express dreams, fears and fantasies through sand tray therapy, arts and crafts, modelling clay, playing musical instruments, and body movement. In addition stories and myths are used for illustrating feelings and working out problems.

SOCIETIES AND CONCLUDING COMMENT

In 1922 a Jung club was established in London and, in 1946, a Society of Analytical Psychology (SAP) was founded in Britain. There is an International Association of Analytical Psychology that, as of 2009, had 3,000 certified analyst members in 32 countries worldwide (Casement, 2009).

Particularly in the Western world, interest in Jungian psychology remains strong. Jung has been called a 'homo religiosus' by Gerhard Adler, the founder of the Association of Jungian Analysts (Casement, 2007), and a 'theologian manqué' (McLynn, 1996). His work has continuing appeal to many of those who are dissatisfied with the narrowness of scientific psychology and who seek to understand human beings in their wholeness.

REVIEW AND PERSONAL QUESTIONS

REVIEW QUESTIONS

1. Describe consciousness and the ego.
2. Describe the personal unconscious and its complexes.

3. Describe the collective unconscious and its archetypes.
4. What are Jungian psychodynamics and how do they differ from Freudian psychodynamics?
5. What are Jung's views on psychological types?
6. What are the four stages of life and how do the tasks of life's morning and afternoon differ?
7. How do people maintain levels of adaptation lower than is desirable?
8. Describe the goals and process of analytic therapy.
9. Describe Jung's ideas on the analysis of the transference.
10. Describe as best you can how Jung approached the task of dream analysis.
11. Describe some ideas of the developmental school of analytical therapy.

PERSONAL QUESTIONS

1. Do Jung's ideas of the personal unconscious and the collective unconscious resonate in terms of your own life? If so, please elaborate.
2. What are some aspects of your shadow and what do you intend doing about them?
3. What do you consider is your personality type and why?
4. Try using Jung's method of active imagination.
5. Take one of your dreams and, to the best of your ability, apply Jung's methods of dream analysis to it.
6. What goals would you set for yourself if you were to be a client in either classical or developmental Jungian analysis?

ANNOTATED BIBLIOGRAPHY

C. G. Jung (1968) *Analytical Psychology: Its Theory and Practice*. New York: Vintage Books.
This book presents the five lectures, plus discussion, that Jung gave at the Tavistock Clinic in London in 1935. Topics covered include the structure of the mind, word association and psychological types, and the methods of active imagination, dream analysis and the analysis of the transference. The book provides an excellent concise introduction to analytical psychology.

C. G. Jung (1966) *The Practice of Psychotherapy* (2nd ed.). London: Routledge (Volume 16 in *The Collected Works of C. G. Jung*)
This book is divided into two parts. Part one, entitled 'General problems of psychotherapy', contains nine papers, including one on the aims of psychotherapy. Part two, entitled 'Specific problems of psychotherapy', contains Jung's ideas on the therapeutic value of abreaction, the practical use of dream analysis, and the psychology of the transference. Some useful case study material is included in an appendix, entitled 'The realities of practical psychotherapy'.

C. G. Jung (1961) *Memories, Dreams, Reflections*. London: Fontana Press.
Jung regarded his life as a story of the realization of the unconscious. In this book compiled at the end of his life Jung tells his personal myth, an inner journey structured around the following chapter headings: first years, school

years, student years, psychiatric activities, Sigmund Freud, confrontation with the unconscious, the work, the tower, travels, visions, on life after death, and late thoughts. Some controversy exists over the extent of Jung's secretary's contribution to this book rather than it being solely a primary source.

C. G. Jung. (1971) *Psychological Types*. London: Routledge.
This book, Volume 6 in the *Collected Works*, was originally published in 1921 after Jung's fallow period. It starts with a scholarly discussion of the notion of psychological types drawing on material from literature, aesthetics, religion and philosophy as well as from psychology. Jung then presents his ideas on attitudes, functions and psychological types. The book ends with an appendix containing four papers on psychological typology.

REFERENCES AND FURTHER READING

Casement, A. (2001) *Carl Gustav Jung*. London: Sage.
Casement, A. (2007) Psychodynamic therapy: The Jungian approach. In W. Dryden (ed.) *Dryden's Handbook of Individual Therapy* (5th ed.). London: Sage, pp. 84–111.
Casement, A. (2014) Jungian and post-Jungian approaches. In W. Dryden and A. Reeves (eds) *The Handbook of Individual Therapy* (6th ed.). London: Sage, pp. 75–100.
Casement, A. (2009) Private correspondence, 30.10.2009.
Casement, A. and Tacey, D. (2006) *The Idea of the Numinous: Contemporary Jungian and Psychoanalytic Perspectives*. London: Brunner-Routledge.
Douglas, C. (2008) 'Analytical psychotherapy'. In R. J. Corsini and D. Wedding (eds) *Current Psychotherapies* (8th ed.). Belmont, CA: Thomson Brooks/Cole, pp. 107–40.
Fordham, M. (1957) *New Developments in Analytical Psychology*. London: Routledge & Kegan Paul.
Fordham, M. (1976) *The Self and Autism*. London: Heinemann.
Fordham, M. (1993) *The Making of an Analyst*. London: Free Association Books.
Hall, C. S. and Nordby, B. J. (1973) *A Primer of Jungian Psychology*. New York: New American Library.
Jung, C. G. (1961) *Memories, Dreams, Reflections*. London: Fontana Press.
Jung, C. G. (1966) *The Practice of Psychotherapy* (2nd ed.). London: Routledge.
Jung, C. G. (1967) *Symbols of Transformation* (2nd ed.). Princeton, NJ: Princeton University Press.
Jung, C. G. (1968) *Analytical Psychology: Its Theory and Practice*. New York: Vintage Books.
Jung, C. G. (1971) *Psychological Types*. London: Routledge.
Jung, C. G. (1976a) The concept of the collective unconscious. In J. Campbell (ed.) *The Portable Jung*. London: Penguin Books, pp. 59–70.
Jung, C. G. (1976b) The relations between the ego and the unconscious. In J. Campbell (ed.) *The Portable Jung*. London: Penguin Books, pp. 70–138.

Jung, C. G. (1976c) The transcendent function. In J. Campbell (ed.) *The Portable Jung*. London: Penguin Books, pp. 273–300.

Jung, C. G. (1981) *The Development of Personality: Papers on Child Psychology, Education and Related Subjects*. London: Routledge.

Jung, C. G. (1982) *Aspects of the Feminine*. London: Ark Paperbacks.

Jung, C. G. (1983) Fundamental concepts of libido theory. In A. Storr (ed.) *The Essential Jung*. Princeton, NJ: Princeton University Press, pp. 59–64.

Jung, C. G. (1989) *Aspects of the Masculine*. Princeton, NJ: Princeton University Press.

McLynn, F. (1996) *Carl Gustav Jung: A Biography*. London: Bantam Press.

Papadopoulos, R. (ed.) *The Handbook of Jungian Psychology: Theory, Practice and Applications*. London: Brunner-Routledge.

Safran, J. D. and Kris, A. (2014) Psychoanalytic psychotherapies. In D. Wedding and R. J. Corsini (eds) *Current Psychotherapies* (10th ed.). Belmont, CA: Thomson Brooks/Cole, pp. 19–54.

Samuels, A. (1985) *Jung and the Post-Jungians*. London: Routledge & Kegan Paul.

Samuels, A. (2001) *Politics on the Couch: Citizenship and the Internal Life*. New York: Karnac Books.

Shamdasani, S. (ed.) (2009) *The Red Book: Liber Novus. C. G. Jung*. New York: W. W. Norton.

This part of the book presents four theoretical positions under the heading of humanistic-existential therapies. Chapter 4 presents Carl Rogers' person-centred therapy. Rogers was the originator of an approach to counselling and therapy that aims to help clients fulfill their unique potential and become their own persons. His approach was partly an attempt to get away from the interpretive psychodynamic therapies described in the previous two chapters. In addition, Rogers was trying to emancipate people from the overbearing influence that parents of his time often had on the thoughts, feelings and actions of their offspring. In the early part of the twentieth century when Rogers was growing up, parents exercised much more power in the home than they do now. Rogers' person-centred therapy challenged authoritarian tendencies in both therapy and parenting and championed the rights of clients to discover their own directions.

Chapter 5 reviews Fritz Perls' gestalt therapy. Perls regarded it as an existential approach 'not just occupied with dealing with symptoms or character structure, but with the total existence of a person' (Perls, 1969, p. 71). Toward the end of his life Perls (1969) wrote that he considered gestalt therapy one of the three then-existing types of existential therapy: the two others being Frankl's logotherapy and Binswanger's daseins therapy. Clients who come for gestalt therapy are in states of existential crisis and need to learn to take responsibility for their existences.

Chapter 6 presents Eric Berne's transactional analysis. Although Berne was strongly influenced by Freud, the theory and practice of transactional analysis are very different from those of psychoanalysis. Berne saw an element of his approach, called script analysis, as being 'para-Freudian' rather than anti-Freudian (Berne, 1970, p. 400), and conceivably the same might be said for the whole of transactional analysis. Berne differed from other humanistic theorists and from Freud in his greater emphasis on social psychiatry, which he defined as 'the study of the psychiatric aspects of specific transactions or sets of transactions which take place between two or more particular individuals at a given time and place' (Berne, 1961, p. 12). Berne analysed what was going on in people's internal worlds when they came into contact with, influenced and were influenced by others in their external worlds.

There are many existential approaches to therapy from different countries. Chapter 7 describes the theory and practice of the American Yalom and May's existential therapy. which assists clients to confront the basic issues of their existence: namely, death, freedom, isolation and meaninglessness. Each of these issues has the potential to generate 'existence pain' (Yalom, 1989). Existential therapy takes place in a relationship in which the therapist strives to offer presence, authenticity and commitment. Little time is spent focusing on clients' pasts, rather therapists try to understand their current situations and enveloping fears. Existential therapists may intervene in many different ways depending on which of the ultimate concerns they and their clients focus.

REFERENCES

Berne, E. (1961) *Transactional Analysis in Psychotherapy*. New York: Grove Press.
Berne, E. (1970) *Sex in Human Loving*. Harmondsworth: Penguin.
Perls, F. S. (1969) *Gestalt Therapy Verbatim*. New York: Bantam Books.
Yalom, I. D. (1989) *Love's Executioner and Other Tales of Psychotherapy*. London: Bloomsbury.

PERSON-CENTRED THERAPY 4

INTRODUCTION

On 11 December, 1940, Carl Rogers gave a presentation at the University of Minnesota entitled 'Some newer concepts in psychotherapy' that is the single event most often identified with the birth of client-centred therapy (Raskin et al., 2014). In 1974, Rogers and his colleagues changed its name from 'client-centred' to 'person-centred'. They believed that the new name would more adequately describe the human values and the mutuality underlying their approach and would apply to contexts other than counselling and psycho-therapy. However, Thorne observes: 'Rogers never completely jettisoned the term client-centred therapy. He uses client-centred and person-centred inter-changeably when talking about counselling and psychotherapy but always employs the term "the person-centred approach" when referring to activities outside the one-to-one therapy situation.' (B. Thorne, personal communica-tion, 15 March, 1994).

This chapter is drawn mainly from Rogers' writings. However, he encouraged colleagues and associates to develop it and, consequently, regarded his theory as a group enterprise (Rogers, 1959). Rogers was influenced by psychologists like Combs, Snygg and Maslow. I incorporate the ideas of Rogers' collaborators when they help to add to or clarify his position. In addition, the chapter ends with some recent contributions to person-centred therapy, mainly from Britain.

CARL ROGERS (1902–87)

Carl Ransom Rogers was born in Illinois, America, the fourth of six children. His father was a civil engineer and contractor who had a successful construction business. A rather sickly boy, Rogers lived his childhood in a close-knit family in which hard work and a highly conservative, almost fundamentalist Protestant Christianity were almost equally revered. Rogers was a shy boy who was teased a lot at home. Included among reasons for the teasing were that he was rather a bookworm and extremely absent-minded; in fact, his family called him 'Professor Moony' after a famous comic-strip character (Cohen, 1997).

When Rogers was twelve his parents bought a farm and this became the family home. Rogers regarded his parents as masters of the art of subtle, loving control.

He shared little of his private thoughts and feelings with them because he knew these would have been judged and found wanting. Until Rogers went to college he was a loner who read incessantly and who adopted his parents' attitude toward the outside world, summed up in the statement: 'Other persons behave in dubious ways which we do not approve in our family' (Rogers, 1980, p. 28). Such dubious ways included playing cards, going to the cinema, smoking, dancing, drinking and engaging in other even less mentionable activities. He was socially incompetent in other than superficial contacts and, while at high school, had only two dates with girls. He relates that his fantasies during this period were bizarre and would probably have been classified as schizoid by a psychological diagnostician.

Rogers entered the University of Wisconsin to study agriculture, but before the end of his sophomore year he changed to history, feeling that this would be a better preparation for his emerging professional goal of becoming a minister of religion. His first real experience of fellowship was in a group there who met in a YMCA class. When he was 20, Rogers went to China for an international World Student Christian Federation Conference in Peking. He stayed in China for more than six months and, for the first time, emancipated himself from the religious thinking of his parents, a fundamental step towards becoming an independent person. Also, at about this time he fell in love with Helen Elliott, who was an artist. In August 1924, two months after completing college, he married her.

In 1924, Rogers went to Union Theological Seminary, but after two years moved to study for his degree in clinical and educational psychology at Teachers College, Columbia University. Here he was exposed to the instrumentalist philosophy of John Dewey, the highly statistical and Thorndikean behavioural approaches of Teachers College, and the Freudian orientation of the Institute for Child Guidance where he had an internship. Along with his formal learning, he was starting to understand relationships with others better, and was beginning to realize that, in close relationships, the elements that 'cannot' be shared are those that are the most important and rewarding to share.

In 1928 Rogers received an MA from Columbia University and then spent twelve years as an administrator and a practising psychologist in a community child guidance clinic in Rochester, New York. In 1931, he received his PhD from Columbia University with his thesis consisting of developing a test for measuring the personality adjustment of nine to thirteen-year-old children. In 1939 Rogers published his first book, entitled *The Clinical Treatment of the Problem Child*. During this period he felt that he was becoming more competent as a therapist, not least because his experience with clients was providing him with valuable learning and insights that contributed to a shift from diagnosis to listening. Furthermore, such a relationship approach met his own needs, since, stemming from his early loneliness, the therapy interview was a socially approved way of getting really close to people without the pains and longer time-span of the friendship process outside therapy.

In 1940, Rogers accepted a position as a professor of psychology at Ohio State University and two years later published *Counseling and Psychotherapy: Newer*

Concepts in Practice the contents of which were derived primarily from his work as a counsellor rather than as an academic psychologist. After initial poor sales, the book became well known because it offered a way to work with veterans returning from the Second World War. From 1942, Rogers had undertaken consultancies relating to the war effort, including training counsellors. After leaving Ohio State University, he spent a very brief spell as director of counselling for the United Services Organization, a serviceman's welfare organization. From 1945 to 1957 Rogers was professor of psychology and executive secretary of the counselling centre at the University of Chicago, where non-directive, or client-centred therapy, as it came to be called, was further developed and researched. In 1951, Rogers published *Client-Centered Therapy*, which contained a theoretical statement as well as a series of chapters related to client-centred practice.

In 1957 Rogers was appointed professor of psychology and psychiatry at the University of Wisconsin, where he examined the impact of the client-centred approach on hospitalized schizophrenics. Thorne writes: 'He went to Wisconsin to make an impact, and he notably failed' (Thorne with Sanders, 2013, p. 18). However, in 1959, he produced by far the most thorough statement of his theoretical position (Rogers, 1959) and in 1961, *On Becoming a Person*, his most commercially successful book was published.

From 1962 to 1963 Rogers was a fellow at the Center for Advanced Study in the Behavioral Sciences at Stanford University. In 1964 he went to the Western Behavioral Sciences Institute at La Jolla, California, as a resident fellow. Then, in 1968, with some colleagues, Rogers formed the Center for Studies of the Person at La Jolla, where he was a resident fellow until his death. During the latter part of his career Rogers developed a great interest in the application of person-centred ideas to group work, community change, and preventing 'nuclear, planetary suicide' and ran many large-scale workshops around the world (Kirschenbaum and Henderson, 1990). In addition, as he grew older, having earlier firmly rejected his Christian past, he realized he had underestimated the mystical or spiritual dimension in life.

From the age of 13, Rogers had viewed himself as a scientist. He was a committed researcher and pioneered the use of tape-recorders to study counselling and therapy processes. In 1956, he received the American Psychological Association's Award for Distinguished Scientific Contributions. Rogers was also an author with a deep commitment to clear and cogent communication. When he was 75, he observed: 'Yet there is, I believe, a much more important reason for my writing. It seems to me that I am still – inside – the shy boy who found communication very difficult in interpersonal situations ...' (Rogers, 1980, p. 80). As well as those already mentioned, his books include *Freedom to Learn* (1969), *Encounter Groups* (1970), *Becoming Partners* (1973), *Carl Rogers on Personal Power* (1977) and *A Way of Being* (1980). A chronological bibliography of Rogers' books and articles published in the period 1930–1980 is printed at the end of *A Way of Being*.

Although the years since 1940 were, on the whole, very successful for Rogers and his ideas, they also contained professional and personal struggles. Two professional struggles were those with psychiatry and with behavioural psychology. Rogers fought for psychologists, as contrasted with psychiatrists, to be allowed to practise psychotherapy and to have administrative responsibility over 'mental health' work. He also constantly highlighted the philosophical and practical issues involved in a humanistic or person-centred as against a behavioural view of human beings.

On a more personal level, Rogers continued striving to become a more real, open and growing person. He struggled, with varying degrees of success, with some personal crises and difficulties. During his Chicago period, with counselling help, he worked through a crisis arising from a 'badly bungled therapeutic relationship' (Rogers, 1980, p. 39) with a particularly demanding and highly disturbed female client (Thorne with Sanders, 2013). In the 1970s, Rogers faced the strains of his wife's long illness – from 1972 she was intermittently in a wheelchair and in 1979 she died. In the last years of her life, there was much pain in his relationship with Helen. Nevertheless Rogers movingly talks of how he was able to express his appreciation and love for her two days before she died (Rogers, 1980). Toward the end his life Rogers was increasingly aware of his 'capacity for love, my sensuality, my sexuality' (Rogers, 1980, p. 96) and wished to have loving relationships outside of marriage. In August 1975, Rogers met and fell in love with a much younger divorcee called Bernice Todres, but the relationship was never sexually consummated. In December 1979 this only intermittently satisfactory and episodic relationship finally ended.

Rogers was a complex mixture of high intelligence, high energy, ambition, competitiveness, Protestant work ethic, strength, vulnerability, charisma, idealism, altruism, self-centredness, caring, shyness, sensitivity, warmth, and ability to touch others deeply. Arguably, as his career developed, he allowed the need to become and maintain the professional persona of Carl Rogers to get in the way of his becoming a more highly developed person. Clearly very conscious of his place in the history of American counselling and therapy, Rogers left the United States Library of Congress 140 boxes of his papers as well as tapes and films of his work.

Even as an old man Rogers was still prone to blame his parents for making him feel that he did not deserve to be loved (Cohen, 1997). A wounded theorist, he was influenced by his own early emotional deprivations to design a counselling approach to overcome their effects and hence to meet his own companionship and growth needs. Other sources of learning included his clients and the stimulus provided by younger colleagues. Rogers claimed that serendipity or 'the faculty of making fortunate and unexpected discoveries by accident' had also been important (Rogers, 1980, p. 64).

THEORY

BASIC CONCEPTS

In 1951 Rogers presented his theory of personality and behaviour as the final chapter of *Client-Centered Therapy*. Eight years later, in an edited publication entitled *Psychology: A Study of Science,* he presented an updated version that he regarded as his major and most rigorous theoretical statement and 'the most thoroughly ignored of anything I have written' (Rogers, 1980, p. 60). Later, with collaborators, Rogers restated his theory, but did not significantly alter it (for instance, Raskin et al., 2014). Rogers thought that this and any theory should be a stimulus for further creative thinking rather than a dogma of truth.

PERCEPTUAL OR SUBJECTIVE FRAME OF REFERENCE

Combs and Snygg (1959) state that, broadly speaking, behaviour may be observed from either the point of view of outsiders or the point of view of the behavers themselves. It is sometimes stated that the former is viewing behaviour from the external frame of reference while the latter is viewing behaviour from the internal, subjective or perceptual frame of reference. Rogers writes of his fundamental belief in the subjective, observing that 'Man lives essentially in his own personal and subjective world, and even his most objective functioning, in science, mathematics, and the like, is the result of subjective purpose and subjective choice' (Rogers, 1959, p. 191). It is this emphasis on the subjective, perceptual view of clients that led to the term 'client-centred'. The perceptions of clients are viewed as their versions of reality.

Later, Rogers was again to stress that the only reality people can possibly know is the world that they individually perceive and experience at this moment. The notion that there is a 'real world', the definition of which can be agreed upon by everyone, is a luxury that the human race cannot afford, since it leads to false beliefs, like faith in technology, which have brought our species to the brink of annihilation. His alternative hypothesis is that there are as many realities as there are people. Furthermore, people are increasingly 'inwardly and organismically rejecting the view of one single, culture-approved reality' (Rogers, 1980, p. 26).

ACTUALIZING TENDENCY

The actualizing tendency is the single basic motivating drive. It is an active process representing the inherent tendency of the organism to develop its capacities in the direction of maintaining, enhancing and reproducing itself. The actualizing tendency is operative at all times in all organisms and is the distinguishing feature of whether a given organism is alive or dead. The organism is always up to something. In addition, the actualizing tendency involves a development towards the differentiation of organs and functions.

Rogers observes, from his experiences with individual and group counselling and from his attempts to provide students in classes with 'freedom to learn', that 'the most impressive fact about the individual human being seems to be the directional tendency toward wholeness, toward actualization of potentialities' (Rogers, 1977, p. 240). Furthermore, he cited support for the actualizing tendency both in his observations of the natural world, for instance the behaviour of sea-weed and of children learning to walk, and in empirical research, be it on sea urchins, rats, human infants and brain-damaged war veterans. The cornerstone of both Rogers' therapeutic work and his political thinking was that, because of their actualizing tendency, people move towards self-regulation and their own enhancement and away from control by external forces. The actualizing tendency is basically positive. It represents Rogers' trust in the wisdom of the organism and its constructive directional flow towards the realization of each individual's full potential.

Maslow (1970) reiterates this assessment of people's basic nature when he writes that the human being does seem to have instinct remnants and that clinical and other evidence suggests that those weak instinctoid tendencies are good, desirable and worth saving. Often, however, people appear to have two motivational systems, their organismic actualizing tendency and their conscious self. Maslow (1962) writes of the basic conflict in humans between defensive forces and growth trends and observes that the actualizing tendency may involve both deficiency and growth motivations. However, given a certain emotional environment, growth motivations will become increasingly strong.

ORGANISMIC VALUING PROCESS

The concept of an organismic valuing process is central to the idea of a real or true and unique self. A person's organismic valuing process relates to the continuous weighing of experience and the placing of values on that experience in terms of their ability to satisfy the organism. For instance, the behaviour of infants indicates that they prefer those experiences, such as curiosity and security, which maintain and enhance their organism and reject those, such as pain and hunger, which do not. This weighing of experience is an organismic rather than a conscious symbolic process. The source of the valuing process or values placed on the various experiences seems clearly to be in the infants, who react to their own sensory and visceral evidence. As people grow older, their valuing process is effective in helping them to achieve self-actualizing to the degree that they are able to be aware of and perceive the experiencing which is going on within them.

EXPERIENCE AND EXPERIENCING

Rogers uses the term 'sensory and visceral experience' in a psychological rather than a physiological sense. Perhaps another way of stating sensory and visceral experience is the undergoing of facts and events, which are potentially available to conscious awareness, by the organism's sensory and visceral equipment. People may be unaware of much of their experiencing. For instance, when sitting, you may not be aware of the sensation on your buttocks until your attention is drawn to it. Another example is that you may not be aware of the physiological aspects of hunger because you are so fascinated by work or play. However, this experience is potentially available to conscious awareness. The total range of experience at any given moment may be called the 'experiential', 'perceptual' or 'phenomenal' field. Rogers stressed that physiological events such as neuron discharges or changes in blood sugar are not included in his psychological definition of experience.

The verb experiencing means that the organism is receiving the impact of any sensory or visceral experiences that happen at the moment. Experiencing a feeling includes receiving both the emotional content and the personal meaning or cognitive content 'as they are experienced inseparably in the moment' (Rogers, 1959, p. 198). Experiencing a feeling fully means that experiencing, awareness and expression of the feeling are all congruent.

PERCEPTION AND AWARENESS

Perception and awareness are virtually synonymous in person-centred theory. When an experience is perceived, this means that it is in conscious awareness, however dimly, though it need not be expressed in verbal symbols. Another way of stating this is that 'perceiving' is 'becoming aware of stimuli or experiences'. Rogers viewed all perception and awareness as transactional in nature, being a construction from past experience and a hypothesis or prediction of the future. Perception or awareness may or may not correspond with experience or 'reality'. When an experience is symbolized accurately in awareness, this means that the hypothesis implicit in the awareness will be borne out if tested by acting on it. Many experiences may not be symbolized accurately in awareness because of defensive denials and distortions. Other experiences, such as buttocks sitting on a chair, may not be perceived, since they may be unimportant to the organism.

Awareness, or conscious attention, is one of the latest evolutionary developments of the human species. One way in which Rogers regarded it was as 'a tiny peak of awareness, of symbolizing capacity, topping a vast pyramid of non-conscious organismic functioning' (Rogers, 1977, p. 244). Figure 4.1 attempts to illustrate this. When a person is functioning well, awareness is a reflection of part of the flow of the organism at that moment. However, all too often people are not functioning well, and organismically they are moving in one direction while their aware or conscious lives are struggling in another.

ACQUISITION

Person-centred theory may become clearer to the reader by maintaining a distinction between self and self-concept. The self may be viewed as the real, underlying, organismic self expressed in popular sayings such as 'To thine own self be true' and 'To be that self which one truly is'. People's self-concepts are their perceptions

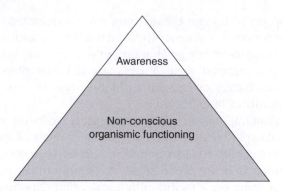

Figure 4.1 Pyramidal view of awareness and non-conscious organismic functioning

of themselves, which do not always correspond with their own experiencing or organismic selves. Thus, ideally the actualizing tendency refers to self-actualizing where aspects of self and of self-concept are synonymous or congruent. However, where self and self-concept are incongruent, the desire to actualize the self-concept may work against the deeper need to actualize the organismic self. In Rogers' writings, the above distinction is always implicit, if not always explicit.

EARLY DEVELOPMENT OF SELF-CONCEPT

The self-concept is the self as perceived and the values attached to these perceptions, or what a person refers to as 'I' or 'me'. Initially, the self-concept may be made up largely of self-experiences, events in the phenomenal field discriminated by the individual as 'I', 'me', or 'self', albeit in a pre-verbal way. For instance, infants who discover their toes may incorporate the fact that they have toes into their self-concept. Also, infants who are hungry may incorporate into their self-concepts the fact that they negatively value hunger. As young people interact with the environment, more and more experience may become symbolized in awareness as self-experience. Not least through interaction with significant others who treat them as a separate self, they develop a self-concept which includes both their perceptions about themselves and the varying positive and negative values attached to these self-perceptions.

CONDITIONS OF WORTH

A need for positive regard from others is a learned need developed in early infancy. Positive regard means here the perception of experiencing oneself as making a positive difference in the experiential field of another. It is likely that, on many occasions, young people's behaviour and experiencing of their behaviour will coincide with positive regard from others and hence meet their need for positive regard. For instance, smiling at parents may reflect a pleasurable experience as well as generating positive regard.

However, on other occasions, young people may feel that their experiencing conflicts with their need for positive regard from significant others. Rogers gives the example of the child who experiences satisfaction at hitting his baby brother, but who experiences the words and actions of his parents as saying 'You are bad, the behaviour is bad, and you are not loved or lovable when you behave this way'. An outcome of this may be that the child does not acknowledge the pleasurable value of hitting his baby brother emanating from his own experience, but comes to place a negative value on the experience because of the attitudes held by his parents and his need for positive regard. Thus, instead of an accurate symbolization of the experience, such as 'While I experience the behaviour as satisfying, my parents experience it as unsatisfying', there may come a distorted symbolization, such as 'I perceive this behaviour as unsatisfying' (Rogers, 1951, p. 500). Such values, which are based on others' evaluations rather than on the individual's own organismic valuing process, are called conditions of worth. Conditions of worth are prevalent because all too often 'individuals are culturally conditioned, rewarded, reinforced, for behaviors that are in fact perversions of the natural directions of the unitary actualizing tendency' (Rogers, 1977, p. 247).

The concept of conditions of worth is important because it means that people develop a second valuing process. The first is the organismic valuing process that truly reflects the actualizing tendency. The second is a conditions of worth process, based on the internalization or 'introjection' of others' evaluations, which does not truly reflect the actualizing tendency but may serve to impede it. However, people possess a false awareness in regard to this second valuing process, since they feel that decisions based on it are in fact based on their organismic valuing process. Thus experiences may be sought or avoided to meet false rather than real needs.

FAMILY LIFE

The adequacy of the self-concepts of parents affects the ways in which they relate to their children. Thomas Gordon, a contributor to Rogers' 1951 book *Client-Centered Therapy*, has emphasized that the level of self-acceptance or self-regard of parents may be related to their degree of acceptance of the behaviour of their children, though this is not something which is static. Rogers observed that parents are able to feel unconditional positive regard for a child only to the extent that they experience unconditional self-regard. By 'unconditional positive regard' Rogers meant prizing a child even though the parent may not value equally all of his or her behaviours. The greater the degree of unconditional positive regard that parents experience towards the child, the fewer the conditions of worth in the child and the higher the level of its psychological adjustment. Put simply, high-functioning parents create the conditions for the development of high-functioning children. In 1970, Gordon published *Parent Effectiveness Training* based on person-centred principles. This book attempts to teach parents how to listen to and talk with their children, thus helping the attitude of prizing to be communicated to them.

THE EFFECT OF CONDITIONS OF WORTH ON SELF-CONCEPT

People differ in the degree to which they internalize conditions of worth depending not only on the degree of unconditional positive regard they are offered by significant others, but also on the degree of empathic understanding and congruence shown to them. In addition the extent of their need for positive regard influences their vulnerability to introjecting conditions of worth. For some, their self-concepts will develop so as to allow much of their experience to be accurately perceived. However, even the most fortunate are likely to internalize some conditions of worth, and the less fortunate are fated to internalize many.

Examples of conditions of worth are: 'Achievement is very important and I am less of a person if I do not achieve' and 'Making money is very important and, if I do not make much money, then I am a failure'. Thus conditions of worth entail not only internalized evaluations of how people should be, but also internalized evaluations about how they should feel about themselves if they perceive that they are not the way they should be. Rogers believed that it is common for most people to have their values largely introjected, held as fixed concepts and rarely examined or tested. Thus, not only are these people estranged from their experiencing, but their level of self-regard is lowered and they are unable to prize themselves fully. Furthermore, by internalizing conditions of worth, they have internalized a process by which they come to be the agents of lowering their own level of self-regard or, more colloquially, of 'self-oppression'.

MARRIAGE AND EDUCATION

The person-centred view is that the conditions for the development of adequate self-concepts and those for remedying inadequate self-concepts are essentially the same. Both contain the characteristics of good and loving interpersonal relationships. Implicit in this is the notion that significant experiences for the development of adequate and, regrettably, also of inadequate self-concepts are neither restricted to childhood and adolescence nor to family life.

Rogers saw contributions to the development of adequate self-concepts as potentially available in many other human situations. Most people are less self-actualizing than desirable because they are cluttered up with conditions of worth. Rogers increasingly turned his attentions to the problems of the less disturbed. Relationships between partners, whether marital or otherwise, can have growth-inducing properties in which conditions of worth dissolve and the level of self-regard increases. In *Becoming Partners*, Rogers (1973) gave a moving case study involving Joe's steady and healing concern for and trust in Irene's potential, despite her initial self-conception that 'I don't let you see this little, black, rotten, ugly ball I have buried down inside that's really me, that's unlovable and unacceptable' (Rogers, 1973, p. 100).

Rogers also turned his attention to the under-realized potential of educational institutions for creating emotional climates for the development of healthy self-concepts. He particularly favoured significant experiential learning that was self-initiated and reflected the concerns of students rather than those of teachers or administrators (Rogers, 1969). In addition, he focused on the politics of interpersonal and inter-group relationships and saw his faith in the actualizing tendency as indicating a more democratic sharing of power and control (Rogers, 1977).

MAINTENANCE

For practising counsellors and therapists the question is not so much how clients become the way they are, as what currently causes them to maintain behaviour that does not meet their current needs. The concept of maintenance or of how maladjusted behaviour and perceptions are perpetuated, often in the face of conflicting evidence, is critical to a full understanding of person-centred theory and practice. Person-centred theory may be viewed as a theory of human information processing or of the processing of experiences into perceptions. This is a process in which, especially for those who are disturbed, conditions of worth play a large part.

PROCESSING OF EXPERIENCE

Rogers observed that when experiences occur in people's lives there are four possible outcomes. First, like the sensation of sitting, they may be ignored. Second, they may be accurately perceived and organized into some relationship with the self-concept either because they meet a need of the self or because they are consistent with the self-concept and thus reinforce it. Third, their perception may be distorted in such a way as to resolve the conflict between self-concept and experiencing. For instance, students with low academic self-concepts may receive some positive feedback about their essays and perceive 'The teacher did not read it properly', or 'The teacher must have low standards'. Fourth, the experiences may be denied or not perceived at all. For example, people may have had their self-concepts deeply influenced by strict moral upbringings and thus be unable to perceive their cravings for sexual satisfaction.

Figure 4.2 represents the processing of experience by low-functioning and high-functioning people. Previously I mentioned that people have two valuing processes, their own organismic valuing process and an internalized process based on conditions of worth. Low-functioning people are out of touch with their own valuing process for large areas of their experiencing. In these areas their self-concepts are based on conditions of worth that cause them to distort and deny much of their experiencing. On the other hand, high-functioning people have fewer conditions of worth and thus are able to perceive most of their experiences accurately.

Both high-functioning and low-functioning people are motivated by the actualizing tendency. The self-concepts of high-functioning people allow them to perceive most significant sensory and visceral experiences and thus their self-actualizing entails no significant blockages to their actualizing tendency. However, with low-functioning people a split occurs and 'the general tendency to actualize the organism may work at cross purposes with the subsystem of that motive, the tendency to actualize the self' (Rogers, 1959, p. 197). Low-functioning people engage in a process of actualizing insufficiently based on their organism's own valuing process. Consequently, while high-functioning people are able to interact with others and their environments on the basis of largely realistic information, low-functioning people do not have that capacity to any great extent.

INCONGRUENCE BETWEEN SELF-CONCEPT AND EXPERIENCE

When experiences are accurately symbolized and included in the self-concept, there is a state of congruence between self-concept and experience or, stated another way, between the self-concept and the organismic valuing process. When, however, experience is denied and distorted, there exists a state of incongruence between self-concept and experience. This state of incongruence

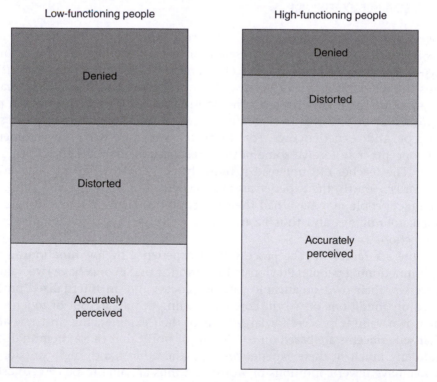

Figure 4.2   Processing of experience by low-functioning and high-functioning people

may exist where experiences are positive as well as where they are negative. Counselling and therapy clients tend to have low self-concepts and frequently deny and distort positive feedback from outside as well as inhibit positive feelings from within.

THREAT, ANXIETY AND SUBCEPTION

Rogers uses the concept of subception or pre-perception to explain the mechanism by which sensory and visceral experiences relevant to the actualizing tendency may be denied or inaccurately perceived. He quotes McCleary and Lazarus' finding that 'Even when a subject is unable to report a visual discrimination he is still able to make a stimulus discrimination at some level below that required for conscious recognition' (1949, p. 178). Subception involves a filtering of experience in such a way that experiences contradictory and threatening to the self-concept may be excluded or altered. Thus the organism may discriminate the meaning of an experience without using the higher nerve centres involved in conscious awareness or perception. The process of subception is the mechanism of defence of the self-concept in response to threats to its current structure or set of self-conceptions.

Anxiety is a state of uneasiness or tension that is the response of the organism to the 'subception' that a discrepancy or incongruence between self-concept and experience may enter perception or awareness, thus forcing a change in the currently prevailing self-concept. The term 'intensionality' is used to describe characteristics of the individual who is in a defensive state. Intensional reactions include seeing experience in absolute and rigid terms, overgeneralization, confusing facts and evaluation, and relying on abstractions rather than on reality testing.

BREAKDOWN AND DISORGANIZATION

This section relates to serious disturbance. The self-concepts of very low-functioning people block their accurate perception of large areas of their significant sensory and visceral experience. If, however, a situation develops in which a significant experience occurs suddenly, or very obviously, in an area of high incongruence, the process of defence may be unable to operate successfully. Thus, not only may anxiety be experienced to the extent to which the self-concept is threatened, but, with the process of defence being unsuccessful, the experience may be accurately symbolized in awareness. People are brought face-to-face with more of their denied experiences than they can handle, with an ensuing state of disorganization and the possibility of a psychotic breakdown. Rogers mentioned that he had known psychotic breakdowns to occur when people sought 'therapy' from many different sources simultaneously and also when clients were prematurely faced with material revealed under the influence of sodium pentathol. Once acute psychotic behaviours have been exhibited, the defensive processes may work to protect people against the pain and anxiety generated by the perception of the incongruence.

IMPORTANCE OF SELF-CONCEPT

A person's self-concept, especially certain self-perceptions that are viewed as central, has been demonstrated to be fundamental to understanding how psychological maladjustment is maintained. The self-concept is so important to people because it is the constellation of their perceptions about themselves and, as such, the means by which they interact with life in such a way as to meet their needs. Effective self-concepts allow people to perceive their experiences realistically, whether they originate within their organisms or in their environments; in other words, such self-concepts allow them open access to their experiences.

Ineffective self-concepts may be maintained tenaciously for a number of reasons. First, as with the effective self-concepts, ineffective self-concepts are perceived as the means of need gratification and the source of personal adequacy. Second, ineffective self-concepts contain within them many conditions of worth which may have been functional at one stage of people's lives, but which have outgrown any usefulness they once possessed. Nevertheless, because they originate from people's need for positive regard, they may be deeply embedded in the structure of their self-concepts as a kind of 'emotional baggage'. Third, the more deeply embedded such conditions of worth have become the more tenaciously they are maintained, since to alter them would involve the anxiety of perceiving the incongruence between these self-perceptions and experiencing. Fourth, the conditions of worth have the effect of lowering people's sense of worth and thus making it less likely that they will have the confidence to acknowledge and face their areas of incongruence. There is a threshold area for both high-functioning and low-functioning people in which they may be able to assimilate incongruent perceptions into their self-concepts. This threshold area appears to be narrower and more tightly defined for low-functioning people.

CHARACTERISTICS OF SELF-CONCEPT

Since the idea of self-concept, sometimes expressed as 'self-structure', 'perceived self', 'phenomenal self', or just 'self', is so fundamental to person-centred theory, I briefly review some of its characteristics.

- *Content areas*: People's self-concepts are unique complexes of many different self-conceptions that constitute their way of describing and distinguishing themselves. Some content areas of people's self-concepts include bodily, social, sexual feelings and emotions, tastes and preferences, work, recreation, intellectual activity, and philosophy and values. People vary in the importance they attach to these various areas and also in the kinds of self-conceptions they have in them. For instance, one person may feel the shape of their nose as important while another may be scarcely aware of it. The self-concept may be described in self-referent statements such as 'I am a good carpenter', 'I like ice-cream' and 'Meeting new people makes me nervous'.

- *Structure or process*: The self-concept may be viewed as a structure made up of different self-conceptions related to each other in various ways. The self-concept is also the means or process by which people interact with the environment and by which they ignore, deny, distort or accurately perceive experience.

- *Central–peripheral*: Combs and Snygg (1959) distinguish between the phenomenal self, the organization or pattern of all those aspects which people refer to as 'I' or 'me', and the self-concept, those perceptions about self which are most vital to people themselves and which may be regarded as their very essence. For all people, some self-conceptions are much more central than others, and everyone has their unique way of ordering self-conceptions as central or peripheral, even though this is often more implicit than explicit.

- *Congruence–incongruence*: Many self-conceptions may match the reality of people's experiencing, in which case there is congruence between self-conception and experience. Other self-conceptions may be different in varying degrees from the reality of their experiencing, in which case a state of incongruence exists.

- *Conditions of worth*: Incongruence implies that a self-conception is based on a condition of worth rather than on the organism's own valuing process. For example, an incongruent self-conception for a person may be 'I want to be a doctor', whereas a congruent self-conception may be 'I want to be an artist'. Being a doctor may be based on values internalized from parents, whereas being an artist represents the organism's own valuing process.

- *Subception and defence*: This is an area of self-concept as a process. Experiences may be denied or distorted by the process of subception. This process defends existing self-conceptions by preventing the person from perceiving incongruence and hence possibly changing both self-conceptions and behaviour.

- *Intensionality–extensionality*: Intensionality describes characteristics of a self-concept in a defensive state, for example rigidity and absence of adequate reality testing. Extensionality describes characteristics of a mature self-concept, such as seeing experience in limited, differentiated terms and testing inferences and abstractions against reality.

- *Level of self-regard*: Another way of expressing level of self-regard is the degree to which individuals prize themselves. Rogers stated that when people's self-concepts were such that no self-experience could be discriminated as more or less worthy of positive regard than any other, then they were experiencing unconditional positive self-regard. Level of self-acceptance is another way of stating level of self-regard.

- *Real–ideal*: Whereas real self-conceptions represent my perceptions of how I am, ideal self-conceptions represent my conceptions of how I would most like to be. Both real and ideal self-conceptions form parts of people's self-concept complex.

THERAPY

THERAPEUTIC GOALS

The question of goals in the person-centred framework can be addressed in two ways: first, the goals of individual clients in therapy and, second, overall goals reflecting the human potential for growth. Clients in person-centred therapy are responsible for having their own purposes and goals.

Therapists do not tell clients where they should be going or how to get there. At the start of therapy there is no process of assessment and goal setting. Rather clients may come with some goals and then, within the context of a safe thera- peutic relationship, may choose to reveal further goals and, as therapy pro- gresses, still different goals may emerge. Much of person-centred therapy focuses on helping clients become more in touch with their feelings and organismic valuing process. During this process clients may evolve a greater sense of what truly are their goals. For some clients, working through to what are personal goals, as contrasted with goals that are 'hand-me-downs' from significant oth- ers, may take many therapy sessions.

Much of the time Rogers saw overall goals in terms of characteristics of the fully functioning person (Rogers, 1959, 1961). However, he also wrote a later statement on the qualities of the person of tomorrow who can live in a vastly changed world (Rogers, 1980). He considered that a paradigm shift was taking place from old to new ways of conceptualizing the person. Table 4.1 presents characteristics, albeit overlapping, of the fully functioning person and the per- son of tomorrow.

Here I identify six main dimensions or themes concerning goals in Rogers' writings, including the scale he developed with some colleagues to measure process changes in psychotherapy (Walker, Rablen and Rogers, 1960). Clients might come into therapy at differing levels on these dimensions and then, dur- ing the course of successful therapy, move forward to higher levels of functioning.

OPENNESS TO EXPERIENCE

A self-concept that allows all significant sensory and visceral experiences to be perceived is the basis for effective functioning. Rogers frequently used the term 'openness to experience' to describe the capacity for realistic perception and observed that 'There is no need for the mechanism of "subception" whereby the organism is forewarned of experiences threatening to the self' (Rogers, 1959, p. 206). Openness to experience makes for more efficient behaviour in that people have a wider perceptual field and are able to behave more often from choice than from necessity. Openness to experience may also increase the possibility of spontaneity and creativity, since people are less bound by the straitjacket of conditions of worth. In other words, openness to experience enables people to engage in an existential process of living where they are alive, able to handle change, and alert to the range of their choices for creating their lives.

RATIONALITY

A feature of openness to experience is that it allows for rationality. When people are in touch with their organismic experiencing their behaviour is likely to be rational in terms of maintaining and enhancing their organism. Rogers thought

Table 4.1 Characteristics of the fully functioning person and the person of tomorrow

The fully functioning person	The person of tomorrow
Open to experience and able to perceive realistically	Openness to the world, both inner and outer
Desire for authenticity	Scepticism regarding science and technology
Rational and not defensive	
Engaged in existential process of living	Desire for wholeness as a human being
Trusts in organismic valuing process	The wish for intimacy
Construes experience in extensional manner	Process persons
	Cares for others
Accepts responsibility for being different	Attitude of closeness toward nature
Accepts responsibility for own behaviour	Anti-institutional
Relates creatively to the environment	Trusts the authority within
Accepts others as unique individuals	Material things unimportant
Prizes himself or herself	A yearning for the spiritual
Prizes others	
Relates openly and freely on the basis of immediate experiencing	
Communicates rich self-awareness when desired	

it tragic that the defences of most people kept them out of touch with how rational they could be. What was earlier described as extensionality rather than intensionality is a characteristic of this rationality.

PERSONAL RESPONSIBILITY

The term personal responsibility refers to people's taking responsibility *for* their own personal development and not just feeling responsible to others. This covers Rogers' ideas of individuals' trust in their organismic valuing process, trust of the authority within, acceptance of responsibility for their own behaviour, and also acceptance of responsibility for being different from others. Personally responsible people, within the existential parameters of death and destiny, are capable of taking control of their lives. The person-centred philosophy in many aspects is one of self-control, self-help and personal power, hopefully within the context of caring relationships. Acknowledgment of personal responsibility is a central part of the self-concepts of effective people.

SELF-REGARD

Self-regard is another important part of the self-concepts of effective people. One way of expressing this is that a person possesses a high degree of unconditional self-regard, or self-acceptance. It is a self-regard based on their organismic valuing process rather than on the praise and needs of others. People with a high degree of unconditional self-regard will prize themselves, even though they may not prize all their behaviours and attributes.

CAPACITY FOR GOOD PERSONAL RELATIONSHIPS

Self-acceptance means that people are less likely to be defensive and hence more likely to accept others. The capacity for good personal relationships incorporates Rogers' notions of accepting others as unique individuals, prizing others, relating openly and freely to them on the basis of immediate experiencing, and having the capacity, when appropriate, to communicate a rich self-awareness. These relationships are characterized by mutual concern for both persons' development. Rogers considered congruence, genuineness, or 'realness' to be probably the most important element in the ordinary interactions of life, while empathy has the highest priority where the other person is anxious and vulnerable.

ETHICAL LIVING

Person-centred theory is based on a view that people, at their core, are trustworthy organisms. This shows itself in the social relations of well functioning people in at least two ways. First, they are capable of a wide identification with other human beings, so they are likely to seek others' development along with their own. Consequently, they are careful not to infringe on the rights of others while pursuing their own ends. Second, they appear to be able to distinguish sharply between ends and means and between good and evil. Qualities which are likely to contribute to such people's ethical living are trust in internal rather than in external authority; an indifference to material things, such as money and status symbols; an attitude of closeness to and reverence for nature; and a yearning and seeking for spiritual values that are greater than the individual.

PROCESS OF THERAPY

The process of person-centred therapy is built on a basic trust of the client's ability, within a growth-promoting climate, to actualize her or his human potential. Right from the beginning Rogers would encourage clients to assume responsibility for the contents of the therapy sessions. Therapy starts with an invitation indicating that the therapist will be an interested listener to whatever the clients wants to share. Following is Rogers' opening statement from a demonstration interview conducted in his later years.

> I don't know what you might want to talk about, but I'm very ready to hear. We have half an hour, and I hope that in that half an hour we can get to know each other as deeply as possible, but we don't need to strive for anything, I guess that's my feeling. Do you want to tell me whatever is on your mind? (Raskin and Rogers, 2005, p. 147).

There is no formal assessment in person-centred therapy since all clients are viewed as being out of touch with their experience on account of their conditions of worth. If therapists were, from their own external frames of reference, to assess clients they would risk replicating the circumstances that had led the latter to acquire and maintain their conditions of worth. In addition, therapists avoid any interpretations or placing external constructions on what the client reveals. Rather they act as companions as clients share whatever seems important at the time. In particular, Rogers would assist clients to express, experience and explore feelings, be they positive, negative, ambivalent or confused, at a rate comfortable for them.

Rogers would define his and the client's role not only by his opening remarks but also by how he listened carefully to what clients communicated without trying to judge or influence their stream of talk in any direction other than their own. Furthermore, Rogers would refuse to allow clients to place him in roles that allowed him to assume responsibility for directing and leading them. For example, if a client said: 'What do you think I should do?' Rogers would show acceptance and understanding of the client's feeling of really wanting an answer about what to do without usurping the client's authority and supplying the answer. In such situations, Rogers might indicate that, without having the answers himself, he hoped he could assist the client to find an answer than was right for her or him. The initial session would end without any attempt to summarize the session or tie up loose ends before closing. Therapist and client would respectfully take their leave of one another.

Person-centred therapy is a process that goes on between as well as within sessions. Though no formal homework is set, most often clients continue the process of therapy by means of their thoughts, feelings and actions between sessions. Subsequent sessions start with clients being allowed to assume responsibility about where to begin: for instance, with an opening remark such as 'Where would you like to start today?' Again, Rogers would attempt to provide a growth promoting climate as clients attempted to get in touch with and experience their own feelings, explore the circumstances of their lives, and settle upon goals and directions that seemed appropriate for them. The same growth promoting climate allows clients, when ready, to address the issue of terminating therapy and how best to lead their lives afterwards.

A more poetic impression of the process of person-centred therapy can be gathered from one of Rogers' favourite sayings from Lao-Tse.

> It is as though he listened
> and such listening as his enfolds us in a silence
> in which at last we begin to hear
> what we are meant to be.

THE THERAPEUTIC RELATIONSHIP

How is a growth promoting relationship achieved? Person-centred therapy does not rely on techniques or on doing things to clients. Rogers believed that in therapy 'it is the *quality* of the interpersonal encounter with the client which is the most significant element in determining effectiveness' (Rogers, 1962, p. 416). Person-centred therapy is a process that can intensely involve the thoughts and feelings of clients and therapists. There is a coherence between how person-centred therapists see the origins of clients' self-aliena-tion and inner schisms and how they can assist them to grow and become healed. Person-centred therapists try to provide the attitudinal conditions that are the antidote to the emotional deprivations that their clients have experienced.

What are the conditions for client growth and reintegration? In 1957, Rogers presented his six necessary and sufficient conditions for therapeutic personality change. He stated that the following conditions had to exist and continue over a period of time for constructive personality change to occur. Also, that 'No other conditions are necessary' (Rogers, 1957, p. 96). First, two people need to be in psychological contact. Second, the client is in a state of incongruence and is vulnerable or anxious. Third, the therapist 'is congruent or integrated in the relationship'. Fourth and fifth, the therapist experiences 'unconditional positive regard for the client', and 'an empathic understanding of the client's internal frame of reference and endeavours to communicate this to the client' (p. 96). Sixth, the therapist is minimally successful in communicating empathic under-standing and unconditional positive regard to the client. Rogers regarded con-gruence, unconditional positive regard and empathy as 'the attitudinal conditions that foster therapeutic growth ...' (Rogers and Sanford, 1985, p. 1379). He stressed that they were not all or none conditions, but exist on continua.

CONGRUENCE

Other words for congruence are genuineness, realness, openness, transparency and presence. Congruence is the most basic of the attitudinal conditions. Therapists need to be in touch with the feelings that they experience, have them available to awareness, and 'to live these feelings, be them in the relation-ship, and ... communicate them if appropriate' (Rogers, 1962, p. 417). Therapists should encounter their clients in direct person-to-person contact. They should avoid an intellectual approach in which clients get treated as objects. Congruent therapists are not playing roles, being polite, or putting on professional façades.

Rogers acknowledged that no one fully achieves congruence all the time. Imperfect human beings can be of assistance to clients. It is enough for thera-pists, in particular moments in immediate relationships with specific persons to be completely and fully themselves with their experiences accurately sym-bolized into their self-concepts.

Congruence does not mean that therapists 'blurt out impulsively every pass-ing feeling ...' (Rogers, 1962, p. 418). Nor does it mean that they allow their sessions to become therapist-centred rather than client-centred. However, it can mean that they take the risk of sharing a feeling or giving feedback that might improve the relationship because it is expressed genuinely. An example is that of therapists sharing their experience of fatigue rather than trying to cover it up. Such openness may restore the therapist's energy level and allow the client to see that they are dealing with a real person. Another example is that Rogers thought that, if he felt persistently bored with a client, he owed it to the client and their relationship to share the feeling. He would own the bored feeling as located in himself rather than make it into an accusatory statement. He would share his discomfort at sharing the feeling and communicate that he would like to be more in touch with the client. Rogers strove to overcome the barrier between them by being real, imperfect and sharing his genuine feeling. He would hope that the client could use this as a stepping-stone to speak more genuinely.

Another insight into congruence may be obtained from what Rogers says about the concept of *presence*. In therapy, both therapists and clients can attain altered states of consciousness in which they feel they are in touch with and grasp the meaning of the underlying evolutionary flow. There can be a mystical and spiritual dimension in counselling and therapy. Rogers considered that he was at his best as a therapist when he was closest to his inner intuitive self and 'when perhaps I am in a slightly altered state of consciousness. Then simply my *presence* is releasing and helpful to the other' (Rogers, 1980, p. 129). In such a state, behaviours that may be strange, impulsive, and hard to justify rationally turn out to be right. Rogers wrote: 'it seems that my inner spirit has reached out and touched the inner spirit of the other. Our relationship transcends itself and becomes a part of something larger. Profound growth and healing and energy are present' (Rogers, 1980, p. 129). Rogers stated that he may behave in strange and unexpected ways which have nothing to do with his thought processes. It is as though his inner spirit has reached out and touched the inner spirit of the other. He considered that he had underestimated the importance of this mystical, spiritual dimension in therapy and in groups.

UNCONDITIONAL POSITIVE REGARD

Other terms used to describe this condition include non-possessive warmth, caring, prizing, acceptance and respect. Unconditional positive regard relates to Rogers' deep trust in his clients' capacity for constructive change if provided with the right nurturing conditions. Rogers stressed the importance of the therapist's attitude towards the worth and significance of each person. The therapist's own struggles for personal integration are relevant to unconditional positive regard since they can be only respectful of clients' capacities to achieve constructive self-direction if that respect is an integral part of their own personality make-ups.

Unconditional positive regard involves the therapist's willingness for clients 'to *be* whatever immediate feeling is going on – confusion, resentment, fear, anger, courage, love, or pride …' (Rogers, 1986a, p. 198). This respect is equivalent to the love expressed by the Christian concept of 'agape', without any romantic or possessive connotations. Rogers makes the analogy between the kind of love parents can feel for their children, prizing them as people regardless of their particular behaviours at any moment. Therapists do not show positive regard for their clients – *if*. If they are smarter, less defensive, less vulnerable and so on. Person-centred theory explains the need for clients to seek therapy because in their pasts they were shown positive regard – *if*.

There are boundaries to showing unconditional positive regard, for instance where a client were to physically threaten a therapist. Unconditional positive regard does not mean that therapists need, from their frames of reference, to approve of all their clients' behaviours. Rather, unconditional positive regard is an attitude and philosophical orientation, reflected in therapist behaviour, that clients are more likely to move forward if they feel prized for their humanity and they experience an emotional climate of safety and freedom in which, without losing their therapist's acceptance, they can show feelings and relate events.

EMPATHY

Other terms for empathy include accurate empathy, empathic understanding, empathic responsiveness, an empathic way of being, an empathic stance, and an empathic attitude. Rogers (1957) wrote: 'To sense the client's private world as if it were your own, but without ever losing the "as if" quality – this is empathy ...' (p. 99). There are various facets to an empathic way of being with clients. Therapists need to 'get into the shoes of' and 'get under the skin' of their clients to understand their private subjective worlds. They need to be sensitive to the moment-by-moment flow of experiencing that goes on both in clients and themselves. They need the capacity to pick up nuances and sense meanings of which clients are scarcely aware. With tact, sensitivity and awareness of what clients can handle, they need to communicate their understandings of their sensings of clients' worlds and personal meanings.

Therapists should communicate their commitment to understanding their clients' worlds by frequently checking the accuracy of their understandings and showing their willingness to be corrected. Empathy is an active process in which therapists desire to know and reach out to receive clients' communications and meanings (Barrett-Lennard, 1998). An empathic attitude creates an emotional climate in which clients can assist their therapists to understand them more accurately.

Responding to individual client statements is a process of listening and observing, resonating, discriminating, communicating and checking your understanding. Needless to say, the final dimension is that the client has, to some extent, perceived the therapist's empathy. Even better is that the therapist's empathy has enabled the client to get more in touch with the flow of her or his experiencing. Box 4.1, taken from a demonstration film with Rogers as the therapist (Rogers, 1965), illustrates this process. The client, Gloria, is talking about how her father could never show he cared for her the way she would have liked.

BOX 4.1   DIMENSIONS OF THE EMPATHY PROCESS

Gloria's statement: 'I don't know what it is. You know when I talk about it feels more flip. If I just sit still a minute, it feels like a great big hurt down there. Instead, I feel cheated.'

Rogers' responding processes

Observing and listening: Observes and listens to the client's verbal, vocal and bodily communication.

Resonating: Feels some of the emotion the client experiences.

Discriminating: Discriminates what is really important to the client and formulates this into a response.

Communicating: 'It's much easier to be a little flip because then you don't feel that big lump inside of hurt.'
Communicates a response that attempts to show understanding of the client's thoughts, feelings and personal meanings. Accompanies verbal with good vocal and bodily communication.

Checking: In this instance, Gloria quickly made her next statement that followed the train of her experiencing and thought. However, Rogers could either have waited and allowed Gloria space to respond or could have enquired if his response was accurate.

Gloria's perception of Rogers' responding

How Gloria reacted indicated she perceived that Rogers showed excellent empathy and that she was able to continue getting more in touch with her experiencing.

Though the next example of empathy comes from an encounter group (Rogers, 1975, p. 3), the empathic process it demonstrates holds true for working with individual clients. A man has been making vaguely negative statements about his father. First, the facilitator enquires whether he might be angry with his father. When the man says he doesn't think so, the facilitator says 'Possibly dissatisfied with him?', to which the man rather doubtfully responds 'Well, yes, perhaps.' Then the facilitator enquires whether the man is disappointed in his father, to which he quickly responds 'That's it! I *am* disappointed that he's not a strong person. I think I've always been disappointed in him ever since I was a boy.'

In the above example, the facilitator is not interpreting the client, nor would Rogers. Rather the facilitator progressively checks out his understanding to grasp exactly what the man wishes to say. Gendlin (1988) mentions how Rogers would take in each correction until the client indicated 'Yes, that's how it is.

That's what I feel.' (p. 127). Characteristically this statement would be followed by a silence in which the client fully received the empathic understanding. Very often during these silences, clients would get in touch with something deeper.

A word now about what empathy is not. True empathy does not have any judgemental or diagnostic quality about it. Empathy is most definitely not a 'wooden technique of pseudo-understanding in which the counselor "reflects back what the client has just said"' (Rogers, 1962, p. 420). In his 1975 article on empathy, Rogers observed how at first he found it helpful to think that the best response was to 'reflect' feelings back to clients, but that later on in his career the word 'reflect' made him cringe. Still unhappy with the term reflection of feelings, Rogers later suggested that therapists' mirroring responses be better labelled as 'testing understanding' or 'checking perceptions' (Rogers, 1986b). To Rogers, empathy was an attitude, a very special form of companionship, a gentle and sensitive way of being with clients. However well intended, mechanical reflections form no part of offering empathy.

THERAPEUTIC INTERVENTIONS

Person-centred therapy is unique among the therapies covered in this book in that Rogers considered a growth promoting relationship characterized by the attitudinal conditions necessary and sufficient for client change to occur. The same attitudinal conditions are relevant when dealing with clients' feelings towards therapists. Rogers considered that some client feelings towards their therapists were understandable responses to therapist behaviour, whereas other feelings were projections 'transferred' from previous relationships. Even in dealing with clients' transference feelings, there was no call for special interventions, such as interpreting the transference. Rogers observed, whether the feelings be therapist-caused or transference reactions, 'If the therapist is sensitively understanding and genuinely acceptant and non-judgmental, then therapy will move forward through these feelings' (Rogers, 1990, p. 130).

CASE MATERIAL

Rogers was very diligent in providing case material and researching the processes and outcomes of person-centred therapy. Readers are encouraged to explore primary sources to get a feel of how Rogers worked. Following are some suggestions about where to look. In *Counseling and Psychotherapy*, Rogers provides a transcript plus some commentary for each of his eight sessions with Herbert Bryan, a young man in his late twenties whom he regarded as definitely neurotic (Rogers, 1942). In *On Becoming a Person*, Rogers provides two excerpts from the case of Mrs Oak, a housewife in her late thirties who was experiencing difficulties in marital and family relationships (Rogers, 1961). This case write-up is also available in *Case Studies in Psychotherapy* (Rogers,

2005). Rogers' work with Gloria is both on film (Rogers, 1965) and part of it is written up as a case example (Raskin and Rogers, 2005). Raskin and Rogers (2005) also provide an example of the first and final thirds of a demonstration interview conducted by Rogers in 1983 illustrating the process of therapy, followed by a brief commentary. Elsewhere Rogers presented excerpts and commentary from another demonstration interview, with a woman called Jan, conducted before a workshop of six hundred participants in Johannesburg, South Africa (Rogers, 1986a).

Thorne (2007) provides a person-centred case study in which he works with Jeremy a man in his early thirties. This case study demonstrates the strength of the therapeutic relationship and the therapist's commitment to his client who at one stage, without getting in touch, did not appear for a session. Thorne (2007) also presents a case example, with Caroline Kitcatt as therapist, in which the client was a woman in her late thirties who came to counselling six months after the break up of her marriage. As part of the process, the client was helped to work through to a more accepting relationship with her mother. Mearns et al. (2013) provide a case example in which the counsellor, Mearns, and the client, a 27-year-old married woman, attain relational depth during the course of their 17 sessions together. Raskin et al. (2014) present and comment upon a demonstration interview by Dr Barbara Temaner Brodley, conducted in 1986 at a cross-cultural workshop in Hungary, with a young European woman who had recently earned a masters degree in the United States. Though only approximately 20 minutes long, this interview demonstrates how, even in a relatively short time, a client can learn in a trusting relationship from material which she is helped to reveal.

FURTHER DEVELOPMENTS

Person-centred therapy has been presented here in relation to individual work. However, Rogers interests and influence were much more extensive. Rogers championed the use of person-centred principles in encounter groups, classroom teaching, management, and peace and conflict resolution.

Rogers has also influenced other people to develop his ideas. For example, in Britain, Mearns and Thorne (2013) have expanded Rogers' notion of self into configurations of self. Their initial working definition is: 'A configuration is a hypothetical construct denoting a coherent pattern of feelings, thoughts and preferred behavioural responses symbolized or pre-symbolized by the person as reflective of a dimension of existence within the self' (2000, p. 102). Though it is the experience of some clients, Mearns and Thorne have not yet found the need to hypothesize a 'governing' configuration. Configurations of self can be growthful, but sometimes are 'not for growth'. For example, a client repeatedly abused by her partner says: 'I know I should leave him, but a big part of me does not want to do that'. Some configurations may well be inconsistent with other parts of the self and carry restricted access to being 'owned' by the individual. Therapists must maintain a therapeutic relationship with both the 'growth' and 'not for growth' configurations in the 'family of selves'. Therapists should remember that some clients symbolize themselves in pluralist terms and others do not. Consequently, they should not insert pluralist conceptions that have not come from clients.

Mearns and Thorne (2000, 2013) also advocate an *actualizing process* which is described by a psychological homeostasis where the balance is under 'dual control', with the drive of the actualizing tendency and the restraint of *social mediation* both able to exercise power. Social mediation is a restraining force within the person that seeks to articulate with the person's social contexts. Though not relevant for the majority of clients, therapists should avoid differentially reinforcing the prompting of the actualizing tendency against the forces of social mediation. Therapists need to beware of being partial to some configurations of self and not to others and need to attend equally to those parts of the client which might be expressing a 'not for growth' imperative.

Regarding the therapeutic relationship, Mearns and Thorne (1999) see its development as containing three elements: trust, intimacy and mutuality. Developing trust is important not only at the start of therapy relationships, but as they continue. Intimacy can contribute to developing therapeutic relationships. Many moments of intimacy correspond to times when the client experiences the therapist as demonstrating complete understanding and valuing. As the relationship develops, mutuality may become established with both therapist and client regarding their work as truly shared. Intimacy comes easily and there is an absence of defensiveness. Therapists can release their empathic sensitivity in whatever ways are most congruent to them. Establishing mutuality is likely to be a time when clients increasingly trust their inner locus of evaluation.

The mutuality element echoes Mearns' (1997, 2003; Mearns and Cooper, 2005; Mearns and Thorne, 2013) idea of meeting the client at relational depth. Therapists who are willing to work with clients at relational depth try to leave aside conventional ways of responding and project themselves fully into the clients' experiencing. Clients, too, may make suggestions as to how therapy may proceed. If and when clients feel convinced of their therapists' ability to meet them at relational depth, they may feel the safety and companionship that allows them to share their very existence as they are experiencing it. Mearns and Cooper describe relational depth as: 'A state of profound contact and engagement between two people, in which each person is fully real with the other, and able to value and understand the other's experience at a high level' (2005, p xii). Relational depth is more than the sum of the core conditions. In meeting clients at relational depth, the maxim of person-centred counselling that it is more about *being* than about *doing* holds true.

The Canadian psychologist David Rennie has developed what he terms an experiential approach to person-centred therapy (Rennie, 1998). Rennie's approach revolves around clients' and therapists' *reflexivity*, which he defines as self-awareness and agency within that self-awareness. Rennie's approach goes beyond empathic responding to focus on both client and therapist processes. Two elements of process work are process *identification*, 'I notice that you seem to have come to a halt'; and process *direction*, 'I don't know if it would be useful or not, but one thing you could try would be to see if you can make contact with the feeling of *being* stuck' (Rennie, 1998, p. 119).

Rogers' daughter, Natalie, has developed person-centred expressive therapy. She 'proposed a connection between all forms of creative expression, from movement through making music, sculpting, painting and writing' (Thorne with Sanders, 2013). Empathy is at the heart of a journey of creative discovery. Her methods can also be used in groups and fosters a social perspective when so used (Rogers, N., 2011).

Rogers has influenced theories sufficiently conceptualized to stand alone: such as Gendlin's experiential or focusing-oriented therapy (Gendlin, 1996) and Greenberg's emotion-focused therapy (Greenberg, 2002; Raskin et al., 2014). Rogers' influence pervades the work of therapists of other theoretical orientations: for example, now all competent cognitive and cognitive-behaviour therapists heavily emphasize the quality of the relationship when assessing clients and delivering interventions. Rogers has also influenced many therapists who describe themselves as eclectic. For example, some eclectic therapists might use a person-centred approach as the treatment of choice for some clients either at the start of therapy or throughout therapy. Furthermore, eclectic therapists can also integrate a more client-focused approach into how they apply interventions derived from many other theoretical positions. However, for many person-centred therapists such eclecticism or integration of person-centred ideas and practices constitutes a violation of the person-centred approach as a coherent functional philosophy.

The development of person-centred therapy and therapists proceeds by means of journals and training centres. Journals devoted to Rogers' approach include *The Person-Centered Journal* and *Person-Centered and Experiential Psychotherapy*.

In 2000, the World Association for Person-Centered and Experiential Psychotherapies and Counseling (WAPCEPC) was established. In 1989 the British Association for the Person-Centred Approach (BAPCA) was founded and there is also the Association for Person-Centred Therapy in Scotland. Training opportunities for developing person-centred counselling and therapy skills are provided in numerous countries throughout the world. The centre of gravity for person-centred work appears to be moving from the United States, where since Rogers' death its influence has rapidly disappeared, 'despite small signs of resurgence in more recent times' (Thorne with Sanders, 2013, p. x), to Europe. The person-centred approach is firmly established in professional and institutional therapy domains in Holland, Germany, Belgium and Britain (Mearns and Thorne, 2000). It is also prominent in Austria (Mearns, Thorne with McLeod, 2013). Furthermore there is continuing interest in the approach in South America, the Far East, and Australia.

REVIEW AND PERSONAL QUESTIONS

REVIEW QUESTIONS

1. Critically review Rogers' concept of the actualizing tendency. What evidence might support or negate Rogers' views about the concept?
2. What does Rogers mean by organismic valuing process?
3. What does Rogers mean by the terms experience, experiencing and awareness?
4. What are conditions of worth and how do they develop?
5. Specify how low-functioning people process their experiences differently from high-functioning people.
6. With reference to a person's self-concept and experience, what does Rogers mean by the term incongruence? Provide an example.
7. Why does Rogers present how to conduct therapy in terms of growth promoting attitudinal conditions rather than techniques?
8. Describe each of the three therapist offered growth promoting attitudinal conditions.
9. In what ways do clients change both during and at the end of successful person-centred therapy?
10. What do you consider the strengths and weaknesses of Rogers' model of the person?
11. What do you consider the strengths and weaknesses of Rogers' model of therapy?

PERSONAL QUESTIONS

1. Are you aware of any of your conditions of worth? If so, what are they and how did you acquire each of them?
2. Examine a past or current relationship that you think has helped or is helping you to attain a more adequate self-concept. What characteristics of the other person were or are helpful?
3. Examine a past or current relationship that you think has hindered you from attaining a more adequate self-concept. What characteristics of the other person were or are harmful?
4. Assess yourself on each of the following attributes of fully functioning or self-actualizing people: openness to experience, rationality, personal responsibility, self-regard, capacity for good personal relationships, and ethical living.
5. If you conduct therapy, how congruent are you and how do you know?
6. If you conduct therapy, how well do you offer unconditional positive regard and how do you know?
7. If you conduct therapy, how empathic are you and how do you know?
8. What relevance, if any, has the theory and practice of person-centred therapy for how you conduct therapy?
9. What relevance, if any, has the theory and practice of person-centred therapy for how you live?

ANNOTATED BIBLIOGRAPHY

Rogers, C. R. (1959) A theory of therapy, personality, and interpersonal relationships, as developed in the client-centred framework. In S. Koch (ed.),

Psychology: A Study of Science (Study 1, Volume 3, pp. 184–256). New York: McGraw-Hill.
Rogers regarded this chapter as one of his most significant publications. He worked for three or four years on it and was proud of its thoroughness and rigour. He endeavoured to make every major statement in it something that could be tested by research. This chapter is a major reference for readers wishing to understand Rogerian theory.

Rogers, C. R. (1951) *Client-Centered Therapy*. Boston: Houghton Mifflin.
This book describes the attitudinal orientation of the counsellor, the therapeutic relationship experienced by the client, the process of counselling and various issues and applications of the client-centred approach. The book concludes with an important nineteen proposition statement of Rogers' theory of personality and behaviour.

Rogers, C. R. (1957) The necessary and sufficient conditions of therapeutic personality change. *Journal of Consulting Psychology, 21*, 95–103.
Regarded also by Rogers as one of his most significant publications, this article presents and discusses six conditions for effective counselling practice. The paper elaborates the counsellor conditions of congruence, unconditional positive regard and empathic understanding.

Rogers C. R. (1961) *On Becoming a Person*. Boston: Houghton Miflin.
Another publication regarded by Rogers as one of his most significant. Rogers acknowledged the book as certainly his most popular and thought it had spoken to people all over the world. The book comprises seven parts: speaking personally; how can I be of help?; the process of becoming a person; a philosophy of persons; the place of research in psychotherapy; what are the implications for living?; and the behavioural sciences and the person.

Rogers C. R. (1975) Empathic: An unappreciated way of being. *The Counseling Psychologist, 5*, 2–10.
This paper, reprinted in *A Way of Being*, is Rogers' re-evaluation of the attitudinal condition of empathy. It is his major statement on the subject.

Rogers, C. R. (1980) *A Way of Being*. Boston: Houghton Mifflin.
A collection of fifteen papers written between 1960 and 1980, this book is divided into four parts: personal experiences and perspectives; aspects of a person-centred approach; the process of education – and its future; and looking ahead – a person-centred scenario. This book is written in the same reader-friendly style as *On Becoming a Person*.

Raskin, N. J., Rogers, C. R. and Witty, M. C. (2014) Client-centered therapy. In D. Wedding and R. J. Corsini (eds) *Current Psychotherapies* (10th ed.). Belmont, CA: Brooks/Cole, pp. 95–150.

An authoritative overview of the theory and practice of client-centred therapy based on a chapter originally written by Rogers.

Mearns, D. and Cooper, M. (2005) *Working at Relational Depth in Counselling and Psychotherapy*. London: Sage.
This book describes relational depth both as specific moments in an encounter and also as a particular quality of a relationship. It highlights how different aspects of the therapist combine to facilitate relationally-deep encounters and various personal 'blocks' which may be experienced.

Mearns, D., Thorne, B. with McLeod, J. (2013) *Person-Centred Counselling in Action* (4th ed.). London: Sage.
Engagingly written this best selling text introduces person-centred theory and practice in a way that clearly and sensitively brings to life the processes going on within and between counsellors and clients. Mearns and Thorne write the book's first nine chapters, whose titles are: basic theory of the person-centred approach: recent developments in person-centred theory, the counsellor's use of the self, empathy, unconditonal positive regard, congruence, 'beginnings', 'middles', and 'endings'. The tenth and final chapter, written by McLeod, is titled: research on person-centred counselling.

REFERENCES AND FURTHER READING

Barrett-Lennard, G. T. (1998) *Carl Rogers' Helping System: Journey and Substance*. London: Sage.
Cohen, D. (1997) *Carl Rogers: A Critical Biography*. London: Constable.
Combs, A. W. and Snygg, D. (1959) *Individual Behavior* (rev. ed.). New York: Harper and Row.
Gendlin, E. T. (1988) Carl Rogers (1902–1987). *American Psychologist, 43*, 127–8.
Gendlin, E. T. (1996) *Focusing-oriented Psychotherapy*. New York: Guilford Press.
Gordon, T. (1970) *Parent Effectiveness Training: The Tested New Way to Raise Responsible Children*. New York: Wyden.
Greenberg, L. S. (2002) *Emotion-focused Therapy: Coaching Clients to Work Through their Feelings*. Washington, DC: American Psychological Association.
Kirschenbaum, H. and Henderson, V. L. (eds) (1990) *The Carl Rogers Reader*. London: Constable.
Maslow, A. H. (1962) *Toward a Psychology of Being*. Princeton, NJ: Van Nostrand.
Maslow, A. H. (1970) *Motivation and Personality* (2nd ed.). New York: Harper and Row.
McCleary, R. A. and Lazarus, R. S. (1949) Autonomic discrimination without awareness. *Journal of Personality, 18*, 171–9.
Mearns, D. (1997) *Person-Centred Counselling Training*. London: Sage.
Mearns, D. (2003) *Developing Person-Centred Counselling*. London: Sage.
Mearns, D. and Cooper, M. (2005) *Working at Relational Depth in Counselling and Psychotherapy*. London: Sage.

Mearns, D. and Thorne, B. (1999) *Person-Centred Counselling in Action* (2nd ed.). London: Sage.

Mearns, D. and Thorne, B. (2000) *Person-Centred Therapy Today: New Frontiers in Theory and Practice.* London: Sage.

Mearns, D., Thorne, B. with McLeod, J. (2013) *Person-Centred Counselling in Action* (4th ed.). London: Sage.

Raskin, N. J. and Rogers, C. R. (2005) Person-centered therapy. In R. J. Corsini and D. Wedding (eds) *Current Psychotherapies.* (7th ed.). Belmont, CA: Thomson Brooks/Cole, pp. 130–65.

Raskin, N. J., Rogers, C. R. and Witty, M. C. (2014) Client-centered therapy. In D. Wedding and R. J. Corsini (eds) *Current Psychotherapies.* (10th ed.). Belmont, CA: Brooks/Cole, pp. 95–150.

Rennie, D. L. (1998) *Person-Centred Counselling: An Experiential Approach.* London: Sage.

Rogers, C. R. (1939) *The Clinical Treatment of the Problem Child.* Boston: Houghton Mifflin.

Rogers, C. R. (1942) *Counseling and Psychotherapy: Newer Concepts in Practice.* Boston: Houghton Mifflin.

Rogers, C. R. (1951) *Client-Centered Therapy.* Boston: Houghton Mifflin.

Rogers, C. R. (1957) The necessary and sufficient conditions of therapeutic personality change. *Journal of Consulting Psychology, 21,* 95–103.

Rogers, C. R. (1959) A theory of therapy, personality, and interpersonal relationships, as developed in the client-centered framework. In S. Koch (ed.), *Psychology: A Study of Science* (Study 1, Volume 3, pp. 184–256). New York: McGraw-Hill.

Rogers C. R. (1961) *On Becoming a Person.* Boston: Houghton Miflin.

Rogers, C. R. (1962) The interpersonal relationship: The core of guidance. *Harvard Educational Review, 32,* 416–29.

Rogers, C. R. (1969) *Freedom to Learn.* Columbus, Ohio: Charles E. Merrill.

Rogers, C. R. (1970) *Encounter Groups.* London: Penguin.

Rogers, C. R. (1973) *Becoming Partners: Marriage and its Alternatives.* London: Constable.

Rogers, C. R. (1974) In retrospect: Forty-six years. *American Psychologist, 29,* 115–23.

Rogers C. R. (1975) Empathic: An unappreciated way of being. *The Counseling Psychologist, 5,* 2–10.

Rogers, C. R. (1977) *Carl Rogers on Personal Power.* London: Constable.

Rogers, C. R. (1980) *A Way of Being.* Boston: Houghton Mifflin.

Rogers, C. R. (1986a) A client-centered/person-centered approach to therapy. In I. Kutash and A. Wolf (eds) *Psychotherapist's Casebook: Theory and Technique in the Practice of Modern Therapies.* San Francisco: Jossey Bass, pp. 197–208. Reproduced in H. Kirschenbaum and V. Henderson (eds) *The Carl Rogers Reader.* London: Constable, pp. 135–52.

Rogers, C. R. (1986b) Reflection of feelings. *Person-Centred Review,* 1, 375–7.

Rogers, C. R. (1990) Reflection of feelings and transference. In H. Kirschenbaum and V. Henderson (eds) *The Carl Rogers Reader.* London: Constable, pp. 127–34.

Rogers, C. R. (2005) The case of Mrs Oak. In D. Wedding and R. Corsini (eds) *Case Studies in Psychotherapy* (4th ed.). Belmont, CA: Thomson Brooks/Cole, pp. 55–76.

Rogers, C. R. and Sanford, R. A. (1985) Client-centered psychotherapy. In H. I. Kaplan, B. J. Sadock, and A. M. Friedman (eds) *Comprehensive Textbook of Psychiatry* (4th ed.). Baltimore, MD: William & Wilkins, pp. 1374–88.

Rogers, C. R. and Russell, D. E. (2002) *The Quiet Revolutionary – An Oral History*. Roseville, CA: Penmarin Books.

Rogers, N. (2011) *The Creative Connection for Groups: Person-centred Expressive Arts for Healing and Social Change*. Palo Alto, CA: Science and Behavior Books.

Thorne, B. (2007) Person-centered Therapy. In W. Dryden (ed.) *Dryden's Handbook of Individual Therapy* (5th ed.). London: Sage, pp. 144–72.

Thorne, B. with Sanders, P. (2013) *Carl Rogers* (3rd ed.). London: Sage.

Walker, A. M., Rablen, R. A. and Rogers, C. R. (1960) Development of a scale to measure process changes in psychotherapy. *Journal of Clinical Psychology, 16*, 79–85.

ROGERS ON FILM

Rogers, C. R. (1965) Client-centered therapy. In E. Shostrom (ed.) *Three Approaches to Psychotherapy*. Santa Ana, CA: Psychological Films.

WEBSITES

Association for the Person-Centered Approach (ADPCA): www.adpca.org
British Association for the Person-Centred Approach: www. bapca.co.uk
Center for the Studies of the Person: www.centerfortheperson.org/
World Association for Person-Centered and Experiential Psychotherapy and Counseling (WAPCEPC): www.pce.world.org

COLLECTIONS

The Department of Special Collections at the Davidson Library, University of California, Santa Barbara, contains selected papers, photographs and audio and video tapes of Carl Rogers. To access any of these materials, visit the Carl Rogers Archives website at: www.oac.cdlib.org/cgi-bin/oac/ucsb/rogers

The Library of Congress, Washington, DC, holds all of Rogers' earlier material. To access the library catalogue, go to: http://catalog.loc.gov/

GESTALT THERAPY 5

INTRODUCTION

Fritz Perls considered all other existential philosophies borrowed concepts from other sources: for example, Binswanger from psychoanalysis, Tillich from Protestantism, and Satre from Communism. Gestalt therapy is the only existential approach that has support in its own formation since gestalt formation, the emergence of needs, is a primary biological phenomenon. He observed: 'Gestalt therapy is a philosophy that tries to be in harmony, in alignment with everything else, with medicine, with science, with the universe, with what *is*' (Perls, 1969a, p. 17). This chapter ends with some more recent developments in gestalt therapy.

FRITZ PERLS (1893–1970)

Friederich (Frederick or Fritz) Soloman Perls, was born in Berlin, the son of a Jewish travelling salesman of Palestinian wines. He grew up with his two sisters in a disturbed family in which his parents had many bitter fights, both verbal and physical. Perls' mother used carpet-beating rods on him but he claims she did not break his spirit rather he broke the carpet-beaters. He saw his father as a hypocrite who preached one thing and lived another and who progressively isolated himself from his family. Perls wrote: 'Basically I hated him and his pompous righteousness, but he could also be loving and warm. How much my attitude was influenced by my mother's hatred of him, how much she poisoned us children with it, I could not say' (Perls, 1969b, pp. 250–1). During his puberty years, a period during which he was initiated into both sex and acting, Perls was the black sheep of his family. Throughout his life Perls was a rebel rather than a complier, a man with a very quick eye for others' phoniness and pseudo-authenticity, and somewhat of an exhibitionist himself. His early experiences of rejection and insecurity may have deeply influenced his later life.

Perls' ideas were largely formed in the Austro-Germanic world. On leaving high school, he enrolled as a medical student at Berlin University. At the start of the First World War, Perls had been declared physically unfit for active service. However, by 1916 fitness requirements were much lower and Perls interrupted his medical studies to serve as a medical officer, including a spell in the trenches from 1916 to 1917.

In 1918 Perls returned to being a student at the universities of Freiburg and Berlin, and in 1920, he received his M.D. from the latter institution.

In 1926 Perls moved to Frankfurt where he accepted a post as assistant to the gestalt psychologist Kurt Goldstein at the Frankfurt Neurological Institute. Also in 1926, Perls met Laura Posner, whom he was to marry in 1929. Together they shared a strong interest in gestalt psychology. Perls considered he had a peculiar relationship with the gestalt psychologists, admiring much of their work, but unable to go along with them when they became logical positivists. He did not read any of their textbooks, but had read some papers by Lewin, Wertheimer and Kohler. He observed: 'Most important for me was the idea of the unfinished situation, the incomplete gestalt' (Perls, 1969b, p. 62). The academic gestaltists never accepted Perls and he did not regard himself as a pure gestaltist.

For some years, Perls had been undergoing training as a Freudian psychoanalyst. He moved to Vienna in 1927 and a year later completed his analytical training. On returning to Germany, from 1928 to 1933 Perls worked as a certified Freudian psychoanalyst mainly in Berlin.

In addition to gestalt psychology and Freudian psychoanalysis there were numerous other influences on Perls. He had a love of acting and, early in life, studied under Max Reinhardt, the noted director of the Deutsche Theater. Reinhardt insisted that his students observe very closely how people express emotions through their voice and gestures (Clarkson and Mackewn, 1993). Perls was also interested in Reich's idea of character armour, whereby repressions and resistances became total organismic functions. Later influences were to include Moreno, with his ideas on therapy by means of psychodrama, American humanistic psychology and Eastern religion, especially Zen Buddhism.

In 1933, with the rise of Hitler, Perls fled from Germany to Holland. Apart from being Jews, Fritz and Laura Perls had to leave quickly to avoid being rounded up by the Nazis because of their left wing political activism. At the time of his departure Perls' analyst was Wilhelm Reich and his supervisors were Otto Fenichel and Karen Horney. He wrote: 'From Fenichel I got confusion; from Reich, brazenness; from Horney, human involvement without terminology' (Perls, 1969b, p. 39). In 1934, on the recommendation of Ernest Jones, Freud's friend and biographer, accompanied by wife and young daughter, Renate, Perls moved to Johannesburg as a training analyst. In 1935, despite Fritz wanting her to abort her pregnancy, Laura gave birth to their son Stephen, who came to regard him as a distant and disengaged father very much wrapped up in his own world (Perls, 1993).

Fritz and Laura Perls soon had successful private practices and, in 1935, they established the South African Institute for Psychoanalysis. From 1942 to 1945, Perls worked as a South African army medical officer and psychiatrist near Pretoria in the war against the Nazis. During his South African years Perls was influenced by the holism of Jan Smuts, the South African general, prime minister and philosopher. Smuts wrote about the way individuals and the universe are actively 'whole-making' and introduced the idea from physics that everything has a field and that things and organisms must be considered in relation to their fields (Smuts, 1987). In 1942 Perls' first book *Ego, Hunger and Aggression* was published in South Africa, with the British edition being published in 1947, with the sub-title *A Revision of Freud's Theory and Method*. Perls' wife Laura authored several chapters in this book and she was an important collaborator in the founding of gestalt therapy (Yontef and Jacobs, 2014).

Fritz and Laura Perls became increasingly concerned at the beginning of apartheid policies in South Africa. In 1946 Perls emigrated to the United States and established a private practice in New York City. Laura and their two children joined him in the autumn of 1947. In 1951 Perls published *Gestalt Therapy: Excitement and Growth in the Human Personality*, a book co-authored by Ralph Hefferline, Professor of Psychology at Columbia University, and Paul Goodman, a social philosopher and writer. Some view Goodman, an uninhibited and radical bisexual, as the third co-founder of gestalt therapy (Clarkson and Mackewn, 1993).

In 1952 Perls established the New York Institute of Gestalt Therapy and, in 1954, the Cleveland Institute for Gestalt Psychotherapy. Between 1952 and 1956, Perls had increasing differences of opinion with Laura Perls and Paul Goodman about directions for gestalt therapy. In 1957, partly for health reasons due to a recently diagnosed heart condition, Perls moved to the milder climate of Miami and was never again to live with Laura for any length of time. In Miami Perls became friends and lovers with Marty Fromm, even as she continued to be in therapy with him (Clarkson and MacKewn, 1993).

In 1960 Perls moved to the West Coast of the United States and, in 1964, joined the staff of the Esalen Institute at Big Sur, California, as resident associate psychiatrist. During this period, he began doing gestalt demonstrations on stage in front of increasingly large groups, including illustrating his hot seat technique. However, Perls realized that large group gestalt demonstrations were not gestalt therapy proper. In May 1969, Perls moved to Cowichan on Vancouver Island in British Columbia where he was establishing a gestalt community. Here he was very happy and finally at peace with the world. In December 1969 Perls left Cowichan for what was to be the last time, went to Europe, but was clearly unwell on his return. After a brief illness Perls died in a Chicago hospital of a heart attack on March 14, 1970, at the age of 76. During his last illness, Laura had flown to join him only to find Perls sometimes confiding in her and sometimes shouting at and ignoring her.

In 1969, Perls had published *Gestalt Therapy Verbatim* and the autobiographical pot-pourri of prose, poetry and psychology entitled *In and Out of the Garbage Pail*. At the time of his death Perls was working on two books *The Gestalt Approach* and *Eye Witness to Therapy* and these were published posthumously in 1973 as a single book entitled *The Gestalt Approach & Eye Witness to Therapy*.

THEORY

BASIC CONCEPTS

Perls (1973) wrote in his introduction to *The Gestalt Approach & Eyewitness to Therapy* that gestalt theory was grounded in experience and observation, had changed with years of practice and application and was still growing. The following presentation is almost exclusively based on Perls own writings, some in conjunction with collaborators. Though, as shown later, others have developed gestalt therapy after Perls' death, no other really major figure has emerged since then.

GESTALT

The German noun *gestalt* means form or shape and among the meanings of the verb *gestalten* are to shape, to form, to fashion, to organize and to structure. Other terms for gestalt include pattern, configuration or organized whole. The major thrust of the experimental work of the gestalt psychologists was to show that humans do not perceive things in isolation but organize them through their perceptual processes into meaningful wholes (for example, a row of dots may be perceived as a straight line).

People's visual fields are structured in terms of 'figure' and 'background' or 'ground'. Whereas 'figure' is the focus of interest (an object or pattern etc.), 'ground' is the setting or context. Perls and his colleagues (Perls et al., 1951) noted that the interplay between figure and ground was dynamic. For instance, the same ground may with differing interests and shifts of attention give rise to different figures. A given figure may itself become ground in the event that some detail of its own becomes figure. The relation between that which stands out (figure) and the context (ground) is meaning, which in a good gestalt is clear (Yontef and Jacobs, 2014).

THE HOLISTIC DOCTRINE

The human organism is a unified whole. In particular Perls objected to the old mind–body split. The emergence of psychosomatic medicine made the close relationship of mental and physical activity increasingly apparent. In fact mental activity seemed to be an activity of the whole person carried out at a lower energy level than those activities called physical. Human beings are wholes engaging in fantasizing, play-acting and doing. For instance, people's actions provide clues as to their thoughts and their thoughts provide clues concerning what they would like to do. In short, people do not have organisms but *are* organisms engaged in activities of the same order that are often wrongly dichotomized into mental and physical activities.

Another erroneous dichotomy is that between self and external world. Individuals are not self-sufficient but can only exist in an environmental field. Environments do not create individuals nor do individuals create environments. Rather each is what it is because of its relationship to the other and the whole. For instance, in the example of a person seeing a tree, there is no sight without something to be seen nor is anything seen if there is no eye to see it.

There are numerous other false dichotomies such as those between emotional (subjective) and real (objective), infantile and mature, biological and cultural, love and aggression, and conscious and unconscious. For instance, regarding the split between infantile and mature, it is often lack of certain childhood traits that devital-izes adults while other traits called infantile may be the introjections of adult neu-roses. A consistent theme of the gestalt approach is to search for the overall pattern rather than for false dichotomies.

CONTACT BOUNDARY AND CONTACT

Earlier I mentioned that Perls disdained the split between self and the external world considering that the organism and the environment stood in a relation-ship of mutuality to one another. The contact boundary is the boundary between organism and environment and it is at this boundary that psycho-logical events take place. Perls and his colleagues (1951, p. 229) considered that 'psychology studies the operation of the contact-boundary in the organism/environment field'. Such 'contact' or 'being in touch with' involves both sen-sory awareness and motor behaviour. The organism's sensory system provides it with a means of orientation, with the motor system providing a means of manipulation. Both orientation and manipulation take place at the contact boundary. In healthy functioning, once the system of orientation has per-formed its function, the organism manipulates itself and the environment in such a way that organismic balance is restored and the gestalt is closed.

All thoughts, feelings and actions take place at the contact boundary. In healthy functioning, people have an effective contact-withdrawal rhythm or means of meeting psychological events at the contact boundary. Contacting the environment represents forming a gestalt, whereas withdrawal is either closing a gestalt completely or mobilizing resources to make closure possible. More simply contact and withdrawal may respectively be viewed as acceptance and rejection of the environment. The components of contact and withdrawal are almost invariably present, but the neurotic person has a reduced capacity to discrimi-nate between the appropriateness of these dialectical elements and consequently behaves with reduced effectiveness as will be seen in the later section on inter-ruptions of contact.

HOMEOSTASIS AND BALANCE

The basic tendency of every organism is to strive for balance. The organism is continuously faced with an imbalance that is disturbing through either external (demands from the environment) or internal (needs) factors. Life is characterized by a continuous interplay of balance and imbalance in the organism. Homeostasis or organismic self-regulation is the process by which the organism satisfies its needs by restoring balance when faced with a demand or need that upsets its equilibrium. Health constitutes the appropri-ate operation of the homeostatic process, whereas sickness means that for too long a time the organism has remained in a state of disequilibrium, of being unable to satisfy its needs. Death constitutes a total breakdown of the homeostatic process.

Though psychological and physiological are interrelated, the organism may be perceived as having psychological as well as physiological contact needs. A simple example of a physiological need is that, for the organism to be in good health, the water content of the blood must be kept at a certain level, neither too low nor excessive. If, for instance, the water content of the blood falls too low the individual feels thirst, with its symptoms of dry mouth and restlessness and the wish to restore the imbalance by drinking. A possible example of a more psychological need is that of mothers to keep their children happy and contented. Consequently, even when sleeping, they may be very sensitive to the cries and whimpers of their offspring.

The homeostatic process also operates where several needs are experienced simultaneously. However here a selective process takes place based on the organism's need for survival and for self-actualization; with the simultaneous experiencing of many needs, the individual attends to the dominant survival and self-actualization need before attending to the others. Put another way, the dominant need or the need that presses most sharply for satisfaction becomes the foreground figure while the other needs recede, at least momentarily, into the background. Perls (1969a) wrote about doing away with the whole of instinct theory and simply considering the organism as a system that needs balance if it is to function properly. Though practically people have hundreds of unfinished situations in them, the most urgent situation always emerges. Individuals, to be able to satisfy their needs (to complete or to close incomplete *gestalten*) must be able both to sense what they need and to manipulate themselves and their environments to obtain what is necessary.

Life is basically an infinite number of unfinished situations or incomplete gestalts, with no sooner than one gestalt being completed than another comes up. The homeostatic process is the means by which the organism maintains itself 'and the only law which is constant is the forming of gestalts – wholes, completeness. A gestalt is an organic function. A gestalt is an ultimate experiential unit' (Perls, 1969a, p. 16). With the introduction of the concept of the homeostatic process, it was possible to see gestalt formation as a primary biological drive, with the gestalt being the basic experiential unit having such properties as figure and ground and completeness or incompleteness.

THE SELF AND SELF-ACTUALIZATION

The self is the system of contacts at the contact boundary at any moment. The self exists where there are boundaries of contact and its activity is that of forming figures and grounds. The self always integrates the senses, motor coordination and organic needs. It is the integrator or artist of life and though it 'is only a small factor in the total organism/environment interaction … it plays the crucial role of finding and making the meanings that we grow by' (Perls et al., 1951, p. 235).

The self consists of the identifications and alienations at the contact boundary. For instance, individuals may identify with their families, but feel alien to people from different countries. Inside the boundary tends to be perceived as good and outside as bad. Self-actualization may be viewed as the expression of appropriate identifications and alienations. Healthy functioning involves identifying with one's forming organismic self, not inhibiting one's creative excitement, yet alienating what is not organismically one's own. Sickness involves restricting one's areas of contact through alienating parts of one's forming organismic self by means of false identifications.

Perhaps a more accessible way of stating this is to make a distinction between self-actualizing based on the existential principle that 'a rose is a rose is a rose' and self-image actualizing in which people live for their image of how they should be rather than how they are. Perls (1969a) considered that 'Every external control, even *internalized* external control – "you should" – interferes with the healthy working of the organism. There is only one thing that should control: the *situation*' (p. 20). If people understand the situations they are in, and let these situations control their actions, then they learn how to cope with life. An even more simple view of Perls' ideas on self-actualization may be gained from his dictum: 'So lose your mind and come to your senses' (Perls, 1970a, p. 38).

EXCITEMENT

Humans secure their energy from the food and air they take in. Perls emphasized vitality and the need to integrate the social being and the animal being. Perls used the word excitement to describe the energy we create, because it coincides with the physiological function of excitation. This life force or *élan vital* is at the heart of the gestalt approach. Perls observed: 'Now normally the *élan vital*, the life force, energizes by sensing, by listening, by scouting, by describing the world – how is the world there. Now this life force first mobilizes the center – *if* you have a center. And the center of the personality is what used to be called the soul: the emotions, the feelings, the spirit' (Perls, 1969a, p. 68).

Excitement varies according to the task on the basis of hormonal differentiation: for instance, it gets tinged with some other substance, for example adrenalin for anger or sexual hormones for erotic contact. Much of our excitement goes into energizing the motor system because the muscles link people with the environment. Even for most emotional events, emotion is transferred into movement. However, some excitement goes into energizing the senses. Healthy people allow their excitement to get to their senses and muscles, but unfortunately many people allow much of their excitement to be drained off into their fantasy life, into their computer (unproductive thinking), and into self-image actualization. Perls (1969a) believed that modern humans live in a state of low grade vitality in which the average person at most lives only 5 to 15 per cent of their potential and the person who has even 25 per cent of their potential available is considered a genius.

EMOTION

Emotion, which is the organism's direct evaluative experience of the organism/environment field, is immediate rather than being regulated by thoughts and verbal judgements. Emotion is a continuous process since all instances in people's lives carry some feeling tone of pleasantness or unpleasantness. Excitement is modified into specific emotions according to the situation that has to be met and the emotions mobilize the sensory and motor system so that needs may be satisfied. Gestalt therapy attaches great importance to the emotions which are not only essential as energy or excitement regulators but are also 'unique deliveries of experience which have no substitute – they are the way we become aware of our concerns, and, therefore, of what we are and what the world is' (Perls et al., 1951, p. 96).

ACQUISITION

AGGRESSION, ASSIMILATION AND INTROJECTION

An aggressive attitude towards experience is necessary if it is really to be assimilated or made the organism's own. An analogy may be made between the aggression required for eating and that required for assimilating experience. Food needs to be destroyed or de-structured before that which is valuable to the organism can be retained and undesirable substances can be eliminated. Undesirable substances that are not eliminated may be poisonous and detrimental to the organism. Every organism in an environmental field grows by incorporating, digesting or destructuring, and assimilating or absorbing selectively new matter whether it is food, lectures or parental influence. Loving parents are likely to provide their children with experiences which they will assimilate since they are relevant to their own needs as they grow from environmental support to self-support.

Not all experience, however, goes through the destructuring and assimilation process required for healthy functioning. Introjections are experiences that are swallowed as wholes rather than being properly digested. The outcome of introjection is that undesirable as well as desirable substances have been retained, thus weakening the organism. Hateful parents are likely to provide their children with experiences that have to be introjected or taken in whole even though they are contrary to the needs of the organism.

FRUSTRATION AND MANIPULATION

The young baby is virtually totally dependent on its mother, but as time goes by the child learns to communicate, to crawl and walk, to bite and chew, and to accept and reject. In short the child learns to realize some part of its potential for existence. Growth comes about through learning to overcome frustrations by mobilizing one's innate resources to manipulate the environment to satisfy needs. The term manipulation refers to a person's ways of mobilizing and using the environment to satisfy needs. Both healthy and unhealthy organisms manipulate the environment, with healthy organisms manipulating it on an underlying basis of self-support, whereas unhealthy organisms are seeking environmental rather than self-support.

Perls wrote: 'Without frustration there is no need, no reason to mobilize your resources, to discover that you might be able to do something on your own, and in order not to be frustrated, which is a pretty painful experience, the child learns to manipulate the environment' (Perls, 1969a, p. 35). Perhaps it would be more accurate to say that with the right kind of frustrations the child learns to manipulate the environment in such a way as to meet its needs and restore effective organismic balance. However with lack of frustration (the spoiled child) or with frustrations which block or are beyond the child's coping capacity, the outcome is likely to be that the child starts to mobilize the environment by playing phony roles and games: for instance playing stupid, playing helpless, playing weak and flattering. These false manipulations cause individuals to alienate parts of themselves, be it their eyes, ears or genitals.

INTERRUPTIONS OF CONTACT

Humans are forced to learn much more through education than by using their biologically based instincts. Consequently much of the animal's intuition as to what is the 'right' procedure is either missing or blocked. Instead there is a whole range of composite fantasies, handed down and modified through the generations, as to what constitutes the 'right' procedures. These procedures perform mostly support functions for social contacts (viz. manners and ethics) and have the disadvantage of not necessarily being biologically based. Consequently there are frequently interruptions in the contact provided by ongoing organismic processes that, if left alone, would be conducive to self-support. Examples of such interruptions are 'Don't touch that' or 'Don't do this'. Even withdrawals may be interrupted as in the example 'You stay here now, keep your mind on your homework and don't dream'. People often incorporate their parents' interruptions as introjections in their own lives, for example 'Grown men don't cry'. Unhealthy organisms or neurotics are self-interrupters who need to become aware both of the fact that they are interrupting themselves and also of what they are interrupting.

SUPPRESSION OF EMOTION

Suppression of emotion is a major way in which adults interrupt the contact of their children. Such adults, who frequently have been brought up in environments in which 'the authorities' were afraid of emotion, tend to squelch the emotions of their children and thus prevent their emotions from undergoing natural development and differentiation. This is mainly achieved through an overemphasis of the 'external world' and the demands of 'reality' and a belittling of organismic needs and emotions. The outcome of this is that children 'adjust' to such unremitting pressure by dulling their body-sense and losing some of their vitality. However, because emotions are inherent to the organism, this suppression of emotions does not eliminate 'undesirable' emotions rather it disturbs 'the intricate organism/environment field by setting up a great number of situations which, *unless avoided, are immensely emotion-arousing!*' (Perls et al., 1951, p. 97).

MAINTENANCE

Though Perls often used the terms neurosis and neurotic, he considered that problems of poor gestalt formation and closure were extremely widespread. In this section I examine the gestalt view of how people maintain their contact deficiencies. Needless to say, people's difficulties are compounded because they live in cultures or environments where self-image actualizing rather than self-actualizing is common.

ZONES OF AWARENESS

There are three zones or layers of awareness: outer, self and intermediate (see Box 5.1). Perls sometimes used the Indian word *maya* to describe the intermediate zone or DMZ. *Maya* means illusion or fantasy and is a kind of dream or trance. More colloquial and crude is Perls use of the term 'mind-f**king' to describe the activity of the DMZ which hinders people from coming to their senses.

BOX 5.1   THE THREE ZONES OF AWARENESS

THE OUTER ZONE (OZ)

This zone consists of awareness of the world, of those things, facts and processes that are available to everyone.

THE SELF ZONE (SZ)

This zone is the place within the skin, our authentic organismic selves.

THE INTERMEDIATE ZONE (DMZ)

This zone, which is located within the self zone, is often called 'mind' or consciousness which prevents people from good contact or being 'in touch' with themselves or the world. The DMZ is a zone of fantasy activity that consumes excitement and leaves little energy over for being in touch with reality.

ANXIETY AND STAGE FRIGHT

Gestalt theory has both a physiological and psychological definition of anxiety. The physiological definition is: 'Anxiety is the experience of breathing difficulty during any blocked excitement' (Perls et al., 1951, p. 128). The idea underlying this definition is that heightened energy mobilization, with the need for more air (an increase in the rate and amplitude of breathing), occurs whenever there is strong concern and contact. As such it is a healthy way of being in erotic, aggressive, creative and other sorts of exciting or energy mobilizing situations. A less healthy response is to control, interfere with and interrupt the excitement by trying to continue breathing at the rate that was adequate prior to it. This leads to a narrowing of the chest to force exhalation in order to create a vacuum into which fresh air can rush. Anxiety, derived from the Latin word 'angustia', meaning narrowness, is the product of an emergency measure caused by the conflict between excitement and control.

The psychological definition of anxiety is that it is 'the gap between the now and the later' or 'stage fright' (Perls, 1969a, pp. 32–3). As such it is the result of the fantasy activity of the DMZ. This fantasy activity is rehearsing for a future that people do not really want to have because they are afraid of it. Perls wrote: 'We fill in the gap where there should be a future with insurance policies, status quo, sameness, *anything* so as not to experience the possibility of openness towards the future' (Perls, 1969a, pp. 48–9). People who are in the now and have access to their senses are unlikely to be anxious because their excitement can flow immediately into the kind of spontaneous, creative and inventive activity which achieves solutions to unfinished situations. They are not blocked from good contact with themselves and the environment by *maya* or fantasies, prejudices, apprehensions and so on. They are prepared to take reasonable risks in living. Perls distinguished between catastrophic fantasies, which entail too much precaution, and anastrophic fantasies that entail too little. He thought some people managed a balance between catastrophic and anastrophic fantasies, thus having both perspective and rational daring.

NEUROSIS

Neurotic individuals allow society to impinge too heavily on them. They cannot clearly distinguish their own needs and see society as larger than life and themselves as smaller. Society can consist of any one of a number of groups, for example, the family, the state, the social circle and co-workers. When the neurotic and one or more of these groups simultaneously experience different needs, the neurotic is incapable of distinguishing which need is dominant and thus can make neither a good contact nor a good withdrawal. Consequently one or more of the contact boundary disturbances of neurosis seem the most effective way to maintain balance and a sense of self-regulation in situations where the odds appear to be overwhelmingly adverse.

Perls distinguished between health, psychosis and neurosis. In health, people are in touch with the realities both of themselves and the world. In psychosis, people are out of touch with reality and in touch with *maya*, especially fantasies about megalomania and worthlessness. In neurosis a continual fight is taking place between *maya* and reality.

CONTACT BOUNDARY DISTURBANCES

The neuroses, which entail significant contact boundary disturbances, operate primarily through four mechanisms, albeit interrelated. These neurotic boundary disturbances are 'nagging, chronic, daily interferences with the processes of growth and self-recognition' (Perls, 1973, p. 32). Introjection, projection, confluence and retroflection are the four mechanisms of contact boundary disturbance. However, these mechanisms are only neurotic when used chronically and inappropriately. They are useful and healthy when authentically chosen and used temporarily in particular circumstances not by compulsion, but by choice.

INTROJECTION

I have already mentioned *introjection* as the process by which material from outside is swallowed whole rather than digested properly, with the valuable elements being assimilated and the undesirable or toxic elements discarded. Introjects, or undigested thoughts, feelings and behaviour, are the results of the process of introjection. Introjection may be viewed as the tendency to 'own' as part of the self what actually is part of the environment. Two outcomes of introjection are first, that the introjects prevent individuals from getting in touch with their own reality because all the time they are having to contend with these foreign bodies and, second, that the introjects may be incompatible with one another and thus contribute to personality disintegration.

PROJECTION

Projection is the reverse of introjection in that it is the tendency to 'own' as part of the environment what actually is part of the self. Projection can take place on two levels: in relation to the outer environment and in relation to the self. Perhaps most commonly, projection involves shifting those parts of ourselves that we dislike and devalue onto others rather than recognizing and dealing with the tendencies in ourselves. Projections are associated with introjects because people usually devalue themselves in relation to introjected self-standards, whose unacceptable derivatives in terms of self-evaluations are then projected onto the environment.

Projection in relation to the self takes place when people disown as part of themselves either areas in which or certain impulses that arise. For instance, people may say of their anger 'It took control of me' whereby the anger is given an objective existence outside of themselves so that they can make it responsible for their troubles and avoid full recognition of the fact that *it* is part of *her* or *him*.

CONFLUENCE

With *confluence*, the individual lacks any distinction or experiences no boundary at all between self and environment. People who are unaware of the contact boundaries between themselves and others are neither able to make good contact with them nor, where appropriate, to withdraw. A feature of confluence is demanding likeness and refusal to tolerate differences. Two examples of confluence are marital partners and parents who, respectively, refuse to see their spouses and children as different from themselves.

RETROFLECTION

In *retroflection*, the individual fails to discriminate between self and others accurately and treats themselves the way they originally wanted to treat other people or objects. For instance, the harassed mother at the end of a long day in which everything has gone wrong may turn her destructive impulses against herself. Retroflection means literally 'to turn sharply back against'. When people retroflect they redirect their activity inward and substitute themselves instead of the environment as the targets of their behaviour. Retroflection is not necessarily neurotic. In certain situations it may be to the individual's advantage to suppress particular responses. However retroflection is pathological when it is chronic, habitual and out of control.

Perls was sensitive to the use of language both in representing and helping to sustain contact boundary disturbances. For example, in introjection the personal pronoun 'I' is used when the real meaning is 'they', in projection the pronouns 'they' or 'it' are used when the real meaning is 'I', in confluence the pronoun 'we' is used when there may really be differentness, and retroflection uses the reflexive 'myself' as in the statement 'I am ashamed of myself'.

The following is Perls' succinct summary of the lacks of discrimination, interferences and interruptions entailed in the four main contact boundary disturbances:

> The introjector does as others would like him to do, the projector does unto others what he accuses them of doing to him, the man in pathological confluence doesn't know who is doing what to whom, and the retroflector does to himself what he would like to do to others (1973, p. 40).

LAYERS OF NEUROSIS

Perls (1969a, 1970a) came to see the structure of neurosis as consisting of five layers, each of which is described in Box 5.2. A major feature in the maintenance of neuroses is that people are not willing to undergo the pain of the impasse, the feeling of being stuck and lost. An example involving the later layers of neurosis is that of a young woman who had recently lost her child and who needed to be able to face her nothingness and her grief to be able to came back to life and make real contact with the world.

BOX 5.2   THE FIVE LAYERS OF NEUROSIS

THE CLICHE LAYER

For example, the meaningless tokens of meeting, such as a handshake or 'Good morning'.

THE ERIC BERNE OR SIGMUND FREUD LAYER

The layer in which people engage in the counter-productive manipulations of phony roles and games (for example the bully, the very important person, the cry baby, the nice little girl, the good boy and so on).

THE IMPASSE

When the role-playing layer is worked through, then therapist and client come to the third layer called the impasse or sometimes the sick-point. This layer is characterized by a phobic attitude manifested in avoidance and flight from authentic living. In particular suffering is avoided, especially the suffering of frustration.

THE DEATH OR IMPLOSIVE LAYER

Behind the impasse is the death or implosive layer, which appears either as fear of death or a feeling of not being alive. Here people implode by contracting and compressing themselves.

THE EXPLOSION

The explosion is the final neurotic layer. There are four basic kinds of explosions from the death layer: into grief, if a person works through a loss that has not been assimilated; into orgasm, for sexually blocked people; into anger; and into joy. The explosions, which may be mild depending on the amount of energy invested in the implosive layer, connect with the authentic, organismic person.

THERAPY

THERAPEUTIC GOALS

Clients come to gestalt therapy because they are in existential crises. Perls had a rather cynical view of their motivation stating: 'Anybody who goes to a therapist has something up his sleeve. I would say roughly 90% don't go to a therapist to be cured, but to be more adequate in their neuroses' (Perls, 1969a, p. 79). Gestalt therapy goals revolve around the client's movement from environmental support to self-support. Beginning clients are mainly concerned with solving problems. Gestalt therapists assist clients to support themselves not only in solving current problems, but in living more authentically. In order to be self-supporting clients need to be in touch with their organismic existential centres ('I am what I am'). People who are in touch with their organismic selves or with their senses are self-actualizing or self-supporting.

The process of self-actualizing involves an effective balance of contact and withdrawal at the contact boundary and the ability to use energy or excitement to meet real rather than phony needs. Furthermore, self-actualizing involves being able to withstand frustration until a solution emerges. Self-supporting people take responsibility for their existences and possess *response-ability* or freedom of choice. They are able appropriately to use aggression to assimilate their experiences and they are largely free from the neurotic contact boundary disturbances of introjection, projection, retroflection and confluence. They possess relatively little self-destructive unfinished business since they are good at forming and closing strong gestalts.

Yontef and Jacobs (2014) observe that the only goal of gestalt therapy is awareness. Clients require awareness both in particular areas, awareness of content, and also of the processes or automatic habits by which they block awareness, awareness of process. This latter self-reflective kind of awareness, sometimes called 'awareness of awareness', enables clients to use their skills in awareness to rectify disturbances in the awareness process.

PROCESS OF THERAPY

It is important to distinguish how Perls worked in groups towards the end of his life and the practice of ongoing individual gestalt therapy, which is its most common form today. Perls was a showman who conducted gestalt therapy in workshops at Esalen that included communal baths as an adjunct. He required six elements for his performance: '1) My skill 2) Kleenex 3) The hot seat 4) The empty chair 5) Cigarettes 6) An ashtray' (Perls, 1969b, p. 227). Perls viewed all therapy interviews as experimental. Therapists need to try things out to help clients become aware of how they are now functioning as persons and organisms. Sometimes he would do mass experiments or exercises, but mostly he worked with a series of single people, or sometimes couples, in front of the group.

In ongoing individual gestalt therapy assessment can be done as part of the therapeutic process rather than as an initial diagnostic procedure, though some therapists also undertake initial assessments. Clients need to be willing to work within the gestalt therapy framework and feel that their therapist is someone whom they can trust. In the initial session therapists are likely to discuss details of fees, cancellation of sessions policy and other pertinent practical matters.

Gestalt therapists' offices are designed to be friendly and comfortable and avoid having desks or tables between therapists and clients. Where possible, space is available for movement and experimentation. In addition, every effort is make to ensure privacy both in terms of soundproofing and safeguarding of records.

Sessions are usually once weekly which gives clients time to digest what happened in the previous session. Though more frequent sessions are possible, gestalt therapists take care to encourage self-support rather than dependency by not becoming too available. Often individual therapy is combined with group therapy, couples therapy, family therapy, workshops, and with meditation or biofeedback training.

Evaluation of therapeutic process and outcomes occurs as part of therapy and both therapists and clients participate. Beginning clients may be most concerned with solving problems and relief of psychological discomfort. Therapists encourage their clients to assume responsibility for self-support in addressing their problems and resultant discomfort. Initially clients may talk about problems but show little insight into the how of their behaviour. As therapy progresses, clients become more aware both of how they behave and of how unaware they have hitherto been. As therapy continues, client and therapist may pay more attention to general personality issues and the general patterns and conditions that contribute to clients' insufficient awareness. The idea is that clients increasingly carry their higher levels of awareness into their everyday lives and maintain and build upon them after therapy ends.

THE THERAPEUTIC RELATIONSHIP

There are at least two ways of looking at the therapist–client relationship in gestalt therapy: that of Perls in his demonstrations and workshops and that of other important practitioners, for instance Laura Perls, Gary Yontef and Lynne Jacobs. The relationship and style of Perls' Esalen workshops is often called 'Perlsism' or 'Perlsian Gestalt' to differentiate it from the relationship and style of therapy practised by those other leading gestalt therapists.

Perls was a charismatic and dominating personality who, once he became well known, may have attracted clients who felt they might benefit from his confronting approach. Though ostensibly he advocated a democratic dialogue between therapist and client, the reality was that much of the time he was controlling the therapeutic process. Perls' son Stephen was to observe that his father did not know how to relate to another person on an equal basis (Perls, 1993). Perls' relationships with clients contained the paradox of advocating personal responsibility at the same time as assuming the major responsibility for the therapeutic process himself.

At his best Perls was so concerned with helping clients that he would not allow them to sabotage their growth by being phony, an important word in his vocabulary. A contemporary phrase for Perls' relationships with clients is tough love. Other leading practitioners have conducted gestalt therapy within the context of more equal or horizontal therapist–client relationships.

In gestalt therapy relationships, therapists concentrate on what clients do moment-to-moment and on what is happening between therapist and client. Therapists attend closely to what clients experience because they believe that the client's subjective experience is as real and valid as the therapist's 'reality' (Yontef and Jacobs, 2014).

All gestalt therapists regard the therapeutic relationship as a 'working' rather than a 'talking' relationship. In this working relationship, both therapists and clients are self-responsible: therapists for the quality of their presence and self-awareness, their knowledge and skills in relating to the client, and for maintaining an open and non-defensive stance; and clients for their commitment to working to become more in charge of their lives through developing greater self-awareness. Furthermore, therapists are responsible for not colluding in clients' manipulations to get them to do what clients fear they cannot do for themselves. Instead, therapists should relate to clients in a warm, respectful, direct and honest manner.

THERAPEUTIC INTERVENTIONS

The use of gestalt therapy interventions 'hinges on questions of *when, with whom,* and *in what situation*' (Shepherd, 1970, p. 324). In 'Perlsian' therapy, he would be likely to intervene without much, if any, consultation. With most gestalt therapists, appropriate interventions are decided upon in an ongoing dialogue between therapist and client. Such interventions are considered as experiments. A major purpose of encouraging clients to experiment with different ways of thinking and acting is to collect information to achieve genuine understanding rather than mere changes in behaviour. Repeatedly clients are encouraged to 'Try this and see what you experience' (Yontef and Jacobs, 2014). Creativity from therapists and clients in setting up and carrying out appropriate experiments is highly valued. Parlett and Denham observe that, within the gestalt therapy approach, 'each therapist applies gestalt principles in individual ways and uses different methods according to her/his professional background and personal style' (2007, p. 242). The following are some interventions and experiments used by Perls.

AWARENESS TECHNIQUE

Gestalt therapy is an experiential rather than a verbal or interpretive approach. Assessment data about how clients' interrupt their contact with life are collected as therapists and clients work together. Gestalt therapy demands that clients experience themselves as fully as possible in the here-and-now both to understand their present manipulations and contact boundary disturbances and also to re-experience the unfinished business of past problems and traumas.

Perls (1973) regarded the simple phrase 'Now I am aware' as the foundation of the gestalt approach. The 'now' because it keeps therapists and clients in the present and reinforces the fact that experience can only take place in the present. The 'aware' because it gives both therapists and clients the best picture of the latter's present resources. Awareness always takes place in the present and opens up possibilities for action.

Clients are asked to become aware of their body language, their breathing, their voice quality and their emotions as much as of any pressing thoughts. Below are some examples of Perls directing Gloria's attention to her non-verbal behaviour taken from the *Three Approaches to Psychotherapy* film series (Dolliver, 1991, p. 299; Perls, 1965).

> *'What are you doing with your feet now?'*
> *'Are you aware of your smile?'*
> *'You didn't squirm for the last minute.'*
> *'Are you aware that your eyes are moist?'*
> *'Are you aware of your facial expression?'*

One way of following up a client's awareness report is for the therapist to say 'Stay with it' or 'Feel it out'. Such instructions can encourage clients to more fully experience and work through feelings to completion. For example, staying with moist eyes may lead to further experiencing and then identifying the reasons for feeling sad and for crying.

Exaggeration, which may focus on either movement and gesture or on verbal statements, is another way of heightening clients' awareness of how they communicate. In each instance, clients are asked progressively and repeatedly to exaggerate the behaviour. Examples of exaggeration requests from Perls' interview with Gloria are as follows (Dolliver, 1991, p. 300; Perls, 1965).

> *'Can you develop this movement?'*
> *'Develop it as if you were dancing.'*
> *'Now exaggerate this.'*
> *'What you just said, talk to me like this.'*
> *'Do this more.'*

Yet another way of heightening clients' awareness of their here-and-now communication is to ask them to use the phrase *'I take responsibility for it'*. For instance, 'I am aware that I am moving my leg and I take responsibility for it'.

When using awareness techniques, therapists may self-disclose and provide here-and-now feedback about how they see clients communicating. Furthermore, therapists can judiciously share how they are affected.

Since clients are self-interrupters they often find it difficult to remain in the here-and-now. The awareness technique is really a concentration technique, sometimes called focal awareness, by which clients learn to experience each now and each need and also how their feelings and behaviour in one area are related to feelings and behaviour in other areas. Thus they come to an awareness not only of the fact that they are interrupting their contact with themselves and the world, but also of what they are interrupting and how they are doing it through the neurotic mechanisms of introjection, projection and so on. Clients are also asked to do some homework that consists of reviewing the session in terms of a systematic application of the awareness technique.

SYMPATHY AND FRUSTRATION

Empathizing with clients is insufficient since the therapists are withholding themselves and at worst allowing confluence. Sympathy alone spoils clients. What is needed is a combination of sympathy and of frustration. Clients must be frustrated in their efforts to control the therapist by neurotic manipulations and instead learn to use their powers of manipulation to meet their real needs. The therapist focuses on getting clients to become more aware and not to become phobic when they start feeling uncomfortable.

Perls provided situations in which his clients experienced being stuck in frustration and then frustrated their avoidances still further until they were willing to mobilize their *own* resources. He repeatedly frustrated clients until they were face to face with their blocks, inhibitions, and ways of avoiding having eyes, ears, muscles, authority, and security in themselves. Frustration often leads to the discovery that the phobic impasse does not exist in reality but in fantasy, in that clients have been preventing themselves from using their own available resources through catastrophic expectations. Furthermore frustration helps clients to express their needs and requests directly rather than to cover them over with neurotic manipulations. The imperative is the primary form of communication and clients who can actually state what they need and mean what they state have made the most important step in their therapy.

ELICITING FANTASIES

A limitation of the awareness technique is its slowness. In order to speed up therapy Perls made considerable use of fantasizing, be it verbal, written down or acted out as a drama. Below is an example taken from the *Three Approaches to Psychotherapy* film series in which Perls encourages Gloria to describe a fantasy (Dolliver, 1991, p. 300; Perls, 1965).

> 'Can you describe the corner you'd like to go to?'
> 'Imagine you are in this corner and you are perfectly safe. Now what would
> you do in that corner?'
> 'What should I do when you are in that corner?'

During the interview, Perls also asked Gloria to describe her fantasies about him (Dolliver, 1991, p. 301).

> 'Now what can I do to you?'
> 'How old must I be?' (for Gloria to scold him)
> 'How should I be? Give me a fantasy. How could I show my concern for you?'
> 'What would I do? How would I conceal my feelings?'

Dolliver observes that whenever Gloria offered Perls feedback about her experience of him, Perls always regarded it as a transference fantasy representing her projected attributes.

DRAMA TECHNIQUES

'Monotherapy', perhaps better termed monodrama, is a form of psychodrama with a difference. In monotherapy, instead of having other people as well as the client involved in the drama, the client creates his own stage and plays all the roles under his or her own direction and expression.

In the *shuttle* technique clients are asked to shuttle their attention from one area to another. For instance, a client can shuttle between the visualization of a memory and the organismic reliving of it in the here-and-now. Another example involves getting clients to shuttle between their feelings in and about an incident and their projections in the incident. For example, a client who feels angry with a colleague for 'apple-polishing' his boss may shuttle to experiencing his own needs and desires for approval from the boss. A further example is that of getting clients to shuttle between talking and listening to themselves. After each sentence, clients are asked: 'Are you aware of this sentence?'. The purpose here is to help clients stop compulsive talking which interrupts their experiencing of themselves and listening to others.

Drama and fantasy work can involve both the *hot seat* and the *empty chair*. The individual with whom the counsellor works in front of the group occupies the hot seat. The empty chair is a second chair which is a 'projection-identification gimmick ... waiting to be filled with fantasized people and things' (Perls, 1969b, p. 224). Essentially it is a method of highlighting the shuttling process by getting clients to change chairs as they shuttle between parts of themselves or between different people in a drama.

Topdog–underdog dialogues are one of the main examples of the use of the shuttle technique involving both fantasy work and the empty chair. Perls considered that in their fantasies many people played self-torture games in which they were fragmented into an inner conflict between controller (topdog) and controlled (underdog). The topdog (or super ego) is righteous, authoritarian, full of 'shoulds' and 'should nots', perfectionistic and manipulates with threats of catastrophe if his demands are not carried out. The underdog (or intra ego) is cunning and manipulates with being wheedling, defensive, apologetic, playing the cry baby and so on. Typical underdog statements are 'Mañana', 'I try my best' and 'I have such good intentions'. Through shuttling between these polarities, clients are helped to understand the structure of their behaviour and also to reconcile these two fighting clowns by becoming more in touch with their organismic selves.

DREAMWORK

Perls (1970b) regarded dreams as the royal road to integration. Dreams are existential messages, not just unfinished situations, current problems or symptoms. Especially if the dreams are repetitive, a very important existential issue for the client is likely to be involved. There are four stages to dreamwork (see Box 5.3).

BOX 5.3   THE FOUR STAGES OF DREAMWORK

Stage 1   **Sharing the dream:** The client relates the dream.

Stage 2   **Retelling the dream in the present tense:** The client retells the dream or a section of it as a drama by changing the past tense into the present tense, for example 'I was climbing a mountain' becomes 'I am climbing a mountain'. Perls would ask clients to say their dreams, or parts of their dreams, again 'in the *present tense*: as if you were dreaming it *now*?' (Perls, 1970b, p. 205, emphasis in original).

Stage 3   **Talking to the different actors in the dream:** The client becomes the stage director and sets the scene and talks to the different actors in the dream or section of it. For example, when working with Mary Anne's dream, Perls introduced the action element with the statement: 'Now let's start acting it out. Tell this to the man. Talk to the man – express your resentment' (Perls, 1970b, p. 206). The client is encouraged to become the different actors, the props and all that is there. Clients do not have to work with a whole dream for even if they re-identify with just one or a few items in the dream the exercise is valuable.

Stage 4   **Conducting a dialogue between different elements in the dream:** The fourth stage of dreamwork may be facilitated by the empty chair technique to allow for dialogues between the different people, objects or parts of the self that are encountering each other. These dreamwork encounters provide opportunity for two things: the integration of conflicts and reidentification with those parts of the self that are alienated, especially the assimilation of projections. Dreamwork is an excellent way of finding the holes in a client's personality. These tend to be manifested as voids and blank spaces that are accompanied by nervousness and confusion.

RESPONSIBILITY LANGUAGE

Perls was interested in semantics and he was conscious of how clients could interfere with self-support through poor use of language (Levitsky and Perls, 1970; Perls, 1970a). Using verbs that acknowledge choice and personal agency is one example of using responsibility language: for example, rephrasing 'I can't do that' to 'I *won't* do that'. In addition, clients can be alerted to use the personal pronoun 'I' rather than 'It' or 'They' and send messages directly to their therapists and to others. Furthermore, if clients ask the kind of questions that manipulate the environment for support, therapists can encourage them to change those passive questions into more active and self-supporting statements.

CASE MATERIAL

Since gestalt therapists both differ in how they work and also work with many different here-and-now techniques, it is hard to get an overall feel for the approach from reading case material. Perls' book *Gestalt Therapy Verbatim* (1969a) is primarily made up of verbatim transcripts from his large-scale weekend dreamwork seminars between 1966 and 1968 and from an intensive four week gestalt therapy workshop in 1968, all of which were held at Esalen. Perls presents his therapy with a number of different clients from the seminars and the workshop, including working with dreams in the case of Jane (Perls, 2005). In addition, the *Eyewitness* part of *The Gestalt Approach & Eyewitness to Therapy* (1973) contains transcripts, that Perls considered had great teaching potential, taken from his conducting therapy films. In the 'Gestalt therapy' film in the earlier *Three Approaches to Psychotherapy* series, Perls introduces his approach, conducts a brief interview with Gloria and then summarizes his impressions of the session (Perls, 1965).

Anther example of gestalt therapy is that of Laura Perls working first with a 25-year-old black woman and then with a 47-year-old Central European Jewish refugee (Perls, 1968). Joen Fagan (1974) presents transcripts with commentary for three sessions with Iris, who had agreed to be videotaped and had no previous experience with gestalt therapy.

Clarkson, with Cavicchia, (2013) illustrates the various stages of long-term gestalt therapy with a progressive case example, contributed by Sue Fish, where the client is Gary, a university senior lecturer. As therapy progressed, Gary left a relationship that had become unsatisfactory. He became more able to mobilize and use his own resources, including supporting himself in an interdependent relationship with a new girlfriend, Jessica.

Parlett and Denham (2007) provide a case example of a client, Dave, who was seen by Denham. Dave had been unable to talk to his parents about being abused as a child and also felt suffocated by his mother who kept him under her wing. Gestalt procedures used included Dave experimenting telling the therapist about ways in which they disagreed and two-chair work with his 'mother'. Mann (2014) discusses his work with Michelle, aged 44, who, despite having seen a few therapists, continued to suffer from depression. Experiments included a dialogue forming sentences with the two words 'I' and 'You' in them, and therapist and client alternating between asking each other 'Who are you?' As a result of therapy, Michelle began to experiment with new ways of being in her life.

Yontef and Jacobs (2014) present an excerpt taken from the fourth year of therapy with Miriam, whose world was characterized by extreme isolation due to terrifying and degrading childhood abuse. In this session, the therapist gently and gradually accedes to the client's wish for touch by touching her fingertips at the same time as helping her talk about the experience.

FURTHER DEVELOPMENTS

I have already mentioned that many other leading gestalt therapists developed more horizontal relationships with clients than did Perls. Since Perls' death, the practice of gestalt therapy has altered in many other ways and continues to develop (Clarkson with Cavicchia, 2013; Mann, 2014; Parlett and Denham, 2007; Yontef and Jacobs, 2014). Contemporary gestalt therapists are more supportive, compassionate and kind. There is less emphasis on frustration and abrasively confronting those clients perceived as manipulative. When using confrontation, gestalt therapists take great care not to humiliate or re-traumatize clients by triggering unnecessary shame in them.

Therapists are less likely to pose as experts and more likely to show their humanity, including their fears, defensiveness and confusions. Mann (2014) observes that, with financial constraints, gestalt therapists need to offer brief as well as long-term psychotherapy. He contends that most people can benefit from gestalt brief psychotherapy, while acknowledging the limitations of what change is possible in the available time.

Gestalt therapists are encouraged to make 'I' statements to enhance their contact with clients and clients' focusing. In describing how she works, Laura Perls (1970c) provides examples of disclosing her awareness and feelings, sharing personal problems and life experiences, and using physical contact. Her guiding principle is to use such disclosures only if they might help clients take their next steps.

Many contemporary gestalt therapists attempt to exemplify Buber's (1937/58) concept of the 'I – Thou' relationship in which two unique people encounter and openly respect one another's essential humanity. 'I – Thou' relationships are here-and-now person-to-person existential encounters in which therapist and client are open to being changed by the other (Clarkson, 1997). Such relationships may be contrasted with 'I – It' relationships in which others are treated as objects to be used and manipulated.

Contemporary gestalt therapy tends to be highly individual with a different therapy being tailor made for each client (Yontef and Jacobs, 2014). Therapists and clients creatively generate and carry out appropriate experiments as therapy progresses. However, Mann (2014) writes: 'Some therapists are highly experimental and dramatic using plenty of physical movement, whilst others engage more verbally and are more contained in their relational style' (pp. 192–3).

Clarkson, with Cavicchia, (2013) provide a good example of how a gestalt therapist can work. They present a seven-stage cycle of gestalt formation and production: sensation, awareness, mobilization, action, final contact, satisfaction, and withdrawal. The cycle's last six stages are then used as a framework for illustrating the gestalt therapy process. The authors suggest some appropriate experiments for each stage.

Another development is that, drawing on gestalt therapy's empty chair technique, Greenberg and colleagues have devised an empty chair dialogue intervention geared to the resolution of 'unfinished business' with significant others (Greenberg, Rice and Elliott, 1993). Such unresolved negative feelings can contribute to anxiety and depression as well as be transferred into other relationships where they are inappropriate. This intervention 'in which the client engages in an imaginary dialogue with the significant other, is designed to access restricted feelings allowing them to run their course and be restructured in the safety of the therapy environment' (Pavio and Greenberg, 1995, p. 419).

Some gestalt therapists may openly use psychoanalytic formulations to describe character structure (Yontef, 1988). When conducting groups the trend is for gestalt therapists to make greater use of the interactions between and contributions from group members than Perls did, though a minority mainly still follow Perls' working with individuals in front of the group style. Making use of interactions can be done either by getting participants to talk to each other with an emphasis on direct here-and-now communication or by mixing Perls' style with direct here-and-now communication between participants (Yontef and Jacobs, 2014). A further development is that gestalt therapy techniques have been integrated into other approaches. For example, gestalt techniques and experiments are commonly used in conjunction with transactional analysis (Dusay and Dusay, 1989; James and Jongeward, 1971).

Parlett and Denham observe: 'Basic to all training of gestalt psychotherapists is that all trainees have prolonged individual and group therapy themselves' (2007, p. 243). Gestalt therapy has training institutes in every major city of the United States and in most countries of Europe and South America as well as in Australia. Training standards for gestalt therapists in Britain are among the most stringent in the United Kingdom Council for Psychotherapy. In Britain there are several hundred psychotherapists who primarily identify themselves as gestalt therapists. However, in Britain and elsewhere, there are also many people who call themselves gestalt therapists after attending a few workshops and without adequate academic preparation (Yontef and Jacobs, 2014).

There are national gestalt therapy associations in many countries. There is also a European Association for Gestalt Therapy and an Australian and New Zealand association, GANZ. There are now four English language gestalt journals: the *International Gestalt Journal*, the *Gestalt Review*, the *British Gestalt Journal* and the *Gestalt Journal of Australia and New Zealand*. In addition, gestalt therapy literature is prominent in much of the world.

REVIEW AND PERSONAL QUESTIONS

REVIEW QUESTIONS

1. What did Perls mean by gestalt formation?
2. Why did Perls consider it important for people to take an aggressive attitude to experience?
3. In growing up what is the role of frustration?
4. Describe each of Perls' three layers of awareness.
5. Describe each of the following mechanisms of contact boundary disturbance: introjection, projection, retroflection, and confluence.
6. What are the goals of gestalt therapy?
7. How and why do gestalt therapists use awareness techniques?
8. How and why do gestalt therapists use sympathy and frustration?
9. How and why do gestalt therapists use drama techniques?

10. What is the purpose of dreamwork and what are its four stages?
11. What is 'Perlsian' gestalt therapy and how does it differ from the way some of Perls collaborators and many contemporary therapists practise gestalt therapy?

PERSONAL QUESTIONS

1. What specific events in your life may have influenced you to come to your mind and lose your senses?
2. Assess how you relate to your environment in terms of each of Perls' mechanisms of contact boundary disturbance: introjection, projection, confluence and retroflection.
3. What are the phony roles and games that you use to obtain environmental support rather than rely on self-support?
4. Sit in a comfortable chair and, for the next three minutes, say to yourself 'Now I am aware …' each time you become aware of your body language, your breathing, your emotions, and any pressing thoughts. For example, 'Now I am aware I'm uncrossing my legs.'
5. Spend the next three minutes focusing on your response-ability for your life by staying in the now and saying to yourself about all your current behaviour '… and I take responsibility for it.'
6. Use the shuttle technique and change chairs as you shuttle between different parts of yourself or between yourself and another person.
7. What is your fantasy of how it would be like for you to be in the hot seat being in therapy with a gestalt therapist like Perls?
8. What relevance, if any, has the theory and practice of gestalt therapy for how you conduct therapy?
9. What relevance, if any, has the theory and practice of gestalt therapy for how you live?

ANNOTATED BIBLIOGRAPHY

Perls, F. S., Hefferline, R. F. and Goodman, P. (1951) *Gestalt Therapy: Excitement and Growth in the Human Personality.* London: Souvenir Press.
This book contains an introduction and two volumes. Volume 1 is a series of eighteen experiments: experiments 1 to 11 focus on contacting the environment, technique of awareness, and directed awareness; experiments 12 to 18 focus on retroflection, introjection, and projections. Volume 2 is a major statement of gestalt theory consisting of three parts: introduction; reality, human nature, and society; and theory of the self. This detailed book is for serious students and therapists.

Perls, F. S. (1969a) *Gestalt Therapy Verbatim.* New York: Bantam Books.
This book consists of three parts: talk, dreamwork seminar, and intensive workshop. The talk and dreamwork seminar parts are selected and edited material from audio tapes made at weekend dreamwork seminars conducted by Perls at the Esalen Institute, Big Sur, California between 1966 and 1968. The intensive workshop part is taken from audio tapes of a four-week intensive workshop

conducted in 1968. The talk part of the book provides an easily readable introduction to gestalt theory.

Perls, F. S. (1969b) *In and Out of the Garbage Pail*. New York: Bantam Books.
As the book's cover says 'Joy. Sorrow. Chaos. Wisdom. The free-floating autobiography of the man who developed Gestalt Therapy.' A pot-pourri of self-
disclosure by means of prose and poetry. This book is a good way to meet Perls,
the man.

Perls, F. S. (1973) *The Gestalt Approach & Eyewitness to Therapy*. New York:
    Bantam Books.
This book is a combination of two projects that Perls was working on at the time
of his death. *The Gestalt Approach* is Perls' final statement of his theory and was
written because he regarded his two previous theoretical works *Ego, Hunger and
Aggression* and *Gestalt Therapy* as too outdated and difficult to read. *Eyewitness to
Therapy* provides descriptions of gestalt therapy in action.

Clarkson, P. with Cavicchia, S. (2013) *Gestalt Counselling in Action* (4th ed.).
    London: Sage.
This book starts by introducing gestalt approach and the fundamentals of
gestalt practice. A seven-stage cycle of gestalt formation and production is presented and, using the cycle as a framework, the practice of gestalt counselling
is reviewed. This engaging and well-written book is a rich source of ideas about
how to integrate experiments into gestalt practice.

Mann, D. (2014) Gestalt therapy. In W. Dryden and A. Reeves (eds) *The
    Handbook of Individual Therapy* (6th ed.). London: Sage, pp. 179–205.
A sound introductory chapter on modern gestalt therapy.

Yontef, G. and Jacobs, L. (2014) Gestalt therapy. In D. Wedding and R. J.
    Corsini (eds), *Current Psychotherapies* (10th ed.). Belmont, CA:Brooks/Cole,
    pp. 299–338.
This chapter provides a good overview of a contemporary approach to gestalt
therapy.

REFERENCES AND FURTHER READING

Buber, M. (1937/1958) *I and Thou* (2nd ed.). Edinburgh: T and T Clark.
Clarkson, P. (1997) Variations on I and thou. *Gestalt Review, 1* (1), 56–70.
Clarkson, P. with Cavicchia, S. (2013) *Gestalt Counselling in Action* (4th ed.).
    London: Sage.
Clarkson, P. and Mackewn, J. (1993) *Fritz Perls*. London: Sage.
Dolliver, R. H. (1991) Perls with Gloria re-viewed: Gestalt techniques and Perls'
    practices. *Journal of Counseling and Development, 69*, 299–304.

Dusay, J. M. and Dusay, K. M. (1989) Transactional analysis. In R. J. Corsini and D. Wedding (eds), *Current Psychotherapies* (4th ed.). Itasca, IL: Peacock, pp. 405–53.

Fagan, J. (1974) Three sessions with Iris. *The Counseling Psychologist, 4* (4), 42–60.

Fagan, J. and Shepherd, I. L. (eds) (1970) *Gestalt Therapy Now: Theory, Techniques, Applications*. Palo Alto, CA: Science & Behavior Books.

Greenberg, L. S., Rice, L. N. and Elliott, R. (1993) *Facilitating Emotional Change: The Moment by Moment Process*. New York: Guilford Press.

James, M. and Jongeward, D. (1971) *Born to Win: Transactional Analysis with Gestalt Experiments*. Reading, MA: Addison-Wesley.

Levitsky, A. and Perls, F. S. (1970) The rules and games of gestalt therapy. In Fagan, J. and Shepherd, I. L. (eds), *Gestalt Therapy Now: Theory, Techniques, Applications*. Palo Alto, CA: Science & Behavior Books, pp. 140–9.

Mackewn, J. (1994) Modern Gestalt – An integrative and ethical approach to counselling and psychotherapy. *Counselling, 5* (2),105–8.

Mann, D. (2014) Gestalt therapy. In W. Dryden and A. Reeves (eds), *The Handbook of Individual Therapy* (6th ed.). London: Sage, pp. 179–205.

Parlett, M. and Denham, J. (2007) Gestalt therapy. In W. Dryden (ed.), *Dryden's Handbook of Individual Therapy* (5th ed.). London: Sage, pp. 227–55.

Pavio, S. C. and Greenberg, L. S. (1995) Resolving 'unfinished business': Efficacy of experimental therapy using empty-chair dialogue. *Journal of Consulting and Clinical Psychology, 63*, 419–25.

Perls, F. S. (1947) *Ego, Hunger and Aggression: A Revision of Freud's Theory and Method*. London: Allen and Unwin.

Perls, F. S. (1969a) *Gestalt Therapy Verbatim*. New York: Bantam Books.

Perls, F. S. (1969b) *In and Out of the Garbage Pail*. New York: Bantam Books.

Perls, F. S. (1970a) Four lectures. In Fagan, J. and Shepherd, I. L. (eds), *Gestalt Therapy Now: Theory, Techniques, Applications*. Palo Alto, CA: Science & Behavior Books, pp. 14–38.

Perls, F. S. (1970b) Dream seminars. In Fagan, J., & Shepherd, I. L. (eds), *Gestalt Therapy Now: Theory, Techniques and Applications*. Palo Alto, CA: Science & Behavior Books, pp. 204–33.

Perls, F. S. (1973) *The Gestalt Approach & Eyewitness to Therapy*. New York: Bantam Books.

Perls, F. S. (2005) The case of Jane. In D. Wedding and R. Corsini (eds) *Case Studies in Psychotherapy* (4th ed.). Belmont, CA: Thomson Brooks/Cole, pp. 157–75.

Perls, F. S., Hefferline, R. F. and Goodman, P. (1951) *Gestalt Therapy: Excitement and Growth in the Human Personality*. London: Souvenir Press.

Perls, L. P. (1968) Two instances of Gestalt therapy. In P. D. Pursglove (ed.), *Recognition in Gestalt Therapy*. New York: Funk & Wagnalls, pp. 42–68.

Perls, L. P. (1970c). One gestalt therapist's approach. In J. Fagan and I. L. Shepherd (eds), *Gestalt Therapy Now: Theory, Techniques, Applications*. Palo Alto, CA: Science & Behavior Books, pp. 125–9.

Perls, S. (1993) Frederick Perls: A son's reflections. Talk given by Stephen Perls on April 23 at the Fifteenth Annual Conference on the Theory and Practice of Gestalt Therapy, Hotel du Parc, Montreal, Canada (the text of this talk is available on www.gestalt.org).

Shepard, I. L. (1970) Limitations and cautions in the Gestalt approach. In J. Fagan and I. L. Shepherd (eds), *Gestalt Therapy Now: Theory, Techniques, Applications*. Palo Alto, CA: Science & Behavior Books, pp. 234–8.

Smuts, J. (1987) *Holism and Evolution*. Cape Town: N & S Press. First published in 1926.

Yontef, G. M. (1988) Assimilating diagnostic and psychoanalytic perspectives into Gestalt therapy. *Gestalt Journal, 11* (1), 5–32.

Yontef, G. and Jacobs, L. (2014) Gestalt therapy. In D. Wedding and R. J. Corsini (eds), *Current Psychotherapies* (10th ed.). Belmont, CA: Brooks/Cole, pp. 299–338.

PERLS ON FILM AND AUDIO AND IN BOOKS AND ARTICLES

Perls, F. (1965) Gestalt therapy. In E. Shostrom (ed.) *Three Approaches to Psychotherapy*. Santa Ana, CA: Psychological Films.

The Gestalt Journal Press lists a comprehensive bibliography of gestalt books, articles, videos and audio recordings (go to www.gestalt.org for more information).

TRANSACTIONAL ANALYSIS 6

INTRODUCTION

Eric Berne, the originator of transactional analysis (TA), stated that the criterion distinguishing his approach from other approaches was that it was based on the personality theory of Child, Parent and Adult ego states. Throughout this chapter Parent, Adult and Child start with a capital letter when describing ego states. The dividing line between what was and what was not transactional analysis rested on whether or not human behaviour was explained in terms of such ego states.

In Chapter 1, I mentioned that one of the functions of counselling and psychotherapy theories is to provide languages for conducting the therapeutic conversation. Berne was a leader in realizing the importance of therapists and clients using the same language. Transactional analysis provides an easily understood language that therapists and clients can use together to analyse and work on problems and transactions in the interests of clients' achieving greater autonomy and intimacy. This chapter mainly focuses on traditional or classical Bernian transactional analysis. However, at the end of the chapter, I present some more recent TA developments.

ERIC BERNE (1910–70)

In 1910, Eric Berne was born Eric Lennard Bernstein in Montreal, Canada, and he grew up in a poor Jewish section of the city. His father appears to have been a dedicated general practitioner who often took Berne on his rounds. His mother, Sara, was a professional writer and editor who, after her husband died in 1921, supported Berne and his sister by her writing. Berne dedicated his first book to his mother who was probably influential in developing his writing interest and skills.

Berne's interest in medicine stemmed more from his father's example. James (1977) considers that the little Child in Berne was traumatized by his father's death. Certainly his father appears to have had a strong influence on Berne, whose goal was always to cure patients. This influence is reflected in the Latin dedication in Berne's seminal book *Transactional Analysis in Psychotherapy,* a translation of which is 'In Memory of My Father David, Doctor of Medicine, Master of Surgery, and Doctor to the Poor' (Berne, 1961).

Berne studied English, psychology and pre-medicine at McGill University in Montreal and received his BA in 1931. In 1935 he obtained his MD and Master of Surgery degree from the same institution. Berne then went to the United States, where he became an American citizen. After an internship at Englewood Hospital in New Jersey, he became a psychiatric resident at Yale University School of Medicine. Reacting to the anti-Semitism of this period, he changed his name to Berne and began a private psychiatric practice in Norwalk, Connecticut. He also contracted the first of three marriages, each of which ended in divorce. Berne became Clinical Assistant at Mt Zion Hospital in New York and, in 1941, began training at the New York Psychoanalytic Institute, being analysed by Paul Federn, a former colleague of Freud.

In 1943 Berne entered the Army Medical Corps as a psychiatrist and it was during the war period that he started working with groups. On his discharge in 1946 he moved to Carmel, California, and finished *The Mind in Action,* since extensively revised and now published as *A Layman's Guide to Psychiatry and Psychoanalysis.* He also resumed his psychoanalytic education at the San Francisco Psychoanalytic Institute and underwent a training analysis with Erik Erikson. In 1950 he took a position at Mt Zion Hospital, San Francisco, and restarted private practice. For the remainder of his life he worked both in San Francisco and in Carmel, 125 miles away.

From his days in the army, Berne developed a research interest in intuition and developed the concept of ego image, which is a therapist's intuitive image of a person that in some ways describes his ego. Ego images are largely based on observation and listening to what patients say about themselves. During the period 1954 to 1958 Berne developed his ideas on the diagnosis of ego states or structural analysis; the analysis of individual transactions; the analysis of a series of transactions with covert as well as overt content, otherwise known as game analysis; and the longitudinal view of a patient's whole life from which it was possible to extrapolate her or his future, now called script analysis. In September 1954 Berne started his first transactional analysis group. His ideas were developed further in a series of regular seminars in Carmel that, in 1958, were succeeded by the San Francisco Social Psychiatry Seminars, later called the Eric Berne Seminars.

Berne was moving away from orthodox psychoanalysis and, in 1956, his application for membership of the Psychoanalytic Institute of San Francisco was rejected for the third time. Of this event he comments: '... after fifteen years the psychoanalytic movement and the writer officially parted company (on the most friendly terms) ...' (Berne, 1961, p. 13). When, some years later, the Psychoanalytic Institute offered him membership, he declined with thanks. Berne had increasingly felt that the effective therapist had to be more active than was allowed in orthodox psychoanalysis and had to practise transaction-ally rather than from the head of a couch.

At the November 1957 Western Regional Meeting of the American Group Psychotherapy Association in Los Angeles Berne presented a paper entitled 'Transactional analysis: a new and effective method of group therapy', which was published in 1958. During three successive summers he broadened his experience by going to the South Pacific to study socialization and mental illness in various island cultures. By 1961 he had visited mental hospitals in about 30 different countries in Europe, Asia, Africa and the islands of the Atlantic and Pacific to test his ideas in various racial and cultural settings.

In 1961 Berne's most systematic statement *Transactional Analysis in Psychotherapy* was published. In 1963 he published a discussion of the application of transactional analysis to groups in *The Structure and Dynamics of Organizations and Groups.* In 1964 his ideas on analysing psychological games were publicly presented in *Games People Play: The Psychology of Human Relationships,* though these ideas had appeared three years earlier in a private edition of the book. The principles of transactional analysis for therapists were explained in his 1966 book *Principles of Group Treatment,* and his ideas on script analysis were developed in *What Do You Say After You Say Hello?,* published posthumously in 1972. Berne also wrote *The Happy Valley* for children and *Sex in Human Loving* for both non-professionals and professionals

During the 1960s, along with his writing and private practice, Berne held a number of appointments. These included Consultant in Psychiatry to the Surgeon General, US Army; Attending Psychiatrist to the Veterans Administration Mental Hygiene Clinic; Lecturer in Group Therapy, Langley-Porter Neuropsychiatric Clinic; Visiting Lecturer in Group Therapy, Stanford Psychiatric Clinic; and Adjunct Psychiatrist, Mt Zion Hospital, San Francisco. Early in 1970 Berne and his third wife were divorced. He died of a heart attack on 15 July the same year. Berne's work was continued by a number of his colleagues who attended the San Francisco seminars, including Claude Steiner, who developed script analysis.

It is interesting to speculate on Berne's own life script. The son of a doctor and a writer, he spent his life curing and writing about curing people. Some idea of his professional ideals may be gleaned from the introduction to his *Principles of Group Treatment,* which is written for those who wish to become 'real doctors' as contrasted with the 'non-real' or 'unreal' variety. A 'real doctor':

(a) *has the overriding consideration throughout his practice of curing his patients;*
(b) *plans his treatment so that at each phase he knows what he is doing and why he is doing it;*
(c) *clearly distinguishes research and experimentation from good medical or surgical care, the former always being subsidiary to the latter; and*
(d) *takes complete responsibility for the welfare of his patients (Berne, 1966, p. xvii).*

The development of transactional analysis represents Berne's own commitment to being a 'real doctor'.

THEORY

BASIC CONCEPTS

Berne saw transactional analysis both as a theory of personality and social interaction and as a method of therapy. Some of his assumptions and basic concepts are presented below.

THE FUNDAMENTAL OK POSITION

Berne had a positive view of human nature which is stated in the transactional-analytic position 'I am OK; you are OK'. Another way he expressed this is by his statement 'Every human being is born a prince or a princess; early experiences convince some that they are frogs, and the rest of the pathological development follows from this' (Berne, 1966, pp. 289–90).

Related to the basic assumption of human OK-ness are two further assumptions. First, Berne regarded practically every human being as possessing the complete neurological apparatus for adequate reality-oriented or Adult functioning. The only exceptions were those with the most severe type of organic brain injuries. Thus the therapeutic task is that of how to strengthen this already existing apparatus so that it may take its normal place in the client's psychic organization. Second, Berne believed that people have a built-in drive to both mental and physical health. The transactional analyst's job is to help nature by removing obstructions to patients' emotional and mental development, so letting them grow in their own directions.

EGO STATES

The fundamental building block of transactional analysis is the concept of ego states. Berne defined an ego state as 'a consistent pattern of feeling and experience directly related to a corresponding consistent pattern of behavior' (Berne, 1966, p. 364). Each human being exhibits three kinds of ego states, Parent, Adult and Child. At any given moment any individual in a social grouping will predominantly exhibit one or another of these states. The three ego states, depicted in Figure 6.1, are described as follows:

- *Parent:* The Parent ego state is a 'set of feelings, attitudes, and behavior patterns which resemble those of a parental figure' (Berne, 1961, p. 66). It is both an accumulation of data and a way of relating to people. The Parent ego state may be seen behaviourally in one of two forms. The *controlling* or prejudicial Parent is manifested as a set of seemingly arbitrary and rigid rules, usually prohibitive, which may either agree or disagree with the rules of a person's culture. The *nurturing* Parent is manifested as sympathy and care for another individual or for oneself. Thus the Parent can be over-controlling and inhibiting or supportive and growth enhancing. The Parent ego state may also influence a person's Adult or Child ego states. The function of the Parent is to conserve energy and to diminish anxiety by making certain decisions automatic.
- *Adult:* The Adult ego state is 'an autonomous set of feelings, attitudes, and behavior patterns which are adapted to the current reality' (Berne, 1961, p. 67). Characteristics by which an Adult ego state may be recognized include organization, adaptability and intelligence.
- *Child:* The Child ego state is 'a set of feelings, thoughts, attitudes and behavior patterns which are relics of the individual's own childhood' (Berne, 1961, p. 69). Berne considered that we all carry within ourselves a little boy or girl who feels, thinks, acts and responds just as we did when we were children of a certain age. The Child ego state is exhibited

behaviourally in two major forms. The *adapted* Child is manifested by feelings and behaviour that inferentially are under parental influence, such as sulking, compliance, rebelliousness, withdrawal and inhibition. The *natural* Child is manifested by spontaneous expression such as self-indulgence or creativity. Berne considered the natural Child to be the most valuable part of the personality. The proper function of a 'healthy' Child is to motivate the Adult so as to obtain the greatest amount of gratification for itself. This it does by letting the Adult know what it wants and by consulting the Parent about its appropriateness.

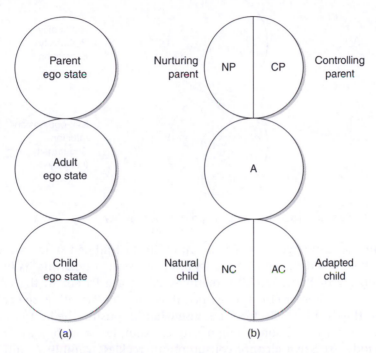

Figure 6.1   (a) Structural and (b) descriptive diagrams of personality

STRUCTURAL ANALYSIS OF EGO STATES

Structural analysis consists of diagnosing and separating one feeling-thinking-and-behaviour pattern or ego state from another. Further analysis of ego states does not provide new ego states, but rather subdivisions of the existing ones. Such analysis is called second-order structural analysis and can get very detailed. In particular, it focuses on further analysis of the Parent and Child.

In Figure 6.2 the Parent is divided into two components, one derived from the father and one derived from the mother. Children incorporate some characteristics of each parent into their Parent ego state, including the ways in which their parents exhibited thinking and feeling when expressing values. Consequently, second-order structural analysis includes the Parent, Adult and Child ego states of both parents.

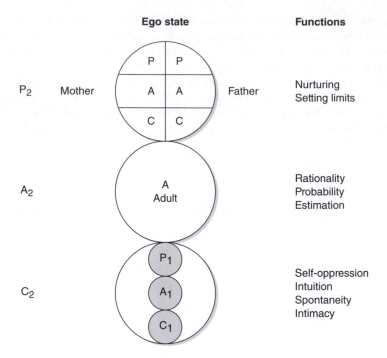

Ego state   **Functions**

P_2 Mother |P|P| Father
         |A|A| Nurturing
         |C|C| Setting limits

A_2 A
            Adult   Rationality
                             Probability
                             Estimation

C_2 P_1 Self-oppression
              A_1 Intuition
              C_1 Spontaneity
                             Intimacy

Figure 6.2   Second-order structural diagram of personality

Within the Child ego state, Parent, Adult and Child ego states, which were already there when the child made its basic decision concerning its life script, can be observed. Berne (1972) sometimes called the Parent in the Child the 'electrode', and Steiner (1974) described it as the 'Pig Parent'. Berne called the Parent in the Child the electrode because when it 'pushes the button', the person automatically does something negative. Examples of such negative behaviour include excessive alcohol consumption, reckless gambling, and getting sexually turned off if coming on too strong.

Berne saw the Adult in the Child as a keen and perceptive student of human nature, which he called the Professor (Berne, 1961). Steiner calls the Adult in the Child the Little Professor and observes that it is the ego state which Berne himself used in his studies on intuition, when he would guess the occupations of people using his own intuition (Steiner, 1974). The Adult in the Child is the source both of intuitive and creative thinking and of delusion, since it may not always be right. The Child in the Child ego state is the source of innate wants and feelings. Spontaneity is a central characteristic of the Child in the Child, but sometimes this spontaneity can be self-destructive.

PSYCHIC ENERGY AND CATHEXIS

Transactional analysis is a dynamic theory of personality in that it uses the concepts of psychic energy and of cathexis or distribution of energy. At a given moment the ego state that is most strongly cathected will have executive power. Berne wrote of the flow of cathexis which gives rise to shifts in ego states. He considered that the most convenient way of acknowledging the differentiation of ego states was to view each state as having a boundary that separates it from other ego states. Under most conditions ego-state boundaries are semi-permeable. Shifts in ego state depend on three factors:

1. the forces acting on each state;
2. the permeability of the boundaries between ego states; and
3. the cathectic capacity of each ego state.

Berne (1961) observed that it is the quantitative balance between these three factors that determines the clinical condition of the client and thus indicates the therapy procedures.

STIMULUS, RECOGNITION AND STRUCTURE HUNGER

The psychobiological basis of social psychiatry is that the ability of human beings to maintain coherent ego states depends on a changing flow of sensory stimuli. Berne cited Spitz's (1945) work, which demonstrated that sensory deprivation in infants resulted not only in psychological changes, but also in organic deterioration. Berne posited that there were three principal forms of drive, hunger or motivation: stimulus, recognition and structure hunger.

- *Stimulus hunger:* The most favoured forms of stimuli are those offered by physical intimacy. Berne acknowledged the dangers of over-stimulation as well as of under-stimulation.
- *Recognition hunger:* Recognition hunger may be viewed as a partial transformation of infantile stimulus hunger. Berne used the term 'stroking' to denote any act implying recognition of another's presence. There are numerous rituals, such as saying 'Hello!', which imply recognition and give gratification. Biologically, even negative recognition has an advantage over no recognition at all. Put colloquially, 'Folks need strokes!'
- *Structure hunger:* Structure hunger addresses the everyday problem of how to structure one's waking hours. Such time structuring is concerned only with social time or the time people spend with others.

TIME STRUCTURING

Berne observed that if two or more people were in a room together they had six possible kinds of social behaviour or time structuring from which to choose. These are discussed below.

- *Withdrawal:* Here two people do not overtly communicate with one another, for example if they are on a bus or are withdrawn schizophrenics. In withdrawal, people remain wrapped up in their own thoughts.
- *Rituals:* Rituals are stylized signs of mutual recognition dictated by tradition and social custom. At the simplest level, two people saying 'Good morning' engage in a ritual.

- *Activities:* Activities, more commonly called work, are not just concerned with dealing with the material means of survival. They also have a social significance in that they offer a framework for various kinds of recognition and satisfactions. Berne considered that work transactions were typically Adult-to-Adult, oriented mainly towards external reality.
- *Pastimes:* Pastimes are semi-ritualistic, topical conversations that last longer than rituals but are still mainly socially programmed. They might include 'Ain't it Awful' and 'General Motors' types of conversations. The focus of pastimes tends to be external to the participants rather than directly self-referent.
- *Games:* Games, in contrast to pastimes, are sequences of transactions which are based more on individual than on social programming. A psychological game is a set of covert or ulterior as well as overt transactions that lead to a predictable outcome or payoff. Frequently these payoffs involve negative feelings or 'rackets' such as anger and depression. Collecting racket feelings is known as collecting 'trading stamps', which may some day be cashed in for behaviours, such as a good cry or going out and buying some new clothes. More drastically, 'trading stamps' may be cashed in for divorce or attempted suicide. Each game has a motto by which it can be recognized, for example 'Why don't you? – Yes but' and 'If it weren't for you' (Berne, 1964).
- *Intimacy:* Berne defined bilateral intimacy as 'a candid, game-free relationship, with mutual free giving and receiving and without exploitation' (1972, p. 25). Intimacy represents individual and instinctual programming in which social programming and ulterior motivations are largely, if not totally, suspended. Intimacy is the most satisfying solution to stimulus, recognition, and structure hunger, but unfortunately it is not very common for people to live as 'princes' and 'princesses'. Berne's idea of intimacy included, but was not restricted to, sexual intimacy.

TYPES OF TRANSACTIONS

In transactional analysis a stroke or unit of recognition is viewed as the fundamental unit of social interaction. An exchange of strokes constitutes a transaction. Thus rituals, activities, pastimes, games and intimacy may all be viewed as involving transactions. During transactions, at any given time each person is likely to have one of their three ego states predominantly energized or cathected. Thus transactions take place between ego states and, at its simplest level, transactional analysis involves diagnosing the ego states involved in a stimulus and response exchange. In other words, the transactional stimulus may come from the Parent, Adult or Child of one person and the transactional response from the Parent, Adult or Child of the other person.

There are three main types of transactions: complementary, crossed and ulterior.

COMPLEMENTARY TRANSACTIONS

Complementary transactions are ones in which the directions of the stimulus-response transactions are consistent, such as discussing the ills of the world (Parent–Parent), talking about work (Adult–Adult), or having fun together (Child–Child). Another way of stating this is that complementary transactions

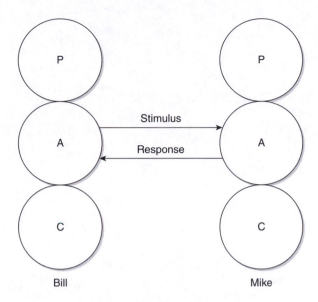

Figure 6.3   Example of a complementary transaction

are ones in which people receive a response from the ego state that they have
addressed. An example of a complementary transaction is given in Figure 6.3.
There are nine possible types of complementary transactions (PP, PA, PC, AP,
AA, AC, CP, CA, CC). Berne's first rule of communication was that communication will proceed smoothly as long as transactions are complementary. In the
example in Figure 6.3 Mike responds (a) from the ego state addressed by Bill
and (b) to the ego state from which Bill addressed him.

CROSSED TRANSACTIONS

In a crossed transaction the transactional response (a) comes from an ego state
different from the one addressed, and/or (b) may go to an ego state that did not
send the original stimulus. Berne's second or converse rule of communication
was that communication is broken off when a crossed transaction occurs. In
fact, the break may be only slight and momentary. However, at the other
extreme, communication may be broken off completely. Figure 6.4 is an example of a crossed transaction. There are 72 possible types of crossed transactions,
but only a few occur frequently.

ULTERIOR TRANSACTIONS

An ulterior transaction is where, under the guise of an overt and socially more
acceptable communication, an individual engages in an underlying and
socially more risky communication. Another way of viewing this is that in
much human interaction there is an underlying psychological as well as an

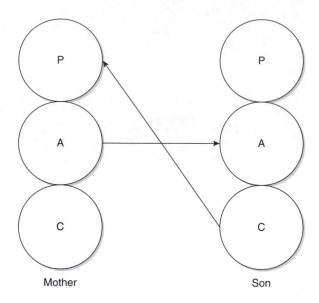

Figure 6.4   Example of a crossed transaction

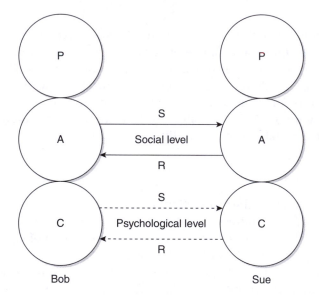

Figure 6.5   Example of an ulterior transaction

overt social agenda. Psychological games, by definition, involve ulterior transactions.

Ulterior transactions may occur in everyday situations such as when a salesman says to a customer, 'Perhaps you shouldn't buy that beautiful and expensive coat', when his psychological message is 'Come on, I want you to buy it'. Potential sexual situations are other everyday situations in which ulterior transactions may occur. Figure 6.5 illustrates such an ulterior transaction.

ACQUISITION

THE SCRIPT

Berne defined a script as: 'A life plan based on a decision made in childhood, reinforced by the parents, justified by subsequent events, and culminating in a chosen alternative' (1972, p. 445). He regarded scripts as preconscious life plans by which people structure their time. Scripts determine people's destinies, including their approach to relationships and to tasks. He considered that scripts are usually based on childlike illusions that may persist throughout a whole lifetime. People's scripts are the product of parental programming plus the decisions they made in response to that. Children seek out parental programming for three reasons:

1. to give a purpose in life which otherwise might be wanting;
2. to provide a way of structuring their time acceptable to their parents; and
3. since people have to be told how to do things (Berne, 1972).

Scripts lead people to have an illusion of personal autonomy when in fact they are carrying out, often unthinkingly, the directives of their scripts. At times, however, some people may question their scripts and this may cause identity crises that may or may not be resolved satisfactorily by removal of some of the blockages to genuine autonomy and a well-functioning Adult. Berne's view of human life, as contrasted with human nature, was pessimistic, as he tended to see humans as driven by script directives which led to ways of time structuring seriously detrimental to attaining autonomy and creative activity.

THE SCRIPT MATRIX

The script matrix is a diagram used to help understand the development of people's scripts. It is helpful to an understanding of the transmission of scripts if the matrix depicts a second-order structural breakdown of the Child. Figure 6.6 depicts such a script matrix for a hypothetical person, Mary. The diagram aims to show how script directives are transmitted to her. Although, during her upbringing, it is desirable for Mary to experience much of the nurturing Parent ego state of her parents and also their reasoning Adult and spontaneous Child, she may also be experiencing negative directives from the Parent in the Child ego state of one or both of her parents. As depicted in Box 6.6, the directives to Mary may be contradictory.

Although a chapter in Berne's 1961 book *Transactional Analysis in Psychotherapy* is devoted to analysis of scripts, he acknowledged the valuable work of Steiner in devising the script matrix and in helping to develop script theory. Berne proposed that it was the parent of the opposite sex who usually tells the child what to do and the parent of the same sex who usually demonstrates how to do it. Steiner (1974) added that it was the Child in the Parent who gives the restrictive directives or injunctions and the Adult in the Parent who gives the child the pattern or programme of behaviour.

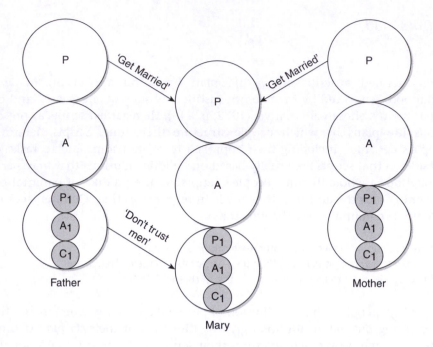

Figure 6.6   Script matrix showing transmission of script directives

INJUNCTIONS, ATTRIBUTIONS AND DISCOUNTS

Although directives from parents can be nurturing and conducive to the child's emotional development, they can also be restrictive, reflecting the fears and insecurities of the Child in the parent.

INJUNCTIONS

Injunctions are expressed as messages beginning with 'Don't'. They can be relatively mild or highly restrictive. Steiner (1974) gives the following as injunctions by which people learn to block intimacy:

- do not give strokes if you have them to give,
- do not ask for strokes when you need them,
- do not accept strokes if you want them,
- do not reject strokes when you do not want them, and
- do not give yourself strokes.

He considers that the above injunctions are the basis of depression. Other injunctions may stop people from thinking, especially perhaps if they are female. Still others may interfere with the capacity to experience feelings, especially perhaps for males.

Box 6.1 presents 12 injunctions that Mary and Robert Goulding repeatedly found when analysing scripts (Goulding and Goulding, 1979, pp. 34–9; Stewart, 1996a).

BOX 6.1   LIST OF COMMON SCRIPT INJUNCTIONS

- 'Don't exist'
- 'Don't be you' (sometimes, 'Don't be the sex you are')
- 'Don't be a child' (or 'Don't enjoy')
- 'Don't grow up' (or 'Don't leave me')
- 'Don't make it' ('Don't succeed')
- 'Don't' (i.e.'Don't do anything')
- 'Don't be important'
- 'Don't belong'
- 'Don't be close'
- 'Don't be well (or 'Don't be sane')
- 'Don't think'
- 'Don't feel'

ATTRIBUTIONS

Steiner states that children are also strongly influenced by attributions, or being told what they are and what they must do, and how they are feeling. Family reinforcement schedules tend to reward children who follow attributions and punish children who disobey injunctions.

DISCOUNTS

Children are also liable to receive discounts from their parents. Steiner regards a discount as a crossed transaction in which a person says something from an Adult ego state to another person's Adult and the other person responds from his or her Parent or Child. For instance, children's inquisitiveness may be discounted by parental rebuffs. More generally, a discount in TA is the minimization of some aspect of oneself, another person, or a situation.

DECISIONS

On the basis of early transactions related to feeding, toilet training, weaning and family relationships, the young person starts developing a view of the world. Where children are given unconditional protection they are less likely to develop restrictive scripts. However, when parents make their nurturing conditional on their child's submission to their injunctions and attributions, the child may make a conscious decision to adhere to parental wishes even though this means the sacrifice of autonomy. These decisions tend to be made in the pre-school years and are as realistic as the capacity of the Adult in the Child or Little Professor at the time of the decision. As a result of this decision, however, the child tends to take a different and more negative position and also develops a script. Berne acknowledged that some scripts could be winner's scripts.

LIFE POSITIONS

The fundamental assumption of transactional analysis is that of human OK-ness as expressed in the statement or life position 'I'm OK – You're OK'. By making a decision children move out of this position. Instead, they adopt one of three other life positions, namely: 'I'm not-OK – You're OK'; 'I'm OK – You're not-OK'; and 'I'm not-OK – You're not-OK'. Each of these three 'not-OK' positions reflects and sustains impaired ego state development. 'Not-OK' positions militate against the development of intimacy and are the bases on which individuals play out their games. Just as stimulus, recognition and structure hunger can be viewed as motivators, it is also possible to view the need to justify a basic life position as a motivator. Perhaps, though, it is more accurate to consider position hunger as a refinement of the other motivators, indicating how their fulfillment is to be attained. Box 6.2 is an example of a decision leading to a life position in the case of Rita (Berne, 1966).

BOX 6.2   RITA: AN EXAMPLE OF A DECISION LEADING TO A LIFE POSITION

When she was a little girl, Rita used to run to greet her father when he came home from work. As time went on her father's behaviour became erratic because of his drinking and he would push Rita away. One day her father had a particularly bad row with her mother. Rita, who was 6 years, 2 months and 23 days, was bewildered and frightened and at 5 p.m. that afternoon she made a decision that she would never again love a man. In order to maintain her decision, Rita took a position regarding her father that, even when amiable and sober, he was fundamentally bad. Over time she generalized her position to most other men, the not-OK-ness of whom she epitomized in the slogan 'All men are beasts'. Her position also became the basis of a game in which her seductive behaviour provoked 'decent' men to make advances, which she then rejected. Berne observed that Rita's seductive manoeuvres were an attempt to establish an intimate relationship that she was unable to carry through.

DEVELOPMENT OF GAMES

During children's upbringing they are taught the rituals, activities and pastimes appropriate to their situations in life. They also learn games through significant experiences in their family life from their earliest months. Berne (1964) gave as an example of how a game might be learned the case of three-year-old Mike who, when his seven-year-old brother was allowed to leave the dinner table and lie down because of a stomach-ache, said 'I have a stomach-ache too', as though he wanted the same consideration. Mike's parents, however, did not co-operate and thus may have saved him from the game of pleading illness (social transaction) in order to gain some privilege for himself (ulterior or psychological transaction). Berne considered that games are imitative in nature, and also that they are deliberately initiated by the neopsychic Adult or Little Professor in the Child, frequently between the ages of two and eight. As illustrated by Rita, games are often formulated to help justify a life position.

THE COUNTERSCRIPT

In the development of a script, the person is given not only script injunctions and attributions from their parents' Parent in the Child, but also counterscript messages from their parents' Parent. Berne (1972) used the word 'prescription' for counterscript messages and observed that prescriptions were usually transmitted from grandparents. Examples of prescriptions are 'Be a good boy (or girl)!' and 'Work hard'. Script injunctions and counterscript prescriptions are sometimes contradictory, and life may involve an alternation between compliance first to one and then to the other. The counterscript may lead to a period of time in which an unhappy life plan gives way to a happier period. However, in the end the script injunctions always prevail, though again the possibility of winner's scripts should be acknowledged.

Steiner (1974) indicates that an alcoholic's Parent may give the counterscript 'Be sober' while the parent in the Child is giving the injunction 'Don't think! Drink'. In Figure 6.6 Mary's parents' Parent counterscript prescription was 'Get married' while her father's Parent in the Child injunction was 'Don't trust men'. Frequently injunctions are transmitted non-verbally by approval or disapproval of certain kinds of behaviour, and this may make them harder to bring into awareness than when they are transmitted more openly.

MAINTENANCE

In the preceding section the ways in which people acquire scripts and games were described. The question to be answered in this section is why people persist in acting out scripts and playing games rather than enjoying autonomy and intimacy, or, in other words, why people stay frogs when it might seem more rewarding to revert to being princes or princesses? Part of the answer is that both scripts and games have their rewards or payoffs.

SCRIPT PAYOFFS

Berne (1972) defined the script payoff as the ultimate destiny or final display that marks the end of a life plan. He considered that there were four main payoffs in clinical practice: be a loner, be a bum, go crazy or drop dead. While these ultimate destinies are one way of viewing the concept of script payoff, another way is to look at it in terms of current as contrasted with ultimate rewards. Steiner (1974) observes that when people enter their counterscript phase, despite a superficial sense of wellbeing, they experience a deep visceral discomfort. However, people experience visceral comfort when reverting to script behaviour. This is because adherence to script injunctions represents acquiescence to parental wishes, albeit the parental Parent in the Child, and thus is associated with the wellbeing and comfort of parental protection. Steiner notes that an alcoholic, even in the pain of a hangover, is receiving approval for acquiescing to the parental Child's injunction 'Don't think! Drink'. Steiner is perhaps more pessimistic about scripts than many other TA therapists

GAME PAYOFFS

Games too have their payoffs, which are related to the life positions adopted in their players' scripts. For instance, the payoff in Rita's script was manipulating men to boorish behaviour that confirmed her position that men are not-OK. Berne (1964) observed that, beyond their social function of time structuring, games are urgently needed by some people to keep their health. Their life positions are so tenaciously maintained that to interfere with or deprive them of the payoffs from their games may cause disturbance, or even psychosis. Thus game analysis must be approached cautiously.

   An example of a game with a payoff is 'If it weren't for you'. A person can complain endlessly that if it were not for a husband, wife, child, boss or some other person, they could engage in an activity from which at present they feel restricted. Sometimes, however, these other people are being used to defend the person against the realization that, if it were not for them, she or he might be unable to perform a difficult or anxiety-evoking task. If the task were performed, it would no longer be possible to cause the other person discomfort by saying 'If it weren't for you'. This game validates the life-position that others are not-OK.

THE ILLUSION OF AUTONOMY

Berne (1972) considered that only the strongest can live without illusions and that one of the illusions which is the hardest to relinquish is that of autonomy or self-determination. An autonomous person knows what is practical and Adult, what he accepts that comes from others, and what he does that is determined by early impulses. The illusion of autonomy is where a person does not acknowledge feelings and behaviours coming from his Child and Parent ego states, but instead believes that they come from the Adult ego state.

   Berne distinguished between delusions and illusions, both of which are contaminations of the Adult ego state and, as such, prevent it from effectively dealing with here-and-now situations. Delusions are the prejudices and directives from parents that a person treats as though they were his own ideas.

Illusions are those wishful ideas, impulses and early tastes coming from the Child which are accepted as Adult and rational. The significance of the illusion of autonomy is that an individual, being unaware of the delusions and illusions that are causing 'frog-like' behaviour, lacks the necessary insight and motivation for change. Thus destructive ways of time structuring are sustained rather than ameliorated. What is needed is a re-alignment and strengthening of the Adult ego-boundary to allow accurate processing of all relevant information.

CONTAMINATION AND EXCLUSION

With a truly autonomous person the ego-boundaries are strong, yet appropriately permeable to allow psychic energy to move between Parent, Adult and Child ego states. The illusion of autonomy indicates a structure where ego-boundaries are insufficiently well defined and the Adult ego state is being contaminated by the Parent and/or Child ego states. Exclusion, on the other hand, occurs in situations where psychic energy becomes exclusively cathected in a constant Parent, a constant Adult, or a constant Child (Berne, 1961). Thus one ego state is strongly cathected while the other two are decommissioned.

Berne considered that the excluding Parent is to be found in 'compensated' schizophrenics, where exclusion is the principal defence against confused Child or archaeopsychic activity. He gave as an example of an excluding Adult, Dr Quint, who had a sincere commitment to data processing as a way of life, yet possessed no healthy Child or Parent characteristics. Narcissistic impulsive personalities exhibit the excluding Child, where both rational and nurturing and limit-setting ego states are avoided. The excluding Parent, Adult or Child may defend itself; for instance, by the use of intellectualization in the case of the excluding Adult.

INADEQUATE INFORMATION

The last point to be made regarding the maintenance of maladaptive behaviour is that the effectiveness of the Adult is dependent on the adequacy of the information available to it. Furthermore, the Adult may need to develop some skills of effective Adult functioning, including the ability to collect and adequately assess relevant information. James and Jongeward (1971) state that the computer phrase 'Garbage in, garbage out' applies to the Adult or, for that matter, to any other ego state.

THERAPY

THERAPEUTIC GOALS

FOUR CATEGORIES OF GOALS

Transactional analysis seeks to help clients obtain an 'I am OK, you are OK' life position. For clients who have been turned by their life's experiences from princes and princesses into frogs, Berne saw four possible goals (Berne 1961; 1972). Stewart views these goals as progressive stages in the direction of cure (Stewart, 1996a).

1. *Social control.* Though still feeling distress, clients can control their symptoms in their interactions with others.
2. *Symptomatic relief.* Getting better, or 'progress', that Berne regarded as making clients into more comfortable frogs.
3. *Transference cure.* Here clients can stay out of their scripts so long as they can keep their therapists either literally or mentally around.
4. *Autonomy.* Clients cast off the frog skin and take up once more the interrupted development of the prince or princess (Berne, 1966). The client's Adult takes over the role of the therapist as the client attains autonomy. Autonomy refers to the capacity for 'non-script' behaviour 'with no particular time schedule, developed later in life, and not under parental influence' (Berne, 1972, p. 418).

Autonomous behaviour is the opposite of script behaviour. It involves the total or partial overthrow of (a) the weight of a whole tribal or family historical tradition, (b) the influence of the individual's parental, social and cultural backgrounds, and (c) seeking ulterior payoffs from games. Furthermore, autonomy consists of the active development of personal and social control so that significant behaviour becomes a matter of free choice. Berne summarized the process of the attainment of autonomy as 'obtaining a friendly divorce from one's parents (and from other Parental influences) so that they may be agreeably visited on occasion, but are no longer dominant' (Berne, 1964, p. 183).

The attainment of autonomy involves the person's regaining three basic capacities of the fundamental OK position: awareness, spontaneity and intimacy.

- *Awareness.* Awareness means the capacity to see and hear directly and not in the way in which one was brought up. It means living in the here-and-now, open to the sensations coming from the environment in the way a painter, poet or musician might be.
- *Spontaneity.* Spontaneity means the capacity to feel directly and to express feelings directly and not in the way in which one was brought up. The spontaneous person can choose feelings, be they Parent, Adult or Child feelings.
- *Intimacy.* Intimacy means the capacity to relate to another person or persons in an aware, spontaneous, loving and game-free way. Berne regarded intimacy as essentially a function of the natural, uncorrupted Child.

CONTRACTUAL THERAPY GOALS

Transactional analysis takes a contractual approach to therapy. A key question in such an approach is 'How will both you and I know when you get what you came for?' (Dusay and Dusay, 1989, p. 427). Therapist and client negotiate a contract that defines both treatment goals and mutual responsibilities in achieving the goals. Contract goals can focus on outcomes and actions.

Outcome goals include: physiological changes, for instance lowering of dias-tolic blood pressure; and relief of psychological symptoms, such as impotence or a specific phobia. Action goals specify behaviour changes, for instance not hitting children, refraining from alcohol or drugs, or holding a job for a speci-fied time period. Stewart (1996a, p. 68) suggests the following principles for establishing contracts:

1. *Contracts in TA may be either for outcomes or for actions.*
2. *However, any contract for an outcome must be supported by at least one contract for a related action.*

Contracts are open to amendment as therapy proceeds. Updates and changes of goals are frequent. Furthermore, the therapist's or the client's ultimate goal may differ from the set of operational criteria for improvement stated as initial goals. During therapy, transactional analysts always observe determi-nants underlying symptoms and responses. Berne (1966) gave the example of the therapist, who wished to investigate a client's archaic attitudes towards parental figures, stating goals in terms of alleviation of symptoms first and later proposing an amendment to the contract that focused on the goal of altering attitudes towards parental figures.

PROCESS OF THERAPY

Settings for transactional analysis range from home-like surroundings to more business-like offices. Since body language clues are important in conducting transactional analysis, in most therapists' offices there are no tables or chairs that block therapist and client views of one another. The majority of TA settings include whiteboards, blackboards or giant paper pads that both therapists and clients can use to illustrate transactions and games and other relevant matters. Some therapists employ audiovisual aids to provide feedback and heighten clients' awareness.

In the initial session or sessions, therapists work in a number of ways. They introduce and use a simple common vocabulary. During therapy there is no gossiping or small talk. Ground rules for the therapeutic contact are agreed, such as no violence or threats of violence, and no use of alcohol or mind alter-ing drugs. Furthermore, an initial fee-for-service business contract may be established. Therapists conduct an initial assessment of clients and work with them to establish contract goals, including a time frame for ending therapy.

THE THERAPEUTIC RELATIONSHIP

Transactional analysts provide supportive and nurturing relationships condu-cive to clients assuming greater personal responsibility for their lives. Within the framework of a common and easily understandable language, therapists provide permission for clients to play an active role in therapy. Therapists support clients as they reveal and analyse themselves more fully and try out more Adult patterns of feeling, thinking and behaving.

Transactional analysis, as originally formulated by Berne, is largely an educational process and thus the therapist–client relationship resembles a democratic teacher–learner relationship. Early on in therapy, therapist and clients establish ground rules and define the elements of their working or learning contract. Therapists train clients in the skills of analysing ego states, transactions, games and scripts. Furthermore they encourage and assist clients to identify Adult options for dealing with people, problems and situations in their lives. As indicated earlier, more often than not therapists' offices contain educational aids such as whiteboards and large writing pads.

Therapists are sensitive to clues regarding clients' inauthentic ways of relating to others, including their therapists. Where there are problems in the therapeutic relationship, such as non-payment of fees or missed appointments, therapists view these transactions as psychological games and provide therapy accordingly (Dusay and Dusay, 1989).

THERAPEUTIC INTERVENTIONS

Berne regarded transactional analysis as an umbrella term for four different, but interrelated, approaches to treatment. These approaches are structural analysis, transactional analysis, game analysis and script analysis. Berne (1961) saw a progression from structural analysis, through transactional and game analysis, to script analysis, though he realized that the script analysis state was not always attained.

STRUCTURAL ANALYSIS

As mentioned earlier, structural analysis consists of diagnosing and separating one feeling-thinking-and-behaviour pattern or ego state from another. Structural analysis helps clients to identify and become aware of both the existence and the contents of their ego states. Its aim is to free people to have appropriate access to all their ego states without debilitating exclusions and contaminations. A related aim is to help the Adult to remain in control of the personality in stressful situations.

TRANSACTIONAL ANALYSIS

Berne (1961) saw one aim of transactional analysis as social control or the ability of the Adult to decide when to release the Parent or Child and when to resume the executive. If a person does not have social control, others can consciously or unconsciously activate that person's Parent or Child ego states in ways that may not be helpful. Transactional analysis proper, as Berne (1972) called it, is the analysis of single transactions by means of transactional diagrams. Clients are helped to understand the ego state transactions involved in situations and relationships in which they are experiencing difficulty as a means towards greater competence in handling them.

GAME ANALYSIS

Game analysis is another way of attaining social control. Just as an understanding of structural analysis is a prerequisite of transactional analysis, so an understanding of analysis of single transactions is a prerequisite of understanding the more complex series of transactions called games. In game analysis the client is encouraged to learn more satisfying ways of structuring time and acquiring strokes. The methods of game analysis include helping a client to see what game she or he is playing, what the moves are, what the racket or bad feeling payoffs are, and how the games justify a life position. It is also important to help the client to express constructively the natural Child need or feeling that she or he has been discounting.

SCRIPT ANALYSIS

The script analyst must take care not to behave in ways that promote a client's script. The purpose of script analysis is to help clients to get out of their script and thus to behave autonomously. The therapist needs to listen carefully to and observe the client's verbal and non-verbal behaviour for script signs or signals. Additionally, script analysis may involve the use of a script checklist to help both analyst and client to know the client's script (Berne, 1972). Script analysis aims to help clients to abandon their early decisions, *previously* made in different circumstances and with an incomplete neopsychic or Adult apparatus, by *now* making and enacting re-decisions for change.

A script antithesis is a therapeutic intervention that directly contradicts a parental injunction and thus brings temporary or permanent release from a script. Berne (1972) considered that the final common pathway of a patient's behaviour is the preconscious dialogue between Parent, Adult and Child, or voices in the head, which can easily be brought into consciousness. Re-decision can be helped by getting into the client's head another voice, that of the therapist. This process involves the three 'Ps' of script antithesis: potency, permission and protection.

Potency is defined by whether the therapist's voice in the client's head has been powerful enough to prevail over the voices or injunctions of the client's Parents in the Child. Permissions can be positive or negative. Positive permissions or licences involve the therapist saying 'Let her/him do it!', whereas with negative permissions or releases the therapist is saying 'Stop pushing her/him into it!'. When clients follow a script antithesis and go against a parental injunction, their Child may get very anxious. Protection means that during the period of change the client can call upon their therapists to exercise their potency again in time of need.

BASIC INTERVENTIONS AND INTERPOSITIONS

Berne originally designed transactional analysis as a group therapy adjunct to psychoanalysis. Berne (1966, pp. 233–47) identified eight categories of basic therapeutic techniques that have relevance for individual, couples and family work as well as for groups of 7 to 8 clients. He divided these basic techniques into interventions and interpositions. Dusay and Dusay observe that interpositions go beyond interventions by being 'an attempt by the therapist to interpose something between the patient's Adult and other ego states and to stabilize the Adult and make it more difficult to slide into Parent or Child activity' (1989, p. 441).

INTERVENTIONS

1. *Interrogation*: Therapists use interrogation primarily to clarify, pin down and document specific points that might be clinically useful in future. Examples of interrogation are 'Did you actually steal the money?' and 'Did you really hit her?' Therapists who ask too many questions may find clients happy to play 'Psychiatric history'.
2. *Specification*: Specification is intended to fix something in both the therapist's and the client's minds so that it can be referred to later in therapy. Examples are: 'So you always wanted to buy more expensive things' and 'I'm hearing that you felt angry'.
3. *Confrontation*: In confrontation therapists use information previously elicited and specified in order to point out an inconsistency and, thereby, to disconcert a client's Parent, Child or contaminated Adult. Therapists should not use confrontation when genuinely convinced that clients are incapable of seeing the inconsistency.
4. *Explanation*: Therapists use explanation to strengthen, decontaminate or reorient the client's Adult. An example is: 'So you see the Child in you was threatening to become active, and when that happens your Adult fades out and your Parent takes over and that's when you shout at the children'.

INTERPOSITIONS

1. *Illustration*: Illustrations are anecdotes, similes or comparisons that follow a successful confrontation for the purpose of reinforcing it and softening any undesirable after effects. Illustrations are attempts by therapists to interpose something between the client's Adult and the other ego states to make it more difficult for her/him to slide into Parent or Child activity.
2. *Confirmation*: When clients provide confirmatory evidence after confrontations, therapists can use confirmation to stabilize the client's Adult. For example, if a client were to say 'I just can't do this – Oops, I mean I won't do it' the therapist will immediately confirm the client's greater self-awareness (Dusay and Dusay, 1989, p. 441).
3. *Interpretation*: Therapists use the preceding interventions and interpositions with the primary object of cathecting and decontminating the Adult. Interpretations are not always necessary for treatment to be successful. However, in some cases the therapist may choose to postpone moving on to crystallization until the Child has been deconfused by psychodynamic interpretation. Alternatively, therapists may first use

crystallization to establish Adult control and then undertake the analytic deconfusion of the Child.

4. *Crystallization*: Transactional analysis aims to bring clients to the point where crystallizing statements from therapists are effective. A crystallization is a statement of a client's position from the therapist's Adult to the client's Adult. An example of a crystallization is: 'So you are now in a position to stop playing that game if you want to.'

Berne (1966) stressed that therapists using interventions and interpositions should:

- never get ahead of the clinical material offered by clients;
- never miss a legitimate opportunity to forge ahead; and
- never push against resistance except for testing purposes based on well-thought-out concrete hypotheses.

CASE MATERIAL

As an appendix to *Transactional Analysis in Psychotherapy*, Berne (1961) presents 'A terminated case with follow-up'. The client, a 34-year-old woman called Mrs Enatosky had complained initially of depression, though Berne stated the formal diagnosis was best stated as schizo-hysteria. The client showed a special aptitude for structural and transactional analysis and soon began to exert social control for the games that went on between her, her husband and her 13-year-old son. In *Games People Play*, Berne (1964) illustrated the characteristics of games in general by choosing the most common game between spouses, colloquially called 'If It Weren't for You' (IWFY). Towards the end *of What Do You Say After You Say Hello?*, Berne (1972) presented three brief case histories that illustrate working with scripts.

Those who have developed Berne's work have also presented case material. Dusay's (1978) book *Egograms* illustrates the functional aspects of ego states and presents many examples of how energy imbalance in clients is treated by redecision and exercises. The case of Judd, who had been diagnosed as a hypochondriac by many physicians, illustrates the use of egograms in TA group work (Dusay and Dusay, 1989). In another example drawn from group therapy, the Gouldings (1978) present the case of Tim, which demonstrates in detail combining transactional analysis and gestalt, a fairly common practice.

More recently, Stewart (2014) presents an extended case study of John that runs through the second part of his book. Tudor and Hobbes (2007) provide a case example of Simon that demonstrates how to assist integrating Child and Parent ego state material into the Adult ego state. Sills (2013) presents the case of Stan, aged 39, whose life was devoid of passion and stimulation, which included a continuing exploration of his Child ego states. Joines and Stewart (2002) provide another substantial source of case material in their book *Personality Adaptations*.

FURTHER DEVELOPMENTS

Since Eric Berne's death in 1970, there has been considerable expansion in TA's theory and practice. Dusay and Dusay state that, to date, there have been four transactional analysis phases: the ego state phase (1955–62); the transactions and games phase (1962–66); the script analysis phase (1966–70); and a fourth post-Berne phase 'stimulated by the action techniques of the human-potential movement, gestalt, psychodrama, encounter, and many of the other explosive, energy-liberating systems' (1989, p. 448). Stewart and Joines (2012) observe that in the 1970s three main schools emerged in TA: the classical (Bernian) school; the redecision school; and the Cathexis (Schiffian) school. These three styles of TA are often known as 'traditional schools'. Since then further developments have included both a focus on the Process Model and personality adaptations and also a renewed interest in the psychodynamic ideas that provided the original base for transactional analysis. Below I selectively overview some developments that have taken place after Berne's untimely early death.

THE USE OF EGOGRAMS

Ego states may be viewed not only in terms of their content, but also in terms of the degree to which they are cathected both before and after treatment. Dusay (1972; Dusay and Dusay, 1989) devised a diagram called the egogram that graphs the extent to which each of a person's ego states are cathected. An egogram shows in bar-graph form how much of a person's energy exists in the five functional ego states: Critical Parent (CP); Nurturing Parent (NP); Adult (A); Free Child (FC); and Adapted Child (AC). A bar graph profile identifies what may be the client's probable types of problems and where their strengths and weaknesses lie. Figure 6.7 is an example of an egogram.

Dusay (1972) suggested a constancy hypothesis: namely, that the amount of psychic energy within a person is constant and that if energy is taken away from one ego state more will be available for other ego states. Thus, as treatment progresses, the AC ego state may be less strongly cathected, while the A and FC ego states may attain stronger cathexes. In terms of the Figure 6.7 egogram, the height of AC would become lower, with the amount taken away distributed between raising the heights of A and FC.

Dusay and Dusay (1989) observe that each person has different ego-state imbalances. They use a variety of techniques and exercises for people needing to raise or lower the energy cathected in specific ego states: for example, assertiveness techniques for those low in Critical Parent; empathy techniques for those low in Nurturing Parent; thinking exercises for those low in Adult; creative and intuitive activities for those low in Free Child; and compromise and getting along with others exercises for those low in Adapted Child.

Figure 6.7   Example of an egogram

THE CATHEXIS SCHOOL AND REPARENTING

Stewart and Joines (2012) identify a *Schiffian* or *Cathexis* school of transactional analysis based on the Schiffs' reparenting work with schizophrenics (Schiff, 1969, 1970, 1975). This is performed in residential treatment centres, where severely disturbed clients with a tendency to regress and relive early childhood experiences are 'reparented' by positive parents. This level of intense and continuing therapeutic involvement is not appropriate for non-psychotic clients. Nevertheless, therapists may act as 'replacement parents' for less disturbed clients giving them positive messages and permissions to replace restrictive injunctions received from their natural parents.

THE REDECISION SCHOOL AND INCORPORATION OF GESTALT METHODS

Gestalt and psychodrama methods may be used in conjunction with transactional analysis. The Gouldings (Goulding, 1974; Goulding and Goulding, 1976; 1979) developed an approach called *redecision therapy* that combines TA and gestalt theory and practice. They consider that early decisions are made from a feeling rather than a thinking position. Therefore, to get out of script decisions, people must get in touch with their original Child feelings at the time of the decisions, deal with unfinished emotional business, and 'change the early decision for a new and more appropriate *redecision*' (Stewart and Joines, 2012, p. 299). The Gouldings see impasses as developing between ego states. They use the gestalt empty chair technique to enable clients to have dialogues between ego states. During this process, clients may connect with and reveal strong feelings suppressed since childhood.

Another example of the incorporation into TA of gestalt techniques are the exercises and experiments in James and Jongeward's (1971) book *Born to Win*. For instance, as part of an exercise on the Adapted Child, readers are asked 'Can you admit to any top-dog and/or under-dog positions with yourself?' and 'Can you relate these to your Parent and Child ego states?' (p. 155).

THE PROCESS MODEL AND PERSONALITY ADAPTATIONS

The Process Model developed by Kahler (2008, Stewart and Joines, 2012) rests upon Berne's idea that people might enact their scripts within extremely short time periods. By focusing on the process rather than the content of clients' communication, therapists can identify driver behaviours. In the TA tradition, Kahler has given his five drivers colloquial names: 'Be Perfect', 'Be Strong', 'Try Hard', 'Please You' and 'Hurry Up'. Driver behaviours are so called because they have a 'driven' quality about them. While over time everyone shows all five driver behaviours, most people have a primary driver that they show most often and first in any interaction. Stewart (1996a) regards driver behaviours as the 'gateway to the script'. Drivers are external indicators or early warning signals that the person may be replaying a specific script belief internally. Clients always enact driver behaviours just before they move into their scripts.

Ware (1983) presents six personality adaptations: obsessive-compulsive, paranoid, schizoid, passive-aggressive, hysteric and antisocial. Since each adaptation contains a specific set of script beliefs about the world, correct identification of a client's adaptation assists the therapist to plan the most appropriate treatment. Being able to spot a client's primary driver, helps therapists reliably diagnose her or his main personality adaptation. With each of the adaptations, often primary drivers are accompanied by secondary drivers. For example, clients, whose primary driver is 'Try Hard' will have the passive-aggressive personality adaptation. Clients who have the driver behaviours 'Be Perfect' and 'Be Strong' shown with approximately equal intensity will have the paranoid adaptation (Stewart, 1996b). Combining the Process Model with personality adaptations provides a powerful means of analysing and treating scripts.

THE RELATIONAL APPROACH

The relational approach, usually performed in individual as contrasted with group psychotherapy, heavily stresses the importance of the relationship between therapist and client (Cornell and Hargaden, 2005; Fowlie and Sills, 2011; Hargaden and Sills, 2002). However, the model of ego states is still central to relational TA's theory.

The relational approach represents a rapprochement between TA and psychoanalysis (Stewart, 2014). It emphasizes that the therapeutic relationship continually contains unconscious processes. Stewart and Joines (2012) write: 'The task of the relational therapist is to remain open to her responses to the client as the unconscious dialogue between them develops. Moment by moment client and therapist are seen as co-creating whatever happens in the process of therapy' (p. 301). This differs from more traditional approaches to TA where there tends to be a planned movement towards highly specific contracts. Instead, the relational approach assumes that therapeutic change occurs mainly at an unconscious level. Such change materializes as, between them, therapist and client work out the unconscious issues arising in the relationship.

JOURNALS, ASSOCIATIONS AND TRAINING

The *Transactional Analysis Bulletin* started in 1962 with Berne as editor. In 1964 the International Transactional Analysis Association (ITAA) was formed as a training and accreditation body for transactional analysis. It now produces the *Transactional Analysis Journal* along with a bi-monthly online newsletter *The Script*. In 2010, the online *International Journal of Transactional Analysis* was launched (www.ijtar.org).

The ITAA has seen its numbers fall from almost 11,000 members in 1976 to 1,169 in 2010. However, there is a European Association for Transactional Analysis (EATA) that performs training and accreditation functions. Stewart and Joines (2012) observe that, in 2010, its membership was over 7,500 people. They continue: 'Add to that the number of people belonging to TA organizations outside Europe, and the worldwide total must come close to the figure of some 11,000 ITAA members that marked the peak of mass popularity of TA in 1976' (p. 319). There is also the UK Association for Transactional Analysis (UKATA), formed in 1974, the Scottish Transactional Analysis Association (STTA), formed in 2010, and an Australian Federation of TA Associations (FTAA).

The past 25 years have seen a growing number of TA courses gaining validation for university awards. TA is recognized as an established modality by the European Association for Psychotherapy (EAP), the UK Council for Psychotherapy and the British Association for Counselling and Psychotherapy (Stewart and Joines, 2012).

REVIEW AND PERSONAL QUESTIONS

REVIEW QUESTIONS

1. Describe each of the following ego states:

   - Parent
   - Adult
   - Child.

2. Why is transactional analysis a dynamic theory of personality?
3. What are stimulus, recognition and structure hungers?
4. What did Berne mean by time structuring and what are the ways in which people can structure time?

5. Provide an example of and draw a diagram for each of the following types of transactions:

   - complementary
   - crossed
   - ulterior.

6. What did Berne mean by a script?
7. What are games and how do people develop them?
8. What are script payoffs and game payoffs?
9. What are the goals of transactional analysis?
10. Describe briefly each of the following:

   - structural analysis
   - transactional analysis
   - game analysis
   - script analysis.

PERSONAL QUESTIONS

1. Do a first-order PAC structural analysis on yourself (Figure 6.1 (a)) indicating thoughts, feelings and behaviours belonging to your:

   - Parent ego state;
   - Adult ego state;
   - Child ego state.

2. Assume that you have 100 units of energy to divide among your Critical Parent, Nurturing Parent, Adult, Free Child, and Adapted Child ego states. In terms of the way you usually feel and behave, draw an egogram distributing the 100 units of energy among the five ego states.

3. Provide an example from your own life of each of the following types of transactions:

   - complementary
   - crossed
   - ulterior.

4. Take a relationship with a significant other in your life (parent, spouse, child, colleague, etc.) and analyse one or more of the transactions in it in terms of the Parent, Adult and Child ego state, or states, cathected in each person.

5. Identify some of the games you play, including the moves involved and their negative feeling payoff or your racket. Suggest an easily remembered name for each of your games.

6. Draw a script matrix for yourself as in Figure 6.6 and indicate some of the main script injunctions and counterscript prescriptions you received from your parents.

7. Identify any early decisions you made which are no longer appropriate. Formulate appropriate statements of redecision that will allow you to change the ways in which you are currently scripted to feel and behave.

8. What relevance, if any, has the theory and practice of transactional analysis for how you conduct therapy?

9. What relevance, if any, has the theory and practice of transactional analysis for how you live?

ANNOTATED BIBLIOGRAPHY

Berne, E. (1961) *Transactional Analysis in Psychotherapy*. New York: Grove Press.
This book is Berne's major statement of structural analysis and transactional analysis. It consists of four parts: psychiatry of the individual and structural analysis; social psychiatry and transactional analysis; psychotherapy; and frontiers of transactional analysis. A case study is provided as an appendix.

Berne, E. (1964) *Games People Play: The Psychology of Human Relationships*. New York: Grove Press.
This book is Berne's international best-seller. It consists of three parts: analysis of games; a thesaurus of games; and beyond games. The chapters in the thesaurus of games cover: life, marital, party, sexual, underworld, consulting room, and good games. Berne gave each game a catchy title.

Berne, E. (1966) *Principles of Group Treatment*. New York: Grove Press.
This book is a systematic treatise on the use of transactional analysis in groups. The book's first part describes the basic principles of group treatment. The focus of the book's second part is transactional analysis, its general principles and basic techniques, and the handling of the more common games that occur in the course of group treatment.

Berne, E. (1972) *What Do You Say After You Say Hello?* London: Corgi Books.
Published posthumously, this book elaborates Berne's ideas on scripts. The book is divided into five parts: general considerations; parental programming; the script in action; the script in clinical practice; and scientific approaches to script theory.

Steiner, C. M. (1974) *Scripts People Live*. New York: Grove Press.
A comprehensive discussion of script theory by the creator of the script matrix. There is a special focus on political and social institutions.

Stewart, I. and Joines, V. (2012) *TA Today: A New Introduction to Transactional Analysis* (2nd ed.). Melton Mowbray: Lifespace Publishing.
This textbook explains current TA ideas in straightforward language, starting from basic principles. It covers all the topics in the 'Official 101' introductory exam in TA. The teaching material is reinforced by numerous examples and exercises.

Stewart, I. (2014) *Transactional Analysis Counselling in Action* (4th ed.). London: Sage.
Part 1 of the book focuses on The TA Framework. Part 2, which contains about three-quarters of the book, is about The Process of Counselling with TA. The systematic process of TA is illustrated by a case study from the client's first contact and intake, through diagnosis and treatment planning, to contract-making and the implementation of the planned treatment sequence. Skills Practices, Space for Reflection, and Further Reading are placed at the end of chapters.

REFERENCES AND FURTHER READING

Berne, E. (1958) Transactional analysis: A new and effective method of group therapy. *American Journal of Psychotherapy, 12,* 735–43.

Berne, E. (1961) *Transactional Analysis in Psychotherapy.* New York: Grove Press.

Berne, E. (1963) *The Structure and Dynamics of Organizations and Groups.* Philadelphia J. B. Lippincott Co.

Berne, E. (1964) *Games People Play: The Psychology of Human Relationships.* New York: Grove Press.

Berne, E. (1966) *Principles of Group Treatment.* New York: Grove Press.

Berne, E. (1968) *A Layman's Guide to Psychiatry and Psychoanalysis.* Harmondsworth: Penguin Books. First published in 1947 as *The Mind in Action.*

Berne, E. (1968) *The Happy Valley.* New York: Grove Press.

Berne, E. (1970) *Sex in Human Loving.* Harmondsworth: Penguin Books.

Berne, E. (1972) *What Do You Say After You Say Hello?* London: Corgi Books.

Cornell, W. and Hargaden, H. (eds) (2005) *From Transactions to Relations: The Emergence of a Relational Tradition in Transactional Analysis.* Chadlington: Haddon Press.

Dusay, J. M. (1972) Egograms and the 'constancy hypothesis'. *Transactional Analysis Journal, 2,* 27–41.

Dusay, J. M. (1978) *Egograms.* New York: Harper & Row.

Dusay, J. M. and Dusay, K. M. (1989) Transactional analysis. In R. J. Corsini and D. Wedding (eds) *Current Psychotherapies* (4th ed.). Itasca, IL: Peacock, pp. 405–53.

Fowlie, H. and Sills, C. (eds) (2011) *Relational Transactional Analysis: Principles in Practice.* London: Karnac.

Goulding, M. and Goulding, R. E. (1979) *Changing Lives through Redecision Therapy.* New York: Brunner Mazel.

Goulding, R. E. (1974) Thinking and feeling in psychotherapy (three impsses). *Voices, 10,* 11–13.

Goulding, R. E. and Goulding, M. (1976) Injunctions, decisions and redecisions. *Transactional Analysis Journal, 6,* 41–8.

Goulding, R. E. and Goulding, M. (1978) The case of Tim. *The Power is in the Patient: A Transactional Analysis/Gestalt Approach to Psychotherapy.* San Franscisco: TA Press, pp. 43–55.

Hargaden, H. and Sills, C. (2002) *Transactional Analysis: A Relational Perspective.* London: Routledge.

James, M. and Jongeward, D. (1971) *Born to Win.* Reading, MA: Addison Wesley.

James, M. and Contributors (1977) *Techniques in Transactional Analysis: For Psychotherapists and Counselors.* Reading, MA: Addison-Wesley.

Joines, V. and Stewart, I. (2002) *Personality Adaptations.* Nottingham: Lifespace Publishing.

Kahler, T. (2008) *The Process Therapy Model.* Little Rock, AR: Taibi Kahler Associates Inc.

Schiff, J. (1969) Reparenting schizophrenics. *Transactional Analysis Bulletin, 8,* 158–64.

Schiff, J. (1970) *All My Children.* New York: Evans.

Schiff, J. (1975) *The Cathexis Reader.* New York: Harper & Row.

Sills, C. (2013) Transactional analysis. In W. Dryden and A. Reeves (eds), *Handbook of Individual Therapy* (6th ed.). London: Sage, pp. 207–39.

Spitz, R. (1945) Hospitalism, genesis of psychiatric conditions in early childhood. *Psychoanalytic Study of the Child, 1,* 53–74.

Steiner, C. M. (1974) *Scripts People Live.* New York: Bantam Books.

Stewart, I. (1996a) *Developing Transactional Analysis Counselling.* London: Sage.

Stewart, I. (1996b) Developments in transactional analysis. In Dryden, W. (ed.), *Developments in Psychotherapy: Historical Perspectives.* London: Sage, pp. 62–90.

Stewart, I. (2014) *Transactional Analysis Counselling in Action* (4th ed.). London: Sage.

Stewart, I. and Joines, V. (2012) *TA Today: A New Introduction to Transactional Analysis* (2nd ed.). Melton Mowbray: Lifespace Publishing.

Tudor, K. and Hobbes, R. (2007) Transactional analysis. In W. Dryden (ed.), *Dryden's Handbook of Individual Therapy.* London: Sage, pp. 256–86.

Ware, P. (1983) Personality adaptations. *Transactional Analysis Journal, 13* (1), 11–19.

WEBSITE

The website if the International Transactional Analysis Association (ITAA) is www.itaa-world.org

7 EXISTENTIAL THERAPY

INTRODUCTION

Yalom (2001) writes: *'Existential psychotherapy is a dynamic therapeutic approach that focuses on concerns rooted in existence'* (p. xvi). The word existence is derived from the Latin word *existere*, literally meaning 'to stand out, to emerge.' People struggle not only with their biological genetic substrate, their repressed instinctual strivings, with internalized significant adults who may be uncaring, unloving or neurotic, with disordered forms of thinking, with current crises involving *their* career and relationship with significant others, but also with a confrontation with their existence. Yalom does not consider existential therapy to be a freestanding ideological school. Rather 'a well trained therapist who has knowledge of and skills from many therapeutic approaches *should also be trained to have a sensibility to existential issues'* (Yalom, 2008, p. 202). However, this sensibility is rarely sufficient for an overall positive outcome.

IRVIN YALOM AND ROLLO MAY

IRVIN YALOM (1931–)

In 1931, Irvin Yalom was born Washington DC, the son of Russian immigrant parents who, in the 1920s, had arrived penniless in the United States. His parents had virtually no formal education, never read books and struggled to survive economically by running a grocery store. The family lived in a roach-infested apartment above the store, in a poor, black neighbourhood of Washington. Though he admired his father, Yalom 'spent too many hours in my childhood silently hating my mother's vicious tongue' (Yalom, 1989, p. 147). For instance, when Yalom was fourteen years old, his father suffered a serious coronary in the early hours of the morning. As mother, father and son waited for the family physician to arrive: '"It's all your fault," she shouted, "you did this – all the aggravation, all the grief you gave him – you did this to him. You. You"' (Yalom 1998, p. 437). When his mother grew old, she lost her fangs and his relationship with her became much closer (Yalom, 2001). Yalom grew up in facing two additional existential perils because 'In the streets, the black attacked me for my whiteness, and in school, the white attacked me for my Jewishness' (Yalom,

1989, p. 88). However, reading – especially reading fiction – provided a refuge from the external harshness and, early in life, Yalom developed the notion that writing fiction was the finest thing a person could do (Yalom, 2005a).

The visit of a kindly physician when his father had his coronary influenced Yalom 'to be a physician and to pass onto others the comfort he had given me' (Yalom, 2008, p. 144). In 1952, he received a BA degree from George Washington University and, in 1956, obtained a M.D. from Boston University. During the next six years, Yalom served as an intern at New York's Mt Sinai Hospital, a psychiatric resident at Baltimore's Johns Hopkins Hospital, a consultant at the Patuxent Institution in Maryland, and a US Army Captain in Honolulu. In 1962, Yalom was appointed an instructor in psychiatry at Stanford University School of Medicine, a decision partly made to put 3,000 miles between his mother and himself (Yalom, 2001). He became an assistant professor, associate professor and professor in 1963, 1968, and 1973, respectively. In 1994, Yalom retired and became an Emeritus Professor of Psychiatry at Stanford. He now devotes much of his time to writing psychotherapy novels and stories.

Throughout a fifty-year career so far, Yalom has undergone personal therapy including being in 750 hours of five-time-a-week orthodox Freudian analysis, two years of gestalt therapy, three years with Rollo May, when he developed death anxiety during his work with patients with cancer (Yalom, 2008), as well as many brief stints with other approaches including behaviour therapy, bioenergetics, Rolfing, marital-couples work and numerous encounter groups.

In 1963 Yalom married his wife Marilyn, whom he had known since the age of fifteen. She received a PhD in Comparative Literature from Johns Hopkins and went on to become a university professor. The Yaloms have four grown-up children and an increasing number of grandchildren.

Yalom has published numerous scientific papers. In addition, his professional writing includes: *The Theory and Practice of Group Psychotherapy* (Yalom and Leszcz, 2005), *Existential Psychotherapy* (1980), *Inpatient Group Psychotherapy* (1983), and co-authorship of *Everyday Gets a Little Closer* (1974), *The Gift of Therapy: Reflections on Being a Therapist* (2001) and *Staring at the Sun: Overcoming the Dread of Death* (2008).

Yalom's psychological novels and non-fiction stories include: *Love's Executioner and Other Tales of Psychotherapy* (1989), *When Nietzsche Wept* (1991) – which won the Commonwealth Club's Gold Medal for Fiction for the Best Novel of 1992, *Lying on the Couch* (1996), *Momma and the Meaning of Life* (1999), *The Schopenhauer Cure* (2005a) and *The Spinoza Problem* (2012). Yalom intends these best-selling books both as entertainment and as pedagogical works representing a new genre of teaching psychotherapy by novels and stories. A Yalom compilation, entitled *The Yalom Reader* (1998), combines material illustrating his three major interests: group psychotherapy, existential psychotherapy and writing. Yalom concludes: 'In sum, I feel that in my life and profession I have fulfilled myself and realized my potential' (Yalom, 2008, p. 164).

ROLLO MAY (1909–94)

In 1909, Rollo May was born in Ohio. One of seven children, his father was a YMCA secretary who moved his family quite often. May's parents' relationship was discordant and his family life unhappy, a stimulus for his later interest in therapy. May describes his mother as a 'bitch-kitty on wheels' (Rabinowitz, Good, and Cozad, 1989, p. 437). His only sister, who was older than him, was psychotic and spent some time in a mental hospital. May obtained relief from family misery by sitting and playing on the shores of the St. Clair river.

A rebel during high school, May studied liberal arts at Oberlin College, obtaining his BA in 1930. May then went to Greece for three years where he taught boys aged 12 to 18 in a gymnasium and studied ancient Greek civilization. In addition, one summer vacation he went to Vienna where he studied individual psychology with Alfred Adler. In 1938, May received his B.D. from Union Theological Seminary, where he met and developed an ongoing friendship with Paul Tillich, who had recently been expelled from Nazi Germany, and who was a major influence on his thinking. In 1949 May obtained his PhD in clinical psychology from Teachers College of Columbia University.

While pursuing his doctoral degree, May came down with tuberculosis. His recovery involved spending nearly two years bed-ridden in an upstate New York sanatorium where he spend much time reading and thinking about the nature of anxiety. Ultimately, this work led to his writing *The Meaning of Anxiety* (1950). During his New York City years, May conducted a private practice, authored books and articles, was an adjunct professor at the New School of Social Research and New York University, and served as a training analyst and supervisor at the William Alanson White Institute. May then lived in San Franscisco where he wrote, taught and saw clients. May was divorced twice and, in 1989, confided 'I've always had good friends and lovers, but I'm scared to death of marriage' (Rabinowitz, Good and Cozad, 1989, p. 437). He died on 22 October, 1994, at the age of 84.

Reflecting his early interest in English literature, May was a prolific author of books and articles. Over a long period he was at the forefront of applying existential and humanistic ideas to psychotherapy. May's books include *The Art of Counseling* (1939), *The Meaning of Anxiety* (1950), his co-edited book *Existence* (which includes two important chapters by him: May, Angel and Ellenberger, 1958)), *Psychology and the Human Dilemma* (1967), *Love and Will* (1969), *Power and Innocence: A Search for Sources of Violence* (1973), *The Courage to Create* (1975), *Freedom and Destiny* (1981) and *My Quest for Beauty* (1985). Though he enjoyed his twilight years, towards the end of his life May observed: 'I wouldn't want to go through this life again. I mean, one time is enough. I don't know that I'd do anything differently, but it would be too boring' (Rabinowitz, Good, and Cozad, 1989, p. 439).

THEORY

BASIC CONCEPTS

BEING AND NON-BEING

May (May et al., 1958) observed that being as a participle of a verb and implies that someone is in the process of becoming something. He stated that, when used as a noun being means *potentia*, the source of potential. An analogy is that the acorn has the potential to become an oak. This analogy is only partially accurate for humans since they have the capacity for self-consciousness. Humans can choose their own being. The choices that they make about being are not just concerned with whether or not to commit suicide, but are relevant to every instant of their lives.

Because of widespread collectivist and conformist trends in society, modern humans have repressed their sense of being. People's sense of being refers to their whole experience of existence, both conscious and unconscious. They need to experience themselves as beings in the world and have a basic 'I-Am' experience, expressed by one of May's clients as 'Since, I Am, I have the right to be' (May et al., 1958, p. 43). The 'I-Am' experience is not the solution, but rather the precondition for the solution to clients' problems.

The opposite of being is non-being or nothingness. Existence implies the possibility of not existing. Death is the most obvious form of non-being. However, there are numerous other threats to being in the form of loss of potentiality through anxiety and conformity and through lack of clear self-awareness. In addition, destructive hostility and physical sickness can pose threats to being. However, people who are able to confront non-being can emerge with a heightened sense of being including a greater awareness not only of themselves, but of others and the world around them.

THE THREE FORMS OF BEING-IN-THE-WORLD

Existential therapy distinguishes three modes of world that characterize people's existence as being-in-the-world. First, there is the *Umwelt*, the 'world around'. The *Umwelt* represents the natural world, the laws of nature and the environment. For animals and human beings alike, the *Umwelt* includes biological needs, drives and instincts. It also includes each organism's daily and life cycles. The natural world is accepted as real.

Second, there is the *Mitwelt*, the 'with-world'. This is the social world of relating to fellow humans singly and in groups. Both in personal and group relationships people influence each other and the structure of meaning that develops. May writes: '*The essence of relationship is that in the encounter both persons are changed*' (May et al., 1958, p. 63). How people relate in intimate relationships, for instance their degree of commitment, influences the meaning of the relationships for them. Similarly, how much of themselves people put into groups influences the meaning of the groups for them.

Third, there is the *Eigenwelt,* or 'own world'. The *Eigenwelt* is uniquely present in humans and entails self-consciousness and self-awareness. Also, the *Eigenwelt* entails grasping the personal meaning of a thing or person. Individuals need own their relationships to things and people: for instance, 'This flower is beautiful' means 'For me, this flower is beautiful'.

The three modes of being are interrelated. For instance, love entails more than the biological drives of the *Umwelt.* Furthermore, it entails more than the social or interpersonal relationship of the *Mitwelt.* In addition, love requires the *Eigenwelt,* in that, when relating to another, people need to be sufficient to themselves.

NORMAL AND NEUROTIC ANXIETY

To be human is to be anxious. Anxiety is an unavoidable part of human life. May (1950) distinguishes between normal and neurotic anxiety. He defines anxiety as 'the threat to our existence or to values we identify with our existence' (May, 1977, p. 205). In the course of normal development everyone experiences various threats to their existence. One source of normal anxiety is humans' existential vulnerability to Nature, sickness and death. Another source is the need to progressively become independent from parents with the tensions and crises that this process can create. However, people can use such threats constructively as learning experiences and continue to develop.

The reaction of normal anxiety has three characteristics. First, it is proportionate to the objective threat in the situation being confronted. Second, it does not involve repression. Third, it can be used creatively to identify and confront the conditions bringing it about. Existential therapists view their main function as helping clients come to terms with the normal anxieties that are part of human existence.

Neurotic anxiety possesses the opposite characteristics to normal anxiety. Neurotic anxiety is a disproportionate reaction to an objective threat, involves repression, and is destructive rather than constructive. Another way of viewing neurotic anxiety is that people subjectively react to objective threats in terms of their inner psychological patterns and conflicts. The repression and blocking of awareness involved in neurotic anxiety leaves people more vulnerable to threats since they lose access to important information with which to distinguish and deal with the threats.

NORMAL, NEUROTIC AND EXISTENTIAL GUILT

Like anxiety, guilt is part of human existence. A distinction may be drawn between normal and neurotic guilt. Neurotic guilt derives from *imagined* transgressions against others, parental injunctions, and societal conventions. Normal guilt is a call to conscience and sensitizes people to the ethical aspects of their behaviour.

Existential or ontological guilt represents another form of guilt. May distinguishes between three forms of existential guilt. The first form, which corresponds to *Eigenwelt,* is failure to live up to potential. As such, people can be guilty of transgressions against themselves. The second form, which corresponds to *Mitwelt,* relates to distorting the reality of one's fellow humans. The third form of existential guilt, which involves *Umwelt* as well as the other two modes-of-being, is 'separation guilt' in relation to nature as a whole.

Existential guilt is universal. It is rooted in self-awareness and does not arise from violation of parental injunctions, 'but arises from the fact that I can see myself as the one who can choose or fail to choose' (May et al., 1958, p. 55). Thus existential guilt is inexorably linked with the notion of personal responsibility. Existential guilt is not in itself a form of neurotic guilt, though it possesses the potential to turn into neurotic guilt. However, if correctly addressed, existential guilt can have constructive outcomes both in terms of greater humility and sensitivity to others and in increased creativity.

TRANSCENDENCE

Humans' unique capacity to think and talk in symbols allows them the possibility of transcending time and space. Humans can project themselves into the past and into the future. In addition they can transcend themselves in their social relations and see themselves as others see them and give appropriate weight to others' perceptions. The capacity to transcend immediate concrete situations provides humans with the basis of both their freedom and their responsibility.

Transcendence is derived from the Latin word *transcendere,* meaning 'to climb over and beyond'. The ability to transcend immediate situations is part of the ontological nature of human beings. Existing involves humans in a continuous process of emerging in that they transcend their pasts and presents to create their futures. Unless seriously ill or blocked by anxiety or despair, all humans engage in this process.

EXISTENTIAL ULTIMATE CONCERNS

Yalom (1980) has identified four existential ultimate concerns – death, freedom, isolation, and meaninglessness – with considerable relevance for counselling and therapy. Though the fear of death is the most prominent ultimate concern, as therapy progresses concerns about freedom, isolation and meaning in life emerge as well (Yalom, 2008). Each concern begets a different existential conflict.

DEATH

The first existential conflict is that between awareness of the inevitability of death and the wish to continue to live: the conflict between fear of non-being and wishing to be. Life and death, being and non-being, are interdependent rather than concurrent. Death is the fundamental source of anxiety, whether it be neurotic, normal or existential. Perhaps the term death terror denotes the force of death concern better than death anxiety. Death anxiety, the fear of ceasing to be, can be both conscious and unconscious. From early in their lives children are extremely preoccupied with death. Strong death anxiety is likely to be repressed. To cope with the terror of potential non-being, people erect denial-based defences against death anxiety. To a large extent psychopathology has its origins in failed attempts to transcend death.

FREEDOM

The second existential conflict is that between people's confrontation with groundlessness and freedom and their wish for ground and structure. Humans are 'condemned to freedom' (Sartre, 1956, p. 631); they do not live in a well-ordered and structured universe. There is no secure ground under-girding existence. Rather there is lack of structure and groundlessness that generates both anxiety and dread. Because of their freedom, humans are also condemned to responsibility. They are not only responsible for imbuing the world with significance, but entirely responsible for their lives, for their actions and their failures to act.

ISOLATION

The third existential conflict is that between people's awareness of their fundamental isolation and their wish for contact, protection and to be a part of a larger whole. There are three forms of isolation.

- *Interpersonal isolation,* often experienced as loneliness, means that people are in varying degrees cut off from others. This may be through deficient social skills, psychopathology or by choice and of necessity.
- *Intrapersonal isolation* means that people are blocked from awareness of or dissociated from parts of themselves. Whereas interpersonal isolation may not contain pathology, intrapersonal isolation does so by definition.
- *Existential isolation* is rooted in the human condition in that each person enters, lives in, and leaves the world alone. Ultimately there is an unbridgeable gap between self and others. Yalom (1980) observes that existential isolation refers to an even more fundamental form of isolation, namely 'Separation from the world' (p. 355).

MEANINGLESSNESS

The fourth existential conflict is that of humans confronting their need for meaning in an indifferent world that has no meaning. What is the meaning of life? Humans require coherence, purpose and significance. They organize random stimuli into figure and ground. They are neuro-psychologically organized to seek patterns and meaning. However, the human paradox is that of existence in an indifferent universe with no predetermined meaning. A distinction may be made between cosmic meaning, whether human life fits into some overall cosmic pattern, and terrestrial meaning, the meaning of my life. With the decline in religious beliefs, modern humans are faced with the need to discover secular personal meaning in the absence of cosmic meaning.

EXISTENTIAL PSYCHODYNAMICS

In personality theory, the term dynamics relates to the concept of energy or force. The notion of psychodynamic conflict relates to the clash between opposing forces. The Freudian model of dynamic conflict was that of the clash between ego and instinctual sexual and aggressive drives. To Freud, the deeper conflicts were associated with the earliest psychosexual conflicts.

Existential psychodynamics differ in two important ways from Freudian psychodynamics. First, existential conflicts and existential anxiety flow from people's inescapable confrontations with the givens of existence: death, freedom, isolation and meaninglessness. Second, existential dynamics do not assume a developmental or archaeological model where first is synonymous with deep. When existential therapists and clients explore deeply, they do so not by focusing on everyday concerns, but thinking deeply about existential ultimate concerns.

ACQUISITION

Despite existential anxieties and conflicts being inescapable parts of life, the question still remains of how people develop different modes of dealing with the ultimate concerns of existence?

DEATH

Young children, even though not intellectually equipped to understand what death means, grasp its essence. Yalom (1980) believes that children then deny their first knowledge of death. Mechanisms of denial include such beliefs as death is temporary, children do not die, I will not die because I am special, and that there is an ultimate rescuer. Coming to terms with the concept of death is a major developmental task which some children handle better than others.

Exposure to death can be for good or ill. Factors likely to be helpful include the presence of already existing ego resources, good genes, and supportive adults able to deal with their own death anxieties. However, exposure to death can be traumatic when these factors are insufficiently present. Deaths of siblings and of parents can be especially frightening and exceed children's coping resources. Research indicates that both neurotic and psychotic psychiatric patients have lost a parent more frequently than the general population. The degree of cultural acceptance of death also influences how much anxiety death will generate in both adults and children.

The quality of death education that parents offer to their children affects their awareness and acceptance of death. Children are often shielded from death by misinformation, denial, fairy tales, euphemisms, and assurances that children do not die. As with sex, children do not ignore the issue, but turn to other sources of information of varying degrees of reliability. Western cultures offer no real guidelines about how parents should educate their children about death. Many adults, who seek comfort in child-like beliefs, do not help this state of affairs.

FREEDOM

The modern day emphasis on freedom and responsibility as existential concerns derives from the breaking down of traditional belief systems, religions, rituals and rules. In the 20th and continuing into the early 21st century, there has been a rapid disintegration of structures and values. Permissive parenting has now left many young people with the need to choose but without clear guidelines as to how or what to choose. Numerous people are unprepared for the freedom they now have. Frequently, when confronted with the existential fact of their responsibility for their lives, they experience difficulty in handling this realization. Now people are less faced with what they 'must' do, instead the emphasis is on what they want to do. In what may be a transitional period between old and new ways of being in the world, many people have failed to learn adequately how to wish, how to will and how to decide and stay committed to their decisions.

ISOLATION

Isolation is acquired in the following ways.

- *Interpersonal isolation*: Cultural and technological change plays a large part in the creation of this form of isolation. In the United States and other Western cultures there has been a decline in community links – churches, local shops, neighbours who know each other and have local roots, family doctors and so on.
- *Intrapersonal isolation* stems from obstructions and frustrations that occur early in life and threaten some vital aspect of the individual's nascent sense of self.
- *Existential isolation* is closely interwoven with interpersonal isolation. Many people fail to develop the inner strength, confidence and sense of identity that enables them to face existential isolation. Never having received genuine growth-inducing love, they do not know how to offer it to others. If committed and authentic therapist–client relationships can help clients confront and come to terms with their existential isolation, it can safely be inferred that clients have insufficiently experienced such relationships in their pasts.

MEANINGLESSNESS

Many factors in contemporary culture contribute to people having a diminished sense of life's meaning compared to their forebears in the pre-industrial agricultural world. First, instead of meaning being supplied by religion, now most people neither believe in religion nor go to church. Second, the spread of urbanization and industrialization has contributed to people losing a sense of meaning through their contact with nature. No longer are most people closely connected with the cycles of the land and of farm animals. Third, most contemporary humans no longer belong to and have roles in rural communities, but instead often live in relatively impersonal urban communities.

Fourth, many contemporary humans are alienated from their work and think that they engage in mechanical and routine tasks of little intrinsic interest. Fifth, contemporary humans are less beset with basic survival needs, such as food, shelter, and water. Their greater security and leisure confronts them much more with the abyss of meaninglessness. Time on their hands means time to be haunted by issues of meaning. In addition, in economic recessions, many people are confronted by unemployment with the loss of and need for meaning. Sixth, contemporary humans face the possibility of nuclear annihilation and global environmental destruction. If the world is not going to last, why bother?

MAINTENANCE

EXISTENTIAL MODEL OF DEFENCE MECHANISMS

How do people maintain insufficient awareness and psychopathological behaviour within the existential framework? They evolve both conscious and unconscious psychological operations to deal with the anxiety generated by existential ultimate concerns. These psychological operations or *defence mechanisms* are of two types. First, there are conventional defence mechanisms, such as projection, which defend people against anxiety regardless of its source. Second, there are specific defences for each of the four ultimate concerns that defend people against these fundamental fears. These defence mechanisms may not only be relevant to individual clients, but they may be reinforced by whole cultures colluding in them.

Figure 7.1 depicts the existential model of defence mechanisms in reaction to awareness at some level of an inner conflict raised by an ultimate concern. Such defence mechanisms provide a modicum of psychological safety at the expense of restricting people's potential for growth and of generating existential guilt.

Figure 7.1 Existential model of defence mechanisms

DEATH ANXIETY DEFENCES

Though the specific defences for each ultimate concern are mentioned separately, they may overlap. Furthermore, they require recombining or merging into an overall existential model of psychopathology. Children's modes of coping with death awareness and death terror involve denial. For children and adults alike, Yalom (1980) has identified two major death anxiety defence mechanisms.

- *Specialness* While at the conscious level most people accept their lives as finite, deep down they can develop irrational beliefs about their own immortality and inviolability. Where this defence is weak or absent, then people may develop one of a number of clinical syndromes, including compulsive heroism, being a 'workaholic' and turning a deaf ear to time's message, narcissism, and the drive for power and control. Frequently, such people seek therapy when they no longer can ward off their death anxiety through these pretences.
- *Belief in an ultimate rescuer.* This defence represents the belief that, however bad things may get, the individual is not alone in an indifferent universe and some omnipresent servant will come to the rescue. People using the defence of the ultimate rescuer may restrict their lives by locating and serving a 'dominant other'. Most people do not acknowledge their belief system until it fails to serve its purpose: for instance, if they acquire a fatal illness or their 'dominant other' dies or psychologically withdraws.

FREEDOM ANXIETY DEFENCES

Freedom anxiety defences protect individuals from awareness of their responsibility for the authorship of their lives. Awareness of responsibility entails being 'aware of creating one's own self, destiny, life predicament, feelings and, if such be the case, one's own suffering' (Yalom, 1980, p. 218). Compulsivity is one defence against responsibility awareness. Yalom gives the example of Bernard a 25-year-old salesman who was compulsively driven in his sex, work, and leisure lives. His compulsivity obliterated choice, yet Bernard was responsible for creating as well as maintaining his compulsivity. Other defences against freedom anxiety include: displacing responsibility on to others, including therapists; denying responsibility by posing as the innocent victim or losing control; avoidance of autonomous behaviour; and pathology in wishing, willing and deciding.

ISOLATION ANXIETY DEFENCES

In isolation anxiety defences people do not relate to others in their own right, but use them for defensive functions. One defence against ultimate aloneness is to exist and seek affirmation in others' eyes. Such people exist so far as they are part of others' consciousness and receive approval from them. Frequently, under the guise of loving, they can hide their inability to love. However, ultimately others are likely to get fed up with meeting their needs for affirmation. Fusion with an individual or group is another isolation anxiety defence. Rather than confront and come to terms with their fundamental isolation, people feel and think they are not alone because they are part of others. In addition, compulsive sexuality is a defence against isolation anxiety. Sexually compulsive people treat their partners as objects rather than persons. They do not take the time to know and be known. Instead, their serial relationships are caricatures of the real thing.

MEANINGLESSNESS ANXIETY DEFENCES

People handle meaninglessness anxiety in different ways. Compulsive activity is one way of avoiding a confrontation with meaninglessness. Individuals compulsively engage in any of a range of activities as a reaction to an underlying deep sense of purposelessness. Sooner or later many individuals who have compulsively sought money, pleasure, power, recognition and status start questioning their values. Crusadism is a form of compulsive activity where people seek out issues that they can make into time and energy consuming crusades. Nihilism is another defence against meaninglessness anxiety. Here people avoid confronting meaninglessness, by disparaging all sources of meaning that others find in their lives, for instance love or service.

THERAPY

THERAPEUTIC GOALS

Existential therapy is more a mode of viewing human beings than a rigorous system. In the final analysis, existential therapists view clienthood as ubiquitous. However, generally clients are more troubled than their therapists.

   Yalom and Josselson write: 'The existential therapist hopes to alleviate crippling levels of anxiety, but not to eliminate it. Life cannot be lived (nor death faced) without anxiety' (2014, p. 279). The overriding goal of existential therapy is that clients experience their existence as real. The underlying assumption is that the fundamental neurotic process is the repression of the ontological sense, thus involving the loss of a sense of being and the truncation of awareness and potential. Since therapy is primarily concerned with helping clients experience their existence, any symptomatic 'cure' is a by-product or secondary goal. Existential therapists attempt to avoid a technical, mechanical approach to clients that can lead to the latter obtaining a symptomatic 'cure' at the expense of constricting their existence. Great stress is placed in viewing clients in human rather than behavioural terms and on authentic therapist–client relationships.

More specifically, existential therapy entails assisting clients to embark on a journey of self-investigation, whose goals are

- to understand the unconscious conflict;
- to identify the maladaptive defence mechanisms;
- to discover their destructive influence;
- to diminish secondary anxiety by correcting restrictive modes of dealing with self and others, and
- to develop other ways of coping with primary anxiety.

PROCESS OF THERAPY

Existential therapists respect the individuality of each client and approach each client with the aim of sharing the story they have to tell. Yalom observes:

> … the therapy process I ultimately developed is closely linked to the creative process, to the reading and writing of fiction: *reading* in that I always listen for the unique fascinating story of each patient's life; *writing* in that I believe, with Jung, that therapy is a creative act and the effective therapist must invent a new therapy for each patient. (Yalom, 1998, p. 307)

Existential therapy stresses that, existential issues are important to some clients at some, but not all stages of therapy. Clear instances of when to use of the existential approach to therapy are when clients face boundary situations associated with ultimate concerns. Such existential crises include death, personal and work transitions, irreversible decisions, and becoming unexpectedly isolated among others. The decision to work on existential conflicts should be a joint therapist–client decision.

Existential therapists seek to assist clients to understand their inner conflicts in relation to the ultimate existential concerns of death, freedom, isolation and meaninglessness. They continually focus on how clients avoid assuming personal responsibility for their distress. They attempt to identify clients' maladaptive defence mechanisms and help raise awareness of their negative consequences. As well as assisting clients to develop other ways of coping with primary or existential anxiety, existential therapists work to lessen secondary anxiety by helping clients alter limiting ways of relating to self and others. For this purpose therapists may use a variety of interventions employed by other therapeutic approaches so long as they are consistent with a basic existential framework.

Long-term therapy is most appropriate for thoroughly addressing existential issues that affect deeper layers of the individual's mode of being in the world. However, aspects of an existential approach, for instance an emphasis on responsibility and authenticity, can still be incorporated into briefer therapy.

THE THERAPEUTIC RELATIONSHIP

The quality of the therapist–client relationship is central to existential therapy. Yalom (2001) writes: 'Therapists must convey to the patient that their paramount task is to build a relationship together that will itself become the agent of change' (p. 34). The therapy relationship is not viewed in terms of transference and little time is spent trying to dig up clients' pasts. Since existential therapists emphasize the depth of confrontations with ultimate concerns at the given moment, they try to understand their clients' *current* situations and enveloping fears.

Yalom and Josselson (2014) write: 'Existential therapists experience and present themselves as real, self-revealing *fellow-travellers*' (p. 287). Empathy, presence, authenticity, and commitment are words that describe the quality of relationship that existential therapists strive to offer. Yalom (2001) also uses the terms engagement, openness and egalitarianism. Existential therapy conducted on an individual basis takes place between two real people. The existential therapist is not a shadowy reflector, but a live human who tries to understand and experience the client's being.

Therapists who are present to clients do not impose their own thoughts and feelings on them. Nor do they transfer to clients' thoughts and feelings coming from previous relationships, what is sometimes called *countertransference*. Yalom (1989) recalls that he had always been repelled by fat women and had to work through these feelings to be fully present to a grossly overweight client who entered his office. Furthermore, existential therapists are conscious that clients have many ways of inviting involvement with their therapists in order to avoid focusing on personal problems.

Yalom (1980) talks about surreptitious 'throw-ins' making all the difference in therapy. He cites a number of critical incidents in therapy in which therapists showed their commitment and engaged their clients in human rather than stereotyped encounters. An example is that of a therapist seeing an acutely ill client for a long emergency session on a Saturday afternoon. In Yalom's case study *Every Day Gets a Little Closer* (Yalom and Elkins, 1974), written from both therapist's and client's perspectives, he was struck by the importance his client attached to small personal touches: such as warm looks and compliments about the way she looked. In addition to presence, characteristics of good therapist–client relationships include caring, extending oneself, touching clients at a profound level, and wisdom (Yalom, 1980). Therapists help clients 'by being lovingly present with that person; by being trustworthy, interested; and by believing that their joint activity will ultimately be redemptive and healing' (Yalom, 1989, p. 227).

SELF-DISCLOSURE

Therapist self-disclosure is an important issue in existential therapy. The overriding goal is that of an authentic relationship in the client's best interests.

Existential therapists can use two kinds of self-disclosure. First, they can disclose about their personal struggles to come to terms with existential ultimate concerns and be human. Yalom (1989) regards himself as having erred on the side of too little self-disclosure and writes that 'whenever I have shared a great deal of myself, patients have invariably profited ...'(p. 164).

Second and more important, existential therapists can have a process as contrasted with a content focus. They can use their thoughts and feelings about what is going on in the here-and-now to try to improve the therapeutic relationship. Such disclosures need to be well-processed, tactful and never impulsive. For instance, Yalom (1989, 2005b) felt bored with his fat lady client, Betty. Initially he tried to sort out how much of his boredom was countertransference. However, he pinpointed two reasons for his boredom, that Betty was always revealing something that occurred elsewhere and that she hid behind a mask of false gaity. He tactfully confronted Betty by pointing out that he thought she masked her pain by staying jolly and asking her permission to interrupt and point out when she was entertaining him the moment it occurred. This self-disclosure acted as a springboard for deepening their relationship. Yalom writes that often he might say something like 'I've found that I can be more helpful to you by focusing on the one relationship where I have the most accurate information – the relationship between you and me' (Yalom, 2001, p. 86).

THERAPEUTIC INTERVENTIONS

Each of the ultimate concerns has implications for which therapeutic interventions may be appropriate.

THERAPY AND DEATH

Increased awareness of death can lead to heightened appreciation of life. Terminally ill cancer patients react to the diagnosis in varying ways. Many do not fully hear what their doctors say. Some are flooded with existential terror. Others acknowledge the news briefly, regroup their defences, engage in internal processing, and then are ready for more information. Many cancer patients are able to use their illness as an awakening experience – an opportunity for personal growth. They reassess priorities, choose not to do the trivial, gain an enhanced sense of living in the present, become more in touch with nature, communicate more deeply with loved ones, and have fewer interpersonal fears about rejection and taking risks. Mechanisms for change in cancer patients include the beliefs that existence cannot be postponed and the wisdom of counting your blessings. Increased death awareness can also bring about a radical shift in perspective in clients who are not terminally ill.

Yalom states that a good working rule for clinicians is 'death anxiety is inversely proportional to life satisfaction' (Yalom, 1980, p. 207). Interventions for increasing death awareness may increase clients' anxiety in the short term. The objective is not to anaesthetize the anxiety, but to help clients come to terms with it and use it constructively. Following are some methods that existential therapists use to increase client's death awareness.

GIVING PERMISSION

Existential therapists can cue clients that discussion of issues concerning death is valued in therapy. Some of this cueing may be by encouraging and showing interest in clients' disclosures in the area. Yalom (2001) early in therapy makes a point of obtaining a history of the clients' experiences with death. He asks questions such as 'When did you first become aware of death?', 'What deaths have you experienced?', and 'How have your attitudes about death changed during your life?'. Clients raise the topic of death more frequently once therapists demonstrate that they are comfortable with the topic.

Another part of giving permission is that of avoiding colluding in clients' denial of death. Therapists can play active roles in keeping therapy superficial. They require the ability to tolerate their own death anxiety to follow adequately clients' leads. Some therapists may require further personal therapy until they work through personally and professionally debilitating death anxiety blockages.

IDENTIFYING DEFENCE MECHANISMS

Two of the main defence mechanisms against death anxiety are the belief in specialness and the belief in the existence of an ultimate rescuer. Existential therapists collaborate with clients to identify such maladaptive defence mechanisms and their negative consequences. Clients are assisted to acknowledge the reality of their finiteness rather than deny it. Existential therapists require tact, persistence and good timing to help clients to identify and relinquish childlike ways of viewing death.

WORKING WITH DREAMS

Existential therapists encourage clients to share their dreams. In dreams and nightmares unconscious themes can appear without being repressed or heavily edited. Death themes are common in dreams and nightmares. Discussion and analysis of dreams relates to clients' current existential conflicts. However, clients are not always ready to deal with the material revealed in their dreams. Box 7.1 illustrated a nightmare of Marvin, a 64-year-old client of Yalom's, Yalom's private reflections about it, and what happened afterwards (Yalom, 1989, pp. 242–46).

BOX 7.1   EXAMPLE OF WORKING WITH A DREAM

MARVIN'S NIGHTMARE

The two men are tall, pale and very gaunt. In a dark meadow they glide along in silence. They are dressed entirely in black. With tall black stovepipe hats, long-tailed coats, black spats and shoes, they resemble Victorian undertakers or temperance workers. Suddenly they come upon a carriage, ebony black, cradling a baby girl swaddled in black gauze. Wordlessly, one of the men begins to push the carriage. After a short distance he stops, walks around to the front, and, with his black cane, which now has a glowing white tip, he leans over, parts the gauze, and methodically inserts the white tip into the baby's vagina.

YALOM'S PRIVATE REFLECTIONS ABOUT THE MEANING MARVIN'S NIGHTMARE

I am old. I am at the end of my life's work. I have no children, and I approach death full of dread. I am choking on darkness. I am choking on the silence of death. I think I know a way. I try to pierce the blackness with my sexual talisman. But it is not enough.

WHAT HAPPENED AFTERWARDS

Afterwards, when Yalom asked Marvin to associate to his dream he said nothing. When Marvin was then asked what he made of all the death imagery, he preferred to discuss the dream from the perspective of sex rather than of death.

WORKING WITH REMINDERS OF FINITENESS

Therapists can assist clients to identify and constructively deal with their death anxiety by being 'tuned-into' the signs of mortality that are parts of normal life. The death of loved ones can be a powerful reminder of personal mortality. The death of parents means that ours is the next generation to die. The death of children can invoke a sense of powerlessness in relation to cosmic indifference. Also, where it is an only child who dies, parents realize that they will not be immortal through passing on their seed. In addition, severe illness can confront clients with their finiteness and vulnerability.

Transitions remind clients of their mortality. Such transitions include the passage from adolescence to adulthood, commitment to a permanent relationship, children leaving home, and marital separation and divorce. In middle age many clients become more aware of deaths, realizing that they are no longer growing up, but instead growing old. In addition, retirement or unexpected career threats can powerfully increase death awareness.

In daily life reminders of the passage of time are ever present. Physical signs of aging – for instance graying, wrinkling, skin plaques, stiffening of the joints, loss of stamina, poorer eyesight – shatter the illusion of permanent youthfulness. Going to reunions shows that everyone else is aging. Frequently, since they are milestones of the aging process, birthdays and anniversaries can generate existence pain as well as or instead of joy.

AIDS TO INCREASING DEATH AWARENESS

While many existential therapists would not use artificial aids to increase clients' death awareness, some therapists do. Clients can be asked to write their obituaries or fill out death anxiety questionnaires. In addition they can be taken on guided fantasies regarding their deaths, imagining 'where', 'when', 'how', and their funeral. Yalom (1980) describes two different ways of getting clients to interact with the dying: observing a group of terminally ill people and introducing a person with terminal cancer into an everyday therapy group.

DESENSITIZING CLIENTS TO DEATH

Therapists can assist clients to deal with death terror by exposing them over and over to the fear in lessened doses. Yalom (1980) cites that in working with groups of cancer patients, he has seen many times their dread gradually diminish through sheer familiarity.

UNDERSTANDING ANXIETIES ASSOCIATED WITH DEATH

Therapists may break down and identify the anxieties associated with death. A distinction needs be made between the true helplessness arising from the fundamental existential fact of death and the ancillary feelings of helplessness. Clients can be encouraged to regain more of a sense of control over aspects of their lives they can influence. Also, they can be helped to identify and rationally confront their ancillary fears, such as having a painful death, loneliness and concern over loved ones. In the adult's unconscious dwell childlike irrational terrors about death. Such terrors can be brought into the open and assessed realistically.

RIPPLING

Yalom observes that rippling can be singularly powerful in countering a patient's death anxiety and distress at the transience of life. Each person creates concentric circles of influence that may affect others for years and even for generations. He writes: 'Rippling ... refers ... to leaving behind something from your life experience; some trait; some piece of wisdom, guidance, virtue, comfort that passes on to others, known or unknown' (Yalom, 2008, pp. 83–4). An example of rippling, albeit at one remove, is that of Barbara, who when her mother died, could feel aspects of her mother that had rippled into friends, who in turn would pass the ripples on to their children and children's children.

THERAPY AND FREEDOM

Therapy in relation to the ultimate concern of freedom focuses on increasing clients' awareness of their responsibility for their lives and on assisting them to assume this responsibility. The therapist has to look at the clients' rather than other people's roles in their lives, because that is where they can be of most help. Yalom (2001) writes 'Responsibility assumption is the essential first step in the therapeutic process' (p. 141). He reports that all the research data suggest that through successful therapy clients become more aware of their personal responsibility for their lives (Yalom, 1980). Therapists can use a wide variety of techniques to assist responsibility awareness and assumption.

IDENTIFYING DEFENCES AND METHODS OF RESPONSIBILITY AVOIDANCE

Therapists can help clients to understand the functions of some of their behaviours, for instance compulsiveness, in avoiding responsibility for choices. In addition, therapists can explore with and, if necessary, confront clients with their responsibility for their own distress. For instance, when lonely clients keep belittling others, the therapist can say 'And you are lonely'. A general guideline is that when clients complain about their situations, therapists inquire about how they created them. In addition, therapists can focus on how clients use responsibility avoidance language: for instance, saying 'I can't' instead of 'I won't'.

IDENTIFYING RESPONSIBILITY AVOIDANCE IN THE HERE-AND-NOW

Clients' responsibility avoidances can manifest themselves in the therapist–client relationship. Therapists need awareness of their own feelings about clients to identify how they might elicit similar reactions from others. For instance, a woman with a history of relating to abusive men may distort her perception of her male therapist and behave toward him in ways that, in another context, might elicit the abuse she dreaded. Therapists can also confront clients with their here-and-now attempts to transfer responsibility for what happens either inside or outside of therapy on to them. If so, therapists may need to work through clients' resistances such as 'If I knew what to do, I wouldn't need to be here.'

CONFRONTING REALISTIC LIMITATIONS

All human beings have realistic adverse circumstances with which to deal. Therapy can help clients to change their attitude to or re-construe external circumstances that they cannot alter. In addition, therapists can assist clients in identifying areas in their lives that they can influence. For instance, therapists dealing with cancer patients can assist them to assume more responsibility for their relationships to their doctors, such as assertively requesting information about their illness.

CONFRONTING EXISTENTIAL GUILT

Existential therapists view one of the functions of anxiety as a call to conscience. One source of anxiety is guilt about failure to actualize potential. For instance, a client who engaged in compulsive sexual behaviour also had difficulty being assertive in his business life. Identifying how he transgressed his potential as a human being through limiting his life through compulsive sex, was the springboard for his gaining the confidence to become more assertive. No longer was the client inwardly terrified about exposure of all the shameful episodes in his life. As his compulsiveness declined, his sense of being a chooser increased. A distinction exists between guilt for bad choices made in the past and refusal to make new choices. So long as clients continue to behave in the present as they did in the past, then they cannot forgive themselves for their past choices.

FREEING UP WISHING

Wishing precedes willing (May, 1969). However, for clients to wish they need to be in touch with how they feel. Working with affect-blocked clients can be a slow and repetitive process. Dramatic breakthrough methods are avoided since their effects tend not to be sustained. Instead, within the context of authentic relationships, existential therapists explore the source and nature of clients' blocks and the underlying feelings they try to express. In addition, therapists repeatedly ask affect-blocked clients questions like 'What do you feel?' and 'What do you want?'.

FACILITATING DECIDING

Existential therapists encourage clients to see that every action is preceded by a decision. Decisions are difficult because alternatives exclude. As such, decisions are boundary situations in which people create themselves, despite their fundamental groundlessness. Many clients paralyze their decision-making capacity through 'what-ifs': for instance, 'What if I lose my job and can't find another?' Therapists can assist clients to explore the ramifications of each 'what-if' and analyse the feelings they generate. While ensuring that responsibility for decisions remains with clients, therapists can assist them to generate and evaluate decision options. Therapists can encourage clients to make decisions actively in ways that reinforce acceptance of their power and resources.

Where necessary, existential therapists try to disencumber their clients' wills. Therapist acceptance is crucial for clients learning to trust their wills and gain the belief that they have a right to act. Following are 'insights' that existential therapists commonly offer to will-stifled clients: 'Only I can change the world I have created', 'There is no danger in change', 'To get what I really want, I must change', and 'I have the power to change'. Decisions to change may take place over a considerable period of time.

THERAPY AND ISOLATION

The following are ways in which existential therapists can assist clients in confronting and dealing better with the ultimate concern of isolation.

CONFRONTING ISOLATION

Therapists can help clients realize that ultimately everyone is alone. Clients can learn both what they can and what they cannot obtain from relationships. Therapists can ask clients to experiment with periods of self-enforced isolation in appropriate doses. Benefits of this experiment can include increased awareness both of the terror of loneliness and of hidden resources and courage.

IDENTIFYING DEFENCE MECHANISMS

Clients can be helped to identify the defences they use to cope with the conflict of the need to belong and the fact of existential isolation. Becoming aware that existing in the eyes of others, fusion with others, and compulsive sexuality are defence mechanisms against existential anxiety can act as a springboard for doing something about them.

IDENTIFYING INTERPERSONAL PATHOLOGY

Using the ideal of a need-free or 'I-Thou' relationship as a yardstick, clients' ways of avoiding real relationships with others can be identified. To what extent do they relate to others as objects to satisfy their wants and needs? How well can they love others? How good are they at listening and revealing themselves? What are their specific distancing operations? Therapists can instruct clients in 'the ABCs of the language of intimacy ...' (Yalom 1989, p. 43). Such ABCs include how to own and express feelings.

USING THE THERAPIST–CLIENT RELATIONSHIP TO ILLUMINATE PATHOLOGY

Existential therapists have reservations about seeing clients as transferring feelings and attitudes from important past relationships on to them. Instead they prefer to use the therapist–client relationship to illuminate pathology that may interfere with current and future relationships. Frequently clients distort aspects of their relationship with their therapists. Therapists can raise clients' awareness of such distortions, including their consequences for other relationships.

THE HEALING RELATIONSHIP

As mentioned earlier, existential therapists strive to develop real relationships with clients. Even though therapist–client relationships are temporary, the experience of intimacy can be permanent. The relationship can be powerfully affirming for clients because someone whom they respect and who *really* knows them fully accepts them. Therapists who have deep relationships with clients can help them face their existential isolation. Also, they help clients realize that they alone are responsible for their lives.

THERAPY AND MEANINGLESSNESS

The following are some ways in which existential therapists can work with clients complaining of lack of meaning in their lives.

REDEFINING THE PROBLEM

When clients complain that 'life has no meaning', they appear to assume that life has a meaning that they cannot find. The existential position is that people are meaning-giving rather than meaning-getting. Existential therapists raise clients' awareness that there is no inherent meaning in life, rather they are responsible for creating their own meaning. Frequently, what is subsumed under meaninglessness, is best pursued under the other ultimate concerns of death, freedom and isolation.

IDENTIFYING MEANINGLESSNESS ANXIETY DEFENCES

Existential therapists can assist clients to become more aware of their meaninglessness anxiety defences. To what extent does their search for money, pleasure, power, recognition and status flow from their failure to confront the existential issue of meaninglessness? Clients can be helped to recognize the consequences and costs of their defences. Their defences against meaninglessness may contribute to their leading superficial lives that create the very problems that consciously or unconsciously they seek to avoid.

ASSISTING ENGAGEMENT IN LIFE

Therapists should approach the problem of meaninglessness by assisting their clients to become more engaged in the stream of life. They should assume that the desire to engage in life is always present in clients. Therapists can offer clients authentic relationships that demonstrate their own engagement in the therapeutic process. They can explore clients' long-range hopes and goals, belief systems, capacity to love and attempts to express themselves creatively. In addition, they can identify and try to remove blocks in the clients' progress towards engagement. Clients may find insufficient meaning in their relationships, work, leisure, creative pursuits and religious strivings. Each area can be analysed for obstacles that clients can then work to remove.

CASE MATERIAL

May gives an example of existential therapy with Mercedes, a black woman who moved during therapy from almost complete impotence to self-esteem and the capacity for aggression. Being black and a woman were two contributing factors in Mercedes' sense of powerlessness (May, 1973, pp. 81–89; reproduced in Wedding and Corsini, 1995). A further case example, that of David a 50-year-old scientist highly anxious about confronting his wife of 27 years about his decision to separate from her, is provided toward the end of Yalom and Josselson's summary chapter on existential psychotherapy (Yalom and Josselson, 2014). Numerous brief case illustrations illuminate Yalom's (1980) *Existential Psychotherapy* and his *Staring at the Sun* (2008). In addition, in *Everyday Gets a Little Closer,* Yalom as therapist and Ginny Elkins as client share their end of session thoughts over the course of long-term therapy (Yalom and Elkins, 1974).

Yalom's use of literature as a teaching device also sheds light on the processes of and issues in conducting existential therapy. Yalom is acutely aware that effective therapists need to be humanly involved when relating to clients, a point well illustrated in his books of therapeutic short stories *Love's Executioner* (Yalom, 1989) and *Momma and the Meaning of Life* (Yalom, 1999). In addition, in *Lying on the Couch*, he illustrates issues of therapist and client transparency, therapeutic boundaries, and the use of dreams in existential therapy (Yalom, 1996).

FURTHER DEVELOPMENTS

Yalom writes: 'I considered revising *Existential Psychotherapy* but in the end rejected that plan – there was no tradition of an evolving literature, no research to update and review. Besides it seemed silly to update a book that purported to deal with timeless elements of the human condition' (Yalom, 1998, p. 339). In addition, further developments in May and Yalom's existential therapy have been forestalled somewhat by Rollo May's death in 1994 and Irvin Yalom's spending more time writing psychotherapy fiction.

Though primarily an individual approach, existential therapy is sometimes conducted in groups of eight to ten members. Therapy groups provide here-and-now information on members' ways of avoiding or assuming responsibility. Also, the interactional format of groups gives therapists and members opportunities to observe and work on interpersonal distortions and maladaptive behaviours. Existential group therapists attempt to take group members through the following sequence: learning how their behaviour: (1) is viewed by others, (2) makes others feel, (3) creates the opinions others have of them, and (4) influences their opinions of themselves. In groups, clients can see how they create in others the very reactions that trouble them in their outside lives (Josselson, 2007). In addition, groups can work on issues surrounding the ultimate concerns of death and meaninglessness. For instance, in groups of cancer patients the issue of confronting death is likely to be a major area for work.

CONCLUDING COMMENT

Yalom and Josselson end their chapter summarizing existential therapy with the following observation:

> Our present age is one of disintegration of cultural and historical mores, of love and marriage, the family, inherited religions, and so forth. Given these realities, the existential emphasis on meaning, responsibility, and living a finite life fully will become increasingly important. (2014, p. 296)

REVIEW AND PERSONAL QUESTIONS

REVIEW QUESTIONS

1. What does the word existential mean?
2. What are the characteristics of and inner conflicts associated with each of the four existential ultimate concerns: death, freedom, isolation and meaninglessness?
3. What are existential psychodynamics and what is the existential model of defence mechanisms?
4. What are some defences for anxiety attached to each ultimate concern?
5. What are the goals of existential therapy?
6. What are desirable characteristics in existential therapist–client relationships?
7. Describe some interventions existential therapists can use for working with clients' death anxiety.
8. Describe some interventions existential therapists can use for enhancing clients' responsibility awareness and assumption.
9. Describe some interventions existential therapists can use for working with clients' problems of existential isolation.
10. Describe some interventions existential therapists can use for working with clients' problems of meaninglessness.

PERSONAL QUESTIONS

1. To what extent do you experience your existence as real? Answer as specifically as possible.

2. To what extent and in what ways do you experience existential anxiety? What are some of your main defences against existential anxiety?

3. Assess the degree to which you currently take personal responsibility for making or creating your existence. In what ways might you engage in less responsibility avoidance and in greater responsibility assumption?

4. Do you consider that meaninglessness is a major problem for people in Western society? If so, how does this affect you personally?

5. What relevance, if any, has the theory and practice of Yalom and May's existential therapy for how you conduct therapy?

6. What relevance, if any, has the theory and practice of Yalom and May's existential counselling and therapy for how you live?

ANNOTATED BIBLIOGRAPHY

Yalom, I. D. (1980) *Existential Psychotherapy*. New York: Basic Books.
This book is a major contribution to the counselling and therapy literature. It develops a psychodynamic theory of existential anxiety centred on humans' confrontations with the ultimate concerns of death, freedom, isolation and meaninglessness. The book suggests ways in which existential therapists can assist clients to confront and come to terms with each of these sources of existential anxiety. Both theory and practice are illuminated by numerous vignettes and case examples.

Yalom, I. D. and Josselson, R (2014) Existential psychotherapy. In D. Wedding and R. J. Corsini (eds), *Current Psychotherapies* (10th ed.). Belmont CA: Brooks/Cole, pp. 265–98.
An authoritative and relatively concise statement of the theory and practice of existential psychotherapy.

Yalom, I. D. (2008) *Staring at the Sun: Overcoming the Dread of Death*. London: Piatkus.
This book is a personal journey stemming from Yalom's confrontation with death. The book contains what he has learned about overcoming the terror of death from his own experience, his therapeutic work, and the thoughts of writers who have informed his work.

Yalom, I. D. (2001) *The Gift of Therapy*. London: Piatkus.
A series of eighty-five brief offerings covering the therapist–patient relationship; methods of exploring death, meaning and freedom; a variety of issues in the everyday conduct of therapy; the use of dreams in therapy; and the hazards and privileges of being a therapist.

Yalom, I. D. (1998) *The Yalom Reader: Selections from the Work of a Master Therapist and Story Teller*. New York: Basic Books.

This book charts Yalom's writing career as it has progressed from texts of psychotherapy to novels of psychotherapy. The material selected for the book's three parts address each of Yalom's major interests: (1) group therapy; (2) existential psychotherapy; and (3) writing.

Yalom, I. D. (1989) *Love's Executioner and Other Tales of Psychotherapy*. London: Bloomsbury.
The human face of existential therapy. A series of beautifully written case studies in which Yalom works with his clients. Both therapist and clients come alive as real people struggling with the concerns of existence. The book provides Yalom's insights into 'grey areas' regarding their own behaviour existential therapists are likely to face.

REFERENCES AND FURTHER READING

Josselson, R. (2007) *Playing Pygmalion: How People Create One Another*. New York: Rowman and Littlefield.
May, R. (1939) *The Art of Counseling*. Nashville: Cokesbury.
May, R. (1950) *The Meaning of Anxiety*. New York: Ronald Press.
May, R. (1953) *Man's Search for Himself*. New York: W. W. Norton.
May, R. (1967) *Psychology and the Human Dilemma*. Princeton, NJ: Van Nostrand.
May, R. (1969) *Love and Will*. New York: Norton.
May, R. (1973) *Power and Innocence: A Search for the Sources of Violence*. New York W. W. Norton.
May, R. (1975) *The Courage to Create*. New York: Norton.
May, R. (1977) *The Meaning of Anxiety* (rev. ed.). New York: Norton.
May, R. (1981) *Freedom and Destiny*. New York: Norton.
May. R. (1985) *My Quest for Beauty*. New York: Norton.
May, R., Angel, E. and Ellenberger, H. F. (eds) (1958) *Existence: A New Dimension in Psychiatry and Psychology*. New York: Basic Books.
Rabinowitz, F. E., Good, G. and Cozard, L. (1989) Rollo May: A man of myth and meaning. *Journal of Counseling and Development, 67*, 436–41. (Interview with Rollo May)
Sartre, J. P. (1956) *Being and Nothingness*. New York: PhilosophicalLibrary.
Wedding, D. and Corsini, R. (1995) *Case Studies in Psychotherapy*. Itasca, IL: F. E. Peacock.
Yalom, I. D. (1980) *Existential Psychotherapy*. New York: Basic Books.
Yalom, I. D. (1983) *Inpatient Group Psychotherapy*. New York: Basic Books.
Yalom, I. D. (1989) *Love's Executioner and Other Tales of Psychotherapy*. London: Bloomsbury.
Yalom, I. D. (1991) *When Nietzsche Wept*. New York: Basic Books/Harper. Paperback: Harper Collins, 1992.
Yalom, I. D. (1996) *Lying on the Couch*. New York: HarperPerennial.

Yalom, I. D. (1998) *The Yalom Reader: Selections from the Work of a Master Therapist and Story Teller.* New York: Basic Books.

Yalom. I. D. (1999) *Momma and the Meaning of Life.* New York: Basic Books.

Yalom, I. D. (2001) *The Gift of Therapy: Reflections on being a Therapist.* London: Piatkus.

Yalom, I. D. (2005a) *The Schopenhauer Cure: A Novel.* New York: HarperCollins.

Yalom. I. D. (2005b) Existential psychotherapy: Fat lady. In D. Wedding and R. Corsini (eds), *Case Studies in Psychotherapy* (4th ed.). Belmont, CA: Thomson Brooks/Cole, pp. 133–55.

Yalom, I.D. (2008) *Staring at the Sun: Overcoming the Denial of Death.* London: Piatkus.

Yalom, I. D. (2012) *The Spinoza Problem.* New York: Basic Books.

Yalom, I. D. (2013) Autobiographical information. www.yalom.com

Yalom, I. D. and Elkins, G. (1974) *Every Day Gets a Little Closer.* New York: Basic Books.

Yalom, I. D. and Josselson, R (2014) Existential psychotherapy. In D. Wedding and R. J. Corsini (eds), *Current Psychotherapies* (10th ed.). Belmont CA: Brooks/Cole, pp. 265–98.

Yalom, I. D. and Leszcz, M. (2005) *The Theory and Practice of Group Psychotherapy* (5th ed.). New York: Basic Books.

Adherents of behaviour therapy view their practice as firmly rooted in experimentally derived principles of learning. However, behavioural theory is an overall theory as well as an experimentally based attempt to describe the specific laws or principles of human behaviour. As an overall theory the distinctive emphasis is on the overwhelming role of environmental contingencies in influencing the acquisition and maintenance of behaviour. In its most radical form the behavioural model sees human actions as derived solely from three sources: biological deprivations, such as hunger and sexual tension; the individual's learning history; and the characteristics of and contingencies provided by environmental contexts. There is no place for concepts such as mind and free will. However, a distinction has emerged in behaviour therapy between approaches based on conditioning, radical behaviour therapy, and those which emphasize cognitive mediating variables, cognitive behaviour therapy. The latter emphasis is less deterministic than the former.

Chapter 8, 'Behavior Therapy', focuses mainly on radical behaviour therapy. The theory section focuses on the work of five leading behavioural theorists: Pavlov's classical conditioning, Watson's conditioned behaviourism, Skinner's operant conditioning, Wolpe's reciprocal inhibition, and Bandura's social cognitive theory. The practice part of the chapter focuses predominantly on conditioning methods for altering observable behaviour rather than on approaches to altering behaviour by means of altering cognitions. Practitioners of radical behaviour therapy are a declining breed. Now most therapists using the methods described in this chapter, especially the younger ones, are more likely to view themselves as cognitive behaviour therapists rather than as straight behaviour therapists.

Chapters 9 to 11 focus on cognitive behaviour therapies. Chapter 9 describes rational emotive behaviour therapy. When he first developed it in 1955 Albert Ellis termed his approach rational therapy (RT). In 1961, he changed its name to rational emotive therapy (RET). In 1993, Ellis further changed its name to rational emotive behaviour therapy (REBT). What Ellis means by 'rational' is cognition that is effective in self-helping rather than cognition merely empirically and logically valid. He wished that he had used the word cognitive from the start since many people narrowly restrict the word rational to mean intellectual or logico-empirical. People's rationality rests on judging soundly which of their desires or preferences to follow and, therefore, is based on thoughts, emotions and feelings. Ellis introduced 'behaviour' into his approach's name for the sake of accuracy. From its start, the approach has strongly emphasized behaviour along with cognition and emotion.

Chapter 10 presents cognitive therapy, which was initially developed in the early 1960s by Dr Aaron Beck, but has continuously evolved since then. The theory postulates that during clients' cognitive development they learn incorrect habits of processing and interpreting information. Cognitive therapists attempt to unravel clients' distortions and help them to learn different and more realistic ways of processing and reality-testing information. Influences on the practice of cognitive therapy include Rogers, Ellis and the behaviour therapists. The gentle style of questioning and emphasis on unconditional acceptance owes much to person-centred therapy. The emphasis on finding solutions to conscious problems resembles rational emotive behaviour therapy. Setting goals and session agendas, testing hypotheses, using specific behaviour change procedures, and assigning homework are among the contributions from behaviour therapy.

Chapter 11 describes Arnold Lazarus's multimodal therapy. Lazarus (2008) observed that the multimodal orientation transcends the behavioural tradition by adding unique assessment procedures and by dealing in great depth and detail with sensory, imagery, cognitive, and interpersonal factors and their interactive effects. Clients' needs are often better served if therapists work in multimodal rather than unimodal or bimodal fashions. Multimodal therapy rests heavily on multimodal assessment to choose the most appropriate techniques for particular clients with their unique psychological profiles and circumstances. Lazarus observed about the term multimodal therapy, 'It might have been better to call it "multimodal assessment and comprehensive psychotherapy" or something like that.' (Dryden, 1991, p. 107). Nevertheless, the approach is presented here in this part along with other cognitive behaviour approaches.

REFERENCES

Dryden, W. (1991) *A Dialogue with Arnold Lazarus: 'It Depends'*. Milton Keynes: Open University Press.

Lazarus, A. A. (2008) Multimodal therapy. In R. J. Corsini and D. Wedding (eds) *Current Psychotherapies* (8th ed.). Belmont, CA: Thomson Brooks/Cole, pp. 368–401.

BEHAVIOUR THERAPY 8

INTRODUCTION

Much of the research on which the behavioural model is based has been performed on animals such as dogs, cats and pigeons. This raises issues of the generalizability of a model derived largely from non-human animals in laboratory settings to humans in natural settings. Nevertheless, the point remains that, at the molecular level or level of observations of specific behaviours, behavioural psychologists and researchers have made a distinctive contribution to developing a theoretical framework for psychotherapy.

This chapter differs from that of the preceding ones. The theory section aims to introduce the reader to some key behavioural concepts through discussing selectively the ideas and experimental work of five leading theorists. The practice section of the chapter provides an introduction to some basic methods mainly of radical or traditional behaviour therapy. Wolpe viewed behaviour therapy as a conditioning therapy and his approach is based largely on classical conditioning in which unadaptive habits are weakened or eliminated and adaptive habits are initiated and strengthened. Traditional behaviour therapy also incorporates operant conditioning assumptions and practices.

THEORY

PAVLOV'S CLASSICAL CONDITIONING

IVAN PETROVICH PAVLOV (1849–1936)

In 1870 Pavlov matriculated at the Faculty of Physical-Mathematical Sciences of the University of St Petersberg. In 1883, he was awarded an MD degree by the Imperial Military-Medical Academy in St Petersberg. In 1890, he was appointed a professor of pharmacology and then, in 1895, became a professor of physiology at the Imperial Military-Medical Academy.

Beginning in 1891 Pavlov made fundamental discoveries concerning the nature and physiology of digestion and, in 1904, received the Nobel Prize in physiology and medicine for this work. In 1901, Pavlov redirected his research interests from the digestive processes to the functioning of the cerebral hemispheres of dogs by means of the salivary reflex conditioning method. He spent the remainder of his life on this research, eventually with a large staff. Pavlov's books include *The Work of the Digestive Glands* (1897/1902) *Conditioned Reflexes: An Investigation of the Physiological Activity of the Cerebral Cortex* (1927).

CLASSICAL CONDITIONING

Pavlov considered that both instincts and reflexes were alike in being inevitable responses of the organism to internal and external stimuli. 'Reflex' was the preferred term since it had been used from the beginning with a scientific connotation. The whole nervous activity of animals is based on inborn reflexes, which may be either excitatory or inhibitory. Such reflexes 'are regular causal connections between certain definite external stimuli acting on the organism and its necessary reflex reaction' (Pavlov, 1927, p. 16). The inborn reflexes alone are inadequate to ensure the continued existence of the organism, with the more specialized interaction between the animal and the environment provided through the medium of the cerebral hemispheres. The 'most general function of the hemispheres is that of reacting to signals presented by innumerable stimuli of interchangeable signification' (Pavlov, 1927, p. 16).

In his book *Conditioned Reflexes,* subtitled 'An investigation of the physiological activity of the cerebral cortex', Pavlov describes the precautions taken to build a laboratory so as to eliminate, as far as possible, any stimuli outside his control. In order to register the intensity of the salivary reflex, all the dogs used in his experiments were subjected to a minor operation that consisted of transferring the opening of the salivary duct from the mucous membrane of the mouth to the outside skin. In the experimental laboratory a dog would be harnessed to a stand in one section of a double chamber, while the experimenter was in the other section.

Box 8.1 diagrammatically depicts Pavlov's metronome experiments, with the term 'response' substituted for 'reflex'. Food in the mouth is an unconditioned stimulus (UCS), which automatically elicits the inborn response of salivation (UCR). Through repeated reinforcement consisting of stimulation by beating the metronome followed by feeding, the metronome becomes a conditioned stimulus (CS), thus becoming a signal for food and eliciting the conditioned response of salivation (CR). However, if the metronome (CS) is no longer reinforced by feeding, then the conditioned response (CR) undergoes extinction and diminishes, or even disappears (ECR).

Learning a conditioned response in the above manner has come to be termed classical or respondent conditioning. Pavlov and his colleagues explored many other areas, such as conditioned inhibition and the generalization of stimuli, but these researches are not described here. Pavlov's researches into the conditioned reflex were essential to the founding of behaviour therapy.

BOX 8.1 THE CONDITIONING AND EXTINCTION OF A DOG'S SALIVARY RESPONSE TO THE BEATING OF A METRONOME

Stage one

Unconditioned Stimulus (UCS) ⟶ Unconditioned Response (UCR)
(food)   (salivation)

Stage two

Conditioned Stimulus (CS)
(metronome)
reinforced by
Unconditioned Stimulus (UCS) ⟶ Unconditioned Response (UCR)
(food)   (salivation)

Stage three

Conditioned Stimulus (CS) ⟶ Conditioned Response (CR)
(metronome)   (salivation)

Stage four

Conditioned Stimulus (CS) ⟶ Extinguished Conditioned
(metronome, no longer   Response (ECR)
reinforced by feeding)   (diminution/absence of salivation)

WATSON'S CONDITIONED BEHAVIOURISM

JOHN BROADUS WATSON (1878–1958)

Watson, sometimes viewed as the founder of behaviourism, was born in Greenville, South Carolina, to an energetic and religious mother and a philandering father, who left home when Watson was 13 years old. He was educated at Furman University in Greenville and at the University of Chicago, where his doctoral thesis was on animal education. Watson married when he was 25 years old. At 30, he became professor of psychology at Johns Hopkins University in Baltimore and, at 36, he was elected president of the American Psychological Association. During the 1910s, Watson moved his emphasis from animal to human observation and experimentation. From 1913 Watson worked hard at establishing behaviourism as a method of psychology.

In 1919 Watson, who was then 41, met a l9-year-old graduate student called Rosalie Raynor. In 1920, he was forced to resign from Johns Hopkins University on the grounds of adultery with a student and no other university would employ him. Divorced in late 1920, Watson married Rosalie in January 1921 and lived happily with her until her tragic death from illness in 1936.

After leaving university life Watson became a highly successful advertising executive. In the 1920s, Watson conducted some research on children with Mary Cover Jones and also did some popular psychological writing. Watson's books include *Animal Education* (1903), *Behavior* (1914), *Psychology from the Standpoint of a Behaviorist* (1919), *The Psychological Care of the Infant and Child* (1928) and *Behaviorism* (1931).

CONDITIONED BEHAVIOURISM

What is observable is the real field of psychology and what can be observed is what the organism does or says, that is to say its behaviour. Watson considered that there were two points of view dominant in the American psychological thinking of his time: introspective or subjective psychology, which he termed the old psychology, and the new and objective psychology of behaviourism. As the behaviour of animals can be investigated without referring to conscious-ness, so can the behaviour of man. In fact 'the behaviour of man and the behaviour of animals must be considered on the same plane; as being equally essential to a general understanding of behaviour' (Watson, 1913, p. 176).

STIMULUS, RESPONSE AND CONDITIONING

The Watsonian behaviourist sees all psychological problems and their solutions as being schematized in *stimulus* (or the more complex *situation*) and *response* terms, often abbreviated to S-R terms. In the ideal behaviourist world, given the response the stimuli can be predicted and given the stimuli the response can be predicted.

Stimuli may be unconditioned in that from birth they call forth definite responses, such as the responses of turning the eyes away from or closing the eyes to light. On the other hand, most stimuli to which humans respond are conditioned or learned, for example all the printed words to which humans respond. Similarly, responses may be unconditioned, as in the above light example, but very frequently they are conditioned, as in the case of a two-year-old child who has learned to substitute screaming for laughter at the sight of a dog. Watson observed that the whole body of man is built around the keynote 'rapid, and when needed, complicated reactions to simple and complex stimuli' (Watson, 1931, p. 91).

The Watsonian behaviourist is a strict determinist. Watson considered that, given total control over a dozen healthy infants from birth, he could take any one at random and train this person to become any type of specialist he might select, including doctor, lawyer, artist, beggar-man and thief. Inheritance of capacity, talent, temperament, mental constitution and characteristics does not really exist, since these things depend on training.

Habit formation probably starts in embryonic life and is very rapid after birth. The development of emotional habits will be used to illustrate the importance of conditioning.

CONDITIONING OF EMOTIONS

Watson states that there are three types of unlearned beginnings of emotional reactions, or unlearned emotional responses, to stimuli. These responses are fear, rage and love. These emotional reactions might be viewed as unconditioned reflexes or responses. For instance, a loud sound is a fundamental stimulus for eliciting the fear response.

Watson and Raynor did a series of experiments on an 11-month-old boy called Albert. (Watson and Raynor, 1920). The first experiment involved the establishment of a conditioned emotional response of fear to a white rat. This was achieved by linking on some trials the loud sound of the striking of a bar with Albert's touching the white rat. When later the white rat was presented alone, Albert exhibited fear responses of crying, falling over and crawling away.

A second experiment showed that there was a transfer of the conditioned fear response, though less strong, from the white rat to other furry animals (rabbit, dog) and objects (fur coat, cotton wool) when five days later they were presented to him. The above tests were carried out on a table covered with a mattress in a small, well-lit room.

A further experiment indicated, after 31 days, the persistence in a less intense form of both the conditioned fear response to the rat and the transferred fear responses to the fur coat and the rabbit. Watson and Raynor concluded that it was probable that many of the phobias in psychopathology are conditioned emotional reactions of either the direct or the transferred type. Emotional disturbances can be retraced to conditioned and transferred responses set up in infancy and childhood to all three of the fundamental human emotions.

Watson and Raynor did not remove Albert's conditioned emotional responses prior to his discharge from hospital, to be adopted by a family that lived outside Baltimore. However, Mary Cover Jones, an associate of Watson's, conducted an experiment in which Peter, a boy of about three years, was unconditioned or reconditioned of his 'home grown' fears of a rabbit, a white rat and related stimuli (Jones, 1924).

The experimenters were given permission to give Peter his lunch of crackers and a glass of milk. Just as he began to eat his lunch, the rabbit was displayed in a cage of wire mesh just far enough away not to disturb his eating. Gradually the rabbit was brought closer and closer and finally Peter would eat with one hand and play with the rabbit with the other. There was a transfer of unconditioning of fear responses to other furry objects, with degrees of success varying from total to greatly improved.

Watson contended that human emotional life is the result of the wear and tear of environmental forces. Through experiments such as those described above, an initial understanding was developing of how emotional reactions could be conditioned and unconditioned. He considered that there is no need to introduce the concept of mind into the so-called mental diseases. Diagnosis should involve an analysis of behaviour alone. Personality problems are behaviour disturbances and habit conflicts that need to be cured by unconditioning and conditioning.

SKINNER'S OPERANT BEHAVIOURISM

BURRHUS FREDERICK SKINNER (1904–90)

Skinner was born in Susquehanna, Pennsylvania. In 1926 he graduated from Hamilton College where, majoring in English, he had planned to become a writer. In 1928, after unsuccessful trial period at writing, Skinner entered Harvard University as a graduate student in psychology, obtaining his doctorate in 1931. From 1931 to 1936, he worked as a postdoctoral fellow in the laboratory of W. J. Crozier, a distinguished experimental biologist.

Skinner held early academic appointments, from 1936 to 1945, at the University of Minnesota and, from 1945 to 1948, at Indiana University. In 1948, he became professor of psychology at Harvard where he retired from active teaching in 1974. Throughout the remainder of his life Skinner continued writing and lecturing. Among his numerous awards, in 1958 Skinner received the American Psychological Association's Award for Distinguished Scientific Contributions.

Skinner's 19 books include his seminal work *The Behavior of Organisms* (1938), *Science and Human Behavior* (1953), *Verbal Behavior* (1957) which he considered his most important book, and *Schedules of Reinforcement* (Ferster and Skinner, 1957).

OPERANT BEHAVIOURISM

Skinner's distinctive contribution to psychology has been to elaborate the importance of the after-effects or consequences of behaviour. A response that has occurred cannot be predicted or controlled, but all that can be predicted is the probability of a similar response occurring in the future. The unit of a predictive science of behaviour is an operant. The term 'operant' emphasizes the fact that behaviour *operates* on the environment to generate consequences. Thus the consequences define the properties with respect to which responses are viewed as similar. Skinner used the term 'operant' both as an adjective, as in operant behaviour, and as a noun, which indicates the behaviour defined by a given consequence. The critical difference with Pavlov is that in Pavlov's work the reinforcer is paired with the *stimulus,* whereas in operant behaviour it is contingent upon a *response.* Classical and operant conditioning are the only two possible kinds of conditioning.

CONTINGENCIES OF REINFORCEMENT

Skinner stressed the role of the environment in shaping and maintaining behaviour. Behaviour both operates on the environment to produce consequences and also is controlled or contingent upon the consequences produced by that environment. Any adequate description of the interaction between an organism and its environment must specify three elements:

1. the occasion on which a response occurs;
2. the response itself; and
3. the reinforcing consequences.

The interrelationship of these three elements constitutes the contingencies of reinforcement. For example, in an experiment with pigeons, any stimuli deriving from the experimental space, such as sound or light, and from the operanda of the experiment, such as a translucent disc on the wall that may be pecked, and from any special stimulating devices prior to the response, are the 'occasion' of the response. The response itself might be pecking the disc and the reinforcing consequence might be food provided at a time when the pigeon is hungry.

POSITIVE AND NEGATIVE REINFORCEMENT

The probability of a response is increased after both positive and negative reinforcement. Positive reinforcements consist of presenting something, such as food, water or sexual contact, in a situation. Negative reinforcements consist of removing something, such as a bright light or an electric shock, from the situation. Thus the difference between positive and negative reinforcement hinges on whether it is the presence or absence of a given reinforcer that increases the probability of a response. The withdrawal of a positive reinforcer has the same effect as the presentation of a negative reinforcer.

PRIMARY AND CONDITIONED REINFORCERS

Skinner considered that all reinforcers eventually derive their power from evolutionary selection and that it is part of 'human nature' to be reinforced in particular ways by particular things. For instance, both the positive reinforcer of food and the negative reinforcer of escape from a dangerous situation have obvious survival value. Only a small part of behaviour is immediately reinforced by food, water, sexual contact or other reinforcers of evident biological significance. Such reinforcers are the primary or unconditioned ones.

Most behaviour is emitted in response to reinforcers that have become associated with or conditioned to primary reinforcers. For instance, if each time food is given to a hungry pigeon a light is turned on, the light eventually becomes a conditioned reinforcer. The light may then be used to condition an operant in the same way as food. A conditioned reinforcer is generalized when it is paired with more than one primary reinforcer. The importance of this is that a generalized conditioned reinforcer, such as money, is useful because it is not attached to just one state of deprivation, such as hunger, but to many. Therefore, under this kind of reinforcement, a response is more likely to occur. Other generalized conditioned reinforcers are attention, approval and affection.

SCHEDULES OF REINFORCEMENT

Ferster and Skinner (1957) observed that many significant features of the shaping and maintenance of behaviour can be explained only by reference to the properties of schedules of reinforcement, and also that intermittent reinforcement can be a very important source of reinforcement in its own right and not just the poor relation of inevitable or continuous reinforcement. Box 8.2 depicts non-intermittent and intermittent reinforcement schedules.

BOX 8.2   SCHEDULES OF REINFORCEMENT

NON-INTERMITTENT SCHEDULES OF REINFORCEMENT

- *Continuous reinforcement*, where every response emitted is reinforced.
- *Extinction*, where no responses are reinforced.

Intermittent schedules of reinforcement

- *Fixed interval*, in which the first response occurring after a given period of time (for example, five minutes) is reinforced, with another period beginning immediately after the reinforcement.
- *Fixed ratio*, in which every *nth* response is reinforced. (The word 'ratio' refers to the ratio between responses and reinforcements.)
- *Variable interval*, in which reinforcements are scheduled according to a random series of intervals having a given mean and lying between arbitrary values.
- *Variable ratio*, in which reinforcements are scheduled according to a random series of ratios having a given mean and lying between arbitrary values.
- *Multiple*, in which one schedule of reinforcement is in force in the presence of one stimulus and a different schedule in the presence of another stimulus. For instance, there is a fixed interval when the key in the pigeon's experimental box is red, and a variable interval when the key is green.
- *Differential reinforcement of rate of response*, in which a response is reinforced only if it follows the preceding response after a specified interval of time (for example, three minutes) or before the end of a given interval (for example, half a second).

MAINTENANCE AND EXTINCTION

Skinner did not consider the term 'learning' to be equivalent to 'operant conditioning'. Learning emphasizes acquisition of behaviour, whereas operant conditioning focuses on both acquisition and maintenance of behaviour. Thus behaviour continues to have consequences, and if these consequences or reinforcements are not forthcoming then extinction occurs. For instance, when a pigeon's behaviour, such as the lifting of its head, which has been reinforced by the consequence of food, no longer continues to receive this reinforcement, the head lifting tends to occur with a reduced frequency. Similarly, when people engage in behaviour that no longer has rewarding consequences, they find themselves less inclined to behave that way.

Schedules of reinforcement are relevant to extinction. For example, the resistance to extinction generated by intermittent reinforcement may be much greater than that under continuous reinforcement. The task of a science of behaviour is to account for the probability of a response in terms of its history of reinforcement and extinction. Skinner used the term 'operant strength' to indicate the probability of a given response and observes that with humans the condition of low operant strength resulting from extinction often requires treatment. For instance, psychotherapy might sometimes be viewed as a system of reinforcement designed to reinstate extinguished behaviour.

SHAPING AND SUCCESSIVE APPROXIMATION

Behaviour may be shaped by reinforcing successive approximations to the desired response. Skinner gives the example of teaching a pigeon to bowl by swiping, with a sharp sideward movement of its beak, a wooden ball down a miniature alley towards a set of toy pins. When he and his colleagues waited for the complete response, which was to be reinforced by food, nothing happened. Then they decided to reinforce any response that had the slightest resemblance to a swipe and, afterwards, to select responses which more closely approximated the final form. This was a highly successful procedure and within minutes the pigeon was striking the ball as if it had been a champion squash player.

STIMULUS DISCRIMINATION AND CONTROL

Operant behaviour is emitted through important connections with the environment. For instance, in a pigeon experiment, neck stretching is reinforced when a signal light is on and allowed to extinguish when a signal light is off. The contingencies of reinforcement are that a stimulus (the light) is the occasion, the response is stretching the neck, and the reinforcement is food. The process through which the response is eventually more likely to occur when the light is on is called discrimination. Another way of viewing discrimination is to say that a response has come under the control of a discriminative stimulus or, more briefly, under stimulus control. Once an operant discrimination has been conditioned, the probability of the response occurring may be increased or decreased by presenting or removing the discriminative stimulus. An example of the effect of stimulus control on humans is the increased probability of purchasing behaviour through the effective display of merchandise in a shop.

STIMULUS GENERALIZATION

When the reinforcing effect of one stimulus spreads to other stimuli, the effect is that of generalization or induction. For instance, if a response to a round, red spot one square inch in area is reinforced, a yellow spot of the same size and shape may also be reinforcing through the common properties of size and shape. However, by reinforcing only responses to the red spot with the above dimensions, and by extinguishing the response to the yellow spot, the red spot may be given exclusive discriminative control. An example of stimulus generalization in everyday life is reacting to people in a similar way because they resemble someone we know.

WOLPE'S RECIPROCAL INHIBITION

JOSEPH WOLPE (1915–97)

Wolpe was born on April 20, 1915, and educated in Johannesburg, South Africa. From 1948 to 1956 and again from 1957 to 1959 Wolpe was a lecturer in the department of psychiatry at the University of Witwatersrand, Johannesburg as well as conducting a private psychiatric practice.

In the late 1940s, as a result of laboratory experiments with cats as subjects, he developed a method based on reciprocal inhibition for de-conditioning neurotic fear responses. Wolpe then applied his experimental findings in his clinical work, with great success. From 1956–57, Wolpe was a Fellow at the Center for Advanced Study in the Behavioral Sciences at Stanford University in California.

Wolpe later returned to the United States, where, from 1960 to 1965, he was professor of psychiatry at the University of Virginia at Charlottesville, from 1965 to 1984, at Temple University in Pennsylvania and, afterwards, at the Medical College of Pennsylvania in Philadelphia. Wolpe's books *include Psychotherapy by Reciprocal Inhibition* (1958) and *The Practice of Behaviour Therapy* (1990).

RECIPROCAL INHIBITION

Wolpe noted that old habits are often eliminated by allowing new habits to develop in the same situation. The term *reciprocal inhibition* encompasses all situations in which the elicitation of one response appears to bring about a decrement in the strength of evocation of a simultaneous response. He hypothesized that if an incompatible response were to inhibit the conditioned response and lead to much drive reduction, then a significant degree of conditioned inhibition of the original response would be developed. Eventually, his work led to his framing the following general reciprocal inhibition principle:

> If a response antagonistic to anxiety can be made to occur in the presence of anxiety-evoking stimuli so that it is accompanied by a complete or partial suppression of the anxiety responses, the bond between these stimuli and the anxiety responses will be weakened. (Wolpe, 1958, p. 71)

In a later work, Wolpe suggests that the term mutual inhibition might be more comprehensible than reciprocal inhibition (Wolpe and Wolpe, 1988).

THE LEARNING AND UNLEARNING OF NEUROTIC FEARS AND HABITS IN CATS

Wolpe conducted fundamental laboratory research on the learning and unlearning of neurotic fears (Wolpe, 1958). The subjects were 12 domestic cats between the ages of six months and three years. Lasting neurotic effects were induced in all the cats by the administration of several electric shocks in a small experimental cage. Six of the cats were subject to a procedure by which, after control observations, the cat was given five to ten grid shocks preceded by a 'hoot' lasting two to three seconds. The other six cats were subject to a different procedure in which they were first conditioned to perform food-approach responses to a buzzer. This response was strongly reinforced over eight to 16 experimental sessions. The next stage of the procedure involved sounding the buzzer and shocking the cat when it made its food-approach response until it ceased to do so. The mean number of shocks required was four.

The immediate responses of the cats to the shocks included combinations of the following: rushing hither and thither, clawing at the cage, getting up on hind legs, crouching, trembling, howling, pilo-erection and rapid respiration. Persistent responses displayed by all animals were: (a) resistance to being put into the experimental cage; (b) signs of anxiety when inside the cage; and (c) refusal to eat meat pellets anywhere in the cage even after one, two or three days' starvation. The above symptoms were invariably intensified by presentation of the original auditory stimuli. Furthermore, all cats showed some of these symptoms outside the experimental cage.

The learned neurotic reactions of six of the cats were associated with inhibition of feeding. This suggested to Wolpe that under different conditions feeding might inhibit the neurotic reactions. The neurotic anxiety reactions were subsequently removed, or unlearned, in all cats by getting them to eat in the presence of successively larger doses of anxiety-evoking stimuli. The cats were subject to a number of procedures. One procedure was to place the cat in the experimental cage and move pellets of meat towards its mouth on the flat end of a four-inch rod held in the experimenter's hand, in the hope that the human hand would act as a stimulus to overcome the inhibition to eating. After some persistence, four out of the nine cats undergoing this procedure were induced to eat. However, only one of the three cats whose food-approach responses had been shocked was induced to eat in this way. The three cats not subject to the human-hand procedure were induced to eat by Masserman's 'forced solution' procedure. This involved repetitions of a procedure, in the experimental cage, of gradually pushing a hungry, neurotic cat by means of a movable barrier towards an open food box containing appetizing food.

The five cats which remained unaffected by the human-hand method were eventually induced to eat in the experimental cage by a procedure which involved a hierarchy of anxiety-evoking rooms ranging from the most anxiety-evoking, the experimental room or Room A, to the least anxiety-evoking, which turned out to be the passage outside Room D. The five cats initially ate at different points in the hierarchy, but by a method of gradual ascent all cats were eventually induced to eat in Room A and then in the experimental cage. By similar methods the cats' neurotic responses to the conditioned auditory stimuli were inhibited.

Wolpe explained the success of his experiments by stating that, when stimuli to incompatible responses are present simultaneously, the occurrence of the response that is dominant in the circumstances involves the reciprocal inhibition of the other. Thus, as the number of feedings increased, the anxiety responses gradually became weaker, so that to stimuli to which there was initially an anxiety response there was ultimately a feeding response with inhibition of anxiety.

RECIPROCAL INHIBITION IN THERAPY

Wolpe states that: 'The behavior therapist deliberately uses competing responses to overcome useless fears' (Wolpe and Wolpe 1988, p. 27). In overcoming the neurotic reactions of clients or patients, Wolpe considers it vital to conduct a thorough behaviour analysis to determine which stimuli actually or potentially evoke them currently. Wolpe (1958) listed eight incompatible responses at the disposal of therapists through which deliberate intervention for change may be made. These are: assertive responses; sexual responses; relaxation responses; respiratory responses; 'anxiety-relief' responses; competitively conditioned motor responses; 'pleasant' responses in the life situation (with drug enhancement); and (a) interview-induced emotional responses and (b) abreaction. Relaxation, as part of systematic desensitization, is described later in this chapter.

BANDURA'S SOCIAL COGNITIVE THEORY

ALBERT BANDURA (1925–)

Bandura was born and raised in Mundare in northern Alberta, Canada. In 1949, he graduated from the University of British Columbia with a psychology major and in 1952 he received a doctorate in clinical psychology from the University of

Iowa, followed by a one-year postdoctoral internship at the Witchita Guidance Center. Afterwards he went to Stanford University and, in 1964, was appointed a full professor. In 1974, the university awarded him an endowed chair. More recently, Bandura (2009) has used social cognitive theory to try to abate urgent global problems, such as population growth

Bandura's books include: *Principles of Behavior Modification* (1969), *Aggression: A Social Learning Analysis* (1973), *Social Learning Theory* (1977), *Social Foundations of Thought and Action: A Social Cognitive Theory* (1986) and *Self-Efficacy: The Exercise of Control* (1997).

SOCIAL COGNITIVE THEORY

All the theorists presented so far in this chapter focused mainly on conditioning. Though Bandura is often listed among the major behavioural theorists (see for instance, Wilson, 2008), he differs from the other theorists reviewed here in attributing much more influence to human agency, observational learning, and perceived self-efficacy. Bandura's labelling of his theoretical position as 'social cognitive' acknowledges both the social contribution to how people think and act and the importance of cognitive processes to motivation, emotions and actions. For many academics and practitioners Bandura's theoretical and research input has helped broaden behaviour therapy into cognitive behaviour therapy. Bandura's writing is voluminous and is treated very selectively here.

HUMAN AGENCY

Human agency is the capacity to exercise self-direction through control over one's own thought processes, motivation and action. Human agency has been conceptualized in three main ways: autonomous agency, in which people are totally independent agents of their actions; mechanical agency, where agency rests in environmental determinants; and emergent interactive agency, which is the model of social cognitive theory.

Emergent interactive agency is based on a model of triadic reciprocality. Reciprocal refers to mutual causation between the three factors. Behaviour (B), cognitive and personal factors (P), and environmental influences (E) each operate independently as determinants on one another. Figure 8.1 depicts this reciprocal determinism position. The 'influences vary in their selective strength and they do not occur simultaneously' (A. Bandura, personal communication, February 1, 1994). In the final analysis, human behaviour is the result of reciprocal interaction of external events and personal determinants such as genetic endowment, acquired competencies, reflective thought and self-initiative. People are free to the extent that they are able to exercise self-influence and determine their actions.

Social cognitive theory identifies four core features of human agency: intentionality, forethought, self-reactiveness, and self-reflectiveness (Bandura, 2004). Intentionality means that people form intentions that include action plans and

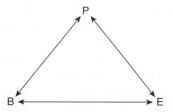

Figure 8.1   Representation of reciprocal determinism

strategies for attaining them. Forethought involves people setting themselves goals and anticipating the likely outcomes of prospective actions for guiding and motivating their efforts. Self-reactiveness means that people are self-regulators who adopt personal standards and monitor and regulate their actions by self-reactive influence: doing things that provide satisfaction and a sense of worth and avoiding actions that bring self-reproach. Self-reflectiveness means that people reflect on their efficacy, the soundness of their thoughts and actions, and adjust or change them, if necessary. The capacity for human agency enables humans to participate, individually and collectively, in shaping their lives and social systems.

OBSERVATIONAL LEARNING

The two main modes of learning are observational learning, learning by watching, and enactive learning, learning by doing. Most human behaviour and cognitive skills are learned from observing models. Functions that observational learning can perform include the following. Modelling can instruct observers in the skills and rules of behaviour. Also, modelling can inhibit and disinhibit behaviour already in people's repertoires. Yet another function is that of response facilitation. Modelled behaviour can serve as prompts and cues for people to perform behaviour already in their repertoires, yet is not initiated. A further function of modelling is that of eliciting emotional arousal. People can perceive and behave differently in states of heightened arousal. In addition, symbolic modelling shapes people's images of social realities by the way in which it portrays human relations and the activities they pursue.

   People can learn thinking skills from observing models. However, often covert thought process are inadequately conveyed by modelled actions. For instance, a model may solve a problem cognitively, but the observer only sees the resulting actions without gaining insight into the thought processes leading up to them. An approach to learning cognitive skills is to have models verbalize aloud how they think as they engage in problem-solving activities. Advantages of combining nonverbal with verbal modelling include the ability of nonverbal modelling to gain and hold attention and the chance of overt behaviour conferring added meaning to cognitive processes. Observers' cognitive skills are likely to improve more with models who demonstrate actions and thought processes rather than demonstrate actions alone.

The social cognitive view is that observational learning does not necessarily require extrinsic reward. Such learning occurs through cognitive processing during modelling and before observers perform any responses. The main role of incentives in observational learning is before rather than after modelling. For instance, observers' attention can be increased by anticipation of rewards from using modelled behaviours. Furthermore, anticipated rewards can motivate them to symbolize and rehearse modelled activities. Incentives are facilitative rather than necessary.

SELF-EFFICACY AND GOALS

Conceptions of personal efficacy are the foundation of human agency. It is not simply a matter of knowing what to do. To enact skilled performance people need both to possess the requisite skills and the self-beliefs of efficacy to use them. Bandura writes: 'Unless people believe they can produce desired effect by their actions they have little incentive to act or to persevere in face of difficulties' (2004, pp. 621–2).

Judgements of personal efficacy are different from response outcome expectations. Perceived self-efficacy refers to beliefs in one's capabilities to organize and execute the courses of action required to manage prospective situations (Bandura, 2008). Outcome expectations are judgements about the likely consequences such behaviour will produce. The judgement that one can jump six feet is an efficacy judgement. However, the anticipated social recognition from jumping six feet is an outcome expectation. Outcomes are consequences of acts not the acts themselves.

Magnitude, generality and strength are three important dimensions of efficacy expectations (Bandura, 1977). Efficacy expectations can vary according to the magnitude or level of difficulty of tasks: for instance, being confident about performing well in easy rather than in difficult tasks. Generality refers to the degree of generalization of mastery expectations beyond the specific treatment situation. Strength refers to the persistence of personal mastery expectations despite disconfirming experiences.

Self-efficacy beliefs determine goals and outcomes and determine how environmental facilitators and impediments are viewed (Bandura, 2004). Efficacy beliefs affect choice behaviour: for instance what to do. Perceived efficacy can foster engagement in activities, whereas perceived inefficacy can lead people to avoid potentially enriching experiences. Furthermore people of high self-efficacy view impediments as surmountable by persevering though effort and by improving their self-management skills. People of low self-efficacy are easily put off from trying in the face of impediments. Traditional behaviourist theory has to answer the question of how organisms capable of forecasting the future have no capacity for self-influence. People can produce their own futures rather than simply foretell it.

There are four major ways of developing a strong sense of efficacy (Bandura, 1997, 2004). Any method of treatment may work with one or more of these sources.

1. *Mastery experiences.* Personal experiences of success provide the most fundamental source of efficacy expectations.
2. *Social modelling.* Efficacy expectations may be altered by observing others and noting the positive and negative consequences of behaviour for them. Efficacy expectations induced by modelling are generally weaker than those induced by successful task performance.
3. *Social persuasion.* Verbal persuasion, such as suggestion and exhortation, may also influence self-efficacy. Persuasion may be most useful where it persuades people to try enough to succeed which in turn enhances their efficacy beliefs.
4. *Physical and emotional state.* Physical and emotional states affect efficacy beliefs in three ways. First, when people are tense and anxious, their physical state or level of emotional arousal can negatively influence their efficacy expectations. Second, mood states affect people's judgement of their personal efficacy: positive moods enhance perceived efficacy and depressed moods diminish it. Third, in activities involving strength and stamina, people judge their fatigue, aches and pain as signs of weak physical efficacy.

Personal agency or intentional regulation of behaviour operates through two cognitively based sources of motivation: first, forethought and, second, goal-setting with self-evaluative reactions to one's behaviour. Bandura observes: 'Human motivation relies on *discrepancy production* as well as *discrepancy reduction*. It requires both *proactive control* and *reactive or feedback control*' (1989, pp. 1179–80). Initially people motivate themselves through setting standards or levels of performance that create a state of disequilibrium and then they strive to attain them. Feedback control involves subsequent adjustments of effort to achieve desired results. Goals act as motivators by specifying the conditions for self-satisfaction with performance.

In addition, goals are important for the development of self-efficacy. They provide people with standards by which to judge their capabilities. Particularly useful are progressively difficult short-term sub-goals. Such sub-goals provide both incentives for action and, when attained, produce efficacy information and confidence to persist. Perceived inefficacy can cause people to lower their goals and thus decrease their dissatisfaction with sub-standard performances.

THERAPY

Nowadays definitions of behaviour therapy differ according to whether the therapist mainly emphasizes learning principles based on classical and operant conditioning, or emphasizes personal agency and cognitive intervening variables as well. Reitman and Drabman (1997) observe: 'radical behaviorists study thinking and other private events from within a contextual scientific framework that places, a priori, all causal events outside the organism itself' (p. 421). In cognitive behaviourism it is the individual's inner cognitions that cause much of their behaviour. This part of the chapter focuses predominantly on conditioning methods for altering observable behaviour, traditional behaviour therapy, rather than on approaches to altering behaviour by means of altering cognitions, cognitive behaviour therapy. Practictioners of traditional behaviour therapy are a declining breed. Now most therapists using the methods described in this chapter, especially the younger ones, are more likely to view themselves as cognitive behaviour therapists rather than behaviour therapists.

THERAPEUTIC GOALS

At the risk of introducing a level of generality which behaviour therapists, with their emphasis on specific goals for individual clients, might find uncongenial, the following is a list of behaviour therapy goals derived from the writings of the five theorists reviewed in this chapter:

- overcoming deficits in behavioural repertoires;
- strengthening adaptive behaviours;
- weakening or eliminating maladaptive behaviours;
- absence of debilitating anxiety reactions;
- the capacity to relax;
- the ability to assert oneself;
- effective social skills;
- adequacy at sexual functioning; and
- capacity for self-control.

PROCESS OF THERAPY

ASSESSMENT

Early on the behaviour therapist invariably conducts a behavioural assessment, sometimes known as a functional analysis, to identify and understand clients' problem areas (Cormier, Nurius and Osborn, 2013; Wolpe, 1990). Adequate behavioural assessments allow therapists to identify the context, antecedents and consequences of the responses they wish to treat, while inadequate behavioural assessments may lead to the wrong methods being applied to the wrong problems. After initial sessions, behavioural assessment aims to assist both in evaluating treatment effectiveness and in deciding whether to continue, discontinue and alter treatment.

When clients make statements like 'I seem to be very depressed these days', 'I don't seem to have many friends' or 'I get very tense at work', behaviour therapists attempt an analysis based on an *SRC* assessment, where S refers to the *stimulus* or *situational antecedents, R* to the *response variables* and *C* to the consequences or *consequent variables*. The purpose of the *SRC* analysis is to search for the key variables that control clients' behaviour. Sometimes these may be masked: for instance, aggression at work may reflect a poor marital relationship. Behavioural assessment aims for a high degree of specificity. For instance, in analysing a response, information on duration, frequency, generality, and strength of the response should be collected. Therapists seldom ask why questions, since those starting with how, when, where and what are more useful (Wilson, 2008).

Behaviour therapists differ in the extent to which they gather historical material concerning how the presenting concerns were learned, though this may be important in obtaining an accurate picture. Wolpe (1990), for instance, gathered historical material on his clients' presenting concerns, family life, educational and occupational development, and sexual development. He also explored his clients' current social relationships.

BEHAVIOURAL OBSERVATION

Sometimes therapists collect behavioural information by asking clients to role-play situations in which they experience difficulty, with the therapists playing the other person. On other occasions therapists go with clients into real-life settings to observe how they behave. An example of this might be going into pubs or restaurants with clients who experience difficulty drinking or eating in public, then observing and discussing their behaviour and emotions as they happen or shortly afterwards. However, when therapists are present, clients may behave differently from usual. Another form of observation in real-life settings is to collect information from significant people who interact with clients in their everyday lives, such as teachers or parents in the case of children, or spouses in the case of married people. Sometimes valid indirect observations in natural settings may be made by making frequency counts of various carefully defined categories of behaviour.

Clients may be asked to collect baseline data by monitoring their current behaviour. One way to go about this is to ask clients to fill in three column daily diary sheets investigating the *SRC* elements of a specific behaviour being monitored – one column heading each for situation, response, and consequences. Such a behavioural monitoring diaries might be kept for a week or however long it takes to obtain the relevant information.

QUESTIONNAIRES

Therapists may ask clients to complete self-report questionnaires. Such measures may focus on overt *behaviour,* or how the client acts, on *emotions,* or how the client feels, and on clients' perceptions of their environments. Perhaps the most commonly used type of questionnaire is the sort that asks clients to indicate the kinds of situations that cause them anxiety. One such questionnaire is Wolpe and Lang's *Fear Survey Schedule* in which clients are provided with five categories, ranging from 'not at all' to 'very much', for rating how disturbed they currently feel in 87 situations, such as 'People in authority', 'Angry people', 'Darkness' and 'Airplanes' (Wolpe, 1990; Wolpe and Lang, 1969). A questionnaire focused on self-report of behaviour is Alberti and Emmons' (2008) *Assertiveness Inventory*, with such items as 'Do you speak out or protest when someone takes your place in line?'. Another kind of questionnaire, which focuses on activities, events and experiences which clients find rewarding, is MacPhillamy and Lewinsohn's *Pleasant Events Schedule* (Lewinsohn, Munoz, Youngren and Zeiss, 1986). Such a questionnaire is useful in identifying actual and potential reinforcers that may be used in conjunction with treatment. There is now a plethora of rating scales, self-report questionnaires, inventories and diary records that facilitate client assessment, ongoing treatment and evaluation of outcomes.

Additional sources of assessment data are: medical information, including obtaining a medical assessment if there is any suspicion of a physiologically based problem or one with medical implications; and records of previous psychological or psychiatric treatment.

TREATMENT

Depending on the specification of goals at the end of the initial behavioural assessment, behaviour therapy offers a range of treatment interventions, including reinforcement procedures, systematic desensitization, exposure and assertive training. Homework assignments are a regular part of behaviour therapy. Behavioural assessment and monitoring take place throughout the course of behaviour therapy.

Most often behaviour therapy treatment is time limited. For instance, a therapist might contract with a client to pursue a treatment plan for two to three months (approximately 8 to 12 sessions) and re-evaluate progress at the end of this period (Wilson, 2008). Antony (2014) writes that, in the majority of studies, behavioural treatment is conducted over a period of 10 to 20 sessions. However, animal phobias are often successfully treated in one session. Therapy lasting from 25 to 50 sessions is also moderately common, though any contact over 100 sessions is rare.

Behaviour therapy sessions vary in length, from the traditional therapeutic hour to 30 minutes or even 15 minutes when specific interventions are in use. Therapy sessions may also be longer than an hour, for instance a therapist-assisted exposure session. Since therapeutic goals have often been stated clearly at the start of therapy, therapist and client can monitor progress in attaining goals and make termination of therapy decisions accordingly.

THE THERAPEUTIC RELATIONSHIP

Behaviour therapists realize that the quality of the therapeutic relationship can significantly influence the success of therapy. They are highly accepting of clients since they view their behaviour as a combination of physical endowment and the effects of experience and of current environmental contexts. Some characteristics of skilled behaviour therapists are that they are concerned, sensitive, warm, sincere, task-oriented, thorough, systematic, flexible and appropriately directive. Frequently, early on in initial sessions, therapists offer clients a rationale for their problems in learning terms along the lines of, since psychological distress results from learning faulty habits, it makes sense to treat it by using scientific knowledge of how habits are made and broken (Wolpe, 1990). Increasingly therapists acknowledge that 'common factors' in the relationship have an impact on the outcomes of therapy.

THERAPEUTIC INTERVENTIONS

Behaviour therapists have a repertoire of interventions that they tailor to assist clients to attain their goals. Where possible, they rely heavily on research findings concerning the effectiveness of an intervention when applied to a particular problem. In those cases where the empirical evidence is insufficiently clear or nonexistent, therapists use clinical acumen and judgement within the framework of behavioural principles.

RELAXATION TRAINING AND SYSTEMATIC DESENSITIZATION

Antony (2014) writes that: 'Although there is evidence supporting systematic desensitization, it is rarely recommended today' (p. 197). However, often the relaxation training part of systematic desensitization is used on its own to reduce the effects of anxiety and stress on the body.

Where behavioural assessments indicate that clients have certain specific anxiety or phobic areas, rather than just general tension, systematic desensitization was often the preferred intervention. Wolpe (1958, 1990; Wolpe and Wolpe, 1988) was the originator of systematic desensitization, a treatment he considered to be based on the reciprocal inhibition principle described earlier in this chapter. Systematic desensitization may be conducted concurrently with other behavioural interventions. It involves three elements: (a) training in deep muscular relaxation; (b) the construction of hierarchies of anxiety-evoking stimuli; and (c) asking the client, when relaxed, to imagine items from the anxiety-evoking hierarchies.

TRAINING IN RELAXATION

Clients may be taught to relax in recliner chairs, or on mattresses or, at the very least, in comfortable upright chairs with headrests. Bernstein and Borkovec (1973) observe that in teaching muscular relaxation there is a succession of events that must be observed with each muscle group. This tension-relax cycle has five elements: (a) *focus*, focusing attention on a specific muscle group; (b) *tense*, tensing the muscle group; (c) *hold*, maintaining the tension for five to seven seconds; (d) *release*, releasing the tension in the muscle group; and (e) *relax*, focusing attention on the letting go of tension and further relaxation of the muscle group. Clients need to learn this *focus-tense-hold-release-relax* cycle so that they may apply it in their homework. Having explained the basic tension-relax cycle, therapists may then demonstrate it by going through the cycle in relation to their own right hand and forearm and at each stage asking their clients to do the same.

Therapists are then likely to take clients through the other muscle groups, demonstrating them as necessary. The 16 muscle groups often used are right hand and forearm; right biceps; left hand and forearm; left biceps; forehead; eyes, nose and upper cheeks; jaw and lower cheeks; neck and throat; chest and shoulders; stomach; right thigh; right calf; right foot; left thigh; left calf; and left foot.

Behaviour therapists differ in the number of sessions they take for relaxation training. Furthermore, clients differ in the speed with which they attain a capacity to relax. Wolpe (1990) taught progressive muscular relaxation in about six lessons and asked his patients to practice at home for two 15-minute sessions per day.

- *Brief muscular relaxation procedures*: When the full muscular relaxation procedures have been learned and clients are able to attain deep relaxation, briefer muscular relaxation procedures may be introduced. Bernstein and Borkovec (1973) provide examples of sequential brief muscular relaxation procedures. One variation is to tense seven muscle groups: the right arm muscles, the left arm muscles and the facial muscles are each tensed as single groups; the neck and throat muscles are tensed as previously; and the chest, shoulder and stomach muscles, the right leg and foot muscles and the left leg and foot muscles are each tensed as single groups. Simultaneous muscular relaxation involves tensing virtually all muscles at once. When ready, brief muscular relaxation procedures should be incorporated into clients' relaxation homework.
- *Mental relaxation*: Often as part of systematic desensitization, clients are encouraged to engage in mental relaxation. Such relaxation usually involves imagining a peaceful scene, such as 'lying in a meadow on a nice warm summer's day, feeling a gentle breeze, watching the clouds'. Frequently, mental relaxation is used after going through a muscular relaxation procedure.

CONSTRUCTING HIERARCHIES

Wolpe (1990) writes: 'An anxiety hierarchy is a thematically related list of anxiety-evoking stimuli, ranked according to the amount of anxiety they evoke' (p. 160). A common way of checking on the anxiety-evoking potential of hierarchy items is to say that zero is a feeling of no anxiety at all, and 100 is the maximum anxiety possible in relation to a particular theme. Thus individual items can be rated according to their positions on this subjective units of disturbance (SUDS) scale. Appropriate hierarchy items can be generated around each theme. During treatment, hierarchy items may need to be re-ordered or reworded, or additional items introduced.

PRESENTING HIERARCHY ITEMS

A desensitization session may start with therapists verbally relaxing clients. When therapists are assured that clients have attained states of deep relaxation, they may start presenting scenes along the lines of 'Now I want you to imagine that you are thinking about exams while revising at your desk three months before exams …'. Therapists start with the least anxiety-evoking scene on hierarchies. Wolpe (1990) used to ask clients to raise their index finger when the scene was clear. Then he would let the scene remain for 5 to 7 seconds and terminate by saying 'Stop the scene'. Next clients would report their SUDS level. After 20 to 30 seconds, clients could be asked to imagine the same scene again. If this caused no anxiety, the therapist could withdraw the scene, possibly spend time further relaxing the client, and move on to the next hierarchy item.

An important assumption underlying systematic desensitization is that once a low anxiety-evoking item, for example ten units, has ceased to cause anxiety, all the other items in the hierarchy become less anxiety-evoking by ten units. Thus the 100-unit item becomes a 90-unit item, and so on. In general, only weak anxiety-evoking stimuli are presented to clients during desensitization sessions. Therapists may work from more than one hierarchy during desensitization sessions. A record is kept of all scene presentations and their outcomes.

EXPOSURE STRATEGIES

Systematic desensitization is a complex treatment presently less used than in the past. Exposure strategies are now increasingly used. In exposure, confrontation with the feared stimulus is direct and continues until the unwanted responses to the stimulus have become reduced. The most common form of exposure is *in vivo exposure*, getting the client to face feared situations in real life. Examples are getting a client who fears driving to practise driving or a client who fears public speaking to do just that repeatedly. If possible, in vivo exposure is likely to be practised in therapy sessions, as well as between sessions for homework.

Though *imaginal exposure* to feared mental imagery was part of Wolpe's systematic desensitization, today imaginal exposure is most likely to be used for clients who tend to suppress and fear their thoughts or mental imagery rather than to reduce fear of an external object or situation. For example clients with post-traumatic stress disorder (PTSD) 'often suppress memories of their trauma (e.g., memories of a sexual assault), and individuals with OCD often suppress intrusive thoughts and images related to their obsessions (e.g., irrational thoughts of harming a loved one)' (Antony, 2014, p. 210).

When using exposure strategies, therapists and clients need to observe certain key principles (Richards, 2007). Since fear does not lessen until it is confronted for a sufficient length of time, exposure to the feared stimulus must be for a long time. Prolonged exposure to the feared stimulus will lead to a gradual reduction in fear over time. Furthermore, the prolonged exposure to the feared stimulus must be repeated. Subsequent confrontations with feared stimuli can lead to a decrease in the initial fear as well as to a more rapid reduction of the fear response. Clients can have further sessions until the reduction in their fear levels both within and between sessions becomes sufficiently reduced and habituated.

In exposure, clients face real-life stimuli that are graded to make up a hierarchy. As they habituate to lower items by means of prolonged and repeated exposures, they work up the hierarchy towards more difficult situations. In those instances, where clients suppress their thoughts and/or it is not possible to use real-life feared stimuli, imaginal exposure may be used.

Systematically graduated real-life exposure can form a central part of the behaviour therapy treatment of agoraphobia (Wilson, 2008). Therapists can accompany clients during the exposure sessions and supply support, encouragement and positive reinforcement. Furthermore, therapists ensure that clients understand the importance of staying in the feared situations until their anxiety decreases. Afterwards, therapists debrief clients about what happened.

ASSERTIVE TRAINING

Often behavioural assessments highlight clients' deficits in the area of assertion. Wolpe (1990) wrote: 'Assertive behavior is the socially appropriate verbal and motor expression of any emotion other than anxiety' (p. 135). An early trend in assertive training was that of standing up for one's rights or what might be termed *oppositional* behaviour. For some time now, assertive training has been extended to include the expression and accurate communication of *affectionate* behaviour, where appropriate. Thus assertive behaviour now encompasses the expression of positive as well as of negative thoughts and feelings (Alberti and Emmons, 2008).

Therapists and clients work together to define what may be appropriate behaviours in specific situations: for instance, asking a boss for a pay rise or a girl for a date. This stage involves the generation and consideration of alternative responses. Additionally, clients may be encouraged to observe effective models. Assertiveness must take into account the styles of individual clients and appropriate assertive behaviour should be as 'natural' for them as possible. Responses that might seem appropriate for therapists may not be appropriate for particular clients. Timing is also important, in that clients should not be encouraged to engage in assertiveness tasks for which they are not ready. Consequently, it may be necessary to construct a hierarchy of progressively more difficult assertion tasks.

Once appropriate responses have been formulated, therapists train clients in assertiveness by means of behaviour rehearsal. Alberti and Emmons (2008) stress that assertive training should not focus only on verbal behaviour, but also on other components such as eye contact, body posture, gestures, facial expression, voice tone, inflection and volume, and fluency and timing of assertion. Therapists need to rehearse and coach their clients in these non-verbal and para-verbal aspects of assertiveness. Behaviour rehearsals can also include rehearsing clients in handling the negative and positive consequences of their assertion as well as in how to handle a variety of situations. Audio- and video-recordings are used by some therapists to provide feedback to clients about their assertive behaviours.

Enactment in real life follows behaviour rehearsal. Clients should be set appropriately difficult assertiveness homework assignments. Monitoring between session assertive behaviour attempts is likely to help them. Feedback from real-life attempts at assertive behaviour indicates the adequacy of the behaviour and where, if necessary, it might be improved.

REINFORCEMENT INTERVENTIONS

Reinforcement interventions aim to modify behaviour by altering its consequences and, as such, reflect operant rather than classical conditioning principles.

IDENTIFYING REINFORCERS

In order to use reinforcement systematically, it is necessary to discover what is reinforcing for individual clients. Ways in which therapists can find out what their clients consider reinforcing include asking them, asking others about them, observing what they say and do in the interview setting, and getting them to observe and monitor themselves outside interviews.

Some self-report questionnaires exist for assessing reinforcers. Cautela (1967a) has devised a *Reinforcement Survey Schedule* to identify possible reinforcing stimuli together with their relative reinforcing values. Another self-report questionnaire is MacPhillamy and Lewinsohn's *Pleasant Events Schedule* (Lewinsohn et al., 1986; MacPhillamy and Lewinshon, 1971). This instrument consists of 320 events and activities generated after an extensive search of possible 'pleasant events'. Subjects rate each item in the schedule on a five-point scale of pleasantness. A shortened version of the *Pleasant Events Schedule* can be derived from those items associated with improved mood for a substantial proportion of people. Lewinsohn and Graf (1973) list 49 such items and suggest that they fall into three categories: social interactional, effects incompatible with depression, and ego supportive, or activities leading to feelings such as adequacy and competence.

BEHAVIOURAL ACTIVATION

Behavioural activation is based on the observation that many clients find it easier to act rather than think themselves out of depression (Martell et al., 2001). It goes beyond Lewinsohn and his colleagues attempts to increase depressed clients' pleasant activities by stating a dual process analysis of depression. Depressed people's ability to feel pleasure reduces and this causes them to withdraw from previously enjoyed activities as these become less positively reinforcing. Along with this, they avoid activities that might be even slightly aversive – for instance contacting others. Thus, they subject themselves both a reduction in positive reinforcement and to negative reinforcement that increases their likelihood of further avoidance and reduces their opportunities for positive experiences still further (Richards, 2007).

Behavioural activation focuses on avoidance as well as on attempting to schedule pleasant activities. Therapists assist clients to schedule a gradually increasing series of activities into their lives in order both to reduce the feelings of aversion and, at the same time, to increase the possibilities for positive reinforcement. Clients are helped to make out hierarchies of items, which reflect both their difficulty and desirability, that they are doing less of due to their depression. Therapists then support clients as they work through their hierarchies, give them feedback and help them to select new activities from their hierarchies.

REINFORCEMENT PROGRAMMES AND TOKEN ECONOMIES

Positive reinforcement is the major method for changing behaviour in applied settings. Positive reinforcement programmes can be used both to increase desirable behaviours and to decrease undesirable behaviours. The second goal can be accomplished by positively reinforcing alternative or incompatible behaviours (Kazdin, 2012).

In designing reinforcement programmes it is particularly important that, when a behaviour is initiated, the reinforcement contingent upon that behaviour is immediate, otherwise its differential effect may be lost. Acquisition of desired behaviours may initially involve reinforcement either of component behaviours or related behaviours and build up to the desired behaviours by successive approximation. Therapists can use continuous reinforcement to establish behaviours initially. Afterwards, they can use intermittent reinforcement, since resistance to extinction is greater if fewer responses are reinforced.

Reinforcement may either be administered directly, by provision of actual reinforcers, or indirectly, by means of tokens which may later be exchanged for reinforcers. Furthermore, clients may be reinforced vicariously by observing models obtain rewards for desired behaviours (Bandura, 1986).

Tokens are tangible conditioned reinforcers that may be exchanged for back-up reinforcers such as prizes, opportunities to engage in special activities, food or other purchases. Token reinforcement programmes need to establish clearly the rules of exchange that specify the number of tokens required to obtain back-up reinforcers (Wilson, 2008). Token economies or token reinforcement programmes have been used with school children, delinquents and hospital patients. Applications of token economies in elementary and secondary school settings have improved students' classroom performance in reading, writing, and arithmetic (Kazdin, 2012).

Kazdin and Bootzin (1972) suggest that extinction of the desired behaviours generally follows removal of token reinforcement. They state that generalization should be planned rather than depended on as an inadvertent consequence of the token economy. Reinforcement programmes and token economies may involve the co-operation and training of significant others in the clients' environments. For instance, therapists may need to work with teachers or parents in devising reinforcement procedures for individuals or groups of children.

TIME OUT AND RESPONSE COSTS

Time out is a procedure frequently recommended by behaviour therapists for use with disruptive children. It involves removal of clients from situations in which they might otherwise be receiving reinforcement. For instance, a child's attention-seeking behaviour in a classroom may be being reinforced by teacher attention and peer approval, neither of which is available when the child is made to leave the classroom for a set period of time. Time out procedures involve a clear instruction, adequate warning that the time out procedure is contingent upon the undesired behaviour and, if this goes unheeded, application of time out in a systematic and unemotional way.

Response costs involve deductions of certain amounts from clients' collections of reinforcers if they perform undesired behaviours. For instance, participants in a token economy may lose some of their tokens. Where possible, response costs should be used in conjunction with positive reinforcement of desirable or alternative behaviours.

HELPING CLIENTS TO OBTAIN REINFORCEMENT

A very important aspect of behavioural treatment may be that of helping clients to increase the number and scope of reinforcers available to them (Cormier, Nurius and Osborn, 2013). Another way of saying this is that, instead of passively relying on others, clients can be helped to identify and actively seek out people, activities and situations that provide the desired reinforcements. Lewinsohn and Libet (1972) assert that a low rate of positive reinforcement is a critical antecedent of depressive behaviours and that improvement is likely to be accompanied by an increase of positive reinforcement.

TRAINING CLIENTS TO USE SELF-REINFORCEMENT

Training clients to use self-reinforcement is often termed a self-control or self-management strategy. It can involve assisting clients to observe their behaviour, set goals for themselves, identify suitable reinforcers, plan graded steps to attain their goals, and specify when to administer consequences (Cormier et al., 2013; Watson and Tharp, 2013). In helping clients to design self-reinforcement programmes, it is important that they perceive both that they have chosen their goals or target behaviours and also that they have the confidence to complete tasks that will bring desired outcomes. Consequently, frequently therapists design self-reinforcement programmes with graded steps to ensure that clients build up their confidence with success experiences. This enhances motivation both initially and later. Some clients may have to build up component skills prior to initiating self-management programmes.

Self-reinforcers can be external or internal. External reinforcers include: (1) self administration of new reinforcers that are outside clients' everyday lives, such as a new item of clothing or a special event; and (2) initial denial of some pleasant everyday experience and later administration of it contingent upon some desired action. Internal reinforcers include self-talk statements such as 'That's great', or 'Well done', or 'I'm glad I made it' that clearly indicate the client's satisfaction with achieving target actions.

STIMULUS CONTROL

Thoresen and Mahoney (1974) indicate that there are two general self-control strategies that clients can use to influence their actions. First they can try modifying their environments to control target actions *prior to* their execution. Second, they can self-administer a reward *following* or *contingent upon* an action or series of actions that achieves either a goal or a subgoal.

Behaviour therapists assist clients to use stimulus control as one form of environmental modification. Stimulus control entails either modifying in advance the stimuli or cues associated with maladaptive responses and/or establishing cues associated with adaptive responses. For example, ways in which behaviour therapists might suggest that people on weight reduction programmes modify their environments to control their food intake include: ensuring that food is placed out of sight and of easy reach; equipping their refrigerators with time locks; only keeping as much food in the house as can be consumed in a short period of time; and, where appropriate, avoiding contact with people associated with excessive eating.

Stimulus control can also be used to enhance adaptive behaviours. For example, students can learn to associate their desks with work if they use them only for that purpose. Some behaviour therapists use stimulus control in treating sleep disorders by having insomniac clients only associate their beds with sleep (Morawetz, 1989).

COVERT SENSITIZATION

Often clients who engage in negative communications/actions deny or rationalize the negative consequences of their behaviour. Therapists can assist clients in gaining greater awareness of the consequences of their negative communications/actions. Covert sensitization, sometimes known as covert conditioning, is an intervention for stopping or lessening clients' unwanted behaviours (Cautela, 1967b). Here therapists administer and assist clients to self-administer aversive consequences in their imaginations: for instance imagining the sight and smell of puking all over themselves if they eat a piece of chocolate cake.

PARTICIPANT MODELLING

Perhaps Bandura's most distinctive contribution to behaviour therapy has been his participant modelling approach (Bandura, Jeffery and Wright, 1974; Bandura, Jeffery and Gadjos, 1975; Cormier et al., 2013). This approach emphasizes in vivo performance of feared tasks, with the consequences generated by successful performance being viewed as the primary vehicle for psychological change. Participant modelling involves a number of stages. First, therapists repeatedly model feared activities, for instance handling snakes or dogs, to show clients both how they can be successfully performed and that the feared consequences do not occur. Second, joint performance with their therapists may enable clients to start engaging in activities that would be too threatening to engage in on their own. Therapists, who function as guides and anxiety inhibitors, use hierarchies of increasingly difficult sub-tasks.

Third, therapists may introduce response induction aids or protective conditions to reduce expectations of feared consequences and thus help clients to perform the desired tasks. For instance, when treating snake phobias, response induction aids might include the model's holding the snake securely by the head and tail, use of protective gloves, and presenting a smaller snake. Fourth, therapists gradually withdraw performance supports to ensure that clients can function effectively without assistance. Fifth, clients may have a period of self-directed performance in which they spend time interacting with the feared object on their own. During the initial period of self-directed performance, therapists may stay in the room with clients, but later withdraw possibly to observe clients behind one-way mirrors. The idea is that clients' confidence is best strengthened by independent achievements in which it is clear that successful consequences are due to their ability to master feared situations on their own.

CASE MATERIAL

With the rise of cognitive behaviourism, it is increasingly difficult to find case material based solely on conditioning assumptions. Case illustrations liberally illustrate Wolpe's (1990) *The Practice of Behavior Therapy*. Wolpe presented vignettes, interview transcripts and also discussed four instructive complex cases: social anxiety, multidimensional automobile phobia, washing compulsion, and reversal of sexual preference.

In *Life Without Fear: Anxiety and its Cure*, Wolpe wrote: 'Complex cases are not at all exceptional; rather, they are the rule' (Wolpe and Wolpe, 1988, p. 95). In this book Wolpe presented some complex cases including: a case of anxiety and depression; fear of marriage; a multifaceted case of depression; fear of being alone based on fear of losing control; an unusual case of male sexual failure; and a many-sided phobia.

Richards (2007) provides a case study whereby he successfully used behavioural activation, with Samina, a depressed 44-year-old woman. Wilson (2008) provides a case study where a therapist, Dr Jones, treated successfully Melissa, a 22-year-old graduate student who had a pattern of binge eating followed by self-induced vomiting which together with her attempts to lose more weight were consistent with buimia nervosa (BN). Treatment included reading a self-help book *Overcoming Binge Eating*, self-monitoring, adopting a regular eating pattern, learning to become more assertive with her boyfriend (she left him and dated someone else developing a caring relationship) and, ultimately, a behavioural experiment in which she stopped all body checking. The final two of 16 sessions focused on relapse prevention.

Antony (2014) provides a case example where the client was a 40-year-old college professor, Simon, who grew increasingly isolated because of his social anxiety. His treatment included five main components: education, cognitive strategies, exposure, reduction of safety behaviours, and social skills training. Sessions 4 to 10 focused on exposure therapy. By the end of treatment Simon reported significant reductions in his anxiety and rarely avoided social situations.

FURTHER DEVELOPMENTS

Traditional or radical behaviour therapy, based on conditioning principles, possibly had its heyday in the 1960s and 1970s. For around 40 years it has been increasingly challenged by cognitive behaviour therapy with its internal cognitive rather than external contextual view of the causation of behaviour. Reitman and Drabman (1997) argue for the value of behaviour therapists valuing the differences between the contextual and the cognitive traditions within their fold. They assert that radical behaviour therapy interventions may turn out to be the treatment of choice for some problems. Indeed, some therapists use either behaviour therapy or cognitive behaviour therapy depending on the client's problem(s).

Behaviour therapy is well represented by associations. In the United States there is the Association for Behavioral and Cognitive Therapies (ABCT); in Britain, the British Association for Behavioural and Cognitive Psychotherapies (BABCP); and in Australia, the Australian Association for Cognitive and Behaviour Therapy (AACBT). In addition, there are active behaviour therapy organizations in many countries of Latin America. Though training in behaviour therapy is widely available, frequently it is more cognitive behavioural rather than behavioural in orientation.

Numerous journals are devoted to behaviour therapy, with two of the most prominent being *Behavior Therapy*, published by the AABT, and *Behaviour*

Research and Therapy. Nowadays, many if not most of the articles in these journals are cognitive behavioural rather than behavioural.

REVIEW AND PERSONAL QUESTIONS

REVIEW QUESTIONS

1. What is meant by classical conditioning?
2. How does Watson view the connection between stimulus and response?
3. What does Skinner mean by each of the following terms?

    (a) *operant conditioning*
    (b) *contingencies of reinforcement*
    (c) *non-intermittent schedules of reinforcement*
    (d) *intermittent schedules of reinforcement*
    (e) *shaping and successive approximation.*

4. Express what Wolpe means by the term reciprocal inhibition.
5. What does the term perceived self-efficacy mean and why is it important?
6. What are the functions of behavioural assessment and how do behaviour therapists collect assessment information?
7. Describe the goals and methods of systematic desensitization.
8. Describe the treatment(s) involving exposure.
9. Describe the goals and methods of assertive training.
10. How can behaviour therapists assist clients in obtaining reinforcement in their daily lives?
11. Describe and illustrate what is meant by participant modelling.

PERSONAL QUESTIONS

1. Practise relaxing yourself for 15 to 20 minutes a day over a period of at least a week. Keep a monitoring log of your relaxation homework. During your relaxation homework cover:

    *   progressive muscular relaxation;
    *   brief muscular relaxation;
    *   mental relaxation; and
    *   if relevant, apply exposure methods to help you manage a feared situation.

2. Pick a specific situation in your life where you consider you could be more assertive. Set yourself verbal and non-verbal behavioural goals for change and self-administer assertiveness training, including rehearsing targeted behaviours, to attain your goals.
3. Design a positive self-reinforcement programme. Specify:

    (a) *your goal in behavioural terms;*
    (b) *how you intend to observe your behaviour, establish a baseline and monitor progress;*
    (c) *the positive reinforcer(s) you intend using;*
    (d) *the precise conditions for self-administering the positive reinforcer(s);*
    (e) *whether and how you intend using graded steps and subgoals to attain your goal; and*
    (f) *a time schedule for your programme.*

5. What is the relevance of the practice of behaviour therapy to how you conduct therapy?
6. What is the relevance of the practice of behaviour therapy to how you lead your life?

ANNOTATED BIBLIOGRAPHY

Pavlov, I. P. (1927) *Conditioned Reflexes: An Investigation of the Physiological Activity of the Cerebral Cortex.* Oxford: Oxford University Press.
In this book Pavlov defines terms such as reflex, describes his experimental laboratory, and gives details of some of his pathfinding experiments into the functioning of the cerebral hemisphere of dogs.

Watson, J. B. (1931) *Behaviorism.* London: Kegan Paul, Trench and Traubner.
This book presents Watson's answer to the question 'What is behaviorism?' and includes his views on conditioning, instincts, thinking, memory, personality and ethics.

Skinner, B. F. (1953) *Science and Human Behavior.* New York: Macmillan.
This book articulates Skinner's ideas on applying the science of behaviour to individuals and groups. In addition, Skinner examines controlling agencies such as government and law, religion, psychotherapy, economic control, and education.

Skinner, B. F. (1957) *Verbal Behavior.* New York: Appleton-Century-Crofts.
Skinner describes his interpretation of language and the uses of language in this book. Verbal behaviour results from the same principles of operant learning as found in other species. Skinner analyses the various controlling relationships in verbal behaviour.

Wolpe, J. (1958) *Psychotherapy by Reciprocal Inhibition.* Stanford, CA: Stanford University Press.
This is Wolpe's seminal book in which he describes his fundamental animal research and its therapeutic applications. The book is a classic in the behaviour therapy literature.

Wolpe, J. (1990) *The Practice of Behavior Therapy* (4th ed.). Oxford: Pergamon Press.
This book describes in detail the author's views on the causes of neurosis, behaviour analysis, and a range of treatment methods including assertiveness training, systematic desensitization and its variations, and operant conditioning. In addition, Wolpe presents some complex cases and provides an evaluation of behaviour therapy.

Bandura, A. (1986) *Social Foundations of Thought and Action: A Social Cognitive Theory.* Englewood Cliffs, NJ: Prentice-Hall.

This huge volume is the definitive statement of Bandura's position. In it he presents a theoretical framework for analysing human motivation, thought, and action from a social cognitive perspective.

Wilson, G. T. (2008) Behavior therapy. In R. J. Corsini and D. Wedding (eds), *Current Psychotherapies* (8th ed.). Belmont, CA: Thomson Brooks/Cole, pp. 223–62.
A chapter by a prominent cognitive behaviour therapist that overviews the theory, practice, development and then current status of behaviour therapy.

Antony, M. M. (2014) Behavior therapy. In D. Wedding and R. J. Corsini (eds), *Current Psychotherapies* (10th ed.). Belmont, CA: Brooks/Cole, pp. 193–229.
A recent chapter overviewing the theory, practice, development and current status of behaviour therapy.

Cormier, S., Nurius, P. S. and Osborn, C.J. (2013) *Interviewing and Change Strategies for Helpers: Fundamental Skills and Cognitive-Behavioral Interventions* (7th ed.). Belmont, CA: Brooks/Cole.
This huge and extremely detailed book presents skills and strategies for major stages of the helping process, including: relationship, assessment and goal setting, strategy selection and implementation, and evaluation and termination.

REFERENCES AND FURTHER READING

Alberti, R. E. and Emmons, M. L. (2008) *Assertiveness and Equality in Your Life and Relationships* (9th ed.). Atascadero, CA: Impact Publishers.
Antony, M. M. (2014) Behavior therapy. In D. Wedding and R. J. Corsini (eds), *Current Psychotherapies* (10th ed.). Belmont, CA: Brooks/Cole, pp. 193–229.
Bandura, A. (1969) *Principles of Behavior Modification*. New York: Holt, Rinehart and Winston.
Bandura, A. (1973) *Aggression: A Social Learning Analysis*. Englewood Cliffs, NJ: Prentice-Hall.
Bandura, A. (1977) *Social Learning Theory*. Englewood Cliffs, NJ: Prentice-Hall.
Bandura, A. (1986) *Social Foundations of Thought and Action: A Social Cognitive Theory*. Englewood Cliffs, NJ: Prentice-Hall.
Bandura, A. (1989) Human agency in social cognitive theory. *American Psychologist, 44*, 1175–84.
Bandura, A. (1997) *Self-Efficacy: The Exercise of Control*. New York: Freeman.
Bandura, A. (2004) Swimming against the mainstream: The early years from chilly tributary to transformative mainstream. *Behaviour Research and Therapy, 42*, 613–30.
Bandura, A. (ed.) (2008) *Self-Efficacy in Changing Societies*. New York: Cambridge University Press.

Bandura, A. (2009) Social cognitive theory goes global. *The Psychologist, 22,* 504–6.

Bandura, A., Jeffery, R. W. and Gadjos, E. (1975) Generalizing change through participant modeling with self-directed mastery. *Behaviour Research and Therapy, 13,* 141–52.

Bandura, A., Jeffery, R. W. and Wright, C. L. (1974) Efficacy of participant modeling as a function of response induction aids. *Journal of Abnormal Psychology, 83,* 56–64.

Bernstein, D. A. and Borkovec, T. D. (1973) *Progressive Relaxation Training: A Manual for the Helping Professions.* Champaign, IL: Research Press.

Cautela, J. (1967a) A Reinforcement Survey Schedule for use in therapy, training and research. *Psychological Reports, 20,* 1115–30.

Cautela, J. (1967b) Covert sensitization. *Psychological Reports, 20,* 459–68.

Cormier, S., Nurius, P. S. and Osborn, C. J. (2013) *Interviewing and Change Strategies for Helpers* (7th ed.). Belmont, CA: Brooks/Cole.

Ferster, C. B. and Skinner, B. F. (1957) *Schedules of Reinforcement.* New York: Appleton-Century-Crofts.

Jones, M. C. (1924) A laboratory study of fear: The case of Peter. *Pedagogical Seminary, 31,* 308–15.

Kazdin, A. E. (2012) *Behavior Modification in Applied Settings* (7th ed.). Long Grove, IL: Waveland Press.

Kazdin, A. E. and Bootzin, R. E. (1972) The token economy: An evaluative review. *Journal of Applied Behavior Analysis, 5,* 343–72.

Lewinsohn, P. M. and Graf, M. (1973) Pleasant activities and depression. *Journal of Consulting and Clinical Psychology, 41,* 261–68.

Lewinsohn, P. M. and Libet, J. (1972) Pleasant events, activity schedules and depression. *Journal of Abnormal Psychology, 79,* 291–95.

Lewinsohn, P. M., Munoz, R. F., Youngren, M. A. and Zeiss, A. M. (1986) *Control Your Depression* (rev. ed). New York: Prentice Hall Press.

MacPhillamy, D. J. and Lewinsohn, P. M. (1971) *Pleasant Events Schedule.* Mimeograph, University of Oregon.

Martell, C. R., Addis, M. E. and Jacobson, N. S. (2001) *Depression in Context: Strategies for Guided Action.* New York: W. W. Norton.

Morawetz, D. (1989) Behavioral self-help treatment for insomnia: A controlled evaluation. *Behavior Therapy, 20,* 365–79.

Pavlov, I. P. (1902/1897) *The Work of the Digestive Glands.* London: Griffin.

Pavlov, I. P. (1927) *Conditioned Reflexes: An Investigation of the Physiological Activity of the Cerebral Cortex.* Oxford: Oxford University Press.

Reitman, D. and Drabman, R. S. (1997) The value of recognizing our differences and promoting healthy competition: The cognitive behavioral debate. *Behavior Therapy, 28,* 419–29.

Richards, D. (2007) Behaviour therapy. In W. Dryden (ed.), *Dryden's Handbook of Individual Therapy* (5th ed.). London: Sage, pp. 327–51.

Skinner, B. F. (1938) *The Behavior of Organisms.* New York: Appleton-Century-Crofts.

Skinner, B. F. (1953) *Science and Human Behavior.* New York: Macmillan.

Skinner, B. F. (1957) *Verbal Behavior.* New York: Appleton-Century-Crofts.

Skinner, B. F. (1958) Reinforcement today. *American Psychologist, 13,* 94–9.

Skinner, B. F. (1969) *Contingencies of Reinforcement.* New York: Appleton-Century-Crofts.

Thoresen, C. E. and Mahoney, M. J. (1974) *Behavioral Self-Control.* New York: Holt, Rinehart & Winston.

Watson, D. L. and Tharp, R. G. (2013) *Self-Directed Behavior: Self-modification for Personal Adjustment.* (10th ed.). Belmont, CA: Brooks/Cole.

Watson, J. B. (1903) *Animal Education.* Chicago: University of Chicago Press.

Watson, J. B. (1913) Psychology as the behaviorist views it. *Psychological Review, 20,* 158–77.

Watson, J. B. (1914) *Behavior.* New York: Holt.

Watson, J. B. (1919) *Psychology from the Standpoint of a Behaviorist.* Philadelphia. Lippincott. 2nd ed. 1924, 3rd ed. 1929.

Watson, J. B. (1928) *The Psychological Care of the Infant and Child.* New York: W. W. Norton

Watson, J. B. (1931) *Behaviorism.* London: Kegan Paul, Trench and Traubner.

Watson, J. B. and Raynor, R. R. (1920) Conditioned emotional reactions. *Journal of Experimental Psychology, 3,* 1–14.

Wilson, G. T. (2008) Behavior therapy. In R. Corsini and D. Wedding (eds), *Current Psychotherapies* (8th ed.). Belmont, CA: Thomson Brooks/Cole, pp. 223–62.

Wolpe, J. (1958) *Psychotherapy by Reciprocal Inhibition.* Stanford, CA: Stanford University Press.

Wolpe, J. (1976) *Theme and Variations: A Behaviour Therapy Casebook.* Oxford: Pergamon Press.

Wolpe, J. (1990) *The Practice of Behavior Therapy* (4th ed.). Oxford: Pergamon Press.

Wolpe, J. and Lang, P. J. (1969) *Fear Survey Schedule.* San Diego, California: Educational and Industrial Testing Service.

Wolpe, J. and Wolpe, D. (1988) *Life Without Fear: Anxiety and Its Cure.* Oakland, CA: New Harbinger Publications.

RATIONAL EMOTIVE BEHAVIOUR THERAPY

9

INTRODUCTION

When first developed in 1955, Albert Ellis termed his approach rational therapy (RT). In 1961, he changed the name to rational emotive therapy (RET). In 1993, Ellis (1993a) further changed the name to rational emotive behaviour therapy (REBT). What Ellis meant by 'rational' is cognition that is effective in self-helping rather than cognition merely empirically and logically valid. He wished that he had used the word cognitive from the start since many people narrowly restrict the word rational to mean intellectual or logico-empirical. People's rationality rests on judging soundly which of their desires or preferences to follow and, therefore, is based on thoughts, emotions and feelings (Ellis, 1990).

Ellis introduced 'behaviour' into his approach's name for the sake of accuracy. From its start, the approach has strongly emphasized behaviour along with cognition and emotion. Ellis wrote: 'So, to correct my previous errors and to set the record straight, I shall from now on call it what it has really always been – rational emotive behavior therapy (REBT)' (Ellis, 1993a, p. 258).

Ellis (Ellis and Ellis, 2014) distinguish between general REBT and preferential REBT. General REBT is virtually the same as cognitive behaviour therapy and aims to teach clients rational or appropriate behaviours. Preferential REBT emphasizes a profound philosophic change. At the same time as including general REBT, it also teaches clients how to dispute irrational ideas and self-defeating behaviours and how to use powerful cognitive-emotive-behavioural methods as self-helping skills. This chapter focuses on preferential REBT, which from now on will be referred to as rational emotive behaviour therapy (REBT).

ALBERT ELLIS (1913–2007)

Albert Ellis was born in in 1913 in Pittsburgh, Pennsylvania, and grew up in New York City. He had a brother and sister who were 19 months and 4 years younger than him, respectively. His travelling salesman father was physically absent much of the time. His Jewish mother was benignly neglectful and 'was much more immersed in her own pleasures and ego-aggrandizing activities than she was in understanding and taking care of her children' (Ellis, 1991a, p. 3). Aged twelve, he discovered that his parents had divorced. Afterwards, although living fairly close, his father came round to visit less than once a year.

Another childhood misfortune was that, aged four and a half, Ellis almost died of nephritis and, until the age of nine, was hospitalized eight times – once for a period of ten months. When young Ellis also had psychological as well as physical problems. He writes: 'It took me almost two decades to talk myself out of that crap of being ingratiating. I was born and reared to be shy and scared. Throughout my childhood and teens I had a real social phobia. I viewed public speaking as a fate worse than public masturbation' (Ellis 1997a, p. 69). Nevertheless, he did very well at school. However, his difficult childhood helped him to 'become a stubborn and pronounced problem solver' (Ellis, 2004a, p. 63). For instance, aged 19, he overcame his terror of public speaking by persisting in giving political talks over a period of three months. Furthermore, to overcome his shyness with women, he forced himself to talk to a hundred girls in a row in the Bronx Botanical Gardens (Ellis, 1997a). As with public speaking he was able to make a 180-degree change in how he performed. These experiences were important precursors to REBT because Ellis discovered the great value of reasoning and self-persuasion in changing his dysfunctional feelings and actions (Ellis, 2010).

Beginning his writing career at the age of 12 Ellis turned out a large number of stories, essays and comic poems and received as many rejection slips too. In 1934, despite his early ambition to become the Great American Novelist, Ellis received a bachelor's degree in business administration from the City University of New York. Early occupations included a business matching trousers to still suitable jackets and being personnel manager of a gift and novelty firm. Ellis devoted much of his spare time to writing fiction. Partly because of difficulties getting his fiction published, Ellis turned exclusively to writing non-fiction, especially focusing on the 'sex-family revolution'.

Discovering that he liked therapy as well as writing, in 1942 Ellis entered the clinical psychology programme at Columbia University, receiving a master's degree in 1943. Soon after obtaining this, he began a small private practice in psychotherapy and marital and sex therapy. In 1947, Ellis received his doctorate from Columbia University with a thesis on personality questionnaires, an earlier thesis on love having been censored before it got off the ground. After his doctorate, Ellis' ambition was to become an outstanding psychoanalyst and so he completed a training analysis with an analyst from the Karen Horney group and began to practise psychoanalysis under his teacher's direction. From 1948 to 1952, Ellis worked for the New Jersey Department of Institutions and Agencies, mainly as chief psychologist of the New Jersey State Diagnostic Center and then as chief psychologist of the entire state of New Jersey. He also continued his private practice in New York.

For some time, Ellis had employed active-directive methods in his psychotherapy, marital and sex therapy. Also, before undergoing analysis, Ellis had worked through many of his own problems by reading and practising the philosophies of Epictetus, Marcus Aurelius, Spinoza and Bertrand Russell, and so he started teaching clients the philosophic principles that had helped him.

Between 1953 and 1955, Ellis increasingly rebelled against psychoanalysis and began calling himself a 'psychotherapist' rather than a 'psychoanalyst'. He wrote: 'I finally wound up, at the beginning of 1955, with RET' (Ellis, 1991a, p. 15). He gave his first paper on it at the American Psychological Association's annual meeting in Chicago on August 31, 1956.

In 1959 he founded The Institute for Rational Living, Inc., now called the Albert Ellis Institute, as a non-profit-making scientific and educational organization to teach the principles of rational living. Afterwards Ellis donated all his royalties and income from clients and workshops to the Institute. In 1964, the Institute bought a large New York townhouse. However, in 2005, Ellis was dismissed from all duties at the Institute and also from its board, of which he was president. In January 2006, the State Supreme Court reinstated him to the board. However from 2005, he could no longer teach in the Institute and so, with his wife Debbie Joffe Ellis, he rented space in the building next door and continued teaching (Ellis and Ellis, 2011).

Ellis was a man of boundless energy, probably a genetic inheritance from his 'two highly energetic parents who both lived reasonably long lives and were active until the last day of their lives' (Dryden, 1989, p. 545). He spent most of his time working. When he was over 83 years old, in a week where he was mainly in New York 'I usually see individual and group clients from 9:30 am to 11pm – with a couple of half hour breaks for meals, and mostly for half hour sessions with individual clients. So during each week I may see over 80 individual clients and over 40 more group clients' (Ellis, 1997b, p. 17). In addition, Ellis held his 7.30–9.00 pm Friday night workshop where he interviewed people in public. On Saturday night and Sunday, he worked on books, writing, researching, attending to correspondence and various other things. Until just before his death, Ellis gave numerous workshops and seminars in America and overseas and used the travel time to write and read.

Ellis' work was his main priority. However, he had 'had two marriages, two living together arrangements (LTAs), many passionate love experiences, and scores of (relatively brief) sexual affairs from my twenty-fourth to my ninetieth year' (Ellis, 2004a, p. 216). In 1964, he met 24-year-old Janet Wolfe and lived with her in an open relationship from 1965 to 2002. During this period he commented that his life 'would be greatly bereft of laughter, warmth, and intimacy without her' (Dryden, 1989, p. 541). Ellis and Janet had no children, since they regarded it as unfair that, due to his work, he would not have much time to spend with them.

Ellis had to work around physical disabilities to attain and maintain his phenomenal productivity level (Ellis, 1997b). From age 19, he was hampered by chronically fatiguable eyes. The upshot of this was that he read rarely for more than 20 minutes and often kept his eyes shut during therapy sessions. Aged 40 Ellis was diagnosed as having full-blown diabetes and had to find ways of minimizing the inconvenience attached to this condition: for instance eating small meals about ten times a day – even three or four times in the middle of the night. In his late 60s Ellis' hearing began to deteriorate and by his mid-70s he had two hearing aids that, even when in good working order, had their limitations. Later in life, Ellis also had to suffer from a bladder that was easily filled but slow to empty, so that peeing became a more lengthy process. However, efficient as ever, Ellis found ways of combining peeing with other activities. In June 2003, Ellis had a colonectomy, and after that had nursing care around the clock. He was 'also greatly helped by my assistant and dearest friend, Debbie Joffe, with whom I enjoy an extremely close and loving connection' (Ellis, 2004a). In 2004, Ellis married Australian psychologist Joffe, whom in the dedication to his autobiography he calls 'The greatest love of my whole life, my whole life' (Ellis, 2010). Ellis died on July 24, 2007, in the arms of his wife.

Ellis' work has been controversial. His REBT ideas challenged psychoanalytic and Rogerian orthodoxies. His ideas on sex challenged conventional morality. In addition, Ellis was not afraid to speak his mind. However, over the past 50 years or so, cognitive behavioural ideas became increasingly fashionable and Ellis regarded himself as the father of REBT and the grandfather of cognitive behaviour therapy.

Ellis was always a prolific writer, even before publishing in the area of psychology. He published over 800 papers in psychological, psychiatric, and sociological journals and anthologies. In addition, Ellis authored or edited over 75 books and monographs including: *Reason and Emotion in Psychotherapy* (1962), *A Guide to Rational Living* (Ellis and Harper, 1997), *The Practice of Rational Emotive Behaviour Therapy* (Ellis and Dryden, 1997), *Rational Emotive Behaviour Therapy: A Therapist's Guide* (Ellis and MacLaren, 2004), *Ask Albert Ellis?: Straight Answers and Sound Advice from America's Best-Known Psychologist* (2003b), *Rational Emotive Behavior Therapy: It Works for Me – It Can Work for You* (2004a), *The Myth of Self-Esteem: How Rational Emotive Behavior Therapy Can Change Your Life Forever* (2005), *All Out: An Autobiography* (2010) and *Rational Emotive Behavior Therapy* (Ellis and Ellis, 2011). Apart from humour, the guiding principles of Ellis' (1991a) work were 'Science, efficiency, honesty, revolutionism, and passionate skepticism' (p. 30).

THEORY

BASIC CONCEPTS

FUNDAMENTAL AND PRIMARY GOALS

Virtually all humans have three fundamental goals (FG): to survive, be relatively free from pain, and to be reasonably satisfied or content. As subgoals or primary goals (PG), humans want to be happy: when by themselves; gregariously with other humans; intimately, with a few selected others; informationally and educationally; vocationally and economically; and recreationally (Ellis, 1991b). Furthermore, people live in a social world and self-interest requires putting others a close second (Ellis and Dryden, 1997).

REBT sees humans' basic goals as preferences or desires rather than needs or necessities. Rational living consists of thinking, feeling and behaving in ways which contribute to the attainment of the chosen goals, whereas irrationality consists of thinking, feeling and behaving in ways which block or interfere with their attainment. Living rationally consists of striking a sensible balance between short-range and long-range hedonism, or between the pleasures of the here-and-now and the longer-range pleasures gained through present discipline. Thus rationality may be defined as the use of reason in pursuit of chosen short-range and long-range hedonism.

EMOTION, COGNITION AND BEHAVIOUR

In an early paper on 'Rational psychotherapy' Ellis (1958) proposed three fundamental hypotheses. First, thinking and emoting are closely related. Second, thinking and emoting are so closely related that they usually accompany each other, act in a circular cause-and-effect relationship, and in certain (though hardly all) respects are essentially the same thing, so that one's thinking becomes one's emotion and emoting becomes one's thought. Third, both thinking and emoting tend to take the form of self-talk or internalized sentences and, for all practical purposes, the sentences that people keep saying to themselves are or become their thoughts and emotions. Thus people's internal self-statements are capable of both generating and modifying their emotions. In addition, Ellis stressed that thinking and emotion interact with behaviour. For instance, people usually act on the basis of thoughts and emotions and their actions influence how they think and feel.

HEALTHY AND UNHEALTHY EMOTIONS

REBT is not an approach of no emotions; rather it emphasizes healthy or appropriate emotions. Negative emotions may be either healthy, unhealthy or mixed (Ellis and MacLaren, 2004). Unhealthy emotions are those that interfere with achieving a sensible balance between short-range and long-range hedonism. For instance, it may be appropriate for people in an alien and difficult world to be fearful, cautious or vigilant so that they may take any necessary steps for realistic protection. However, anxiety and overconcern are unhealthy emotions, since they are based on irrational thinking or unsane beliefs and, in fact, may interfere with or block attaining goals. Similarly, hostility may have a healthy and an unhealthy part. The healthy part of hostility involves acknowledging discomfort or annoyance as a basis for action designed to overcome or minimize the irritation. The unhealthy part of hostility may involve blaming others and the world in such a way as to block effective action and possibly generate even more unhappiness for oneself and further hostility from others.

Pleasurable and enjoyable emotions can also be healthy or unhealthy. For example, people may feel excessive pride when praised by others because they possess an unsane belief about the necessity of others' approval. A sensible balance between achieving short-range and long-range hedonistic goals involves a balance between achieving short-range and long-range appropriate pleasurable emotions.

TWO BIOLOGICAL TENDENCIES

In all people a tension exists between two opposing biological creative tendencies (Ellis and Ellis, 2014). On the one hand, people have innate tendencies to create, develop and actualize themselves as healthy-goal-attaining human beings. They have a great potential to be rational and pleasure producing. On the other hand, they have innate tendencies to create, develop and implement irrational cognitions, unhealthy emotions and dysfunctional behaviours. REBT theorizes that often people are 'biologically predisposed to strongly, passionately, and rigidly construct and hold on to their disturbance-creating musts and other irrational beliefs' (Ellis, 1993b, p. 199). Thus, they possess a huge potential to be destructive of themselves and of others, to be illogical and continually to repeat the same mistakes.

Ellis believed that all the major human irrationalities exist in virtually all humans regardless of culture and educational level. Human fallibility has an inherent source. The fact that people seem so easily conditioned into dysfunctional thinking and behaviour and that these are so hard to modify are both viewed as evidence for an innate tendency to irrationality (Ellis, 1980). People's failure to accept reality almost always causes them to manifest the characteristics of emotional disturbance. However, differences exist in genetic predisposition to irrationality.

People are not only born and raised to be irrational, they also have some degree of free choice in how much they make themselves emotionally disturbed. For example, when growing up, Ellis' younger sister chose to make the worst of her childhood conditions (Ellis, 1991a, 2004a). However, people can use their biological tendency to have some degree of free choice to help as well as to damage themselves. First, they can choose to think differently and act more effectively about what is going on. Second, because they possess the capacity to think about how they think, people can choose to acquire and maintain the cognitive skills for containing and counteracting their tendencies to irrationality.

ABC THEORY OF PERSONALITY

Ellis had an ABC theory of personality to which he added D and E to cover change and the desirable result of change. In addition, the letter G can be placed first provide a context for people's ABCs.

1. **G** Goals, both fundamental and primary;
2. **A** Adversities or activating events in a person's life;
3. **B** Beliefs, both rational and irrational;

4.	**C**	Consequences, both emotional and behavioural;
5.	**D**	Disputing irrational beliefs;
6.	**E**	Effective new philosophy of life.

Just as cognitions, emotions and behaviours interact with each other and are virtually never entirely pure, so do the ABCs of REBT. Goals (G), activating events (A), beliefs (B) and consequences (C) 'all seem to be part of a collaboration with one another' (Ellis, 1991b, p. 145).

RATIONAL AND IRRATIONAL BELIEFS

Ellis (Ellis and Ellis, 2014; Ellis and McLaren, 2004) divided belief systems into two basic categories: rational beliefs and irrational beliefs.

- *Rational beliefs (rBs)* are healthy, productive, adaptive, consistent with social reality, and generally consist of preferences, desires and wants. When thinking rationally about adversities (As) that either block or sabotage their goals (G), people engage in preferential thinking. Preferential as contrasted with demanding thinking involves either explicitly and/or tacitly reacting with their belief systems (Bs) in realistic ways and experiencing appropriate emotional and enacting goal-oriented behavioural consequences (Cs).
- *Irrational beliefs (iBs)* are rigid, dogmatic, unhealthy, maladaptive, mostly get in the way of people's efforts to achieve their goals, and are comprised of demands, musts and shoulds. When thinking irrationally about adversities (As) that either block or sabotage their goals (Gs), people engage in demanding thinking.

In reality, people's responses to adversities (As) mainly result from a combination of rational and irrational beliefs, though often one becomes the 'winning' mode. Ellis (Ellis and Ellis, 2014) observed that a person's self-defeating behaviour usually follows from the interaction of A (Adversity) and B (Belief about A) and that C (disturbed Consequences) generally follow the formula A x B = C. Box 9.1 contrasts ABCs for preferential and demanding thinking.

BOX 9.1 ABCS OF PREFERENTIAL AND DEMANDING THINKING

PREFERENTIAL THINKING

- A   Adversity or activating event perceived as blocking or sabotaging goals
- B   Belief system involving preferential thinking: 'I prefer to have my important Goals unblocked and fulfilled!'
- C   Consequences: emotional – frustration and unhappiness; behavioural – avoiding or trying to eliminate the adversity.

(Continued)

(Continued)

DEMANDING THINKING

A   Adversity or activating event perceived as blocking or sabotaging goals
B   Belief system involving demanding thinking: 'I absolutely must have my impor-
     tant Goals unblocked and fulfilled, but I don't have to get my preference met!'
C   Consequences: emotional – anxiety and/or excessive hostility; behavioural – self-
     defeating overreaction or underreaction to the adversity.

DEMANDING BELIEFS AND THEIR DERIVATIVES

Irrational belief systems often operate on at least four levels: primary demanding belief(s), derivatives of the primary demanding belief(s), secondary
demanding belief(s), and derivatives of the secondary demanding belief(s).

1. *Primary demanding belief(s)*: The primary demanding belief or beliefs involves people's
   main demands and commands in relation to the adversity. Ellis (1980) has coined the
   term 'musturbation' to indicate that these beliefs are usually expressed as musts, shoulds,
   ought tos, have-tos and got-tos. He has identified three major clusters of irrational beliefs
   that create inappropriate emotional and behavioural consequences:

   (a) I must do well and win approval for all my performances.
   (b) Others must treat me considerately and kindly.
   (c) Conditions under which I live must be arranged so that I get practically everything I
        want comfortably, quickly and easily.

2. *Derivatives of the primary demanding belief(s)*: People usually create highly unrealistic
   and over-generalized inferences and attributions as derivatives of their musturbatory
   and absolutistic demands. Three common irrational derivatives often accompany their
   musturbatory beliefs (Ellis, 1991b; Ellis and MacLaren, 2004):

   (a) *Awfulizing* 'If I don't have my important Goals unblocked and fulfilled as I must, it's
        awful!' In this context, 'awful' means totally bad or more than bad.
   (b) *I can't-stand-it-itis* 'If I don't have my important Goals unblocked and fulfilled as I
        must, I can't stand it!'
   (c) *Damning oneself and others* 'If I don't have my important Goals unblocked and ful-
        filled as I must, I'm a stupid, worthless person.' 'Others are bad people for blocking
        my important goals.'

3. *Secondary demanding belief(s)*: Once people make themselves miserable at C, they tend to
   exacerbate their misery by making themselves miserable about being miserable. In other
   words, they transform the negative consequence (C) of the primary demanding belief ABC
   into an adversity or activating event (A) for a secondary level demanding belief ABC. Box 9.2
   provides an example of such chaining. Frequently, people make themselves anxious about
   being anxious, depressed about being depressed, guilty about feeling guilty, and so on.

BOX 9.2   ABCS FOR PRIMARY AND SECONDARY DEMANDING BELIEFS

PRIMARY ABC

A1   'I did poorly on my job today.'
B1   'Since I must do well, isn't that horrible!'
C1   'I feel anxious, depressed and worthless.'

SECONDARY ABC

A2(C1)   'I feel anxious, depressed and worthless.'
B2   'Since I must not feel anxious, depressed and worthless, isn't that horrible!'
C2   'I feel even more anxious, depressed and worthless.'

---

4. *Derivatives of secondary demanding belief(s)*: People can now choose to create and derive awfulizing, I can't-stand-it-itis, and damning oneself and others from their secondary as well as their primary musturbatory beliefs. They now have two negative consequences and their derivatives for the price of one. Also, in an ever spiraling cycle, they can intensify the unhappiness they create with their beautiful hang-ups.

EGO DISTURBANCE AND LOW FRUSTRATION TOLERANCE

Ellis (1988) proposed that neurotic problems can be grouped in two main headings according to the three main musturbatory beliefs and their derivatives: (1) ego disturbance (self-damning) and (2) low frustration tolerance (LFT) or discomfort disturbance. *Ego disturbance* arises from the belief that 'I *must* do well and win approval for all my performances' because it leads to people thinking and feeling that they are inadequate and undeserving persons when they do not do as well as they must. He regarded this as godlike grandiosity since people demand that they be special, perfect, outstanding, and superhuman.

Low frustration tolerance arises from the grandiose belief that people think they are so special that conditions must be easy and satisfying for them. They then progress to holding either or both the irrational beliefs that 'Others must treat me considerately and kindly' and 'Conditions under which I live *must* be arranged so that I get practically everything I want comfortably, quickly and easily.' Awfulizing and I can't-stand-it-itis are derivatives of such beliefs. Basically in ego disturbance and low frustration tolerance what people are insisting is that 'I must have an easy life, I must be perfect, and people and conditions should always cater to *me, me, me, me* !' (Ellis, 1988, p. 119).

ACQUISITION

How do people acquire rational and irrational beliefs? Ellis' emphasis was much more on how people sustained their irrationality than on how they initially acquired it. The past cannot be undone and it is counterproductive to excessively focus on how people feel about the past. Ellis advised people to 'Forget your "Godawful" past' (Ellis, 1988, p. 69). He considered that psychology has focused on how people originally become illogical and that this by no means indicates how people maintain or perpetuate their illogical behaviour, or what they should do to change it. Consequently, Ellis' treatment of the development of irrational cognitions and musturbatory beliefs was cursory. However, three main strands may be identified: biology, social learning and choosing irrational cognitions. Since, biological or innate tendencies to irrationality have been previously discussed, the main focus here is on social learning and choosing.

SOCIAL LEARNING

Given that human beings are born with a distinct proneness to irrationality, this tendency is frequently exacerbated by their environment, especially early in life, when people are most vulnerable to outside influences. Ellis saw humans as basically highly suggestible, but acknowledged innate differences. Irrational ideas, which once might have been appropriate in view of the helpless state of the child, are acquired for a number of reasons (Ellis, 1991b; Ellis and Ellis, 2014; Ellis and Harper, 1997). First, young children are unable to think clearly, in particular insisting on immediate rather than on future gratification and being unable accurately to distinguish real from imagined fears. However, as they grow older, normal children become less insistent on having their desires and demands immediately gratified. Second, frequently childish demands can be assuaged by magic, for instance parents saying that a fairy godmother will satisfy them. Third, children are dependent on the planning and thinking of others and their suggestibility or conditionability is greatest when they are very young. Fourth, parents and members of the family group themselves have irrational tendencies, prejudices and superstitions which they inculcate into their children. Fifth, this process is exacerbated by the indoctrinations of the mass media. Lastly, cultures and religions can impart irrational, self-defeating and society-defeating views.

CHOOSING IRRATIONAL COGNITIONS

The process of acquiring irrationality is not simply a matter of reacting to how others behave. Humans largely create their own emotional disturbances through not developing and exercising their capacity for rational choice. Negative social learning experiences do not in themselves lead to people acquiring irrational cognitions. Many people who have had negative upbringings choose not to disturb themselves unduly. Still others, with or without support, work through their problems. The reverse is also true. Favourable social learning experiences do not in themselves lead to rational cognitions. Many people who have had favourable upbringings develop significant irrational beliefs. While social learning experiences influence people for good or ill, they still have the capacity to choose how they react to them. Ellis and Dryden concluded: 'Thus, the REBT theory of acquisition can be summed up by the view that as humans we are not disturbed simply by our experiences; rather we bring our ability to disturb ourselves to our experiences' (1997, p. 21).

MAINTENANCE

Why do people persist in holding their irrational beliefs and their derivatives? People not only become irrational, they stay irrational. In fact, often they become even more irrational. Staying rational in an irrational world is a struggle. Once acquired, people tend to repeat their irrational beliefs again and again and again. Ellis continually stressed that people have strong tendencies to re-indoctrinate themselves with their self-defeating ideas. People's irrational beliefs do not continue because they were once 'conditioned' and so now hold them 'automatically'. Instead, people still, here and now, actively reinforce them, and their present active self-propagandizations and constructions keep these beliefs alive (Ellis and Ellis, 2014).

REASONS CONTRIBUTING TO HUMANS STAYING IRRATIONAL

Following are some reasons that contribute to humans staying irrational, often at great personal cost to themselves, others and to society.

BIOLOGICAL TENDENCIES

Human's biological tendencies to irrationality do not go away with maturation, but are part of their life-long genetic inheritance. Ellis stressed that humans: 'are powerfully predisposed to unconsciously and habitually prolong their mental dysfunctioning and to fight like hell to give it up' (1987, p. 365). Rather than strike a realistic balance between short-range and long-range hedonism, humans mostly embrace short-range hedonism. This preference for the pleasures of the moment is a main source of resistance to change.

EMOTIONAL CONTRIBUTIONS

Absolutistic musts are often 'hot' cognitions that have a strong evaluative-feeling component in them. Such cognitions are held strongly and powerfully and, as such, can be difficult to change. In addition, people then not only develop derivatives of their primary irrational beliefs, but also secondary irrational beliefs and their derivatives. As a result they raise the level of their emotionality and then may think even more irrationally. They may fail to see how upset they are. Furthermore, they are now so upset that they fail to reality-test and dispute their irrational beliefs in ways that they might otherwise do. Instead of making people better the consequences of irrational beliefs make them worse.

INSUFFICIENT SCIENTIFIC THINKING

People continue to disturb themselves because they fail to think scientifically about what is going on in the world. To think scientifically people need constantly to observe and check the 'facts' so see the extent to which they are 'true' and whether or not they have changed. Scientific thinking is flexible and requires evidence to uphold or negate viewpoints. Also, the scientific method is sceptical that the universe has any absolute standards of 'good' and 'bad'. Science does not have absolute rules in regard to human behaviour.

REINFORCING CONSEQUENCES

People can emotionally, cognitively and behaviourally reinforce their irrational beliefs. Emotionally, absolutistic musturbatory beliefs lead to strong negative feelings – such as severe anger and depression – that make them seem true. Cognitively and behaviourally, people reinforce their beliefs in different ways according to the belief. For instance, people who must be socially approved avoid taking social risks, and by doing so, convince themselves that it is too difficult and dangerous to do otherwise. Furthermore, when avoiding social situations, they may feel a sense of emotional relief. The combination of their emotional, cognitive and behavioural reactions makes them more rather than less socially anxious.

EMPHASIZING ONE'S 'GODAWFUL' PAST

Ellis stated as an REBT insight: *'Your early childhood experiences and your past conditioning did not originally make you disturbed. You did'* (Ellis, 1988, p. 70). People maintain their emotional disturbance by looking for causes in their pasts. Focusing on the past interferes with people focusing on the present in which they still may be upsetting themselves with the same irrational beliefs with which they upset themselves in their pasts. People cannot undo their pasts, but they can change their presents and futures. Furthermore, often focusing on the past leads to an overemphasis not only on the past relative to the present, but also to an overemphasis on other people's behaviour relative to one's own.

UNREALISTIC BELIEFS ABOUT CHANGE

People's low frustration tolerance can be both cause and consequence of unrealistic beliefs about working to change, with or without professional assistance, their thoughts, feelings and actions. Irrational beliefs about change include (Ellis, 1987, 1993b):

- 'I must be able to change with little discomfort, work and practice on my part.'
- 'Changing how I think, feel and behave shouldn't be so hard.'
- 'I must change quickly and profoundly.'
- 'When changing, I must not have any setbacks.'

OTHER COGNITIVE FACTORS

Following are some other factors and processes whereby people maintain and worsen their irrational beliefs and emotional disturbances (Ellis 1987; Ellis and Dryden, 1997).

- *Naivety*: People can have and hang on to hugely naive personal theories about the nature of their psychological problems and how they are maintained.
- *Ignorance*: People, including therapists, can consider that it is statistically normal and healthy for them to be unnecessarily upset. They fail to distinguish between healthy and unhealthy thoughts, feelings and behaviours.
- *Stupidity*: Many people are too unintelligent to work effectively on their emotional problems. They fail to gain sufficient insight into the fact that that they create their own disturbances.
- *Unperceptiveness*: Without therapy, many disturbed people rarely look at their irrational beliefs and ideas and how these create and drive their upset-ness. Even when pointed out to them in therapy, many disturbed people are still incapable of grasping how they upset themselves.
- *Rigidity*: Even when they acknowledge their self-defeating irrational beliefs, many people rigidly stick to their musturbatory beliefs and their derivatives, for instance awfulizing and I can't-stand-it-itis. Some such people may be psychotic or have borderline personality disorders, whereas others are simply rigid thinkers.
- *Defensiveness*: Humans are prone to avoid facing and dealing directly with their problems. They use various methods of distorting and denying problems, for instance rationalization and avoidance.
- *Pollyannaism and indifference*: Some people who are prone to extreme anxiety and suffer from a serious illness, such as heart disease or cancer, may deal with it by denying its seriousness. Sometimes, such defensive manoeuvres may help people to cope. However, on many occasions, such thinking may block efforts to attain physical health and psychological change.
- *Changing the situation*: For many, the easy way out is to change the situation, for instance, obtain a divorce, rather than try to change themselves and then consider whether or not to change the situation. For every neurotic who really tries to have a fundamental shift in the way they think, there are probably ten times as many trying to *feel* better by changing the situations in which they behave self-defeatingly rather than to *get* better. This ratio holds true whether or not people come for therapy.
- *Other palliative means*: People and their would-be helpers resort to many palliative means of dealing with emotional disturbances rather than get to the root of them. Many clients and potential clients use distraction techniques such as progressive relaxation, biofeedback, meditation and yoga. Some try superficial positive thinking. Many people lose themselves in

political, religious and mystical cults. Short-term feel-good remedies like alcohol and drugs are very common. In brief, many disturbed people seek low-level and palliative remedies rather than more rigorous and long-lasting solutions.

INSUFFICIENTLY CHALLENGING BELIEFS THROUGH ACTION

People may reinforce their beliefs through unwillingness to change their actions. Their 'tried and true' self-defeating ways may bring short-term relief at the expense of long-term gain. An Ellis insight is: *'You can change irrational beliefs (iB's) by acting against them: by performing behaviours that contradict them'* (1988, p. 109). Why then don't people change their actions to challenge their beliefs? One reason is that they may not have insight into their irrational beliefs, their derivatives, and their emotional and behavioural consequences. Another reason is that people resist the risk and effort involved in taking action. Some people may not be clear on what to do. Still others may know what to do, but lack the skills, confidence and support to do it. Another category is people who change their actions, but lack the staying power to maintain them, especially when faced with difficulties and setbacks. Such people suffer from low frustration tolerance.

THERAPY

THERAPEUTIC GOALS

Earlier in this chapter, I presented Ellis' GABCDE outline. There are two meanings to E depending on whether the change goals of REBT are inelegant or elegant.

INELEGANT CHANGE GOALS

Ellis wrote: 'Inelegant change largely consists of some kind of symptom removal' (1980, p. 13). Here, at D, REBT targets the cognitions, emotions and behaviours that accompany self-defeating feelings, like anxiety and depression, and dysfunctional behaviours, like avoiding social and public speaking situations. The goal of focused or inelegant REBT is that of focused or inelegant change. Here the letter E stands for an effective new philosophy focused on one or more specific symptoms or problems. Effectiveness in relation to these symptoms can be cognitive (similar to rational beliefs), emotional (healthy feelings), and behavioural (desirable behaviours).

ELEGANT CHANGE GOALS

In contrast to inelegant change, elegant change involves clients with disturbances making 'a profound ideational and philosophic change – which means that it tries to help them acquire several core attitudes that they can use to undisturb themselves in a large variety of situations, and not merely with the emotional-behavioral problem with which they mainly came to psychotherapy' (Ellis, 2003a, p. 233). In elegant change, E goes further than an effective new philosophy that supports the removal of specific symptoms to assist clients to develop and implement an effective philosophy of life. Ellis wrote: 'To do this, clients need to acknowledge how often and how strongly they escalate their healthy goals, desires, and preferences into arrogant and grandiose *must*-urba-tion – and apply themselves to anti-*must*urbatory thinking' (1997c, p. 337). Thus E stands for the goal of effective new philosophies for specific symptoms in inelegant REBT and for the goal of an effective philosophy of life (which includes effective new philosophies for specific symptoms) in elegant REBT.

As part of teaching anti-*must*urbatory thinking, Ellis actively encouraged practically all his clients to achieve three highly important cognitive-emotional-behavioural states or goals (Ellis, 1999a, 2003a; Ellis and Ellis, 2011).

- *Unconditional self-acceptance (USA)*: Clients can always choose to accept themselves just because they are alive and human, whether or not they perform well or are approved of by others.
- *Unconditional other acceptance (UOA)*: Whatever other people do and however abomina-bly they act, clients can choose to accept the sinner, though not their sins, to try to help them behave better, and to refuse to damn them as people.
- *Unconditional life acceptance (ULA)*: Otherwise known as high frustration tolerance (HFT), unconditional life acceptance means that clients can choose to acknowledge that their desires are not needs, adversities are not awful but can be highly inconvenient, they can stand what they do not like, and 'long-range hedonism, or striving for today's pleasures, without neglecting tomorrow's, will often get them more of what they want and less of what they dislike' (Ellis, 1999a, p. 39).

PROCESS OF THERAPY

Right from the start, therapists show clients that REBT is an active-directive structured therapy focusing on helping clients not only to feel better, but by changing their thinking and behaviour, to get better. Orientation or induction can be by way of pre-therapy demonstrations, brief explanatory lectures at the start of therapy, and using clients' problem material to illustrate the application of REBT (Ellis and Dryden, 1997).

Before commencing therapy some REBT therapists like clients to fill out a basic biographical information form that also elicits information about their present-ing problems (see Ellis and Dryden, 1997, pp. 88–95). In addition, therapists may ask clients to fill out a personality data form which asks clients questions about their feelings in the following areas: acceptance, frustration, injustice, achieve-ment, worth, control, certainty and catastrophizing (1997, pp. 36–9).

Clients are encouraged to focus on specific problems right from the start. Early in therapy Ellis frequently read out the client's answer to item 23 in the biographical information questionnaire which asks: 'Briefly list (PRINT) your present main complaints, symptoms and problems'. Then clients were asked to discuss what problem is most bothersome. Probably the main form of assessment in REBT is that which comes from having a number of sessions with clients and working with the material that they share. Towards the end of the initial phase of REBT, both therapist and client should have an understanding of the client's main emotional and behavioural problems and have started to prioritize these to provide a structure for their future work together.

The middle phase of REBT is focused on therapists adopting an educational approach to teaching clients how to strengthen their rational beliefs and weaken the irrational ones. This phase of REBT has two main agendas: helping clients solve their particular emotional and behavioural problems and teaching them the skills of identifying and solving problems. In general, in addition to focusing on what clients have been most bothered about during the previous week, therapists encourage them to work through a consistent problem before moving on to the next. Homework tasks are assigned and particular attention is paid to what the client has learned or failed to learn between sessions so that blocks to the learning process can be addressed. Frequently, clients are asked to fill out REBT self-help forms as part of homework assignments. Hard and persistent challenging of irrational beliefs tends to be a prominent feature of the middle phase. REBT 'realistically and unromantically now says: Yes, strongly persuade and push your clients to strongly persuade themselves in the direction of their main goals and preferences and against sabotaging their own purposes' (Ellis, 2003a, p. 238).

The main object of the end phase of REBT is to help clients become their own therapists. Termination may take place not when clients have worked through all their problems using REBT skills, but when they feel confident that they can use these skills to address the remaining problems on their own. Therapists work towards termination either by decreasing the frequency of sessions or by negotiating a specific termination date. During the end phase, therapists can work with clients to anticipate problems and difficulties and articulate how they might use their REBT skills to deal with these problems. Most REBT therapists schedule follow-up sessions to monitor client progress.

REBT is committed to assisting clients to maintain their changes. However, Ellis (1988) acknowledged the likelihood of backsliding. Right from the start, clients are taught that they can only change and maintain change with work and practice. Throughout therapy, homework assignments are used to help clients build skills for both outside and after therapy. When clients find themselves backsliding, they are told to go back to the ABCs and see what they did to fall back into their old patterns. Then they are encouraged to forcefully dispute (D) these irrational beliefs. They are advised to try again and again until they genuinely replace their irrational beliefs with their effective new philosophies (E).

Most often therapists see clients for weekly individual sessions. Ellis' own therapy sessions often lasted for 30 minutes. Clients normally have 5 to 50 sessions. Brief therapy of 1 to 10 sessions is used for clients who have specific problems or for those only prepared to stay in therapy for a short time (Ellis, 1996). Individuals who are not too generally disturbed can usually attain the inelegant change of symptom removal in brief therapy. Preferably, individuals with severe problems should come for individual and/or group therapy for at least 6 months so that they can practise what they learn.

REBT can be used with most kinds of clients, ranging from those who are mildly disturbed to juvenile delinquents, borderline personality disorders, psychotics when they have some contact with reality and individuals with higher grade mental deficiency. Normally, Ellis did not consider REBT suitable for clients who were out of contact with reality, in a highly manic state, seriously autistic or brain injured, and in the lower ranges of mental deficiency. He often referred seriously disturbed clients for medication in addition to REBT.

REBT is significantly more effective with mildly disturbed clients and with those who have a single major symptom, say sexual inadequacy, than with strongly disturbed clients. Therapists find it much more difficult to assist the latter to change since REBT theory hypothesizes that the causes of musturbatory thinking and emotional disturbance are largely innate.

THE THERAPEUTIC RELATIONSHIP

In REBT, the main role of the therapist is that of an authoritative, but not authoritarian, teacher who strives to impart to clients self-helping skills conducive to thinking rationally, feeling appropriately and behaving effectively so that they can attain their goals. REBT practitioners often employ a fairly rapid-fire active-directive-persuasive-philosophic methodology. In most instances, they quickly pin clients down to a few basic dysfunctional beliefs (Ellis and Ellis, 2014).

What kind of a therapeutic relationship best supports this active-directive teaching role? Therapists try to build rapport with clients by using empathic listening, including reflecting feelings. Ellis and Dryden (1997) distinguished between *affective* empathy, understanding how clients feel, and *philosophic* empathy, understanding the philosophies or thinking underlying these feelings. Therapists attempt to offer both kinds of empathy. In addition, therapists offer clients unconditional other acceptance (UOA), accepting them as fallible human beings and not judging the goodness or badness of their personhood against predetermined moral standards. However frequently, if appropriate, therapists will share their reactions to clients' negative behaviours.

REBT therapists do not show undue warmth to most of their clients. They are wary of colluding in clients' dire needs for approval. They try to encourage clients to confront their own problems and assume responsibility for finding their own warmth and happiness rather than seeking it from therapists. Often clients perceive REBT therapists as warm and caring because of their commitment to their welfare and tolerance for all individuals.

Particularly during early sessions, therapists do most of the talking. They do not hesitate to confront clients with how they contribute to their own distress.

They forcefully dispute and debate their clients' illogical thinking as well as helping clients to do this for themselves. They freely share their opinions and self-disclose, so long as this is not detrimental to clients. Furthermore they use humour, but never at their clients' expense, since they consider that many of them take themselves and their problems far too seriously. Therapists also use humour to attack disturbance-producing ideas.

A distinction exists between REBT content and the therapist's style of working with clients. Ellis' therapeutic style, like that of many of his followers, was hard-hitting and forceful. However, Ellis might well have gone more slowly and gently before doing any vigorous disputing when working with clients who suffered from extreme traumas, such as rape or child abuse. Other REBT practitioners, either with specific clients or with all of their clients, choose varying degrees of passive and gentle styles.

THERAPEUTIC INTERVENTIONS

DETECTING IRRATIONAL BELIEFS AND THEIR DERIVATIVES

Therapists as teachers detect clients' irrational beliefs, their musturbations, and their derivatives – for instance awfulizing. Furthermore, they teach clients how to do this for themselves. In order to relinquish demandingness, it helps if clients' can acknowledge that they may possess this characteristic. Ellis taught them his ABC system. Within the ABC system, irrational beliefs can be traced cognitively, emotionally and behaviourally. Cognitively, irrational beliefs can be detected through overt or implicit signs of demandingness. In particular, Ellis looked for 'musts', 'shoulds', 'oughts', 'have tos' and 'got tos' that signal clients' musturbatory absolutistic beliefs. In addition, he looked for explicit and implicit phrases such as 'That is horrible!' and 'I can't stand it' that indicate derivatives of possessing primary and secondary irrational beliefs.

Emotionally, irrational beliefs are signalled by unhealthy feelings, such as panic and depression. Behaviourally, self-defeating actions offer clues to irrational beliefs. Sometimes the cognitive, emotional and behavioural clues are obvious to both therapists and clients. On other occasions, though obvious to therapists, clients may resist acknowledging the evidence. In still other instances clients may hold irrational beliefs in subtle and tricky ways that make them seem natural (Ellis, 1987). Such beliefs can challenge therapists' powers of detection.

DISPUTING IRRATIONAL BELIEFS AND THEIR DERIVATIVES

Acknowledging musts and their derivatives is insufficient for them to disappear. Instead, therapists and clients combine to fight them by disputing them. The technique of disputing is the most typical and perhaps the most often used method of REBT. Disputing involves challenging and questioning unsubstantiated hypotheses that clients hold about themselves, others and the world. In most instances, REBT therapists quickly pin clients down to a few central irrational ideas and their derivatives that they then challenge and dispute. In addition, they teach clients how to dispute their own beliefs. Cognitions, feelings and behaviours interact in how people create and maintain irrational beliefs. Therefore, when disputing irrational beliefs and their derivatives, therapists are likely to be more effective if they work in all three of the cognitive, emotional/experiential and behavioural modalities rather than in one or two. However, no modality is entirely pure or free from the others.

COGNITIVE INTERVENTIONS

SCIENTIFIC QUESTIONING

Disputing may be approached using either a didactic or a Socratic style. In a didactic or lecturing style, therapists can provide explanations and illustrations. In a Socratic or scientific questioning approach, through a series of leading questions therapists attempt to pinpoint where clients' thinking, feeling and behaving is becoming problematic. Such questions are not only for therapists to ask clients, but for clients to learn to ask themselves. When practising disputing, it is very important that clients do so outside of stressful situations to give them the chance to build up and fine-tune their skills for the actual situations.

Box 9.3 illustrates four areas of cognitive disputing (Ellis and MacLaren, 2004).

BOX 9.3   FOUR AREAS OF COGNITIVE DISPUTING

FUNCTIONAL DISPUTES

Functional disputing aims to point out to clients that their beliefs may be interfering with their attaining their goals. Typical questions are:

- 'Is it helping you?'
- 'How is continuing to think this way (or behave, or feel this way) affecting your life?'

EMPIRICAL DISPUTES

Empirical disputing aims to help clients evaluate the factual components of their beliefs. Typical questions are:

- 'Where is the evidence that you must succeed at all important tasks?'
- 'Where is the proof that it is accurate?'
- 'Where is it written?'

(Continued)

(Continued)

LOGICAL DISPUTES

Logical disputing aims to highlight illogical leaps that clients make from desires and preferences to demands when thinking irrationally. Typical questions are:

- 'How does it follow that just because you'd like this thing to be true and it would be very convenient, it *should* be?'
- 'How is it logical that because you sometimes *act* badly that makes you a *bad person*?'

PHILOSOPHICAL DISPUTES

Philosophical disputing aims to address the meaning of and satisfaction in life issues. Often clients get so focused on identified problems that they lose perspective on other areas of life. A typical question might be:

- 'Despite the fact that things will probably not go the way you want some/most of the time in this area, can you still derive some satisfaction from your life?'

The desired cognitive outcome of disputing specific irrational beliefs and their derivatives is a sound set of preferential beliefs or effective new philosophies (E) related to each belief. Desirable emotional and behavioural effects should stem from and interact with the effective new philosophies. For clients seeking elegant change, the desirable effect of learning how to dispute irrational beliefs is an effective new philosophy that can be applied both now and in future. Box 9.4 provides an ABCDE example, which includes disputing and its effects (Ellis, 1988).

BOX 9.4   AN ABCDE EXAMPLE OF COGNITIVE DISPUTING

- **A** I go for an interview and fail to get the job.
- **B** 'I must never get rejected.'

  - o 'How awful to get rejected!'
  - o 'I can't stand the rejection!'
  - o 'This rejection makes me a rotten person'

- **C** Undesirable emotional consequences: depression, worthlessness, anxiety, anger.

   Undesirable behavioural consequences: Refusing to go for other job interviews. Functioning poorly on job interviews through anxiety.

- **D** 'Why must I never get rejected?'

  o 'Why is it awful to get rejected for a job?'
  o 'Why can't I stand this rejection?'
  o 'How does this rejection make me a rotten person?'
  o 'Why must I always do poorly on job interviews?'

- **E** 'I'd prefer to have got this job, but there is no evidence that I absolutely must have it.'

  o 'Nothing makes it awful to get rejected, though I find it highly inconvenient.'
  o 'I can stand rejection, though I'll never like it.'
  o 'Rejection never makes me a rotten person, but a person with some unfortunate traits.'
  o 'I don't always have to do poorly on job interviews, especially if I try to learn from my errors.'

  Illustrative emotional effect: feeling sorrowful, but not depressed.
  Illustrative behavioural effect: I went for some more job interviews.

RATIONAL COPING STATEMENTS

Therapist and client can formulate rational coping statements. This step is usually taken after forceful disputing of irrational beliefs, but sometimes it can accompany such disputing. Some coping statements can be simple encouragements: for instance, 'I can accomplish this task' or 'I don't have to get upset in these situations'. Rational coping statements can also address areas of irrational thinking: for example, statements such as 'I'd prefer to have got this job, but there is no evidence that I absolutely must have it' and 'Nothing makes it awful to get rejected, though I find it highly inconvenient' illustrated in area E of Box 9.4.

DISCUSSION

Therapists can discuss with clients various aspects of their irrational thinking. For instance, with Roger a 24-year-old computer programmer afraid of public speaking, Ellis (1991e) discussed the harm of self-rating and how he could choose to unconditionally accept himself whether or not he failed at speaking and whether or not he was anxious about failing and showed his anxiety to others.

COGNITIVE HOMEWORK

Clients need repeatedly to challenge their irrational beliefs and to practise their disputing skills both to learn them and also to reinforce their new rational philosophies. REBT uses various homework techniques to develop disputing skills.

- *Recordings of sessions*: Therapists encourage clients to record sessions and listen to each one several times.
- *Self-help forms*: Clients are encouraged to fill out self-help forms. Therapists check the forms to see how accurately clients dispute their irrational beliefs. For instance in Sichel and Ellis' (1984) form, clients identify an activating event (A) and the consequences or conditions (C) they would like to change. Then the form consists of three columns. In the first column, clients circle which of 13 irrational beliefs (B), for instance 'I MUST do well or very well!' and 'People MUST live up to my expectations or it is TERRIBLE!' lead to their consequences (C). In addition, they can add other relevant irrational beliefs. In the second column, there is space for them to dispute (D) each circled irrational belief. In the third column, they write in effective rational beliefs (E) to replace their irrational beliefs. After the columns there is a space (F) where they can write in feelings and behaviours experienced after arriving at their effective rational beliefs. The form ends with the following self-statement about the necessity of work and practice: 'I WILL WORK HARD TO REPEAT MY EFFECTIVE RATIONAL BELIEFS FORCEFULLY TO MYSELF ON MANY OCCASIONS SO THAT I CAN MAKE MYSELF LESS DISTURBED NOW AND ACT LESS SELF-DEFEATINGLY IN THE FUTURE' (Sichel and Ellis, 1984, p. 2).

  Another self-help form is known as DIBS (Disputing Irrational Beliefs). DIBS consists of six questions about: the belief I want to dispute, whether the belief can be rationally supported, existing evidence for the belief, existing evidence against the belief, the worst that could happen to me if I never achieved what I wanted in respect to the belief, and good things that might happen if I never achieved what I wanted (Dryden and Ellis, 1986). A further self-help form is Dryden and colleagues' self-help form that takes clients through the ABCDE sequence (Dryden, Walker and Ellis, 1992; Ellis and Dryden, 1997).
- *Reminder cards*: Clients can write out rational coping statements on 3 x 5 inch cards and repeat them at various times between sessions.
- *Referenting*: Referenting is a term for asking clients to do a cost benefit analysis in which they list the real advantages and disadvantages of changing their irrational thoughts and behaviours.
- *Practising REBT on others*: Encouraging clients to practise talking their friends and relatives out of their disturbances.
- *Visualizing*: Clients can be shown how to visualize themselves competently performing situations that they currently fear.
- *Bibliotherapy*: Assigning clients self-help books to read, for instance Ellis (1999b, 2003b), Ellis and Crawford (2000) and Ellis and Harper (1997). Ellis (1993d) is keenly aware of the advantages and disadvantages of self-help materials.
- *Self-help recordings*: Ellis made innumerable audio-cassettes, including *Solving Emotional Problems* (Ellis, 1982), *How to be Happy though Human* (1984) and *How to Stop Worrying and Start Living* (1987b). In addition, clients can watch videotapes of therapists working with clients in areas such as coping with anger and overcoming low frustration tolerance. Many clients find listening to cassettes and observing videotapes to be helpful.

PROBLEM SOLVING

Clients bring their goals (G) to the activating events and adversities (A) in their lives. These goals present many practical or reality problems for them to try to solve: for instance, obtaining a good education, finding a mate, getting a job and succeeding at work. Clients have a choice about whether they solve these reality problems or choose to upset themselves about them. If clients upset themselves, then they have an emotional problem about their reality problem. In such cases, therapists can assist them to detect and actively dispute the relevant irrational beliefs. Sometimes it is better that clients do not address practical difficulties until they have worked through related emotional difficulties. For instance, an individual or couple might defer a decision to divorce until they have given themselves sufficient chance to see whether or not, with a lessening of their irrational beliefs, they might happily live together.

Therapists willingly assist clients to solve reality problems. However, where necessary, they also insist on vigorously detecting and disputing accompanying irrational beliefs. In assisting problem solving, therapists help clients to state problems and goals clearly, generate and evaluate alternative strategies, outline the steps to attain goals, identify resources and supports, and develop the requisite practical skills for success.

EMOTIVE/EXPERIENTIAL INTERVENTIONS

REBT therapists use emotional/experiential interventions to supplement and reinforce cognitive interventions (Ellis and MacLaren, 2004). Such interventions include the following.

- *Rational emotive imagery*: In rational emotive imagery (REI), clients are encouraged to imagine one of the worst activating event or adversities (A) that could happen to them, for instance, rejection by someone whose approval they really want (Ellis, 1993f; Ellis and MacLaren, 2004). They vividly imagine this adversity occurring and bringing a host of problems into their life.

  Then they are encouraged to get in touch with the undesirable negative emotional consequence triggered by this adversity (A) – for instance, anxiety, depression, rage, self-hatred or self pity – and really, really feel it (C1). They should spontaneously feel what they feel and not what they are supposed to feel. Once they feel unhealthily upset at C1, they should hold on to this feeling for a minute or two. Then, keeping the same adversity (A) in their imagination, they should work on changing their disturbed negative feeling to a prescribed healthy negative feeling consequence (C2), such as sorrow, disappointment, regret, frustration, irritation or displeasure. The way to do this is by telling themselves strongly and repetitively sensible rational beliefs or coping statements: for example, 'Yes, they really did treat me shabbily and unfairly, which I wish they wouldn't have done. But there is no reason why they must treat me fairly, however *preferable* that would be ...' (Ellis, 1993f, p. 9). Clients should persist with their imagery and rational statements until they change their unhealthy feeling (C1) to a healthy negative feeling (C2) – it usually takes only a few minutes. They should have the homework assignment of carrying out this imagery procedure daily for about 30 days for each disturbed feeling they are trying to change.
- *Forceful disputing*: Forceful disputing may be performed both by therapists on clients and by clients on themselves (Ellis, 1993e). Since, many irrational beliefs involve hot cognitions that possess a large emotional component, they require forceful and vigorous disputing. Often therapists need to strongly argue, persuade and point out the

shaky logic of their clients' beliefs. Weak or moderately strong disputing may be insufficient. Ellis showed Roger, the computer programmer, how to create strong anti-worrying statements about public speaking and say them to himself forcefully: for example 'I NEVER, NEVER, NEVER have to speak well or unnervously in public, though it would be nice if I did!' (Ellis, 1991e, p. 454). In addition, Ellis worked out with Roger a dialogue with himself in which he recorded some of his potent irrational beliefs, such as 'I'm a nervous slob who deserves to be mute rather than risk making a fool of myself in public!' and in which he vigorously, forcefully and heatedly disputed them. Clients can make, and remake more powerfully, such recordings for themselves as homework. Then they can play them back to themselves, their therapists and, if in therapy groups, to the other group members.

- *Role playing*: Ellis uses role playing as a way of showing clients what their false ideas are and how they affect relating to others. In role playing, therapists place clients in simulated situations and offer assistance in thinking more effectively in them. For instance, Roger role played giving a difficult talk in front of Ellis and the therapy group he had joined as an adjunct to individual sessions. When Roger appeared anxious during the role-play, Ellis stopped the performance to let Roger ask himself 'What am I telling myself right now to *make* myself anxious? And what can I do right now to think and feel away this anxiety?' (Ellis, 1991e, p. 454).
- *Reverse role playing*: Reverse role playing is another REBT forceful disputing technique. Client and therapist switch roles, so clients are now in a position to dispute actively their own irrational beliefs, which the therapist holds on to as strongly as the client did in earlier sessions. For example, Ellis role played Roger tenaciously holding on to some of his irrational beliefs so that Roger could practise forcefully attacking them (Ellis, 1993e).
- *Unconditional acceptance*: The therapist's basic acceptance of them as people helps clients feel and think that they are acceptable, despite any negative characteristics.
- *Humour*: The judicious use of humour can help reduce clients' irrational beliefs and self-defeating behaviours to absurdity. Therapists frequently exaggerate clients' nutty ideas and use 'various kinds of puns, witticisms, irony, whimsy, evocative language, slang, and deliberate use of sprightly obscenity ...' (Ellis, 1980, p. 26). For example, Ellis said to Roger, his public speaking phobia client: 'You really should feel ashamed of avoiding making speeches. Every other person your age speaks fluently and has no anxiety. What a unique jerk you are!' (Ellis, 1991e, p. 454). Encouraging clients to sing to themselves rational humorous songs and telling amusing anecdotes are further methods to counteract clients' tendencies to take themselves, others and the world too seriously.

BEHAVIOURAL INTERVENTIONS

As with emotional/experiential interventions, REBT therapists use behavioural interventions to supplement and reinforce cognitive interventions. Ellis doubted whether people ever truly change their irrational beliefs until they act many times against them. When young, Ellis suffered from severe fears of public speaking and meeting new women. He forced himself to repetitively engage in activities, giving political talks and talking to women on a park bench in the Bronx Botanical Garden, that challenged his fears. In both instances his actions helped rid him of his irrational fears (Ellis, 1997a, 2004a, 2010). Following are some REBT behavioural interventions.

- *Assignments that challenge demandingness*: Clients who have musturbatory beliefs about approval and derivatives of these beliefs about the awfulness of rejection may be encouraged to ask someone for a date or force themselves to socialize. Simultaneously they convince themselves that it is not awful, but only inconvenient to get rejected. Clients who have perfectionist beliefs may have the assignment of deliberately making a real attempt to speak badly in public.

  Clients are encouraged to do their assignments *repetitively*. For instance, Roger the speech anxious client, was asked to speak in public as often as he could, once or twice a week (Ellis, 1991e). Often clients are asked to do their assignments *floodingly*, staying in situations they perceive as highly dangerous until they see that their 'danger' is largely imagined. For instance, clients afraid of riding on buses or underground trains are urged to do this immediately, many times a day in rush hours, if that is what they most fear. Concurrently, in all instances where clients dispute their musturbatory beliefs behaviourally, they can dispute them cognitively too.

- *Shame attacking exercises*: Ellis hypothesizes that ego anxiety is highly related to feelings of shame, guilt, embarrassment and humiliation. Consequently, the more people confront the irrational beliefs behind these feelings, the less they are likely to disturb themselves. Clients are encouraged to do things in public that they regard as particularly shameful or embarrassing. Examples are yelling out the stops on elevators, buses or underground trains or asking for sex-related items in loud voices in chemist shops.

  After explaining the principle of shame attacking exercises, REBT therapists can negotiate exercises with clients. The purpose of these exercises is to prove that these behaviours in themselves are really not shameful and that they can be done with relative comfort and self-acceptance. In addition, clients are urged to disclose more about what they perceive, or what they perceive others' perceive, as shameful. Box 9.5 provides an example of a shame attacking exercise (Ellis, 1996, pp. 91–4).

BOX 9.5   EXAMPLE OF A SHAME ATTACKING EXERCISE

THE THERAPIST

Albert Ellis

THE CLIENT

Chana, who was anxious about test-taking, kept procrastinating on her studies, and refused to take some important subjects at school because she knew that taking them would entail several tests during the term. Chana was afraid of people finding out how poorly she did on tests.

THE SHAME ATTACKING EXERCISE

Chana chose the exercise of asking strangers for a dollar bill. Ellis instructed Chana, when asking strangers for dollar bills, to work on possible feelings of humiliation and embarrassment and then choose not to make herself feel unashamed and unembarrassed.

(Continued)

(Continued)

During the exercise

At first Chana felt very nervous and tongue-tied about going up to a stranger. However, she reminded herself that she did not need the stranger's approval and, by the third time she tried it, she really began to feel shameless and, by the fifth time, started enjoying the exercise.

After the exercise

As a result of the exercise Chana saw that she could do shame attacking exercises with people who knew her in which she talked about her test-taking problems. As part of this process, Chana developed the effective new philosophy: 'I don't need their god-damned approval. Let them think what they think!'

- *Skills training*: The distinction between behavioural skills and cognitive skills is imprecise. Always, when therapists assist clients with behavioural skills – for instance assertion and communication skills – they train clients cognitively in disputing the accompanying irrational beliefs and derivative self-statements. Sometimes, clients are asked to seek additional training experiences to acquire relevant skills. Ellis thought that speech anxious Roger showed insufficient assertion skills at work, for instance not refusing to do presentations when genuinely unprepared. Ellis encouraged Roger to attend a six-week assertion course at his Institute as well as take a five-month public speaking course at a local college (Ellis, 1991e).
- *Use of rewards and penalties*: REBT therapists use rewards and penalties to encourage clients to do homework and implement self-change programmes (Ellis, 1980; Ellis and Dryden, 1997). For instance, every time Roger filled out an RET Self-Help Report or gave a public speech, he would reward himself by listening to one of his favourite CDs. Whenever he failed to carry out an assignment he would talk to his boring aunt for 30 minutes. Two doses of this excruciating penalty cured Roger of not doing assignments! (Ellis, 1991e).

OVERCOMING RESISTANCE

When clients resist following therapy procedures and doing homework assignments, they mainly do so because of the following irrational beliefs (Ellis, 1986a): (1) 'I *must* do well at changing myself.'; (2) 'You (the therapist and others) *must* help me change.'; and (3) 'Changing myself *must* occur quickly and easily.' Stemming from such beliefs (iB), resisters have negative feelings consequences, for instance depression self-pity, and behavioural consequences, such as procrastination and withdrawal. In addition, they employ derivatives of irrational beliefs, such as awfulizing. The main REBT approach to resistant clients is to teach them to find and forcefully dispute the main irrational beliefs contributing to their resistance.

Therapists can encourage resistant clients to use rational coping statements, for instance 'Therapy doesn't have to be easy. I can, in fact, enjoy its difficulty and its challenge' (Ellis, 1986a, p. 262). In addition, therapists can ask clients to list the disadvantages of resisting and the advantages of working at therapy and then regularly reviewing and thinking about these lists. Furthermore, some resistant clients can be helped by proselytizing REBT and using it on friends and relatives.

CASE MATERIAL

Ellis was conscientious about providing case demonstrations of REBT in action, only some of which are mentioned here. Ellis presented a case example containing verbatim transcripts of the first, second and fourth sessions with a 23-year-old woman who came to therapy because she was self-punishing, impulsive and compulsive, afraid of males, had no goals in life, and was guilty about her relationship with her parents (Ellis, 1971, Ellis, 2008).

Ellis provided a verbatim transcript, plus commentary, of his conducting a first session of REBT brief therapy with Ted, a 38-year-old African-American, married 20 years, with two children who became panicked whenever he took the train to work or back to his office and whenever he thought about having intercourse with his wife (Ellis, 1996). Another verbatim transcript case example is that of the first fifteen minutes of an initial interview Ellis conducted with a 25-year-old single woman, Sara, who worked as the head of a computer programming section in her firm and who without any traumatic or violent history, was very insecure and self-denigrating (Ellis and Ellis, 2014). Ellis also discussed Sara's overall treatment of a further six sessions of individual work, followed by 24 weeks of REBT group therapy and one weekend of a rational encounter marathon group.

A further verbatim transcript case example is that of Ellis working with a woman therapist who volunteers to bring up problems of feeling inadequate as a therapist and as a person. Ellis and Dryden then reviewed the transcript and analysed its REBT aspects (Ellis and Dryden, 1997). In yet another case examples of REBT, though this time without transcripts, Ellis illustrated the cognitive, emotive and behavioural methods he used during therapy with Jane, a 27-year-old woman afflicted with severe social and work anxiety (Ellis and Dryden, 1997).

Ellis may also be seen conducting therapy. An early example is his work with Gloria in the *Three Approaches to Psychotherapy* film series (Ellis, 1965). In addition, videos of Ellis and other prominent REBT therapists conducting sessions are available. For example, Ellis made a videotape in which he conducted therapy with a woman dealing with guilt over her husband's suicide. In another videotape, entitled *Dealing with Addictions*, Ellis interviewed a 32-year-old man with low frustration tolerance, short-term hedonism and polyabuse. Ann Vernon provides a good example of how REBT looks in practice in the DVD *Rational Emotive Behavior Therapy Over Time* (Vernon, 2011).

FURTHER DEVELOPMENTS

Other applications of REBT include group therapy and marathons either along with individual counselling or instead of it (Ellis, 1992, Ellis and Dryden, 1997). In group REBT, members are taught to apply detecting and disputing irrational beliefs on one another (Ellis and Ellis, 2014). They also get practice at attacking their ego disturbance irrational beliefs through disclosing material that they perceive as risky. In addition clients in groups, while working on assertion and other communication skills, can partake in role-plays.

Ellis had a major interest in the application of REBT to marital, couples and family relationship problems (Ellis, 1986b, 1991c, 1991d, 1993c, 2005; Ellis and Crawford, 2000; Ellis and Dryden, 1997). Therapists usually see marital or love partners together, listen to their complaints, and then teach them that even though their complaints may accurately describe behaviour at A, their upsetness at C is not justified. In particular, work focuses on musturbatory beliefs generating hostility. Also, frequently, therapists teach partners compromising and relationship skills. In family REBT, tolerance for oneself and others, independent of how obnoxious specific behaviours may be, is repeatedly taught to both parents and children.

Ellis is possibly the most influential English-speaking psychological educator of the twentieth and early twenty-first century in terms of helping ordinary people learn how to overcome their emotional disturbances and become more self-actualizing. Through his books and cassettes, he made a major contribution to educating the public in America and elsewhere on how to live more effectively. He also influenced numerous other writers of self-help books.

REBT is practised widely throughout the world, with institutes or centres established in Britain, Australia, the United States, France, Germany, Holland, Italy, India, Israel and Mexico. Ellis concluded that REBT is what its name implies: rational and emotive, realistic and visionary, empirical and humanistic. Such an approach befits humans in all their complexity (Ellis and Ellis, 2014).

REVIEW AND PERSONAL QUESTIONS

REVIEW QUESTIONS

1. Why does Ellis now call his approach rational emotive behaviour therapy?
2. Describe the differences between healthy or appropriate and unhealthy or inappropriate emotions.
3. What does Ellis consider to be the biological basis of personality?
4. Give an example of Ellis' ABC theory where B represents

   (a) demanding musturbatory thinking
   (b) preferential thinking.

5. Critically discuss Ellis' ideas about the derivatives of irrational beliefs.
6. Discuss the roles of social learning and free choice in acquiring irrational beliefs.
7. Describe the contribution of each of the following factors to maintaining, and possibly strengthening, irrational beliefs:

   (a) biological tendencies
   (b) emotional contributions
   (c) insufficient scientific thinking
   (d) reinforcing consequences
   (e) emphasising one's 'Godawful' past
   (f) unrealistic beliefs about change
   (g) insufficiently challenging beliefs through action.

8. What are the differences between inelegant and elegant therapy goals?
9. Outline the process of REBT individual therapy.
10. What is the nature of the therapist–client relationship in REBT?
11. Give at least one example of each of the following ways of disputing irrational beliefs: functional, empirical, logical and philosophical. Apart from scientific questioning, what other cognitive interventions do REBT therapists use?
12. Describe emotional/experiential interventions used in REBT.
13. Describe behavioural interventions used in REBT.
14. Critically discuss the issue of overcoming resistance in REBT.

PERSONAL QUESTIONS

1. Identify at least two of your irrational beliefs based on absolutistic demanding thinking in relation to each of the following:

   (a) yourself
   (b) others
   (c) the conditions under which you live.

2. For one of the irrational beliefs you identified above state

   (a) how you acquired it
   (b) how you maintain it.

3. From your own life, give an example of each of the following:

   (a) the ABCs of rational thinking
   (b) the ABCs of irrational thinking.

4. Choose one of your irrational beliefs (B) that you wish to change. How could you dispute (D) it by:

   (a) cognitive methods?
   (b) emotive/experiential methods?
   (c) behavioural methods?

   What new effective new philosophy (E) would you arrive at?

5. What relevance, if any, has the theory and practice of rational emotive behaviour therapy for how you conduct therapy?

6. What relevance, if any, has the theory and practice of rational emotive behaviour therapy for how you live?

ANNOTATED BIBLIOGRAPHY

Ellis, A and Ellis, D. J. (2011) *Rational Emotive Behavior Therapy.* Washington DC: American Psychological Association.
This was one of the final books that Dr Albert Ellis worked on, with his wife Debbie Joffe Ellis, before his death in 2007. It consists of seven chapters: 1. Introduction; 2. History; 3. Theory; 4. The therapy process: primary change mechanisms; 5. Evaluation; 6. Future developments; and 7. Summary.

Ellis, A. and Ellis, D. J. (2014) Rational emotive behavior therapy. In D. Wedding and R. J. Corsini (eds), *Current Psychotherapies* (10th ed.). Belmont, CA: Brooks/ Cole, pp. 151–91.
An authoritative overview of the theory and practice of rational emotive behaviour therapy almost exclusively written by its originator.

Ellis, A. and MacLaren, C. (2004) *Rational Emotive Behavior Therapy: A Therapist's Guide* (rev. ed). San Luis Obispo, CA: Impact Publishers.
Practical and accessible, this REBT therapist guide includes chapters on the philosophical and personality theory foundations of REBT, its theory of personality disturbance and change, assessment, cognitive techniques, emotive/experiential techniques, behavioural techniques and the integration of REBT with other systems of therapy.

Ellis, A. and Harper, R. A. (1997) *A Guide to Rational Living.* North Hollywood, CA: Wilshire Books.
This is a completely revised and rewritten version of the REBT self-help classic that is often recommended by cognitive behaviour therapists to clients. The book is a succinct, straightforward approach to REBT based on self-questioning and homework and shows how readers can help themselves with various emotional problems.

Ellis, A. (1999b) *How to Make Yourself Happy and Remarkably Less Disturbable.* Atascadero, CA: Impact Publishers.
Every therapist is at risk of crooked thinking. An excellent way to learn about REBT is to apply it to yourself. This entertaining self-help book presents Ellis' views on emotional disturbance and on the importance of scientific thinking. Readers are then presented with a series of chapters showing them in simple language 'how to' take and maintain more control of their thoughts, feelings and actions.

Neenan, M and Dryden, W. (2010)) *Rational Emotive Behaviour Therapy in a Nutshell* (2nd ed.). London: Sage.

This introductory book concisely presents the theory and practice of REBT. The book's contents are: the distinctive features of rational emotive behaviour therapy; the REBT 'Situational ABC' model; assessment; disputing; homework; and working through and promoting self-change.

REFERENCES AD FURTHER READING

Dryden, W. (1989) Albert Ellis: An efficient and passionate life. *Journal of Counseling and Development, 67,* 539–46.

Dryden, W. and Ellis, A. (1986) Rational-emotive therapy (RET). In W. Dryden and W. Golden (eds), *Cognitive-Behavioural Approaches to Psychotherapy.* London: Harper & Row, pp. 129–68.

Dryden, W. and Neenan, M. (2004) *Rational Emotive Behavioural Counselling in Action* (3rd ed.). London: Sage.

Dryden, W., Walker, J. and Ellis, A. (1992) *REBT Self-Help Form.* New York: Albert Ellis Institute for Rational Emotive Behavior Therapy.

Ellis, A. (1958) Rational psychotherapy. *Journal of General Psychology, 59,* 35–49.

Ellis, A. (1962) *Reason and Emotion in Psychotherapy.* Secaucus, NJ: Citadel.

Ellis, A. (1971) A twenty-three year-old woman, guilty about not following her parents' rules. In A. Ellis, *Growth Through Reason: Verbatim Cases in Rational-Emotive Therapy.* Hollywood: Wilshire Books, pp. 223–86.

Ellis, A. (1977) *Anger: How to Live With and Without It.* Sydney: MacMillan Sun Books.

Ellis, A. (1980) Overview of the clinical theory of rational-emotive therapy. In R. Grieger and J. Boyd (eds), *Rational-Emotive Therapy: A Skills-based Approach.* New York: Van Nostrand Reinhold, pp. 1–31.

Ellis, A. (1986a) Rational-emotive therapy approaches to overcoming resistance. In A. Ellis and R. M Grieger (eds), *Handbook of Rational-Emotive Therapy* (Vol. 2). New York: Springer, pp. 246–74.

Ellis, A. (1986b) Application of rational-emotive therapy to love problems. A. Ellis and R. M. Grieger (eds), *Handbook of Rational-Emotive Therapy* (Vol. 2, pp. 162–182). New York: Springer.

Ellis, A. (1987) The impossibility of achieving consistently good mental health. *American Psychologist, 42,* 364–375.

Ellis, A. (1988) *How to Stubbornly Refuse to Make Yourself Miserable about Anything, Yes Anything!* Sydney: Pan MacMillan.

Ellis, A. (1990) Is Rational-Emotive Therapy (RET) 'Rationalist' or 'Constructivist'? In A. Ellis and W. Dryden, *The Essential Albert Ellis* (pp. 114–141). New York: Springer.

Ellis, A. (1991a) My life in clinical psychology. In C. E. Walker (ed.), *The History of Clinical Psychology in Autobiography.* Vol.1 (pp. 1–37). Pacific Grove, CA: Brooks/Cole.

Ellis, A. (1991b) The revised ABC's of Rational-emotive therapy (RET). *Journal of Rational-Emotive & Cognitive Behavior Therapy, 9,* 139–72.

Ellis, A. (1991c) Using RET effectively: Reflections and interview. In M. E. Bernard (ed.), *Using Rational-Emotive Therapy Effectively*. New York: Plenum, pp. 1–33.

Ellis, A. (1991d) Rational-emotive behavior marriage and family therapy. In A. M. Horne (ed.), *Family Counseling and Therapy* (3rd ed.). Itasca IL: Peacock, pp. 489–513.

Ellis, A. (1991e) Rational-emotive treatment of simple phobias. *Psychotherapy, 28,* 452–6.

Ellis, (1992) Group rational-emotive and cognitive-behavioral therapy. *International Journal of Group Psychotherapy, 42,* 63–80.

Ellis, A. (1993a) Changing Rational-Emotive Therapy (RET) to Rational Emotive Behavior Therapy (REBT). *The Behavior Therapist, 16,* 257–258.

Ellis, A (1993b) Reflections on rational-emotive therapy. *Journal of Consulting and Clinical Psychology, 61,* 199–201.

Ellis, (1993c) The rational-emotive therapy (RET) approach to marital and family therapy. *The Family Journal: Counselling and Therapy for Couples and Families, 1,* 292–307.

Ellis, A. (1993d) The advantages and disadvantages of self-help therapy materials. *Professional Psychology: Research and Practice, 24,* 335–9.

Ellis. A. (1993e) Vigorous RET disputing. In M. E. Bernard and J. L. Wolfe (eds), *The RET Resource Book for Practitioners*. New York: Institute for Rational-Emotive Therapy, p. 7.

Ellis, A. (1993f) Rational-emotive imagery: RET version. In M. E. Bernard and J. L. Wolfe (eds), *The RET Resource Book for Practitioners*. New York: Institute for Rational-Emotive Therapy, pp. 8–10.

Ellis, A. (1994) *Reason and Emotion in Psychotherapy* (rev. ed). Secaucus, NJ: Citadel.

Ellis, A. (1996) *Better, Deeper and More Enduring Brief Therapy: The Rational Emotive Behavior Approach*. New York: Brunner/Mazel.

Ellis, A. (1997a) The Evolution of Albert Ellis and Rational Emotive Behavior Therapy. In J. K. Zeig (ed.), *The Evolution of Psychotherapy: The Third Conference*. New York: Brunner/Mazel, pp. 69–82.

Ellis, A. (1997b) Using rational emotive behavior therapy techniques to cope with disability. *Professional Psychology Research and Practice, 28,* 17–22.

Ellis, A. (1997c) Extending the goals of behavior therapy and of cognitive behavior therapy. *Behavior Therapy, 28,* 333–9.

Ellis, A. (1999a) Three methods of rational emotive behavior therapy that make my psychotherapy effective. *Psychotherapy Bulletin, 34,* 38–9.

Ellis, A. (1999b) *How to Make Yourself Happy and Remarkably Less Disturbable*. Atascadero, CA: Impact Publishers.

Ellis, A. (2001) *Feeling Better, Getting Better, Staying Better: Profound Self-help for Your Emotions*. Atascadero, CA: Impact.

Ellis, A. (2003a) Similarities and differences between rational emotive behavior therapy and cognitive therapy. *Journal of Cognitive Therapy: An International Quarterly, 17,* 225–40.

Ellis, A. (2003b) *Ask Albert Ellis?: Straight Answers and Sound Advice from America's Best-Known Psychologist*. Atascadero, CA: Impact.

Ellis, A. (2003c) *Overcoming Resistance: A Rational Emotive Behavior Therapy Integrated Approach*. New York: Springer.

Ellis, A. (2004a) *Rational Emotive Behavior Therapy: It Works for Me – It Can Work for You*. Amherst, NY: Prometheus Books.

Ellis, A. (2004b) *Sex Without Guilt in the Twenty-first Century*. New York: Barricade Books.

Ellis, A. (2005) *The Myth of Self-Esteem: How Rational Emotive Behavior Therapy Can Change Your Life Forever*. Amherst, NY: Prometheus Books.

Ellis, A. (2008) A twenty-three-year-old woman guilty about not following her parents rules. In Wedding, D. and Corsini, R. (eds), *Case Studies in Psychotherapy* (5th ed.). Belmont, CA: Thomson Brooks/Cole, pp. 67–85.

Ellis, A. (2010) *All Out: An Autobiography*. Amherst, New York: Prometheus Books.

Ellis, A. and Crawford, T. (2000) *Making Intimate Connections: 7 Guidelines for Great Relationships and Better Communication*. Atascadero, CA: Impact.

Ellis, A. and Dryden. W. (1997) *The Practice of Rational Emotive Behaviour Therapy*. London: Free Association Books and New York: Springer.

Ellis, A and Ellis, D. J. (2011) *Rational Emotive Behavior Therapy*. Washington DC: American Psychological Association.

Ellis, A. and Ellis, D. J. (2014) Rational emotive behavior therapy. In D. Wedding and R. J. Corsini (Eds), *Current Psychotherapies* (10th ed.). Belmont, CA: Brooks/Cole, pp. 151–91.

Ellis, A. and Harper, R. A. (1997) *A Guide to Rational Living*. North Hollywood, CA: Wilshire Books.

Ellis, A. and MacLaren, C. (2004) *Rational Emotive Behavior Therapy: A Therapist's Guide* (rev. ed). San Luis Obispo, CA: Impact Publishers.

Neenan, M. and Dryden, W. (2010) *Rational Emotive Behaviour Therapy in a Nutshell* (2nd ed). London: Sage.

Sichel, J. and Ellis, A. (1984) *RET self-help form*. New York: Institute for Rational-Emotive Therapy.

ELLIS ON CASSETTE (ILLUSTRATIVE)

Ellis, A. (1977b) *A Garland of Rational Songs* (with songbook). New York: Institute for Rational Emotive Behavior Therapy.

Ellis, A. (1982) *Solving Emotional Problems*. New York: Institute for Rational Emotive Behavior Therapy.

Ellis, A. (1984) *How to Be Happy though Human*. New York: Institute for Rational Emotive Behavior Therapy.

Ellis, A. (1987b) *How to Stop Worrying and Start Living*. Washington, DC: Psychology Today Tapes.

ELLIS ON FILM

Ellis, A. (1965) Rational-emotive therapy. In E. Shostrom (ed.). *Three Approaches to Psychotherapy.* Santa Ana, CA: Psychological Films.

ELLIS ON VIDEOTAPE (ILLUSTRATIVE)

Coping with the Suicide of a Loved One (49 mins)
Dealing with Addictions (55 mins)

ADDITIONAL DVD

Vernon, A. (2011) *Rational Emotive Behavior Therapy Over Time.* Washington DC: American Psychological Association.

WEBSITES

Dr Debbie Joffe Ellis: www.debbiejoffeellis.com
EllisREBT: www.ellisrebt.com
REBT Network: www.rebtnetwork.org

COGNITIVE THERAPY 10

INTRODUCTION

Cognitive therapy was initially developed in the early 1960s by Dr Aaron Beck of the University of Pennsylvania. The theory postulates that during clients' cognitive development they learn incorrect habits of processing and interpreting information. Cognitive therapists attempt to unravel clients' distortions and help them to learn different and more realistic ways of processing and reality-testing information.

Cognitive therapy's theoretical underpinnings come from three main sources (Beck and Weishaar, 2014). First, the phenomenological approach to psychology, which posits that the individual's view of self and personal world are central to how they behave. Second, structural theory and depth psychology; in particular Freud's theory contributed to Beck's structuring cognition into primary and secondary processes. Third, the work of early cognitive psychologists like Allport, Piaget and George Kelly in particular influenced Beck (Padesky and Beck, 2003). For example, Kelly's concept of personal constructs is similar to Beck's idea of schemas. The practice of cognitive therapy also owes much to Rogers, Ellis and the behaviour therapists.

AARON BECK (1921–)

Aaron Temkin 'Tim' Beck was born on July 18, 1921, in Providence, Rhode Island, the fourth, but third surviving, son of Russian Jewish immigrant parents. In 1919, Beck's parents lost their only daughter in an influenza epidemic, an event that precipitated a deep depression in his mother that lasted off and on for the rest of her life. Aged seven, Beck had a near fatal illness that reinforced his mother's over-protectiveness. While his father was tranquil, Beck did not like his mother's moody, inconsistent and excitable behaviour. Beck's father, who ran a printing business, encouraged his interest in science and nature. At high school, Beck edited the school paper and graduated first in his class. When growing up, he developed many anxieties and phobias, including fears of abandonment, surgery, suffocation, public speaking and heights (Weishaar, 1993).

In 1942, Beck graduated from Brown University, having majored in English and political science. Beck took pre-medical courses both before and after graduating and, in 1946, received his MD from Yale University School of Medicine. From 1946 to 1948, he served a rotating internship and a residency in pathology at the Rhode Island Hospital. From 1950 he started a neurology residency at the Cushing Veterans Administration Hospital in Framingham, Massachusetts. Due to a shortage of psychiatry residents, against his wishes Beck was forced to complete a six-month rotation in psychiatry. Deciding to remain in psychiatry, from 1950 to 1952, he was a Fellow in psychiatry at the Austen Riggs Center in Stockbridge, Massachusetts. In 1953, the American Board of Psychiatry and Neurology certified Beck in psychiatry and, in 1958, Beck graduated from the Philadelphia Psychoanalytic Institute. Since 1954, Beck has been a faculty member in the University of Pennsylvania's Department of Psychiatry. Currently he is University Professor Emeritus of Psychiatry and President of the independent Beck Institute for Cognitive Therapy and Research, where staff are affiliated with the University Psychiatry Department.

In the late 1950s, Beck began research on the dreams of depressed patients to test the psychoanalytic theory that depression was anger turned inward. The data did not support psychoanalytic theory, so Beck continued to collect data to construct a more empirically derived model of depression (Padesky and Beck, 2003). The period from 1960 to 1963 saw the development of cognitive therapy. Beck observes: 'There's nothing that I've been associated with since 1963 the seeds of which were not in the 1962 to 1964 articles. That was the critical period: changing from psychoanalysis to developing a new theory of therapy' (Weishaar, 1993, p. 21).

Beck's process of developing theory is that he first observes patients, then develops ways of measuring these observations, then formulates a theory if the observations are validated by a number of cases, then designs interventions congruent with the theory, then over time and through further experimentation continues to assess whether the theory is confirmed or negated and to refine it. When developing theory, Beck also uses self-observation. Finally, treatment protocols are tested via outcome studies, including examination of relapse and post-treatment course (Padesky and Beck, 2003). Beck and others continue to evolve cognitive therapy based on new research.

Beck has authored or co-authored over 375 articles in professional and scientific journals. His books include *Cognitive Therapy and the Emotional Disorders* (1976), *Cognitive Therapy of Depression* (Beck et al., 1979b), *Anxiety Disorders and Phobias* (Beck and Emery, 1985), *Love is Never Enough* (1988), *Cognitive Therapy of Personality Disorders* (Beck et al., 2003), *The Integrative Power of Cognitive Therapy* (Alford and Beck, 1997), *Scientific Foundations of Cognitive Theory and Therapy of Depression* (Clark et al., 1999), *Prisoners of Hate: The Cognitive Basis of Anger, Hostility and Violence* (1999) and *Cognitive Therapy of Anxiety Disorders: Science and Practice* (Clark and Beck, 2010). Tests and measures that Beck has developed with colleagues include the *Beck Depression Inventory*, the *Beck*

Hopelessness Scale, the *Suicide Intent Scale*, the *Suicide Ideation Scale*, the *Beck Self-Concept Test*, the *Beck Youth Inventories*, and the *Clark-Beck Obsessive-Compulsive Inventory*.

In 1950 Beck married his wife Phyllis, a continuing source of strength and support, who developed her own career by becoming a Pennsylvania Superior Court Judge. The Becks have four children and many grandchildren.

THEORY

BASIC CONCEPTS

Cognition is the key to understanding and treating psychological disorders. Alford and Beck write: 'Cognition' is defined as that function that involves inferences about one's experiences and about the occurrence and control of future events' (1997, p. 14). Humans need to adapt to changing environmental circumstances. Cognition includes the processes involved in identifying and predicting complex relations among events for the purposes of adaptation. Humans have the capacity both for primal/primitive and for higher level cognitive processing.

SCHEMAS

Schemas are structures that consist of people's fundamental beliefs and assumptions. Schemas are meaning-making cognitive structures. There are two categories of meaning: first, the objective or public meaning of an event, which may have few significant implications for the individual; and second, its personal or private meaning. Meaning assignment controls the psychological systems, such as behavioural, emotional, attentional and memory, so that the individual can activate strategies for adaptation.

Schemas are relatively stable cognitive patterns that influence, through their beliefs, how people select and synthesize incoming information. They are developed early in life from personal experiences and identifications with significant others and reinforced by further learning experiences. Schemas are not pathological by definition – they may be adaptive or maladaptive. They are analogous to George Kelly's (1955) formulation of personal constructs. People categorize and evaluate their experiences through a matrix of schemas.

Schemas possess structural qualities such as degree of breadth, flexibility, and their relative prominence in a person's cognitive organization. In addition, according to the degree of energy invested in them at any time, schemas can range from latent to predominant. When schemas are hypervalent, they are pre-potent and easily triggered. Psychopathology is characterized not only by the activation of inappropriate schemas but, in all probability, by their crowding out or inhibiting more adaptive schemas.

MODES

Contemporary cognitive theory stresses the concept of modes. Modes are networks of cognitive, affective, motivational and behavioural schemas. Modes are fundamental to personality since they interpret and adapt to emerging and ongoing situations (Beck and Weishaar, 2014). In earlier writings, cognitions were viewed as the mediating variable that triggered people's affective, motivational and behavioural systems. Now, instead of a linear relationship, all aspects of human functioning are viewed as acting together as a mode. Alford and Beck observe: 'The operation of a mode (e.g, anger, attack) across diverse psychological systems (emotion, motivation) is determined by the idiosyncratic schematic processing derived from an individual's genetic programming and internalised cultural/social beliefs' (1997, p. 10).

Modes can be primal, which means that they are universal and linked to survival. Anxiety is an example of a primal mode. Examples of modes under conscious control include conversing and studying. Primal modes include primary process thinking that is primitive and that conceptualizes situations in global, rigid, biased and relatively crude ways. Primal modes of thinking may originally have been adaptive in an evolutionary sense, yet they can become maladaptive in everyday life when triggered by systematically biased thinking and misinterpretations.

In addition, humans are capable of higher levels of cognitive processing which tests reality and corrects primal, global conceptualizations. However, in psychopathology, these corrective functions become impaired and primary responses can escalate into full-blown psychiatric disorders. Nevertheless, conscious or higher level thinking can override primal thinking and make it more flexible and realistic. Cognitive therapy approaches dysfunctional modes by deactivating them, modifying their content and structure, and by constructing adaptive modes to neutralize them.

COGNITIVE VULNERABILITY

The term *cognitive vulnerability* refers to human cognitive frailty. Because of their schemas, each person has a set of unique vulnerabilities and sensitivities that predispose them to psychological distress. People's schemas and beliefs influence the way they process data about themselves. When they exhibit psychological problems, their dysfunctional schemas and beliefs lead them systematically to bias information in unhelpful ways.

Beck (Beck et al., 2003) gives the example of Sue, who heard noises coming from the next room where her boyfriend Tom was working on some chores. Sues first thought was that 'Tom is making a lot of noise'. However Sue's information processing continued and she made the following interpretation of her experience: 'Tom is making a lot of noise *because he's angry at me.*' Her attribution of causality was produced by a conditional schema or belief that 'If an intimate of mine is noisy, it means he is angry at me.' Further down her hierarchy were the beliefs that 'If people reject me, I will be all alone' and 'Being alone will be devastating.' At the most basic level Sue had the belief or schema that 'I am unlovable.' When activated, Sue's basic belief (or schema) 'I am unlovable' acted as a 'feed-forward' mechanism moulding the information about Tom's behaviour in a way to fit the schema. Beck provides an alternative explanation that might have better fitted the information available to Sue, namely that 'Loud hammering is a sound of exuberance.'

AUTOMATIC THOUGHTS

Automatic thoughts are less accessible to awareness than voluntary thoughts, but not so deeply buried as beliefs and schemas. These thoughts are similar to what Freud termed 'preconscious' thinking and what Ellis terms 'self-statements'. People's self-evaluations and self-instructions appear to be derived from deeper structures – their self-schemas. Automatic thoughts reflect schema content – deeper beliefs and assumptions. In normal functioning self-appraisals and self-evaluations operate more or less automatically to help people stay on course. However, in psychopathology certain automatic thoughts operate to help people stay off course. Most psychological disorders are characterized by specific systematic biases in processing information. For example, depressive disorders are characterized by a negative view of self, experience and the future, and anxiety disorders by fear of physical or psychological danger.

The following are some salient characteristics of automatic thoughts. Automatic thoughts:

- are part of people's internal monologue – what and how they talk to themselves;
- can take the form of words, images, or both;
- occur very rapidly and usually at the fringe of awareness;
- can precede and accompany emotions, including feelings and inhibitions – for instance, people's emotional responses to each other's actions follow from their interpretations rather than from the actions themselves;
- are generally plausible to people who assume that they are accurate;
- have a recurring quality, despite people trying to block them out;
- affect tone of voice, facial expression and gestures, even though they may not be expressed verbally;
- can be linked together with more subtle thoughts underlying more obvious thoughts – for instance, when a husband boasts about his wife's cooking, his wife's secondary obvious automatic thought is 'He's fishing for a compliment', while her primary subtle automatic thought is 'They'll think that's all I'm good for.' (Beck, 1988); and
- though often hard to identify, therapists can train clients to pinpoint these thoughts with great accuracy.

COGNITIVE DISTORTIONS

Dysfunctional beliefs embedded in cognitive schemas contribute to systematic cognitive distortions, more accessible in automatic thoughts, that both characterize and maintain psychological distress. Box 10.1 includes some of the main cognitive distortions (Beck and Weishaar, 2014):

BOX 10.1   COGNITIVE DISTORTIONS

ARBITRARY INFERENCE

The process of drawing specific conclusions without supporting evidence and sometimes in the face of contradictory evidence. An example of arbitrary inference is that of the working mother who after a busy day concludes, 'I am a terrible mother.'

SELECTIVE ABSTRACTION

Selectively attending to a detail taken out of context at the same time as ignoring other more salient information. An example of selective abstraction is that of the boyfriend who becomes jealous at seeing his girlfriend tilt her head toward a man at a noisy party in order to hear him better.

OVERGENERALIZATION

Drawing a general rule or conclusion from one or a few isolated incidents and then applying the rule too broadly to unrelated situations. An example of overgeneralization is the woman who concludes after a disappointing date, 'All men are alike. I'll always be rejected.'

MAGNIFICATION AND MINIMIZATION

Evaluating particular events as far more or far less important than they really are. An example of magnification is the student who catastrophizes 'If I appear the least bit nervous in class it will mean disaster.' An example of minimization is that of a man describing his terminally ill mother as having a 'cold'.

PERSONALIZATION

Having a tendency without adequate evidence to relate external events to oneself. For instance concluding, when an acquaintance walking down the opposite side of a busy street does not acknowledge a wave of greeting, 'I must have done something to offend him/her.'

DICHOTOMOUS THINKING

Black-and-white, either-or, and polarized thinking are other terms for dichotomous thinking. Thinking in extreme terms, for instance 'Unless I do extremely well on this exam, I am a total failure.'

EVOLUTIONARY AND GENETIC FACTORS

The cognitive structures and schemas relevant to depression, anxiety disorders and personality disorders reflect our evolutionary history (Beck, 1991; Beck et al., 2003).

It is reasonable to consider that the notion of long-standing cognitive-affective motivational processes influence people's automatic processes: the way we construe events, what we feel, and how we are disposed to act. Much animal behaviour is regarded as programmed, with underlying processes reflected in overt behaviour. Though there are risks in extrapolating from animal to human ethology, similar developmental processes may be operative in humans. Animal analogies may clarify many aspects of normal and abnormal human behaviour. For instance, observations of primate behaviour seem highly relevant to depressed behaviour in humans.

'Strategies' are forms of programmed behaviour designed to serve biological goals. Regarding anxiety and anger, Beck (Beck and Emery, 1985) suggests four 'primal' survival strategies – fight, flight, freeze and faint – to perceptions of threat. Also, he proposes that strategies associated with traditional personality disorders may have possible antecedents in our evolutionary past (Beck et al., 2003). The dramatic strategy of the histrionic personality may have roots in the display rituals of non-human animals. The attack strategy of the antisocial personality may have roots in predatory behaviour.

Human strategies may be adaptive or maladaptive depending on their circumstances. The strategies adopted by people with personality disorders are maladaptive exaggerations of normal strategies. For instance, with the dependent personality disorder the cognitive substrate or basic belief is 'I am helpless' which leads to a strategy of attachment based on fear of abandonment. With the avoidant personality disorder, the basic belief is 'I may get hurt' which leads to a strategy of avoidance.

Mention has already been made of the role of evolution in laying the foundation for cognitive schemas and behavioural strategies. In addition, biological factors, such as variation in the gene pool, differentiate individuals in terms of their vulnerability to different kinds of distress. For instance, predisposing factors in depression are hereditary susceptibility and diseases that cause persistent neurochemical abnormalities.

Beck (Beck et al., 2003) regards the evidence as strong for relatively stable temperamental and behavioural differences being present at birth. These innate 'tendencies' can be strengthened or weakened by experience. For instance, because of the quality of their interpersonal interactions and learning experiences, not all shy children become shy adults. Furthermore, mutually reinforcing cycles can be established between people's innate tendencies and others' reactions to them. For instance, individuals with innate care-eliciting tendencies can elicit care-producing behaviour in others, even beyond the age when such behaviour is adaptive.

ACQUISITION

This section on acquisition seeks to answer two main, yet interrelated, questions. First, how are cognitive schemas, automatic thoughts and cognitive distortions initially acquired? Second, how are symptoms of psychiatric and other disorders activated? Here my focus is on dysfunctional cognitions and behaviour, though much of what follows is relevant to acquiring adaptive cognitions and behaviour.

ACQUISITION OF VULNERABILITY

Cognitive therapy views the acquisition of the potential for psychological distress as the result of many interacting factors: evolutionary, biological, developmental and environmental. Though many of the factors are common across individuals, each individual has their unique variations and way of attaching personal meaning to events. Below are some ways in which people acquire vulnerabilities.

CHILDHOOD TRAUMAS

Specific affect-laden incidents in childhood may create the potential for later distress by generating dysfunctional underlying beliefs (Beck and Emery, 1985). One example is the client who suffered a sense of doom and dread every Christmas season. His earliest memory of this feeling was when, aged seven, he saw his mother taken away to a tuberculosis sanatorium. His underlying belief became 'Something bad is going to happen over the Christmas holidays.' Another example is the five year old, who went away on a trip and returned to find the family dog dead, developing the belief that 'When I'm not physically close to others, something bad will happen to them.' A further example is that of the seven year old whose father left the family permanently after a marital fight developing the underlying belief that 'If I make others angry they will leave me.'

NEGATIVE TREATMENT IN CHILDHOOD

Children can be subject to ongoing negative treatment that affects their self-esteem and later makes them vulnerable to psychological distress. Furthermore, parents and significant others can model abusive behaviour which their children later use against others. Box 10.2 provides examples of acquiring cognitive vulnerability in childhood (Beck, 1988; Beck et al., 2003).

BOX 10.2   CHILDHOOD ABUSE AND LATER COGNITIVE VULNERABILITY

EXAMPLE 1   DYSFUNCTIONAL BELIEF: 'I AM A WIMP'

Gary had periodic violent outbursts against Beverley, whom he perceived as needling him all the time for not doing chores. Gary had suffered from being brought up in a household where people controlled each other through power and might. His father and older brother intimidated him and Gary developed a core schema 'I am a wimp.' To compensate

---

for this belief, Gary adopted an interpersonal strategy of intimidation to control other peo-ple's inclination to dominate him like his family had earlier done.

EXAMPLE 2 DYSFUNCTIONAL BELIEF: 'I AM A BAD KID'

In her childhood, a 28-year-old single woman who now suffered from panic disorder, had come home from school early one day and her mother screamed at her for waking her up saying 'How dare you interrupt my sleep!' Despite the fact that her mother drank a lot and was irritable and unpredictable, the woman developed the beliefs 'I am a bad kid' and 'I am wrong because I upset my mother.'

EXAMPLE 3 DYSFUNCTIONAL TENDENCY TO SELF-CRITICISM

A female client kept criticizing herself unnecessarily. She lessened her self-criticism when she re-experienced childhood scenes of criticism and obtained the insight 'I criticize myself now not because it's right to do so, but because my mother always criticized me and I took this over from her.'

SOCIAL LEARNING

Beck endorses social learning theory. However, he also stresses that individuals have unique learning histories and idiosyncratic ways of attaching meanings to earlier events. Many reasons exist for personality disorders – for example, obsessive-compulsive and paranoid behaviour may develop either as a compensation for or from fear. However, the reinforcement of relevant strategies by parents and significant others is among the reasons for specific personality disorders. For instance, the dependent personality's help-seeking and clinging strategies may have been rewarded and attempts at self-sufficiency and mobility discouraged. Identification with other family members can be important in what personality disorder strategies get developed. In addition, negative life experiences may worsen an initial predisposition so that, for instance, the shy child turns into an avoidant personality.

Modelling is a key process in social learning theory. For example, marital partners have memories about how their parents behaved. Parental modelling provides a basis for rules, shoulds and should nots, that they bring into their own marriages. Beck (1988) provides the example of Wendy and Hal who married very young and had trouble freeing themselves from parental model-ling and reinforcement. Wendy had absorbed her mother's traditional rule that 'The role of a wife is to take care of her husband.' When Wendy failed to live up to the rule, she disparaged herself. Hal's father had stressed and rewarded perfectionism so much that Hal had developed the belief 'I can never do anything right.' His mother reinforced his self-doubts because she had a negative attitude toward men: 'Men can't do anything – they're weak and helpless.' Hal's rules and beliefs made him vulnerable both to creating and dealing with difficulties in his marriage.

INADEQUATE EXPERIENCES FOR LEARNING COPING SKILLS

People may have been inadequately provided with personal experiences to learn coping skills. For example, an element in the anxious person's assessment of a threat is their ability to cope with the threat. A boy who has developed the coping skills of dealing with a bully is likely to feel less anxious about the bully because of this. People who fail to develop adequate assertion skills may be more prone to depression: first, they may lose self-esteem through others' actions and, second, they may then disparage themselves for lack of assertion. Most couples have learned insufficient skills in marital communication 'and so unwittingly produce continual abrasions, misunderstandings, and frustrations' (Beck, 1988, p. 275).

ACTIVATION OF VULNERABILITY

The term *cognitive shift* describes the shift of energy away from normal or higher level cognitive processing to a predominance of processing by pathological primal schemas. According to the disorder, energy is used to activate and inhibit unconscious patterns. For instance, in depression, generalized anxiety disorders, and panic attacks, the depressive, danger and panic modes are energized, respectively. The concept of mode reflects the manner in which a schema is expressed. For example, a schema such as 'I'm inadequate' may lead to a predominance of catastrophizing cognitions when the anxiety mode is activated and to a predominance of self-blame and hopelessness cognitions when the depressed mode is activated.

Thinking and behaving in ways that indicate vulnerability is a matter of degree. The *continuity hypothesis* suggests that anxiety, depression and personality disorders are exaggerated mechanisms of normal functioning. People can acquire dysfunctional schemas, rules, automatic thoughts and behaviours and not have them activated so that they become full-blown disorders or highly damaging factors in marital relationships.

The *cognitive shift* gets triggered when people perceive that their vital interests are at stake or have been affected. Often, initially, the shift into psychopathology is activated in response to major life stressors. Later the shift may be activated by less severe stressors. With repeated activations over the life span, people become increasingly sensitive to triggers so that it takes objectively less severe or salient stressors to precipitate a shift.

In non-endogenous unipolar depression, people have a cognitive vulnerability that is triggered by stressful life events or a series of traumatic experiences. An example of the development of vulnerability to activation of the cognitive shift is that of a person with recurrent depression whose first episode may have been precipitated by a severe life stressor (e.g., losing a job). Later episodes may be precipitated by relatively minor and less directly relevant stressors (e.g., hearing of a friend in another field being fired) that take on inordinate meaning due to prior experiences.

Three activating or precipitating factors are proposed for generalized anxiety disorders (Beck and Emery, 1985). First, people may face increased demands, for instance after the birth of a child or a job promotion. Second, there may be increased threat in an area of a person's life, for example, a new mother having a baby susceptible to infections, or an employee getting a hostile new boss. Third, stressful events and reversals may undermine confidence. An example is that of a young lawyer who failed his bar examination and, at about the same time, was told by his girlfriend that she did not love him. Fearing for his future as a lawyer and family man, he became chronically anxious.

MAINTENANCE

When people's cognitive vulnerabilities get activated and their cognitive processes go awry, why do they stay that way? Many people cope with the activation of their cognitive vulnerabilities by instigating adaptive cognitive and behavioural strategies. However, those with psychopathological disorders and those with deeply distressed marriages may remain stuck in faulty patterns of information processing and behaviour, to their own and other people's great disadvantage. There is no single cause why people continue to process information inefficiently. The evolutionary history of the species and genetic influences play a part. Also, the extent and depth of people's experiences of childhood traumas, negative treatment in childhood, faulty social learning and inadequate experiences of learning coping skills play their parts too.

FAILURE TO TURN OFF PREDOMINANT MODES

The type of schema that is evoked may be determined by the mode that is active at any given time. Normally there is a balance between modes so that when one predominates or is hypervalent for a long time, an opposing mode is activated. For instance, during a period of elation a person may become aware of negative feedback, or hostility may be counterbalanced by anxiety. In psychopathological disorders there seems to be an interference in the turn-off of the dominant mode. This results in systematically biased interpretations of negative events in depression, of positive events in mania and of dangerous events in anxiety disorders. Beck considers the reasons are obscure as to why the opponent mode remains relatively inactive, thus failing to contribute to a more balanced view of reality. One possibility is that neurochemical disturbances either stimulate a prolonged over-activity of the dominant mode or fail to stimulate sufficient activity in the opposing mode.

INABILITY TO REALITY-TEST DYSFUNCTIONAL INTERPRETATIONS

Since clients accept their dysfunctional beliefs so readily during anxiety and depression, Beck believes that they have temporarily lost their ability to reality-test their interpretations. Their information processing, based on dysfunctional schemas and beliefs, is permeated with automatic thoughts containing cognitive distortions. Cognitive distortions are not only manifestations of psychopathology, they serve to maintain it by interfering with clients' ability to test the reality of their thinking. Clients think in rigid, stereotypical terms. They fail to distinguish adequately between fact and inference. Instead of viewing the content of their thoughts as testable hypotheses, they jump to conclusions on inadequate evidence and then view their conclusions as facts. They insufficiently take into account any feedback that might modify or negate their thoughts and perceptions. Thus information processing systems become closed, instead of remaining open to assessing new data as they become available.

RESISTANCES TO CHANGE

Many reasons exist for why clients resist changing. For instance, clients may be fearful of the negative effects of their changing on others. Marta was a 42-year-old woman living with her mother and diagnosed as having a dependent personality disorder. Whenever she thought of moving she feared that this would kill her mother – and her mother reinforced this thinking (Beck et al., 2003). Many highly anxious, depressed and suicidal clients fear change as an unknown. Sometimes clients fear the positive as well as the negative consequences of change, for instance having to deal with the added responsibility of a promotion or marriage.

Beck (1988) considers that partners in distressed relationships may need to confront many beliefs, possibly expressed in the form of automatic thoughts, which weaken their motivation for change. Such thoughts include: 'My partner is incapable of change' and 'She/he hurt me. She/he deserves to be hurt.'

COGNITIVE MODELS

A systematic bias in information processing characterizes most psychological disorders. Overviews of Beck's cognitive models of depression, anxiety disorders, anger and distressed couple relationships are now presented.

THE COGNITIVE MODEL OF DEPRESSION

Beck views *depression* not just as a mood state, but a cognitive state as well (Beck, 1991; Beck et al., 1979b). Depression entails clients activating three major cognitive patterns known as *the cognitive triad*, involving negative views of:

- *themselves* as unlovable, worthless, helpless and lacking in the ability to attain happiness;
- *their past and present experiencing of the world* – their personal world is extremely demanding and presents huge obstacles to achieving goals;
- *the future* which is viewed as hopeless and unlikely to improve – this hopelessness may bring about ideas of suicide.

These cognitive patterns lead to the motivational, behavioural and physical symptoms of depression. An illustrative motivational symptom is *paralysis of will* created by the belief that one lacks the ability to cope or control an event's outcome. Inertia and fatigue are illustrative behavioural and physical symptoms, respectively.

Depressive schemas are formed early in life. Situations of loss similar to those originally embedding the schema may trigger a depression. Series of traumatic events may also activate depressions. As the depression worsens, depressive schemas become hypervalent to the point where clients may become unable to view their negative thoughts objectively and find themselves completely preoccupied with repetitive negative thoughts. As dysfunctional schemas become more activated, so does the incidence of systematic cognitive distortions.

THE COGNITIVE MODEL OF ANXIETY DISORDERS

The main cognitive theme in *anxiety disorders* is danger. Anxiety is a strategy in response to threat. In anxiety disorders the normal evolutionary survival mechanism of anxiety becomes exaggerated and malfunctioning. Beck and Emery (1985) adopts Lazarus' (1966) distinction between primary and secondary appraisal. Primary appraisal is the first impression of a situation that suggests the situation is noxious. Then successive reappraisals are made concerning the nature and relevance of the threat to a person's vital interests, including physical and psychological injury. Secondary appraisal involves the person assessing his or her resources for dealing with the threat. This process takes place at the same time as evaluating the nature of the threat. As with depression a person's underlying dysfunctional schemas and beliefs may predispose them to anxiety. Their dysfunctional beliefs may be activated by increased demands, threats and stresses that may interact with previous problems. Cognitive distortions reflecting dysfunctional schema include overestimating the probability and severity of the threat, magnification of the negative consequences (catastrophizing), underestimating one's resources for dealing with the threat, and insufficiently taking into account support factors, for instance the presence of others who might help. In brief, anxious individuals maximize the likelihood of harm and minimize their ability to cope.

THE COGNITIVE MODEL OF ANGER

The evoking of *anger* depends upon the inference that a person has been wronged in some way (Beck, 1999). Many reasons may contribute to this perception. People may insufficiently apply the rules of evidence by looking at all the pros and cons relevant to their interpretation of a situation. They may inadequately consider alternative explanations. Instead of problem solving, people attend to their own subjective meaning of an event. In addition they may possess beliefs that lead to distress: for instance, 'If a person criticizes me, it means she or he doesn't respect me' and 'If I don't receive respect, then I am open to further assaults.' In addition people may have unrealistic rules and imperatives: for instance, the desire 'I wish my wife was more respectful' can get transferred into an absolute rule 'My wife *should* be more respectful.'

People may gloss over unpleasant feelings immediately following the negative interpretation of an experience and be more aware of their subsequent angry feelings. For instance, they may feel sad or anxious and such feelings may need to be acknowledged and understood. In addition anger-prone people place an excessive emphasis on protection of their rights. They can remain unaware that other people may have a different view of their entitlements and that the rigid assertion of their rights leads to distress and non-productive anger. Though a degree of anger has information value, the powerful nature of some people's angry feelings can draw their attention away from the specific nature of their problems and thus interfere with solving them. Frequently, angry people need to be trained in communication skills. They also may need training in how to deal with violent impulses. A man who acquires insight into the labile nature of his self-esteem, can then work to substitute more realistic beliefs that leave his self-esteem less vulnerable. For instance, instead of 'A man does not take any crap' he can think 'A man can take the crap without allowing it to get to him.' In addition, the permissions that violent people give themselves can be elicited, challenged and changed.

THE COGNITIVE MODEL OF DISTRESSED COUPLE RELATIONSHIPS

Beck observes 'what attracts partners to each other is rarely enough to sustain a relationship' (Beck, 1988, p. 46). Poor communication skills are one reason for marital difficulties. In addition partners bring much personal baggage into the relationship in terms of hidden expectations of each other and the relationship. The expectations in marriage are less flexible than in uncommitted relationships. Furthermore, much behaviour in marriage has idiosyncratic symbolic meanings attached to it revolving around symbols of love or rejection, security or insecurity.

When disappointment in a relationship sets in and emotions run high, partners lose some or virtually all of their ability to reality-test their interpretations of their own and each other's thoughts, feelings and actions. Instead they react to their 'invisible reality' that is likely to be based more on their internal states, fears and expectations than on what actually happens. Dysfunctional schemas and beliefs can be triggered leading to a negative cognitive set about the other person. A distressed couple's voluntary and automatic thinking contains numerous cognitive distortions. Partners tend to fixate on what is wrong in their relationship rather than on what is right. They misperceive and misinterpret what the other says or does, engage in mind reading and attribute undesirable and malicious motives to each other, and fail to check out the accuracy of their negative explanations and illogical conclusions.

In addition, partners send each other barbed messages that trigger hurt and anger. They perceive they have been wronged, get angry, and feel impelled to attack and attack. Hostility is part of a primitive fight-flight survival mechanism. However, acting on the primitive urge to attack is often destructive to the relationship. It increases the level of threat in the relationship and hence partner's tendencies to think in rigid and erroneous ways. Furthermore, hostility can increase partners' resistances to working on their relationship.

THERAPY

THERAPEUTIC GOALS

Cognitive therapy aims explicitly to reenergize the reality-testing system. In varying degrees, clients with psychopathological disorders and couples in distressed relationships have lost the ability to reality-test dysfunctional interpretations. Cognitive therapy teaches clients adaptive meta-cognition – how to think about their thinking – so that they can correct faulty cognitive processing and develop assumptions that allow them to cope. While cognitive therapy may initially address symptom relief, its ultimate goal is to remove systematic biases in how clients think. In addition, cognitive therapy aims to impart behavioural skills relevant to clients' problems, for instance, listening and communication skills for distressed couples or assertion skills for shy people.

Clients are told that a goal of cognitive therapy is for them to learn to become their own therapists (Beck and Weishaar, 2014). When working with clients' cognitions, goals include teaching them to:

1. monitor their negative automatic thoughts;
2. recognize the connections between cognition, affect and behaviour;
3. examine and reality-test the evidence for and against distorted automatic thoughts;
4. substitute more realistic interpretations for biased cognitions; and
5. learn to identify and alter the beliefs that predispose them to distort their experiences (Beck et al., 1979b).

Clients need not be highly intelligent to gain from cognitive therapy – in fact Beck's researches show no relationship between intelligence and cognitive therapy outcomes.

Cognitive therapy 'is ideally suited to patients who can focus on their automatic thoughts, accept the therapist–patient roles, are willing to tolerate anxiety in order to do experiments, can alter assumptions permanently, take responsibility for their problems, and are willing to postpone gratification in order to complete therapy' (Beck and Wesihaar, 2014, p. 250). Cognitive therapy can also be effective for hallucinations and delusions. It is not recommended for clients with impaired memory and reasoning abilities, such as with organic brain syndromes. For some disorders, such as recurrent major depressive episodes, a combination of cognitive therapy and medication is recommended.

PROCESS OF THERAPY

At the Beck Institute for Cognitive Therapy and Research in suburban Philadelphia, clients undergo a three-hour intake protocol consisting of a clinical interview and psychological tests. The clinical interview provides a thorough history of the background factors contributing to the client's distress. The interview also assesses current level of functioning, prominent symptoms and expectations for therapy. The *Beck Depression Inventory* (Beck et al., 1961), the *Anxiety Checklist* (Beck, 1978), and the *Dysfunctional Attitudes Scale* (Weissman, 1979) are prominent among the psychological tests used during the intake protocol.

The initial interview has many purposes: initiating a relationship, providing a rationale for cognitive therapy, producing symptom relief and eliciting important information. Right from the start therapists impart to clients the expectation that cognitive therapy will be time-limited. During the initial interview, therapists start to define problems. Definitions of problems entail both functional and cognitive analyses.

The *functional* analysis seeks to answer questions such as: 'What are the component parts of the problem?', 'How is it manifested?', 'In what situations does it occur?', 'What is its frequency, intensity and duration?', and 'What are its consequences?'

The *cognitive* analysis identifies the client's thoughts and images when an emotion is triggered, the extent to which the client feels in control of thoughts and images, and predictions about the likelihood of the problem occurring and what will happen. From the beginning, therapists train clients to monitor their feelings, thoughts and behaviour and to recognize the connections between them. *Homework* is a feature throughout cognitive therapy. An example of an early homework assignment might be asking clients to record their automatic thoughts when distressed.

During initial sessions, therapists and clients draw up *problem lists*. Problem lists can consist of specific symptoms, behaviours or pervasive problems. Their function is to assign treatment priorities. Considerations in prioritizing treatment include magnitude of distress, symptom severity, and pervasiveness of theme. Therapists approach each problem by choosing the appropriate cognitive and behavioural techniques to apply. Therapists always offer a rationale for each technique. In addition, both when suggesting and implementing techniques, therapists elicit feedback from clients.

While the early stages of therapy may focus on symptom removal, middle and later stages are more likely to emphasize changing clients' patterns of thinking. Clients are helped to understand the interrelationships between their thoughts, feelings and behaviours. Once they can evaluate automatic thoughts that interfere with effective functioning, then they can identify and examine the underlying assumptions or beliefs generating such thoughts. Assumptions may be revealed as themes in automatic thoughts across time and across situations. Once assumptions and core beliefs have been identified and their disruptive power understood, then cognitive therapy aims to assist clients to examine their validity and current usefulness and then discard or amend them, as appropriate.

As cognitive therapy progresses, clients develop their skills of being their own therapists and assume more responsibility for identifying problems, analysing their thinking and creating suitable homework assignments. The role of the therapist shifts from being fairly didactic to facilitating clients as they develop their cognitive self-helping skills. The frequency of sessions decreases as clients become more proficient.

Being mainly a short-term structured approach, cognitive therapy tends to have its ending built into its beginning. Therapy ends when goals are reached and clients feel confident about implementing their new skills. From the outset therapists discuss with clients criteria and expectations for termination. There are a number of ways of assessing progress including: relief from symptoms, changes in reported and observed behaviour, and changes in thinking both inside and outside therapy. Performance in homework assignments, such as filling in the *The Thought Record* and carrying out specific tasks and experiments, also assists in assessing progress. In particular, therapists look out for clients' ability to reality-test and, if necessary, modify or discard distorted interpretations. Termination is often gradual, say from weekly to biweekly sessions, followed by booster sessions one and two months after termination. The purpose of such sessions is to consolidate gains and assist clients to keep employing their new skills (Beck and Weishaar, 2014).

Cognitive therapy sessions generally last for 45 minutes. The standard treatment length for unipolar depression is 8 to 16 sessions at weekly intervals. Moderately to severely depressed clients may be seen twice a week for the first two or three weeks. Clients with anxiety disorders generally receive from 5 to 15 sessions (Clark and Beck, 1988). The treatment of personality disorders generally takes longer and may last for a year or more.

THE THERAPEUTIC RELATIONSHIP

Cognitive therapy is an educational process in which therapists are active in developing relationships with clients and using their expertise in helping clients examine and modify beliefs and behaviour. The quality of the therapist–client relationship is an important medium for improvement. Cognitive therapy is not an impersonal approach, but one in which therapists seek to understand their clients as individuals. Beck regards his therapeutic style as somewhat Rogerian. Therapists strive to create an emotional climate of personal regard, genuine warmth and non-judgemental acceptance. Furthermore, cognitive therapists give clients their phone numbers in case of emergency.

Cognitive therapists attempt to demystify therapy by using a language that clients can understand. They treat clients with respect by offering rationales both for their overall approach and for each technique that they propose. In addition, they share responsibility for what happens in therapy by discussing case conceptualizations and involving clients in setting goals and session agendas. Cognitive therapists also elicit feedback from clients about both their suggestions and their behaviour. Therapists are sensitive to signs of transference and allow clients' reactions to them to be aired. Therapists can use these transference reactions to identify and work with clients' automatic thoughts and interpersonal distortions.

With most personality-disordered clients, cognitive therapists offer a closer and warmer relationship than in acute disorders, such as anxiety and depression. Therapists can face problems of non-collaboration from clients, especially those with personality disorders (Beck et al., 2003).

SERVING AS CO-INVESTIGATOR – COLLABORATIVE EMPIRICISM

In addition to offering accepting and warm relationships, cognitive therapists play an active role in the therapy process and encourage clients to play an active role too. All of the client's cognitions are viewed as testable hypotheses. Therapists and clients collaborate together in the scientific endeavour of examining the evidence to confirm or negate the client's cognitions. Based on what clients say and how they say it, therapists develop hypotheses that can identify cognitive errors as well as underlying assumptions and beliefs. Therapists then ask clients to comment on whether their hypotheses fit the facts. By these means, clients are encouraged both to view their thoughts as personal views of reality and to build their skills of evaluating their validity. Throughout the process of identifying and exploring the evidence for biased thinking, as appropriate either the therapist or the client takes the more active role.

SERVING AS A GUIDE – GUIDED DISCOVERY

There are a number of different facets to guided discovery. Therapists can operate as guides to assist clients to discover the themes that run through their present automatic thoughts and beliefs. This can be taken one stage further where therapists and clients link the beliefs to analogous experiences in the past and collaboratively piece together the developmental history of the beliefs. Another use of guided discovery is that therapists act as guides in assisting clients to reality-test their possible errors in logic by designing new experiences that involve the client experimenting with different behaviour. Therapists do not use cajoling, disputation and indoctrination to assist clients to reality-test their thinking and adopt new beliefs. Rather they encourage clients to develop their own skills of using and assessing information, facts, and probabilities in order to obtain more realistic perspectives than sometimes offered by their initial thoughts.

THERAPEUTIC INTERVENTIONS

Both cognitive and behavioural interventions are used in cognitive therapy. The interventions selected depend on such factors as the nature of the client's problems, the therapeutic goals, and how well they are functioning.

COGNITIVE INTERVENTIONS

The following are some of the main cognitive interventions used by cognitive therapists to assist clients to replace their distorted automatic thoughts and beliefs with more realistic ways of processing information.

ELICITING AND IDENTIFYING AUTOMATIC THOUGHTS

In order to change their thinking, clients need first become aware of their thought processes. Included below are some specific interventions for eliciting and identifying automatic thoughts.

1. *Providing reasons*: Therapists can provide reasons for the importance of examining the connections between how clients think, feel and act. Furthermore, they can introduce the concept of automatic thoughts and provide an example of how underlying perceptions influence feelings. In addition, therapists can communicate that a major assumption of cognitive therapy is that clients are experiencing difficulties in reality-testing the validity of their interpretations. Box 10.3 provides an example of a cognitive therapist showing the relationship between cognition, affect and behaviour (Beck et al., 1979b, pp. 147–8).

BOX 10.3   EXAMPLE OF SHOWING THE INFLUENCE OF COGNITIONS ON AFFECT AND BEHAVIOUR

THE CLIENT

A 43-year-old depressed male patient.

THE SCENE

The therapist instructed the client to imagine a person was home alone one night and heard a crash in another room.

(Continued)

(Continued)

INTERPRETATION 1

This person thinks 'There's a burglar in the room'.

Possible consequences of interpretation 1

The therapist then asked the client

- 'How do you think this person would feel?', to which the client answered 'Very anxious, terrified'.
- 'And how might he behave?', to which the client replied 'He might hide or phone the police'.

INTERPRETATION 2

The therapist then instructed the client to imagine that the person heard the same noise and thought: 'The windows have been left open and the wind has caused something to fall over.'

Possible consequences of interpretation 2

The therapist then asked the client

- 'How would he feel?', to which the client replied the person wouldn't be afraid, though he might be sad if he thought something valuable had been broken.
- 'And would his behaviour be different following this thought?', to which the client replied it would be different in that he would probably go and see what the problem was and certainly wouldn't phone the police.

MAIN TEACHING POINTS

The therapist emphasized that this example showed

- that usually there were a number of ways the client could interpret a situation, and
- the way he interpreted a situation would affect how he felt and behaved.

2. *Questioning*: Clients may be questioned about automatic thoughts that occur during upsetting situations. Where clients experience difficulty recalling thoughts, imagery or role-playing may be used. When questioning, therapists observe clients carefully for signs of affect that may offer leads for further questioning.
3. *Encouraging clients to engage in feared activities*: Frequently, during sessions, clients are encouraged to engage in anxiety-evoking activities: for instance, making phone calls or writing letters they had been putting off. As they perform the activity, therapists can ask the question 'What is going through your mind right now?' Therapists can also go with clients into real-life situations where they experience difficulty, for instance crowded places, and get them to verbalize what they think.

4. *Focusing on imagery*: Gathering information about imagery can be an important way of accessing automatic thoughts. Though individual differences exist, clinical observations suggest that many people visualizing scenes react to them as though they were real.
5. *Self-monitoring of thoughts*: Clients may be set homework in which they record their thoughts. They may complete a *Thought Record* in which they record in their respective columns:

   (a) *date*;
   (b) *situation* leading to negative emotion(s);
   (c) *emotion(s)* felt and their degree on a 0–100 per cent scale;
   (d) *automatic thought(s)* and a rating of how strongly they believed the automatic thought(s) on a 0–100 per cent scale.

Therapists may encourage some clients to use wrist counters to help them learn to recognize automatic thoughts as they occur.

REALITY-TESTING AND CORRECTING AUTOMATIC THOUGHTS

Interventions for assisting clients to treat their thoughts as hypotheses that require testing against reality and, if necessary, discarding, modifying or replacing include the following.

1. *Conducting Socratic dialogues*: Questions comprise the largest category of verbal statements in cognitive therapy. Questions reflect the basic empirical orientation of the approach and have the immediate goal of converting clients' closed belief systems into open systems. Beck and Weishaar state: 'The purposes of the therapists' questions are generally to (1) clarify or define problems; (2) assist in the identification of thoughts, images, and assumptions; (3) examine the meanings of events for the patient; and (4) assess the consequences of maintaining maladaptive thoughts and behaviors' (2014, p. 247). More specifically questions seek to help clients: become aware of what their thoughts are; examine them for cognitive distortions; substitute more balanced thoughts; and make plans to develop new thought patterns. A basic raising awareness question is to ask clients ' What is going through your mind right now?'

   Therapists use questioning rather than indoctrination and disputation. Conducted in an emotional climate of warmth and acceptance, the Socratic style of questioning assists clients to expand and evaluate how they think (Beck, 2011). Typical questions are:

   (a) 'Where is the evidence?'
   (b) 'What is the evidence that supports this idea?'
   (c) 'What is the evidence against this idea?'
   (d) 'Is here an alternative explanation?'
   (e) 'What is the worst that could happen? Could I live through it?'
   (f) 'What is the best that could happen?'
   (g) 'What is the most realistic outcome?'
   (h) 'What is the effect of my believing the automatic thought?'
   (i) 'What could be the effect of changing my thinking?'
   (j) 'What should I do about it?' and
   (k) 'What would I tell _____ (a friend) if he or she *were in the same situation?*'

Clients learn to ask themselves the same questions that their therapists have asked. For instance, however plausible their automatic thoughts may 'feel', clients in distressed relationships can question their validity by asking themselves the following series of questions:

(a)   'What is the evidence *in favour of* my interpretation?'
(b)   'What evidence is *contrary* to my interpretation?'
(c)   'Does it *logically* follow from my spouse's actions that my spouse has the motive that I assign to him or her?' and
(d)   'Is there an *alternative* explanation for his or her behaviour?' (Beck, 1988).

Box 10.4 provides an example of some of Beck's questions to evaluate a client's thinking (Beck, 1976, pp. 249–52).

BOX 10.4   CASE EXAMPLE: EVALUATING THE THOUGHT THAT 'FAILURE IS A CATASTROPHE'

THE CLIENT

A medical student inhibited in numerous situations where assertion was essential. Here the therapist focuses on the client's fears of giving a talk in front of his class tomorrow.

THE THERAPIST'S QUESTIONS

- 'What are you afraid of?'
- 'Suppose you do make a fool of yourself, why is that so bad?'
- 'Now look here, suppose they ridicule you, can you die from it?'
- 'Suppose they decide that you are the worst public speaker that ever lived, will this ruin your career?'
- 'But if you flubbed it would your wife or parents disown you?'
- 'Well what would be so awful about it?'

When the client answers that he would feel pretty bad, the therapist asks: 'For how long?' and the client replies 'For about a day or two' and the therapist then says: 'And then what?', to which the client replies 'Then I'd be O.K.'

THE THERAPIST'S SUMMARY

The therapist pointed out to the client that, somewhere along the line his thinking got fouled up, and that he tended to regard failure as a catastrophe. The client needed to start challenging his wrong premises and to label failures accurately as failures to attain goals and not as disasters.

SUBSEQUENT THERAPY SESSIONS

As therapy proceeded the therapist coached the client in changing his notion that failure was a catastrophe as well as challenged maladaptive attitudes producing psychological distress in other social situations.

2. *Identifying cognitive distortions*: Therapists can teach clients what the common cognitive distortions are, for instance arbitrary inference and magnification. Both during therapy and as homework clients can be asked to identify the distortions in how they think. Clients may use the three-column technique for this:

   (a) column one – describe a situation that elicits negative emotions;
   (b) column two – identify their automatic thoughts in the situation;
   (c) column three – list the types of distortions in these thoughts.

3. *Decatastrophizing*: In decatastrophizing, the basic question is 'So what if it happens?' Areas covered in this technique include: the event's probability and severity, the client's coping capacity and support factors, and the client's ability to accept and deal with the worst possible outcomes.

4. *Reattribution*: Reattribution techniques test automatic thoughts and underlying beliefs by considering alternative ways of assigning responsibility and cause. Clients can be encouraged to rate on a 0–100 scale the degree of responsibility they feel for negative events and feared outcomes. By means of questioning, the therapist attempts to loosen them up by generating and evaluating alternative explanations.

5. *Redefining*: Redefining problems entails making them more concrete and stating them in terms of what the client might do. For example, a lonely person who feels uncared for may redefine his or her problem as 'I need to reach out to other people and be caring.'

6. *Decentring*: Decentring involves assisting clients to evaluate their belief that everyone is focusing on them. Clients can be encouraged to assess more closely what others are doing: for instance, other students may be daydreaming, looking at their lecturer, or taking notes. In addition, clients can be asked to closely observe how frequently they attend to others. This may help them realize how limited their observations are and, thus infer that other people's observations are the same.

7. *Forming adaptive responses*: Cognitive therapists train clients in how to form more adaptive responses to their automatic thoughts. Again, questioning is an important way to assist clients in learning to use their inner monologue for rather than against themselves. Box 10.5 provides an example of a client providing a counteracting adaptive response to herself (Beck, 1988). Finding an adaptive response can help clients see their automatic thoughts as an interpretation rather than as 'the truth'.

BOX 10.5 EXAMPLE OF FORMING AN ADAPTIVE RESPONSE

THE SITUATION

Wendy who was phoned by her husband Hal to say he was tied up at the office.

- *Emotional reaction*   Anger
- *Automatic thought*   'Its not fair – I have to work too. If he wanted to, he could be home on time.'
- *Adaptive response*   'His job is different. Many of his customers come in after work.'

8. *Daily recording of adaptive responses*: When ready, clients can be encouraged to fill out adaptive response and outcome columns on their *Thought Record*. In the outcome column, clients:

   (a) rerate their beliefs in their automatic thought(s) on a 0–100 per cent scale, and
   (b) specify what their subsequent emotions are and rate them on a 0–100 per cent scale.

9. *Imagery techniques*: Numerous imagery techniques are discussed by Beck and Emery (1985). Among these techniques are assisting clients to gain more realistic perspectives through repeated visualizations of fantasies, through projecting themselves into the future and looking back on their present situations, and by getting them to exaggerate images, for instance of harming others.

IDENTIFYING AND MODIFYING UNDERLYING BELIEFS

Underlying beliefs may be harder for therapists and clients to access than automatic thoughts. Often they fall into one of three main belief clusters centring on issues of:

- *acceptance* – for instance, 'I'm flawed and therefore unacceptable';
- *competence* – for instance, 'I'm inferior'; and
- *control* – for instance, 'I have no control.'

Underlying beliefs are signposted by the themes in clients' automatic thoughts. Clients' behaviour, coping strategies and personal histories are additional sources for therapists to form belief hypotheses. Most clients find it difficult to articulate their beliefs without assistance. Generally therapists present hypotheses to clients for verification. Where clients disagree, therapists can work with them to form more accurate statements of their beliefs.

Nowadays therapists assist clients to respond to their cognitions at both intellectual and emotional levels. The following are some cognitive interventions for modifying beliefs:

1. *Socratic questioning*: Therapists can use questions that encourage clients to examine their beliefs: for instance' 'Does the belief seem reasonable?', 'Can you review the evidence for it?', and 'What are the advantages and disadvantages of maintaining the belief?'
2. *Hypothesis testing*: Together therapists and clients can set up experiments that encourage clients to test the reality of their beliefs. Box 10.6 provides an example of such an experiment (Beck, 1988, p. 224).

BOX 10.6   EXAMPLE OF HYPOTHESIS TESTING CONCERNING A BELIEF

THE CLIENT

Marjorie, who was afraid to make a mental commitment to her spouse, Ken, because she was afraid she might find out that she could not trust him.

MARJORIE'S UNDERLYING BELIEF

'I must never allow myself to be vulnerable.'

Consequence of Marjorie's distorted thinking

Her aloof behaviour and fault finding created distance in their relationship.

THE EXPERIMENT

Beck and Marjorie set up a three-month experiment for her to test the hypothesis: 'If I totally commit myself to the relationship, look for the positive instead of the negative, I will feel more secure.' During the experiment, Marjorie was to change how she thought and acted.

Result of the experiment

Marjorie discovered that she was more secure and had fewer thoughts about leaving Ken.

---

3. *Using imagery*: Imagery can be used to assist clients to 'relive' past traumatic events and so restructure their experiences and the beliefs and emotions derived from them.
4. *Reliving childhood memories*: Beck (Beck et al., 2003) considers that with chronic personality disorders it is crucial to use childhood material to assist clients in reviewing and loosening their underlying beliefs. By recreating 'pathogenic' developmental situations through role playing and role reversal, clients have an opportunity to restructure or modify beliefs and emotions formed during this period.
5. *Refashioning beliefs*: Therapists can assist clients to refashion their beliefs. Beck gives the example of M.K. a director of a research institute at a major university who suffered from a major depressive disorder and generalized anxiety disorder. The client had strong beliefs of inadequacy and rejection which he crystallized as 'I must be *the best* at everything I do.' One of M.K.'s beliefs was refashioned thus: 'It is rewarding to succeed highly, but lesser success is rewarding also and has no bearing on my adequacy or inadequacy. I am adequate no matter what.'

BEHAVIOURAL INTERVENTIONS

Behavioural interventions have many purposes in cognitive therapy. First, behavioural interventions can lay the foundation for later cognitive work. An issue arises whether to focus on behaviour first, cognition first, or both concurrently. Behavioural interventions may sometimes be used before cognitive interventions to promote symptom relief and enhance motivation. For instance, severely depressed clients may be encouraged to perform small tasks to counteract their withdrawal, get them involved in constructive activities, and open their minds to the possibility of gaining satisfaction from previously pleasurable activities.

However, in contrast to normal people, depressed clients can change their behaviour markedly, but do not necessarily change their negative hypervalent cognitions (Beck et al., 1979). In working with couples, Beck (1988) concentrates on changing behaviour first since he regards it as easier to change actions than thinking patterns. In addition, spouses may immediately reward each other's changes in behaviour.

Second, behavioural interventions can be used to assist clients in reality-testing their automatic thoughts and beliefs. A third use of behavioural interventions is, along with cognitive interventions, to assist clients to engage in feared activities. A fourth use is to train clients in specific behavioural skills. Since the uses of behavioural interventions overlap, below they are not categorized according to purpose.

The following are some of the main behavioural interventions used by cognitive therapists:

1. *Activity scheduling*: Activity scheduling is a form of timetabling. Planning specific activities with clients can be important in helping clients to realize that they can control their time. A principle of activity scheduling is to state what activity the client agrees to engage in rather than how much they will accomplish. Clients can set aside time each evening to plan their activities for the next day.
2. *Rating mastery and pleasure*: Using 0–10 scales, clients can rate the degree of mastery and the degree of pleasure they experienced in each activity during the day. Mastery and pleasure ratings can give depressed clients an insight into the activities that reduce their dysphoria.
3. *Hypothesis testing*: Hypothesis testing has both behavioural and cognitive components (Beck and Weishaar, 2014). Especially later in therapy, behavioural experiments may be designed to provide information that may contradict existing automatic thoughts, faulty predictions and underlying beliefs. A young man about to cancel a date because of the fear 'I won't know what to say' was encouraged to go on the date and treat not knowing what to say as an experimental hypothesis. The findings of this particular experiment disproved his hypothesis (Beck and Emery, 1985). In the earlier example Marjorie was engaging in a behavioural as well as a cognitive experiment to test her underlying belief 'I must never allow myself to be vulnerable.'
4. *Rehearsing behaviour and role playing*: Behaviour rehearsal can be used to develop clients' skills for specific social and stressful situations. Demonstration and video feedback can be used as part of skills training. Behaviour rehearsals should have a number of trials and rehearse clients in a variety of responses. Also, clients can rehearse situations by using their imaginations.
5. *Assigning graded tasks*: Often clients fail at tasks because they try to do too much too soon. Therapists and clients can develop hierarchies of feared or difficult situations. Then clients can perform less threatening before moving on to more threatening activities.
6. *Using diversion techniques*: Clients may be encouraged to engage in activities that divert them from their strong negative emotions and thinking. Such activities include work, play, socializing and doing something physical.
7. *Assigning homework*: Homework forms an important part of cognitive therapy. Its purpose is both to shorten the time spent in therapy as well as facilitate the development of cognitive and behavioural skills for use after therapy. Homework assignments include

self-monitoring, activities designed to reality-test automatic thoughts and underlying beliefs, implementing procedures for dealing with specific situations, and activities for developing cognitive skills such as identifying cognitive distortions, rational responding and refashioning beliefs.

CASE MATERIAL

Beck and colleagues (Beck et al., 1979; Beck, 2008), present an initial interview with a depressed 40-year-old female clinical psychologist client who had recently been left by her boyfriend. The interview transcript is broken down into five parts: questioning to elicit vital information, broadening the client's perspective, 'alternative therapy', obtaining more accurate data, and closure. Beck and Young (1985) illustrate in the case example of a depressed young female client how cognitive therapists elicit and evaluate maladaptive thoughts and assumptions throughout treatment. Beck and Weishaar (2014) show both behavioural and cognitive interventions for attaining therapeutic goals in the case example of a 21-year-old male college student who complained of sleep onset insomnia and frequent awakenings, halting speech and stuttering, feelings of nervousness, dizziness, and worrying. Throughout his book *Love is Never Enough*, Beck (1988) provides numerous vignettes of the use of cognitive interventions in relationship therapy.

Other sources of case material include Freeman and Dattilio's edited *Comprehensive Casebook of Cognitive Therapy* (1992); Greenberger and Padesky's *Mind Over Mood* (1995); and Judith Beck's *Cognitive Therapy: Basics and Beyond* (2011).

FURTHER DEVELOPMENTS

Cognitive therapy has been used with all ages, from children to the elderly. Beck reports that several controlled studies have shown it to be at least as effective as antidepressant medication in treating elderly depressed clients. Individual randomized control trials, reviews of the literature of outcome studies, and meta analyses all assert the success of cognitive therapy and cognitive behaviour therapy for treating depression and anxiety disorders in particular (Beck and Weishaar, 2014).

Cognitive therapy has been used for group work with families. Some newer applications of cognitive therapy include working with clients with schizophrenia, post-traumatic stress disorders, substance abuse problems, hypertension and dissociative disorders as well as with clients who have committed sexual offences, such as exhibitionism and incest. Schema-focused approaches to personality disorders have been an important development in cognitive therapy.

The growth of cognitive therapy has been quick because of its empirical basis and demonstrated efficacy. In 2003 Padesky and Beck noted that cognitive therapy had spread more rapidly in recent decades than rational emotive behaviour therapy. Cognitive therapy has been evaluated by thousands of studies that examine its conceptual models, treatment methods, protocols and outcomes. Treatment protocols, such as those for depression and panic disorder, have been in existence for some time. Generally, cognitive therapy does as well or better than other active therapies for these problems. Other problems for which cognitive therapy has proved effective include social phobia, generalized anxiety disorder, post-traumatic stress disorder and obsessive-compulsive disorder. Research also indicates that cognitive therapy leads to lower relapse rates than other active therapies.

Cognitive therapy has been combined with other approaches. For instance mindfulness-based cognitive therapy (Segal, Williams and Teasdale, 2002) unites cognitive therapy with Buddhist-based meditation practices to prevent relapse from depression. Other approaches incorporating cognitive therapy include acceptance and commitment therapy (Hayes, Strosahl and Wilson, 2003), relapse prevention methods for high-risk behaviours (Marlatt, 2002) and compassion strategies (Gilbert, 2009). As well as these therapies incorporating strategies from cognitive therapy, cognitive therapy also incorporates strategies from them.

There are over ten training centres for cognitive therapy in the United States, including the Beck Institute for Cognitive Behavior Therapy, directed by Beck's daughter, Dr Judith Beck. In addition, training in cognitive therapy is widely available elsewhere, including Britain and Australia. In 1985, the *International Cognitive Therapy Newsletter* was started for the exchange of information among cognitive therapists. The main cognitive therapy research journals are *Cognitive Therapy and Research*, the *International Journal of Cognitive Psychotherapy*, and *Cognitive and Behavioral Practice*.

A final thought – with the current emphasis on containing costs through managed care, cognitive therapy's short-term approach will be increasingly popular with both third-party payers and clients (Beck and Weishaar, 2014).

REVIEW AND PERSONAL QUESTIONS

REVIEW QUESTIONS

1. What are schemas and modes and why are they important?
2. What are automatic thoughts and why are they important?
3. What are cognitive distortions and why are they important?
4. What are Beck's views on the following causes of cognitions and behaviour

   - evolutionary causes
   - genetic causes?

5. What is the nature and role of each of the following factors in helping people acquire cognitive vulnerability: childhood traumas, negative treatment in childhood, social learning, and inadequate experiences for learning coping skills?
6. What are some factors relevant to activating cognitive vulnerability?

7. What is the nature and role of each of the following factors in helping people maintain cognitive vulnerability: failure to turn off hypervalent modes, inability to reality-test dysfunctional interpretations, and resistances to change?
8. Critically discuss the goals of cognitive therapy.
9. Describe the nature of the therapist–client relationship in cognitive therapy.
10. Describe the process of cognitive therapy.
11. What are some of the main cognitive interventions used in cognitive therapy for:

   - eliciting and identifying automatic thoughts
   - reality-testing and correcting automatic thoughts
   - identifying and modifying underlying beliefs?

12. What are some of the main behavioural interventions used in cognitive therapy?

PERSONAL QUESTIONS

1. List any significant factors when you were growing up that may have contributed to your acquiring faulty ways of processing information.
2. Think of a specific problem in your life. Elicit and identify some of your automatic thoughts regarding it.
3. Identify characteristic cognitive distortions, if any, in the way you process information.
4. Identify an automatic thought in a problem area and challenge it by means of Socratic questioning.
5. In a problem area, identify a thought that lends itself to being reality-tested through changing your behaviour. Design and implement a behavioural experiment to reality-test your thought.
6. What relevance, if any, has the theory and practice of cognitive therapy for how you conduct therapy?
7. What relevance, if any, has the theory and practice of cognitive therapy for how you live?

ANNOTATED BIBLIOGRAPHY

Beck, A. T. and Weishaar, M. E. (2014) Cognitive therapy. In D. Wedding and R. J. Corsini (eds), *Current Psychotherapies* (10th ed.). Belmont, CA: Brooks/Cole, pp. 231–64.
An authoritative chapter reviewing the theory and practice of contemporary cognitive therapy.

Beck, A. T., Rush, A. J., Shaw, B. F. and Emery, G. (1979) *Cognitive Therapy of Depression.* New York: John Wiley.
This book presents Beck's cognitive model of depression. The bulk of the book is a clinical handbook devoted to practical aspects of treating depressed clients, for instance the therapeutic relationship, the application of both cognitive and behavioural interventions, and problems related to termination and relapse.

Beck, A. T. and Emery, G. (1985) *Anxiety Disorders and Phobias: A Cognitive Perspective.* New York: Basic Books.

Part 1 of the book, written by Beck, is entitled 'Theoretical and clinical aspects' and presents his cognitive model of anxiety. Part 2 of the book, written by Emery, is entitled 'Cognitive therapy: Techniques and applications' and has chapters on the principles of cognitive therapy, techniques for cognitive restructuring, modifying imagery, affect, and behaviour, and on restructuring assumptions.

Beck, A. T. (1988) *Love is Never Enough: How Couples Can Overcome Misunderstandings, Resolve Conflicts, and Solve Relationship Problems Through Cognitive Therapy.* New York: Harper & Row.
This book describes the power of negative and biased thinking in couple relationships. Beck shows how partners can improve their relationship by identifying and modifying their maladaptive automatic thoughts and underlying beliefs.

Beck, J. S. (2011) *Cognitive Therapy: Basics and Beyond* (2nd ed.). New York: Guilford Press.
This 21 chapter book starts with case conceptualization and evaluation. It then proceeds to show how to work with patients' thinking, behaviour and emotions. The book also contains chapters on homework, termination and relapse prevention, and problems in therapy.

Padesky, C. A. and Greenberger, D. (1995) *Clinician's Guide to Mind Over Mood*; and Greenberger, D. and Padesky, C. A. (1995) *Mind Over Mood: Change How You Feel by Changing The Way You Think.* New York: Guilford Press.
These companion volumes are designed as step-by-step guides to the techniques and strategies of cognitive therapy. The manual is designed as a self-help workbook and the clinician's guide provides therapists with instructions on how to incorporate the workbook into individual and group psychotherapy.

Weishaar, M. E. (1993) *Aaron T. Beck.* London: Sage Publications.
Weishaar has been both a student and collaborator of Beck's, so she writes with authority. The five chapters in the book cover: Beck's life, his theoretical contributions, his practical contributions, some criticisms and rebuttals, and Beck's overall influence.

REFERENCES AND FURTHER READING

Alford, B. A. and Beck, A. T. (1997) *The Integrative Power of Cognitive Therapy.* New York: Guildford Press.

Beck, A. T. (1963) Thinking and depression. 1. Idiosyncratic content and cognitive distortions. *Archives of General Psychiatry, 9,* 324–33.

Beck, A. T. (1964) Thinking and depression. 2. Theory and therapy. *Archives of General Psychiatry, 10,* 561–71.

Beck, A. T. (1976) *Cognitive Therapy and the Emotional Disorders.* New York: New American Library.

Beck, A. T. (1978) *Anxiety Checklist.* Philadelphia, PA: Center for Cognitive Therapy.

Beck, A. T. (1988) *Love is Never Enough: How Couples Can Overcome Misunderstandings, Resolve Conflicts, and Solve Relationship Problems Through Cognitive Therapy.* New York: Harper & Row.

Beck, A. T. (1991) Cognitive therapy: A 30-year retrospective. *American Psychologist, 46,* 368–75.

Beck. A. T. (1999) *Prisoners of Hate: The Cognitive Basis of Anger, Hostility and Violence.* New York: Harper Collins.

Beck, A. T. (2005) The current state of cognitive therapy, *Archives of General Psychiatry*, 62, 953–9.

Beck, A. T. (2008) Cognitive therapy: An interview with a depressed and suicidal patient. In D. Wedding and R. J. Corsini (eds) *Case Studies in Psychotherapy* (5th ed.). Belmont, CA: Thomson Brooks/Cole, pp. 97–110.

Beck, A. T. and Emery, G. (1985) *Anxiety Disorders and Phobias: A Cognitive Perspective.* New York: Basic Books.

Beck, A. T., Freeman, A. et al., (2003) *Cognitive Therapy of Personality Disorders* (2nd ed.). New York: Plenum.

Beck, A. T., Kovacs, M. and Weissman, A. (1979a) Assessment of suicide intention: The Scale for Suicide Ideation. *Journal of Consulting and Clinical Psychology, 47,* 343–52.

Beck, A. T., Rush, A. J., Shaw, B. F. and Emery, G. (1979b) *Cognitive Therapy of Depression.* New York: John Wiley.

Beck, A. T., Ward, C. H., Mendelson, M., Mock, J. E., and Erbaugh, J. K. (1961) An inventory for measuring depression. *Archives of General Psychiatry, 4,* 561–71.

Beck, A. T. and Weishaar, M. E. (2014) Cognitive therapy. In D. Wedding and R. J. Corsini (eds), *Current Psychotherapies* (10th ed.). Belmont, CA: Brooks/Cole, pp. 231–64.

Beck. A. T. and Young, J. E. (1985) Cognitive therapy of depression. In D. Barlow (ed.), *Clinical Handbook of Psychological Disorders: A Step-by-Step Treatment Manual.* New York: Guildford Press, pp. 206–44.

Beck, J. S. (2011) *Cognitive Therapy: Basics and Beyond* (2nd ed.). New York: Guilford Press.

Beck, J. S and Beck, A. T. (2002) *Beck Youth Inventories of Emotional and Social Impairment.* San Antonio, TX: The Psychological Corporation.

Clark, D. A. and Beck, A. T. (2002) *Clark-Beck Obsessive-Compulsive Inventory.* San Antonio, TX: The Psychological Corporation.

Clark, D. A. and Beck, A. T. (2010) *Cognitive Therapy of Anxiety Disorders: Science and Practice.* New York: Guilford Press.

Clark, D. M. and Beck, A. T. (1988) Cognitive approaches. In C. G. Last and M. Hersen (eds), *Handbook of Anxiety Disorders.* New York: Pergamon, pp. 362–85.

Clark, D. M., Beck, A. T. and Alford, B. A. (1999) *Scientific Foundations of Cognitive Theory and Therapy of Depression.* Philadelphia: John Wiley.

Freeman, A. and Dattillio, F. M. (eds) (1992) *Comprehensive Casebook of Cognitive Therapy.* New York: Plenum Press.

Gilbert, P. (2009) *The Compassionate Mind*. London: Constable.

Greenberger, D. and Padesky, C. A. (1995) *Mind Over Mood: Change How You Feel by Changing the Way You Think*. New York: Guilford Press.

Hayes, S. C., Strosahl, K. and Wilson, K. G. (2003) *Acceptance and Commitment Therapy: An Experimental Approach to Behavior Change*. New York: Guilford Press.

Kelly, G. (1955) *The Psychology of Personal Constructs*. New York: Norton.

Kendall, P. C., Hollon, S. T., Beck, A. T., Hammen, C. L. and Ingram, R. E. (1987) Issues and recommendations regarding use of the Beck Depression Inventory. *Cognitive Therapy and Research, 11,* 289–99.

Lazarus, R. S. (1966) *Psychological Stress and the Coping Process*. New York: McGraw-Hill.

Marlatt, G. A. (ed.) (2002) *Harm Reduction: Pragmatic Strategies for Managing High Risk Behaviors*. New York: Guilford Press.

Padesky, C. A. and Beck, A. T. (2003) Science and philosophy: Comparison of cognitive therapy and rational emotive behavior therapy. *Journal of Cognitive Psychotherapy, 17,* 211–25.

Padesky, C. A. and Greenberger, D. (1995) *Clinician's Guide to Mind Over Mood*. New York: Guilford Press.

Segal, Z. V., Williams, J. M. G. and Teasdale, J. D. (2002) *Mindfulness-Based Cognitive Therapy for Depression: A New Approach to Preventing Relapse*. New York: Guilford.

Weishaar, M. E. (1993) *Aaron T. Beck*. London: Sage Publications.

Weissman, A. (1979) *The Dysfunctional Attitudes Scale*. Philadelphia, PA: Center for Cognitive Therapy.

BECK ON AUDIO AND VIDEO

Beck, A. T. (1977) *Demonstration of the Cognitive Therapy of depression: Interview#1 (Patient with family problem)*. Audio and video available.

Beck, A. T. (1979) *Cognitive Therapy of Depression: Interview#1 (Patient with a hopelessness problem)*. Audio and video available.

Beck, A. T. (1985) *Cognitive Therapy of Anxiety and Panic Disorders: First Interview Techniques*. Audio and video available.

Beck, A. T. (1990) *Cognitive Therapy of an Aviodant Personality*. Two audio-cassette set.

USEFUL ADDRESS

The Beck Institute for Cognitive Behavior Therapy
1 Belmont Avenue #700
Bala Cynwyd
PA 19004
USA
Website: www.beckinstitute.org

MULTIMODAL THERAPY 11

INTRODUCTION

Multimodal therapy is an approach developed by Arnold A. Lazarus, a clinical psychologist, in response to the constraints of traditional behaviour therapy. Lazarus' first book on multimodal therapy was entitled *Multimodal Behavior Therapy* (1976). However, he considered including the word behaviour in the title to be misleading, since it did not take into account working with other modalities, such as cognition and imagery. Consequently, he shortened the name to multimodal therapy.

ARNOLD A. LAZARUS (1932–2013)

Arnold Lazarus was born in Johannesburg, South Africa on January 27, 1932, the youngest of four children. His father ran a small retail business. At the time of his birth his two sisters were aged 14 and 17 and his brother was aged 8. Lazarus grew up feeling that as the youngest family member 'I was typically ignored and my opinion was considered unimportant' (Dryden, 1991, p. 101). This contributed to his feeling shy, inadequate and hypersensitive. Lazarus was a 'skinny kid who was bullied a lot' (Dryden, 1991, p. 1), and, consequently, spent much time on body-building activities. He exhibited an early interest in writing and, in his teens, had some stories published in local newspapers. Another youthful writing assignment was that of Associate Editor of a South African body-building magazine. When Lazarus was growing up, broadening experiences included: attending several high schools, spending time on a farm, working in a department store and selling houses.

Lazarus started university with a view to becoming a journalist and writer. However, on discovering that he could be a psychotherapist without going through a formal medical education, he became seriously interested in psychology and psychotherapy. In 1955 Lazarus received a BA with psychology and sociology majors, in 1956 a BA Honours in Psychology, in 1957 an MA in Experimental Psychology, and in 1960 a PhD in Clinical Psychology, all degrees conferred by the University of the Witwatersrand in Johannesburg. His PhD research on 'New group techniques in the treatment of phobic conditions' used group systematic desensitization. Joseph Wolpe was chairperson of his dissertation committee.

Lazarus' occupational history started with a part-time psychologist position in 1958–59 with the Mental Health Society in Johannesburg. From 1959 to 1963 and then from 1964 to 1966 he was in private practice as well as being a part-time lecturer at Witwatersrand Medical School. Albert Bandura, on the basis of seeing a write-up of Lazarus' PhD findings in the *Journal of Abnormal and Social Psychology* (Lazarus, 1961), invited him to Stanford University where, from 1963 to 1964, he was Visiting Assistant Professor in the Psychology Department. Uneasy with apartheid and the South African political situation, in 1966 Lazarus and his family returned to the United States, where in 1976 he became a naturalized American citizen.

From 1966 to 1967, Lazarus directed the Behavior Therapy Institute in Sausalito California. From 1967 to 1970, he was a Professor of Psychology in the Department of Behavioral Science in Temple University Medical School, Philadelphia. Joseph Wolpe, his former supervisor, was also at Temple University but he and Lazarus had an acrimonious falling out when Wolpe perceived Lazarus' views on the broadening of behaviour therapy to include cognition and 'technical eclecticism' as heretical and threatening to what he was propounding. From 1970 to 1972, Lazarus was Visiting Professor and Director of Clinical Training in Yale University's Department of Psychology. In 1972, he moved to Rutgers University in New Jersey being from 1972 to 1974 a Professor in and Chairman of the Psychology Department, from 1974 to 1998, a Distinguished Professor in the Graduate School of Applied and Professional Psychology, and then Distinguished Professor Emeritus of Clinical Psychology. Until his death on October 1, 2013, in addition to his private practice, he was President of the Lazarus Institute in Skillman, New Jersey, where his clinical psychologist son Clifford is the Executive Director and his licensed clinical social worker daughter-in-law Donna is the Clinical Director.

By 2013, Lazarus had authored or co-authored around 18 books and over 350 journal articles and book chapters. His books include *Behavior Therapy Techniques* (Wolpe and Lazarus, 1966), *Behavior Therapy and Beyond* (1971), *Clinical Behavior Therapy* (as editor and contributor (1972)), *Multimodal Behavior Therapy* (1976), *In the Mind's Eye: The Power of Imagery for Personal Enrichment* (1984), *Marital Myths Revisited* (2001), *Don't Believe It For a Minute!* (Lazarus, Lazarus and Fay, 1993), *The 60-Second Shrink: 101 Strategies for Staying Sane in a Crazy World* (Lazarus and Lazarus, 1997), *The Practice of Multimodal Therapy: Systematic, Comprehensive and Effective Psychotherapy* (1989b) and *Brief but Comprehensive Psychotherapy: The Multimodal Way* (2006).

In 1956, Lazarus married Daphne, and in 1959 Linda was born, followed in 1961 by Clifford. His priorities were: first, wife and family; second, meaningful friendships and the pursuit of fun (plays, music, brisk walks etc.); and third, work. By work, he meant intellectual stimulation, making a social contribution and surviving economically.

Regarding his professional work, Lazarus mentioned three contributions: first, showing that behaviour therapy could be more humanistic; second, broadening behaviour therapy's horizons to include cognitions, thus developing cognitive behaviour therapy; and third, developing 'an even broader and more systematic framework in my writings on multimodal methods' (Dryden, 1991, p. 112).

THEORY

BASIC CONCEPTS

TECHNICAL ECLECTICISM

Eclecticism is not a unitary construct (Lazarus, 1989a). Instead there are many different kinds of eclecticism. Lazarus distinguished unsystematic eclecticism, where therapists require neither a coherent rationale nor empirical validation for the techniques they use, and systematic (technical) eclecticism, where therapists are guided by a preferred theory but also draw techniques from other orientations.

Lazarus also distinguished theoretical eclecticism from technical eclecticism. Unlike their theoretically eclectic counterparts, technically eclectic therapists use procedures from different sources without necessarily subscribing to the theories or disciplines that spawned them (Lazarus, 2008a). Systematic technical eclectics neither choose techniques that 'feel right' nor hop from theory to theory. Lazarus wrote: 'The hallmark of technical eclecticism is the use of prescriptive treatments based on empirical evidence and client need, rather than theoretical and personal predisposition' (Lazarus, 1989a, p. 252). Technical eclectics mainly use cognitive behavioural ideas and techniques. In addition, they may draw from Adlerian, Rogerian, Eriksonian, psychodrama, gestalt, reality and transactional analysis schools, but without embracing any of these diverse theories. They regard as excess baggage the needless addition or multiplication of explanatory principles.

An important distinction exists between observations and theories. Theories are essentially speculations trying to account for various phenomena. Observations reflect clinical data without trying to offer explanations. Lazarus gave these examples: 'Adolescents tend to imitate the behavior of peers whom they respect', which is a statement based on observation; and 'They do so unconsciously due to inadequate parental introjects', a statement based on theory (Lazarus and Messer, 1991). Though acknowledging that clinical practice cannot be totally atheoretical, his technically eclectic therapy is governed by many observations (not theories) from different sources.

Unlike technical eclecticism, theoretical integration attempts to synthesize different therapy techniques as well as the theories underlying change from different orientations. Lazarus saw technical eclecticism as a step towards eventual integrationism. However, he urged caution in proceeding with integrationism. There is the danger of superficially merging theoretical tenets that are intrinsically incompatible (Lazarus, Beutler and Norcross, 1992; Lazarus, 2006).

Furthermore, therapists can become more intent on attaching theoretical labels to what they do than on precisely stating both what they do with each client and how they select what they do.

THRESHOLDS

Physiologically, people react to a variety of arousing stimuli with differing and distinctive patterns of autonomic nervous system activity. Lazarus (2006, 2008a) used the term threshold to describe people's differing capacities to tolerate negative stimuli such as pain, frustration, stress, cold, noise and pollution. People whose autonomic nervous systems are stable, which usually indicates high thresholds to many events, have a different personality pattern and are likely to be less anxiety prone than those whose autonomic reactions are labile, which usually correlates with low thresholds.

Thresholds, with their large innate component, can limit the effectiveness of psychological interventions. Lazarus gives the example of the limitations of hypnosis and other psychological techniques on a person with extremely low pain tolerance. While their pain tolerance may be raised, their innate threshold to overreact to pain stimuli nevertheless remains.

THE SEVEN MODALITIES: BASIC ID

The concept of modalities is the bedrock of comprehensive multimodal assessment and treatment. Human personality can be divided into seven discrete, yet interacting, modalities or dimensions. Lazarus wrote: 'These modalities exist in a state of reciprocal transaction and flux, connected by complex chains of behavior and other psychophysiological processes' (1992, p. 236). Box 11.1 presents the seven modalities, each illustrated by its description in the Structural Profile, a multimodal self-assessment questionnaire (Lazarus, 2006, pp. 143–4). The acronym BASIC ID is formed by using the first letter of each modality. This provides a useful shorthand descriptor of the seven modalities. In addition, the acronym serves as an *aide memoire*.

BOX 11.1 THE SEVEN BASIC ID MODALITIES

1. *Behaviour*: 'Some people may be described as "doers" – they are action oriented, like to keep busy, get things done and take on various projects. How much of a doer are you?'
2. *Affect*: 'Some people are very emotional and may or may not express it. How emotional are you? How deeply do you feel things? How passionate are you?'
3. *Sensation*: 'Some people attach a lot of value to sensory experiences, such as sex, food, music, art and other "sensory delights." Others are very much aware of minor aches, pains, and discomforts. How "tuned in to" your sensations are you?'

4. *Imagery*: 'How much fantasy or daydreaming do you engage in? This is separate from thinking or planning. This is "thinking in pictures", visualizing real or imagined experiences, letting your mind roam. How much are you into imagery?'
5. *Cognition*: 'Some people are very analytical, like to plan things and reason things through. How much of a "thinker" and "planner" are you?'
6. *Interpersonal*: 'How important are other people to you? This is your self-rating as a social being. How important are close friendships to you, the tendency to gravitate toward people, the desire for intimacy? The opposite of this is being a "loner."'
7. *Drugs/biology*: 'Are you healthy and health-conscious? Do you avoid bad habits like smoking, too much alcohol, drinking a lot of coffee, overeating and so on? Do you exercise regularly, get enough sleep, avoid junk foods and generally take care of your body?'

Lazarus acknowledged that people's behaviour is specific to situations and to other people. Nevertheless, people have tendencies, usually evident in the first decade of their lives, to favour some BASIC ID modalities over others. People's BASIC ID tendencies determine the tone and quality of how they function. For instance, to call someone an 'imagery reactor' means that their most highly valued and predominant modality is visual. Though they may not do so all the time, they are inclined to respond to and organize the world in terms of mental images. On the other hand, 'cognitive reactors' respond to the world from their intellects. In terms of brain research, the right hemisphere is probably dominant for imagery reactors and the left the hemisphere for cognitive reactors. Sensory reactors may be subdivided according to the predominance of each of the five basic senses. Lazarus observed: 'To "know" or to "understand" another person is to have full access to his or her BASIC ID. Self-knowledge implies an awareness of the content of one's own BASIC ID as well as insight into the interactive effects therein' (1989b, pp. 16–7).

Thresholds and preferred modalities interact. For example, the person with low pain tolerance, high frustration tolerance, high activity, and vivid imagery is very different from a person with low frustration tolerance, moderate activity, highly analytical (cognition), and capable of only forming fleeting images (Lazarus, 2008a).

ACQUISITION

Lazarus never developed a full theoretical statement regarding how people acquire and maintain their BASIC ID modalities and their personality strengths and weaknesses. Instead he preferred to be more of an empiricist and leave the theorizing to others. Nevertheless, he endeavoured to understand other theorists' frameworks and principles to see which were the best scientifically proven ideas upon which he could draw. Lazarus studiously avoided theoretical integration and stressed that multimodal therapy is not a conglomeration of psychoanalysis, behaviour therapy and many other systems (Lazarus, 2008a).

People's personalities stem from their genetic endowment, physical environment and social learning history. Multimodal therapy is not atheoretical: instead its technically eclectic stance operates within a consistent *social cognitive learning theory* (Bandura, 1986). However, when dealing with dyadic and family, and other complex interactions, Lazarus added explanatory concepts from communication and systems theory (Kwee and Lazarus, 1986).

According to Lazarus (1992, 2006), seven key constructs shape and maintain human personality:

1. associations and relations among events;
2. modelling and imitation;
3. non-conscious processes;
4. defensive reactions;
5. private events;
6. meta-communications; and
7. thresholds.

ASSOCIATIONS AND RELATIONS AMONG EVENTS

Association, in the form of events occurring simultaneously or in close succession, is important in all learning processes. Much human behaviour is the result of classical and operant conditioning. For instance, many aversions appear to originate from *classical conditioning*. Lazarus (2008a) provided the example of the client who had experienced post-operative nausea a few years previously and been in a hospital bed next to a man who kept playing a cassette of Beethoven's *Moonlight Sonata*. Later the client became sick to his stomach any time he heard that music.

Operant conditioning, where the probability of behaviour recurring is mediated by its consequences, is another major social learning process. For instance, a depressed woman can reinforce her depression by locking herself up in her bedroom and avoiding rewarding social contacts (Kwee and Lazarus, 1986). Another example is that of a woman who states 'I now realize that my headaches were in large part due to the fact that the only time my husband showed me any real caring was when I was in pain' (Lazarus, 2008a).

MODELLING AND IMITATION

Modelling and vicarious processes are also important in learning. People learn from observing and imitating what others do. Furthermore, they learn from perceiving the positive and negative consequences of others' behaviour.

NON-CONSCIOUS PROCESSES

Much learning is neither conscious nor deliberate. Non-conscious processes are not to be confused with the Freudian notion of the unconscious. What Lazarus meant by non-conscious processes is that 'people have different levels and degrees of awareness, and that unrecognized – subliminal – stimuli can influence one's thoughts, feelings, and behaviors ...' (1992, p. 235). Frequent demonstrations have illustrated that, during altered states of consciousness, people have access to memories and skills that are unavailable to conscious recall.

DEFENSIVE REACTIONS

Through their social learning experiences people may acquire a variety of unnecessary defensive reactions. Defensive reactions are avoidance responses attenuating pain, discomfort, anxiety depression and guilt (Lazarus, 2006). Such reactions entail people lessening their awareness, denying or distorting their perceptions and mislabelling their feelings. Included among defensive reactions are: denial; over-intellectualization and rationalization; projection, wrongly attributing one's feelings to others; and displacement, for instance of aggression towards other people, animals or things.

PRIVATE EVENTS

People filter and can override their conditioning and modelling because of their intervening thoughts about these stimuli. They do not respond to the real environment, but to their *perceived* environment. Factors influencing their perceptions include: idiosyncratic use of language, selective attention, problem-solving competencies, goals, performance standards, attributions, self-efficacy, expectancies, and values, attitudes and beliefs. Such thoughts determine which stimuli are noticed, how they are perceived and valued and how long they are remembered.

Misinformation and missing information are two of the major means through which people's private thoughts lead to emotional problems and disorders (Dryden, 1991). With *misinformation*, people have learned incorrect assumptions and beliefs about life and living. One area of misinformation encompasses the perfectionist beliefs held in Western society, for instance that life-long happiness results from fame and fortune. Other areas of misinformation include: the inability of people to realize that their lives are mainly controlled by their own thoughts and perceptions rather than by external events; the belief that it is good to ventilate anger; the belief in the importance of pleasing others; and the idea that it is better to play safe by leading a life where there are no risks. Marital misinformation includes the myths that 'Romantic love makes a good marriage' and 'If you feel guilty, confess' (Lazarus, 2001).

With misinformation, people have acquired erroneous ideas. With *missing information*, people do possess the information to enact basic skills required for successful living. Social skills provide an important area of missing information about such matters as eye contact and how to converse. In addition, many people lack information on how to handle job interviews and present themselves favourably.

Lazarus regarded as terrifying the amount of ignorance pervading the world. Even events such as international terrorism and drug smuggling can be 'tied into extreme misinformation and missing information that people have about the sort of values and skills that could make for a happier world' (Dryden, 1991, p. 15).

META-COMMUNICATION

Humans can both communicate and communicate about their communications, otherwise known as meta-communication. People can step back and examine the content and processes of their own relationships and patterns of communication. For example, in couples therapy partners can either skillfully or unskillfully explore and discuss the processes of their relationship, including identifying unhelpful communication patterns. The ability to meta-communicate characterizes all high quality relationships between friends, relatives and lovers.

THRESHOLDS

For a review of Lazarus' ideas on thresholds, the reader is referred back to the relevant section earlier in this chapter on p. 312.

MAINTENANCE

People's personalities are not only acquired but also maintained through the interaction of genetic endowment, social learning, and environmental influences. For example, people's genetic endowment persists in the form of different thresholds and favoured BASIC ID modalities. Social learning influences the maintenance of personality in a number of ways. People learn maladaptive habits or conditioned emotional reactions 'through various associations and unfortunate connections of events' (Dryden, 1991, p. 9). Such habits may be simple or complex and persist in interfering with their happiness. In addition, through conditioning and modelling, they learn not only behaviours, but also perceptions of self-efficacy, performance standards and goals that they maintain for good or ill. In addition, people's environments can continue to offer reinforcements and models that contribute to maintaining their thoughts, feelings and behaviours.

Non-conscious processes influence maintenance of personality. People may remain unaware of what they have learned and keep learning from others. Consequently, such thoughts, feelings and behaviours are less easy to change. Once learned, defensive reactions act as habits that block people from full awareness of how they and others behave. Defensive reactions make it harder for people to work on their problems since they lack insight both into their defensive reactions and into their negative consequences. Consequently, defensive reactions are both part of and serve to maintain unhelpful aspects of people's BASIC IDs.

Lazarus assigned a pivotal role to misinformation and missing information in maintaining behaviour and in causing people to become therapy clients. Gaps in people's repertoires, because they were never given necessary information and essential coping processes, render them ill-equipped to deal with societal demands (Lazarus, 2008a). In addition, people can communicate about their communication in ways that maintain rather than solve problems, for instance by blaming one another.

The following are other factors, interacting with those already mentioned, that can contribute to people maintaining dysfunctional thoughts, feelings and behaviours (Dryden, 1991).

- *Conflicting or ambivalent feelings or reactions*: People can possess approach-approach or avoidance-avoidance conflicts resulting in extreme indecisiveness. Their prior learning experiences have contributed to their indecision and inertia. Their indecisiveness may be both self-maintaining and also contribute to their inability to change aspects of how they function.
- *Interpersonal inquietude*: Many people remain upset because of undue dependencies, excessive hates and misplaced loves. Lazarus saw such interpersonal inquietude stemming from skills deficits and from unrealistic demands that people impose upon each other.
- *Poor self-acceptance*: People maintain negative feelings about themselves because they do not understand the difference between accepting their totality as human beings and functionally evaluating specific shortcomings and personal limitations. Self-acceptance means 'Don't put your ego on the line, accept yourself, your totality, even though there might be lots of little "i's" as part of the big "I", that are less than exemplary' (Dryden, 1991, p. 13). For instance, people can make mistakes and possess skills weaknesses without feeling totally crushed as persons.

THERAPY

The practice of multimodal therapy possesses six distinctive features:

1. 'The specific and comprehensive attention given to the entire BASIC ID
2. The use of Second-Order BASIC ID assessments
3. The use of Modality Profiles
4. The use of Structural Profiles
5. Tracking the modality firing order
6. Deliberate bridging procedures' (Lazarus, 1992, p. 250).

Though not in the order listed above, this section reviews how each of these distinctive features form part of multimodal therapy.

THERAPEUTIC GOALS

Long-range hedonism is a guiding philosophy (Dryden, 1991). Though Lazarus did not define fun, a major goal for most humans is to have fun while alive. However, people need to attain a good balance between long-range and short-range hedonism.

Though individuals differ in their predominant modalities, the BASIC ID suggests illustrative subgoals for effective functioning:

- *Behaviour*: Taking effective actions in pursuit of realistic goals.
- *Affect*: Acknowledging, clarifying and recognizing feelings; coping with negative feelings and enhancing positive ones.
- *Sensation*: Being in touch with and enjoying one's senses.
- Imagery: Being in touch with one's imagination; using coping images.
- *Cognition*: Possessing sufficiently accurate and complete information; thinking realistically.
- *Interpersonal*: Possessing good relating skills, for instance assertion and conversational skills; capacity for healthy interdependency.
- *Drugs/biology*: Taking good care of one's body and physical health; eating and drinking in moderation.

People can have weaknesses in one or more of the above modalities and still be happy. Humans are fallible with a biological penchant sometimes to be self-defeating. However, people can feel self-acceptance, accept their fallibility, at the same time as attempting to be less fallible.

Multimodal therapy goals are tailored to particular clients and take into account their 'goals, coping behaviors, situational contexts, affective reactions, "resistances", and basic beliefs' (Lazarus, 1992, p. 237). Rigidity is to be avoided in all aspects of therapy, including assessment and goal-setting. In some instances, clients' main problems are obvious and a thorough assessment of all seven BASIC ID modalities is unnecessary.

In most cases, multimodal therapy rests on a thorough assessment of the BASIC ID that leads to constructing a Modality Profile listing salient problems and recommended treatments within each modality. Outcome goals, namely overcoming or coping with the problem, are implicit for each problem listed by modality in the profile. For instance, depression is one of the problems listed in the Affect section of a client's Modality Profile. An outcome goal for this problem relates to a lessening of the client's depressed feelings, preferably in some measurable way. Inasmuch as Modality Profiles also list recommended interventions, decision and process goals are implicit in them. A therapist decision-making goal is to select the most effective treatments of choice for each problem. Could the therapist have selected better treatments of choice for the client's depression problem than the recommended interventions of coping imagery and increasing rewarding activities? Once chosen, to what extent does each intervention, on its own or in combination, contribute to the problem or outcome goal of lessening the client's depression?

PROCESS OF THERAPY

Multimodal therapy may be conducted in either complete or brief forms. The average duration of a complete course of multimodal therapy is approximately 50 one-hour-long sessions (weekly sessions for about a year). Lazarus (2008a) observed that fewer than 30 per cent of the clients seen at the various Multimodal Therapy Institutes seem to require or are willing to participate in 50 hours of therapy. The majority favour brief therapy consisting of about 1 to 15 hour-long sessions, which may take place either over a short period of time or extend over many months (Lazarus, 2006). Lazarus contended that by using the multimodal framework, therapy can be both brief and comprehensive.

INITIAL SESSIONS

Initial sessions follow no rigid format. Therapists may meet with individuals, couples, or families. They may begin with small talk and collecting basic information, for instance address and phone number, before embarking on a more detailed enquiry. Two main questions relating to clients' presenting complaints are: 'What has led to the current situation?' and 'Who or what is maintaining it?' (Lazarus, 1992, 2008a). In addition, therapists look for signs of psychosis, organic problems, and depression. From the start, therapists are attuned to noting information about which modalities of the BASIC ID their clients' complaints apply to. In addition, they try to assess clients' expectations about therapy and the most appropriate kind of relationship style to adopt. Furthermore, they look for clients' strengths and positive attributes. Quite often in initial interviews therapists use specific interventions, for instance cognitive disputation. At the end of the initial interview, therapists give most adult clients the 15-page *Multimodal Life History Inventory* (Lazarus and Lazarus, 1991; Lazarus, 2006). This inventory asks numerous questions about antecedent events and maintaining factors with the answers being divided into BASIC ID categories.

An important multimodal therapy principle is 'Know your own limitations and other clinicians' strengths' (Dryden, 1991, p. 30). Referrals should be made where other therapists have skills that the therapist does not possess or more appropriate personal styles for particular clients. Lazarus did not consider himself particularly good at working with seriously disturbed people – for instance schizophrenics, substance abusers, and people with anti-social personality disorders. He sought out more expert or gifted people for such clients. Often referrals to other therapists are best made before bonding with the original therapist occurs. Lazarus also refered clients to self-help groups, such as Alcoholics Anonymous, Self Management and Recovery Training (SMART), Overeaters Anonymous and Parents Without Partners.

THE MODALITY PROFILE

Lazarus (1992) wrote: 'the mainstay of multimodal assessment centers on Modality Profiles and Structural Profiles' (p. 246). A Modality Profile is a BASIC ID chart listing problems and interventions within each modality. Lazarus only drew up such profiles when therapy was not going quickly enough and unforeseen problems arose. Around the start of the third session, therapists have usually gleaned enough information from interviews and the *Life History Inventory*

Table 11.1   Example of a Modality Profile

Modality	Problem	Intervention
Behaviour	Procrastination	Contingency contracting
	Tends to pout or withdraw when frustrated	Modelling and role playing of assertiveness skills
	Volatile and explosive	Relaxation and communication training
Affect	Anxiety	Breathing and deep muscle relaxation; stress inoculation training
	Depression	Coping imagery; increase rewarding activities
Sensation	Tension (esp. in jaws and neck)	Relaxation training
	Lower-back pain	Orthopaedic exercises
Imagery	Lonely images	Picturing various coping responses
	Images of failure	
Cognition	Perfectionism	Cognitive restructuring
	Negative scanning	
	Dichotomous thinking	
	Self-downing	
Interpersonal relationships	Passive-aggressive	Social skills and assertiveness training
	Unassertive	
	Has few friends	
Drugs/biology	Insufficient exercise	Healthy lifestyle programme
	Overweight	

to spend 15 to 20 minutes drafting a preliminary Modality Profile for the client. Sometimes clients are asked to draft their own Modality Profiles separately from their therapists and then the two compare notes. Multimodal therapists treat their clients' Modality Profiles as sets of hypotheses. Modality Profiles are shared and discussed with clients.

Table 11.1 provides an example of a Modality Profile for a 37-year-old man in therapy for generalized anxiety (Lazarus, 1992, p. 242).

THE STRUCTURAL PROFILE

The Structural Profile comes towards the end of the *Multimodal Life History Inventory*. Here clients are asked to rate themselves across each of the BASIC ID modalities on a 7-point scale with 1 being the lowest and 7 being the highest. The descriptions for each modality were provided earlier in this chapter when introducing the seven BASIC ID modalities. The Structural Profile provides useful additional information to both therapist and client about how the client interacts with the world. It can be easily depicted on a bar graph.

In addition, to the 7 questions that form part of the *Multimodal Life History Inventory,* Lazarus developed a 35-item standardized instrument called the *Structural Profile Inventory* (SPI) (1989b, 2006). In 1995 an Expanded Structural Profile was developed by Lazarus' son Clifford (Lazarus, 2006, pp. 145–8).

The SPI has proved very useful in couples therapy. The profiles pinpoint reasons for misunderstanding and can lead to fruitful discussions of what to do about them. Sometimes the profiles may indicate that divorce therapy is a more realistic prospect than marital therapy. For instance, where one partner values affective expression and interpersonal intimacy and is low on behaviour and cognition, and the other partner has the opposite profile.

TRACKING

Clients have fairly reliable patterns or orderings of modalities in how they generate negative affect, though on occasion these patterns may vary. Tracking refers to the careful assessment of the 'firing order', the ordering of the chain reaction of the different modalities. For instance, one client may generate negative emotions through dwelling first on sensations (S) (e.g. heart palpitations) that 'fire' cognitions (C) (e.g. 'I may get very ill or die') that 'fire' aversive images (I) (e.g. pictures of catastrophic disease) that 'fire' maladaptive behaviour (B) (e.g. extreme withdrawal) (Lazarus, 2008a). Another client, instead of the SCIB firing order outlined above may display a CISB pattern (cognitive-imagery-sensation-behaviour).

One purpose of tracking is to provide clients with insight into the precise processes by which they generate negative affect so that they can intervene appropriately. Another purpose is to assist therapists in selecting and prioritizing treatment interventions. Box 11.2 provides an example of a female client tracking her firing order and then the therapist planning treatment accordingly (Lazarus, 2008a). Had the client a different firing order, the therapist would have trained her in a different sequence and encouraged her to use this different sequence in real life.

BOX 11.2   EXAMPLE OF TRACKING

TRACKING THE FIRING ORDER

An agoraphobic woman tracked in herself a CISA firing order:

- an illustrative cognition (C) was 'What if I pass out?',
- followed by mental images (I) of herself hyperventilating and fainting,

(Continued)

(Continued)

- which fired sensations (S) of light-headedness and sweaty palms,
- which fired feelings (A) of panic and anxiety.

TREATMENT BASED ON THE CLIENT'S FIRING ORDER

Following the client's firing order, her therapist:

- first provided her with self-instructional training (Meichenbaum, 1977) to counter-act her self-defeating cognitions;
- next, the therapist taught her coping imagery in which she vividly imagined herself remaining calm and controlled in feared situations (such as shopping in a supermarket); and
- taught her in the sensory modality, slow abdominal breathing and differential muscle relaxation.

The client was instructed to practise her training in real life. When shopping in a supermarket, she was to follow the sequence of:

- using positive self-instructions (C)
- then adding coping imagery (I)
- and then using abdominal breathing while deliberately relaxing muscles not in use at the time (S).

SECOND-ORDER BASIC ID ASSESSMENTS

When impasses occur in treating clients, therapists may perform second-order BASIC ID assessments. Such assessments allow a more detailed review of behaviours, affective responses, sensory reactions, images, cognitions, interpersonal factions, and drugs and biological factors in relation to the area in which change is proving difficult. For instance, unassertive behaviours may persist, despite role playing, behaviour rehearsal, modelling and other relevant training. When, as part of her second-order assessment, one client was asked for her BASIC ID associations to the concept of assertiveness, her answers were as follows: behaviour, attacking; affect, angry; sensation, tension; imagery, bombs bursting; cognition, get even; interpersonal, hurting; and drugs/biologicals, high blood pressure (Lazarus, 2008a). Although the therapist had attempted to convey to her the difference between assertion and aggression, the second-order BASIC ID showed that she still regarded assertive responses as tantamount to vicious attacks. Box 11.3 provides another example of a second-order BASIC ID profile (Lazarus, 2006, pp. 58–9).

BOX 11.3 EXAMPLE OF A SECOND-ORDER BASIC ID PROFILE

THE CLIENT

The client had an established alcohol addiction, and one of the items on his Modality Profile was 'Urges to Use Alcohol or Cravings'.

HIS SECOND-ORDER BASIC ID PROFILE

When asked about the impact of these urges or cravings across the BASIC ID, the following profile emerged:

- *Behaviour*   Clenches jaw;
                     Starts pacing or wringing hands.
- *Affect*   Anxiety;
                     Depression.
- *Sensation*   Muscle tension;
                     Dry mouth.
- *Imagery*   Visualizes drinking alcohol;
                     Imagines smell and taste of drink;
                     Pictures sense of intoxication.
- *Cognition*   Thoughts of unfairness;
                     Belief that craving will never subside;
                     Idea that intake can be controlled;
                     Various other rationalizations.
- *Interpersonal*   Withdraws from social interaction or
                     lashes out irritably at others.
- *Drugs/biology*   Smokes a cigarette or has a cup of coffee.

POSSIBLE STRATEGIES

The most obvious strategies based on this profile include:

1. more attention to deep muscle relaxation;
2. successful images of turning away from alcohol; and
3. cognitive disputation.

SELECTION OF INTERVENTIONS

Multimodal therapy 'is an open system in which the principle of technical eclecticism encourages the constant introduction of new techniques and the refinement or elimination of existing ones, but never in a random or shotgun manner' (Lazarus, 2008a, p. 396). A fundamental premise of the multimodal approach is that clients are usually troubled by a multitude of specific problems that should be dealt with by a multitude of specific treatments. How do multimodal therapists select treatment interventions? Table 11.1 provided, as part of a Modality Profile, the techniques selected for a man in therapy for generalized anxiety. Multimodal therapists need to be aware of and skilled in a wide repertoire of techniques or interventions. If unaware of or unskilled in certain interventions they are unlikely to help clients with certain conditions. The first or main requirement for selecting interventions is the extent to which there are research data to support them. Empirical data exist for documenting treatments of choice across a variety of conditions including 'bulimia nervosa, compulsive rituals, social skill deficits, bipolar depression, schizophrenic delusions, focal phobias, tics and habit disorders, pain management, hyperventilation, panic disorders, autism, enuresis, vaginisimus and other sexual dysfunctions, and a variety of stress-related disorders...' (Lazarus et al., 1992). However, probably some 'grey areas' will always exist. Practising therapists should familiarize themselves with the research outcome literature.

Multimodal therapists take a number of other factors into account in selecting and prioritizing interventions. Such factors include clients' priorities, firing orders, and the desirability of early success experiences. Careful consideration is given to answers to the following three items on page 4 of the *Multimodal Life History Inventory*: 'In a few words, what do you think therapy is about?', 'How long do you think your therapy should last?', and 'What personal qualities do you think the ideal therapist should possess?' (Lazarus, 1992, pp. 242–3). For instance, clients thinking the ideal therapist is an active listener may take unkindly to active-directive, task-oriented therapists.

Multimodal therapists start 'with the most obvious and logical procedures.' (Kwee and Lazarus, 1986, p. 335). Once selected, therapists still need to accommodate their chosen interventions to the unique characteristics of each client in order to promote adherence and compliance. While the initial selection of interventions may be relatively straightforward, their implementation 'requires clinical experience, acumen, and artistry' (Kwee and Lazarus, 1986, p. 337). If the initially selected interventions did not work, Lazarus might draw on other well-researched interventions. Sometimes he went beyond well-researched interventions to try other interventions that might help specific clients: for example, the technique of shrinking the feared object down to size from neurolinguistic programming (NLP) or using the conceptualization of Parent, Adult and Child from Transactional Analysis (Dryden, 1991). In addition, second-order BASIC ID assessments may be conducted to look for significant factors that may have been overlooked in initial assessment procedures.

PROGRESS EVALUATIONS

Ongoing evaluations of progress are integral to multimodal therapy. Since Modality Profiles are commonly drawn up, therapists can evaluate progress for each problem within each of the seven BASIC ID dimensions. Such information is relevant both during therapy and for making termination of therapy decisions. Lazarus provided the following example how a multimodal therapist specified a client's gains and achievements (2008a, p. 390):

Behaviour:	Less withdrawn; less compulsive; more outspoken
Affect:	More warm, less hostile; less depressed
Sensation:	Enjoys more pleasures; less tense, more relaxed
Imagery:	Fewer nightmares; better self-image
Cognition:	Less self-downing; more positive self-statements
Interpersonal:	Goes out on dates; expresses wishes and desires
Drugs/biology:	Has stopped smoking; sleeps well; exercises regularly

THE THERAPEUTIC RELATIONSHIP

The therapeutic relationship can be divided into relationship behaviours that are universal and those that differ for specific clients. One universal relationship behaviour is the attempt to develop a collaborative alliance whenever possible. Multimodal therapists endeavour to work together with clients. A second relationship universal is never to attack a client's sense of dignity as a person, though their maladptive behaviours may be assailed.

'"Relationships of choice" are no less important than "techniques of choice" for effective psychotherapy' (Lazarus, 1993, p. 404). For most clients the purpose of the therapeutic relationship is to provide 'the soil that enables the techniques to take root' (Dryden, 1991, p. 17). Unlike Rogers who would offer the same kind of 'carefully cultivated warmth, genuineness and empathy to all his clients' (p. 18), Lazarus tried not only to match the nature of the relationship to the client, but also to the clients' observed needs at different times in therapy. For some clients, good listening is sufficient. However, many clients require therapists to select and use specific techniques to help them develop coping skills for problems identified in their Modality Profiles. Thus, therapists need to offer relationships that go beyond good listening.

Lazarus emphasized flexibility and versatility and used the metaphor of the 'authentic chameleon' (Lazarus, 1993, 2006) to indicate that multimodal therapists vary their relationship styles to fit with clients' expectations, personalities, problems and goals. He described four different, yet overlapping, ways of varying relationships with clients.

1. *The relationship continuum*: Multimodal therapists view helping relationships on a continuum from 'a very close-knit, dependent bonding at the one end, to a rather formal, businesslike involvement at the other' (Kwee and Lazarus, 1986, p. 333). Throughout therapy, the relationship is used flexibly to fit each client's expectancies and preferred modalities. For instance, some people do not respond well to therapist warmth and empathy and like a more businesslike approach.

2. *Matching therapist styles*: Therapist styles that Lazarus sought to match to individual clients included: 'whether and when to be cold, warm, or tepid; when and whether not to be confrontational; when and whether to be earthy, chummy, casual and informal rather than "professional"; when to self-disclose or remain enigmatic; when to be soft-nosed, gentle and tender, and when to come on like a tough army sergeant; and how to adjust my levels of supportiveness and directiveness' (Lazarus, 1993, p. 405).

3. *Supportivness and directiveness dimensions*: During therapy, multimodal therapists continually ask themselves how supportive and how directive they need be with their clients. Four possibilities are: high direction–high support, low direction–low support, low direction–high support and high direction–high support. Effective therapists switch among and between all four modes 'in the chameleon sense' (Dryden, 1991, p. 19). Lazarus worked mostly in the high direction–high support mode, since he saw therapy as an educational process in which the therapist's main role is that of a clinical teacher. Furthermore, clients change most rapidly when ready for high direction and high support.

4. *Relationships differing with selected techniques*: Lazarus used techniques that drew upon the work of Freud, Rogers, Perls, Ellis, Adler, Haley, and the behaviourists among others. As part of tailoring his interventions to the needs of each client, he also flexibly utilized the kind of relationship implicit in these techniques (Lazarus, 1989b). For instance, he might use Rogerian reflection, gestalt psychodrama and imagery techniques, or behavioural assertiveness training, and accordingly adjust the kind of relationship he offered.

The two *client* variables that most influenced Lazarus' relationship style were his perceptions of their readiness for change and of their reactance level. Ongoing therapy interactions play a dominant part in selecting relationship of choice. For instance, Lazarus adopted an extremely gentle stance in which he was almost whispering to a very timid and shy young woman who expressed strong reactions about her dealings with 'loud, pushy, or obnoxious people' (Lazarus, 1993, p. 406). The outcome was that the client, who had poor relationships with her two previous therapists, co-operated well with him.

BRIDGING

Bridging is a rapport enhancement technique that illustrates the flexibility of the multimodal therapy relationship. When bridging, therapists deliberately tune into the clients' preferred modalities before gently helping them cross bridges into other modalities that may prove more productive (Lazarus, 1992, 2006, 2008a). Clients are more likely to feel understood by therapists who first respond within their preferred representational system. Other ways of describing bridging are that therapists first 'talk their clients' language' or 'start from where they are' before moving into less preferred modalities. An advantage of doing this is that clients then become less resistant to working in these other modalities. Box 11.4 provides an example of bridging (Lazarus, 1992, pp. 247–9).

BOX 11.4   EXAMPLE OF BRIDGING

The multimodal therapist is interested in understanding an initial emotional reaction.

ORIGINAL INTERACTION

Therapist: 'How did you feel about your father's decision to leave home?'
Client: 'My father tended to put his needs first, and neither my mother nor I were factored into the equation.'

STAYING IN THE COGNITIVE MODALITY

Rather than pressure the client into the affective modality the therapist might first join with the client in the cognitive modality.

BRIDGING INTO THE SENSORY MODALITY

Then, after about five minutes, the therapist could bridge into a modality that was less threatening than the affective modality, for instance the sensory modality with a question like:

Therapist: 'By the way can you tune into some sensations anywhere in your body?'

BRIDGING INTO THE AFFECTIVE MODALITY

Then, after discussing sensations, the therapist could bridge into the affective modality with a question such as:

Therapist: 'I really wonder how you feel about the things your father has done?'

By now the client should be much less defensive about revealing feelings.

THERAPEUTIC INTERVENTIONS

The following are principal multimodal interventions or techniques for each BASIC ID dimension (Kwee and Lazarus, 1986; Lazarus, 1989b, 2008a). Frequently, these interventions are used in combination. Interventions should be used sparingly according to the assessed needs of individual clients.

BEHAVIOUR

- *Behaviour rehearsal*: Therapists, who start by playing the other person, repeatedly rehearse clients in how to behave in specific situations. Dialogues are either audio- or video-recorded and played back. When ready, clients enact their skills in the actual situations.

- *Modelling*: Therapists provide role models for specific behaviours clients are encouraged to imitate. Therapists may model behaviours in real-life settings: for instance assertively returning faulty goods to a shop.
- *Non-reinforcement*: By not attending to specific client behaviours, therapists and others in clients' social environments can facilitate their extinction.
- *Positive reinforcement*: To strengthen specific client behaviours, therapists can dispense social reinforcers such as praise, recognition and encouragement. With children and adolescents therapists may use tangible reinforcers, such as food and money. Therapists may also use tokens that may be exchanged for tangible rewards.
- *Recording and self-monitoring*: Therapists encourage clients to engage in the systematic recording, charting and/or counting of targeted behaviours.
- *Stimulus control*: The absence or presence of certain stimuli is related to the frequency of behaviours. For example, people trying to lose weight can keep snacks and desserts out of their homes. Students trying to increase study behaviours can arrange their desks without distracting stimuli and only sit at them when studying.
- *Systematic exposure*: Therapists encourage clients to expose themselves step-by-step to their feared situations. Many additional techniques, for instance *goal rehearsal or coping imagery*, may be used to overcome avoidances in conjunction with systematic exposure.

AFFECT

- *Anger expression*: Anger-expression means assisting clients to own and express their anger. It is not an end in itself and clients may require *behaviour rehearsal* in how to express anger assertively. Techniques to get clients in touch with angry feelings include coaxing them to say louder and louder 'I am angry' and getting them to pummel and kick foam rubber cushions, pillows and inflatable objects.
- *Anxiety management training*: First, therapists teach clients general *relaxation training* and *goal-rehearsal or coping imagery*. Then they teach clients to generate anxiety-evoking cognitions and imagery and immediately after to relax and dwell on calm sensations, picture serene images, dispute irrational ideas, and concentrate on optimistic and relaxing thoughts.
- *Feeling-identification*: Labelling feelings accurately is one area of feeling-identification: for instance, clients may say they are 'depressed' when their symptoms are more those of 'anxiety'. The main area of feeling-identification is on exploring the client's affective domain to help them identify significant feelings that might be unclear or misdirected.
- *The empty chair*: The client faces an empty chair and imagines it occupied by a significant other. The client starts a dialogue with this other person and then switches chairs back and forth to conduct both parts of the dialogue. Therapists may offer prompts about what to say, for instance, 'Ask her to tell you exactly how she would have wanted you to respond.' As well as assisting clients to own and express feelings, the empty chair helps them appreciate others' viewpoints.

SENSATION

- *Biofeedback*: There are biofeedback devices that can help clients to monitor and modify physiological functions like muscular tension, heart rate, brain wave activity, galvanic skin response and skin temperature. For example, for a client suffering from painful tension in the jaw, the therapist can attach electrodes to the jaw muscles that are wired to a machine that provides tonal feedback (the more tension the louder the sound) according to the degree of muscular tension. Clients can learn to maintain a low decibel level or eliminate the tone altogether.

- *Focusing*: Therapists encourage clients in contemplative and relaxed states to tune into their spontaneous thoughts and feelings until one major felt bodily expression emerges. After several minutes of intense focusing, clients are asked to extract something new from their sensations, images and emotions.
- *Hypnosis*: Therapists can usefully learn several methods for inducing trances to maximize their chances of success with individual clients. Hypnotic-induction techniques mostly involve sensory fixation (for example, focusing on a spot on the ceiling) and monotonous repetitions, such as 'calm and relaxed'.
- *Meditation*: Therapists can teach clients meditation, for instance sitting down, gradually closing their eyes, and inwardly repeating a 'mantra' such as the word 'in' on inhaling and the word 'out' on exhaling. As thoughts float in and out of awareness, the meditator continues to think the words 'in' and 'out'. Often two daily twenty-minute sessions are advocated. However, some clients gain most from mini-meditations of two or three-minute sessions several times daily.
- *Relaxation training*: Clients can learn total relaxation and/or differential relaxation. Total relaxation is another term for progressive muscular relaxation involving alternate tensing and letting go of each major muscle area. Differential relaxation entails learning to relax those muscles not in use when performing various tasks. For instance, a person tensing their jaw, shoulders and neck and holding their breath when sitting and writing can deliberately relax the tense muscles and breathe abdominally in a slow and rhythmic fashion.
- *Sensate focus training*: Usually prescribed for sexually dysfunctional couples, sensate focus refers to sensual rather than to sexual pleasuring. The pleasuring partner is forbidden to touch the genitals or female breasts and no pressures for sexual performance are permitted. Instead the pleasuring partner massages, touches and stimulates the part of the body that the recipient enjoys having stimulated. Afterwards, partners can reverse roles.
- *Threshold training*: Threshold training is a common technique for the treatment of premature or rapid ejaculation. The female manually stimulates the man's penis. When he feels a pre-orgasmic sensation he says 'stop' and/or removes her hand until the sensation abates. This procedure is repeated. Later more advanced variations can be added: for instance manual stimulation using a lubricant, and effecting vaginal entry and withdrawing on feeling a pre-orgasmic urge. Within a few weeks, many males can delay ejaculation for long periods.

IMAGERY

- *Anti-future shock imagery*: This intervention helps prepare clients for changes likely to happen in the coming months or years: for instance, becoming a parent, being promoted, or moving to a new location. Clients are encouraged to visualize themselves coping with these changes.
- *Associated imagery*: When clients experience unwanted emotions for which they are unable to account, therapists can ask them to focus immediately on any image that comes to mind and see it as vividly as possible. New images that emerge are to be visualized as clearly as possible. If no new images emerge, the original image is to be examined as if through a zoom lens, with this process often eliciting other images for tracking. Frequently clients report significant insights from using this technique.

- *Aversive imagery*: Clients can learn to associate unpleasant images with behaviour that is unwanted, yet self-reinforcing (for example, alcoholism, sexual deviations, overeating). For instance, clients on diets can be trained to imagine that someone has vomited over the rich food they wish to eat.
- *Goal rehearsal or coping imagery*: Clients are trained to break down the steps involved in difficult upcoming events. For each step, they visualize themselves faltering, but coping. For instance, a woman with an aversion to hospitals had the goal of visiting and supporting a sick friend. She imagined herself coping with the difficulties involved in the hospital visit and her sense of achievement for helping her friend.
- *Positive imagery*: Positive imagery entails visualizing a pleasant scene, real or imagined, past, present or future. Beneficial effects of positive imagery include: reducing tension, inhibiting anxiety and enhancing enjoyment.
- *The step-up technique*: Clients unduly anxious about upcoming events, for instance a public speech, are asked to picture the worst thing imaginable and then imagine themselves coping with the situation and surviving the most negative outcomes. Some clients require *self-instructional training* along with the step-up technique.
- *Time projection (forward or backward)*: Time projection or 'time tripping' can be used to help clients relive and work through past events. In addition, clients can imagine both what might happen in the future, for instance depressed clients picturing themselves engaging in more and more rewarding activities; and how the present might look from the vantage point of the future, for instance picturing an event after a few months and realizing the temporary nature of the current problem.

COGNITION

- *Bibliotherapy*: A well-chosen self-help book 'can be worth more than a dozen sessions' (Lazarus, 1989b, p. 243). Books should be thoroughly read, even summarized in notebooks, and readings discussed during sessions.
- *Correcting misconceptions*: Therapists can provide clients with factual information to correct misconceptions about society, other people and themselves. Sexual misconceptions are common. Therapists should learn the relevant facts and realities. Bibliotherapy can form an important component of correcting misconceptions.
- *Ellis' ABCDE paradigm*: Therapists can teach clients Ellis' A (activating event), B (beliefs), C (consequences), D (disputing) and E (effects) paradigm. Clients can learn to identify their irrational beliefs (B) about activating events (A) that lead to negative consequences (C). Disputing these irrational beliefs (D) can result in the effect (E) of the diminution or elimination of negative consequences.
- *Problem solving*: Clients can learn to apply the rudiments of scientific methodology to problems. Problem solving involves generating plausible hypotheses that can be strengthened or weakened by gathering relevant information. Decisions are made on the basis of facts and probability rather than by mysticism or chance.
- *Self-instructional training*: Therapists can train clients to replace negative self-statements with positive, task-oriented statements that facilitate coping. For instance, clients anxious about a forthcoming event could instruct themselves to: develop a plan; handle the situation one step at a time; if anxious to pause and take a few deep breaths; remind themselves that they only have to keep fear manageable rather than eliminate it; focus on what they need to do; acknowledge the link between controlling self-talk and controlling fear; and recognize that it gets easier each time they use their self-instructions.

- *Thought blocking*: Thought blocking is a technique to combat obsessive and intrusive thoughts. Clients can be taught to sub-vocally scream 'STOP!' over and over again. A variation of thought blocking is for clients to flick their wrists with a rubber band when they scream 'STOP!'. Some clients find it helps to picture huge neon signs flashing the letters ' STOP ' on and off.

INTERPERSONAL

- *Communication training*: Therapists can train clients in how to send and receive communications. Sending skills include eye contact, body posture, voice projection and the use of simple concrete terms. Receiving skills include active listening and rewarding senders for communicating. Role playing and behaviour rehearsal are especially useful in communication training.
- *Contingency contracting*: Clients agree to make rewards or negative consequences (usually self-imposed) contingent upon increasing, decreasing or maintaining a specific behaviour.
- *Friendship training*: In friendship training, therapists identify and train clients in how to interact in pro-social and affectionate ways. Skills that therapists emphasize include empathy, showing caring and concern, self-disclosing, positive reinforcement and give-and-take. Clients are taught to avoid competitiveness and self-aggrandizement.
- *Graded sexual approaches*: Partners are advised to engage in sensual and sexual activities only so long as pleasurable feelings predominate. They terminate such activities when anxious feelings erupt. With each encounter, anxieties can recede and greater sexual arousal and intimacy become possible.
- *Paradoxical strategies*: Symptom prescription, for instance therapists telling compulsive clients to increase their checking and ritualistic behaviours, is a common paradoxical strategy. Clients may decrease their unwanted behaviours if their therapists prescribe that they exaggerate symptoms. Another common paradoxical strategy is that of forbidding a desired response. An example is that of therapists forbidding men with erectile difficulties to have intercourse until they get specific permission. Clients whose desired responses are forbidden may be more likely to enact them, for instance by engaging in sexual intercourse.
- *Social skills and assertiveness training*: Four specific assertive response patterns or abilities that therapists can train clients in are: saying 'no'; asking for favours and making requests; expressing positive and negative feelings; and initiating, continuing and terminating conversations. Behaviour rehearsal and modelling are two major techniques employed in social skills and assertiveness training.

DRUGS/BIOLOGY

Multimodal therapists encourage clients take responsibility for their health and to develop good habits of eating nutritionally, exercising and engaging in recreational activities. Therapists refer clients to physicians where they suspect organic problems or consider biological interventions, such as anti-depressant medication, indicated.

STRATEGIES FOR SAVING TIME

In therapy, especially brief therapy, it is important that therapists do not waste their clients' and their own time. In brief therapy it is most important to select clearly defined goals quickly and to move into specific problem-solving interventions as soon as possible. Sometimes the application of an intervention may come well before assessment has been completed.

Clients can be educated as to the benefits of brief therapy. Furthermore, therapists can use time between sessions to good effect by thinking about clients' progress and, where necessary, revising their game plans. In addition, therapists can use phone calls, letters and email to amend homework assignments or make sympathetic enquiries.

Brief therapy requires an educational stance and should avoid conversational therapy. Lazarus (2006) observed: 'Passive and reflective therapists are anathema to the process of brief and effective psychotherapy' (p. 67). He disabused clients of the widespread overvaluation of insight and the need to focus heavily on the past. Multimodal therapists as educators may use bibliography and prime clients as to the importance of practising homework assignments. Furthermore, Lazarus was not afraid to prompt clients with ideas, strategies and solutions rather than wait for these to emerge from clients themselves.

CASE MATERIAL

Case studies presented by Lazarus include his work with George a 32-year-old agoraphobic patient who had previously been treated without success by a number of therapists (Lazarus, 1989b, 2005). Another example of Lazarus work is that with Al and Lisa, the former presenting with inhibited sexual desire (Lazarus, 2006). Lazarus conducted two initial conjoint sessions, 8 individual sessions with Al, 6 individual sessions with Lisa, and then 3 final conjoint sessions in improving this couple's emotional and sexual relationship. A further case study is Lazarus' work over eight months with a 33-year-old woman, married to a successful company president, who was afraid of becoming pregnant, insecure and unassertive (Lazarus, 2008a). Lazarus (2008b) also presents his work over a period of years with Ben, a twice-divorced man who headed the editorial department of a large publishing house. During therapy, several events called for interventions that had not been part of the original plan. Additional case material is contained in a chapter providing an example of the multimodal assessment and treatment of a case of panic, anxiety, and social phobia, and a marital therapy case compounded by depression (Lazarus, Hasson, and Glat, 1991). In 1985, *A Casebook of Multimodal Therapy* edited by Lazarus was published. This book describes 14 different case studies in a variety of settings and situations.

FURTHER DEVELOPMENTS

Multimodal therapy, with its BASIC ID assessment and interventions, has been applied in many areas in addition to individual personal therapy. Multimodal therapy has been used in marital work and in group work. In addition, multimodal therapy has provided a framework for career counselling and for Employee Assistance Programme (EAP) counselling. Other areas of application of multimodal principles include working with children in classroom settings, developing gifted adolescents, parent training, working with inpatients in mental hospital, and counselling and therapy education. Thus multimodal therapy, at the same time as espousing breadth in how therapists assess and treat clients, has broad applicability to a wide range of areas.

Since 1972, training in multimodal therapy has been a formal aspect of the clinical psychology doctoral programme at Rutgers University in the United States. There are several multimodal therapy institutes in the United States as well as some smaller centres. Multimodal therapy is also taught and practised in Britain and in other countries in Europe: for instance, in the Netherlands under the auspices of Dr M. G. T. Kwee, several therapists are using the approach. Books, articles and chapters on multimodal therapy have been written or translated into German, Italian, Portuguese, Spanish and Dutch. Multimodal therapy is also taught in South America. For example, in Argentina, Dr Roberto Kertesz and his colleagues have practised multimodal therapy, offered training seminars, and translated many of Lazarus' books into Spanish (Lazarus, 2006). Thus, the influence of multimodal therapy spreads well beyond the United States.

REVIEW AND PERSONAL QUESTIONS

REVIEW QUESTIONS

1. Why does Lazarus call his approach multimodal?
2. What does the term technical eclecticism mean?
3. What seven key constructs does Lazarus use to explain how human personality is shaped and maintained?
4. To what extent does multimodal therapy have a theoretical base? Why is Lazarus afraid of his approach being too closely tied to any theory?
5. What are the goals of multimodal therapy?
6. What is the role of assessment in multimodal therapy and how do therapists go about it?
7. Critically discuss the role of the therapist–client relationship in multimodal therapy.
8. What does Lazarus mean by bridging and tracking? Provide examples.
9. How do multimodal therapists select interventions?
10. What are some principal multimodal interventions for changing

    - behaviour
    - affect
    - sensation
    - imagery
    - cognition
    - the interpersonal modality
    - the drugs/biology modality?

11. How do multimodal therapists evaluate clients' progress?

PERSONAL QUESTIONS

1. Identify a specific problem area in your life. To what extent do each of Lazarus' seven key factors for explaining how human personality is shaped and maintained contribute to your acquiring and maintaining your problem?
2. Develop your Structural Profile by rating yourself, by using a 7-point scale (1 2 3 4 5 6 7), on each of the BASIC ID modalities.
3. Develop a Modality Profile for yourself.
4. Select and implement interventions to help you with one of your problems.
5. What relevance, if any, has the theory and practice of multimodal therapy for how you conduct therapy?
6. What relevance, if any, has the theory and practice of multimodal therapy for how you live?

ANNOTATED BIBLIOGRAPHY

Lazarus, A. A. (2006) *Brief but Comprehensive Psychotherapy: The Multimodal Way.* New York: Springer.
Based on the central message 'Don't waste time', this book succinctly sets out the main rationale and distinctive assessment and therapy techniques employed in brief *and* comprehensive multimodal therapy. Elements of effective brevity are identified and case examples are provided from individual and couples therapy.

Lazarus, A. A. (1989b) *The Practice of Multimodal Therapy: Systematic, Comprehensive and Effective Psychotherapy* (rev. ed.). Baltimore, MA: The Johns Hopkins University Press.
This book is exactly the same as the 1981 version apart from a 1989 epilogue and the addition of the 35-item Structural Profile Inventory as Appendix 4. The book includes chapters on multimodal therapy's basic rationale, its basic concepts for practice, the initial interview, multimodal assessment-therapy connections, relationship factors and the selection of techniques. In addition, there are chapters on multimodal marriage therapy, multimodal sex therapy, and multimodal therapy in special situations, for instance working with children. In addition to the Structural Profile Inventory appendix, the book has appendices containing a glossary of 37 principal techniques, the Multimodal Life History Questionnaire, and the Marital Satisfaction Questionnaire.

Lazarus, A. A. (2008a) Multimodal therapy. In R. Corsini and D. Wedding (eds), *Current Psychotherapies* (8th ed.). Belmont, CA: Thomson Brooks/Cole, pp. 338–401.
This chapter includes material on multimodal therapy's basic concepts, history and current status, theory of personality, theory of psychotherapy, process and mechanisms of therapy, applications and evaluation. A case example is provided.

Lazarus, A. A. (1992) Multimodal therapy: Technical eclecticism with minimal integration. In J. C. Norcross and M. R. Goldfried (eds), *Handbook of Psychotherapy Integration.* New York: Basic Books, pp. 231–63.

This chapter presents Lazarus' ideas on systematic (technical) eclecticism and the risks of integration. Lazarus describes the distinctive features of the multimodal approach and how it differs from other eclectic approaches. Research findings are reviewed and suggestions made for clinical training and desirable future directions for psychotherapy.

Lazarus, A. A. (1984) *In the Mind's Eye: The Power of Imagery for Personal Enrichment.* New York: The Guilford Press.
This is a well-written book of imagery techniques that therapists can use with clients and people can use for self-help. The book is divided into four parts: the power of imagery; using imagery to build confidence and skill; using imagery to overcome problems; and some additional imagery exercises.

REFERENCES AND FURTHER READING

Bandura, A. (1986) *Social Foundations of Thought and Action: A Social Cognitive Theory.* Englewood Cliffs, NJ: Prentice-Hall.

Dryden, W. (1991) *A Dialogue with Arnold Lazarus: 'It Depends'.* Milton Keynes: Open University Press.

Kwee, M. G. T. and Lazarus, A. A. (1986) Multimodal therapy: The cognitive-behavioural tradition and beyond. In W. Dryden and W. Golden (eds), *Cognitive-Behavioural Approaches to Psychotherapy.* London: Harper & Row, pp. 320–55.

Lazarus, A. A. (1961) Group therapy for phobic disorders by systematic desensitization. *Journal of Abnormal and Social Psychology, 63,* 505–10.

Lazarus, A. A. (1971) *Behavior Therapy and Beyond.* New York: McGraw-Hill.

Lazarus, A. A. (ed.) (1972) *Clinical Behavior Therapy.* New York: Brunner/Mazel.

Lazarus, A. A. (1976) *Multimodal Behavior Therapy.* New York: Springer.

Lazarus, A. A. (1981) *The Practice of Multimodal Therapy.* New York: McGraw-Hill.

Lazarus, A. A. (1984) *In the Mind's Eye: The Power of Imagery for Personal Enrichment.* New York: The Guilford Press.

Lazarus, A. A. (ed.) (1985) *Casebook of Multimodal Therapy.* New York: Guilford.

Lazarus, A. A. (1989a) Why I am an eclectic (not an integrationist). *British Journal of Guidance and Counselling, 17,* 248–58.

Lazarus, A. A. (1989b) *The Practice of Multimodal Therapy: Systematic, Comprehensive and Effective Psychotherapy* (rev. ed.). Baltimore, MA: The Johns Hopkins University Press.

Lazarus, A. A. (1992) Multimodal therapy: Technical eclecticism with minimal integration. In J. C. Norcross and M. R. Goldfried (eds), *Handbook of Psychotherapy Integration.* New York: Basic Books, pp. 231–63.

Lazarus, A. A. (1993) Tailoring the therapeutic relationship, or being an authentic chameleon. *Psychotherapy, 30,* 404–7.

Lazarus, A. A. (2001) *Marital Myths Revisited: A Fresh Look at Two Dozen Mistaken Beliefs About Marriage.* Atascadero, CA: Impact Publishers.

Lazarus, A. A. (2003) Multimodal behavior therapy. In W. O'Donohue, J. E. Fisher and S. C. Hayes (eds), *Cognitive Behavior Therapy*. Hoboken, NJ: Wiley, pp. 261–5.

Lazarus, A. A. (2004) Private communication to the author, September 27.

Lazarus, A. A. (2005) The case of George. In D. Wedding and R. J. Corsini (eds), *Case Studies in Psychotherapy* (4th ed.). Belmont, CA: Thomson Brooks/Cole, pp. 177–87.

Lazarus, A. A. (2006) *Brief but Comprehensive Psychotherapy: The Multimodal Way.* New York: Springer.

Lazarus, A. A. (2008a) Multimodal therapy. In R. J. Corsini and D. Wedding (eds), *Current Psychotherapies* (8th ed.). Belmont, CA: Thomson Brooks/Cole, pp. 338–401.

Lazarus, A. A. (2008b) Multimodal therapy: The case of Ben. In D. Wedding and R. J.Corsini (eds) *Case Studies in Psychotherapy* (5th ed.). Belmont, CA: Thomson Brooks/Cole, pp. 147–58.

Lazarus, A. A. and Lazarus, C. N. (1991) *Multimodal Life History Inventory.* Champaign, IL: Research Press.

Lazarus, A. A. and Lazarus, C. N. (1997) *The 60-Second Shrink: 101 Strategies for Staying Sane in a Crazy World.* San Luis Obispo, CA: Impact Publishers.

Lazarus, A. A. and Messer, S. B. (1991) Does chaos prevail? An exchange on technical eclecticism and assimilative integration. *Journal of Psychotherapy Integration, 1,* 143–58.

Lazarus, A. A., Beutler, L. E. and Norcross, J. C. (1992) The future of technical eclecticism. *Psychotherapy, 29,* 11–20.

Lazarus, A. A., Hasson, C. and Glat, M. (1991) Multimodal therapy. In K. N. Anchor (ed.), *Handbook of Medical Psychotherapy*. Toronto: Hogrefe & Huber, pp. 123–40.

Lazarus, A. A., Lazarus, C. N. and Fay, A. (1993) *Don't Believe it for a Minute!* San Luis Obispo, CA: Impact Publishers.

Meichenbaum, D. H. (1977) *Cognitive-Behavior Modification.* New York: Plenum.

Wolpe, J. and Lazarus, A. A. (1966) *Behaviour Therapy Techniques.* Oxford: Pergamon Press.

LAZARUS ON AUDIO AND VIDEO

Lazarus, A. A. (1976) *Learning to Relax.* New York: Institute for Rational Living.

Lazarus, A. A. (1982) *Personal Enrichment through Imagery* (3 cassettes plus workbook). New York: BMA Audio Cassette Publications.

Lazarus, A. A. (1984a) *Mental Imagery: Your Hidden Potential.* Washington DC: American Psychological Association (Psychology Today).

Lazarus, A. A. (1984b) *Mental Imagery: Techniques and Exercises.* Washington, DC: American Psychological Association (Psychology Today).

Lazarus, A. A. (2006) *Live Case Consultation.* California: psychotherapy.net

Videotapes of Lazarus doing multimodal therapy have been published by the American Psychological Association and by Allyn & Bacon.

This part of the book presents four more recent theoretical positions. Chapters 12 and 13 come under the heading postmodern therapies. Postmodern therapies are situated in a tradition of thought that questions or rejects 'certain knowledge' in areas of human life, including theories that assume the actuality of therapist expertise in psychological causes and functioning.

Chapter 12 is devoted to solution-focused therapy (SFT) that was developed in the 1980s by Steve de Shazer and Insoo Kim Berg of the Brief Family Therapy Center in Milwaukee, USA. The central assumption is that the goals for therapy will be chosen by attenders or clients who themselves have resources which they will use in making changes. A detailed history is not essential. However, if a story has never been told before, then it may need to be listened to before continuing. 'Problem talk' and speculation about motives or 'purposes' of symptoms are avoided. Therapists adopt clients' vocabulary for problems and track their use of language.

A solution-focused interview will contain certain specific elements. Problems and goals are defined in practical terms that enable attenders to focus on solutions. Asking about pre-session changes, exceptions to the problem, scaling the problem from 0 to 10, and asking the 'miracle question' keep the focus on effective solutions. At the end of the session, feedback encourages change. Tasks such as 'Do more of what is working already' or 'It is time to try something different' help to maintain change afterwards.

Sufficient improvement is often achieved within three to five sessions and about 25 per cent of clients require one session. As with other psychotherapies, problems of long standing are less responsive to treatment.

Chapter 13 is on narrative therapy that, as a postmodern therapy, has a great deal in common with solution-oriented work. Narrative therapy is wholly appropriate for work with individuals and couples, but its origins are in family therapy. When Michael White left the Australian public health system in the 1970s, he and a colleague established an independent practice in family therapy, their work strongly influenced by the writings of Gregory Bateson and the Milan school. White and David Epston met at a conference, where they recognized common ground in their attitudes and beliefs and in their unconventional approaches to assisting troubled families. Epston, an anthropologist born in Canada, trained in social work and established a family therapy centre in Auckland.

Family therapy was also the main activity of the Dulwich Centre in Adelaide, founded and co-directed by Michael and Cheryl White, although it also had a strong commitment to community work both locally and in deprived communities outside Australia. Over three decades, until White's death in 2008, he and his colleagues developed narrative approaches, published books and a journal, provided increasingly detailed training, and organized international conferences. The Dulwich Centre continues these activities. As White and Epston's ideas spread, family therapists worldwide took up their practices and promoted narrative therapy through many workshops, conferences, articles and other writings.

Chapter 14 covers possibly the most recent addition to the therapeutic approaches, positive therapy. Positive therapy, involves the application of the new field of positive psychology to the alleviation of distress by focusing much of the therapeutic effort on actively promoting the client's wellbeing. The rationale is that many of the problems and distressing conditions that beset people have effects (such as reduced energy, lowered self-confidence and reduced social contact) that serve to maintain or deepen the person's suffering. The therapy aims to reverse the effects of multiple vicious circles by promoting virtuous circle effects that enable clients to experience frequent positive emotions, to see things in a realistically positive way, and to recognize and use their personal strengths.

Positive therapy involves a strong psycho-educational component and helps clients to use and to develop their emotional intelligence: the ability to understand and manage their own and other people's emotions. This component can be delivered in many ways, including in educational group settings. The approach has ambitious goals that include the aim of helping clients to achieve meaning, fulfilment and happiness. Drawing on evidence from many studies, the idea is that clients can be helped to gain knowledge and skills that will not only enable them to survive and to deal with current distress but will also provide them with 'skills for life' that will increase their resilience in the longer term and enable them to thrive and to flourish.

Chapter 15, mindfuless in therapy, explores a mindfulness-based approach as an integrative approach to therapy. This approach differs from most traditional approaches in that the theoretical background that underpins it is drawn from Buddhist psychology. Mindfulness meditation supports the therapist in bringing an embodied, attuned presence to the therapeutic relationship. Short meditation practices may be brought into the therapy sessions as a resource for insight and for supporting the client in finding a way to respond differently to what has brought them to therapy.

There is an emphasis on cultivating moment-to-moment awareness of experience as it arises, and on bringing a reflective enquiry process to experience that invites understanding of the patterns that are recurrent for clients. Embedded at the core of a mindfulness approach is an attitude of compassion and acceptance of whatever is here, and of developing understanding and skills in turning towards and being with the difficulties they experience in their lives.

SOLUTION-FOCUSED THERAPY

Alasdair Macdonald

INTRODUCTION

Solution-focused therapy is generally considered to have become a discrete model with the publication of 'Brief therapy: focused solution development' by de Shazer and colleagues in 1986. The work of the Mental Research Institute (MRI) in California, had led to strategic therapy, aiming at change rather than explanation of problems. Solution-focused therapy followed on from this work, emphasizing the resources of the individual seeking help and using language as the vehicle for change and reframing. The leading theorists were Steve de Shazer and Insoo Kim Berg. They had worked together at the Mental Research Institute and had become partners in life and work. They moved to Milwaukee, initially proposing to establish 'the MRI of the North'.

Thereafter they worked with numerous eminent therapists including Eve Lipchik, Elam Nunnally and Wallace Gingerich. They modified existing brief therapies by using feedback about successful outcomes. The result was a therapy process in which response to the attending individuals is considered more important than working from a theory of causation.

STEVE DE SHAZER (1940–2005)

The son of an engineer and an opera singer, Steve was brought up in Milwaukee, USA. He enjoyed baseball, cooking and daily walks. He read many philosophy tracts in German and French, listened to jazz and delighted in assessing the beers of many countries. Having studied classical music, he played several instruments professionally, including working as a saxophonist on the jazz circuit. Other qualifications included visual arts and social work. Meeting with the late John Weakland at the Mental Research Institute (MRI) in Palo Alto led to a long friendship. By the end of his life de Shazer was regarded as an authority on the writings of Ludwig Wittgenstein.

His friend and colleague Yvonne Dolan describes him (Dolan 2005):

> de Shazer was an iconoclast and creative genius known for a minimalist philosophy and a view of the process of change as an inevitable and dynamic part of everyday life. He was widely recognized as the author of the first book on Solution-focused Brief Therapy, as a pioneer in the field of family therapy, and as a primary developer of what has become internationally recognized as the solution-focused approach.

De Shazer published several important new therapy texts as well as many chapters and articles (see References). He gave workshops all over the world and was on the editorial boards of several international journals. His work is available in several languages. He had been heard to say that he travelled so much that all his friends lived outside his home town.

Having been unwell with a blood disease for some time, he died while travelling to teach in Wien, Austria. Insoo was able to be with him at the end.

INSOO KIM BERG (1934–2007)

The daughter of a wealthy Korean family, Insoo spent her childhood in Seoul. The family lost much from Allied bombing during the Korean War. After study at Ewha Women's University in Seoul she moved to the USA in 1957 where she obtained BS and MSSW degrees in Milwaukee. Postgraduate studies at the Family Institute of Chicago and the Menninger Foundation led her to join the MRI in Palo Alto where she was mentored by John Weakland and met Steve de Shazer.

Within Milwaukee Family Services Berg consulted to a very wide variety of institutions and programmes. De Shazer and she were co-founders and directors of the Brief Family Therapy Center (BFTC) in Milwaukee. They and their colleagues developed solution-focused brief therapy by eliminating any elements of psychotherapy which did not seem to lead to useful change for their clients. In their subsequent travels they trained therapists and management consultants around the world.

Berg was a fluent writer who wrote many articles and ten books describing solution-focused brief therapy and its applications. Most of her books have been translated into other languages. She served on the editorial boards of four major journals in the United States. She was a founder member of the Solution-Focused Brief Therapy Association of North America and a supervisor for the American Association for Marriage and Family Therapy. She had connections with the Wisconsin Association for Marriage and Family Therapy, the National Association of Social Workers (USA) and the European Brief Therapy Association. Her speeches were much in demand at international conferences. Like many from her homeland, Berg was a hard-working person who took obvious pleasure in her work and rarely had holidays. She enjoyed walking, stretching exercises and gardening. Her yoga skills surpassed that of fellow classmates half her age. Reading novels and listening to classical music were relaxations for her as well as the everyday pleasures of satisfying conversation, good food and a good night's sleep.

Everyone who knew Berg accepted that she was a profoundly gifted clinician. Her intellectual achievements were counter-balanced by compassion for others and her relaxed and casual demeanour. She had a ready smile and a warm sense of humour with infectious optimism. She respected the talents of others and affected others both personally and professionally. She radiated undeniable respect and absolute confidence in the self-expertise of each individual person. Insoo Kim Berg died suddenly in Milwaukee in 2007, having led life to the full right up to the last moment.

Berg encapsulated her professional values thus: 'Knowing when to push, when to let go, what to listen to and what to ignore. All these skills are based on profound respect for human dignity and working to restore a sense of who they are and what they want to be' (Berg, 2006).

THEORY

BASIC CONCEPTS

There are a number of differences between solution-focused therapy and traditional psychodynamic and behavioural psychotherapies. The central assumptions are that the goals for therapy will be chosen by the attender and that the attenders themselves have resources which they will use in making changes. It is assumed that attenders seek help because they have run out of ideas for dealing with a problem or have become stuck with a particular pattern of response that is not proving effective. The therapeutic conversation aims at restoring hope and self-esteem, while reducing anxiety to a point where people become able to think more widely and creatively about solutions. The experience of thinking differently and with hope about a problem improves the chance that new solutions will be imagined and pursued.

Because anxiety can restrict cognition and attention to additional factors, it is possible to take the view that a lack of solutions is the result of anxiety in every case. Taking that view, the work of solution-focused therapy and all other therapies is to reduce anxiety in order to allow wider thinking about possible approaches to the problem. In solution-focused therapy this is achieved by the quick establishment of an alliance with the attender through the use of language. Topics such as exceptions, scaling and the 'miracle question' are used to promote a sense that the problem is solvable. Once anxiety is reduced, the attender becomes able to mobilize their existing strengths and resources to address their desired goals.

A detailed history is not essential for solution-focused therapy. However, if a story has never been told before then it may need to be listened to before continuing. 'Problem talk' and speculation about motives or 'purposes' of symptoms are avoided. The therapist adopts the attender's vocabulary for the problem and tracks their use of language.

It is preferable that any prior assumptions about hidden motives and unconscious mechanisms on the part of the therapist do not interfere with attention to the content of the attender's discourse. In de Shazer's words (1994), the interview is 'text-focused'; that is, the information comes from the material offered by the attender and it is their understanding and language that are employed. The alternative, applied in traditional therapies, is a 'reader focus', in which the reader/therapist has special knowledge and only needs enough from the attender to make a fit with the preconceived ideas and plans of the therapist. This concept of therapy as text-focused links well with Wittgenstein's (1965) view of language as the essential tool for thought. The attender has the text and the language so ideas in the mind of the therapist should not intrude on this material. The lack of technical language is both a consequence of this view of therapy and an asset in communicating with attenders.

A central element of psychodynamic training is the need for personal therapy for therapists. This is expensive for the trainee in money and emotional energy and has not been shown to correlate with becoming a better therapist. McAskill's review (1988) concluded that damage to self or to relationships occurs in up to 10 per cent of trainees during personal therapy. It has also been suggested that trainees are less effective as therapists while undergoing personal work (Garfield and Bergin, 1971).

To the solution-focused therapist, personal therapy as a part of training is unnecessary and irrelevant. The focus on the attender and their needs means that therapist issues should enter into the process as little as possible. There are ethical standards for members of society and for healthcare professions that need to be followed. However, personal therapy for therapists has no effect on such standards, which are not a personal matter. Sometimes the attender's goals may seem strange or unlikely, but as long as they are not illegal or dangerous to self or others then they can be a legitimate goal for therapy. If the therapist has objections to working with certain persons or goals then they need to pass the person to someone who can work with them. This is not directly connected with personal therapy, since all therapists have areas of relative skill or lack of skill.

ACQUISITION AND MAINTENANCE

Every person has their own values and beliefs, which may have served them well in the past. The acquisition and maintenance of these is only of relevance to the solution-focused therapist insofar as they are applied to any specific problem of life. Values and beliefs may change as new ways of solving problems are developed, for example by changing from aggressive responses to dialogues.

THERAPY

THERAPEUTIC GOALS

The therapist adopts a non-expert or 'not-knowing' stance, in which the individual and not the therapist selects goals and the means to meet these goals. A therapist may negotiate goals with the attender, for example if the goals are unrealistic ('We will never argue again'; 'The baby will not cry any more'). In work with offenders, some goals may be unethical, for example a goal of more effective burglary. A goal to avoid return to court or jail may be acceptable if the means to that goal include a reduction in offending behaviour. However strange or unlikely, a goal may turn out to be achievable, or may be replaced as the situation improves.

De Shazer used to say that he wanted to retain the word 'brief' in 'solution-focused brief therapy' because he said that it is the only word which is clearly understood by attenders. By brief in this context is meant 'not one more session than is necessary'. Redundant conversations are not useful to therapist or attender, but 'solution-forced' therapy is not useful either (Nylund and Corsiglia, 1994). Worldwide, research shows that many persons only require one session but the average is three to six-and-a-half sessions. For some attenders there may be many sessions or many courses of therapy spanning years.

PROCESS OF THERAPY

A solution-focused interview will contain certain specific elements. 'What do you want to get out of being here today?' or 'What are your best hopes for this session?' begin the process of collaboration between therapist and attenders. Problems and goals are defined in practical terms that enable the attender to focus on solutions. Questions aim at defining the problem in terms of frequency and length, thus making it practical and measurable rather than overwhelming.

It can be confusing for the therapist if the individual tries to work on more than one problem at a time. If there is more than one problem it can be useful to ask 'Which is the biggest problem at the moment?' or 'Which problem would you like to work on first?'. Often, solving one problem releases enough energy for the individual to solve the remainder without specific therapy.

Problem-free talk is used to enhance the relationship. It often reduces anxiety and guilt if an individual finds that the therapist enquires about their successes and interests as well as the problems. It is helpful in widening the conversation away from the problem and hence indirectly encourages thinking about solutions.

Psychodynamic therapists say that if an emotion is named in a session, then that emotion will soon appear, often accompanied by memories and experiences connected to it. Therefore it is unwise to introduce topics or emotions into the session unless the attender has done so first. In our practice we ask 'What do you think about that?', not 'What do you feel about that?', because an answer about feeling will be less precise, less behavioural and less open to change by direct means.

PRE-SESSION CHANGES AND EXCEPTIONS

Asking about pre-session changes and exceptions to the problem identifies resources, strengths and coping abilities that may have passed unnoticed previously. Asking about exceptions is particularly useful with goals that are normally viewed as resistant to change, such as alcohol and drug misuse or domestic violence. Attenders may be feeling quite hopeless about their ability to change or control their situation and are surprised to find that there are small exceptions where they clearly control or delay behaviours. This improves their sense of self-mastery and their ability to plan further small steps.

SCALING

Scaling questions are one of the great assets of the solution-focused therapist. They help the attender to move from all-or-nothing goals towards less daunting steps. Scaling the problem from 0 to 10 encourages a focus on small identifiable steps rather than the wish for 'instant relief'. The scale has no reality outside the conversation with the therapist but is an instantly usable means of tracking progress. Scales also increase clarity of communication with other professionals who may be involved with the attender. Any move up the scale suggests that something is effective.

It is sometimes suggested that solution-focused work ignores feelings. However, it is common for the first response to 'How will you recognize when you are one point further up the scale?' to take the form 'I will feel …'. Acknowledging this feeling, it can then be expanded into the behaviours that go with this feeling and the reactions of others to these changes: 'When you feel X, what else will be different?'.

Scaling can also be used in other ways. For example, 'How confident are you of reaching the number you have chosen as a goal?'. People who have come to therapy only as a last resort may be able to identify goals but initially have no confidence that they can reach them. In relationship problems it is useful to ask 'On a scale of 0 to 10, how confident are you that you will be together in two years' time?'. Attenders often learn from their own replies, whether the partner is present or not. If both are present then the same question can be helpful to them. If one says '2' and the other says '10', then they have learned something about how they are communicating with each other. It is not always necessary for the therapist to comment on this directly. Scaling can be done with percentages or lines of toys or by holding up fingers. The scale needs to have enough points for small changes to be possible: 'better, the same or worse' is not an effective scale.

MIRACLE QUESTION

Asking the miracle question brings in a sense of optimism and play, allowing creative thinking to emerge and confirming the goals already identified:

> I'm going to ask you a kind of strange question now. Suppose [*pause*] you go to bed and to sleep tonight as usual [*pause*] and while you are asleep a miracle happens [*pause*] and the problem that brought you here today [*look round all present*] is solved [*pause*]. But you are asleep and don't know that it has been solved [*pause*].

What will be the first small signs that this miracle has happened and that the problem is solved?

It is best to wait a few moments without moving or speaking, as the question is a complex one and individuals may need time to reflect before answering. After about 10 seconds you can prompt them with practical questions, for example 'Will you wake at the same time when the miracle has happened?'. Then amplify the story with 'what else' questions and contributions from others present. It is usually best not to direct the person in any specific ways beyond general enquiries about the effects of the miracle at home, school or elsewhere.

When the miracle question is not suitable, perhaps for reasons of comprehension or cultural difference, other future-focused questions can be equally effective. Perhaps 'When you send us a video of your family in five years' time when the problems are gone, what will we see in the video?'.

BREAKS OR NOT?

The founders of SFT and many therapists who come from a family therapy tradition believe that it is useful to take a break in order to compose the feedback. It is a common experience that appropriate responses occur to us just after we have left a situation. It is in the nature of human interaction that we are affected by one another's emotions and this is one of the pleasures of human existence. However, when attenders are anxious and unable to reflect, we will be affected by this if we are in close contact with them. Leaving the room and/or entering another conversation with colleagues or supervisors allows us the cognitive space to think more clearly about their situation and about what comments will be the most useful. In traditional therapy this thinking takes place between sessions or in supervision. A break gives the attenders the advantage of this process of reflection within the same session.

Some therapists ask attenders on their return if they have remembered anything important during the break. This is best avoided because it restarts the exploratory dialogue instead of punctuating the end of the session. Some therapists regard a break as unnecessary and as causing an interruption in the therapeutic dialogue. If I am in a situation where a break is impractical because of time or the setting in which I am working, I say, 'You have told me about a complicated situation. Please let me think for a few minutes before I give you some feedback about it.' Attenders appear to see this as respectful of their situation and are content to sit quietly.

Before giving the feedback or before going for a break it is important to ask this closing question: 'Before we finish, is there anything else you want to mention that we have not covered?'. As well as punctuating the session, this is a safety question. It gives the attender an opportunity to raise any matter at all, which may not be connected with the ostensible reason for attendance. They have had the duration of the session to decide if the therapist can be trusted enough to reveal matters that they may not have wished to disclose previously. If their response requires further questions, about self-harm or danger to others, then this can be done at once. If a major new topic is produced then it may need to be carried forward to a future session.

FEEDBACK

Each session ends with feedback to the attenders. A structured format is useful to both attenders and therapists. Attenders appear anxious about what feedback they are going to receive. However good the initial relationship, they appear to anticipate criticism. As a rule this anxiety lessens in subsequent sessions. First, the problem is acknowledged briefly: specifically or in general. This confirms to the attender that the therapist is not ignoring or underestimating the problem. Compliments follow: at least one by name for each person present. In some cultures it is acceptable to include some compliments during the earlier part of the session. However, this runs the risk of appearing to underestimate the seriousness of the situation. In UK practice it seems acceptable to give compliments only at the feedback stage. It is useful to use session notes to highlight possible compliments for use in the feedback. Sometimes several positives can be combined, for example if the attender is talkative, has attempted several pre-session changes and holds two jobs, these could be combined into 'You are energetic' or 'You are a determined person.' It may be that compliments that identify enduring characteristics rather than single events are more likely to produce change. However, children often prefer compliments that refer to specific events.

The number of compliments is also dictated by local custom. In the United States people are accustomed to compliments so the compliments can be numerous. In the UK more than three compliments for one person seems to be regarded with suspicion. With couples or families it is practical to offer one compliment for each person present, followed by an additional compliment about the relationship or family.

If the client has no specific plans by the end of the session, the therapist may suggest a task such as one of the following.

1. 'Think or discuss what in your present life you want to keep the same.' This is useful if the situation is not clear or if there has not been time to complete the session in full. It is safer than advising any change prematurely.
2. 'You have several good ideas already for reaching your goals. We think that you should do more of what you are already doing.'
3. 'You have tried many ideas already, with limited results. It is time to try something completely new. You will know best yourselves what to try after you have thought about it.' Attenders come up with some remarkable and unexpected ideas when given this task.
4. 'Each evening predict where you will be on the scale tomorrow and check next evening if you were right.' A good day is a success whether they predicted it or not, so that the overall chance of an exception of some kind is increased.

5. 'Pretend on one day each week that the miracle has happened but do not tell anyone which day you have chosen.' This can be useful for couples and families as they have to attend to each other to see if they can tell when the other is pretending that good things are happening. This leaves them looking for positives in each other's behaviour instead of negatives.

According to psychotherapy research, attenders expect therapists to give advice or provide tasks and it helps the therapeutic alliance if this is done. Whether the attenders do the task or not does not affect outcome. It is best not to describe the task as 'homework', a word that has a negative connotation for many people.

It is sometimes appropriate to include normalizing information as a part of the intervention, for example whether all toddlers are dry at night or whether most adolescents will be difficult at some stage in their maturation.

> *Therapist*: [*Acknowledging the problem*] You have been worrying a lot about your drinking. [*Compliments*] I am really impressed that you have begun to cut it down. You work really hard and you know what you want out of life. You have lots of good ideas about how to cut down your drinking. You have thought of some practical steps such as not going out with drinking friends, working long hours at the weekend, taking less money when you go out, and not mixing drinks while you are out. [*Task*] You plan to try some of these before next time.

Watch for nods and open postures as signs of engagement with the intervention. Non-verbal responses are a much more reliable guide than verbal comments. In our experience it is best not to allow any discussion of the feedback. If questions are asked, simply repeat a part of the feedback or say that they can revisit the topic at their next visit.

Following the feedback, ask if they want to make another appointment and how soon that should be. Attenders often want enough time to think about what has been said and to try out changes before they return. Anything other than a definite 'No' should be taken as a cue for making an appointment 'which you can cancel if you do not need it'. People often fail to cancel and simply do not attend. Nevertheless, this is a better course than failing to offer another appointment. It is not useful for attenders or therapists if someone must create a crisis simply to obtain another appointment.

RETURN VISITS

All return visits begin with the question 'What has been better since we last met?'. Although problems will be reported in many cases, starting with optimism allows a more flexible dialogue later.

It is important to give the attender credit for all positive events. Similarly, it is helpful to speak as if negative events are external and not the fault of the attender. For example, if an attender reports having assaulted someone, 'How come that happened?' or 'How did that come about?' may uncover useful information whereas direct criticism of their actions is less likely to do so.

It is best not to ask about the tasks from the previous session. They may report on it spontaneously, in which case it can be built on or repeated in the feedback if it was helpful. It is important to give the credit to the attender and not to the therapist. If they did it and it failed, the therapist can apologize for choosing the wrong task or the wrong moment for suggesting it. If they did not do it, asking about it will not improve co-operation; the issue is whether things are better, not what happened with the task.

Questions for return visits:

What has been better for you since you were last here?
(If positive events have happened) How did you do that?
(If negative events have happened) How did that come about? How did you cope with that?
Where are you on your scale from 0 to 10 today?
What comes next to be up one point on the scale? (Get a practical description.)

Give feedback in the same structured form as used in the first session (see previous section on feedback).

It is unusual to remind attenders where they placed themselves on the scale at their last visit, unless they ask specifically. The scale is an internal measure and so the numbers in themselves are not significant. The current score and the next step are what matter. If their score is the same on the scale or lower than at the last visit then a reminder about this can be experienced as criticism. If they are higher now than before, then it is more important to explore this achievement than to make comparisons with the past, which cannot be changed in any case.

Return visits are commonly shorter than first sessions for individuals. Couples and families usually require more time as there are two or more accounts of events.

In solution-focused work individuals, couples or families may be seen; the sessions follow a similar pattern with each. As with other psychotherapies, problems of long standing are less responsive to treatment. Medication and other treatments can be combined with solution-focused therapy. Hospital stays and waiting lists are reduced when a solution-focused approach is adopted, since it focuses on empowering service users.

THE THERAPEUTIC RELATIONSHIP

In general the therapist seeks to maintain respectful curiosity about the attender's situation, keeping to the 'not-knowing' position. In some cases the therapists may provide knowledge or information, if this is requested or seems likely to be of value. For example, an issue of bed-wetting in a child may be assisted if the therapist can provide information about normal development in different age groups. However, it is common to find that attenders already have the information or that they disregard the therapist's comments.

The therapist assumes that change is possible or even inevitable, given the nature of human existence. Yvonne Dolan, in working with adult survivors of sexual abuse, talks of entering each session with 'an almost psychotic optimism'. Equally, the responsibility for change rests with the attender. We can change ourselves and no one else. Others may respond constructively to changed behaviour but this cannot be forced.

Language matching or language tracking means using the attender's words for events and situations. In solution-focused therapy, language tracking is a central part of the therapist's skill for building relationships and mutual comprehension. Ideally, every statement made by the therapist should contain a word or phrase used by the attender in their last statement. If this is not feasible, for example if the attender is silent or monosyllabic, then at the very least, another phrase used earlier can be incorporated. This technique was originally developed within solution-focused therapy but is valuable in any conversation. It is especially useful where language may be compromised, in children, the elderly or those speaking a second language or through an interpreter.

Like Buddhists and Quakers, solution-focused therapists believe that every word spoken is important and has significance. Not every word can be explored in detail; therapy has many interesting byways and hints that are not relevant to the goal of helping the attender move forward. Part of the skill of the therapist is to select words for attention that lead to useful information and to positive events. Meaning is a shared experience, heavily influenced by language (in the widest sense). Think of a married couple who say to you 'We fight every week'. Until you know whether 'fight' means verbal disagreement or physical combat, neither safety assessment nor joint therapy can proceed.

Therapists often experience practice in solution-focused therapy as being more respectful and less stressful than other forms of therapy. As a result therapist allegiance to the model is often strong. Such allegiance is one factor that is known to predict a good outcome in many therapies. A large proportion of solution-focused therapists have experience with other models but prefer solution-focused therapy. However, therapists highly skilled in other models sometimes accept the basics of solution-focused therapy but prefer to continue with their existing skills.

A number of solution-focused therapists have emphasized the role of post-hypnotic suggestions in the effects of solution-focused therapy. The management consultant Fletcher Peacock (2001) points out the difference between the instructions 'Don't drop that' and 'Carry that carefully'. One mental picture promotes dropping, and the other promotes careful carrying. He believes that we are all affected by phrasing changes such as this every day. Mahlberg and Sjoblom (2004) have enlarged on the practical uses of such ideas in work with children in alternative schooling.

Language is itself one aspect of behaviour. Studies have shown that language has a direct effect on physical behaviour. Hausdorff and colleagues (1999) have shown that elderly people exposed to positive comments about ageing showed fewer disturbances of gait thereafter than those exposed to negative comments. In a detailed study, Rosenkranz and colleagues (2005) showed that when asthmatics heard asthma-related words such as 'wheeze' then their brain and lung functions changed at once towards patterns associated with illness.

The concept of 'resistance', found in many schools of therapy, assumes that if therapy is not making progress then attenders are failing to co-operate for conscious or unconscious reasons of their own. This largely absolves the therapist of responsibility and implicitly or explicitly blames the attender. In an early paper on 'The death of resistance', de Shazer (1984) criticized this position. He maintained that there is no such thing as resistance, only the attender's unique way of co-operating. It is part of the therapist's task to seek ways to engage with the attender successfully. If the attender did not do a task, then the fault is with the task and its timing or presentation, not with the attender.

THERAPEUTIC INTERVENTIONS

To solution-focused therapists, all questions are both part of the assessment and part of the intervention. Like the eminent founder of person-centred therapy Carl Rogers, they see the person as the greatest resource available, and the only one who can make change happen. For any one individual, different questions may have the crucial effect in stimulating change. As far as possible, challenging beliefs or offering suggestions is framed as respectful questions to the person. For example, asking 'How will that help?', 'Has that worked for you before?', or 'What will you do if that does not work?'.

There is an emphasis on detail in solution-focused therapy that has some resemblance to behavioural techniques. This moves problems from an amorphous source of distress to a defined and specific place in the attender's life. 'We fight all the time' is more alarming than 'Verbal quarrels with some swearing by both parties lasting 15 minutes and occurring five days weekly for the last six months.' Knowing this, it is possible to seek extenuating ('not in front of the children') or precipitating factors ('always after a few drinks') and to talk about times when such behaviour does not happen or when it occurs less often. It is also easier for the therapist to remark on progress when the frequency of the behaviours is registered in this fashion.

General words such as 'everybody' and 'people' are worth unpacking. Usually this means a person, or persons, whose opinion is very important to the attender and who acts as a social reinforcer of certain behaviours. Knowing who this is and how they respond is helpful to the therapy process. It may be useful to involve this person in the therapy sessions.

The question 'What else?' is invaluable. It implies that you are following the story closely and that you know that there is more to come. It is surprising how often attenders will react to this simple query by producing more information and ideas. To avoid being repetitive, you can extend the question by adding it to their last response: 'As well as X, what else is happening then?' or 'As well as X, what else helps?'. Linguistically, 'What else?' implies a continuous dialogue, so it helps to maintain the relationship with the attender even if the therapist is not yet clear about the situation. The same phrase can be useful in dealing with distressed attenders where little information has been forthcoming. Once new information stops or if time is precious, to ask 'Anything else?' will imply that this element of the discussion is coming to an end.

Another useful word is 'instead'. Any statement containing a negative can be reversed easily to 'So what will you be doing instead of X?' This one change can make an enormous difference to the information offered and to the atmosphere of the session.

'Should' is a verb with two meanings. It can imply a formal duty by another, for example, 'The Finance Department should pay you on Fridays.' In problem talk it often means 'Someone else should do something about this problem, not me.' So it is useful to pay attention when this word is used.

It is valuable for the therapist to use the future direct tense as often as possible: 'What will be different when ...', not the conditional tense 'What would be different if ...'. Direct tenses are more likely to lead to action. Once something has been spoken then it is more likely to happen. If the therapist uses these tenses, the attender is likely to copy them and confidence and action are more likely to follow.

The physiological components of emotional arousal are often very similar but are given different names by those experiencing them. Anger, excitement, anxiety and grief all have much in common. To reframe a feeling as 'anticipation' or 'energy' can often have a useful effect in increasing positive self-perception.

A discussion about the 'Yes, but ...' construction in the English language took place in 2005 on the solution-focused discussion forum on the internet (sft-l@listserv). The discussion is accessible in the archive of the sft-l list. The consensus was that when this construction is used, everything said before 'but' can be disregarded. In other words, 'Yes, but ...' generally means 'No'. Also, 'I don't want to criticize, but ...' means 'I am criticizing ...'. As a therapist, if you find yourself using this construction, you can consider whether you can express your reservations differently and more clearly. For example, instead of saying 'You say that relapse will not happen, but it has happened three times already', it would be clearer to say 'Relapse has already been a problem for you' or 'How will you deal with it if relapse does happen in spite of your hopes?'

MOVING TOWARDS CONCLUDING THERAPY

Once people have had time to review their progress, they often decide that a return visit is not needed. Follow-up studies eventually reveal that many attenders have done well, but there is some anxiety for the therapist when someone fails to attend without notice. If no message is received then a standard letter is sent to the attender with a copy to the referring agent. 'We were sorry not to see you for your appointment today. We hope that this means that things are going better for you (both, all). We will not send further appointments unless we hear that it is necessary.' It is not appropriate to pursue non-attenders with offers of therapy unless other information suggests that safety assessment needs to be undertaken. This standard letter respects their decision and makes no criticism of their absence. It makes it clear to them and to the referring agent that they bear the responsibility for any further action, such as requesting another appointment.

Most attenders will be ready for discharge when they have reached seven or above on their scale. Some studies have found that 25 per cent of attenders only require one session. However, the average from all published studies of solution-focused therapy is that three to six sessions are usual. De Shazer (2005) suggested that 'If you tell the attender there will be four to six sessions, then they will wait until session five before doing anything.' In many cases the gap between sessions can become longer as they move towards discharge from therapy. Many brief therapists work to a notional limit of 10 or 12 sessions. If success is not forthcoming after 10 sessions, it may be that solution-focused therapy, or this particular therapist, is not the best form of help for the attender at this time. However, people make changes at different speeds, so a fixed limit is not always appropriate. Some chronic or long-term problems can require many more sessions. De Shazer's rule is: 'Not one session more than is necessary' (Macdonald, 2011, p.35).

One strength of solution-focused brief therapy seems to be that it does no harm. Even if attenders do not improve, the questioning process appears to be harmless and compliments are usually appreciated. It is often easier to choose a suitable alternative treatment after solution-focused discussions about the attender's goals and preferences. With other therapies it can take much longer to determine whether or not therapy is going to be effective. Solution-focused therapy can often be completed before the attender has reached the top of the waiting list for other treatment. If they have not improved with solution-focused work then they can move on to other treatments. This is another argument for early access to solution-focused work. In general, around 70 per cent of attenders will improve with solution-focused work. Thus only those 30 per cent who do not respond to solution-focused brief therapy need to be passed on to specialists in other therapies, thus making better use of scarce resources.

In the case of attenders who are clearly doing well but are reluctant to be formally discharged, it can be useful to propose that, 'Because you have made changes so quickly, you have not used up all the sessions available. You have sessions in reserve, so if necessary you can call us directly to arrange another session.' This reassures many attenders and it is rare for them to use the 'sessions in reserve'. In our clinic we usually close the case for administrative purposes if we have not heard from the attender after six months.

CASE MATERIAL

Because language and interaction are seen as central to solution-focused therapy, there is a strong emphasis on the study of interviews and on experiential

355

training. Therefore, every one of the books by de Shazer, Berg and other solution-focused therapists includes case material and often transcripts of sessions. For the interested reader, some of the best interview transcripts can be found in de Shazer's *Words Were Originally Magic* (1994). There are line-by-line accounts of first and subsequent sessions with several attenders. It is possible to examine both the attender's contribution and the immediate response of the therapist.

For training tools, DeJong and Berg's *Interviewing for Solutions* (2012) demonstrates the clinical method, broken down into different sections and adapted to various situations. There is an accompanying set of demonstrations available on video, which allows non-verbal aspects of the interactions to be studied also.

De Shazer and Berg also released a number of videos and DVDs which include interviews with families, persons with unusual beliefs, drug users and the terminally ill. Since the deaths of de Shazer and Berg these are available from the Solution Focused Brief Therapy Association of America. Because of ethical considerations in releasing clinical material for worldwide use, many of the tapes show actors who are basing their performance on tapes and transcripts from the real attenders.

In teaching situations, trainees seeing these videos are intrigued by the apparently casual and formless style of de Shazer, which nevertheless leads the attender directly to possibilities and solutions. Berg shows personal charm and endless respectful curiosity in highly charged situations, sometimes with as many as seven family members of all ages present.

Other workers have also released useful multimedia teaching aids. However, the work of the originators of the method is an invaluable guide to the way in which the founding theorists actually practised, or at least to what they wished to show to the world as their preferred practice.

FURTHER DEVELOPMENTS

Unlike other psychological therapies, solution-focused therapy has been found in a number of studies to be equally effective for all social classes (de Shazer and Isebaert, 2003; Knekt et al., 2012; Macdonald, 2005). This is perhaps because of its relative lack of theory and jargon. It is an important finding because of the implications for a world that is short of resources and helping agencies. Unlike many Western psychotherapies, the techniques have been reported to work well in other cultural settings. Workers in China, Taiwan, Japan, Korea, India and the Middle East have made use of the method in healthcare services and in management.

The UK Department for Education and Science has policy documents on bullying and leadership commissioned from solution-focused specialists. SFT is used by services for learning disability and substance misuse and success has been reported by those who work with acquired brain injury and Asperger's syndrome (Bliss and Edmonds, 2007). It has been beneficial within the criminal justice system, including domestic violence.

Research in many countries and languages shows a significant evidence base for solution-focused therapy. There were 1,600 publications in 2013. At the time of writing, there are 130 relevant published studies from around the world, including two meta-analyses and five systematic reviews. Twenty-six randomized controlled trials show benefit from solution-focused brief therapy including 13 which show benefit compared to existing treatments. Of 47 comparison studies, 38 favour solution-focused therapy. Effectiveness data are also available in naturalistic studies of more than 5,000 cases with a success rate exceeding 60 per cent; requiring an average of three to five sessions of therapy time. The topics studied include emotional and mental health problems in adults and children, substance misuse, violence and offending behaviour, physical ill-health and unemployment.

Management consultancy is beginning to adopt postmodern techniques including solution-focused models. There are numerous quantitative studies of the use of solution-focused techniques in the workplace, which distinguishes this model from other consultancy techniques (for example, Hoffman et al., 2006; Mussman, 2006).

There are numerous accredited training modules available in UK colleges. The UK Association for Solution Focused Practice is the forum for SFT therapists in the UK. The European Brief Therapy Association (EBTA) has established an annual world conference, which has been held since 1993. The EBTA awards research grants annually, which has led to the completion and publication of a number of projects of importance.

REVIEW AND PERSONAL QUESTIONS

REVIEW QUESTIONS

1. What are the effects of beginning a first consultation by asking about goals for the session?
2. Does knowing the attender's goal for therapy assist the therapist?
3. Does defining a goal for therapy assist the attender?
4. What are the effects of problem-free talk in a first consultation?
5. What advantage does scaling offer in terms of assessing progress?
6. What changes in a person's thinking about a problem can arise from the use of scaling?
7. What are the effects of the miracle question, or any similar future-focused question, on a person's view of the problem?
8. If you know a method for achieving a goal, such as reducing anxiety, is it ethical not to tell the attender what you know unless/until they ask specifically for such advice?
9. If you know 50 methods for achieving a goal, such as reducing anxiety, is it ethical not to tell the attender all of them?

PERSONAL QUESTIONS

Think of a recent success of yours at home or at work.

1. What skills did you use to achieve this?
2. Who else noticed this success?
3. Had you used these skills before?

4. How did you know that you had these skills?
5. Where did these skills come from?
6. What can you do to improve these skills?
7. How will that improvement show itself?
8. Who else will notice that you have improved these skills?
9. How will they tell that your skills have improved?

ANNOTATED BIBLIOGRAPHY

Berg, I. K. and Dolan Y. (2001) *Tales of Solutions: A Collection of Hope-Inspiring Stories*. New York: Norton.
Berg and Dolan collected a variety of case examples from many therapists around the world. Each case represents different ways of managing situations and problems. This book is easy to read, which makes it an excellent first text for learning solution-focused therapy

DeJong, P. and Berg, I. K. (2012) *Interviewing for Solutions* (4th ed.). San Francisco, CA: Brooks/Cole.
This book and accompanying video offer a basic teaching text for solution-focused therapy. Although the examples are from the US context they form a good introduction that can be combined with training programmes.

De Shazer, S. (1994) *Words Were Originally Magic*. New York: Norton.
In this book de Shazer gives a clear exposition of his then views about the theoretical/philosophical basis for solution-focused therapy. The second part of the book contains several transcripts of real interviews which demonstrate the model as used by its leading theoretician.

De Shazer, S., Berg, I. K., Korman, H., Dolan, Y. and Trepper, T. (2007) *More Than Miracles: The State of the Art of Solution-Focused Brief Therapy*. New York: Haworth Press.
This recent text focuses on the interview process and the use of language in solution-focused therapy. It was in draft when Steve de Shazer died and has been completed by leading experts within the model. Many of the concepts can usefully be applied in other models of therapy.

Franklin, C., Trepper, T. S., Gingerich, W. J. and McCollum, E. E. (eds) (2011) *Solution-Focused Brief Therapy: A Handbook of Evidence-Based Practice*. New York: Oxford University Press.
This book is a vital guide to the present state of knowledge about solution-focused therapy research.

Macdonald, A. J. (2011) *Solution-Focused Therapy: Theory, Research and Practice* (2nd ed.). London: Sage.
An introduction to the method, followed by chapters on its application within specialist areas such as mental health and organizational work.

REFERENCES AND FURTHER READING

Berg, I. K. (1994) *Family Based Services: A Solution-Focused Approach.* New York: Norton.

Berg, I. K. (2006) Keynote speaker, 1st Asia Pacific Solution Focused Approach Conference, Furama Riverfront Hotel, Singapore; 17–18 August.

Berg, I. K. and Dolan, Y. (2001) *Tales of Solutions: A Collection of Hope-Inspiring Stories.* New York: Norton.

Berg, I. K. and Reuss, N. H. (1998) *Solutions Step by Step: A Substance Abuse Treatment Manual.* New York: Norton.

Berg, I. K. and Steiner, T. (2003) *Children's Solutions Work.* New York: Norton.

Berg, I. K. and Szabo, P. (2005) *Brief Coaching for Lasting Solutions.* New York: Norton Professional.

Bliss, E. V. and Edmonds, G. (2007) *A Self-Determined Future with Asperger Syndrome: Solution Focused Approaches.* London: Jessica Kingsley.

DeJong, P. and Berg, I. K. (2012) *Interviewing for Solutions.* (4th ed.). San Francisco, CA: Brooks/Cole.

De Shazer, S. (1982) *Patterns of Brief Family Therapy.* New York: Guilford.

De Shazer, S. (1984) The death of resistance. *Family Process, 23,* 30–40.

De Shazer, S. (1985) *Keys to Solutions in Brief Therapy.* New York: Norton. pp. 147–57.

De Shazer, S. (1988) *Clues: Investigating Solutions in Brief Therapy.* New York: Norton.

De Shazer, S. (1991) *Putting Difference to Work.* New York: Norton.

De Shazer, S. (1994) *Words Were Originally Magic.* New York: Norton.

De Shazer, S. (2005) Masterclass, BRIEF, London, 8–9 September.

De Shazer, S. and Isebaert, L. (2003) The Bruges Model: a solution-focused approach to problem drinking. *Journal of Family Psychotherapy, 14,* 43–52.

De Shazer, S., Berg, I. K., Korman, H., Dolan, Y. and Trepper, T. (2007) *More Than Miracles: The State of the Art of Solution-Focused Brief Therapy.* New York: Haworth Press.

De Shazer, S., Berg, I. K., Lipchik, E., Nunnally, E., Molnar, A., Gingerich, W. and Weiner-Davis, M. (1986) Brief therapy: Focused solution development. *Family Process, 25,* 207–22.

Dolan, Y. (2005) Obituary for Steve de Shazer. Personal communication by email, 20 November 2005.

Garfield, S. L. and Bergin, A. E. (1971) Personal therapy, outcome and some therapist variables. *Psychotherapy: Theory, Research and Practice, 8,* 251–3.

Hausdorff, J. M., Levy, B. R. and Wei, J. Y. (1999) The power of ageism on physical function of older persons: reversibility of age-related gait changes. *Journal of the American Geriatrics Society, 47,* 1346–9.

Hoffman, K., Lueger, G. and Luisser, P. (2006) Effects of solution-focused training on productivity and behaviour. In G. Lueger, and H-P. Korn (eds), *Solution-Focused Management.* Munich: Rainer Hampp, pp. 89–97.

Jackson, P. Z. and McKergow, M. (2002) *The Solutions Focus: The Simple Way to Positive Change*. London: Nicholas Brearley.

Knekt, P., Lindfors, O., Virtala, E., Härkänen, T., Sares-Jäske, L. and Laaksonen, M. A. (2012) The effectiveness of short- and long-term psychotherapy during a 7-year follow-up. *European Psychiatry 27, Supplement 1*, 1-x.

McAskill, N. (1988) Personal therapy in the training of the psychotherapist: Is it effective? *British Journal of Psychotherapy, 4*, 219–26.

Macdonald, A. J. (2005) Brief therapy in adult psychiatry: Results from 15 years of practice. *Journal of Family Therapy, 27*, 65–75.

Macdonald, A. J. (2011) *Solution-Focused Therapy: Theory, Research and Practice* (2nd ed.). London: Sage.

Mahlberg, K. and Sjoblom, M. (2004) *Solution-Focused Education*. Stockholm: Mahlberg & Sjoblom.

Mussman, C. (2006) Solution-focused leadership: The range between theory and practical application. In G. Lueger and H-P. Korn (eds), *Solution-Focused Management*. Munich: Rainer Hampp, pp. 99–110.

Nylund, D. and Corsiglia, V. (1994) Becoming solution-focused in brief therapy: Remembering something we already know. *Journal of Systemic Therapies, 13*, 5–11.

Peacock, F. (2001) *Water the Flowers, Not the Weeds*. Montreal: Open Heart.

Rosenkranz, M. A., Busse, W. W., Johnstone, T., Swenson, C. A., Crisafi, G. M., Jackson, M. M., Bosch, J. A., Sheridan, J. F. and Davidson, R. J. (2005) Neural circuitry underlying the interaction between emotion and asthma symptom exacerbation. *Proceedings of the National Academy of Sciences, 102*, 13319–24.

Watzlawick, P., Weakland, J. II. and Fisch, R. (1974) *Change: Principles of Problem Formation and Problem Resolution*. New York: Norton.

Wittgenstein, L. (1965) *The Blue and Brown Books: Preliminary Studies for the 'Philosophical Investigations'*. New York: Harper.

Alasdair Macdonald has been a Consultant Psychiatrist in the United Kingdom (UK) since 1980 and currently holds a temporary contract with Dorset HealthCare University Foundation NHS Trust. He is the former Research Coordinator, President and Secretary of the European Brief Therapy Association. He is a psychotherapy supervisor in Dorset.

13 NARRATIVE THERAPY

Martin Payne

INTRODUCTION

Narrative therapy was developed by family therapists Michael White at the Dulwich Centre in Adelaide, South Australia, and David Epston at the Auckland Family Centre in New Zealand. Their work swiftly became respected by family therapists, and is now being recognized more widely, with articles appearing in counselling publications, and with training organizations offering workshops and longer courses.

Although White and Epston re-thought many aspects of family therapy, narrative therapy is nevertheless rooted in this modality, and counsellors who work with individuals or couples may be surprised, even dismayed, by aspects such as the use of reflecting teams and the focus on asking questions. However many, including the author of this chapter, have discovered in narrative therapy a breath of fresh air in the ways it has re-examined many taken-for-granted assumptions of traditional therapy.

DAVID EPSTON (1944–) AND MICHAEL WHITE (1949–2008)

Epston and White always identified the conceptualization and development of narrative therapy as their equal and joint endeavour. Epston was born in Canada in 1944 and originally trained as an anthropologist. He became a social worker, and emigrated to New Zealand where he worked with children, young people and their families in an Auckland hospital before leaving the public health system to set up a private practice. He was influenced by Milton Erikson, who based much of his therapeutic technique on telling stories to clients, implicitly inviting them to interpret these stories in relation to their own lives and difficulties (Rosen, 1982). Epston's anthropological perspective, with its awareness of cultural influences on behaviour, was brought to bear in how he assisted families, paving the way for narrative therapy's non-pathologizing practices. Contemporary anthropology also anticipates narrative therapy's enquiring what people's experience means to them rather than interpreting this experience according to preconceived 'professional' ideas – 'the trick is to figure out what the devil *they* think they are up to' (Geertz, 1983, pp. 58, emphasis added).

In 1981 Epston, who was then little known in the family therapy field, met White, who was already established in Australia. They discovered much in common in their unconventional approaches to the work, and began an

> enduring friendship and intellectual partnership that was characterized by unshakeable optimism, a passion over ideas, what seemed like boundless energy, and a real dedication to assist the families with whom they were working … It seemed like every week there was a new development … a joy in offering (new ideas) out to a world that was looking for new ways of working. (Cheryl White, 2009)

Michael White was born in Adelaide in 1948, into a working-class family with Irish origins. On leaving school he worked for a time in a draughtsman's office, which he hated. After various unskilled jobs his growing commitment to social justice led him to train in social work. White found that many social work tutors in Australia habitually questioned the genuineness of students' commitment, assuming their motivation arose from unconscious needs and conflicts. White's indignation at what he saw as a pathologizing, patronizing and demeaning attitude profoundly influenced his approach to therapy.

On qualifying he worked in an Adelaide children's hospital as a clinical social worker. His egalitarian and socially aware attitudes made him critical both of the dehumanizing ways in which clients were treated by the hospital, and of the rigidly hierarchical nature of the hospital's staff structure. He was soon in conflict with management. When White published a paper on his successful work with young patients diagnosed as anorectic, he was forbidden to work with these people and their families on the grounds that he was not a highly qualified medical practitioner. He ignored this order, whereupon, on management instructions, the chairs in his room were removed – but White and his clients continued to meet, sitting on the floor. Management's next step was to punish him by assigning only children who had a long history of unresolved soiling. White riposted by devising (and publicizing) techniques, later central to narrative therapy, which had a 99 per cent success rate in eliminating soiling in an average of four days. When working part time in another psychiatric hospital, White and his team never read the most bulky case files of referred clients, presumably so as to avoid preconceptions based on other professionals' comments and assessments (Epston, 2009, pp. 3–4).

In the mid-1980s White and a colleague set up the independent Dulwich Centre for Narrative Therapy and Community Work, in Adelaide. White's wife Cheryl, whose feminism influenced her husband's ideas and practices, ran Dulwich Centre Publications, which has published many of White's and Epston's writings as well as those of other narrative therapists. A quarterly newsletter evolved into the *International Journal of Narrative Therapy and Community Work*. When the co-director withdrew from the Centre, Cheryl became co-director. It is now an internationally respected and influential base for narrative therapy and for a number of years has organized well-attended conferences in both hemispheres. In addition to his work at the Centre, Michael White gave presentations in many countries.

The Dulwich Centre is also important as a centre for community work and social activism, with a particular commitment to the Aboriginal communities so marginalized and oppressed in Australia's history and in the present.

In 1990, Norton published White and Epston's jointly authored *Narrative Means to Therapeutic Ends*. This became a seminal text, reaching a wide audience through translation into many languages. Epston and White also co-authored *Experience, Contradiction, Narrative and Imagination* (1992). Epston's books include *Collected Papers* (1989), *Down Under and Up Over* (Bowen (ed.), 2009), and titles written in collaboration with colleagues: *Playful Approaches to Serious Problems* (Epston, Freeman and Lobovits, 1997) and *'Catching up' with David Epston* (1998).

White is generally considered the more influential of the two originators. As well as many articles in professional journals he published *Selected Papers* (1989), *Re-Authoring Lives* (1995), *Narratives of Therapists' Lives* (1997), *Reflections on Narrative Practice* (2000), *Narrative Practice and Exotic Lives* (2004), and *Maps of Narrative Practice* (2007).

At a point of personal and professional change in his life, including a project to set up a new therapy centre in Adelaide, Michael White died of a heart attack in 2008 at the age of 59.

THEORY

BASIC CONCEPTS

'FIT'

In his early years as a therapist White was powerfully influenced by the anthropologist Gregory Bateson's concepts of how people come to understand the world and how these understandings influence their lives (White, 1989, pp. 37–8). Although White's later writing seldom mentions Bateson, his influence remained throughout the development of White's thinking and practice. One of Bateson's concepts is 'fit' – a deceptively simple idea which has implications for many human activities including education, training and therapy. When we are faced with unfamiliar ideas, we cannot grasp them unless we can to some extent fit them into our existing knowledge and preconceptions; otherwise these new ideas are meaningless, become distorted, and are immediately forgotten or misinterpreted. We experience bafflement when someone knowledgeable about an unfamiliar specialist subject, perhaps computer technology or the workings of the world economy, tries to explain it in ways that are outside our own basis of comprehension. The speaker may assume that simply telling us what they themselves know will be enough for this knowledge to be transferred to our understanding.

White proposed that therapy must take into account that awareness is 'interpretative', meaning, in postmodern mode, that we do not see the world 'as it is' but inevitably interpret the world through the filter of our preconceptions. These preconceptions govern the initial material clients bring to therapy and should be respected and believed as their genuine apprehension of experience. However, more helpful perspectives are possible if clients are sensitively encouraged to search their experience for aspects beyond their preconceptions, at a pace and in a way that allow these discoveries gradually to be absorbed and integrated into existing awareness.

INSTITUTIONAL POWER

The American sociologist Erving Goffman also influenced White. *Asylums* (1951/1968), Goffman's devastating study of the culture of mental institutions, chimed with White's own experience of working in psychiatric hospitals. He adopted Goffman's term 'unique outcomes' for a key concept of narrative therapy – occasions when persons act, think or feel in ways that are not conditioned by institutional or social expectations but are unique to themselves as individuals. But perhaps the most powerful influence on White's thinking was the French historian of ideas, Michel Foucault. White and Epston emphasise Foucault's recurring theme of how power and knowledge are intertwined, and embodied in institutions as a form of social control (1990, pp. 18–27). In the modern world this power is held by self-elected 'experts' who possess carefully guarded specialist knowledge, and who encourage people to 'self-censor' by continually and critically measuring themselves against the norms and values of those institutions. Foucault analysed many social and cultural systems in this light including the law and prisons, Western norms of sexuality, and 'clinics' (a general term for systems devoted to health, including psychiatry), and the social structures through which those institutions' norms are promoted and validated. White agreed with Foucault that these processes produce stressful pressure on people to become 'docile bodies' subservient to so-called expert diagnoses and judgement, leading to their *judging themselves* as damaged or inadequate. White saw narrative therapy and narrative community work as means of countering the debilitating effects of such power-based processes.

NARRATIVE

The French philosopher Paul Ricoeur, in his seminal book *Time and Narrative* (1984), written when White and Epston were beginning to formulate their ideas, proposed that the concept of 'narrative' is at the centre of human awareness. Narrative is the core structuring process by which we define our relationship to the movement of the earth in relation to the sun, to our time perspective as reflected in the creation of the calendar, and to our sense of our lives as moving from past to present to future.

Many different, equally valid narratives can be told out of the rich subject matter of our lives. Like a good novel, but with subject matter far more detailed and complex, our lives contain an infinite number of potential plots, subplots and episodes which can be, and are, isolated from the teeming complexity of memory and told to ourselves subjectively, and to others verbally, as 'stories'. We do this frequently, from day to day. Usually our self-stories are brief, relatively trivial and soon forgotten by ourselves and our hearers ('We had a good time at the fairground and spent far too much! It was nice until Joe felt sick after the roller-coaster and we had to take him home. But I expect we'll go again next year').

Self-narratives, like this invented example, are fleeting, but others are emotionally loaded, central to our lives, repeated endlessly, and bound up with our sense of identity and our ways of thinking, feeling and acting. When they describe distressing, troubling or painful aspects of life they may come to dominate our thoughts and consciousness. We may endlessly ruminate over, and also share with others who are willing to listen, narratives on topics such as how we met and committed to a person as a life companion and how this relationship has fallen into disillusion and conflict; that our parents never seemed to love us very much but preferred a sibling who even today is their favourite; details of our involvement in a road accident when we thought we were going to die, with images of that event now haunting our dreams and waking moments; how we learned that after enjoying good health all our life we have a dangerous and possibly fatal disease; our inability to shake off sadness at a loved person's death, spending secret hours in tears.

These are not neutral and passive accounts – they are powerfully influential on how we see ourselves, interpret our experience, and define our relationships. They are self-fulfilling and self-reinforcing. And because received cultural norms, including those of the modern therapy culture, tend to define the reactions we describe in deficit-based medical language (such as 'unhealthy' or 'out of touch with our feelings' or 'traumatic'), we may further interiorize hopelessness. Telling our stories to a sympathetic listener may bring some sense of relief, but this relief is likely to be temporary. If the listener tries to cheer us up, to give advice, or in any other way to suggest an alternative way of looking at things, it is more likely to add to our distress, because we cannot relate these comments to how we are actually thinking and feeling. The suggestions will not 'fit' our dominant stories, which will reassert themselves and possibly lead to a vicious circle of hopelessness, leading to further hopelessness.

BOX 13.1 THE NARRATIVE METAPHOR

1. We represent our lives to ourselves and others in the form of self-stories, or narratives, comprising the mental images by which we link our past, present and future.
2. Self-stories are influenced by our relationships and by sociocultural norms, expectations and assumed truths.

3. Self-stories omit much of our lived experience, being formed from selective memory.
4. Self-stories powerfully influence our identity and actions.
5. When we are troubled, our self-stories can become 'problem-saturated' and dislocated from our full experience as lived.

'TEXT'

White was stimulated by ideas from literary theory in the writings of the psychologist Jerome Bruner, and by postmodernist literary theorists including Wolfgang Iser. White elaborates Bruner's suggestion that a parallel exists between the ways in which people understand and remember written stories and novels, and how they understand and remember their lives (White and Epston, 1990, pp. 9–15). Both life and fiction comprise acts, thoughts and feelings over time. Novels and stories, and events in our lives, are remembered selectively.

We bring preconceptions to written stories, so our reading is different from others' experience of the same story. Someone sensitive to nuances of language may focus on how the author portrays atmosphere through evocative phrasing, how the author's 'voice' subtly conveys attitudes such as irony, and the psychological perceptions demonstrated by the characters' reactions and changing relationships. Another reader may simply enjoy the story as a tension-filled series of puzzles gradually resolved, and another may primarily be aware of social or historical factors in the text. Once read, a story's specific details gradually blur in the memory, which is why we can return with pleasure to stories we have read previously.

If we attempt to re-tell a story, even immediately after we have read it, our version will not only be different to other people's similar attempts, but it will considerably differ from the author's text (Bruner, 1986, pp. 161–71). Nevertheless, the effort of recalling the story in the process of retelling it to a listener will make our repeat version more coherent than the uncoordinated and out-of-sequence memories of the text by which we represented it to ourselves in our unspoken memory. If the listener persists with questions about the story we are likely to recall more details, until our account comes to correspond more closely to the original – although it will never duplicate the original, and will always remain a simplification of its subtleties and actuality.

Iser (1978) writes about 'gaps in the text' – those unstated aspects of a story which the author omits, but implies, so that the reader is made to create them for him/herself. White, following Bruner, suggests that the 'text analogy' is a useful way of understanding the process of therapy; the client's life is the text, his/her story of life is the memory of it that is told to the therapist. Gaps in the text are those aspects of the person's life that have been unrecognized or forgotten, but which can throw a light on the problem, or on the person's response to it, in previously unrecognized ways. Questions asked by the therapist about events, actions, thoughts and feelings are instrumental in enabling clients to structure their memories into a sequence, and in so doing to recall their lives more completely. In this way the initial, 'thin' narrative told to the therapist, an account dominated by the problem, becomes 'thickened', that is, extended and enriched. The original story, when enriched, will then include elements – perhaps at this stage tentatively recalled, fragile and apparently minor – which can be recognized, acknowledged and built on so as eventually to allow a more complete, varied and helpful perspective to emerge. This enriched story is the material from which change derives, whether changes in action, attitude, feelings, thinking or sense of self; or in all of these (White, 1989, pp. 37–46).

EDUCATIONAL THEORY

Towards the end of his life White adapted ideas from the educational theorist Lev Vygotsky into an explanatory 'map' for narrative therapy (2007, pp. 271–5). Vygotsky proposed that learning must take place by slow stages where existing knowledge is gradually built on and enlarged, encouraged by a teacher. From his reading of Vygotsky, White developed a therapeutic structure which he called 'scaffolding conversations' or 'distancing conversations', where the therapist assists clients gradually to move away from their initial perception of the problem and to take on board aspects of remembered experience which have been ignored, forgotten or not noticed. In other words, to 'distance' themselves from the limitations of their initial perceptions, and to build a 'scaffolding' of ideas and discoveries which will support their newly developed awareness of unrecognized complexity, with its concomitant growth of hope and a revised self-view.

POST-STRUCTURALISM (OR NON-STRUCTURALISM)

'Post-structuralism' is a reaction against a type of thought called 'structuralism', which was prevalent in European intellectual circles in the middle years of the twentieth century. Structuralists such as the anthropologist Claude Lévi-Strauss proposed that apparently diverse human cultures all derive from the same universal mental processes. Psychoanalytic theory was called on, with Freud's concepts of the structure of the mind, and his expositions of the behaviour produced by the interactional dynamics of these elements, being attributed to all people in all cultures at all times no matter what 'superficial' differences might exist between those cultures. 'Deep structures' were said to exist 'below the surface' of all human activity, and structuralism claimed to be able to reveal these – for example, a limited number of identifiable thematic structures were claimed to exist in all folk tales, no matter what their cultural or geographical origins (Eagleton, 1996, p. 9).

As the name implies, *post*-structuralism has a different perspective. Narrative theory is firmly in the post-structuralist camp (although White preferred the term 'non-structuralist', implying that this way of thinking is not just a reaction to a previous way, but is valid in its own right). For example, Carl Rogers' structuralist concept of a 'core self' has no place in White's theories. Rather, White proposes that a client's loss of a sense of 'who he/she is' reflects that identity is fluid and learned, formed by interpersonal interaction within specific social and cultural contexts. To narrative therapists, the task of counselling people who have a lost or diminished sense of identity is not to assist an assumed core self to re-emerge, but to assist the client to regain a sense of self which has been formed in social interactions. The focus is often on identifying, validating and enlarging clients' memories of people who valued them.

White does not use structuralist 'surface and depth' metaphors to describe mental functioning, and this is consistent with his refusal to assume expert professional insight into hypothesized unconscious motives and dynamics. He prefers metaphors of 'thin' and 'thick' in describing the extent to which people's sense of their lives is partial and attenuated, or close to their full, lived experience. And although he fully concedes that humanism (the Western historical focus on people as bounded individuals) has had positive political and social results, he follows Foucault in claiming that it is no longer possible 'to know and speak of the "truth" of who we are – of the essence of our being, of our human nature' (1997, p. 220). A non-structuralist attitude towards people and their difficulties underpins White's respect for, and focus on, clients' conscious values, purposes and intentions.

ACQUISITION

INFLUENCE OF 'PROFESSIONALS'

White suggests that mental health professionals' dominating ways of acting towards people, and the distancing, pseudo-scientific vocabulary with which they speak about people's lives, give those professionals 'moral worth' and esteem in the eyes of their colleagues, open the door to career advancement and financial remuneration, establish a linguistic code that claims to define realities while actually obscuring the effects of such language on the people who consult them, and help to maintain a monopoly of power and influence by their apparent scientific objectivity (1995, pp. 114–15). These practices 'imply aberration' in people who seek help, and establish and maintain those people's sense of malfunctioning and inadequacy (1995, pp. 115–16).

These power/knowledge aspects of society are not restricted to the mental health professions. White, following Foucault, proposes that they are widespread, and responsible for much of the misery of identity crisis felt by people who seek therapy:

> ... people are active in the policing of their own and each other's lives, and are deeply implicated in the mechanisms of social control that are characteristic of modern power ... that employs various schemes and continuums of normality/abnormality, tables of performance, scales for the rating of every human expression imaginable, and formulae for the ranking of persons in relation to each other. (2004, p. 169)

'THIN' SELF-STORIES

People have always found ways of coping with and overcoming difficult aspects of life by their own unaided efforts, by consultation with friends, relatives and other respected persons, and by gaining comfort in adversity from various religious or philosophical beliefs. The modern Western invention of psychotherapy in its various forms has offered an additional means of resolving painful situations. Since these practices initially arose in medical contexts, for the most part they have retained a 'medical' or remedial assumption that persons who seek the help of therapists have *deficits* which either comprise the problem, or are instrumental in restricting them from overcoming their conflicted or distressing life situations. Clients are, for example, seen by some therapists as subject to the workings of unconscious and unresolved repressed conflicts; or acting according to learned, inappropriate behavioural responses; or disconnected from their core self and true feelings; or thinking illogically. According to these premises the therapist's task is curative; the deficits must be put right by means of the therapist's skill. Certainly it is assumed that clients have an innate capacity to respond to the therapist's expertise, but nevertheless the underlying assumption is that *there is something amiss in them.*

Postmodern models such as solution-focused therapy and narrative therapy do not share this premise. White insists that 'in our work we do not construct problems in terms of disease and do not imagine that we do anything that relates to "a cure"' (1990, p. 14). In a key passage, which also suggests a therapeutic approach implied by the nature of the acquisition process, White explains that he and Epston

> make the assumption that persons experience problems, for which they frequently seek therapy, when the narratives in which they are 'storying' their experience and/or in which they are having their experience 'storied' by others, do not sufficiently represent their lived experience, and that, in these circumstances, there will be significant aspects of their experience that contradict these dominant narratives ... an acceptable outcome [of therapy] would be the identification or generation of alternative stories that enable them to perform new meanings ... that persons will experience as more helpful, satisfying and open-ended. (1990, pp. 14–15)

White is suggesting that a person's *concept* of the problem, rather than any innate psychological deficit when attempting to address it, is what stands in the way of change. The client conceptualizes his/her life, and the problems in that life, in the form of images of events, feelings and thoughts taking place in sequence over time: that is, as a narrative. The client's limited concept is not 'wrong' or 'mistaken' – it corresponds to how he or she really feels and thinks in relation to the problem. But the narrative is partial and selective, having been limited by the problem's power to obscure or blot out memories of life and identity which might assist the client to gain a more helpful perspective, including a recognition of the part played by sociocultural factors. When a wider concept of the situation is acquired and reinforced this can lead to changes in attitudes or actions.

Elements which may influence the limited nature of clients' self-stories include the following.

SOCIOCULTURAL NORMS

Social constructionism influenced White's thinking, especially the writings of the social psychologist Kenneth Gergen. This perspective may be broadly defined as follows: the culture of any society, or subculture within wider society, includes unexamined, taken-for-granted beliefs arising from that culture's history, which are perceived by institutions and individuals as self-evident truths. Such assumed truths are reinforced by social institutions with a vested interest in promoting them, and are further reinforced in individuals through interactions with other people who have interiorized these assumed truths. Many assumed truths are contradicted by clients' actual lived experience, and this dissonance may produce confusion, self-condemnation and distress.

When clients' initial problem-narratives contain instances of distress or self-condemnation because these stories are not in tune with, or do not incorporate, the values and assumptions of their social subgroup or of the wider cultural context, narrative therapists invite clients to think about, and to define, the sociocultural sources of the assumed truths influencing them; to consider how these assumed truths have been propagated and reinforced both socially and personally; and to decide whether those assumed truths stand up to examination in the light of their own beliefs, experiences and values.

BOX 13.2   EXAMPLE OF A CULTURALLY PRODUCED ASSUMED TRUTH

Joanna, aged 36, and her partner Will were happy living together as a committed couple, and each had a demanding but satisfying job. They liked children, but they did not wish to be parents themselves. Much pressure to change this decision was being brought to bear by friends with children, and also by Joanna's parents, who told her that she would be unfulfilled as a woman, claimed to be heartbroken at the prospect of never being grandparents, and bitterly accused Joanna and Will of being selfish. These pressures reflected and were reinforced by the pervasive cultural assumption that families with children are the approved norm. Despite herself, Joanna was having doubts, although every time she imagined children disrupting her and Will's way of life she felt distress. Counselling assisted Joanna to recognize that the assumed norm of having children is a cultural construct; to reconnect with and validate the reasons for her not wanting children; and to reinstate her conviction that being a child-free couple was a wholly legitimate way for her and Will to organize their relationship.

TRAUMA

Trauma is a recurring theme in White's work, especially in relation to recovery from violence or sexual abuse. White was careful not to risk re-traumatizing clients by requesting a detailed account of the original traumatic event or events, and emphatically warned of the dangers in such approaches (1995, pp. 85–7). His focus was on encouraging the client to tell an alternative story around resistance, self-value, self-preservation and signs of recovery. Where abused clients' initial narratives included aspects of self-blame or self-condemnation, White invited them to consider ways in which the perpetrator had been skilled in making the victim feel responsible for triggering the abuse, and assisted them to reconnect with their basic values and beliefs, previously obscured by the diminution of their sense of personal worth (pp. 94–7). In some instances, White would not use the traumatic incident itself as the basis of therapy but would patiently explore other areas of the client's life that suggested the capacity for recovery.

FAMILY INFLUENCES

Family interactions are embodied in White's and Epston's writings and teaching. There is recognition that clients' memories of early experience in their family context, reinforced by themes of family life in their narratives, are often a powerful influence on how they have come to understand themselves, their relationships and their difficulties. This is especially the case when clients have taken on board versions of psychology widely promoted in the popular media, where childhood experience is assumed to be at the root of most, or all, adult attitudes, characteristics and problems. Clients sometimes spontaneously offer the therapist explanations of their problems by relating them to their childhood experiences, and sometimes these explanations can sideline other considerations. They may claim that a perpetrator of violence cannot help this because of a violent childhood, or attribute ill-judged decisions and unsatisfactory ways of life to insecurity stemming from childhood neglect. Clients telling such narratives may benefit from a process that sets such opinions against their actual experience. Of course, this does not imply mistrust of all narratives linking childhood experience to current problems: discrimination is necessary. Adults who as children were sexually abused by a family member may still be finding it hard to disentangle the affection they felt for the abuser, the affection verbally expressed by the abuser, and the nature and effects of acts which overstepped appropriate levels of physical contact.

Current family dynamics, even if well meant, may create or maintain the problem. A parent's anxious attempts to provide advice, support and encouragement to a young person who is trying to change behaviour may diminish the young person's taking responsibility for his or her own decisions, and perpetuate the problem (White, 1989, p. 108). Family stresses may be exacerbated by their contrast with culturally approved images of norms of family life, and problem-narratives will contain elements of personal failure in relation to these assumed norms ('She's dreadfully rude to me, she never comes home on time, and she smokes pot. I must be a really bad parent').

MAINTENANCE

NEGATIVE EXPLANATION

At the level of everyday explanation, maintenance of distress and confusion varies according to the circumstances producing the problem. Someone unhappy and unfulfilled in their work will feel distress and anxiety until they find a more satisfying job; someone affected by depression and grief following the death of a loved partner may take considerable time to reach a point where they feel something like normal life can resume. Since White did not seek to explain the maintenance of problems in terms of persons' deficits or inadequacies, he made no attempt to define innate psychological reasons why clients are unable to resolve problems. He always made a clear distinction between the problem, and the identity of the person affected by it. His writing and teaching implicitly assume that problems come about because sometimes life is like that, and that social and cultural forces (including those that validate destructive attitudes and behaviour) have much to answer for in this respect.

When considering the problem's continuing influence on the person experiencing it, White drew on Gregory Bateson in proposing that rather than looking for *causes* why problems have been maintained, it is more helpful (a) to consider why solutions to the problem have *not* been found; and (b) to examine the 'restraints' which have prevented such solutions – the assumption being that such restraints are usually sociocultural in origin. In the instance of a young woman whose life had been invaded by anorexia nervosa, White suggests that family interactions, governed by culturally assumed truths about how women should ideally look and behave, have contributed to restraining his client from recognizing how change might be possible and desirable, and have created pseudo-explanations for her condition (taken on board by the client and her family) that are profoundly pathologizing, pessimistic and self-defeating:

> The problem is explained in terms of personal inadequacy, incompetence, imperfection and disloyalty ... The failure of the attempted solutions ... serves to reinforce these premises ... Thus, family members are restrained in the search for, and application of, alternative solutions. (1989, p. 66)

> Gender stereotyping is established by various premises that act as restraints ... if a woman is to be appreciated then she should be self-denying and dependent ... Emotional fulfilment is to be achieved by behaviours patterned on nurturing and caring for others ... she must conform to ... an ideal of thinness ... she should preoccupy herself with providing the correct food for others ... Premises that measure a woman's value by her ability to be self-denying, dependent, indirect, thin, and

preoccupied with food provide a context for the selection of anorectic behaviour. An insidious paradox is generated, one that is repeatedly reinforced in various ways: 'discover yourself through losing yourself' and 'find yourself through disappearing'. This easily translates into 'self-actualize through anorexia nervosa' ... Behaviour that does not fit with these premises has no meaning ... and ... cannot be selected out for survival. (1989, p. 69)

DOMINANT SELF-STORIES

White wrote the paper on anorexia before he had identified with the narrative tradition. Later he developed a widely applicable definition of the restraints/ constraints which maintain problems. This definition is that of 'dominant stories'. It unites two key ideas: Foucault's descriptions of culturally influenced self-scrutiny and self-censoring ('normalizing judgement'), and Bateson's concept of restraints that inhibit change by preventing a fit between the client's preconceptions and evidence at variance with those preconceptions.

Clients' dominant stories are the source of dissonance between clients' self-view and the evidence of their full, lived experience. To White, the problem-story, as told repeatedly, with minor variations, by the client, both in interior monologue and literally to others, is the prime source of the problem's maintenance. The client's view of the circumstances and events that contribute to the problem coalesce in his/her awareness, and are self-reinforcing through repetition. In many instances the self-story has become 'problem-saturated' (White and Epston, 1990, pp. 16, 39) and allows no room for (that is, it restrains) any wider or more helpful perspective being entertained.

The maintenance of the dominant problem-story is encouraged by the internalization of values and attitudes concerning distress and confusion deriving from society's assumed truths and established norms. The cultural norm which celebrates bravery, independence and pushing determinedly through difficult times means that clients are likely to see their continuing distress, and their inability to solve their problems, as personal weaknesses. In some subcultures this assumed truth is particularly powerful – for example in sporting circles, the police, the fire service and the armed forces. An inability to feel optimistic, combined with weeping, tiredness, early waking, irritability and longing for solitude, will be hidden from others as far as possible because they are seen as shameful; when defined (perhaps by a doctor) as 'clinical depression' a further dimension of anxiety may be produced because this medical language suggests an innate psychological or psychiatric dimension. In the contemporary culture of 'hard management', stress and fatigue brought about by excessive demands in the workplace are likely to be defined by management as incompetence or inadequacy, and may be interiorized in similar terms by the person affected. Someone grieving for a loved one several years after their death may feel self-condemnation because this goes against society's assumed norm of recovery and 'moving on'. Self-stories reflecting culturally influenced attitudes such as these will be told, reinforced and consolidated into problem-saturated narratives. Turning to a 'professional' for help may be seen as a shameful last resort. The socially reinforced assumed truth that this professional will have the skill to transform the situation by calling on expert superior knowledge will be brought to the consulting room, reflecting and contributing to the power position of that professional and of his/her elite social institution (priesthood, medicine, therapy).

THERAPY

THERAPEUTIC GOALS

The goal of narrative therapy is, simply put, to assist clients to move towards overcoming their problems in living and relating. To call this goal 'therapeutic' in the sense of aiming to define, then to correct or cure, deficits in the client would be wholly misleading.

White did not encourage clients to set goals and monitor progress, since such goals would reflect the mind-set initially brought to therapy (2007, pp. 4–5). A woman experiencing marital problems might set herself the goal of being a more considerate and responsive wife, whereas a less goal-oriented approach might allow her to recognize at an earlier stage that the problem lies elsewhere in the relationship. A man's set, but unfulfilled, goal of gaining promotion in his workplace might restrict him from recognizing that this is not the result of self-imputed limitations, but is derived from the destructiveness of his firm's competitive culture.

However, when clients moved away from their problem-saturated accounts of life to a wider perspective, White did invite them to envisage a time when their problems would be absent, so that images of this 'preferred future' would become part of their revised self-story.

PROCESS OF THERAPY

There is no single book by White or Epston fully outlining narrative therapy, though other narrative therapists have attempted an overview (Freedman and Combs, 1996; Morgan, 2000; Payne, 2006). White and Epston's *Narrative Means to Therapeutic Ends* presented narrative therapy as it stood in 1990, and 17 years later White's *Maps of Narrative Practice* explained his more recent thinking. Between these major texts White and Epston published many papers in family therapy journals, especially the *Dulwich Centre Newsletter* (later the *International Journal of Narrative Therapy and Community Work*), setting out their latest thinking, and practices deriving from it. They also wrote chapters for books edited by other family therapists. Many of these essays and papers later appeared in collections such as White's *Re-Authoring Lives* (1995) and Epston's *'Catching up' with David Epston* (1998) together with material not previously available. There are a few videos of White and Epston at work, varying in technical and therapeutic quality. The scattered nature of these source materials, the wide range of client problems they describe, and the varied means by which these problems were addressed in therapy, make a generalized description of narrative therapeutic processes particularly liable to oversimplification. Within the framework of his 'maps' for therapy White's sessions were flexible, improvised and varied. His priority was always a sensitive response to the individuals, couples and families he counselled (2007, p. 5).

Given these caveats, narrative therapy does incorporate a basic therapeutic process transferable to many varied problems. This process comprises an approximate sequence, though it does not neatly move forward but is conversationally 'natural', subject to back-and-forth questions, restatements, exploratory revisions, and repetitions.

The client's initial problem-story is, through responses to the therapist's questions, gradually modified and explored for meaning. The problem-narrative is 'thickened' or 'enriched' by the gradual inclusion and exploration of *unique outcomes* – White's term, borrowed from Goffman, for significant events, thoughts, feelings and actions, the memory of which has previously been censored out by the power of the problem. Gradually, the client's renewed and enlarged memories produce revised narratives that result in the client's repositioning himself/herself in relation to the problem. Life, problems and identity are seen differently. Dominant, problem-saturated story-elements diminish and more helpful elements become the springboard for change.

BOX 13.3   CORE NARRATIVE THERAPY INTERVENTIONS

- The client tells the problem-story in detail.
- The therapist notes and/or elicits unique outcomes.
- The problem is named, and possibly externalized.
- The therapist encourages the client to give full descriptions of the unique outcomes.
- The client is asked if he/she wishes to commit to change.
- The therapist invites the client to link unique outcomes with his/her history and to explore their meaning.

THE THERAPEUTIC RELATIONSHIP

White related to clients with warmth, acceptance and openness, demonstrating a genuine and concerned interest in their lives and maintaining a friendly, informal and, when appropriate, humour-tinged dialogue. But this was typical of the man in all his dealings with people. White and Epston's writings and teaching deny that the therapist is so central to the client's progress that a unique, temporary relationship of supreme importance must be established. White defined the therapist's relationship with the client in quite different terms than therapists who see this as the central factor promoting change, proposing 'de-centring' of the therapist as an ethical imperative (1997, pp. 200–16).

THERAPIST DE-CENTRING

Therapist de-centring implies consistently placing the client's own knowledge and skills of living firmly at the centre of therapy. The therapist's role is to follow a little behind the client, as the client reconnects with aspects of his or her life that have been clouded in memory by the influence of the dominant story (1995, pp. 36–7). The therapist's questions around these areas of the client's life are genuinely open and exploratory, intended to encourage the client to make his or her own discoveries and to draw his or her own conclusions.

Therapist de-centring involves practices which draw on the client's personal relationships with friends, relatives, mentors and other significant figures, past or present. It is these relationships that are, actually or potentially, genuinely *therapeutic*, as distinct from a temporary relationship with a therapist.

White developed practices promoting therapist de-centring that convey the therapist's ethical position in relation to the client. These include *transparency and accountability*, where the therapist is open about his or her limitations of skill, experience and knowledge, and *taking-it-back practices*, where the therapist affirms that therapy is a two-way process, acknowledges resonances between his/her experience and the client's, and makes clear what he or she has learned from the client.

THERAPEUTIC INTERVENTIONS

(To avoid excessive 'her/him' phrasing, in this section the therapist is female and the client male.)

THE CORE SEQUENCE

ENCOURAGING A FULL DESCRIPTION OF THE PROBLEM AND ITS EFFECTS

The therapist encourages the client to give a very detailed account of the problem, by asking clarifying questions and summarizing the client's responses. How has the problem affected his relationships, including with his family, friends and partner if he has one? Has it invaded his work? Are there health issues linked with the problem? Financial implications? – and so forth. The client feels 'heard', accepted, and gains the human relief of sharing worries with someone who is genuinely interested in his difficulties. By telling a full version of the problem-saturated story, the client is also less likely to return to it later in therapy, when the focus has changed. In subsequent sessions, listening to the problem-story is less emphasized, but time is always given to this if the client wishes to report continuing or new aspects of his difficulties.

NOTING UNIQUE OUTCOMES

The therapist notes elements that appear to stand apart from, or to contradict, the problem-saturated account. In narrative therapy such openings to alternative plot-lines are usually called 'unique outcomes'. A client affected by persistent anxiety may, without assigning it any significance himself, reveal that he attempted a task that anxiety usually prevents him from contemplating. A client whose life has been invaded by depression may mention that he felt slightly better when he went for a walk instead of staying indoors.

NAMING AND EXTERNALIZING THE PROBLEM

A name for the problem is discussed and agreed. The therapist usually encourages the client to choose an 'externalized' definition which linguistically separates the problem from the client's identity, for example 'unwelcome ritual habits' rather than 'my obsessive-compulsive disorder', and 'invasive worries' rather than 'my anxiety'. Thus, the client is encouraged to conceive the problem as something invasive which can be addressed, rather than as an aspect of himself or of his identity, which would imply an innate deficit difficult to dislodge.

Problems are not always externalized, for example when they are relatively minor in relation to larger issues. If they concern deliberately harmful acts they are never externalized, as distancing forms of definition such as 'the violence affecting your relationship' would affirm a perpetrator's tendency to avoid taking responsibility for what he/she does. The temptation to act violently might, however, be externalized, as in 'temptations inviting you to hit her' – implying that temptations can be resisted.

Where the client's internalized view of the problem is imbued with negative self-judgements deriving from cultural norms and expectations, White initiated 'externalizing conversations'. These dialogues go beyond externalizing the problem; they involve dialogue explicitly identifying and examining cultural forces that influence the client's negative self-view. In this way issues of relational and institutional 'politics' are directly addressed, such as the definition of 'success' as career status and monetary gain, or of 'psychological health' as an idealized and probably unachievable level of personal fulfilment.

EXPANDING UNIQUE OUTCOMES

The therapist gains the client's permission to ask questions about aspects of his story which she finds particularly intriguing. If, unusually, there appear to be no unique outcomes implicit in the problem-story, the therapist asks for examples: 'Can you remember a recent time when you didn't follow the rituals quite so completely?' or, 'Are there times when invasive worries have been a little less insistent?'.

She then invites detailed descriptions of the unique outcomes she has noted or elicited. Questions inviting such elaboration are low key, not interrogatory, but nevertheless gently persistent. In this way unique outcomes are expanded into an alternative narrative. This process, called 're-storying' or 're-authoring', is a key technique.

White is adamant that re-storying is not 'pointing out positives' (1995, p. 37). Nothing is pointed out; questions are asked in response to the client's account, with the therapist assisting the client to search his memory for a full description of the nature and circumstances of the unique outcomes. By the client's weaving these new plot-threads into the account of his life, the pessimism of the original problem-account is modified and new possibilities for change become visible.

ESTABLISHING THAT THE CLIENT WISHES TO CONTINUE

Now that a wider perspective is being attained the therapist asks the client whether he wishes to continue with his life as it is at present, or whether he wishes his life to be different. This apparently superfluous question, when answered positively, positions the client in opposition to the problem and affirms his commitment to change.

EXPLORING THE HISTORY AND MEANING OF UNIQUE OUTCOMES

Unique outcomes do not always fit a client's problem-saturated preconceptions, so if the therapist finds that they have no resonance for the client she abandons them. And the identification and description of unique outcomes are not in themselves sufficient for a significant therapeutic process to occur. These descriptions need to be reinforced, and embedded in the client's awareness. Unless the *significance* of unique outcomes for the client is explored he is likely to forget them, or see them as irrelevant, and unless they are linked to his history he may regard them as superficial and temporary.

White's accounts of questions that explore the meaning of unique outcomes give examples such as 'What does this tell you about yourself that it is important for you to know?', 'What difference does knowing this about yourself make to how you feel about yourself?', and 'What do these discoveries tell you about what you want for your life?' (1989, pp. 41–5). Improvising appropriate 'meaning' questions in response to the client's often tentative descriptions of unique outcomes is a core skill of narrative therapy, not easily learned.

OTHER INTERVENTIONS

THERAPEUTIC DOCUMENTS

Clients may forget what was said in the session, especially if the conversation has touched on areas that do not easily fit their assumptions and preconceptions.

White and Epston devised forms of written or other documentation to give to clients, in order to overcome this limitation, including copies of the therapist's session notes, video or sound recordings of sessions, letters summarizing clients' discoveries, 'certificates of achievement', and brief notes of key points using the client's own words (1990, pp. 77–216; White, 1995, pp. 199–213). Clients were also encouraged to create their own documents.

'TELLING AND RETELLING'

White claimed that clients' telling their developing stories to people other than the therapist has great value in reinforcing those stories. Initially he asked clients whom they might like to tell about their discoveries and progress. Friends? Relatives? He progressed to sessions where, with the client's permission, significant others were invited to attend and comment. White also adapted the family therapy practice of 'reflecting teamwork'. In his version, a team of therapists, or of people known to the client personally, listen to the therapist 'interviewing' the client; the client then listens as the therapist interviews the team; the client discusses the team's comments with the therapist while the team listens; finally, all comment on the session. The team members' role is not 'professional' but personal. They are asked not to interpret, congratulate or advise, but to comment on how the client's story has moved them, and whether it resonates with their own life experience (White, 2007, pp. 165–6).

'RE-MEMBERING' CONVERSATIONS

This practice originated in White's work with long-term grieving, where he encouraged clients to 'say hullo again' to their lost loved ones (1989, pp. 29–36). 'Re-membering' unites the meanings of (a) recalling to memory and (b) welcoming back into one's life, in imagination, people from the past who significantly gave support, example, wisdom, love or acceptance. Extending this, people not personally known to the client, such as admired historical figures, sporting heroes, writers or progressive political activists, are sometimes 'membered'. The therapist invites the client to identify such a person or persons, to describe what contribution they made to his life and (where applicable) he to theirs, then to explore what these people might say if they knew of his present difficulties and how he is addressing them. The client's developing self-narrative is enriched by these speculations, with their sense of renewal and continuity. A reverse version is used when clients wish to 'dismiss' from their lives people whose influence was harmful.

CASE MATERIAL

Examples of therapy abound in White's and Epston's writings, often with transcriptions from sessions. Externalizing conversations are engagingly described in White and Epston's accounts of how Nick, aged six, overcame 'Sneaky poo' to learn bowel control (1990, pp. 43–8) and of a young man's gaining a helpful perspective on the machinations of ADHD (White, 2007, pp. 10–23). Therapeutic documents played a large part in Epston's therapy with 17-year-old Ron, whose problem had been diagnosed as uncontrolled anger (1998, pp. 87–94). A client's re-storying of her problem-saturated account by exploring the meaning of a unique outcome, gaining a more positive view of her identity, is movingly illustrated in White's paper on addressing a sense of personal failure (2004, pp. 177–86). This example incorporates re-membering, also found in White's accounts of sessions with colleagues uncertain of their skills (1997, pp. 63–92). Outsider witness sessions are fully described by White (1997, pp. 103–13; 2007, pp. 166–78).

FURTHER DEVELOPMENTS

Narrative therapists continue to build on White and Epston's work. Hedke and Winslade's *Re-membering Lives* (2004) enlarges White's ideas about counselling for grief, and *Ideas for Therapy with Sexual Abuse* (1990), edited by Durrant and Cheryl White, contains contributions from therapists specializing in this area. Studies of narrative practice in wider contexts than the therapy room include Winslade and Monk's *Narrative Counselling in Schools* (1999), their *Narrative Mediation* (2001), and Denborough's *Beyond the Prison* (1996). A feminist perspective is brought to bear in *Working with the Stories of Women's Lives* (2001) edited by Cheryl White. Stephen Madigan has rigorously related narrative theory to practice (Madigan, 2011) and Duvall and Beres (2011) convincingly relate theory, research and practice. A growing number of qualitative research projects on narrative therapy are summarized on the Dulwich Centre website. The 'Just Therapy' team in New Zealand unites counselling and community work through culturally sensitive ways of assisting indigenous communities (Russell, 2003), and narrative practitioners have contributed to community work in Africa, the Middle East and elsewhere. Conferences and training now take place far beyond Australia and New Zealand. In the UK the Institute for Narrative Practice offers workshops and a diploma, and similar organizations exist in other countries. David Epston, via the Dulwich Centre website, is inviting narrative therapists to describe, avoiding narrative therapy jargon, ways in which they have initiated practices not found in the existing literature,

These developments suggest that narrative therapists will resist turning White's legacy into an unchallenged canon, and will continue to honour his spirit by exploring fresh ideas, discoveries and practices.

REVIEW AND PERSONAL QUESTIONS

REVIEW QUESTIONS

1. Which European and American thinkers influenced White and Epston?
2. How has anthropology been important in the development of narrative therapy?
3. What is meant by 'fit'?

4. What is a problem-saturated narrative?
5. What is a unique outcome?
6. How are unique outcomes used in narrative therapy?
7. Why do narrative therapists often define problems in externalizing language?
8. What is a meant by a culturally influenced assumed truth? Give an example.
9. How do narrative therapists see their relationship with clients?
10. What are 'outsider witnesses' and how are they used in narrative therapy?

PERSONAL QUESTIONS

1. Can you think of an idea or concept that is now familiar and understood, but which made little sense to you at first?
2. By what process did it become familiar and understood?
3. Looking back on a difficult period in your life, what helped you to come through that you did not recognize at the time?
4. Who in your past or present might like to hear about how you overcame that problem? What might they say to you about how you addressed it?
5. In your own self-story, what are the most important influences that have made you the person you are today?
6. How do narrative therapy ideas and practices differ from the model with which you are most familiar?
7. What do these models have in common?
8. Do you see the therapist's role as curative or facilitative? How have you reached that conclusion?
9. What conscious commitments, values and purposes led you to take up counselling?
10. Who influenced those commitments, values and purposes?

ANNOTATED BIBLIOGRAPHY

Epston, D. (1998) *'Catching up' with David Epston.* Adelaide: Dulwich Centre Publications.
A stimulating collection of papers; topics include externalizing, re-authoring and working with eating disorders.

White, M. and Epston, D. (1990) *Narrative Means to Therapeutic Ends.* New York: Norton.
This seminal book outlines the core ideas and practices of narrative therapy.

White, M. (1995) *Re-Authoring Lives.* Adelaide: Dulwich Centre Publications.
Possibly White's most popular book, with transcripts of interviews where he explains narrative ideas, and papers on outsider witness practices and reflecting teamwork.

White, M. (1997) *Narratives of Therapists' Lives.* Adelaide: Dulwich Centre Publications.

This book includes chapters on re-membering, the therapeutic relationship, and post-structuralism in relation to traditional therapy.

White, M. (2007) *Maps of Narrative Practice*. New York: Norton.
White's last book contains his most recent guidelines for narrative therapy sessions, illustrated with transcripts.

REFERENCES AND FURTHER READING

Bruner, J. (1986) *Actual Minds, Possible Worlds*. Cambridge, MA: Harvard University Press.

Bruner, J. (1990) *Acts of Meaning*. Cambridge, MA: Harvard University Press.

Denborough, D. (1996) *Beyond the Prison*. Adelaide: Dulwich Centre Publications.

Durrant, M. and White, C. (eds) (1990) *Ideas for Therapy with Sexual Abuse*. Adelaide: Dulwich Centre Publications.

Duvall, J. and Beres, L. (2011) *Innovations in Narrative Therapy*. New York: Norton.

Eagleton, T. (1996) *Literary Theory*. Minneapolis: University of Minnesota Press.

Epston, D. (1989) *Collected Papers*. Adelaide: Dulwich Centre Publications.

Epston, D. (1998) *'Catching up' with David Epston*. Adelaide: Dulwich Centre Publications.

Epston, D. (2009) 'Remembering Michael', *Context*, 105: 3–4.

Epston, D. (ed. Bowen, B.) (2009) *Down Under and Up Over*. London: Association for Family Therapy and Systemic Practice.

Epston, D. and White, M. (1992) *Experience, Contradiction, Narrative and Imagination*. Adelaide: Dulwich Centre Publications.

Epston, D., Freeman, J. and Lobovits, D. (1997) *Playful Approaches to Serious Problems*. New York: Norton.

Freedman, J. and Combs, G. (1996) *Narrative Therapy: The Social Construction of Preferred Realities*. New York: Norton.

Geertz, C. (1983) *Local Knowledge*. New York: Basic Books.

Goffman, E. (1951/1968) *Asylums*. London: Penguin Books.

Hedke, L. and Winslade, J. (2004) *Re-membering Lives*. Amityville, NY: Baywood.

Iser, W. (1978) *The Act of Reading*. Baltimore, MD and London: Johns Hopkins University Press.

Madigan, S. (2011) *Narrative Therapy*. Washington DC: Americal Psychological Association

Morgan, A. (2000) *What is Narrative Therapy?* Adelaide: Dulwich Centre Publications.

Parry, A. and Doan, R. E. (1994) *Story Re-visions*. New York: Guilford.

Payne, M. (2006) *Narrative Therapy: An Introduction for Counsellors*. London: Sage.

Payne, M. (2010) *Couple Counselling: A Practical Guide*. London: Sage.

Ricoeur, P. (1984) *Time and Narrative*. Chicago: University of Chicago Press.

Rosen, S. (ed.) (1982) *My Voice Will Go With You*. New York: Norton.

Russell, S. (ed.) (2003) *Just Therapy*. Adelaide: Dulwich Centre Publications.

White, C. (ed.) (2001) *Working with the Stories of Women's Lives*. Adelaide: Dulwich Centre Publications.

White, C. (2009) 'Where did it all begin?' *Context*, 105: 57–8.

White, M. (1989) *Selected Papers*. Adelaide: Dulwich Centre Publications.

White, M. (1995) *Re-Authoring Lives*. Adelaide: Dulwich Centre Publications.

White, M. (1997) *Narratives of Therapists' Lives*. Adelaide: Dulwich Centre Publications.

White, M. (2000) *Reflections on Narrative Practice*. Adelaide: Dulwich Centre Publications.

White, M. (2004) *Narrative Practice and Exotic Lives*. Adelaide: Dulwich Centre Publications.

White, M. (2007) *Maps of Narrative Practice*. New York: Norton.

White, M. and Epston, D. (1990) *Narrative Means to Therapeutic Ends*. New York: Norton.

Winslade, J. and Monk, G. (1999) *Narrative Counseling in Schools*. Thousand Oaks, CA: Corwin/Sage.

Winslade, J. and Monk, G. (2001) *Narrative Mediation*. San Francisco: Jossey-Bass.

Martin Payne is an independent counsellor working in Norwich.

POSITIVE THERAPY **14**

Neil Frude

INTRODUCTION

Positive psychotherapy (PPT) is a new approach to psychotherapy that stems largely from developments in the field of positive psychology. Although in many ways this is a novel approach, several of the key ideas can be found in well-established forms of psychotherapy, notably solution-focused therapy, person-centred therapy and various 'third wave CBT' approaches, including dialectical behaviour therapy, acceptance and commitment therapy (ACT) and compassion-focused psychotherapy. The fundamental idea behind positive psychotherapy is that there is a reciprocal relationship between distress and wellbeing and that there are important advantages in helping clients to develop skills that will enhance their wellbeing, reinforce their resilience and boost their personal strengths. Thus rather than adopting a problem-solving approach and attempting to reduce distress and symptomatology through direct intervention, positive psychotherapy focuses on helping people to thrive. The idea is that enhancing positive wellbeing will often weaken or eliminate many of the factors that serve to maintain and deepen clinical problems. Such factors include pessimism, low self-confidence and disengagement from social relationships.

MARTIN SELIGMAN (1942–)

Many people have contributed to the ideas and research behind the development of positive psychotherapy and no single person can be properly described as having created PPT in the way in which Albert Ellis is clearly the originator of rational emotive behaviour therapy and Arnold Lazarus the originator of multimodal therapy. However, Martin Seligman is certainly the most conspicuous and energetic figure in the emergence and continuing development of positive psychology, and because PPT is so closely associated with positive psychology, his influence on the development of this therapeutic approach is arguably the most substantial of anyone in the field.

Seligman has a long and distinguished history in clinical psychology. His first major contribution was in the 1970s when, on the basis of a series of animal studies, he put forward a new theory of depression in which he suggested that depression was the result of 'learned helplessness'. This behavioural theory was soon revised by Seligman and colleagues to take into account the cognitive attributions that appeared to play a crucial role in many cases of clinical depression (Abramson et al., 1978). Some people, it was argued, tend to interpret failures and setbacks in ways that are personal, stable and global (for example, 'My poor exam result is a valid reflection of my lack of ability and I expect to get similar pathetic results in my other exams. This just goes to show that I am academically very weak all round'). The revised helplessness theory suggested a clear causal link between a pessimistic outlook and depression, and also suggested that an effective way of preventing or overcoming depression would be to help clients to achieve a more realistic and less negatively biased view of things.

There followed a substantial body of research on 'learned optimism' (Seligman, 1991) which then expanded to a general interest in personal strengths and positivity. Seligman collaborated with others, notably Chris Peterson and Mihalyi Csikszentmihalyi, in emphasising the need for psychology to address positive emotions and personal strengths.

In 1998, Seligman became president of the American Psychological Association and in giving his presidential address he used the opportunity to call for a 'revolution' in psychology to expand and to focus much more on the detailed study of human mental health (not 'ill-health'), wellbeing, strengths and flourishing.

There had been some previous interest in 'positive mental health' (for example, by the British social psychologist Marie Jahoda in the 1950s; Jahoda, 1958) and also some psychological research on happiness (notably by David Myers, as summarized in Myers, 1992), but Seligman's standing, enterprise, forceful argument and sheer hard work, in collaboration with a growing group of highly talented colleagues in several leading universities, ensured that positive psychology soon established a substantial foothold within the discipline.

From its beginning, positive psychology has been developed as an applied science, with key applications in education and organizational functioning as well as in psychotherapy and counselling. Seligman also claimed that positive psychology has provided, for the first time, a coherent theoretical framework for the development of lifestyle coaching (Seligman, 2007).

Seligman published a landmark book *Authentic Happiness* (2002) and followed this with a substantial reworking of his ideas in *Flourish* (2011). Positive psychology is often characterized as 'the science of happiness' but, like several other positive psychologists, Seligman has become uncomfortable with the focus on happiness because many people associate this concept with sensual pleasure and fleeting states of jollity. Such impressions contrast with the idea of happiness as a deep, long-lasting and meaningful positive state that involves such elements as contentment and a sense of purpose.

Following marked contributions to 'positive education' in schools and colleges in several countries, and advising governments on the assessment and development of wellbeing in the general population, Seligman is now leading a major positive psychology project that aims to increase psychological fitness and resilience in the US army.

Among his wide range of positive psychology interests, Seligman has given some attention to therapeutic applications of the field. He has conducted a number of studies and demonstrated strong positive effects of the approach. He has also noted, in common with several other prominent figures in the field, that his involvement in positive psychology has had a profound positive effect on him personally. He concludes that:

> Positive psychology makes people happier. Teaching positive psychology, research-ing positive psychology, using positive psychology in practice as a coach or thera-pist … and just reading about positive psychology all *make people happier.* The people who work in positive psychology are the people with the highest well-being I have ever known (Seligman, 2011, p. vi).

THEORY

BASIC CONCEPTS

WELLBEING AND DISTRESS

The theory behind positive psychotherapy focuses on a reciprocal relation-ship between wellbeing and distress. The main tenet is that enhancing per-sonal wellbeing will decrease a person's vulnerability to distress and will help to relieve the suffering of those who are distressed. Thus rather than being directly focused on the relief of symptoms, positive psychology interventions aim to enhance the person's levels of happiness and wellbeing.

Although distress is often associated with physical ill-health or with mental health conditions such as depression and anxiety, a good deal of human misery comes from conditions and situations that are not recognized as medical syn-dromes. These include chronic loneliness, a sense of personal failure, extreme boredom or the feeling that life is pointless.

Whatever its origins, distress typically leads to a range of negative conse-quences that maintain and deepen the distress. Such effects may include diminished self-confidence, a lack of energy and motivation, a sense of futility, pessimism, disengagement from social contact, a sharp decline in interests and the loss of the ability to find pleasure in things ('anhedonia'). Each of these consequences is likely to form a vicious circle with distress, and together these circles will constitute a systemic pattern that can be labelled a 'vicious daisy', with distress at the centre and the various vicious circles forming the petals. The nature of this system is such that a negative change in any one element (such as a further blow to the person's self-confidence, or difficulties in a key relationship) will lead to an increase in distress that will then radiate through the system, decreasing the person's energy still further as well as increasing such negative aspects as disengagement, pessimism and a sense of futility.

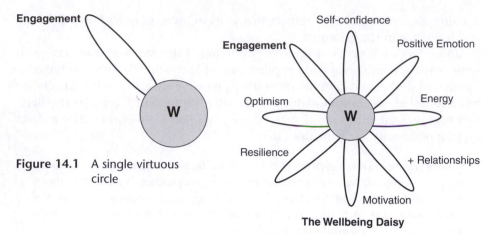

Figure 14.1 A single virtuous circle

The Wellbeing Daisy

Figure 14.2 Lots of virtuous circles together make a daisy

The practice of positive therapy can be seen as involving the reverse of this process, with therapeutic interventions stimulating the action of a 'virtuous daisy' that has wellbeing at its centre. Thus an intervention that enhances optimism, or increased engagement, or higher self-confidence, or positive emotion, will increase general wellbeing and this will then stimulate a range of positive effects. These will include biological, psychological and social benefits, each of which, in their turn, will reverberate throughout the system. Thus an intervention that increases a client's self-confidence, for example, will increase the person's general state of wellbeing, and this in turn is likely to boost their energy levels, to increase their optimism and to heighten their compassion for themselves and other people. According to this model, any successful positive intervention, whatever its specific aim, is likely to have beneficial effects that will radiate throughout the system.

This radiation effect is not only restricted to psychological changes but also crosses into the biological domain. It has long been established that feeling good has a positive effect on a number of health-related biological indicators. Fascinating new research in positive psychology has now demonstrated striking associations between psychological wellbeing and a wide range of biological measures including the efficiency of the immune system (Cohen et al., 2006), cardiovascular functioning (Boehm and Kubzansky, 2012) and hormonal activity (particularly that of oxytocin) (Fredrickson, 2013). Many of these associations have a direct relevance to physical health including cardiovascular health, infection, pain and sleep (Steptoe, Dockray and Wardle, 2009). Finally, there is substantial evidence linking psychological wellbeing to mortality (Chida and Steptoe, 2008). All of this suggests a huge potential for the application of positive psychological interventions to help people whose principal issues relate to their physical health.

WELLBEING

In the context of positive psychotherapy, the term wellbeing refers to a person's subjective wellbeing or how they experience the quality of their life. This experience will reflect both a cognitive evaluation and an emotional response – how good life feels. People with high subjective wellbeing judge their quality of life to be good, they have high life satisfaction and tend to experience positive emotions more often than negative emotions. A person's level of wellbeing will vary considerably over time, often reflecting their circumstances, but such variation tends to be around a general base level which may differ considerably from person to person. People are able to regulate their wellbeing to a large degree, and there is a strong contrary relationship between wellbeing and emotional distress. Positive psychotherapy helps people to reduce their emotional distress by teaching them skills that they can use to enhance their wellbeing.

HAPPINESS

There appears to be a universal desire for personal happiness and the happiness of others, especially those whom we love. Happiness, in this context, does not refer to a fleeting state of pleasure but to something that is both deeper and more stable. This has been referred to by Martin Seligman as 'authentic happiness' and is defined by the leading positive psychologist Sonja Lyubomirsky as: 'The experience of joy, contentment or positive well-being, combined with a sense that one's life is good, meaningful and worthwhile' (Lyubomirsky, 2008, p. 27).

Individual levels of happiness reflect genetic predisposition to a considerable degree, and personal circumstances also play a minor part. But our level of happiness reflects, to a large extent, what we think and what we do. One of the major achievements of positive psychology has been the clear demonstration that people can learn cognitive skills and action skills that will enhance and sustain their happiness and enable them to flourish. The goal of positive psychotherapy, in addition to alleviating emotional distress, is to encourage clients to learn skills that will help them to sustain happiness, to flourish and to thrive. Some of practices that promote such positive change have long been recognized, especially within certain religious traditions, whereas others have emerged very recently from theory and research in positive psychology.

PSYCHOLOGICAL RESILIENCE

Psychological resilience (also sometimes labelled 'emotional resilience', 'hardiness' or 'mental toughness') is a person's ability to withstand the effects of pressure and to 'bounce back' following an experience of adversity, trauma, loss or disappointment. Because resilience is closely related to wellbeing, increasing a person's general level of wellbeing will typically strengthen their resilience.

People who are highly resilient are often skilled at eliciting positive emotions even in times of stress, and because positive emotions often have a neutralizing effect on negative emotions (Fredrickson et al., 2000), this ability can help the person to cope by minimizing negative emotions (Tugade and Fredrickson, 2004). There is good evidence that resilience can be increased by suitable training, and one programme based on positive psychology (the Penn Resiliency Program, Seligman, 2011) has been shown in many studies to be effective in building resilience as well as in reducing depressive symptoms (Brunwasser, Gillham and Kim, 2009).

Resilience is sometimes exhibited as 'post-traumatic growth' whereby the person not only survives emotionally but also actually derives significant benefits from their experience of extreme threat or adversity. This is now a well-established and well-researched phenomenon that has been found to occur in a significant proportion of people who have survived life-threatening situations (Joseph, 2009; Tedeschi and Calhoun, 2004). Post-traumatic growth is associated with changed priorities, an increased appreciation of 'ordinary things', greater compassion and tolerance towards other people, greater appreciation of the importance of relationships and, in many cases, a pervasive sense of wellbeing.

OPTIMISM

Optimism is a style of judgement whereby situations and events are seen primarily in terms of their positive rather than their negative attributes. Thus there is an emphasis on the agreeable and beneficial aspects of a situation rather than on what may be flawed or problematic. Optimistic people also tend to view the future in a hopeful way, and in thinking about the past they are likely to bring to mind more positive than negative aspects. A metaphor commonly used to compare optimists and pessimists suggests that a glass that is half-filled will be seen by optimists as half full and by pessimists as half empty.

A person's outlook, in terms of their optimism or pessimism, has important implications for their behaviour and lifestyle choices. For example, an optimist might follow a failed initial attempt at a task with a hopeful second attempt, whereas a pessimist might well predict repeated failure and therefore give up trying. Such a pessimistic sequence might have highly damaging consequences, for example in job-seeking, dieting or a bid to give up smoking.

Optimism can be regarded as a personality trait and a person's optimistic or pessimistic disposition appears to reflect genetic factors to some degree and personal history to a large degree. However, people can also change their outlook by engaging in strategic practices. Thus people can learn to be more optimistic, and several effective techniques have been devised by positive psychologists to promote such 'learned optimism' (Seligman, 1991; Seligman et al., 2005).

In the context of positive psychology, the term 'optimism' always relates to 'realistic optimism' and this is regarded as a way of correcting an inherent negative bias that often leads people to exaggerate personal flaws and failures as well as external threats. Persistent pessimistic judgements can take a heavy emotional toll and may eventually provoke misery, despair and a sense of hopelessness. This alone indicates the need to promote realistic optimism with clients. Realism is necessary in order to avoid constant disappointment and to enable the person to function effectively. It is clear that effective action is much more likely to follow from a realistic assessment of how things are and of how they are likely to develop than from either a gloomy pessimistic appraisal or a hopelessly over-optimistic view of things.

A substantial and fast-growing research literature has now demonstrated strong associations between optimism and both mental and physical health conditions. For example, optimism has repeatedly been shown to be associated with cardiovascular health (Seligman, 2011) and immunity from infection (Segerstrom and Sephton, 2010).

ACQUISITION AND MAINTENANCE

Positive psychology takes a bio-psycho-social view of human functioning, and therefore recognizes that the original source of distress may be biological (reflecting, for example, dysfunctional brain chemistry), psychological (for example, cognitive distortions) or environmental (abuse in childhood, for example, or chronic work stress). It recognizes that factors from more than one of these domains are likely to be involved in any case of severe distress, and that as a condition progresses it will invariably come to involve biological *and* psychological *and* social (or environmental) elements. Ultimately, a comprehensive understanding of the client's situation almost always calls for a holistic view which appreciates the significance of factors operating at all of these levels.

The approach also recognizes that there are certain human needs which, if not met, are likely to result in a state of languishing. These include a need for social contact (without which, people may suffer from the devastating effects of loneliness), a need for mastery and control over one's life, a need for security, a need for engagement in activities that stimulate interest, and a need to experience positive emotions on a regular basis.

The holistic view recognizes the key significance of vicious circles that prevent recovery and serve to maintain distress at a high level. For example, severe depression can lead to an extreme depletion of energy and motivation, a deepening pessimism, withdrawal from social contact and a loss of interest in any activity that might bring satisfaction and a sense of accomplishment. It is a cruel fact that such effects of depression are the very factors that serve to maintain and deepen depression. And the picture is not dissimilar for other types of distress, including various forms of anxiety, obsessionality and low self-esteem. In each case, the negative effects of the condition serve to maintain and exacerbate the problem.

Positive psychotherapists do not generally assess the client's history in order to develop a detailed formulation of the origins of the client's condition. However, they do make a concerted effort to reverse any maintaining conditions by deliberately stimulating positive activities and changes in outlook in order to replace the prevailing vicious circles with virtuous circles. For example, PPT strategies encourage the client to appreciate and to savour the positive aspects of life, thus attempting to overcome a negative outlook. Other strategies encourage the client to engage in work or social activities that they will find uplifting. All of these interventions aim to increase general wellbeing, thereby destabilizing the processes that are maintaining distress.

THERAPY

THERAPEUTIC GOALS

Much of the therapeutic work in positive psychotherapy focuses on the general objective of increasing wellbeing. It is recognized that there are very many different ways of enhancing wellbeing, and for this reason the specific focus of the intervention may not be regarded as crucial. Some interventions help the client to develop a realistically positive view of themselves, their current situation and their likely future. Other interventions focus on helping clients to manage their lifestyle in order to maximize their engagement and their experience of positive emotions. In terms of the familiar metaphor used to describe cognitive behaviour therapy, that of encouraging clients to see the glass as half full rather than as half empty, positive psychotherapy can be seen as offering novel strategies for achieving this goal while also helping people to put more into the glass (that is, to develop a lifestyle that is happy, fulfilling and meaningful).

Thus the ambition of positive psychotherapists for their clients extends beyond the basic 'therapeutic mission' of reducing distress and includes the aim of helping clients to learn skills of emotional self-management that will stand them in good stead in the future. Part of this can be characterized as building resilience, or as promoting relapse prevention, but their ambition goes further than this and they aim to provide clients with emotional self-management skills that will help them to flourish and to have a life that is enjoyable, meaningful, socially responsible and productive.

PROCESS OF THERAPY

Positive psychotherapy can be delivered in a variety of ways. Delivered as individual therapy, the client will be helped to think about specific issues in a realistically positive way and interventions will be tailored to reflect the client's particular interests and strengths. Individualized homework tasks mean that a good deal of the client's skill development work will take place outside the therapy sessions. Beyond the individual therapy format, the transdiagnostic (or non-diagnostic) nature of PPT, together with its high psycho-education loading, means that it can also be delivered to groups of clients in a didactic fashion (Cheavens et al., 2006; Seligman et al., 2006). The participants in such a group will learn the general principles of wellbeing enhancement and resilience building and will then be encouraged to apply these to their own issues, making use of whatever resources are available to them and reflecting their own individual tastes and preferences. Similarly, positive interventions may be translated into a self-help format and delivered electronically (Schueller and Parks, 2012) or in the form of bibliotherapy (Akhtar, 2012).

Whether individual, group-based, or delivered remotely, PPT is transparent at all times, with the client being fully informed of the rationale underlying both the general process and specific interventions. Most clients find this approach to therapy highly plausible; there is an inherent credibility in the idea that feeling good about oneself and seeing things in a realistically positive way are likely to enhance a general sense of wellbeing and thereby reduce distress.

THE THERAPEUTIC RELATIONSHIP

When positive therapy is delivered in a group format, the idea of 'the therapeutic relationship' needs to be considered in a broad sense. Group sessions are convened as workshops with a substantial didactic component, but it is also recognized that such sessions also offer the opportunity to generate positive emotions (including laughter), friendliness, kindness, mutual appreciation and a sense of achievement. A warm and supportive atmosphere will do much to increase participants' sense of wellbeing. Seligman's observation that teaching positive psychology is invariably uplifting also suggests that the facilitators will also enjoy the sessions and may well benefit from them.

Positive psychotherapy conducted in the form of individual face-to-face sessions allows for the establishment of a close therapeutic relationship. Indeed, the key factors of interpersonal warmth and empathy take on a special significance in the context of positive psychotherapy. It is recognized that a warm relationship will increase the client's wellbeing, and that the therapist's empathy will help to formulate effective interventions.

The very fact that the therapeutic communication will focus mostly on positive aspects (for example, on the client's current strengths and the potential for positive developments in the client's outlook, lifestyle and relationships) means that the atmosphere is likely to be especially agreeable and optimistic. Sessions will include a considerable amount of 'appreciative enquiry' (Cooperrider, Whitney and Stavros, 2005) and the discussion will inevitably lead both therapist and client to discover many positive aspects of the client's character, biography and current circumstances. The therapist's recognition of the client's strengths and achievements will generate opportunities to pay genuine compliments that are like to be especially uplifting for the client. There is good evidence that an appropriate response to positive disclosures is an especially powerful factor in enhancing the closeness of a relationship (Gable et al., 2004).

The positive focus of therapy sessions also gives therapists a greater freedom to self-disclose relevant aspects of their own interests and positive experiences (to speak, for example, about hobbies, favourite films or significant positive biographical events). A comparable degree of self-disclosure might be inappropriate in conversations that focus mainly on despair, anxiety or anger. The increased (although still judicious) disclosure of personal information by the therapist can have a highly significant positive effect on the therapeutic relationship. Indeed, positive therapy sessions may generate the kind of fleeting moments of intense shared positivity that Barbara Frederickson has labelled 'positivity resonance' and which she has shown to bring very substantial emotional benefits for those involved (Fredrickson, 2013).

Several writers in the field have drawn attention to the fact that whereas practising problem-focused therapies may eventually exert a toll on the mental health of the therapist (as evidenced by relatively high rates of depression and burnout), positive psychotherapy would appear to be far less likely to generate such damaging effects (Bannink, 2012; Seligman, 2011).

THERAPEUTIC INTERVENTIONS

Positive therapy interventions have the general aims of helping the client to enhance their wellbeing, to improve their quality of life and to strengthen their resilience. Many of the interventions used to pursue these goals are cognitive in nature, and help the client to recognize, appreciate and savour positive aspects of themselves, their circumstances and their relationships with other people. Other positive interventions are behavioural in nature and help the client to engage in activities that will enable them to experience positive emotions more frequently and to experience their life as meaningful and fulfilling. Because people differ markedly in what they experience as enjoyable and rewarding, the therapist will work with the client to identify the activities and experiences that are likely to make a strong positive impact.

Some clients are already fully aware of the activities and circumstances that evoke positive emotions and give them an 'uplift'. They may have a good appreciation of what stimulates their interest and engagement. Awareness of the nature and self-management of emotions is a key component of emotional intelligence, and many positive therapy interventions can be seen as attempts to develop and apply such intelligence. A valuable component of a positively focused assessment might be an exploration of what triggers the client's positive emotions. Other aspects of a positive assessment include the identification of personal strengths and the recognition of available social and environmental resources.

The extent to which a person can manage their emotions is related not only to an awareness of their own preferences and sensitivities but also to their general understanding of the nature of emotional processes. For this reason, it is often useful to include a substantial psycho-educational component as part of the therapeutic agenda. Because such psycho-education will draw substantially on positive psychology research, the therapist may encourage the client to read an accessible account of the field such as Sonja Lyubomirsky's *The How of Happiness* (2008) or Tal Ben-Shahar's *Happier* (2008).

Examples of useful psycho-educational messages that may be incorporated into therapy sessions are given in Box 14.1.

BOX 14.1 POSITIVE PSYCHO-EDUCATION

Positive psychotherapy often includes a strong psycho-educational element. Informing clients about positive emotions, wellbeing, personal strengths and resilience can help them both to understand and to manage their own emotions. Much of the psycho-educational information given to clients is based directly on positive psychology research.

The following examples indicate the type of knowledge that can be usefully shared with clients:

- Wellbeing and flourishing can be enhanced by skilled actions.
- The relevant skills can be learned.
- Some things can be changed and some cannot.
- People often underestimate how much freedom they have to change.
- People often gain energy by making an effort to be active.
- Emotions are contagious; increasing your own happiness is good for other people in your life.
- Acts of kindness, generosity and forgiveness are beneficial those who act in this way.
- Psychological wellbeing has highly beneficial effects for physical as well as for emotional health.

ADDRESSING CLINICAL ISSUES

The fundamental idea underlying positive psychotherapy is that increasing clients' general wellbeing will invariably reduce their distress and improve their quality of life in many ways. However, in many cases the specific psychological issues and symptoms that clients bring to therapy will also need to be addressed. There is no incongruity in using problem-focused interventions (such as those used in traditional cognitive behaviour therapy) within a positive psychotherapy treatment programme. Equally, therapists working with almost any other therapeutic approach may enrich their practice by including an explicitly positive element in their work with clients.

As an alternative to importing problem-focused techniques, specific clinical problems can also be directly addressed using a positive psychotherapy approach. Typically, this would involve reframing the problematic issue so that the intervention becomes solution-focused rather than problem-focused. Some such interventions make use of the reciprocal inhibition effect, so that they evoke a positive emotion in order to inhibit or neutralize a negative emotion such as anxiety or anger. This technique has a long history in behaviour therapy (for example, relaxation is used to inhibit anxiety in desensitization) and recent experimental research has confirmed the powerful 'undoing' effects that positive emotions can have on negative emotions at both the psychological and the biological levels (Frederickson, 2013).

Thus positive therapy for a client who initially presents with a problem of 'anger management' might involve strategies for increasing her kindness, her tolerance or her ability to remain calm. If a client's problem involves extreme self-criticism, the positive treatment might involve strategies for promoting self-acceptance, self-respect and self-compassion. The problem of deliberate self-harm might be addressed by teaching the client self-soothing techniques. In all such cases, of course, the positive reframing of the issue would be totally transparent to the client and the therapist would collaborate with the client in devising and implementing the intervention.

The range of clinical problems that may be encountered in clinical practice is clearly very wide, and there are equally many different ways in which they can be positively reframed and then addressed using positive interventions. The following overview of positive intervention techniques focuses on their application in enhancing clients' general wellbeing, but it should be recognized that many of the interventions can also be adapted in such a way that they target specific clinical issues.

ENHANCING POSITIVE COGNITIONS

Although individual interventions may be recognized as principally cognitive or behavioural in nature, the distinction is often somewhat arbitrary. For example, on the one hand, interventions that aim to promote a compassionate or charitable outlook (thus focusing on cognitive aspects) would typically also prompt behavioural change. On the other hand, interventions that encourage clients to behave in a kind and generous way would also be expected to increase their kindly outlook and attitude.

Many cognitive interventions are used with the aim of increasing the person's awareness and appreciation of positive aspects of their situation, their lifestyle and themselves. Awareness is increased by encouraging the person to notice, monitor, recall and savour positive features and characteristics. Thus a client may be invited to recall some of the most positive experiences they had in childhood or more recently, perhaps visualizing these in detail, speaking about them to others (including the therapist) and writing about them. In a variation of this, clients may be encouraged to recall situations that evoked particular positive emotions such as pride, contentment, awe or joy. The detailed recall of positive events will often lead the person to re-experience the relevant emotion, and the emotional impact of such recall is often enhanced by sharing the memory with others or by writing about it. Similar enhancement effects can be achieved with day-to-day experiences (for example, through diary-keeping or regular verbal reporting). Contemporaneous monitoring not only increases the person's awareness of the type of event being monitored but also tends to increase the salience of such events. Anticipation of planned future events can also stimulate strong positive emotions, and anticipation may be deliberately enhanced, for example by prompting regular reminders or by engaging in anticipatory savouring, for example by browsing through brochures and guidebooks describing the delights likely to be experienced on a forthcoming holiday.

One of the most frequently used, and frequently researched, positive interventions involves the daily recall, usually in the evening, of three positive things that happened during the day. This is variously described as identifying daily 'blessings', as stimulating feelings of 'gratitude for' good things that have happened, or as heightening the person's sensitivity to positive events. In addition to the benefits that come from the end-of-day recall, this exercise also changes people's cognitive 'set' throughout the day, increasing their appreciation of positive events that might qualify as one of the three good things of the day. If this exercise is repeated regularly (for example, daily for two to three weeks or more) the person may well develop an increased sensitivity to positive events. This in turn may lead to a more optimistic outlook and decrease the extent to which the person regards the world as dangerous and threatening (Lyubomirsky, 2008; Seligman et al., 2005).

ENHANCING SELF-APPRECIATION

Many of the cognitive interventions used in positive psychotherapy help the person to achieve a more realistic appreciation and a more positive view of themselves. Helping people to recognize and value their personal strengths, skills, accomplishments and positive personality characteristics will often move them towards a more realistic self-evaluation and serve to correct a negatively distorted self-image. One intervention that can help to bring about such a change involves the client developing a realistically optimistic image of how they might change in the future (the 'Best Possible Self'; Peters et al., 2010). In a similar activity, the client is invited to construct a reasonable representation of a future lifestyle that would bring them contentment and a sense of fulfilment ('The Life that I'd Like'). These future projections, which are both positive and realistic, are likely to inspire hope and optimism. Other interventions direct the client's attention to positive aspects of their biography. Thus the person may be asked to make a list of some of their successes and notable achievements, and in some cases such an exercise will be extended to take the form of a 'Positive Life Review' or even a 'Positive Obituary' (Seligman, Rashid and Parks, 2006). A focus on the person's current situation may involve the identification of current activities or recent events that highlight their personal values or their character strengths ('Me At My Best').

Another technique used to promote positive self-appreciation involves the use of carefully formulated affirmations. A clear distinction is made between affirmations that are inflexible and unrealistic and those that are reasonable, with only the latter being considered useful (Fredrickson, 2013). Along the same lines, a therapist may help the client to devise a positive and accurate response to the questions that people invariably ask when meeting someone for the first time ('What do you do?'; 'What are you interested in?'). Such questions can be especially daunting for people with a recent history of emotional problems, particularly if these have seriously curtailed their activities, but 'Positive Scripting' can help such people to respond in a truthful yet upbeat fashion. An example of positive scripting is given in Box 14.2.

BOX 14.2   POSITIVE SCRIPTING

In one of her therapy sessions Jane confided that she was dreading a forthcoming social event to be hosted by her husband's company. 'People are bound to ask me what I do', she said, 'and what am I supposed to say – that I don't work because I have a serious mental health problem; that I don't have a job and that I'm ashamed of what I am; that I don't do much except watch a lot of day-time TV; and that I often cry a lot?'.

We worked together to construct an alternative response that would be equally true but would highlight some positive aspects of Jane's biography and current situation. The alternative 'script' that we composed was: 'I'm a qualified nurse, although I'm not working just now. I used to work with dying people but eventually it got to me so I decided to take a break. I've been trying to write a novel, actually, and I want to get back into photography.'

At the next session she reported that the social event had been an uplifting experience for her. She had used the script and found that people were interested, empathic and respectful of her. As well as having helped her to navigate a potentially challenging social occasion, the construction and repetition of this positive script had also had a highly desirable effect on Jane's self-image. It had even stimulated her to look again at her ideas for the novel that had been all but abandoned.

To maintain the client's integrity it is important that all aspects of such a positive script are truthful. The therapist's role is to help the client to identify and to 'cherry-pick' suitable elements from the past, present and realistically hoped-for future to include in such a self-portrait.

Many clients have a pronounced tendency to focus more on their failures than on their successes. Such a negative bias may be corrected by inviting the person to recall personal accomplishments and, especially, incidents in which they demonstrated a certain degree of resilience. If they can be helped to recognize even partial successes, and to fully appreciate the significance of these, this may well lead to substantial gains in self-efficacy and self-respect. For example, when someone is helped to appreciate how well they have coped with some very difficult situations in the past, this is likely to boost their estimate of how resilient they would be in the face of future hardship.

STRENGTHS AND FREEDOM INTERVENTIONS

Interventions that focus on personal strengths typically include both cognitive and behavioural elements. Thus the person is helped both to recognize their existing strengths and to employ them more regularly or to increased effect. There may be a particular focus on enhancing current strengths, reflecting the observation that it is generally much easier, and much more effective, to reinforce existing strengths than to reduce or to eliminate weaknesses. A useful metaphor here is that it is easier to go with the grain than against the grain. Becoming more aware of one's own strengths and 'just noticing' the occasions on which they are used will often increase their salience and encourage their further use.

Freedom Mapping can be a powerful means of developing a person's vision of their potential future and it can be particularly powerful in helping someone to overcome the sense of being trapped in a particular life situation. Mapping out the extent of possible lifestyle changes often provides people with a new sense of freedom. Recognizing the full extent of one's freedom can be highly invigorating, and a huge sense of relief can come from the realization that some of the constraints previously assumed to be permanent can in fact be removed. Clients' judgements regarding the scope of their personal agency and the extent to which they are free to change their life are often grossly inaccurate. The result of this is that they may feel trapped by their life circumstances, sometimes to the point of desperation, because they fail to see how they may be able to exert control and alter their circumstances. Thus a therapist may help a client who is feeling trapped in a distressing and potentially unsustainable situation to devise a 'Plan B' and a 'Plan C'. An example of such an intervention is described in Box 14.3. Many people seriously underestimate the degree to which they are free to change their lifestyle, and such a distorted view may be amplified when someone is experiencing severe and chronic emotional distress.

BOX 14.3   PERSONAL FREEDOM MAPPING – THE CASE OF JAMES

James was 45, a senior engineer in a company that had employed him for 22 years. When another company took over and introduced new ways of working, James found it very difficult to cope. He became frustrated and stressed, his work suffered and eventually he collapsed in tears in a work meeting and had to take time off.

With a large mortgage and a family dependent on his salary, James felt totally trapped. He believed that his only option was to return to work and to 'just get on with it'. But the thought of not being able to cope and of losing his job terrified him and he contemplated suicide. I suggested that he needed a 'Plan B' – a feasible alternative to his current way of life. With my guidance he was able to think realistically about a number of possibilities and, as a result, his sense of being totally trapped ('There's no other way, I just HAVE to go back and stick at it') faded.

Working out one or two feasible alternatives took a lot of pressure off James. He decided that he would return to his job, but he now recognised that he could: 'Always try something else' if things didn't work out. He had reframed his return to work from his original 'This is a matter of do or die' to 'I'll give it a whirl and see what happens.'

Because the possibilities for change are largely shaped by environmental constraints and available resources, the mapping of potential positive change needs to take into account available opportunities and possible hindrances. A client may be encouraged to research such things as local opportunities for volunteering, the availability of online education courses in a particular subject, or local social events. The results of such research can then be discussed with a view to enhancing the client's lifestyle and wellbeing.

Recognition of the extent to which emotions reflect the environmental situation and ongoing activities leads to the simple recommendation: 'Do more of what makes you feel good'. However, the evaluation of things that lead to 'feeling good' needs to take into consideration both the short-term and the long-term costs and benefits. Some things that provide an immediate uplift in mood (such as drinking or gambling) are clearly detrimental to wellbeing in the longer term. Positive psychotherapy encourages clients to be mindful, careful and realistic in managing their activities and to consider effects over an extended time period. This reflects the distinction made in positive psychology between fleeting pleasure and sustained wellbeing ('authentic happiness'; Seligman, 2003).

Active Diary Management refers to a group of behavioural strategies that may be particularly useful in the PPT context. The person is encouraged to reflect on their daily and weekly routine and to consider adjustments that would improve their quality of life. The process often involves a careful consideration of personal preferences and available resources before planning and then implementing changes, initially on a trial basis. Typically, the client would engage in various 'behavioural experiments' and then discuss the outcome of these in further sessions with the therapist. In many cases, such experiments lead to changes that are highly enjoyable, and therefore self-sustaining.

Some clients do relatively little with their time, particularly if they are unemployed, living alone and surviving on a very tight budget. Such clients may feel that they have no particular reason to get out of bed in the morning and it may take considerable ingenuity and a good knowledge of available resources if they are to develop a lifestyle that is interesting and fulfilling. Active Diary Management is essentially lifestyle management and one of the ways in which it can be used to enhance a client's lifestyle is by focusing on their weekly schedule. Some people have no particular activity pattern or special commitments that confer a different mood or feeling on different days of the week. Without work, or regular religious activity, or children to take to school, each day may feel exactly the same as the day before, and this will often lead to boredom and a lack of energy. Clients in this situation can easily be helped to develop a pattern of activities that gives each day a different 'flavour', thereby establishing a weekly rhythm.

Happiness and wellbeing are heightened when people have things to look forward to. Keen anticipation of positive events is an important source of interest and positive emotion. Thus some interventions focus on helping people to 'plant treats in their diary'. Such treats may be rather slight (a visit to a local park, for example, or a visit to the cinema) or they may be more substantial (for example, a holiday). Clients can benefit from understanding how the overall positive experience of an event such as a cinema visit or a holiday can be greatly enhanced by 'active anticipation'. This might involve such activities as reading reviews of a film you are about to see or planning a detailed itinerary for a forthcoming weekend break. Together, 'planting treats' and 'active antici-pation' constitute a powerful recipe by which people can enrich their life experiences.

INTERVENTIONS THAT ENERGIZE

There is a simple, traditional, formula for happiness which, although not derived from positive psychology, is certainly in line with research in the field. The formula states that in order to be happy, a person needs a) something to do, b) something to love, and c) something to look forward to. It is clear that some clients – those who might be described as 'languishing' – come to therapy in a state of a) not having much to do (disengagement), b) having nothing to love (i.e. lacking pas-sion and inspiration) and c) having very little to look forward to (i.e. little hope or positive anticipation). In line with this, positive psychotherapy might be char-acterized as: a) helping clients find rewarding and engaging things to do, b) help-ing clients realize and develop their values and their passions, and c) helping clients to become realistically hopeful and to identify and plan activities that they will be able to anticipate with relish.

One problem frequently encountered when a client has been relatively inac-tive for some time is a lack of energy. Thus a therapist's suggestion that a particu-lar activity could be beneficial might be met with the client's objection that they would not have sufficient mental or physical energy to engage in the task. This presents an opportunity for the therapist to deliver a particular psycho-educa-tional message to the effect that doing nothing is often extremely debilitating whereas becoming more active invariably generates energy. It might be useful to invoke the metaphor of the car which takes a great deal of energy and fuel to move off from a stationary position but requires much less energy to gain further speed once it is moving. Thus re-energizing someone who is in a state of 'psycho-logical paralysis' may start by encouraging them to engage in a very simple task (in extreme cases, this might involve completing a child's jigsaw puzzle, or sim-ply visiting a local shop) and then promoting a sense of achievement when the initial task has been accomplished. It will then be possible to build on this initial success by helping the client to progress to more and more substantial projects, with each success being recognized, appreciated and even celebrated.

A variation of this task-setting strategy involves the therapist 'commission-ing' the client to undertake a homework assignment that makes use of an exist-ing skill or talent that they have not used for some time. Rather than simply encouraging the client to engage in a specific activity at home, the therapist commissions the client to produce a particular piece of work to bring to the next therapy session. Typical commissions would be for an essay, a short story, a list, a poem, a drawing or a photograph. Accepting such a commission is of course optional for the client, but when the strategy is used judiciously it can prove highly motivating and rekindle a dormant interest or talent. The sense of accomplishment that can come from this, together with the therapist's appreciation, can stimulate strong positive emotions that are highly energizing and in some cases will lead the client to revive a dormant skill or talent.

KINDNESS AND GRATITUDE INTERVENTIONS

Another major focus of positive psychotherapy interventions is kindness and gratitude. Again, specific strategies may be cognitive in nature (for example, they may have the aim of 'cultivating a kindly attitude') or behavioural (expressing gratitude, for example, or performing regular acts of kindness) although most of the strategies will stimulate both cognitive and behavioural effects. There is a good deal of evidence demonstrating the beneficial effects of performing acts of kindness as well as of recognizing a debt of gratitude or expressing such gratitude to a third party – perhaps in a letter or face-to-face meeting with the person to whom gratitude is due (Seligman et al., 2005).

One especially powerful intervention involves the regular practice of a 'loving-kindness meditation' (LKM). This is a method for developing compassion and cultivating unconditional love through visualization and the mindful repetition of meditation phrases that generate feelings of warmth and tenderness towards oneself and others. Fredrickson (2013) has shown that practising LKM for just an hour or so every week for a few months transformed people's lives, so that they experienced greater serenity, increased joy, warmer relationships and a higher level of engagement. The practice also produced highly significant biological effects that translated into positive effects on physical health. Mindfulness meditation is also used in positive psychotherapy as it is in several other types of psychotherapy, and the evidence for the positive effects of this practice is substantial and impressive (Marchand, 2012).

The range of positive psychotherapy interventions is very broad and may include, in addition to the strategies described above, a focus on positive interactional skills, relationship enhancement and resilience-building. Therapists working with this approach can work creatively from the general theoretical model to develop their own interventions and to tailor established interventions in response to the specific strengths, interests and preferences of individual clients. The centrality of wellbeing to this approach means that anything that provides an uplift (unless there are longer-term negative consequences) can be regarded as 'therapeutic'. Thus a warm bath can be seen as therapeutic, as can attending a music festival or visiting an art gallery. The model provides a good explanation of how such activities can help to alleviate distress. It would therefore be fully in keeping with positive psychotherapy for the therapist to suggest that a client might enjoy a particular film or a particular piece of music. The extent to which such suggestions will be effective will reflect the therapist's appreciation of the client's specific interests and preferences.

CASE MATERIAL

Several case descriptions are presented in the books listed in the 'Annotated Bibliography' section. However, the literature is not rich in individual case material. More has been written about the general approach and about the specific interventions than about how these have been used with individual clients. Often, of course, the interventions are delivered to groups, or via media. There is a casebook collection (Burns, 2010) and brief examples of individual cases are presented in this chapter, in Boxes 14.2 and 14.3.

FURTHER DEVELOPMENTS

The close connection between PPT and the science of positive psychology means that developments in this therapeutic approach have stayed fairly close to the empirical evidence, much of which derives from experiments conducted in laboratory settings. Relatively little attention has been paid to the skills required of therapists who use this approach, or of what might be characterized as the 'art of positive therapy'. As the approach matures, there may well be useful developments in these aspects. However, the scientific emphasis has generated, very usefully, many carefully devised evaluation studies, so that there is now substantial evidence demonstrating the therapeutic effectiveness of positive interventions (Bolier et al., 2013; Sin and Lyubomirsky, 2009).

Positive psychotherapy overlaps considerably with a number of established therapeutic approaches, including solution-focused therapy and cognitive therapy. There are also a number of particular 'schools' that reflect variations of emphasis between therapists who would be happy to identify themselves broadly as 'positive therapists'. Such variation is evident in developments such as 'Hope Therapy' (Cheavens et al., 2006), 'Quality of Life Therapy' (Frisch, 2006) and 'Well-being Therapy' (Fava and Ruini, 2003). There appears to be growing interest in the use of meditation techniques (mindfulness and the loving-kindness meditation, in particular) as components of positive therapy, and this aligns with a growing emphasis on helping clients to find meaning and fulfilment in their life. Such developments might lead to a recognition that positive psychology in general, and positive psychotherapy in particular, may be moving beyond the current broad bio-psycho-social agenda towards an even broader bio-psycho-social-spiritual agenda.

REVIEW AND PERSONAL QUESTIONS

REVIEW QUESTIONS

1. Consider the relationship between emotional distress and wellbeing, and think about how an increase in wellbeing can help to reduce a person's emotional distress.

2. Why do positive psychotherapists reframe 'problem referrals' into a positive form?
3. Review some methods that are used in positive psychotherapy to help people form a realistically positive view of themselves.
4. Why do positive psychotherapists emphasize the importance of experiencing positive emotions?
5. What is meant by 'active diary management'?
6. What are the advantages of a client being optimistic rather than pessimistic? Why is it important that such optimism be realistic?
7. How would the therapist–client relationship be expected to differ in the context of positive psychotherapy compared with that of a problem-based approach?
8. Identify and discuss similarities and differences between positive psychotherapy and one or two other therapeutic approaches that you have studied.
9. Positive psychotherapy interventions are often delivered to groups of clients in a workshop format. What are the advantages and limitations of delivering this type of therapy in this way?
10. Consider whether (and how) elements of positive psychotherapy might be usefully incorporated into therapy sessions using another particular approach (choose one).

PERSONAL QUESTIONS

1. How aware are you of the strategies that you use, or could use, to manage your own emotions? Think about what you might do in order to:

   (a) Lift your mood if you were feeling down
   (b) Trigger a sense of pride
   (c) Calm yourself if you were feeling anxious
   (d) Evoke a feeling of contentment.

2. Make a list of various things that you are looking forward to:

   (a) later today
   (b) during the next week
   (c) over the next few months
   (d) within the next year.

3. Think about an activity that you really enjoy, and then consider what you could do to enhance your enjoyment of that activity? (In other words, how can you make this good thing better?)
4. Think back through your life and identify someone who went out of their way to help you, encourage you, support you, or maybe even rescue you. Having recognized your indebtedness to this person, allow yourself to feel a deep sense of gratitude to them. And then consider whether there might be some way in which you can express your gratitude to that person.
5. Recall a time when you were really 'up against it' but managed to cope fairly well and to get through the experience without suffering too much long-term distress. Try to recall in detail any strategies that you used in order to exercise resilience.
6. Look back on what has happened to you so far today and identify three positive aspects of what you have experienced. If you want this exercise to make a significant difference to your life, write down these 'three good things' and repeat the exercise daily for the next two or three weeks.

ANNOTATED BIBLIOGRAPHY

Seligman, M. E. P. (2002) *Authentic Happiness: Using the New Positive Psychology to Realize Your Potential for Lasting Fulfilment.* New York: Free Press.
In this book, Martin Seligman provides an analysis of the nature, causes and effects of happiness based on the emerging science of positive psychology. A key message of the book is that people can increase their levels of optimism, wellbeing and happiness by learning and exercising particular skills. This opens up exciting possibilities for applications in many fields, including education and therapy.

Seligman, M. E. P (2011) *Flourish: A New Understanding of Happiness and Wellbeing.* London: Nicholas Brealey Publishing.
Flourish presents Seligman's account of the personal and professional journey that led him to create positive psychology. He also reflects on the current state of the field and shares his vision of how it might develop. He suggests that because positive interventions are easy-to-use and enjoyable, they tend to be self-reinforcing over time. He describes research that shows positive psychotherapy to be highly effective and suggests that a positive approach can also have a preventive effect with respect to both physical and mental health conditions.

Lyubomirsky, S. (2008) *The How of Happiness: A Scientific Approach to Getting the Life You Want.* New York: Penguin.
The How of Happiness is written by a leading positive psychology researcher and draws on her own research findings and those of others to present an intervention programme for increasing happiness and wellbeing. The author suggests that everyone has an innate potential for experiencing joy and happiness but that this is often not realized. The book aims to help people realize that potential.

Fredrickson, B. L. (2009) *Positivity: Groundbreaking Research Reveals How to Embrace the Hidden Strength of Positive Emotions, Overcome Negativity, and Thrive.* New York: Crown.
Frederickson is one of the leading research scientists in the field of positive psychology and in this book she discusses the research evidence relating to positivity. It is clear that positivity builds psychological strengths and resilience, is good for physical health and helps to build strong connections with other people. Positivity can be increased strategically using a wide range of interventions that are detailed in the book.

Bannink, F. (2012) *Practising Positive CBT: From Reducing Stress to Building Success.* Chichester: Wiley-Blackwell.
Bannick characterizes positive psychotherapy as an important new development in cognitive behaviour therapy and also regards it as similar in many ways to solution-focused therapy. The author discusses the issue of why some

therapists are more effective than others and considers the nature of the thera-peutic relationship in positive therapy.

Joseph, S. and Linley, P. A. (2006) *Positive Therapy: A Meta-theory for Positive Psychological Practice.* London: Routledge.
This book introduces positive psychology and discusses the various ways in which developments in that field can be applied in the therapeutic context. The approach is seen as similar in many ways to the humanistic tradition and to person-centred therapy in particular. In line with this, the authors explore the use of positive psychology not just as therapy but also as a means to personal growth. The book is dedicated to both Martin Seligman and Carl Rogers.

Akhtar, M. (2012) *Positive Psychology for Overcoming Depression: Self-help Strategies for Happiness, Inner Strength and Wellbeing.* London: Watkins.
Positive psychotherapy can be delivered in a variety of ways, and this book presents a selection of well-established positive interventions in a self-help for-mat. The book takes 'a positive approach to depression' and shows readers how to apply techniques for learning optimism, building resilience and relating positively to other people.

REFERENCES AND FURTHER READING

Abramson, L. Y., Seligman, M. E. P. and Teasdale, J. D. (1978) Learned helpless-ness in humans: Critique and reformulation. *Journal of Abnormal Psychology, 87,* 49–74.

Akhtar, M. (2012) *Positive Psychology for Overcoming Depression: Self-help Strategies for Happiness, Inner Strength and Wellbeing.* London: Watkins.

Bannink, F. (2012) *Practicing Positive CBT: From Reducing Distress to Building Success.* Chichester: Wiley-Blackwell.

Ben-Shahar, T. (2008) *Happier.* New York: McGraw Hill.

Boehm J. K. and Kubzansky, L. D. (2012) The heart's content: The association between positive psychological well-being and cardiovascular health. *Psychological Bulletin, 138,* 655–91.

Bolier, L., Haverman, M., Westerhof, G. J., Riper, H., Smit, F. and Bohlmeijer, E. (2013) Positive psychology interventions: A meta-analysis of randomized controlled studies. *BMC Public Health, 13,* 119.

Brunwasser, S. M., Gillham, J. E. and Kim, E. S. (2009) A meta-analytic review of the Penn Resiliency Program's effect on depressive symptoms. *Journal of Consulting Clinical Psychology, 77,* 1042–54.

Burns, G. W. (ed.) (2010) *Happiness, Healing, Enhancement: Your Casebook Collection for Applying Positive Psychology in Therapy.* Chichester: John Wiley and Sons.

Cheavens, J. S., Feldman, D. B., Gum, A., Michael, S. T. and Snyder, C. R. (2006a) Hope therapy in a community sample: A pilot investigation. *Social Indicators Research, 77,* 61–78.

Cheavens, J. S., Feldman, D. B., Woodward, J. T. and Snyder, C. R. (2006b) Hope in cognitive psychotherapies: On working with client strengths. *Journal of Cognitive Psychotherapy, 20,* 135–45.

Chida, Y. and Steptoe, A. (2008) Positive psychological well-being and mortality: A quantitative review of prospective observational studies. *Psychosomatic Medicine, 70,* 741–56.

Cohen, S., Alper, C. M., Doyle, W. J., Treanor, J. J. and Turner, R. B. (2006) Positive emotional style predicts resistance to illness after experimental exposure to rhinovirus or influenza virus. *Psychosomatic Medicine, 68,* 809–15.

Cooperrider, D. L., Whitney, D. and Stavros, L. M. (2005) *Appreciative Inquiry: A Positive Revolution in Change.* San Francisco: Berrett-Koehler.

Fava, G. A. and Ruini, C. (2003) Development and characteristics of a well-being enhancing psychotherapeutic strategy: well-being therapy. *Journal of Behavior Therapy and Experimental Psychiatry, 34,* 45–63.

Fredrickson, B. L. (2001) The role of positive emotions in positive psychology. *American Psychologist, 56,* 218–26.

Fredrickson, B. L. (2009) *Positivity: Groundbreaking Research Reveals How to Embrace the Hidden Strength of Positive Emotions, Overcome Negativity, and Thrive.* New York: Crown.

Fredrickson, B. L. (2013) *Love 2.0: How Our Supreme Emotion Affects Everything We Feel, Think, Do, and Become.* New York: Hudson Street Press.

Fredrickson, B. L., Cohn, M. A., Coffey, K. A., Pek, J. and Finkel, S. (2008) Open hearts build lives: Positive emotions, induced through loving-kindness meditation, build consequential personal resources. *Journal of Personality and Social Psychology, 95,* 1045–62.

Fredrickson, B. L., Mancuso, R. A., Branigan, C. and Tugade, M. M. (2000) The undoing effect of positive emotions. *Motivation and Emotion, 24,* 237–58.

Frisch, M. B. (2006) *Quality of Life Therapy: A Life Satisfaction Approach to Positive Psychology and Cognitive Therapy.* Hoboken, NJ: John Wiley and Sons.

Gable, E. L., Reis, H. T., Impett, E. A. and Asher, E. R. (2004) What do you do when things go right? The intrapersonal and interpersonal benefits of sharing positive events. *Journal of Personality and Social Psychology, 87,* 228–45.

Jahoda, M. (1958) *Current Concepts of Positive Mental Health.* New York: Basic Books.

Joseph, S. (2009) Growth following adversity: Positive psychological perspectives on posttraumatic stress. *Psychological Topics, 18,* 335–44.

Joseph, S. and Linley, P. A. (2006) *Positive Therapy: A Meta-theory for Positive Psychological Practice.* London: Routledge.

Lyubomirsky, S. (2008) *The How of Happiness: A Scientific Approach to Getting the Life You Want.* New York: Penguin.

Marchand, W. R. (2012) Mindfulness-based stress reduction, mindfulness-based cognitive therapy, and zen meditation for depression, anxiety, pain, and psychological distress. *Journal of Psychiatric Practice, 18*, 233–52.

Myers, D. G. (1992) *The Pursuit of Happiness: Who is Happy, and Why?* New York: Harper.

Peters, M. L., Flink, I. K., Boersma, K. and Linton, S. J. (2010) Manipulating optimism: Can imagining a best possible self be used to increase positive future expectancies? *Journal of Positive Psychology, 5*, 204–11.

Rasmussen, H., Scheier, M. and Greenhouse, J. (2009) Optimism and physical health: A meta-analytic review. *Annals of Behavioral Medicine, 37*, 239–56.

Schueller, M. S. and Parks, C. A. (2012) Disseminating self-help: Positive psychology exercises in an online trial. *Journal of Medical Internet Research, 14*, e63.

Segerstrom, S. and Sephton, S. (2010) Optimistic expectancies and cell-mediated immunity: The role of positive affect. *Psychological Science, 21*, 448–55.

Seligman, M. E. P. (1991) *Learned Optimism.* New York: Knopf.

Seligman, M. E. P. (2003) *Authentic Happiness: Using the New Positive Psychology to Realise Your Potential for Lasting Fulfilment.* London: Nicholas Brealey Publishing.

Seligman, M. E. P. (2007) Coaching and positive psychology. *Australian Psychologist, 42*, 266–67.

Seligman, M. E. P. (2011) *Flourish: A New Understanding of Happiness and Wellbeing.* London: Nicholas Brealey Publishing.

Seligman, M. E. P., Rashid, T. and Parks, A. C. (2006) Positive psychotherapy. *American Psychologist, 61*, 774–88.

Seligman, M. E. P., Steen, T. A., Park, N. and Peterson, C. (2005) Positive psychology progress: Empirical validations of interventions. *American Psychologist, 60*, 410–21.

Sin, N. L. and Lyubomirsky, S. (2009) Enhancing well-being and alleviating depressive symptoms with positive psychology interventions: A practice-friendly meta-analysis. *Journal of Clinical Psychology, 65*, 467–87.

Steptoe, A., Wardle, J. and Marmot, M. (2005) Positive affect and health-related neuroendocrine, cardiovascular, and inflammatory responses. *Proceedings of the National Academy of Sciences, 102*, 6508–12.

Steptoe, A., Dockray, S. and Wardle, J. (2009) Positive affect and psychobiological processes relevant to health. *Journal of Personality, 77*, 1747–75.

Tedeschi, R. G. and Calhoun, L. G. (2004) Posttraumatic growth: Conceptual foundations and empirical evidence. *Psychological Inquiry, 15*, 1–18.

Tugade, M. M. and Fredrickson, B. L. (2004) Resilient individuals use positive emotions to bounce back from negative emotional experiences. *Journal of Personality and Social Psychology, 86*, 320–33.

Professor Neil Frude is a consultant clinical paychologist based in Cardiff, Wales.

MINDFULNESS IN THERAPY ⬤ 15

Jody Mardula

INTRODUCTION

This chapter on mindfulness and individual therapy covers the roots and developments of mindfulness in the West, and how this ancient Eastern tradition underpins Western mindfulness-based interventions. There are invitations to pause and engage in brief mindfulness practices spaced throughout the chapter, providing an opportunity to engage in reading the chapter mindfully.

A mindfulness-based intervention may arise from learning about mindfulness in a number of ways: reading, downloading talks and meditation practices, attending centres to learn to meditate. However perhaps the most influential therapeutic orientated interventions to date are the Mindfulness-based Stress Reduction (MBSR) (Kabat-Zinn, 1990) and Mindfulness-based Cognitive Therapy (MBCT) eight-week programmes (Segal, Williams and Teasdale, 2002).

Working in a teaching hospital in the USA in the 1980s, Jon Kabat-Zinn developed a secular eight-week programme that brought together mindfulness meditation with yoga and elements of learning from stress physiology, experiential learning, Buddhist psychology and group process. Aimed at patients with chronic pain and a variety of physical and psychological difficulties, the programme involved training in mindfulness, and a teaching style which enabled them to bring mindfulness practices to how they responded to their own difficulties as they experienced them in everyday life. This Mindfulness-based Stress Reduction (MBSR) programme has provided the template for further developments in Mindfulness-based Approaches (MBAs).

Mindfulness-based Cognitive Therapy was developed by Segal, Williams and Teasdale in the late 1990s. Designed as a treatment for people with a history of depression, they adapted the eight-week group format to include a combination of cognitive behaviour therapy with the Kabat-Zinn MBSR course, with the aim of offering a mindfulness-based programme that would contribute to the prevention of depression.

Therapists also began to bring mindfulness and elements from the eight-week courses into their individual work. Two ways of integrating mindfulness with individual therapy emerged, a mindfulness-based therapy and a mindfulness-informed therapy (Germer, Siegel and Fulton, 2005).

THE BUDDHA

The practice of mindfulness is associated with the Buddha, an Indian prince called Siddhattha Gotama, born approximately 2,500 years ago. Living in palace surrounded by luxury, he was deliberately protected from seeing the misery of humanity and the realities of life by his family. Eventually, he became restless and curious and insisted on going out of the palace. Seeing the suffering all around him, he realized that nothing can prevent the inevitable truth of life: we all grow old and experience sickness and death. Loss, unhappiness and impermanence are a part of the human condition, something we all have to face.

Leaving his family and his luxurious life, he went out into the world as a pilgrim, entering into study and periods of isolation and deprivation. After long meditation he became enlightened, and understood the nature of suffering and how to end it. He began to teach his ideas to his followers and became known as the Buddha, meaning the Awakened One (Gethin, 1998).

These ancient teachings, and the wisdom that they present for understanding the human condition, have grown into a body of Buddhist psychological theories. These theories, with their emphasis on attention and awareness meditation practices, are taught today in the twenty-first century through Buddhist ideas and through secular mindfulness-based approaches.

THEORY

BASIC CONCEPTS

TYPES OF THERAPY

A *mindfulness-based therapy* has many of the aspects of group mindfulness-based approaches and involves teaching mindfulness practices and techniques to clients in the therapy session and also as home practice. The emphasis is linked to the therapy issue presented, and in bringing mindfulness to what is happening in the therapy session. The degree to which practices are taught varies from therapist to therapist and is impacted on by their particular therapy model, the environment in which they work and the needs of this particular client at this time.

Mindfulness-informed therapy arises from the therapist's own mindfulness practice, and it may be that mindfulness practices are not directly taught to the client. The emphasis is on the therapist's stance, how they are with themselves, as they sit with their client and in the development of the therapeutic relationship.

Regarding a *mindfulness-informed therapeutic relationship*, there is potential for a deepening of the sense of connection in the dyad, of the felt presence of the client for the therapist and of the close, moment-by-moment accepting attention of the therapist for the client.

The therapeutic style fostered through the therapist's mindful attention to what arises moment by moment during the therapy may in itself lead to the client developing a more accepting attitude towards themselves, finding a way to open to their experience, to begin to turn towards (supported by the presence of an accepting other) what has brought them to therapy.

PAUSE 1.   BRING ATTENTION TO THE BODY

Pause, and become aware that you are sitting here – reading.

Notice how you are sitting, how your body feels.

Perhaps take a few moments to shift your posture in a way that helps you to be supported and present.

Sit for a few moments, aware of your body sitting here.

And move out of this Pause and continue to read.

MINDFULNESS IN INDIVIDUAL THERAPY

Mindfulness cultivates an attitude that people can bring to how they view and live their lives. They can bring a mindful attention to their beliefs about themselves, others and the world, to the sorts of concerns that bring them into therapy. At one level, mindfulness is about staying with the present moment and paying attention to the activity of mind and body, i.e. mindfulness of thoughts, emotions and sensations. The invitation is to notice experience as it unfolds, moment by moment, with an attitude of curiosity, with kindness and to let go of judgements.

At another level it is about noticing how people get caught up in these thoughts and judgements, spend much time thinking about the past or the future, about what they yearn for and what they want to avoid. Often they operate in a mode of autopilot, not even noticing what they are thinking, saying, doing – that they are drinking tea, eating a meal, driving a car – their minds are elsewhere.

As people begin to notice how they tense and judge themselves, how their minds slip into past and future, and into patterns of rumination, they learn that they can bring their attention back to the present, that they can wake up to their experiences, whatever they are. They begin to develop a new perspective on themselves and their lives, supporting and nurturing themselves, bringing fresh eyes to the options they have, less driven by old patterns, ruminative thoughts, projections and transferences.

In bringing a mindfulness attitude to therapy, individuals are also cultivating the attitudinal foundations that underpin mindfulness practice. Kabat-Zinn (1990) describes seven attitudinal qualities that inform both our therapeutic stance and the impact of that stance in the therapy.

- Non-Judging – stance of impartial witness – opening to our inner and outer experience and to the tendency to judge and move away from experience.
- Patience – allowing things unfold in their own time.

- Beginner's Mind – seeing as if for the first time. Bringing a new perspective to experience in each moment rather than seeing it through a fog of preconceptions.
- Trust – in letting the process unfold and trusting the validity of one's own thoughts, feelings and intuition.
- Non-Striving – paying attention to the present moment and not trying to fix or change it.
- Acceptance – a willingness to see whatever is here in the present moment. Opening to new ways of perceiving and acting.
- Letting Go – letting go of the tendency to hold on to what is experienced as pleasant and pushing away the unpleasant. Allowing an attitude of compassion to emerge.

When therapists cultivate these qualities through personal mindfulness practice, they spontaneously bring an embodiment of mindfulness practice into the relational process of therapy (Crane and Elias, 2006). Through the embodiment of these qualities, the therapist is attuned to the process of experiencing as it is happening, developing a more congruent relationship with themselves and so with their client.

Research suggests that therapists, and trainee therapists, who have some training in mindfulness, have more positive outcomes with their clients than therapists who have not had training in mindfulness (Grepmair et al., 2007; Larkin, 2011). This is not surprising as the qualities that are embedded in mindfulness are the kinds of qualities fostered by many therapy approaches: presence, positive regard, empathy, a non-judgemental approach and an attitude of acceptance together with underpinnings of the attitudinal foundations of mindfulness. Both mindfulness and therapy approaches see the mind's tendency to get caught in habitual patterns and scripts which are restricting and self defeating.

Therapists who bring mindfulness to themselves in their work are likely to cultivate a mindful approach to how they care for themselves. This may be in how they structure their day and their sessions, and through engaging in supervision specifically for the mindfulness aspects of their approach, either as a part of or in addition to their clinical supervision. Mindfulness develops the capacity to become increasingly aware of these conditioned patterns and to develop a greater perception of choice as a therapist.

We may be on the threshold of a new, mindfulness-orientated model of psychotherapy. There are treatment strategies that can be derived from mindfulness-orientated therapy. A new model will be developed when effectiveness is established in the empirical literature (Germer et al., 2005).

ACQUISITION

At the heart of a mindful therapeutic approach is an emphasis on present moment awareness. People are often skilled at avoiding the present moment, blocking off their feelings, covering them with anxiety, stress reactions, self harm, addictions, overwork, behaviours that increase suffering.

A mindfulness-based approach emphasises that all experiences are impermanent and often unsatisfactory. People's desire for the things that they want to be permanent can set up a tension between what they actually experience in the moment and how they want things to be. So they have a tendency to want to hang on to the experiences perceived as good, and avoid those perceived as bad, and to be bored, restless or indifferent with experiences perceived as neutral. They operate from a Doing mode of behaviour, staying away from being with their thoughts, feelings and sensations in the moment, Being mode. This creates a resistance to experiencing life as it is (Mardula and Larkin, 2014).

This is illustrated by the well-known Buddhist story of the two arrows. The first arrow causes people pain when it hits them – this could be hearing the news that they have lost a job. The second arrow represents the pain that is caused by their reaction to this first difficulty – the worry about the future, the ruminative self doubt and the anxieties about what others will think about them. They dwell on the pain, worry it may happen again, and create more anxiety and suffering.

Many of the therapy issues that clients work with are like the second arrow; they create their distress through their cravings and aversions, seeking to avoid experiencing whatever it is that they perceive as unpalatable or consider unbearable. They hold on to a belief that if they have enough of whatever gives them pleasure they can find relief from suffering.

This tendency toward suppressing or avoiding what people perceive to be unsafe or unpalatable can become a fixed pattern and impacts on how they habitually respond to difficulties in their lives. Over time these patterns become so internalized that they are unaware of them. People's internal sense of safety depends on this internalization of past events, rather than on a here-and-now evaluation of situations. They develop a bias towards reacting to the present from inappropriate and outdated interpretations, constantly reinforcing and perpetuating unhelpful patterns of behaviour.

Eventually people form an often fixed view of themselves and of how they relate to others and the world. The manner in which they respond to events, the thoughts and feelings that arise, and to the relationships that they build with others are driven by these outdated perceptions and beliefs.

When people experience lack of external support or experience betrayal or what is felt as attack, particularly at an early stage of development, the trauma created has a tendency to remain fixed in the body. A deep, often unconscious, sense of a lack of safety can become entrenched and then built on, creating layers of defences in the body and the mind; what Saki Santorelli calls the 'Bandaged Place' (Santorelli, 1999).

MAINTAINANCE

People see events, experiences and themselves through a distorting lens. They imagine things are permanent and unchanging. Although all around them everything is changing, the weather moves past and across the sky, seasons change, they age. Being unable to see that the distressing present will pass creates another layer of distress and fear. Their tendency to judge is layered onto their perception and the ability to see clearly becomes muddied by past experiences. On the one hand, they may engage unconsciously in reacting to the disliked and unwanted as though it is an attack; pushing it away, avoiding it, harming it. On the other hand they decide that some things are necessary to their happiness and wellbeing, and in the longing and grasping and craving, they develop another layer of distress and suffering.

People get caught up in ruminating about wanting things to be different, fearful that the unpleasant experiences will return. And by doing this, their bodies tend to respond by tightening, their thoughts often get channelled into one direction, their quality of life, the very way that they see themselves and others becomes coloured by their perception and failure to see options.

When people's emotions are strong they tend to suppress them or deny that they are there. They begin to colour how they see themselves as a person, reinforced by their reactive behaviour to try to suppress and avoid what is there. They create more anxious thoughts and feelings. They identify with the behaviour, 'I am an addict', 'I always get things wrong ...'. And so they go on.

People maintain these patterns largely out of conscious awareness. The result is that they continually seek to turn away from what they perceive as painful, difficult and unwanted. It takes a huge amount of energy to maintain these patterns of blocking off. People continue to engage in proliferating and building on their anger, sadness, despair – the second arrow of suffering.

This can be seen as a rupture in their relationship with themselves, a turning away that then impacts on how they relate to others, and of what they seek in coming to therapy. Influenced by early life events and the patterns of attachments that they formed, they perceive their current events through this lens of past relationships and restrict their ability to assess present moment reality and make life-enhancing decisions.

People create their reality from the old stories that arise for them and perpetuation of old scenarios. These stories and how they perceive others are based on projections, stereotyping, judging or idealizing others. This then activates their approach or avoid mode and they are back in that familiar place of suffering, wanting things to be different but unable or unwilling to make that shift.

PAUSE 2.   AWARENESS OF THE BODY AND BREATH

Pause and bring your attention to your body, noticing the sensation of the contact of your feet with the floor, of the weight of your body on the chair. Spend a few moments exploring these sensations. Become fully aware of the body sitting here.

Bring your awareness to your breath as it moves in and out of the body, perhaps feeling the breath against the nostrils or the mouth, or the sensation of the rise and fall of the belly with the in breath and the out breath. Follow the breath for a few moments.

And now come out of this Pause and continue to read.

THERAPY

THERAPEUTIC GOALS

Clients generally come to therapy because they want things to be different. They hope that they can have less of what they dislike and more of what they see as making them happy, in order to become a different person. The goal of a mindful approach is to enable the client to add a cultivation of the supportive attitudes of mindfulness to gradually learning to re-perceive the issues, and patterns and stories that they have brought to therapy, and to develop a way to open towards and tolerate what was previously seen as unendurable and the source of distress.

A mindfulness-informed therapist will bring a non-fixing perspective to the therapy, seeing goals as intentions that develop through the process of the therapy. The therapist aims to help the client relate to their emotional life and all their experience in a different way that does not seek to avoid or eliminate anything. They aim to develop the capacity to notice what is going for the client in the present moment, and to learn to turn towards, rather than turn away from, difficulties that arise.

The therapist adopts an approach that invites a Being mode rather than a Doing mode, with an emphasis on not trying to improve yourself, or to get anywhere else, but simply to realise where you already are, by 'coming to your senses' (Kabat-Zinn, 2005).

This process will be cultivated through inviting the client to:

- notice what is occurring in the present moment – thoughts, sensations and feelings
- bring a non-judgemental attitude to all that they notice
- notice when their mind has wandered off and bring it back to the present
- bring new eyes to their stories, patterns and experiences – re-perceiving
- learn how to come back, over and over again, to the body in the present moment
- notice how they react to experiences they regard as pleasant or unpleasant by avoiding, blocking out or seeking to eliminate them
- become aware of cravings and impulses as they occur
- become aware of how these patterns cause more suffering
- learn to open and turn towards all their experience
- develop an attitude of acceptance of whatever is here, cultivate an accepting, non-judgemental and kindly approach to themselves, others and life.

The attitudinal foundations of mindfulness and the implicit compassion in the practices that are held in the person of the therapist and the therapeutic relationship, support this softening, opening and turning toward the unwanted, difficult, the feared, and an activating of the neural pathways that respond to approach mode by soothing and calming.

PROCESS OF THERAPY

A mindfulness approach may be brought to any human condition. However, the manner in which the therapist chooses to do that will depend on the circumstances of the client at that time, and also some consideration of what approach is most appropriate.

The process of therapy begins from the first contact and assessment session with the client. Clients do not decide to come to see a therapist for meditation but for therapy, so it is important for therapists to pay close attention to why and how they will integrate mindfulness with their primary therapeutic model. They need to consider whether a mindfulness-informed or a mindfulness-based approach is indicated for each client, and build this into their intake and assessment process (Germer et al., 2005).

Before beginning therapy, the client needs to understand the nature of what is being offered to them. With a mindfulness-informed approach, the therapist's way of being with the client is informed and supported by their mindfulness practice. This mindful tone and nature of *how* the therapist is with the client, impacts on the therapy from the outset. The assessment process may not differ from how they would normally assess and organize their client intake and therapeutic agreement. However, where the therapist is considering a mindfulness-based approach of bringing mindfulness practices into the therapy, either through teaching them directly or through encouraging practice between sessions, they need to provide the relevant information about what they are offering. They may choose to do this, and to assess the suitability of the client for this approach through bringing a short practice into the assessment. Teaching a practice gives the client the opportunity to experience how it is to have a meditation practice brought into the therapy, and also allows the therapist to assess the suitability of this approach for this client by observing how they engage in, and are able to reflect on, the practice.

The therapy itself will be conducted through the methodology of whatever school of counselling, psychotherapy, coaching, or other approach the therapist is trained in. The integration of mindfulness into the process is through the attitudinal foundations, the mindfulness-informed presence of the therapist, the addition of a mindful experiential enquiry to the therapy dialogue with pauses to reflect, and perhaps by the inclusion of longer, taught mindfulness practices in a mindfulness-based approach.

The therapist will invite the client to tell their story in their usual manner. The psychological underpinning of mindfulness will emerge through the therapeutic dialogue. For instance, the therapist may invite the client to notice what is going on in their mind and body and how that changes; helping them to link their experience to impermanence, exploring how they spend much of their time on autopilot and linking that to not being in the present moment. This is usually demonstrated through bringing attention to the client's direct experience linked to the therapeutic issue they have brought. Suffering may be alleviated through bringing attention to the experience, observing how thoughts, feelings and sensations unfold in the present, and through developing an understanding of how they are maintained.

Both therapy models and mindfulness invite and support the client in slowing down and reflecting on the patterns that emerge, seeing how they proliferate and get caught in old unhelpful feelings and behaviours. The therapeutic encounter is where people can become aware of these patterns, experience them, understand them and open up alternatives.

A central development of a mindful approach is the development of an acceptance of experience and in particular of the experience that the client has brought to therapy and generally hopes to push away. A mindfulness acceptance does not mean a resignation to what is here, but an acknowledgment of whatever is here. This comes from developing this moment-by-moment awareness of what is arising and then pausing, and of opening to and naming what is here. If there is pain then acknowledging that pain is there, if there is sadness or fear acknowledging that they are here. That is the first step to acceptance, to perceive clearly and to name the experience.

The therapist will, through mindful enquiry and perhaps by teaching short mindfulness practices, together with the client, explore what is arising in the here-and-now of the therapy session, and through the therapist's acceptance of their own and the client's experience, whatever it is, cultivate this process of acceptance. This enables the client to turn towards whatever is here, even to the unwanted and dreaded, and to gradually find that this too can be tolerated, that all things pass, the 'good and the bad', and that in turning towards rather than pushing away, there is a way to be with whatever is here.

Mindfulness fits well into the various schools of psychotherapy

> which have in common the idea that patterns are laid down in people's pasts, becoming solidified through repetition. That this then causes suffering and limits their options for the decisions they may make in their lives. That bringing understanding of these patterns and how they have been developed, and finding out how to shift them is central to therapy. (Barker, 2013, p. 33)

THE THERAPEUTIC RELATIONSHIP

Developing a mindfulness-led therapeutic relationship grows out of the therapist's own mindfulness practice through the regular cultivation of the sort of qualities and attitudes that foster an embodied presence in the therapist (Welwood, 2002). Bringing these qualities to the therapeutic relationship arises naturally from a mindfulness-informed therapy, and can foster the therapist in providing an empathic and authentic relationship which is the basis of good therapy (Keane, 2013).

The therapist holds awareness of their own experience as they sit with the client that includes their felt sense of the client; holding themselves, the client and the therapeutic space between them in awareness (Speeth, 1982). Their therapeutic responses are led by this attuned, embodied awareness of themselves and the other, moment by moment, with an overarching kindly curiosity towards the client and to themselves. In his book *Mindful Therapy* (2006) Bien talks about therapists 'stopping having to intervene and just trying to understand' (p. 56). And within that understanding is also acceptance, of the complete person and of what is here.

Siegal (2010), researching the neuroscience of a mindfulness approach, identifies that the ability to be present with experience depends on having a basic sense of safety. Without this, the way that people usually respond to what they experience as threatening is to fight it, flee from it or to freeze, to cut off from their experience. In doing this, there is a strengthening of the alarm neural pathways which means there is a likelihood of responding in the same way in the future, habits are set down on how to respond to perceived threat. Internal conversation can dominate how internal and external events are perceived. Patterns laid down in the past become solidified. As the therapy progresses, and the client's internal dialogue shifts and they begin to let go and turn toward the previously feared and unwanted, accepting that it is here they activate the secure neural pathways that promote a sense of soothing, calm and safety. Held by the attuned, embodied and compassionate presence of the mindful therapist, they are able to cultivate acceptance of what is here and learn that even this can be explored and experienced, that nothing is outlawed here.

THERAPEUTIC INTERVENTIONS

PAUSE 3.   BREATH AND ENQUIRY

Pause and feel the sensation of both feet on the ground … the movement of the breath in the body … . Follow the sensation of the breath for a few moments. If the mind slips, just gently escort the attention back to the breath, letting go of any judgements you may be having … follow the journey of the in breath and the out breath, and notice the sensation of the movement of the breath in the body.

Now come out of the Pause, and enquire of yourself:

'What did I notice when I paused? Were there any thoughts there? Any feelings or sensations?' Just notice with curiosity, letting go of any judgements. Perhaps just jot down what you noticed.

Therapists may adopt a process of phenomenological enquiry within the therapy conversation, with the intention of exploring with the client their moment-by-moment experience, developing a sense of trust and safety as they open to their experience. 'Mindfulness techniques and practices help to foster a safer more embodied present moment experience that can begin a process of safely turning toward experience … previously experienced as source of distress, pain, and difficulty' (Mardula and Larkin, 2014).

A mindfulness approach can work well integrated into most modes of therapy. Some will adopt a mindfulness approach that comes from the cultivation of the attitudes of mindfulness and the mindful presence of the therapist, and some a more practice-based integration. The interventions of a mindfulness approach are the relationship itself, the phenomenological enquiry process and the teaching of mindfulness practices.

A mindfulness methodology for intervening arises from the development of the mindful therapeutic stance and the embodied presence of the therapist themselves. The therapeutic relationship and dialogue is crucial to bringing mindfulness into the therapy arena and cultivating change. Through the attuned and focused listening embodying the foundations of mindfulness, clients are encouraged to actively develop awareness of their own patterns and processes that are often out of conscious awareness. The aim is for them to notice how they react, to notice what they are feeling in the present moment, or reflect on how they responded at a certain time, in order to be able to choose to respond mindfully rather than automatically in the way they usually do.

This is developed through the therapist adopting a mindful enquiry process that invites clients to notice and describe the different elements of their direct experience in the here-and-now. This invites an experiential here-and-now process rather than the client 'thinking about' things in their usual way. This process allows clients to become aware of and to discriminate between the different elements of their direct experience – of sensation, thought, feelings – both retrospectively tracking these as they arose in their life, or tracking them as they arise in the present.

There are three layers of enquiry, with layer one inviting a noticing of sensations, thoughts and feelings. Layer two invites the client to dialogue about what they noticed, and layer three to link them to the therapeutic issue they have brought or to how they respond to these experiences in their everyday lives.

This process enables clients to engage with the intentions of a mindfulness approach, to see how their minds become caught in particular ways of thinking and relating to experience, or how they habitually interpret events in a certain way, and how their thoughts link them to particular feelings. They begin to perceive how this is relevant to their lives and the issues they are bringing to therapy and how they might respond differently when difficulties arise (Crane, 2009).

This style of dialogue to enquire into and differentiate experiences is invitational, uses open rather than closed questions, and is used in the exploration of a particular experience. Examples of the phrasing and intentions of the enquiry process are:

What did you notice? (For example, focused on physical sensations, sounds, feelings, colours, textures, movement.)
How did that feel?
Where was that occurring in the body?
What else did you notice?
What happened next? (Exploring whether sensation/thoughts changed, moved on, softened, intensified.)
Did you notice any thoughts or emotions connected to that?
When your mind wandered, where did it go?
How did you feel when your mind wandered?
What is happening now?

The order of the enquiry questioning, and where the enquiry is focused varies depending on what the client has brought into the therapy, the direction of the therapy and the sense of curiosity that develops between therapist and client in the moment, a co-creation of the process of the dialogue. This enquiry process may be used to explore with the client their experience as they are relating an account of something that has happened, either recently or in the past; for example, a recent argument that distressed them, or a remembered situation from childhood. The therapist might inquire 'What is happening for you right now as you tell me about … ?'. It may also be used to explore the here-and-now experience, 'What is happening right now as we sit here together … ?', followed by a reflection of what the client notices, and often further exploration.

In a mindfulness-based approach, the therapist may invite the client to pause, and notice what is going on for them, or teach a short practice, and then enquire into what they experienced through the practice. An example of the therapist bringing a mindful enquiry process into a dialogue with a client, is illustrated in how a therapist works with Maggie, who has come to therapy because she is exhausted by loss of sleep and her anxiety about her sleep disturbance is increasing. The therapist helps Maggie to see how as she puts her energy and attention into pushing away sleeplessness, she prolongs it. Later she will invite Maggie to approach her fear of not sleeping by breathing into the sense of fear and anxiety and bring the enquiry process to that experience. This supports the client with a new experience of having the sense of another person present with her as she describes her experience, moment by moment. As she articulates her experience, held in the attuned regard of the therapeutic relationship, and is invited to feel her feet on the floor, to bring herself into a grounded sense of being in the body, she notices how the sensations are not static, they rise and fall, and as she breathes she notices a softening (layer one). The therapist then invites a reflection on what she just noticed and together they gradually move toward a re-perceiving of Maggie's sleeplessness (layer two). Maggie can then bring her new perceptions, and her ability to use a Pause or a Practice to turn towards her unwanted thoughts and feelings as they arise, to the times when she begins to ruminate on sleeplessness, or when she wakes in the night (layer three).

This style of intervention may also be preceded by the therapist leading a longer practice with the client, and the enquiry process that would follow would be more focused on what arose during the practice than the direct experience from the dialogue. The therapist's choice of how and when to enquire, whether to use a Pause, or teach a practice, or to simply use the relationship, will depend on their style, their confidence in the approach, the length of their personal practice and training in a mindfulness approach, and the therapeutic direction arising from their own supervision.

In responding to sleep disturbance it is common practice to encourage getting up and doing something rather than lying there ruminating and becoming fixated on thoughts that keep you awake. This can be very helpful. However a mindfulness perspective would encourage an approach of choosing to turn towards the difficulty, the sense of sleeplessness. And the client needs to gradu-ally learn how to do this and be willing to give it a try.

Many of the situations that clients present with in therapy involve a longing for it to be different and a desire to push away the unwanted. The mindfulness approach, rather than intervening to find ways to avoid this, is to accept that it is here, and find a middle way between enduring and suffering or getting rid of it. Taking care that the intervention is not interpreted as a way to change things, as an invitation to 'relax or calm down', but rather an invitation to accept experience as it is.

Mindfulness teaches affect tolerance, how to sit on the edge of pain and not push it away. Not to drown in the difficulty but to surf it: what Jon Kabat-Zinn termed 'the Full Catastrophe of Living'. It opens new opportunities for clients to relate to themselves, to others and their lives.

PAUSE 4.   A THREE-STEP BREATHING SPACE

Step One. Awareness: Pause, and ask yourself 'what going on for me just now?', and just notice whatever is here, in your thoughts, your sensations and emotions. Just allow them to be here for a few moments.

Step Two. Gathering: Now bring your attention to the breath, and follow the breath as you breathe all the way in and all the way out, follow as one breath follows the other. And if the mind slips off to thinking, just come back to the in breath and the out breath.

Step Three. Expanding: And now expand your attention out to include a sense of your whole body and of your surroundings. Allow the breath to expand and breathe into the whole body, for a few breaths.

And come out of this Breathing Space, and pause again to notice how your body feels now.

CASE MATERIAL

Case vignettes of a mindfulness therapy approach can be found in some of the more recent literature. Meg Barker, in her book *Mindful Counselling and Psychotherapy* (2013) includes case studies on a range of common presenting issues including depression, anxiety, relationships and addictions, and an exploration of how to bring mindfulness into the different schools of therapy. Another source of case examples can be found in Germer and Siegel's *Wisdom and Compassion in Psychotherapy* (2012). Different chapters explore wisdom, compassion and Buddhist psychology underpinning the examples of therapeu-tic practice.

Because the development of approaches to bringing mindfulness into indi-vidual therapy is relatively recent, there is not as yet a large body of recorded case material. Much of the available case material relates to the teaching of mindfulness in the eight-week group format. This material, however, is useful to the therapist, as the therapeutic interventions that bring mindfulness into therapy are present in the taught mindfulness programmes. The therapist exploring how to bring mindfulness into their own therapy approach can benefit from reading these texts as well as case studies from therapy.

FURTHER DEVELOPMENTS

A strong evidence base shown for the efficacy of MBCT for depression led to it being recommended by the National Institute for Health and Clinical Excellence (NICE, 2004 and then 2010) as a treatment of choice for recurrent depression. This was followed by a flowering of MBAs including MBCT for specific clinical populations that include bi-polar, anxiety, cancer, chronic fatigue and insomnia; and other mindfulness-based courses such as Mindfulness-based Relapse Prevention, Mindfulness-based Childbirth and Parenting and MBSR for non-clinical populations.

MBCT for Cancer (Bartley, 2012) has been developed as an eight-week programme that has many of the elements of a relational therapy approach. The Third Wave of CBT approaches includes therapies that bring in elements of mindfulness, such as Acceptance and Commitment Therapy (ACT), Dialectic Behaviour Therapy (DBT), and Compassion Focused Therapy (Gilbert, 2010a and b).

Research into mindfulness in individual therapy is only just emerging. Training courses aimed specifically at therapists are becoming more available. The training for mindfulness practitioners who are supervisors in a mindfulness supervision process has just begun, and, in the UK, a mindfulness supervision protocol is under development between Bangor, Exeter and Oxford Universities. There is an expanding library of books increasingly exploring how to bring mindfulness into therapy, and the empirical research and establishing of a clear model of mindfulness therapy cannot be far behind.

Training processes and organizations for mindfulness teachers are well established. Some of them (Bangor University), focus particularly on training for therapists. Most mindfulness individual therapy courses would require the therapist to have also attended courses on how to teach mindfulness, as the skills embedded in this training are what become integrated into the repertoire of the mindful therapist.

REVIEW AND PERSONAL QUESTIONS

REVIEW QUESTIONS

1. What are the roots of a mindfulness-based approach to therapy?
2. Describe the different ways in which mindfulness may be brought into individual therapy.

3. Discuss how the attitudinal foundations of mindfulness are relevant to an individual therapy.
4. Explore how a mindfulness approach views the acquisition and maintenance of psychological disturbance.
5. Describe and discuss the therapeutic goals of a mindfulness-based approach and the paradox of change in mindfulness.
6. Discuss the relevance of mindfulness within the therapeutic relationship.
7. Describe the therapeutic interventions of a mindfulness approach and how they fit with different schools of therapy.
8. What do you understand by a phenomenological enquiry process? How might you develop this in your therapeutic dialogue?
9. Discuss the relevance of a personal mindfulness practice for therapists. Why might it be important in bringing a mindfulness approach to clients?

PERSONAL QUESTIONS

1. Discuss how you would integrate mindfulness with a therapeutic approach you are familiar with.
2. What methods for developing insight and self reflection are you drawn to? Discuss.
3. What was your experience of engaging in the short practices outlined in the chapter? Give a reflective account of your experience as you read the chapter.
4. Reflect on what ways you get caught in wanting things to be different to how they are. How would a mindfulness approach help and why?
5. What do you think you would personally need to have in place in order to bring a mindful approach to clients?
6. What do you think about the Buddhist concept of suffering? How does this show up in your own life and work?
7. A mindfulness approach sees all mind objects, thoughts, sensations, feelings, as impermanent. What do you notice about impermanence in your life? How might a mindfulness approach help?
8. Mindfulness is a non-fixing approach to therapy. How do you see the difference between fixing and non-fixing in therapy? How would you bring this into your approach?
9. What spoke to you the loudest in reading this chapter about mindfulness? Describe and discuss its relevance to you a person and as a therapist.

ANNOTATED BIBLIOGRAPHY

Barker, M. (2013) *Mindful Counselling and Psychotherapy. Practising Mindfully Across Approaches and Issues.* London: Sage.
This book spells out how a mindfulness approach would approach therapy for common presenting issues. An accessible book that will appeal to counselling and psychotherapy students and experienced therapists.

Crane, R. (2009) *Mindfulness Based Cognitive Therapy.* Abingdon: Routledge.
This book gives a comprehensive and accessible account of a mindfulness cognitive behavioural approach to teaching that can easily be translated into

working in an individual context as a therapist. It includes a short chapter on the mindful enquiry process.

Hick, S. and Bien, T. (eds) (2008) *Mindfulness and the Therapeutic Relationship.* London: Guilford Press.
This book brings an insight into the synthesis of Buddhist and Western therapies, and explores the impact of mindfulness on the therapeutic relationship and development of empathic skills.

Germer, C., Siegel, R. and Fulton, R. (eds) (2005) *Mindfulness and Psychotherapy.* Abingdon: Guilford Press.
A comprehensive book covering bringing mindfulness into contemporary clinical applications with chapters that shine a spotlight on the therapeutic relationship, showing how cultivating mindfulness can inform the therapy relationship and process. The book includes case examples.

Kabat-Zinn, J. (1990) *Full Catastrophe Living: Using the Wisdom of Your Body and Mind to Face Stress, Pain, and Illness.* New York: Dell.
The original book on the development of Mindfulness-based Stress Reduction. This book is an excellent guide to understand how mindfulness-based approaches developed and the intentions and foundations of mindfulness that are so essential to therapy.

Segal, Z., Williams, J. and Teasdale, J. (2002) *Mindfulness Based Cognitive Therapy for Depression: A New Approach for Preventing Relapse.* Abingdon: Guilford Press.
A new edition of the original book outlining the eight-week Mindfulness–based Cognitive Therapy Course. Essential reading for anyone wishing to develop their knowledge and understanding of mindfulness-based approaches.

REFERENCES AND FURTHER READING

Barker, M. (2013) *Mindful Counselling and Psychotherapy. Practising Mindfully Across Approaches and Issues.* London: Sage.
Bartley, T. (2012) *Mindfulness-Based Cognitive Therapy for Cancer.* Wiley-Blackwell.
Bien, T. (2006) *Mindful Therapy: A Guide for Therapists and Helping Professionals.* Boston: Wisdom.
Bowen. S., Chawla N. and Marlatt G. A. (2010) *Mindfulness-Based Relapse Prevention. A Clinician's Guide.* New York: Guildford Press.
Crane, R. (2009) *Mindfulness Based Cognitive Therapy.* Abingdon: Routledge.
Crane, R. and Elias, D. (2006) Being with what is: Mindfulness practice for counsellors and psychotherapists. *Psychotherapy Today*, 31–33.

Crane. R. S., Stanley. S., Rooney. M., Bartley, T., Cooper, C. and Mardula, J. (in preparation) Disciplined Improvisation: Characteristics of inquiry in mindfulness-based teaching. *Psychology and Psychotherapy: Theory, Research and Practice.*

Epstein, M. (1998) *Going to Pieces Without Falling Apart.* New York: Broadway Books.

Germer, C. and Siegel, R. (eds) (2012) *Wisdom and Compassion in Psychotherapy: Deepening Mindfulness in Clinical Practice.* New York: Guilford Press.

Germer, C., Siegel, R. and Fulton, R. (eds) (2005) *Mindfulness and Psychotherapy.* Abingdon: Guilford Press.

Gethin, R. (1998) *The Foundations of Buddhism.* Oxford: Oxford University Press.

Gilbert, P. (2010a) *The Compassionate Mind.* London: Constable.

Gilbert, P. (2010b) *Compassion Focussed Therapy.* London: Routledge.

Grepmair, L., Mitterlehner, F., Loew, T., Bachler, E., Rother, W. and Nickel, M. (2007) Promoting mindfulness in psychotherapists in training influences the treatment results of their patients: A randomized, double-bind, controlled study. *Psychotherapy & Psychosomatics, 76,* 332–8.

Halifax. J. (2009) *Being With Dying: Cultivating Compassion and Fearlessness in the Presence of Death.* London: Shambhala.

Hayes, S. (2005) *Get Out of Your Mind and Into Your Life*: *The New Acceptance and Commitment Therapy.* Oakland, CA: New Harbinger.

Hick, S. and Bien, T. (eds) (2008) *Mindfulness and the Therapeutic Relationship.* London: Guilford Press.

Kabat-Zinn, J. (1990) *Full Catastrophe Living: Using the Wisdom of Your Body and Mind to Face Stress, Pain, and Illness.* New York: Dell Publishing.

Kabat-Zinn, J. (2005) *Coming to Our Senses: Healing Ourselves and the World through Mindfulness.* New York: Hyperion.

Keane, A. (2013) *The Influence of Therapist Mindfulness Practice On Psychotherapeutic Work: A Mixed Methods Study.* Published Online.

Kornfield, J. (1994) *A Path with a Heart.* New York: Bantam.

Larkin, F. (2011) *Mindfulness and Psychotherapy: An Exploration of the Influence of Mindfulness Meditation on the Self of the Psychotherapist and Their Clinical Work.* MA Thesis, for Centre for Mindfulness Research and Practice, School of Psychology, Bangor University, UK.

Levine, P. (1997) *Waking the Tiger: Healing Trauma.* Berkeley, CA: North Atlantic Books.

Mardula, J. and Larkin, F. (2014) Mindfulness in individual therapy. In Dryden, W. and Reeves, A. (eds) *The Handbook for Individual Therapy,* (6th ed.). London: Sage, pp. 445–68.

Santorelli, S. (1999) *Heal Thyself: Lessons on Mindfulness in Medicine.* New York: Bell Tower.

Segal, Z., Williams, J. and Teasdale, J. (2002) *Mindfulness Based Cognitive Therapy for Depression: A New Approach for Preventing Relapse.* New York: Guilford Press.

Siegal, D. (2010) *The Mindful Therapist: A Clinician's Guide to Mindsight and Neural Integration*. New York: Norton.

Speeth, K. R. (1982) On psychotherapeutic attention. *The Journal of Transpersonal Psychology*, 14(2), 141–59.

Swales, M. A. and Head, H. L. (2009) *Dialectical Behaviour Therapy*. London: Routledge.

Wellwood, J. (2002) *Towards a Psychology of Awakening: Buddhism, Psychotherapy, and the Path of Personal and Spiritual Transformation*. Boston, MA: Shambhala.

Jody Mardula is a trainer, teacher and supervisor at Bangor University.

VI

MULTICULTURAL AND GENDER THERAPIES

Over the past forty years or so, there has been growing interest in diversity-sensitive counselling and therapy. The differences on which this burgeoning literature focuses include culture, race, gender, sexual and affectionate orientation, disability, religion, socioeconomic status, and mixtures of these, among others. In the following two chapters, I provide introductory reviews of two dimensions of diversity that affect all therapists and clients: namely, culture and gender.

Sue and Sue (2013) observe that, because no one is immune from inheriting the images and stereotypes of the larger society, most therapists are prisoners of their own cultural conditioning. They may possess and unthinkingly impose stereotypes and preconceived notions on their culturally different clients. Critics of existing counselling and therapy theories assert that their Euro-American cultural bias means that Western oriented therapists may be failing their actual and potential cultural minority group client populations in a number of significant ways. Chapter 16 provides an introduction to the notion of culture, the different goals of multicultural therapy, and to some ways in which counsellors and therapists can provide services for clients with problems that contain a significant cultural component.

In the last third of the twentieth and the beginning of the twenty-first century the rise of feminism and the growth of the men's movement have accelerated the debate over male and female roles. Gender issues permeate therapy: for example, in the gender related assumptions that therapists and clients bring to their personal lives and to therapy. Nevertheless, the fact remains that, with one recent exception, all the main theorists whose work is presented in this book are men and all were educated before the last third of the twentieth century. Chapter 17 aims to provide a brief and basic introduction to some gender issues connected to the theory and practice of counselling and therapy. Of necessity, it is a tour of some of the main points rather than a detailed analysis of any of them.

REFERENCE

Sue, D. W. and Sue, D. (2013) *Counseling the Culturally Diverse: Theory and Practice* (6th ed.). New York: Wiley.

MULTICULTURAL THERAPY 16

INTRODUCTION

Over the past 60 years, there has been a growing interest in diversity sensitive counselling and psychotherapy, which has been stimulated by the perception that the main Western counselling and psychotherapy approaches either insufficiently or wrongly consider the special needs of different groups of clients (Moodley, 2007). Corey (2009) observes that multicultural specialists have asserted that theories of counselling and psychotherapy represent different worldviews, each with its own biases and assumptions about human behaviour. Comas-Diaz (2012) refers to the cultural iceberg, with surface culture, such as appearance and physique, and deep culture, much of which is unconscious, such as worldview orientation (values, beliefs, opinions, attitudes).

Increasingly in Britain and even more so in Australia there are many residents from different cultures. Counselling and psychotherapy services are underutilized by minority groups because of issues like mistrust, perceived irrelevance and cultural insensitivity. Assessment may insufficiently take into account differences in how behaviours are perceived in different cultures. In addition, therapists may fail to understand and address the stresses attached to being in a cultural minority group and the emotional disruption of migration to a different culture. Once psychotherapy begins, apart from obvious language difficulties, therapists may experience difficulty comprehending the communication patterns and personal and social contexts of their clients' problems. If clients have not discontinued already, therapists may establish goals and intervene on the basis of mainstream cultural assumptions that run counter to the cultural norms and personal meanings of their clients. Furthermore, therapists may focus too much on dealing with individuals rather than dealing with individuals in the context of their families and their social networks. In addition the helping professions insufficiently attend to the need for institutional and social change to counteract the oppression of minority groups. For these and other reasons, in recent years there has been an increased interest in and need to take cultural issues into account in psychotherapy.

THE TERMINOLOGY OF CULTURE

Many of the terms associated with culture possess different shadings of meaning according to who does the defining. The following discussion of some key terms and concepts relevant to cultural issues in psychotherapy is illustrative rather than prescriptive. Some of these terms and concepts will be elaborated as the chapter progresses.

- *Culture*: Spindler, who taught the author a course in cultural anthropology at Stanford University, defined culture as 'a patterned system of tradition-derived norms influencing behavior' (Spindler, 1963, p. 7). He went on to observe that cultural norms are in a constant state of flux. Another definition of culture is that it refers to 'an integrated pattern of human behavior that includes thoughts, communications, actions, customs, beliefs, values, and institutions of a racial, ethnic, religious or social group' (Cross et al., 1989, p. iv). A colloquial definition of culture is 'the way we do things here.'
- *Enculturation*: Enculturation refers to the transmission of cultural norms within a given culture. Another way of viewing enculturation is as the socialization process in which younger members learn cultural rules from their elders. Nowadays, there are many different avenues for cultural transmission, for instance the media and the internet.
- *Acculturation*: Acculturation refers to the behavioural and psychological changes that occur in individuals as a result of their interaction with a different culture. For example, all migrants to Britain and Australia undergo acculturation. However, in both countries, migrants acculturate at varying rates and attain different levels of assimilation to the mainstream culture.
- *Culture shock*: Culture shock, of varying levels of severity, is a fairly common reaction to the stresses of adapting to a new culture. Its symptoms can include anxiety, a sense of loss, confusion of roles, feelings of helplessness and a desire for a more familiar and predictable environment. If marked, culture shock can engender pathological symptoms, such as depression and psychological and physical withdrawal.
- *Cultural change*: Cultures are not static. Change can come from within and without, or a mixture of the two. For instance, in Britain and Australia there are traditional mainstream cultures adhered to mainly by the older generation as well as emergent cultures being created predominantly by the younger generation. Intermarrying between different ethnic groups is another stimulus for cultural change coming from within a country.

    In addition, cultural change can come from without: for example, in Britain the influence of other European cultures has increased with entry into the EU and more business, educational and holiday travel to and from other European countries. Similarly, Australian culture changed with the post-Second World War influx of southern European migrants and the post-Vietnam War influx of Southeast Asian migrants. Furthermore the world is increasingly a 'global village' with cultural changes mediated by technological advances such as cable TV and the Internet. Hermans and Kempen observe: 'In an increasingly interconnected world society, the conception of independent, coherent and stable cultures becomes increasingly irrelevant' (1998, p. 1111). Some changes due to globalization may lead to a blurring of cultural distinctions and some lessening of distinctive cultural identities.
- *Multiculturalism*: The central value of multiculturalism is that of cultural puralism and acknowledging that nations like Britain, Australia and America are cultural mosaics rather than cultural melting pots (Sue et al., 1998). Multiculturalism can be contrasted with monoculturalism where high value is attached only to the patterns of behaviour of the dominant or mainstream culture.
- *Cultural cohesion*: Cultural cohesion or social cohesiveness refers to the extent to which the norms of a culture or nation help it to stick together. In Britain, Australia and the United States many of the problems of cultural minorities are those of equality of access

to opportunities within the mainstream culture rather than the fact that a mainstream culture exists. In such culturally diverse countries, a balance needs to be struck between multiculturalism and cultural cohesion. If taken to extremes, in a highly culturally diverse country like Australia, multiculturalism could lead to each ethnic group following its own agenda and so coming into conflict with other ethnic groups. Northern Ireland has provided a good example inadequate cohesion, with its two main cultural groups insufficiently finding common ground.

- *Race*: Race refers to human subgroups possessing physical characteristics that distinguish them from other human subgroups. Such physical characteristics include skin colour, head form, facial features, and amount, colour and texture of body hair. Racial groups include Caucasian, Aboriginal, African, Asian, Polynesian or various combinations of mixed race.
- *Ethnic minority*: A neutral definition of ethnic minorities is that they are groups differentiated from the main population of a country by racial origin and/or cultural background. Another definition of a minority, be it ethnic or otherwise, is that it is a group of people who, because of physical or cultural characteristics, are singled out from others in the society in which they live for differential and unequal treatment, and who therefore regard themselves as objects of collective discrimination.

CULTURE AND DEMOGRAPHY

Some indication of the importance of culture to contemporary counselling can be found in the demographic statistics of various countries. Demography is the study of population sizes, movements and trends, including those concerning ethnic minorities.

In March 2011 the total population of the United Kingdom numbered 62.3 million people (United Kingdom Census, 2012) of whom 53 million were in England, 3.1 million in Wales, 5.3 million in Scotland and 1.8 million in Northern Ireland. In England and Wales, the white ethnic group decreased from 94.1 per cent in 1991, to 91.3 per cent in 2001, to 86 per cent in 2011 (80 per cent of the total population were from the white British group). In London, only 45 per cent out of 8.2 million usual residents were white British. Overall in the United Kingdom the number of Asian people was 4.2 million, the number of black people 1.8 million, and the number of mixed race people 1.2 million. The above figures disguise the full extent of cultural differences in Britain, for instance between the Welsh, Irish, Scots and English as well as between and within the more racially distinguished ethnic groupings. Also, following their accession to the European Union in May 2004, there has been a sharp increase in migrants from central and Eastern European countries, for instance Poland.

Australia is one of the most multicultural and, increasingly, multiracial countries in the world. Australia's population has grown more than six-fold since the beginning of the twentieth century, from 3.77 million to 22.8 million in 2012 (Australian Bureau of Statistics, 2012). Since the end of the Second World War, the proportion of the population born overseas has greatly increased. As well as those from Britain and Ireland, many migrants came from Eastern and Southern Europe, and, more recently, there has been a shift in migration patterns in favour of more migrants from Asia, for instance from Vietnam and China.

Thomas (2004) notes that immigrants from countries outside Asia such as Sudan, Somalia, Iraq and Afghanistan had increased significantly in the previous five years. In 2006, 517,000 people identified themselves as of Aboriginal and Torres Strait Islander descent. By 2021, Australia's indigenous population is expected to exceed 700,000 people.

The United States of America has a long history of multicultural diversity. In 2010 the United States population was 308.7 million (United States Census Bureau, 2011). Though the majority of the population is still white, 63.7 per cent were white-non-Hispanic, they have their ancestry in numerous countries. Of the remainder, 16.2 per cent were white-Hispanic or Latino origin, 12.6 per cent black or African American, and 4.6 per cent were of Asian origin. Demographic projections indicate that non-white will outnumber white persons sometime between the years 2030 and 2050 (Sue et al., 1998). The rapid demographic shift stems from two major trends: immigration and differential birthrates.

THEORY

CULTURE AND FULL HUMANNESS

An important issue in thinking about cultures is the extent to which they are conducive to developing the full humanness of their individual members (Maslow, 1971). The idea that all cultures are equally benign in promoting the human potential of their members is both false and naïve: for example, think of the demeaning position of women when the Taleban ruled Afghanistan. Maslow was cautiously optimistic about the biological nature of human beings. However, he thought that positive aspects of human nature, such as altruistic concern for others, were frequently weak, needed a benign culture for their appearance, and could be inhibited or shattered by bad cultural conditions.

There is a reciprocal interaction between the development or lack of development of individuals and the cultures or societies to which they belong. Maslow considered that 'Individual and social interests under healthy social conditions are synergic and not antagonistic' (1970, p. 85). The multicultural literature must continue addressing how cultures differ in being encouraging, benign, inhibiting or antagonistic to developing both the basic lifeskills and the higher potentials of their members.

CULTURE AND VALUES

One of the main dimensions of a culture is that of values or the underlying principles that guide how people live their lives. However, there is no exact relationship between how people think they ought to behave, their values, and their actual behaviour.

UNIVERSAL VALUES

Schwartz is a prominent researcher in the area of values (Schwartz, 1992; Schwartz and Bilsky, 1990). He classified values into ten types: power, achievement, hedonism, stimulation, self-direction, universalism, benevolence, tradition, conformity and security. Based on information from 20 countries in six continents, Schwartz (1992) confirmed that each of the ten values was found in at least 90 per cent of the countries he surveyed, suggesting that his value types are near universal.

CULTURAL DIMENSIONS

One of the major cross-cultural research endeavours in recent years was the collection of data on work-related attitudes in 50 countries and three regions by the Dutch psychologist Hofstede (1980, 1983). Hofstede identified four cultural dimensions or factors in those countries and regions (see Box 16.1).

BOX 16.1   HOFSTEDE'S FOUR CULTURAL DIMENSIONS

- *Power-distance* refers to social inequality and the amount of authority one person has over others.
- *Uncertainty avoidance* relates to how a culture deals with conflict, especially the creation of beliefs and institutions to deal with disagreements and aggression.
- *Individualism versus collectivism* – individualistic cultures are those in which people only care for themselves and their close relations. In collectivistic cultures, people belong to in-groups or collectives that care for them in return for loyalty.
- *Masculinity-femininity* refers to two opposite sets of cultural values. In masculine cultures, the dominant values are success and money. In feminine cultures, the dominant values evolve around caring for others and quality of life.

Australia was one of the countries Hofstede studied. Of the four dimensions, Australia, relative to other countries, scored very high on individualism, mid-range on uncertainty avoidance and masculinity-femininity, and relatively low on power distance. Southeast Asian countries like Hong Kong, Malaysia and Singapore scored high to very high on power distance, high on uncertainty avoidance and collectivism, and mid-range on masculinity-femininity.

ASIAN VALUES

In Britain, the two main ethnic minorities stem from Southern Asia: namely, Indians and Pakistanis. In Australia, the two main migrant groups are Northeast Asian and Southeast Asian. Though here I present two overlapping versions of Asian values, in reality there are numerous differences between Asian countries and within the populations of each country.

Laungani (1999a) suggests that there are four interrelated core values of factors that distinguish Western from Eastern cultures. In particularly, he focuses on differences between British and Indian cultures. Laungani stresses that the two concepts underlying each of the factors summarized in Box 16.2 should be regarded as extending along a continuum rather than as dichotomous. Note that the one factor which overlaps with Hofstede's four dimensions is that of Individualism–Communalism (Collectivism), which is perhaps the most frequently cited value differentiating Western from Eastern cultures.

BOX 16.2   LAUNGANI'S FOUR CORE VALUES OR FACTORS DISTINGUISHING WESTERN (BRITISH) FROM EASTERN (INDIAN) CULTURES

INDIVIDUALISM – COMMUNALISM (COLLECTIVISM)

Individualism emphasizes self-control, personal responsibility, self-achievement, individuals achieving an identity, and nuclear families.

Communalism (Collectivism) emphasizes dependence on elders and other family members, collective responsibility, collective achievement, family and caste-related identity ascribed at birth, and extended families.

COGNITIVISM – EMOTIONALISM

Cognitivism emphasizes rationality and logic, keeping feelings and emotions in check, work and activity, and relationships based on shared interests.

Emotionalism emphasizes feelings and intuition, expressing emotions openly, relationships as extremely important, and relationships being caste- and family-based.

FREE WILL – DETERMINISM

Free will emphasizes freedom of choice, being proactive, success or failure largely due to effort, self-blame or guilt as a residual consequence of failure, and the possibility of failure leading to blaming the victim.

Determinism emphasizes limited freedom of choice, being reactive, despite success being important it is related to one's karma, no guilt is attached to failure, and no blame is attached to the victim.

MATERIALISM – SPIRITUALISM

Materialism emphasizes the world as 'real' and physical, rejection of contradictory explanations of phenomena, reality is external to the individual and it is perceived through the scientific enterprise.

Spiritualism emphasizes the world as illusory, the co-existence of contradictory phenomena, reality being internal to the individual, and reality being perceived through contemplation and inner reflection.

Ho (1992) lists seven values held in common by Asian cultures that may be operating among Asian Americans, who are predominantly from Southeast and Northeast Asia. These values, which overlap with Laungani's Eastern (Indian) values, are also likely to be held by Southeast Asian and Northeast Asian migrants to Australia. Following is a summary of Ho's seven Asian values.

1. *Filial piety*, or a high degree of respect for parents.
2. *Shame*, or loss of face used as a method of reinforcing proper behaviour.
3. *Self-control*, requiring modesty in behaviour, humbleness in expectations, and hesitation, even when individuals highly desire an object.
4. *Assumption of the middle position*, or the Asian emphasis on consensus as a process that fosters the individual's sense of belonging and togetherness.
5. *Awareness of the social milieu*, involving an awareness and sensitivity to others' opinions and feelings and being prepared to subordinate one's feelings in the interests of solidarity.
6. *Fatalism*, a belief system that accepts events as predetermined.
7. *Inconspicuousness*, based on the fear of attracting attention.

One of the issues of any migrant group is the extent to which the values of the parents who originally migrated are held by their children and grandchildren. Laungani provides some research evidence indicating that maintenance of parental values is the case among British born Indian school children. However, a greater degree of assimilation into mainstream British culture is likely as the generations become further removed from their original migrant ancestors.

Often, conflicts arise *between* migrants, who value their cultures of origin, and their children, who are under considerable pressure to adapt to their host cultures. These conflicts are heightened because the children of migrants often perceive young people in Western cultures as being more independent and free than those in Eastern cultures. Conflicts inevitably also take place *within* the hearts and souls of migrants and their children, all of whom, in varying degrees and in differing ways, experience the pulls and pushes of being caught between two cultures.

THEORETICAL ASSUMPTIONS OF ASIAN THERAPIES

In the above discussion on values, it is apparent that assumptions underlying Asian approaches to therapy will differ from those underlying Western approaches. Arguably, Western therapists have paid too little attention to higher levels of human functioning and contemplation. Wilber (2000) suggests that there are three broad stages of development: pre-personal, personal and transpersonal, also called pre-conventional, conventional, and post-conventional. Limitations on conventional development have been the focus of Western psychotherapy. Walsh (2014) considers that, while capable of addressing lower levels, Asian psychotherapies aim primarily at post-conventional growth and the transpersonal domains.

The concepts of mind and of mental development are central to under-standing Asian therapies, whose starting point is that people's usual state of mind is underdeveloped. Because this state of affairs is so widespread, it often goes unnoticed. People suffer from a case of mistaken identity in that their true nature is something far more remarkable that the self-concept of 'ego' that they mistakenly assume to be their true selves. Psychological suffering is the result of insufficient mental development. It is possible to train and develop the mind both to reduce conventional self-created suffering and to develop supra-normal or post-conventional capacities such as heightened concentration and compassion. Meditation and yoga are included among effective ways of training the mind to function at higher levels and to access a vastly greater unconscious system than that offered by Freudian psychology (Walsh, 2014).

CULTURAL IDENTITY DEVELOPMENT

Cultural identity development theory is based on the assumption that indi-viduals in cultural, racial and other minority groups possess varying levels of consciousness or awareness about their membership both of their minority group and of the wider society. In addition, cultural identity development theory is relevant to mainstream or majority groups in relation to themselves, minority groups and the wider culture.

Helms (1995) presents two racial identity models for the United States, one for members of the white majority culture and another for people of colour. She assumes that whites and coloured people have to work through issues of racism in different ways: for example, many, though not all, whites may start by assuming entitlement to the privileges society offers and many non-whites may perceive their position as one of being oppressed and excluded from equal opportunity. For Helms, the most highly developed white people attain an 'autonomy status', involving an informed and positive commit-ment to racial equality and the capacity to give up the privileges of racism. The most highly developed coloured people attain the 'integrative awareness status' involving a capacity to value their own collective identities as well as the ability to empathize and collaborate with members of other oppressed groups.

A five-stage model of cultural identity development focused on minority rather than majority groups is presented by Cheatham and his colleagues (1997). In this model people start by being 'asleep' in that they have little awareness of themselves as cultural beings and progress to attaining a level of consciousness in which they both possess a knowledgeable pride about their culture and recognize positive dimensions of the mainstream culture. Cheatham and his colleagues' model is summarized in Box 16.3. The model can be extended to deal with the consciousness-raising of other minority groups such as women, and gays and lesbians.

BOX 16.3   A MODEL OF CULTURAL IDENTITY DEVELOPMENT

STAGE 1: NAIVETY

Individuals have little awareness of themselves as cultural beings: for example, children do not distinguish skin colour as an important feature.

STAGE 2: ENCOUNTER

Individuals encounter experiences in their environments that clearly demonstrate that their earlier naïve views were inadequate.

STAGE 3: NAMING

Naming involves identifying one's cultural or minority group and the nature of oppression against it, for instance, Afro-Caribbean-British, Indian-British or Vietnamese-Australian and racism; gays and lesbians and homophobia; women and sexism.

STAGE 4: REFLECTION ON SELF AS A CULTURAL BEING

Individuals develop a keener awareness of themselves as Afro-Caribbean-British, Indian-British or Vietnamese-Australian. Individuals may turn inwards towards their own cultures and away from the majority culture. The developmental task is establishing a definite cultural consciousness.

STAGE 5: MULTI-PERSPECTIVE INTERNALIZATION

Individuals develop pride in their culture, yet accept worthwhile dimensions of the predominant culture. They can use important dimensions of all stages of development.

Therapists and trainees can assess their own level of cultural identity development and, where necessary, take steps to improve their level of awareness of themselves as cultural beings. Therapists need also be aware of their clients' level of cultural identity and, where appropriate, use this knowledge to assist them in attaining higher levels of cultural consciousness. However, therapists need to be careful not to impose cultural agendas on those clients whose concerns lie elsewhere, for instance passing an upcoming test.

A THEORY OF MULTICULTURAL COUNSELLING AND THERAPY

Sue et al. (1996) consider current theories of counselling and therapy too ethnocentric and mono-cultural and lacking conceptual frameworks that incorporate culture as a core concept in the therapeutic relationship. They propose a meta-theory or theory about theories that they call Multicultural Counselling and Therapy (MCT). This meta-theory is intended to offer a framework for understanding the numerous helping approaches that have been developed in both Western and non-Western cultures.

MCT consists of six propositions, each of which has corollaries. The first proposition is that MCT is a meta-theory. The second proposition stresses that therapist and client identities are embedded in many levels of experience and contexts, for example, individual family and culture, and that the totality of these experiences must be the focus on treatment. The third proposition emphasizes the importance of the development of therapist and client cultural identity, including attitudes about dominant–subordinate relationships among culturally different groups. The fourth proposition is that MCT theory is likely to be enhanced when therapists define goals and use modalities consistent with the life experiences and cultural values of their clients. The fifth proposition stresses the importance of multiple helping roles, often involving larger social units, developed by culturally different groups. The final proposition emphasizes that the liberation of consciousness is a basic MCT goal. For example, to develop in clients a critical consciousness, therapists, who draw on both Western and non-Western systems of helping, may often teach clients about the underlying cultural dimensions of their present concerns.

THERAPY

THERAPEUTIC GOALS

There are many different client groups for whom cultural considerations are important: for example, indigenous people, such as Australian Aborigines and Torres Strait Islanders; first generation migrants, with many different reasons for seeking out a life in a new country; descendents of migrants at varying levels of assimilation to the mainstream culture; and members of the mainstream culture, among others. Following are some goals, which may overlap, for working with clients in whose problems issues of culture play a significant role:

- *Support*: Migrants require culture-sensitive support when they first arrive in their new home countries. Think of the cumulative stresses involved in moving to a new culture including change of home, parting from loved ones and previous support networks, language difficulties, climate change, change in physical environment (for instance the countryside and buildings look different), homesickness, loneliness, financial worries, concerns about children's education, and, for many migrants, racist incidents.
- *Dealing with post-traumatic stress*: Many migrants are refugees and some suffer from post-traumatic stress disorders. Reasons for their traumatization include being war victims, witnessing violence, and living through missile attacks, torture, starvation, imprisonment, internment, and rape. Such migrants, may suffer persistent re-experiencing of traumatic events, hyper-arousal, numbing of affect, or oscillate between hyper-arousal and numbing of affect. Traumatized migrants, with their families and support networks, require special culture-sensitive post-traumatic stress disorder therapy.

- *Assisting acculturation and assimilation*: The multicultural literature is often overly negative about the virtues of mainstream cultures such as those in Britain, Australia and America. In addition much the literature seems to insufficiently address the need for cultural cohesion as well as for cultural diversity. Most migrants move because the perceived benefits of their new countries far outweigh those of their former ones. Migration can be a time of great opportunity. However, it is also a time of considerable challenges. Migrants require practical help with such matters as housing, health, education, and employment. Furthermore, all migrants bring psychological strengths and deficiencies to their transitions to a new culture. Some may require culturally sensitive psychological assistance so as not to activate self-defeating patterns for dealing with change and stress, for instance withdrawal, being unwilling to alter old ways of behaving, and aggressively disparaging their new countries.
- *Assisting clients to handle cross-cultural relationships*: Difficulties in cross-cultural relationships can take many forms. Therapists can assist existing members of host countries and first generation migrants to develop skills for accepting difference, reaching out to one another, and for building bridges rather than barriers between cultures. Therapists may also need skills in assisting migrants and their children deal with issues of intergenerational conflict, for instance choice of boyfriends/girlfriends. In a country like Australia, where cross-cultural relationships are common, therapeutic goals can also include helping partners in intimate relationships to understand and accommodate to one another's cultural differences.
- *Consciousness raising and liberation*: For those clients who suffer from discrimination and oppression on account of culture and race, therapeutic goals can and should address issues of cultural identity development. Some readers may also wish to review Box 16.3. Ethnic minority clients can be assisted to take pride in their cultures, liberate themselves from internalized negative stereotypes, and join the broader struggle against external oppression on account of culture and race. Consciousness raising and liberation can also be important therapeutic goals for mainstream culture clients, who require assistance in relinquishing negative aspects of their enculturation, such as a false sense of cultural and racial superiority. Some mainstream culture clients may then also participate in the fight for cultural and racial equality.
- *Avoiding further marginalization*: Therapists need to be aware that, if they pursue cultural agendas clumsily, they can do more harm than good. Where appropriate, therapists can and should help ethnic minority group clients be assertive about attaining their human rights. However, there is a danger that therapists collude when some minority clients further marginalize themselves by unfairly 'demonizing' their host cultures, making their lives out to be worse than they are, and playing the psychological game of 'Ain't it awful', at the same time as doing little positive to change their situations. When dealing with issues of acculturation and change, people of all cultures and races can be inflexible and self-defeating.
- *Attaining higher levels of development*: The goals of some culturally different clients may be more oriented towards growth rather than adaptation to a mainstream culture. What constitutes higher levels of development can vary according to culture and to the therapeutic approach employed. For instance, Eastern cultures stress heightened concentration, mental purification, kindness, compassion, sympathetic joy in one another's accomplishments, equanimity, wisdom and selfless service (Walsh, 2014).
- *The good society*: Arredondo et al. (2008) observe that the etiology of a client's distress is not simply an intrapsychic phenomenon but often a sociocultural and environmental

one. A broader goal of multicultural counselling and psychotherapy is to develop formal and informal norms within societies that are synergistic rather than antagonistic to developing the full human potential of all members. This goal requires therapists to play social engineering and change agent roles, especially in regard to combating institutions and organizations that are instruments of cultural and racial oppression.

THERAPEUTIC APPROACHES

As may be seen from the above list of goals, there are many different considerations in selecting therapeutic approaches for problems that contain a significant cultural component. Also, 'Remember that multicultural clients prefer clinicians to be culturally competent, not necessarily ethnically matched' (Comas-Diaz, 2012). The issue of culturally relevant counselling and therapy can be addressed in at least three different ways: first, by making existing Euro-American therapies more culture-sensitive; second, by therapists developing multicultural counselling and therapy competencies; and third, by engaging in non-Western approaches to counselling and therapy.

MAKING EXISTING EURO-AMERICAN THERAPIES MORE CULTURE-SENSITIVE

To what extent can cultural issues be addressed by modifying the theory and practice of existing Western counselling and therapy approaches so that they become more culture-sensitive? The following discussion addresses some issues in applying person-centred and the cognitive behaviour therapies to minority group and mainstream culture clients.

With mainstream culture clients, person-centred therapists can use Rogerian empathy to assist them to experience and explore their cultural and racial concerns. However, this will only happen in those instances where clients have sufficient awareness and interest to work on such issues. The person-centred concept of empathy can be expanded to include cultural empathy (Ridley and Lingle, 1996). Person-centred therapists who see themselves and their clients as cultural beings can encourage non-Western clients to share their experiences by such methods as listening carefully for and responding to culturally relevant cues rather than not attending to them and also by openly acknowledging that they are from a different culture and then asking their client's assistance in understanding the cultural context of their concerns. When clients reveal experiences, therapists can consciously try to understand the cultural implications of clients' communications. Furthermore, when therapists respond they can be tentative in checking out the extent of their cultural understanding.

There are barriers to Western therapists being perceived as empathic by ethnic minority clients (Laungani, 1999b, Sue and Sue, 2013). For example, Asian clients want to perceive their therapists as expert and expect more direction from them. Furthermore, Asian clients may be reluctant to talk about their problems outside of their families. Communication may be made even more difficult because clients and therapists may not understand the meanings and nuances of one another's spoken and non-verbal communication. In addition, there is a distinct possibility that the Western therapist does not understand the Asian client's cultural worldview, including the importance attached to family relationships, and may project parts of her/his own worldview onto the client. These difficulties can be addressed to some extent, if person-centred therapists, or any other therapists for that matter, are trained to understand the cultures and communication styles of one or more specific cultural groups from whom many of their clients come. However, really getting to grips with the mind-set of any foreign culture is much easier said than done. Ideally, learning about another culture in depth requires learning the relevant language and spending much time immersed in that culture.

The cognitive behaviour therapies provide another example of how it is possible to extend existing Euro-American therapeutic approaches to become more culture-sensitive. Such therapies can be used to help both mainstream clients and minority group clients to think more rationally and realistically regarding culture and race. However there is a paucity of literature regarding how to do this and where the cross-cultural difficulties lie.

Regarding rational emotive behaviour therapy, Ellis (Ellis, 1998) included racial prejudice in his list of prejudice-related irrationalities. In REBT, clients' cultural and racial irrational beliefs and prejudices can be detected, disputed and, where appropriate, restated in preferential and rational terms. Similarly, in cognitive therapy, questioning by skilled therapists can assist clients to identify their underlying cultural and racial automatic thoughts, explore how realistic they are, and formulate more realistic thoughts and perceptions for the future. Regarding multimodal therapy, Palmer (2000) claims it is sufficiently flexible to use with most ethnic minority clients suffering from stress.

MULTICULTURAL COUNSELLING AND THERAPY COMPETENCIES

An American approach to issues of culture and race in counselling and therapy has been to develop a statement of multicultural counselling competencies for culturally skilled counsellors and therapists (Sue et al. 1998). This statement is the work of a committee of the American Psychological Association's Division of Counseling Psychology (since 2003, Society of Counseling Psychology). The committee saw multicultural counselling competencies as having three main dimensions: awareness of own assumptions, values and biases; understanding the worldview of the culturally different client; and developing appropriate strategies and techniques. Each dimension is divided into beliefs and attitudes, knowledge and skills. The United States has a long history of serious, and often brutal, racial oppression that provided one of the main contexts in which this statement was compiled. One of the statement's major assumptions was that of widespread and systematic cultural and racial oppression.

AWARENESS OF OWN ASSUMPTIONS, VALUES AND BIASES

The beliefs held by culturally skilled counsellors and therapists include being sensitive to their own cultural heritage, being comfortable with the differences of clients from other cultures and races, and recognizing the limitations of their competence and expertise. Counsellors and therapists should know about their cultural and racial heritage and how this affects the therapeutic process, understand how oppression, racism and discrimination may affect them personally and in their work, and know about the impact of how they communicate on culturally different clients. Skills include seeking out relevant educational and training experiences, actively understanding oneself as a cultural and racial being, and seeking a non-racial identity.

UNDERSTANDING THE WORLDVIEW OF THE CULTURALLY DIFFERENT CLIENT

Beliefs and attitudes for culturally skilled counsellors and therapists include being aware of their negative emotional reactions and of the stereotypes and preconceived notions that they may hold towards culturally and racially different groups. Therapists should know about the cultural experiences, cultural heritage and historical backgrounds of any particular group with whom they work, acknowledge how culture and race can affect help-seeking behaviour, know how culture and race can influence assessment and the selection and implementation of therapeutic interventions, and know about the oppressive political and environmental influences impinging on the lives of ethnic and racial minorities. Skills include keeping up to date on research findings relevant to the psychological wellbeing of various ethnic and racial groups as well as being actively involved with minorities outside work settings to gain deeper insight into their perspectives.

DEVELOPING APPROPRIATE INTERVENTION STRATEGIES AND TECHNIQUES

Culturally skilled counsellors' and therapists' attitudes and beliefs include respecting clients' religious and spiritual beliefs about physical and mental functioning, respecting indigenous helping practices, and valuing bilingualism. Their knowledge base includes understanding how the culture bound, class bound and monolingual characteristics of counselling clash with the cultural values of various minority groups, being aware of institutional barriers to minority groups using helping services, knowing about the potential for bias in assessment instruments, and understanding minority group family structures, hierarchies, and community characteristics and resources. Skills include the ability to send and receive verbal and non-verbal communication accurately, interacting in the language requested by clients or making appropriate referrals, tailoring the therapeutic relationship and interventions to the clients' stage of cultural and racial identity development, and engaging in a variety of helping roles, beyond being a therapist. Box 16.4 identifies some of these additional helping roles (Atkinson, Thompson and Grant, 1993; Sue and Sue, 2013; Sue et al., 1996).

BOX 16.4   ADDITIONAL ROLES FOR MULTICULTURAL COUNSELLORS AND THERAPISTS

1. *Adviser*: Advising clients how to solve or prevent problems and providing relevant information.
2. *Advocate*: Representing and speaking up for clients' best interests to other individuals, groups or organizations.
3. *Facilitator of indigenous support systems*: Knowing about and appropriately involving support systems, such as the client's extended family and community elders.
4. *Facilitator of indigenous healing systems*: Either referring clients to healers or, if sufficiently knowledgeable and skilled, actually using the indigenous healing methods.
5. *Consultant*: Working collegially with clients to impact or change a third party, including organizational change.
6. *Change agent*: Initiating and implementing action-oriented approaches to changing social environments that may be oppressing clients.

The statement of multicultural competencies is ambitious and has much to recommend it. However, possible reservations include the following. The statement assumes a high degree of cultural and racial oppression by the white mainstream culture, which may not be true in all instances. For example, some of the strongest supporters of minority group rights are white people. Furthermore, many white people are tolerant of and some are very positive about cultural differences, as witnessed by the growing number of cultural and racial intermarriages in countries such as Australia and America (Kerwin and Ponterotto, 1995). In addition, cultural and racial biases are not the sole preserve of white people, and this fact should be more openly acknowledged and addressed.

Despite these reservations, in countries like Britain, Australia and America, both obvious and less obvious oppression of cultural and racial minorities definitely exists. All therapists, regardless of their culture and race, need to address their own level of cultural identity development and their ability to offer culturally sensitive services to all clients, be they from minority groups or from the mainstream culture.

NON-WESTERN APPROACHES TO COUNSELLING AND THERAPY

Non-Western therapies come from many cultures – for instance, Asian and African. Such therapies may be the treatment of choice not only for some ethnic minority group clients, but also for some mainstream culture clients. Sue and Sue (2013) suggest that therapists should also be willing to consult with traditional healers or make use of their services.

Laungani writes of psychotherapy in the East:

> Although western models of therapy continue to be used among the small Westernized clientele to be found mainly in large metropolitan cities, the therapists in Eastern cultures have almost reinvented their ancient indigenous approaches, which range from Astrology and Palmistry, Ayurvedic and Homeopathic treatment, religious therapy pilgrimages, shamanism and exorcism, to yogic exercises and meditation. (2004a, p. 205)

He stresses that these approaches are in keeping with the fundamental value systems of Eastern thinking, including communalism, determinism, emotionalism and spiritualism. The philosophy of individualism, so prominent in Western thinking, holds little sway in Eastern thinking.

In Asia, there is a long tradition of training the mind to foster interdependence, minimize suffering and create happiness. The main teaching of Buddhism, which is a system of psychology as well as a religion, can be summarized in the Buddha's statement: 'Refrain from evil, do good and purify the mind'. Here I use meditation and Naikan therapy to illustrate some Asian approaches to therapy.

MEDITATION

Meditation is a main Asian religious and therapeutic approach. It falls into two main categories: mindfulness of breathing or breath meditation and awareness or insight meditation. All meditation approaches require practice, with perseverance increasing the likelihood of better results. Meditation can be significantly enhanced by attending retreats in which clients engage in continuous meditation practice for days or weeks.

Breathing meditation consists of relaxed concentration on the flow of your breathing, on the in-breaths and on the out-breaths. Breathing meditation may be performed sitting, standing, walking or reclining. Buddhist insight meditations include calmly becoming aware of the impermanence of whatever experiences and sensations arise and meditations that cultivate the four divine abodes of mind – loving kindness, compassion, sympathy and equanimity (Thitavanno, 1995, 2002).

Walsh (2014) observes that meditation can lead to a wide variety of insights and experiences over time. For instance, many clients gain insight into their customary lack of mental control or 'monkey minds'. Meditators come to recognize that everything in their mind is in a state of constant change and that the notion of an unchanging self, or even a self for that matter, is an illusory construction. With this insight egocentricity may be lessened and compassionate identification with others may increase. In advanced states of meditation, supra-normal capacities emerge such as heightened concentration, perceptual sensitivity, and profound peace.

NAIKAN THERAPY

Naikan therapy is a Japanese approach adapted from a more intensive Buddhist meditation practice (Reynolds, 1990). It is aimed at assisting clients to find meaning in their lives, recognize human interdependence, feel and show gratitude, and repair relationships. Naikan therapy assumes that narrowly focusing on oneself creates suffering both for oneself and others.

Clients are encouraged to establish a calm meditative state and then to reflect specifically on three things:

- what another person or other people have done for them,
- how much gratitude is due to them, and
- the difficulties they have caused others and how little they have demonstrated gratitude.

Naikan therapy can elicit various thoughts and feelings, for instance guilt and unworthiness. However, many clients also get in touch with kinder and more generous feelings towards their caregivers. Clients may realize that, despite their weaknesses and failings, they were looked after and helped. Furthermore, they may start feeling very grateful to people in their pasts and want to make amends for their own inadequacies towards them.

CONCLUSION

At present, the main cultures of Britain, Australia and America are insufficiently conducive to developing the full human potential of their members, and this is especially true for those in cultural, racial and other minority groups. The development of culture-sensitive counselling and psychotherapy should not be restricted to any one of the three broad approaches mentioned above. Also, therapists may combine their use of ethnic, indigenous and alternative practices with mainstream treatment (Comas-Diaz, 2012).

Existing Euro-American therapies require further development to deal with the cultural issues pertaining to both minority and mainstream groups. All counsellors and therapists need to develop a set of core multicultural competencies as well as competencies specific to the main ethnic minority and racial groups with which they interact. Much more work is needed in defining, researching and providing good training materials that illustrate these core and culture specific therapeutic competencies. In addition, greater attention needs to be paid to raising Western therapists' awareness of non-Western therapies. Furthermore more research needs to be conducted into the effectiveness of these therapies, either on their own or in combination with Western therapies, with clients from a range of cultures. East, West,

North and South can learn therapeutic insights and skills from one another to the benefit of all.

REVIEW AND PERSONAL QUESTIONS

REVIEW QUESTIONS

1. What is the meaning of each of the following terms?

   - culture
   - enculturation
   - acculturation
   - culture shock
   - cultural change
   - multiculturalism
   - cultural cohesion
   - race
   - ethnic minority?

2. Describe and evaluate each of the following:

   - Schwartz's universal value types
   - Hofstede's four cultural dimensions
   - Laungani's and Ho's views of Asian values.

3. Critically discuss Cheatham et al.'s views of cultural identity development.
4. Critically discuss the goals for culture-sensitive therapy presented in the chapter.
5. What are some ways of making existing Euro-American therapies more culture sensitive?
6. What are multicultural counselling and therapy competencies? What is your reaction to Sue et al.'s statement of competencies?
7. What are some non-Western approaches to counselling and therapy?

PERSONAL QUESTIONS

1. How would you describe

   - the culture of your ancestral background
   - if an ethnic minority group member, the distinguishing features of your culture
   - for all readers, the distinctive features of the mainstream culture in which you live?

2. To what extent do you consider the values you hold are universal and to what extent do you consider they are specific to your culture? Give reasons for your answer.
3. Describe instances, if any, in which you have been

   - the recipient of cultural and/or racial oppression
   - the purveyor of cultural and/or racial oppression.

4. What is your level of cultural identity development? Provide reasons for your answer.
5. To what extent and how can the main counselling and therapy approach you use be adapted for culturally different clients?
6. How can make yourself a more culturally sensitive counsellor or therapist both now and in future?

ANNOTATED BIBLIOGRAPHY

Walsh, R. (2014) Contemplative psychotherapies. In D. Wedding and R. J. Corsini (eds) *Current Psychotherapies* (10th ed.). Belmont, CA: Brooks/Cole, pp. 411–60.
This chapter focuses on contemplation, especially meditation. It shows how contemplative practices can be used by clients, therapists and others to enhance psychological wellbeing and growth, including at higher levels. The chapter includes a case example.

Comas-Diaz, L. (2012) *Multicultural Care: A Clinician's Guide to Cultural Competence.* Washington, DC: American Psychological Association.
This book begins with cultural self-assessment. It then covers such issues as multicultural assessment, cultural analysis, multicultural therapeutic relationships, psychopharmacology, and multicultural treatment – both fostering empowerment and incorporating culture-specific healing. The book ends with a chapter on multicultural consciousness.

Palmer, S. and Laungani, P. (eds) (1999) *Counselling in a Multicultural Society.* London: Sage.
This many authored British book contains eight chapters on such topics as the challenges of counselling in a multiracial society, culture and identity, racial issues, models of counselling and therapy for a multiethnic society, counselling needs of ethnic minorities, client centred or culture centred counselling, and the search for effective counselling across cultures.

D'Ardenne, P. (2013) *Counselling in Transcultural Settings: Priorities for a Restless World.* London: Sage.
Among the issues covered in this book are: anti-discriminatory practice; transcultural counselling for international workers and for refugees; using interpreters; transcultural counselling concerning religion and spirituality and in healthcare; ethics, supervision, and an evidence base for transcultural counselling; and future directions.

D'Ardenne, P. and Mahtani, A. (1999) *Transcultural Counselling in Action* (2nd ed.). London: Sage.
This book is written by two clinical psychologists, one with a white English and the other with an Indian background, working in London's East End. The book introduces the concept of transcultural counselling and then reviews practical issues concerned with clients, counsellors, starting the counselling process, sharing a common language, the therapeutic relationship, change and growth, and ending counselling. The book is illustrated by four case studies with clients with Bangladeshi, English, French and Nigerian cultural backgrounds.

Sue, D. W. and Sue, D. (2013) *Counseling the Culturally Diverse: Theory and Practice* (6th ed.). New York: John Wiley.

This book is focused on the United States. Section One deals with the multiple dimensions of multicultural counselling and therapy. Section Two focuses on multicultural counselling and specific populations.

REFERENCES AND FURTHER READING

Arredondo, P., Tovar-Blank, Z. G. and Parham, T. A. (2008) Challenges and promises of becoming a culturally competent counselor in a sociopolitical era of change and empowerment. *Journal of Counseling & Development, 86,* 261–8.

Atkinson, D. R., Thompson, C. E. and Grant, S. K. (1993). A three dimensional model for counseling racial/ethnic minorities. *The Counseling Psychologist, 21,* 257–77.

Australian Bureau of Statistics (2012) Information available on the Internet.

Cheatham, H., Ivey, A. E., Ivey, M. B., Pedersen, P., Rigazio-DiGillio, S., Simek-Morgan, L., and Sue, D. W. (1997) Multicultural Counselling and Therapy: 1. Metatheory – Taking theory into practice; 2. Integrative practice. In A. E. Ivey, M. B. Ivey and L. Simek-Morgan, *Counseling and Psychotherapy: A Multicultural Perspective* (4th ed.) Boston, MA: Allyn & Bacon, pp. 133–205.

Comas-Diaz, L (2012) *Multicultural Care: A Clinician's Guide to Cultural Competence.* Washington, DC: American Psychological Association.

Corey, G. (2009) *Theory and Practice of Counseling & Psychotherapy* (8th ed.). Belmont, CA: Thomson Brooks/Cole.

Cross, T. L., Bazron, B. J., Dennis, K. W. and Isaacs, M. R. (1989) *Towards a Culturally Competent System of Care.* Washington, DC: Child and Adolescent Service System Technical Assistance Centre.

D'Ardenne, P. (2013) *Counselling in Transcultural Settings: Priorities for a Restless World.* London: Sage.

D'Ardenne, P. and Mahtani, A. (1999) *Transcultural Counselling in Action* (2nd ed.). London: Sage.

Ellis, A. (1998) The biological basis of human irrationality. In A. Ellis and S. Blau (eds) *The Albert Ellis Reader.* Secaucus, NJ: Citadel, pp. 271–91.

Helms, J. E. (1995) An update of Helms's white and people of color racial identity models. In J. G. Ponterotto, J. M. Casas, L. A. Sizuki and C. M. Alexander (eds), *Handbook of Multicultural Counseling.* Thousand Oaks, CA: Sage, pp. 181–98.

Hermans, H. J. M. and Kempen, H. J. G. (1998) Moving cultures: The perilous problems of cultural dichotomies in a globalizing society. *American Psychologist, 53,* 1111–20.

Ho, M. K. (1992) *Minority Children and Adolescents in Therapy.* Newbury Park, CA: Sage.

Hofstede, G. (1980) *Culture's Consequences: International Differences in Work-Related Values.* London: Sage.

Hofstede, G. (1983) Dimensions of national culture in fifty cultures and three regions. In J. B. Deregowski, S. Dziurawiec and R. C. Annis (eds), *Expiscations in Cross-Cultural Psychology*. Lisse, the Netherlands: Swets & Zeitlinger: Sage, pp. 335–55.

Kerwin, C. and Ponterotto, J. G. (1995) Biracial identity development: theory and research. In J. G. Ponterotto, J. M. Casas, L. A. Sizuki and C. M. Alexander (eds), *Handbook of Multicultural Counseling*. Thousand Oaks, CA: Sage, pp. 199–217.

Laungani, P. (1999a) Culture and identity: Implications for counselling. In S. Palmer and P. Laungani, P. (eds), *Counselling in a Multicultural Society*. London: Sage, pp. 35–70.

Laungani, P. (1999b) Client centred or culture centred counselling. In S. Palmer and P. Laungani (eds), *Counselling in a Multicultural Society*. London: Sage, pp. 135–52.

Laungani, P. (2004a) Counselling and therapy in a multi-cultural setting. *Counselling Psychology Quarterly, 17*, 195–207.

Laungani, P. (2004b) *Asian Perspectives in Counselling and Psychotherapy*. London: Routledge.

Maslow, A. H. (1970) *Motivation and Personality* (2nd ed.). New York: Harper & Row.

Maslow, A. H. (1971) *The Farther Reaches of Human Nature*. Harmondsworth: Penguin Books.

Moodley, R. (2007) (Re)placing multiculturalism in counselling and psycho-therapy. *British Journal of Guidance & Counselling, 35*, 1–21.

Palmer, S. (2000) Developing an individual therapeutic programme suitable for use by counselling psychologists in a multicultural society: A multimodal perspective. *Counselling Psychology Review, 15*, 32–50.

Palmer, S. and Laungani, P. (eds) (1999) *Counselling in a Multicultural Society*. London: Sage.

Reynolds, D. (1990) Morita and Naikan therapies – Similarities. *Journal of Morita Therapy, 1*, 159–63.

Ridley, C. R. and Lingle, D. W. (1996) Cultural empathy in multicultural counseling: A multidimensional process. In P. B. Pedersen, J. G. Draguns, W. J. Lonner and J. E. Trimble (eds), *Counseling Across Cultures* (4th ed.). Thousand Oaks, CA: Sage, pp. 21–46.

Schwartz, S. H. (1992) Universals in the content and structure of values: Theoretical advances and empirical tests in 20 countries. In M. Zanna (ed.), *Advances in Experimental Social Psychology*, Vol. 25, New York: Academic Press, pp. 1–65.

Schwartz, S. H. and Bilsky, W. (1990) Toward a theory of the universal content and structure of human values: Extensions and cross-cultural replications. *Journal of Personality and Social Psychology, 53*, 550–62.

Spindler, G. D. (1963) *Education and Culture: Anthropological Approaches*. New York: Holt, Rinehart & Winston.

Sue, D. W., Carter, R. T., Casas, J. M., Fouad, N. A., Ivey, A. E., Jensen, M., LaFromboise, T., Manese, J. E., Ponterotto, J. G., and Vazquez-Nutall, E. (1998) *Multicultural Counseling Competencies: Individual and Organizational Development*. London: Sage.

Sue, D. W., Ivey, A. E. and Pedersen, P. B. (1996) *A Theory of Multicultural Counseling & Therapy.* Pacific Grove, CA: Brooks/Cole.

Sue, D. W. and Sue, D. (2013) *Counseling the Culturally Diverse: Theory and Practice* (6th ed.). New York: John Wiley.

Thitavanno, P. (1995) *Mind Development.* Bangkok: Mahamakut Buddhist University.

Thitavanno, P. (2002) *A Buddhist Way of Mental Training* (2nd ed.). Bangkok: Chuan Printing Press.

Thomas, T. (2004) Psychology in a culturally diverse society. *Australian Psychologist, 39*(2), 103–6.

United Kingdom Census (2012) Information available on the Internet.

United States Census Bureau (2011) Information available on the Internet.

Walsh, R. (2014) Contemplative psychotherapies. In D. Wedding and R. J. Corsini (eds) *Current Psychotherapies* (10th ed.). Belmont, CA: Brooks/Cole, pp. 411–60.

Wilber, K. (2000) *Integral Psychology.* Boston: Shambala.

GENDER THERAPY ⬤17

INTRODUCTION

This chapter is closely related to the previous one, since cultural issues and gender issues overlap. One of the main functions of enculturation is to transmit gender roles from one generation to another. However, to some extent, peer groups may be taking over from parents in performing this central aspect of enculturation (Maccoby, 1990).

A useful distinction may be made between sex, the biological embodiment of differences between men and women, and gender, the social expectations of the feminine and masculine (Tindall, Robinson and Kagan, 2010). Even experiences that are linked to biological sex, for instance a woman's processes of reproduction and fertility, are also socially constructed and, thus, linked to their gender. Both feminist and men's counselling and psychotherapy aim to bring about equality in personal power between men and women and challenge culturally prescribed sex roles.

Gender can be an important aspect of cultural change and conflict, with the changes in women's roles affecting men and vice versa. Many British, Australian and American women strongly feel that they, like ethnic and racial minorities, are oppressed by white male dominated mainstream cultures. An American Psychological Association report on 'Guidelines for Psychological Practice With Girls and Women' has as its first guideline 'Psychologists strive to be aware of socialization, stereotyping, and unique life events on the development of girls and women across diverse cultural groups' (American Psychological Association, 2007, p. 960).

Cultural change can also influence how people learn gender roles: for example, with the movement from agrarian economies stemming from the industrial revolution, many men have spent less time with their families and local communities to the possible psychological impoverishment of all concerned.

THE TERMINOLOGY OF GENDER

Like the terms associated with culture, many of the terms associated with gender possess different shadings of meaning according to who is doing the defining. Below is an introduction to some key terms:

- *Sex*: In this context sex refers to biological aspects about being male or female such as differences in genitals, reproductive functioning, bone structure and size.
- *Gender*: Gender refers to 'psychological, social, and cultural experiences and characteristics associated with the biological aspects of being female or male' (American Psychological Association, 2007, p. 959).
- *Gender role*: The role that a person adopts or that is ascribed to her/him on the dimensions of 'femininity' and 'masculinity'. The concept of gender role incorporates the power relations between men and women.
- *Gender role identity*: The term gender role identity relates to how a person views herself or himself on the dimensions of 'femininity' and 'masculinity'.
- *Gender role socialization*: The processes of enculturation whereby children and adults acquire, internalize and maintain the characteristics, attitudes, values and behaviours associated with femininity, masculinity or a mixture of both.
- *Gender role conflict*: The most common form of gender role conflict within a person is where the gender role the individual either adopts or wishes to adopt is at variance with the gender role prescribed by their culture or reference group. Gender role conflicts between people relate to differences in perceptions regarding appropriate gender roles: for example, different ideas between partners in dual career couples.
- *Sexism*: Sexism refers to external oppression on account of a person's biological sex. Such oppression includes discrimination and/or the systematic denial of resources and can be blatant or subtle (American Psychological Association, 2007). In turn, sexism can become internalized self-oppression. *Individual sexism* relates to any thoughts, feelings and actions that assume the superiority of one sex over the other. *Institutional or organizational sexism* relates to political, institutional and organizational structures that discriminate against, oppress and devalue a person on the grounds of sex. *Heterosexism* extends sexism to focus on individuals and organizations that assume the superiority of heterosexual thoughts, feelings and actions over homosexual or bisexual thoughts, feelings and actions.

THEORY

BIOLOGY AND GENDER

Do gender role differences reflect nature rather than nurture? Underlying the issue of gender roles is the extent to which the sexes are biologically similar. From the viewpoint of evolutionary psychology men and women should share the same characteristics in those situations where they have faced the same or similar adaptive problems. However, men and women would evolve different characteristics in situations where their adaptive demands substantially diverge (Buss, 1995; Darwin, 1871). For example, from the viewpoint of the male, sexual selection involves successfully out-competing members of one's own sex to gain access to more numerous or more desirable mates. From, a female viewpoint sexual selection might involve identifying males willing and able to supply resources and protection through pregnancy and lactation.

Evolutionary psychology emphasizes the interaction between the biological and the social rather than assuming that biological characteristics between the sexes are immutable. For example, the primary difference in the trend towards small changes in cognitive abilities between the sexes is in the area of spatial ability, which is important to being a skilled hunter. However, as men evolve in societies that do not require hunting as a survival skill, this sex difference could gradually diminish.

Moir and Jessell review research indicating that from birth males and females are different. The main behavioural difference is the natural, innate aggression of men. These authors present evidence that the sexes are different because their brains are different and observe: 'To maintain that they are the same in aptitude, skill or behaviour is to build a society based on a biological and scientific lie' (Moir and Jessel, 1989, p. 5). Moir and Jessell report men as being better than women in skills requiring spatial ability. Both aggression and spatial ability skills are characteristics that may originate in male roles at earlier stages of evolution.

There are at least three possibilities for how the nature–nurture controversy can be positively resolved. One possibility is that 'masculinity' and 'femininity' become outmoded concepts because further research indicates that the two sexes are biologically highly similar. Another possibility is that additional research supports Moir and Jessell's assertion that there are important biological sex differences and that men and women then manage to use each other's strengths for everyone's benefit. Still a third possibility is that, over time, men and women evolve, possibly hastened by appropriate nurturing, so that biological sex differences no longer figure so prominently.

WOMEN AND GENDER ROLES

FEMINISM

Feminism has a long history as the advocacy of women's rights on the grounds of equality between the sexes. Betty Frieden (1963) provided an impetus to the modern women's movement with her seminal book *The Feminine Mystique* chronicling the apathy and frustration of many post-Second World War American wives trapped in comfortable domestic concentration camps. Frieden advocated a new life plan for women that would allow them to use their intelligence, enjoy adult company, and undertake serious careers.

Greer asserts that liberation rather than equality is the goal for feminists. She writes: 'If we accept that men are not free, and that masculinity is as partial an account of maleness as femininity is of femaleness, then equality must be seen as a poor substitute for liberation' (Greer, 1999, p. 395). Liberation entails women defining their own values and proudly asserting genuine life-affirming female, as contrasted with feminine, differences from males. Though not heavily stressed by Greer, women's liberation also entails challenging men to assert life-affirming male differences from females.

The unequal distribution of power is a central issue in feminist thinking. While Freud thought that females envied males because they possessed penises, the neo-Freudian analyst Karen Horney considered their envy as being about men's greater power and status in society (Chaplin, 1999).

Over time, the nature of feminist therapy has become more diverse. Enns (Enns, 1993, 2004; Enns and Sinacore, 2001) has identified eight somewhat overlapping philosophies of feminism that cause practitioners to interpret feminist therapy in different ways. Each of these philosophies has a different view on the sources of oppression and what is needed to bring about substantial social transformation (Herlihy and Corey, 2009).

- *Liberal feminists* see women deserving equality because they have the same abilities as men. Major goals of therapy are individual personal empowerment and equality.
- *Cultural feminists* believe in feminizing the culture so that it becomes more nurturing, intuitive, co-operative and relational. A major goal of therapy is the infusion of these feminine values into the culture.
- *Radical feminists* focus on the oppression of women due to patriarchy. Major goals include transforming gender relationships and societal institutions and increasing women's sexual and procreative self-determination.
- *Socialist feminists* consider that solutions to society's problems must take into account class, race, and economics. Their major therapeutic goal is to transform social relationships and institutions.
- *Post-modern feminists* address the issue of what constitutes reality and propose multiple truths as opposed to a single truth. They deconstruct polarities such as masculine–feminine and analyse how such constructs are created.
- *Women of colour feminists* assert that they not only have to deal with gender discrimination, but also with oppression on account of ethnicity, race and class. They consider that feminist theory should pay attention to access to power and privilege and they emphasize activism.
- *Lesbian feminists* sometimes feel that heterosexual feminists do not understand their situation. Lesbian therapists want feminist theory to include an analysis of multiple identities and their relationship to oppression. They also want recognition of the diversity that exists among lesbians.
- *Global-international feminists* take a worldwide perspective and assume that women in different parts of the world live under unique systems of oppression. They challenge Western feminists to understand how racism, sexism, class and economics affect women in different countries.

Despite the fact that there are so many different aspects to feminism, it is still possible to identify a feminist therapist. A feminist therapist believes that gender is central to the practice of therapy and that individual empowerment using feminist therapeutic methods and societal change are crucial goals. Feminist therapists emphasize the commonalities between women while recognizing their different life experiences. However, a large number of women who actively favour women's equality and liberation may not apply the label feminist to themselves. Some of these women even go so far as to hate the word feminism because to them it connotes anger, militancy and lesbianism (Tavris, 1989).

OPPRESSION OF WOMEN

Central to the thinking of many feminists is the idea that men have used their positions of power and influence to oppress women both inside and outside the home. Evans, Kincade and Seem (2011) observe that feminist therapy assumes that the major causes of individuals' problems are external and stem from sexist or oppressive environments. Men are on the inside and women on the outside. Sometimes men's abuse of power blatantly takes place in therapeutic relationships: for instance 'Research indicates that the overwhelming majority of psychologists who have violated professional sexual ethical standards were middle-aged men who had sex with younger female clients' (American Psychological Association, 2007, p. 954).

Sue and Sue (2013) see mainstream white male culture as inherently biased against racial ethnic minorities, women, gays/lesbians and other culturally different groups. They delineate five components of oppression against such minority groups, which I have adapted to focus on the oppression of women. Oppression against women is also prominent in minority groups, so the components of oppression tend to hold good for them too.

1. *Belief in the superiority of men*: Men may possess conscious and unconscious feelings of superiority and consequently of entitlement to better treatment.
2. *Belief in the inferiority of women*: Women can be devalued because their capacities, including their sexuality, are viewed as inferior to those of men.
3. *Power to impose standards*: Men have the power to impose their standards on women. Early examples of this oppression involved excluding women from property and voting rights. Because of their generally having more control over financial resources, men are in a powerful position to impose their standards in the home. Threatened or actual use of greater physical strength can also be used as instruments of control and subjugation of women at home.
4. *Manifestation in institutions*: Chains of command in organizations and institutions favour men over women. Educational and training opportunities favour boys and men over girls and women.
5. *The invisible veil*: Since all people are the products of their cultural conditioning, including their gender role conditioning, their values and beliefs can operate as an invisible veil outside of conscious awareness. Thus even well intentioned individuals may experience difficulty in acknowledging that some of their thoughts, feelings and actions are sexist. Unconsciously and unintentionally, they may collude in perpetuating sexist biases and discrimination. Furthermore, the victims of oppression may fail to see that they have internalized the standards of the mainstream culture and so become the agents of their own oppression.

A final point is that at the heart of feminism are two different, and possibly contradictory, explanations for the past and current oppression of women. One explanation is that oppression results from men's greater power – 'Men did and are doing it to us'. Yet feminists also explain that the best way to gain more equality is through women banding together and being more assertive and socially active – 'We women have the power to bring about change'. One way to reconcile these explanations is to accept that not only men's greater power but also women's prior and possibly present insufficient social action to combat that power maintained, and may still be maintaining, women's oppression.

WOMEN'S EXPERIENCE AND ISSUES

A major criticism of existing counselling and psychotherapy approaches is that they insufficiently address women's experience and issues. The women's movement stresses the importance of women understanding and valuing their own experience. It also stresses the importance of men understanding the extent and ways in which women's experiencing of life is different than theirs. A common theme in the literature on women and gender roles is that women's self-esteem tends to be lower than that of men.

One way of looking at women's experience is in terms of the interaction of the social, the political and the personal. Here concepts like patriarchy, oppression and social action are important. Another way to look at women's experience is in terms of the particular challenges throughout the life span inherent in being a woman: for example, premenstrual tension, infertility and miscarriage, giving birth, post-natal depression, mothering, menopause, and frequently outliving a spouse. Still a further way to look at women's experience is in terms of problems that beset women in varying degrees: for example, domestic violence, sexual harassment, sexual abuse, relentless pressure to be beautiful, anorexia, bulimia, rape, abortion, single parenting, attitudes that constrain career choice, workplace discrimination, and depression and exhaustion resulting from carrying a disproportionate share of work/family responsibilities (Greer, 1999).

A final and practical thought about women's experience is that, in the last ten years, girls' childhood has probably changed. Biddulph (2013) writes: 'To put it bluntly, *our 18 is their 14. Our 14 is their 10'* (p. 6). He asserts that, partly due to a greedy corporate world, girls are being forced out of childhood when they have yet to complete it. Also, girls may not be supported by parents, relatives, friends and society in the way they used to be.

WOMEN'S IDENTITY DEVELOPMENT

Some models of women's identity development exist that are comparable to models of cultural identity development discussed in the previous chapter. Such models take into account and are stimulated by the oppression and subjugation that many women experience and feel. These models trace the development of women's consciousness or awareness from going along with the prevailing gender-role norms to becoming autonomous and socially active. Box 17.1 presents a summary of the five-stage model developed by McNamara and Rickard (1998).

BOX 17.1   A MODEL OF FEMINIST IDENTITY DEVELOPMENT

STAGE 1: PASSIVE-ACCEPTANCE

Passive acceptance of traditional gender roles, men considered superior to women, and prejudice and discrimination denied.

STAGE 2: REVELATION

Sexist events occur that cannot be ignored, an awakening to prejudice and discrimination, anger, dichotomous thinking in that all men are seen as oppressive and all women as positive.

STAGE 3: EMBEDDNESS-EMANATION

Close emotional and supportive relations formed with other women, sharing of emotions, solidifying of feminist identity, less absolutistic thinking regarding men.

STAGE 4: SYNTHESIS

A positive feminist identity is fully developed, less absolutistic thinking about sexism as the cause of all problems, ability to take an independent feminist stance.

STAGE 5: ACTIVE COMMITMENT

Interest in turning attention to making societal changes.

Cheatham and his colleagues (1997) have also presented a five-stage model of women's identity development using the same five stages that they used in their model of cultural identity development: naivety, encounter, naming, reflection on self as a cultural (in this case gender) being, and multi-perspective internalization. Stage models of feminist and of women's identity development are hypotheses that reflect the cultural, historical and political situations at the time of their development. Such models are open to question, for instance radical feminists are uncomfortable with the notion of synthesis in the McNamara and Rickard model.

MEN AND GENDER ROLES

THE MEN'S MOVEMENT

For relationships between the sexes to take place on the basis of genuine equality, both women and men need to change. Partly in response to feminism, there has been a growing men's movement in Western countries. For example, there are thousands of men's groups in the United States (Biddulph, 2003) as well as numerous men's groups in Australia and Britain. In important respects, the men's movement is complementary to rather than in opposition to the women's movement. Both seek equality between the sexes and liberation for persons, whatever their sex, to develop their full humanity without the limitations of rigid gender role prescriptions.

The men's movement has been slower in gaining strength than the women's movement and appears more fragmented. Men's issues have not had prominent advocates as articulate as Betty Frieden and Germaine Greer. Furthermore, the men's movement lags behind the women's movement in publishing books and research articles. However, some women, such as Gloria Steinem, definitely want a men's movement (Biddulph, 2003).

Increasingly the men's movement's emphasis is less about feminizing men and more about developing a positive image of maleness and of men's inner life and experiences. Men who are confident and in touch with their feelings are able to be more flexible in how they deal with others at home and at work rather than live out phony stereotypes of how men should be that fail to meet others' and their own needs.

The overall trend in Western societies is still to bring boys up for the traditional male roles of providers and protectors and, as such, to encourage aggression, competitiveness, self-reliance and not showing vulnerability. Often men are brought up thinking that it is 'sissy' to show weakness, cry, be artistic, and want close relationships with other males. Biddulph (2003) considers that men are a mess, with their three main enemies being isolation, compulsive competition, and life-long emotional timidity.

Another factor in the rise of the men's movement has been anger at the extent to which some feminist writers have successfully portrayed women as victims and men as persecutors. Furthermore, some such advocates appear insensitive to the damage this over-generalized negativity causes to boys and men's self-esteem and to achieving mutually respectful men–women relationships. In addition, those feminist writers who sweepingly portray men as oppressors may insufficiently acknowledge the responsibility of women in their own oppression and women's contribution to socializing both boys and girls into oppressive sex-role stereotypes.

Sometimes there is insufficient recognition in the feminist literature of the pressures and sacrifices many men undergo to provide for their families. Most men are not in positions of great power at work and have to get along as subordinates, sometimes with considerable humiliation and long dull hours, to do as best as they can to support their families. In addition, in areas like domestic violence, men as well as women can be the victims (see for example, Tavris, 1989). However, the outcomes of male violence can be more severe due to their relatively greater strength and, especially in America, their tendencies to use guns and knives. Furthermore, in Australia, Britain and America the criminal statistics are heavily weighted towards male violence.

Men can also be angry or cynical about feminists who seem to 'want it both ways': retaining women's existing privileges at the same time as gaining access to those of men. In addition, men are angered by the phenomenon of men-bashing that occurs in many areas in ways that would probably be considered unacceptable if applied to women (Biddulph, 2003; Tavris, 1989). For instance, in advertising men are often portrayed as jerks in men–women relationships. Anti-male greeting cards are popular and, in Australia, calendars and diaries of the 'All Men Are Bastards' variety have sold well. Another example of men-bashing is that of 'Post-it' notes, with captions such as 'There are only two things wrong with men. Everything they say and everything they do.'

MEN'S GENDER ROLE CONFLICT

Given the limitations of men's enculturation, many men find that they do not fit the mould. O'Neill and his colleagues (1986; 2008) developed a *Gender Role Conflict Scale* (GRCS) that identified four gender role conflict patterns of factors for American men. Box 17.2 briefly describes each of the GRCS's four factors.

BOX 17.2 FACTORS MEASURED BY THE *GENDER ROLE CONFLICT SCALE* (GRCS)

- *Success, power and competition*: This factor represents an emphasis on over-achieve-ment, control, strength, needing to move up the career ladder and being perceived as a 'winner'.
- *Restrictive emotionality*: Here men are frightened of the feminine part of themselves and by feelings that seem womanly. They experience difficulty with their own emo-tional self-disclosure as well as discomfort with the emotional expressiveness of others.
- *Restrictive affectionate behaviour between men*: This is an index of the degree to which men keep other men at a distance by restricting expressions of caring, being wary of friendly male overtures, and protecting themselves from feelings of anxiety or shame about feelings of attraction towards other men that might be interpreted by themselves or others as a gay orientation.
- *Conflict between work and family relations*: This factor measures the level of distress expe-rienced by men due to the impinging of work or study on personal and family life.

The underlying idea behind the GRCS is that the process of male socialization creates conflict, stress and anxiety for men when they deviate from masculine ideals. For example Good and his colleagues (1996) used the GRCS to examine the relation between masculine role conflict and psychological stress in a sam-ple of university counselling centre clients. Their findings supported earlier studies conducted with non-clinical samples of gender role conflict being associ-ated with higher levels of depression and interpersonal sensitivity. In addition, high scores on masculine role conflict significantly predicted paranoia, psy-choticism and obsessive-compulsivity. In another study that compared non-clinical samples of college-aged and middle-aged men, middle-aged men were less conflicted about success, power and competition, but were more conflicted between work and family responsibilities (Cournoyer and Mahalik, 1995). Such studies could be extended to take into account differences in culture and occupation, such as differences between business executives and blue-collar workers.

The work on men's gender role conflict highlights the fact that males as well as females can feel trapped by their gender role socialization. Furthermore, these studies illustrate that wanting to deviate from traditional masculine roles often comes at a psychological price. The role conflict research suggests that there is a place for models of men's as well of women's identity development in regard to gender roles. Currently numerous men remain at low levels of awareness about the effects of gender conditioning on their psychological wellbeing.

MEN'S EXPERIENCE AND ISSUES

Though largely formulated by men, perhaps existing counselling and psycho-therapy approaches are insufficiently sensitive to men's as well as women's experience and issues. A case can also be made for the institutional oppression of men as well as of women. For example, in times of war, men rather than women are called up to the horrors of combat and the possibility of serious injury, if not death. Another example is that some men consider that women are favoured when it comes to taking paid leave for child-care and in divorce court decisions about child custody. Regarding life span problems, men do not have the kind of problems that women do, for instance going through the menopause. However, men's life expectancy is on average five years lower than women's. For instance, 'American men have twice as many vehicle accidents, twice as many deaths from heart attacks, three times as many deaths from injuries, twice the deaths from liver disease. In fact, men exceed women in all thirteen leading causes of death' (Biddulph, 2003, p. 7). Furthermore, American boys commit suicide five times more frequently than American girls (Biddulph, 2008).

There are psychological problems that beset boys and men: for example, behavioural problems in school, hurt stemming from absent or neglectful fathers – sometimes called 'father hunger', work-related stress, alcoholism, being physically violent, pressure to initiate relationships with the opposite sex, pressure to perform sexually (men cannot fake erections), difficulty showing tender feelings and vulnerability, insufficient preparation for fatherhood, insufficient intimacy with same sex friends, pressure to be financially successful, loss of identity through unemployment, and loss of daily contact with children after a relationship break-up. However, there are some positive changes: for instance, Bidduph (2013) found that young fathers spend about three times as much with their children each day than some 40 years previously.

Many men are challenged to adjust to the changes brought about in their partners by the women's movement. Women easily outnumber men as clients in therapy. This imbalance indicates that another problem for men may be their greater unwillingness to admit and seek psychological assistance when experiencing difficulties themselves and creating difficulties for others.

THERAPY

THERAPEUTIC GOALS

Where gender role issues are involved, it is possible to state therapeutic goals for both sexes and for each sex. These general goals include helping individual clients use their strengths and potential, make appropriate choices, remedy poor skills, and develop positive and flexible self-concepts. In addition, therapeutic goals relating to gender roles can often involve both male and female partners: for example, learning to deal with demand/withdraw interaction patterns in marital conflict (Christensen and Heavy, 1993) and handling the numerous issues confronting dual career couples in a time of rapid technological and economic change (Fallon, 1997; Serlin, 1989).

THERAPEUTIC GOALS FOR WOMEN

Worell and Remer (2003) state that the ultimate goal of feminist therapy is to create the kind of society where sexism, along with other kinds of discrimination, is no longer a reality. They consider that many of women's symptoms can be seen as coping or survival strategies rather than as evidence of pathology. Consequently, the goals of feminist therapy are helping them to acquire better strategies, an approach that avoids 'blaming the victim' for her problems. Corey (2012) also mentions that an important goal of feminist therapy is to de-pathologize women's experiencing and to change society so that women's voices are honoured and women's relational qualities are valued.

Chaplin (1999) observes that women and others at the bottom of hierarchies usually have considerable experience of being put down and losing self-esteem. She continues: 'Feminist counselling aims instead to empower people and develop more self-confidence and control over their lives' (p. 8). Along the same lines, Evans et al. (2011) state that feminist therapists should help educate their clients on gender socialization to facilitate four of the major tenets of feminist therapy: the personal is political, valuing women's experiences, striving for an egalitarian relationship, and empowerment.

A study of feminist therapy throws some light on the goals of feminist therapy in practice. Chester (1994) surveyed 140 Australians who considered themselves to be both feminists and counsellors, though just over 14 per cent did not consider themselves feminist counsellors as such. Participants were asked to choose from a list of twenty-six characteristics, which ones they considered essential for feminist counsellors. Box 17.3 presents characteristics that the participants chose as essential. Underneath I have translated these characteristics into goals for feminist counselling, the most essential goals being women valuing themselves on their own terms and becoming free of sex-role stereotypes.

BOX 17.3   CHARACTERISTICS OF AUSTRALIAN FEMINIST COUNSELLORS TRANSLATED INTO GOALS FOR FEMINIST COUNSELLING

Essential feminist counsellor characteristics	%
Encourages women to value themselves on their own terms	92
Encourages clients to free themselves from sex-role stereotypes	83
Encourages female clients to increase their sense of commonality with other women	68
Encourages female clients to work for social change	44
Encourages androgyny	17

Goals for feminist counselling
Valuing herself on her own terms
Freeing herself from sex-role stereotypes
Increased sense of commonality with other women
Working for social change
Androgynous functioning

Statements of therapeutic goals that take women's sex and gender issues into account can focus both on women's life-span issues and on problems that are much more commonly faced by women than men. For example, gender aware and feminist therapists can counsel mid-life women to cope with the menopause constructively (Huffman and Myers, 1999) and, since they on average live longer than men, older women on dealing with old age (American Psychological Association, 2007). In addition, suitably trained and qualified therapists can help women address issues such as insufficient assertion, eating disorders, domestic violence and sexual harassment.

THERAPEUTIC GOALS FOR MEN

Since considerably fewer men than women come for therapy, one broader goal may be to increase the number of men prepared to address their gender role and other problems in therapy. Men, like women, need to free themselves from limiting gender role stereotypes and develop more of their unique potential. Consequently, another therapeutic goal is, where appropriate, to make men aware of the extent to which their thoughts, feelings and behaviours have been and continue to be heavily determined by their past and current gender role socialization.

Therapeutic goals for men can include addressing at least three of the issues identified in the *Gender Role Conflict Scale*: excessive need for success, power and competition; restrictive emotionality; and restrictive affectionate behaviour between men. Though coping with the fourth GRCS factor, conflict between work and family relationships, is a legitimate therapeutic goal, this problem is shared by both sexes – there has been a long term trend towards women's increased participation in the paid workforce, often accompanied by longer hours. Other therapeutic goals for men clients include stopping being physically violent both inside and outside of the home, dealing with work-related stress, and overcoming tendencies to treat women as sexual objects, and developing better health care skills.

Since women are redefining their gender roles faster than men, many men are then put in positions of exploring, understanding and altering their own gender roles. Positive maleness, combining tenderness and toughness and treating women with respect and as equals, is a desirable outcome from this change process. Men as well as women can take pride as they struggle to achieve inner strength and beauty. Boys and men are likely to be more constructive and caring if assisted to become confident in their manhood rather seeking to prove themselves all the time by pretending to be what they are not.

THERAPEUTIC APPROACHES

The above discussion indicates that there are many goals for gender aware counselling and therapy. Here I present four overlapping approaches to women's and men's gender issues and problems: making existing therapies more gender sensitive, developing gender relevant counselling and therapy competencies, feminist therapy, and men's therapy. I end with a note on therapy for lesbian, gay and bisexual clients.

MAKING EXISTING THERAPIES MORE GENDER SENSITIVE

Undoubtedly the rise of feminism and of the men's movement has already had an effect in influencing many therapists of both sexes to perform therapy with a greater focus on healing psychological distress stemming from restrictive gender role socialization and sexism. Of the two psychodynamic approaches presented in this book, Jung's analytical therapy emphasizes the importance of the feminine much more than Freud's psychoanalysis. Jung acknowledged the importance of the mother archetype, which appears in numerous aspects (Jung, 1982). Furthermore, Jung saw people as psychologically bisexual, with men possessing an anima (the personification of the feminine nature in their unconscious) and women possessing an animus (the personification of the masculine nature in their unconscious). Thus Jungian psychology provides a base on which to explore gender role issues at varying levels of consciousness (Schaverin, 1999).

Humanistic counselling and therapy approaches can also be used and adapted to deal with gender role issues. Clients in person-centred therapy can experience and explore issues connected with prior gender role socialization, and current gender role issues and conflicts in an emotional climate of safety and trust. Gestalt therapists can use interventions like awareness experiments, the use of the empty chair, and dream analysis to focus on clients' gender role learnings and behaviours that block excitement and authentic living. Furthermore, in transactional analysis, therapists can assist clients to explore script directives about gender role behaviours and to gain freedom of choice in regard to abandoning damaging ones.

The cognitive behaviour approaches too lend themselves to focusing on gender role issues. For instance, in rational emotive behaviour therapy, gender related irrational beliefs can be detected, disputed and either discarded or restated more rationally. In cognitive therapy, therapists and clients can identify and question the reality of gender related automatic thoughts that confuse fact with inference. Afterwards, where necessary, therapists can work with clients to replace previous sexist and self-oppressing automatic thoughts with conscious and realistic ones.

GENDER RELEVANT COUNSELLING AND THERAPY COMPETENCIES

In the previous chapter, I presented a statement of multicultural counselling and therapy competencies (Sue et al., 1998). This statement can be adapted for gender relevant counselling and therapy competencies which consist of three main dimensions: awareness of own assumptions, values and biases; understanding the worldview of the sex different client; and developing appropriate strategies and techniques. Each dimension is divided into beliefs and attitudes, knowledge, and skills. The basic presumption in stating these competencies is that all therapists need to address their own levels of gender identity development and their ability to offer gender sensitive services.

- *Awareness of own assumptions, values and biases*: The beliefs held by gender skilled therapists include being sensitive to their own gender heritage, being comfortable with differences that exist between them and clients of the other sex, and recognizing the limitations of their competence and expertise. Therapists should know about their gender heritage and how this affects the therapeutic process, understand how sexist oppression and discrimination may affect them personally and in their work, and know about the impact of how they communicate on clients of the other sex. Skills include seeking out relevant educational and training experiences on gender related factors in psychological wellness, actively understanding oneself as a gender being and seeking an autonomous and appropriately flexible gender identity.
- *Understanding the worldview of the sex different client*: Beliefs and attitudes for gender skilled therapists include being aware of their negative emotional reactions and of the stereotypes and preconceived notions that they may hold towards clients of the other sex. Therapists should know about the gender related experiences, heritage and historical backgrounds of any particular group of men or women with whom they work, acknowledge how gender can affect help-seeking behaviour, know how gender can influence assessment and the selection and implementation of therapeutic interventions, and know about the oppressive political and environmental influences impinging on the lives of women and men. Skills include keeping up to date on research findings relevant to the psychological wellbeing of women and men as well as being actively involved with minority and other relevant groups outside work settings to gain deeper insight into their gender perspectives.

- *Developing appropriate intervention strategies and techniques*: Therapists' skills include the ability to send and receive verbal and non-verbal communication accurately, making appropriate referrals to either the same sex or other sex therapists, tailoring the therapeutic relationship and interventions to take into account the gender related dimensions of clients' problems, and engaging in a variety of helping roles, beyond being a therapist, for example, advisor, advocate, consultant and change agent.

FEMINIST THERAPY

Brown (2010) defines feminist therapy as: 'informed by feminist political philosophies and analysis, grounded in multicultural feminist scholarship on the psychology of women and gender, which leads both therapist and client toward strategies and solutions advancing feminist resistance, transformation and social change in daily personal life, and in the relationships with the social, emotional and political environments' (p. 4). Feminist therapists challenge sexism in diagnostic categories and propose alternatives that reflect women's experiences (Herlihy and Corey, 2009). They subscribe to many different theoretical orientations (Chaplin, 1999; Chester, 1994; Corey, 2012).

Feminist therapy can also be described by the values or principles that have emerged from the joining of feminism with therapy. Box 17.4 describes five such central principles underlying feminist therapy (Ballou, 1996; Cheatham et al., 1997).

BOX 17.4 FIVE CENTRAL PRINCIPLES OF FEMINIST THERAPY

1. *Egalitarian relationships*: Feminist therapists are extremely sensitive to issues of power and its distribution. They emphasize sharing power with clients and believe that hierarchical forms of power distribution are inappropriate. Self-disclosure of one's own experiences as a woman can be an important part of the therapeutic process.
2. *Pluralism*: Feminist theory acknowledges and values difference, including complex and multiple-level diversities. Respect for others, including their differences, is a basic tenet of feminist therapy.
3. *Working against oppression*: Feminist therapists work against all forms of oppression: for instance, on the basis of sex, affectional/sexual orientation, race, culture, religious belief, life-style choice, and physical disability.
4. *External emphasis*: External factors, such as social/political/economic structures are crucial to shaping the views of women, how they see themselves and how others see them. Women as individuals are shaped by and interact with political, environmental, institutional and cultural factors.
5. *Valuing women's experiences*: Relying on the actual experiences of women for descriptions of 'reality'. Grounding knowledge claimed about women on the actual women's experience. Valuing highly the experience of women rather than ignoring or discounting it and assuming men's experience to be normative.

What are some specific interventions in dealing with women clients? In gender-role analysis, a feminist therapist explores the impact of past gender-role expectations on the client and together therapist and client use this information to make decisions about future gender-role behaviours (Herlihy and Corey, 2009). Feminist therapists can also make clients aware of the power difference between men and women in society and help them to recognize the different kinds of power that they either possess or to which they have access. For instance, women can learn to appreciate themselves as they are and not rely on men for their sense of worth. Bibliographies of autobiographies, self-help books, counselling and psychology textbooks and other nonfiction books may each be used at appropriate times to learn about gender-role stereotypes and the effects of gender inequality. Other feminist therapy interventions include women's self-help groups, psycho-educational experiences (American Psychological Association, 2007), and suggesting to clients that they participate in social action, for instance providing community education about gender issues or participating in rape crisis centres.

Assertiveness training, gender-role analysis and consciousness raising may be particularly appropriate for the needs of women. Chester (1994) asked her feminist counsellor sample whether they used any techniques or interventions related to their feminism. Ninety-one per cent of the respondents replied in the affirmative. The most commonly cited interventions were challenging sex-role stereotypes and challenging patriarchal norms (each around 15 per cent), assertiveness training, strategies to encourage a sense of empowerment, and self-disclosure (each around 12 per cent). Needless to say, many women clients bring to therapy specific issues, such as procrastination, for which gender-related interventions can be, but not always are, irrelevant.

An issue in feminist therapy is whether and how to confront clients with issues of sexism. It may be important for therapists to assess and take into account the level of gender identity development of clients. In addition, therapists need to help women clients anticipate and deal with the consequences of changing their gender roles. One danger of bringing up issues of sexism too soon is that clients' resist the explanation and do not see its relevance. The opposite is also possible in that clients simplistically latch on to a sexist oppression analysis of their situations, get extremely angry with their partners, and prematurely leave them rather than attempt to work through their relationship issues.

Many feminist therapists develop their own approaches to working with clients. For example, the British therapist Jocelyn Chaplin (1999) has developed a 'cognitive feminism' approach. Chaplin distinguishes between the masculine control model, in which opposites, such as mind-'masculine'-strong and body-'feminine'-vulnerable, are split hierarchically into superior and inferior constructs and the feminine rhythm model. In the rhythm model there is flow and balancing between extremes, for instance alternating between joy and sorrow throughout a day. Each client needs to find her own unique rhythms and balance between her 'active' and 'resting' sides, her 'private' and 'public' sides, and her 'self-expression' and 'caring for others' sides.

Therapy starts with a trust-building mothering stage. Depending on the client, in varying degrees the therapist acts as a container, non-judgemental presence, and provides a space for emotionally letting go. The second stage involves focusing on specific issues, identifying themes and separating out the opposites: for instance the head must rule the heart. The third stage explores the past to understand where the opposites and inner hierarchies came from. The next stage involves dissolving the inner hierarchies, facing ambivalence and accepting opposites. Then therapy progresses to the last stage where clients make decisions and behave differently in the world. During this stage, assertiveness training helps many women express themselves more effectively, for instance by asking clearly for a change.

Feminist therapy may be practised alongside or integrated with other approaches. These include cognitive therapies, psychoanalytic therapies, gestalt therapy, family systems therapies, and psychodrama (Brown, 2010). Also, men have been welcomed as practitioners of feminist therapy, especially since the turn of the century (Brown, 2010).

MEN'S THERAPY

I include a section on men's therapy to highlight the need for more work on therapeutic approaches to men's problems and issues. Many boys and men are suffering psychologically and need assistance to become confident and positive males. Virtually all of negative behaviours towards women chronicled by Greer (1999) are symptomatic of men's psychological wounds and insufficient personal development rather than of their innate badness. Unfortunately, the behaviours of some wounded men, for instance aggression and violence, do little to generate sympathy for their underlying suffering and low self-esteem.

There needs to be a greater development of men's therapy to complement – and definitely not to compete against – responsible feminist therapy. In many books on counselling and therapy (for examples, Sue, Ivey and Pedersen, 1996; Sue and Sue, 2013; Woolfe et al. 2010)), there is more attention paid to women's issues than to men's issues. Much of the existing literature on men's issues focuses on changing negative aspects of men's behaviour, such as curbing domestic violence and sexual abuse. There is a dearth of counselling and therapy books and articles advocating positive maleness and how to achieve it (see Biddulph, 2003). However, the American Psychological Association's relatively new journal *Psychology of Men and Masculinity* may go some way to redressing this deficiency.

Just as the men's movement can be seen as the missing half of the women's movement, men's therapy can be seen as the missing half of feminist therapy. Men's therapy can be conducted both on an individual basis, in men's groups and as part of working with couples and families. In addition, sometimes both men's and women's issues are addressed in mixed sex groups. The goals for men's therapy are like those of feminist therapy: for the man to value himself on his own terms, gain freedom from sex-role stereotypes, gain an increased sense of commonality with other men, and work for social change. With some adaptation, the five central principles of feminist therapy – egalitarian relation-ships, pluralism, working against oppression, external emphasis, and valuing the experience of one's own sex (see Box 17.4) – are highly relevant for men's therapy too. Many therapists need to become more skilled at working with the specific issues facing boys and men. Then they can help these clients to cele-brate, liberate and develop the better parts of their male humanity.

LESBIAN, GAY AND BISEXUAL CLIENTS

To date this chapter has assumed the prevalence of heterosexuality. However gender aware therapists need to deal constructively with homosexuality and bisexuality – for instance, at least one in ten young men is gay or bisexual (Biddulph, 2008). Lesbian, gay and bisexual orientations are not mental ill-nesses. Rather same-sex attractions, feelings and behaviour are normal variants of human sexuality and efforts to change sexual orientation have been shown to be neither effective nor safe (American Psychological Association, 2012).

When working with lesbian, gay and bisexual clients, therapists should remember that sexual orientation and gender identity are distinct characteris-tics of an individual. Avoid seeing gay men and lesbians as particularly likely to manifest gender-nonconforming behaviour. Though all of the above men-tioned approaches to women's and men's gender therapy may be appropriate, therapists should also strive to understand the unique problems and risks that exist for lesbian, gay and bisexual clients. Also, therapists should be aware of any effects of their own sexual orientation and views about sexual orientation may have on how they work with such clients. Just as with heterosexual clients, the therapist's attitude and skills, rather than their own sexual orientation, are most important when working with lesbian, gay and bisexual clients.

CONCLUSION

Though a promising start has been made in developing a counselling and psy-chotherapy literature that takes gender-role issues and their treatment into account, much still remains to be done. There are risks as well as benefits in focusing on gender-role issues. The benefits include a lessening of sexist oppres-sion, a greater chance for people to develop their full human potential rather than lead lives constricted by gender-role stereotypes, and greater attention paid to developing interventions for the specific problems that beset each and both sexes.

There are also risks in changing the current balance of gender roles. For example, 'the masculine supremacy effect' in which masculine values are more honoured in market-driven Western cultures, may lead women to feel under pressure to relinquish some of their feminine virtues, for instance compassion, as they compete in a workforce dominated by masculine values. In addition,

gender role liberation can play into people's selfishness in already highly individualistic Western cultures. Both men and women may sacrifice communal
values, and possibly the welfare of children too, in the interests of their own
individual development.

For the most part, existing counselling and psychotherapy approaches have
insufficiently addressed gender-role socialization and the therapeutic problems and issues arising from it. Feminist therapy is the main example of an
attempt to redress this neglect. There is still considerable scope for originating
new counselling and psychotherapy approaches, as well as for modifying
existing ones, to promote equality between the sexes and to liberate girls,
women, boys and men to become more fully human.

REVIEW AND PERSONAL QUESTIONS

REVIEW QUESTIONS

1. What do each of the following terms mean

   * gender role
   * gender-role identity
   * gender-role socialization
   * gender-role conflict
   * sexism?

2. What is feminism and what are some of the ways in which women are oppressed?
3. What is the men's movement and why is it important?
4. Describe some therapeutic goals that apply

   * to both sexes
   * to women more than men
   * to men more than women?

5. What are some ways of making existing counselling and therapy approaches more applicable to gender-role issues?
6. Describe and critically discuss the idea of gender relevant counselling and therapy competencies.
7. Describe and critically discuss feminist therapy.
8. What role, if any, do you see for men's therapy.

PERSONAL QUESTIONS

1. How would you describe

   * the process of your gender-role socialization
   * the influence of your culture on your gender-role socialization?

2. To what extent do you consider that your attitudes, values and behaviours are masculine,
   feminine or a mixture of both?

3. Describe instances, if any, in which you have been

   • the victim of sexism
   • the purveyor of sexism?

4. To what extent and in what ways do you possess psychological problems involving gender-role issues?
5. Assuming that you possess some psychological problems involving gender-role issues, either what are you doing or what do you intend doing about them?
6. How can you make yourself a more gender sensitive counsellor or therapist both now and in future?

ANNOTATED BIBLIOGRAPHY

Brown, L. S. (2010) *Feminist Therapy*. Washington, DC: American Psychological Association.
This brief book has seven chapters: 1. Introduction to feminist therapy – not for women only; 2. History; 3. Theory; 4. The therapy process; 5. Evaluation; 6. Future developments; and 7. Summary.

Herlihy, B. and Corey, G. (2009) Feminist therapy. In G. Corey *Theory and Practice of Counseling & Psychotherapy* (8th ed.). Belmont, CA: Thomson Brooks/Cole, pp. 339–72.
This textbook chapter provides a history of feminist therapy and reviews some of the key concepts and principles of feminist psychology. It then describes the process of feminist therapy, the role of assessment and diagnosis, and then a review of feminist therapy techniques and strategies. In addition, feminist therapy is discussed from a multicultural perspective and there is a feminist therapy case study.

Chaplin, J. (1999) *Feminist Counselling in Action* (2nd ed.). London: Sage.
This book presents a multi-stage rhythm model of feminist therapy already briefly described in this chapter. Chaplin illustrates each stage of the process is with three case studies.

American Psychological Association (2007) Guidelines for psychological practice with girls and women. *American Psychologist, 62,* 949–79.
The eleven guidelines are divided into three sections: (a) diversity, social context, and power; (b) professional responsibility; and (c) practice applications. Each guideline has two sections: rationale and application.

Biddulph, S. (2008) *Raising Boys* (2nd ed.). Berkeley, CA: Celestial Arts.
This book has ten chapters: 1. What is it with boys?; 2. The three stages of boyhood; 3. Testosterone!; 4. How boy's and girl's brains differ; 5. What dads can do; 6. Mothers and sons; 7. Developing a healthy sexuality; 8. A revolution in schooling; 9. Boys and sports; and 10. A community challenge.

Biddulph, S. (2013) *Raising Girls*. London: HarperThorsons.
Part One of this book is on the five stages of girlhood. Part Two covers the big five risk areas, such as too sexy too soon, and bodies, weight and food, and how to navigate them. Part Three has two chapters: Girls and their mums and Girls and their dads.

Greer, G. (1999) *The Whole Woman*. London: Anchor.
Greer eloquently argues that women throughout the world are still at risk and that, despite gains made by feminism, their lives are becoming more difficult. She provides a comprehensive, irreverent, amusing, earthy and thoroughly one-sided tour of contemporary women's issues in thirty-five self-contained 'chapterkins' divided into four main areas: body, mind, love and power. Feminist therapy is not one of the topics Greer covers.

American Psychological Association (2012) Guidelines for psychological practice with lesbian, gay, and bisexual clients. *American Psychologist*, 67(1), 10–42.
The twenty-one guidelines come under five headings: Attitudes toward homosexuality and bisexuality; Relationships and families; Issues of diversity; Economic and workplace issues; and Research.

REFERENCES AND FURTHER READING

American Psychological Association (2007) Guidelines for Psychological Practice With Girls and Women. *American Psychologist, 62*, 949–79.
American Psychological Association (2012) Guidelines for Psychological Practice with Lesbian, Gay and Bisexual Clients. *American Psychologist, 67*, 10–42.
Ballou, M. (1996) MCT theory and women. In D. W. Sue, A. E. Ivey, and P. B. Pedersen (eds), *A Theory of Multicultural Counseling and Therapy*. Pacific Grove, CA: Books/Cole, pp. 236–46.
Biddulph, S. (2003) *The Secret Life of Men: A Practical Guide to Helping Men Discover Health, Happiness, and Deeper Personal Relationships*. New York: Marlowe.
Biddulph, S. (2008) *Raising Boys: Why Boys Are Different – and How to Help Them Become Happy and Well-Balanced Men* (2nd ed.). Berkley, CA: Celestial Arts.
Biddulph, S. (2013) *Raising Girls*. London: HarperThorsons.
Brown, L. S. (2010) *Feminist Therapy*. Washington, DC: American Psychological Association.
Buss, D. M (1995) Psychological sex differences: Origins through sexual selection. *American Psychologist, 50*, 164–8.
Chaplin, J. (1999) *Feminist Counselling in Action* (2nd ed.). London: Sage.
Cheatham, H., Ivey, A. E., Ivey, M. B., Pedersen, P., Rigazio-DiGillio, S., Simek-Morgan, L. and Sue, D. W. (1997) Multicultural Counseling and Therapy: 1

Metatheory – Taking theory into practice; 2 Integrative practice. In A. E. Ivey, M. B. Ivey and L. Simek-Morgan, *Counseling and Psychotherapy: A Multicultural Perspective* (4th ed.). Boston, MA: Allyn & Bacon, pp. 133–205.

Chester, A. (1994) *Feminist Counselling in Australia.* Unpublished MA (Women's Studies) thesis, University of Melbourne.

Christensen, A. and Heavy, C. L. (1993) Gender differences in marital conflict: The demand/withdraw interaction pattern. In S. Oskamp and M. Constanzo (eds), *Gender Issues in Contemporary Society.* Newbury Park, CA: Sage, pp. 113–41.

Corey, G. (2012) *Theory and Practice of Counseling and Psychotherapy* (9th ed.). Belmont, CA: Brooks/Cole.

Cournoyer, R. J. and Mahalik, J. R. (1995) Cross-sectional study of gender role conflict examining college-aged and middle-aged men. *Journal of Counseling Psychology, 42,* 11–19.

Darwin, C. (1871) *The Descent of Man and Selection in Relation to Sex.* London: Murray.

Enns, C. Z. (1993) Twenty years of feminist counseling and therapy: From naming biases to implementing multifaceted practice. *The Counseling Psychologist, 21* (1), 3–87.

Enns, C. Z. (2004) *Feminist Theories and Feminist Psychotherapies: Origins, Themes, and Diversity* (2nd ed.). New York: Haworth.

Enns, C. Z. and Sinacore, A. L. (2001) Feminist theories. In J. Worell (ed.), *Encyclopedia of Gender* (Vol. 1, pp. 469–80) San Diego, CA: Academic Press.

Evans, K. M., Kincade, E. A. and Seem, S. R. (2011) *Introduction to Feminist Therapy: Strategies for Social and Individual Change.* London: Sage.

Fallon, B. (1997) The balance between paid work and home responsibilities: Personal problem or corporate concern. *Australian Psychologist, 32,* 1–9.

Frieden, B. (1963) *The Feminine Mystique.* London: Penguin Books.

Good. G. E., Robertson, J. M., Fitzgerald, L. F., Stevens, M. and Bartels, K. (1996) The relation between masculine role conflict and psychological distress in male university counseling center clients. *Journal of Counseling & Development, 75,* 44– 9.

Greer, G. (1999) *The Whole Woman.* London: Anchor.

Herlihy, B. and Corey, G. (2009) Feminist therapy. In G. Corey, *Theory and Practice of Counseling & Psychotherapy* (8th ed.). Belmont, CA: Thomson Brooks/Cole, pp. 339–72.

Huffman, S. B. and Myers, J. E. (1999) Counseling women in midlife: An integrative approach to menopause. *Journal of Counseling & Development, 77,* 258–66.

Jung, C. G. (1982) *Aspects of the Feminine.* London: Routledge.

Maccoby, E. (1990) Gender and relationships: A developmental account. *American Psychologist, 45,* 513–20.

McNamara, K. and Rickard, K. M. (1998) Feminist identity development: Implications for feminist therapy with women. In D. R. Atkinson and G. Hackett (eds), *Counseling Diverse Populations.* Boston: McGraw-Hill, pp. 271–82.

Moir, A. and Jessel, D. (1989) *Brain Sex: The Real Difference Between Men & Women.* London: Mandarin.

O'Neill, J. M. (2008) Summarizing 25 years of research on men's gender-role conflict using the Gender Role Conflict Scale: New research paradigms and clinical implications. *The Counseling Psychologist, 36*(3), 358–445.

O'Neill, J. M., Helms, B. J., Gable, R. K., David, L. and Wrightsman, L. S. (1986) Gender Role Conflict Scale: College men's fear of femininity. *Sex Roles, 14,* 335–50.

Schaverin, J. (1999) Jung, the transference and the psychological feminine. In I. B. Seu, and M. C. Heenan (eds), *Feminism & Psychotherapy: Reflections on Contemporary Theories and Practices.* London: Sage, pp. 172–88.

Serlin, B. (1989) Counseling dual-career couples. *Journal of Career Planning & Employment, 50,* 80–6.

Sue, D. W., Carter, R. T., Casas, J. M., Fouad, N. A., Ivey, A. E., Jensen, M., LaFromboise, T., Manese, J. E., Ponterotto, J. G. and Vazquez-Nutall, E. (1998) *Multicultural Counseling Competencies: Individual and Organizational Development.* London: Sage.

Sue, D. W., Ivey, A. E. and Pedersen, P. B. (eds) (1996) *A Theory of Multicultural Counseling and Therapy.* Pacific Grove: Brooks/Cole.

Sue, D. W. and Sue, D. (2013) *Counseling the Culturally Diverse: Theory and Practice* (6th ed.). New York: John Wiley.

Tavris, C. (1989) *Anger: The Misunderstood Emotion* (rev. ed.). New York: Simon & Schuster.

Tindall, C., Robinson, J. and Kagan. C. (2010) Feminist perspectives. In R. Woolfe, S. Strawbridge, B. Douglas and W. Dryden (eds), *Handbook of Counselling Psychology* (3rd ed.). London: Sage, pp. 213–34.

Woolfe, R., Strawbridge, S., Douglas, B. and Dryden, W. (2010) *Handbook of Counselling Psychology* (3rd ed.). London: Sage.

Worell, J. and Remer, R. (2003) *Feminist Perspectives in Therapy: Empowering Diverse Women.* New York: Wiley.

Chapter 18 starts by examining eight key issues in evaluating counselling and therapy theories. These issues are: (1) the relationship between theorists' personal histories and their therapeutic approaches; (2) the influence of theorists' historical and cultural contexts on their therapeutic approaches; (3) the influence of almost all the major theorists being men; (4) the nature of human nature; (5) the extent to which an approach addresses sub-normal, normal and supra-normal functioning; (6) the extent to which an approach fosters self-therapy for afterwards; (7) the role of research in evaluating therapeutic approaches; and (8) how adequately the theory of each therapeutic approach is stated.

I then discuss issues surrounding theoretical and practical eclecticism, including the meaning of the term, the reasons why therapists practise eclectically, how disciplined are the decisions by which therapists practise eclectically, and 'technical eclecticism' or the drawing of therapeutic interventions from different sources without necessarily subscribing to the disciplines that spawned them. I assert that, to date, therapists have worked eclectically rather than in an integrated fashion. The chapter ends with a discussion of reasons for integration and of reasons that slow its accomplishment.

EVALUATION, ECLECTICISM AND INTEGRATION 18

INTRODUCTION

You have now had a chance to read about the many counselling and psychotherapy approaches presented in this book. Undoubtedly, you have already started drawing your own conclusions about the usefulness of the different approaches and how comfortable you would be implementing each of them. In this chapter I want to broaden your perspectives about evaluating the quality of counselling and therapy approaches by reviewing eight key issues.

While there is much to be said for learning about the different theoretical positions separately, in practice most counsellors and therapists use interventions that stem from more than one theoretical position. They find that operating out of one position is too restrictive to help them to understand the range of clients and client problems that they see. Clients who vary according to how responsive they are to different explanations and interventions can also pressure therapists to work more broadly. Consequently in this chapter I also examine issues of eclecticism and of integrating counselling and therapy approaches.

EIGHT KEY EVALUATION ISSUES

ISSUE 1: WHAT IS THE RELATIONSHIP BETWEEN THEORISTS' PERSONAL HISTORIES AND THEIR PSYCHOTHERAPEUTIC APPROACHES?

In Chapter 1 I mentioned that many theorists whose work is described in this book encountered periods of significant psychological suffering in their lives. Furthermore, theorists' suffering motivated them to create psychotherapeutic approaches that would help themselves as well as others. Being highly motivated to develop psychotherapeutic approaches that they could use themselves has both advantages and disadvantages. In evaluating the theory and practice of the different originators, relevant questions are: 'How much of their own problems were or are the theorists projecting onto clients at large?' and 'Is the approach that worked or works for the any particular theorist necessarily that which is best for all clients?' The same sorts of questions can be asked of those studying counselling and psychotherapy approaches. For example, when evaluating the different theoretical approaches, 'How much are your own needs and problems restricting your ability to be objective?'.

ISSUE 2: WHAT IS THE INFLUENCE OF THE THEORISTS' HISTORICAL AND CULTURAL CONTEXTS ON THEIR PSYCHOTHERAPEUTIC APPROACHES?

Undoubtedly theorists are influenced by the historical and cultural contexts in which they live. When evaluating psychotherapeutic approaches, relevant questions here include how much the problems affecting clients change over time and how much across cultures. For instance, the current breakdown of respect for authority may mean that many young people, unlike Rogers, are facing problems of too little rather than too much structure. In addition, the materialism and rampant consumerism of Western societies may be exacerbating people's tendencies to greed and consequent feelings of depression and alienation when their attempts to buy happiness fail. In the twenty-first century, the increasing pace of technological change may also create new sets of problems, which current therapeutic approaches may be insufficiently equipped to address, stemming from changes in how people work and communicate.

As illustrated in the chapter on cultural perspectives, culture influences the creation of theory. To what extent and how are each of the therapeutic approaches presented in this book limited because their Euro-American originators either were or still are wearing cultural blinkers?

ISSUE 3: WHAT IS THE INFLUENCE OF THE FACT THAT ALMOST ALL THE MAJOR THEORISTS ARE MEN?

In *The Female Eunuch*, Germaine Greer observed that Freud was the father of psychoanalysis and that it had no mother (Greer, 1971). Though many women have also been prominent in developing therapeutic approaches, all but one of the major theorists presented in this book are men. In addition, none of the theoretical approaches presented in *Current Psychotherapies* (Wedding and Corsini, 2014), probably the most authoritative American psychotherapy textbook, were mainly developed by women.

A number of interesting questions are raised by the predominance of men in developing major therapeutic approaches such as 'Do some theories contain male bias?'. As mentioned in the previous chapter, Freud's notion of penis envy is uncongenial to many women who envy men their power rather than their penises. Furthermore, if women had been more prominent in theorizing, 'Might we have seen the emergence of different and more humane therapeutic approaches?'. In addition, given equal mental ability between the sexes and possibly women's greater interest than men in relationships, 'Why have women not made more of a contribution to originating major counselling and psychotherapy approaches?' and 'How can the knowledge and talents of women be encouraged so that they make a greater contribution to generating counselling and psychotherapy approaches?'.

ISSUE 4: WHAT IS THE NATURE OF HUMAN NATURE?

Maslow (1971) raised the issue of whether psychology has been based too much on a 'bad animal' rather than a 'good animal' underlying view of human nature. Both Freud and, to a lesser extent Jung, were rather pessimistic about human nature and emphasized the darker individual and collective unconscious forces lying beneath the veneer of civilization. If anything, the psychodynamic theories stress curbing negative instincts and impulses rather than cultivating positive ones.

Traditional behaviourists view people's behaviour as the result of evolutionary drives, for instance for sex, food and shelter, and conditioning. Their mechanistic view of human nature is scarcely flattering to humans. The cognitive behaviourists allow for personal agency. Nevertheless, if anything, theorists like Ellis, with his focus on biological tendencies to irrationality, and Beck, with his underlying maladaptive schemas, have focused more on the negative than on the positive aspects of human nature. Of the theorists in this book, Rogers and Seligmann are perhaps the main one to take predominantly a good animal view of human nature. For Rogers, the actualizing tendency in humans is positive and it only becomes negative to the extent that it is blocked and frustrated by environmental forces. For Seligmann, people have the need and capacity to develop the postive aspects of their human nature.

A fundamental question is evaluating theories is the extent to which they are realistic about human's underlying animal nature. Neither neutrality nor cautious optimism involves the need to deny humans' huge potential for destructive and aggressive behaviours, but they just balance it by also noting humans' huge potential to think, feel, act and communicate constructively. Thus therapy can become a matter of releasing and cultivating higher human potentials as well as of containing and overcoming destructive tendencies.

ISSUE 5: TO WHAT EXTENT DOES THE APPROACH ADDRESS SUB-NORMAL, NORMAL AND SUPRA-NORMAL FUNCTIONING?

When evaluating the different therapeutic approaches, consider the populations for which their originators intended them. You may remember that Jung thought his analytical therapy more suitable for patients searching for meaning in the afternoon of their lives than those requiring help with conventional adaptation in the morning of their lives.

It is possible to look at human functioning in three broad categories – sub-normal, normal and supra-normal – with, at any given moment, individuals being placed somewhere along this continuum. Sub-normal functioning is that where individuals are psychologically distressed and have problems that are more severe than the normal run of the population. Such clients might suffer from the mental disorders that are listed in the American Psychiatric Association's *Diagnostic and Statistical Manual of Mental Disorders* (APA, 2013). Normal functioning is that where people are capable of conventional adaptation to the societies in which they live. Such individuals may still experience problems for which counselling and psychotherapy is appropriate: for instance, relationship problems, stress problems, and study problems.

Some clients who are functioning well may want to function even better. Supra-normal functioning refers to going above, beyond or transcending normal human functioning. Psychotherapy has its origins more in dealing with the problems of the sub-normal and normal that in trying to assist well-functioning people to develop their full human potential. There has yet to be a major therapeutic approach developed by professionals, such as psychiatrists or clinical psychologists, who predominantly deal with normal client populations, let alone superior functioning ones. Perhaps positive therapy comes closest to doing so.

Some theorists in this book, for instance Rogers and Ellis, have paid attention to defining full human functioning. Nevertheless, none of the approaches presented sufficiently addresses helping clients to be compassionate, engage in selfless service and synergistically foster the interests and ideals both of themselves and of human kind. A possible criticism of Western psychotherapy is that it errs too much in the direction of being self-centred therapy. The Austrian psychiatrist, Alfred Adler, with his emphasis on social interest and community feeling, stands out as an advocate of the need to show more concern for others and for the human species (Adler, 1998).

ISSUE 6: TO WHAT EXTENT DOES THE THERAPEUTIC APPROACH FOSTER SELF-THERAPY FOR AFTERWARDS?

Sooner or later all clients are going to part from their therapists. Though a full course of psychoanalysis or of analytical therapy may last for years, that option is for the few. Nowadays there is great pressure from those paying for therapeutic services, for example governments and insurance companies, to encourage short-term managed care. Furthermore, most private clients have limited resources, which makes paying for long-term psychotherapy either difficult or impossible. Even though some clients genuinely require longer-term contact, increasingly most counselling and psychotherapy is short-term, say from 1 to 10 sessions or medium-term, say from 11 to 25 sessions. Important questions then become: 'What are the ingredients of effective time-limited psychotherapy?', 'How can therapeutic gains best be maintained afterwards?' and 'To what extent is the psychotherapy a training in self-therapy?'.

In Chapter 1 I mentioned that one of the functions of theories was to provide languages both for the therapeutic conversation and so that clients can converse with themselves. Choosing from the theories presented here, Freud's psychoanalysis,

Jung's analytical therapy, Rogerian person-centred therapy and Perlsian gestalt therapy appear not to give high priority to sharing the language in which the therapy is conceptualized with clients. For instance, Rogerian therapists do not share concepts like actualizing tendency, conditions of worth, and organismic valuing process with their clients. Though clients in each of these four approaches may end therapy able to lead their lives more skillfully, the skills of so doing tend not to be clearly articulated during therapy. Clients may learn self-therapy skills, but this is more a by-product of the therapy rather than an integral part of it. For example, person-centred therapists assist clients to listen to their feelings and 'inner voices' and in doing so clients can learn to do this better on their own. However, person-centred therapists do not teach these skills directly to clients.

In the cognitive behaviour school the therapist's role is more that of an educator than in either the psychodynamic or the humanistic schools. As part of the therapeutic process the language of the approach gets shared with clients. For instance, in rational emotive behaviour therapy, clients learn to detect, analyse in ABC terms, dispute and restate irrational beliefs both during therapy sessions and when completing homework assignments. In inelegant REBT, this sharing of language may be only in relation to specific symptoms, but in elegant REBT, this sharing can lead to disputing irrational beliefs becoming a way of life.

In cognitive therapy, clients learn that they need to test the reality of their thinking and are taught how to do this. By sharing a common language with clients and educating them in cognitive and, often, in behavioural skills as well, these cognitive behaviour approaches may be more clearly helping clients to become better at self-therapy than those approaches leaving relevant skills to be indirectly acquired and maintained. Perhaps adherents of other than cognitive behaviour approaches might further develop their theory and practice, without losing the essence, so that clients can learn more about how to conduct self-therapy for afterwards.

ISSUE 7: WHAT IS THE ROLE OF RESEARCH IN EVALUATING THERAPEUTIC APPROACHES?

Though counselling and psychotherapy approaches may have different goals, nevertheless a pertinent question in evaluating any approach is always going to be 'Where is the research evidence for its effectiveness?'. Dictionary definitions of research tend to use adjectives like 'careful' and 'systematic' and nouns like 'study', 'inquiry' and 'investigation'. In Chapter 1 I stated that a function of counselling and psychotherapy theories was to provide research hypotheses. Good theory provides good research hypotheses, poor theory provides poor ones.

Research can have a role in laying the scientific base for a therapeutic approach. However, here my emphasis is on the role of research in evaluating the practice of therapeutic approaches. A pertinent question is 'What psychotherapy, conducted by which therapists, is appropriate for which clients, with which problems, under what circumstances?'. Conducting research into therapeutic approaches can be difficult since there are so many considerations to take into account.

RESEARCH VARIABLES

Below are suggestions of variables, albeit sometimes interrelated, that can be explored when researching psychotherapeutic approaches.

- *Therapist variables*: These variables include age, sex, race, culture, professional training, relevant background and experience, and emotional wellbeing.
- *Client variables*: These include age, sex, race, culture, nature of problem or problems, prior history of therapy, severity of disturbance, degree of family and environmental support, and whether any and what medication is involved.
- *Process variables*: These consist of specific details concerning the content and management of therapy. Such variables include frequency and duration of sessions, what interventions were used and how, and how between session time was used.
- *Outcome variables*: These are criteria for measuring what changes occurred at the end of therapy and the degree to which they were maintained. Sources of outcome information include tests and measures, and therapist, client and third-party observations.

RESEARCH METHODS

Methods for evaluating counselling and psychotherapy approaches fall into two main categories: qualitative and quantitative. Qualitative approaches to researching therapeutic approaches include detailed case descriptions and open-ended interviews. Quantitative approaches emphasize the systematic collection and analysis of quantitative information. Both quantitative and qualitative research methods can be used in evaluating psychotherapeutic approaches – they are not mutually exclusive.

In quantitative research, client change can be estimated by comparing information obtained at different times: for example, at the start of therapy, when it ends, and after one or more stipulated follow-up periods. Often quantitative information is in the form of answers to standardized questionnaires measuring variables such as anxiety of depression. Another important source of quantitative information can be recording the frequency and duration of specific thoughts and behaviours.

Quantitative research designs fall into two main categories: comparison group designs and single case designs. In a simple comparison group design, those receiving treatment would form a treatment group and those not receiving treatment would form a control group. Comparison group designs can be more elaborate: for example, as well as a control group, there could be two or three experimental groups each being varied in some clearly defined way.

Increasingly single case designs are being used in counselling and psychotherapy research. Kazdin writes: 'Single case experiments permit inferences to be drawn about intervention effects by using the patient as his or her own control. The impact of treatment is examined in relation to the patient's dys-function over time' (Kazdin, 1986, p. 39). He states that there are four main characteristics of single case designs: clear specification of goals, use of repeated observations, the delineation of time periods in which different conditions (baseline, treatment) apply, and relatively stable data – the more variable the data, the more difficult it is to draw conclusions about intervention effects.

EMPIRICALLY SUPPORTED TREATMENTS

Especially in the United States, research into psychotherapeutic approaches is being used to establish empirically supported treatments (ESTs). In 1993, the Society of Clinical Psychology (Division 12) of the American Psychological Association established a Task Force to identify treatments with scientifically proven effectiveness for particular mental disorders. This Task Force has identi-fied a number of effective, or probably effective, psychological treatments for disorders including depression, eating disorders, marital discord, panic disorder with and without agoraphobia, post-traumatic stress disorder, social phobia, and smoking cessation (Barlow, Levitt and Bufka, 1999).

A number of observations are relevant about empirically supported treat-ments. Where such treatments exist, there is a professional and ethical obliga-tion on the part of therapists to find out about them. Furthermore, unless they have good reason for not doing so in terms of particular clients' circumstances, therapists must seriously consider either implementing the treatments them-selves or referring clients to those competent to do so. Currently, there is a research–practice gap in which therapists under utilize evidence-based treat-ments emanating from the findings of their research-oriented colleagues (McLeod, 2000). One reason for this gap is that some therapists require further training before they can properly implement the protocols for specific empiri-cally supported treatments. Another reason is that the presentation of therapy research findings tends not to be user-friendly to practitioners. Relatively few empirically supported or evidence-based treatments come from outside the area of cognitive behaviour therapy (Lazarus, 1997).

LIMITATIONS OF RESEARCH

Clearly research studies have an important role to play in evaluating psycho-therapeutic approaches. Furthermore, all therapists should be reflective practi-tioners willing to honestly evaluate their own therapeutic processes and outcomes. However, good researchers like good practitioners should acknowledge the limita-tions as well as the strengths of their endeavours. Even in those areas where empirically supported treatments exist, there may be still better ways of treating clients. Skilled researchers not only find out what they know, they often obtain a sharper insight into what remains to be discovered. The concerns of many clients do not fall into circumscribed problem areas and the unavoidable messiness of much of psychotherapeutic practice does not easily lend itself to narrow research studies. In addition, currently some important issues, such as how to encourage supra-normal functioning, obtain scant research attention.

ISSUE 8: HOW ADEQUATELY IS THE THEORY OF EACH PSYCHOTHERAPEUTIC APPROACH STATED?

In Chapter 1, I mentioned that counselling and psychotherapy theories may be viewed as possessing four main dimensions if they are to be stated adequately:

1. a statement of the *basic concepts* or assumptions underlying the theory;
2. an explanation of the *acquisition* of helpful and unhelpful behaviour;
3. an explanation of the *maintenance* of helpful and unhelpful behaviour; and
4. an explanation of how to help clients *change* their behaviour and *consolidate* their gains when therapy ends.

Box 18.1 provides the reader with a basic checklist of questions to ask when assessing how adequately a psychotherapeutic approach's theory is stated.

BOX 18.1   A CHECKLIST FOR ASSESSING A PSYCHOTHERAPEUTIC APPROACH'S THEORETICAL STATEMENT

MODEL OF HUMAN DEVELOPMENT

1. What are the basic concepts of the theory and how adequate are they?
2. How well does the theory say how helpful and unhelpful thoughts, feelings, physical reactions, and communications/actions are acquired?
3. How well does the theory say how helpful and unhelpful thoughts, feelings, physical reactions, and communications/actions are maintained?

MODEL OF PSYCHOTHERAPY

1. How clear and adequate are the approach's therapeutic goals?
2. How clearly articulated and adequate is the approach's process of psychotherapy?
3. What is the nature of the therapeutic relationship and what are its strengths and weaknesses?
4. What interventions are used in the approach and what are their strengths and limitations?
5. To what extent are cultural and gender considerations adequately taken into account in the approach's theory and practice?
6. How consistent is the approach's model of human development with its model of therapeutic practice?
7. What is the research evidence for the effectiveness of the approach with different kinds of clients?

Readers can use the checklist in Box 18.1 to identify gaps in how thoroughly theories are stated. For example, a theoretical statement may be more thorough in assessing how behaviour is maintained than how it was acquired in the first place, or vice versa.

Another way to use the checklist is to evaluate how well the theoretical statement answers each question. For example, one way to answer the question about the basic concepts of the theoretical statement is in terms of how adequately they lay the building blocks for the psychotherapeutic approach. Freud's concepts of levels of consciousness and the tripartite structure of the mental apparatus provide a good foundation for the remainder of his theory and practice.

Another way of reviewing an approach's basic concepts involves assessing its assumptions about human nature. I find that some theoretical statements contain an overly negative view of human nature. Furthermore, I would like to see a clearer statement about the concept of mind and a clearer acknowledgement of the importance of mental development and discipline throughout life in the basic concepts of all theoretical approaches, even rational emotive behaviour therapy and cognitive therapy. Above, I have provided you with a few ideas on how to answer the first question on the checklist. When answering all questions on the checklist, remember to have the courage to think for yourself and to think critically.

ECLECTICISM

The word eclectic means deriving items from various sources, whereas meanings of integrated include made up of parts, whole, complete (Thompson, 1995). Here, I stipulate a definition of integration to mean a complete and coherent theoretical position that is made up of parts. Since such a complete and coherent integrated position has not really been attempted to date, the present discussion will focus on eclecticism, though I return to the issue of integration later.

To say that a therapist is eclectic is a relatively meaningless statement, since there are literally hundreds of theoretical positions that she or he could be using. One way of looking at eclecticism is in the ways in which therapists select the positions out of which they operate. Therapists differ in the ways that they make such choices. For instance, therapists can work eclectically in analytic ways by combining features based on the ideas of Freud, Jung and Melanie Klein. Alternatively, therapists can work eclectically in humanistic ways by combining features of person-centred therapy and gestalt therapy. In addition, therapists can work eclectically in cognitive behaviour ways by combining features of traditional behaviour therapy with rational emotive behaviour therapy and/or cognitive therapy. Other alternatives are to work in ways that combine psychoanalytic, humanistic and cognitive behaviour approaches. In addition, postmodern, Buddhist, multicultural and gender-related approaches can be incorporated into how therapists work.

The reasons why therapists practise eclectically vary and this influences how they practise. One reason is that therapists practise the positions that they are initially exposed to and/or initially find attractive. They may be taught more than one position from the start. Thus, without necessarily admitting it, they are trained to practise eclectically. Then, as therapists work with clients, they may be prompted to learn more about other approaches. For example, someone exposed to and attracted to any approach may find shortcomings in it in practice and seek to supplement it when working with particular clients. The range of clients' problems varies and theoretical positions may seem better for some than for other problems. Furthermore, the range of clients' personalities and backgrounds differs and therapists may feel the need to take this into account when selecting how to intervene.

Related to eclecticism is the issue of how disciplined are the decisions with which the therapist practises it. Arguably, much of the eclecticism practised by therapists is relatively undisciplined. In varying degrees, it is unsystematic eclecticism (Lazarus and Beutler, 1993). Interventions are adopted without being soundly thought through because of the whim of therapists. Increasingly, it is probable that therapists will have to justify more of their psychotherapeutic decisions to funding bodies. This does not mean that they cannot still be eclectic. In fact, sometimes, it may lead to an increase in eclecticism in that the interventions that work for different problems may be derived from different theoretical positions. Lazarus (2008) describes as 'technical eclecticism' the drawing of interventions from different sources without necessarily subscribing to the disciplines that spawned them. The meaning of the term technical eclecticism can be broadened to denote not only specific therapeutic procedures, but also relationship stances (Lazarus, Beutler and Norcross, 1992).

Wherever possible, Lazarus' technically eclectic therapists use treatments based on empirical evidence and client need. Their theoretical leanings are to draw interventions mainly based on social and cognitive learning theory, but they can borrow interventions from other schools, without embracing any of their theories. As research evidence accumulates for various kinds of problems, it is probable that increasing numbers of therapists will be using a technically eclectic framework. Eventually, enough may be understood about the causes of various problems and the most suitable interventions for them that there can be more of a move towards an integrative rather than a technically eclectic approach.

Even technical eclecticism has its limitations. There are still problems that are hard to define in such a way that psychotherapy on them can be researched. For instance, though Yalom is noted as a psychotherapy researcher, his and May's existential psychotherapy lacks a research base because of the highly individualized nature of the issues addressed in it. As people become wealthier, the number with existential concerns is likely to increase. In addition, clients sometimes have combinations of problems that make it difficult, if not impossible, to use the research literature for specific problems with them.

Eclecticism in counselling and psychotherapy will continue to be developed. In future, the nature of clients' problems may vary and the ways of doing psychotherapy with clients may change. For instance, the Internet may be used much more than at present, and face-to-face interactions will be more possible when therapist and client are in different locations. Undoubtedly some existing approaches can be improved and it is also likely that useful new approaches will be created. In addition, improved and new ways will be found for dealing with multicultural, gender and family issues, which tend to evolve over time. Wherever possible, empirical support should be gathered to guide the development of counselling and psychotherapy. Value decisions will also need to be made and re-examined as to what are desirable psychotherapeutic goals and methods of achieving them.

INTEGRATION

To date therapists have worked eclectically rather than in an integrated fashion. Using interventions from more than one theoretical position falls far short of integrating the theoretical positions intellectually. For instance, person-centred therapy does not distinguish to whom and at what stage of therapy the core conditions are offered by therapists. Furthermore, person-centred's theoretical base offers a rationale for approaching therapy this way. Therefore when therapists claim to use a person-centred relationship as part of other therapeutic approaches, for instance in conjunction with cognitive therapy, they are not using it in the way advocated by Rogers. Thus there can be no real integration between Rogers' person-centred therapy and cognitive therapy on the level of either theory or practice. However, such difficulties do not mean that developing an integrated theoretical position is impossible, but that great care needs to be taken over the task.

REASONS FOR INTEGRATION

Present approaches to counselling and psychotherapy may be said to have started with Freud around the turn of the nineteenth into the twentieth century. Much progress has been made since then, but there is still much more to achieve. The world is still a much more troubled and less happy place than it could be, even in the wealthiest countries.

In future, one or more theoretical positions may be developed which are genuinely integrative in that they are complete positions made up of parts that are coherent and based on the same assumptions. The scope of the integrated theoretical position will span across much of the ground covered somewhat separately by today's theoretical positions. For instance, such a psychotherapeutic position will have concepts that cover unconscious and conscious functioning; thinking, feeling and communicating/acting; and take into account multicultural, sex and family differences. It will also take into account how thinking and behaving are acquired, maintained and changed as well as pay attention to feelings and physical reactions. Furthermore, it will pay attention to sub-normal, normal and supra-normal levels of functioning.

There are many reasons for developing one or more integrated theoretical positions. Eventually, world leaders may become fed up with trying to deal with the world's problems by mainly political means, when the problems are basically psychological. Developing a realistic and workable view of the nature of human functioning may become viewed as a task to be undertaken on a world level. If so, funds may become available to develop one or more truly integrated positions about what is basic to humans and how best to bring up, live together and deal with problems that occur.

No existing theoretical position covers the range of human development and of clients' problems. Thus the issue of breadth is inadequately dealt with to date – this is one of the main reasons why eclecticism has flourished. An integrated theoretical position would recognize the commonality of humanity. It would take into account the latest research findings of what can be attributed to nature and to nurture. Its main task would be to identify what is central to being fully human and how best to bring this about both developmentally and psychotherapeutically. In addition, it would recognize differences caused by particular factors such as upbringing, culture, race, social class and gender expectations.

At the moment counselling and psychotherapy deal mainly with people with problems of some degree of severity. However, all people have problems and the need to attain higher levels of functioning is universal. Along with the increase in material wealth, there is the expectation and possibility for people to be happier and more fulfilled than they are presently. A truly integrated theoretical position will take into account the needs of different kinds of people – how to help those with specific problems, how to educate all people, and how to assist people to attain their full potential. In addition, an integrated theoretical position can allow the possibility for people to be different, whether by nature, nurture or by choice.

It is likely that there will be many educational and psychotherapeutic interventions needed to achieve the higher levels suggested by those who fashion an integrated view of human functioning. These interventions will focus on bringing whole nations to higher levels of functioning as well as on the needs of groups, families and individuals. Probably, psychological coaching and education will become both better and more widespread. Counselling and psychotherapy will definitely be needed for the more disturbed elements of the population and may even be used by ordinary people wanting to attain higher levels of functioning more than presently. As technology advances, one can only speculate about the range of ways that counselling and psychotherapy will be offered.

REASONS SLOWING INTEGRATION

The development of one or more integrated approaches to counselling and psychotherapy is unlikely to take place soon. While there might be an increase in approaches like Lazarus' technical eclecticism as more and better research gets done, this falls far short of genuine integration. One of the main barriers is the pride and status of the regulating agencies of the present approaches to psycho-therapy. In differing degrees, they control entry into whether or not one can become a psychotherapist. In addition, much of psychotherapy training takes place in academic institutions and, there, the positions and promotion of staff members depend on their doing relatively narrow research. Another barrier is going to be the hidden theoretical biases, cultural biases, racism, sexism, national-ism and other prejudices that people are likely to bring to the task of developing an integrated theoretical position.

An issue is the degree to which developing one or more integrated theoretical positions can be based on existing concepts and research. If a sound integrative model of the main aspects of human development throughout the lifespan can be arrived at, it may become easier to reach agreement on what might be appro-priate ways to deal with the problems people face in living successfully.

To date, there appears no institution or group of people willing to fund or to undertake the huge task of developing an integrated model of human function-ing and a corresponding integrated model of counselling and psychotherapy. Even if, at some stage in the future, funds do become available, those conducting the task are likely to come to it with blinkers from their cultural upbringing and their previous academic and psychotherapeutic training and experience. Developing an integrated model of counselling and psychotherapy is likely to be a long re-iterative process of testing and refining ideas and practice. Such a model or models will need to take into account how people with different problems and backgrounds can be helped towards functioning not only better, but ultimately at really high levels.

REVIEW AND PERSONAL QUESTIONS

REVIEW QUESTIONS

1. What do you consider the influence of each of the following factors on the development of the counselling and psychotherapy approaches presented in this book:

   - the theorists' personal histories;
   - the theorists' historical and cultural contexts; and
   - the fact that almost all the theorists were or are men?

2. Taken as a group, do you consider the theorists are too negative or positive in their views about human nature? Provide reasons for your answer.
3. Critically discuss the role of research in evaluating psychotherapeutic approaches.
4. Apply the checklist for assessing the adequacy of a psychotherapeutic approaches' theo-retical statement (see Box 18.1) to at least one of the counselling and psychotherapy approaches presented in this book.
5. What are some reasons why therapists can justify practising eclectically?
6. What do you think about the assertion that a genuinely integrative theoretical position has yet to be attempted? Provide reasons for your answer.

PERSONAL QUESTIONS

1. What counselling and psychotherapy approaches covered in this book appeal to you and why?
2. If you favour practising psychotherapy eclectically, how might you do so?

REFERENCES AND FURTHER READING

Adler, A. (1998) *Social Interest: Adler's Key to the Meaning of Life*. Oxford: Oneworld. Original edition 1933.

American Psychiatric Association (2013) *Diagnostic and Statistical Manual of Mental Disorders* (DSM-V). Arlington, VA: APA.

Barlow, D. H. Levitt, J. and Bufka, L. F. (1999) The dissemination of empirically supported treatments: A view to the future. *Behaviour Research and Therapy, 37*, 147–62.

Greer, G. (1971) *The Female Eunuch*. London: Paladin.

Kazdin, A. E. (1986) Research designs and methodology. In S. L. Garfield and A. E. Bergin (eds), *Handbook of Psychotherapy and Behavior Change* (3rd ed.). New York: Wiley, pp. 23–68.

Lazarus, A. A. (1997) *Brief but Comprehensive Psychotherapy: The Multimodal Way*. New York: Springer.

Lazarus, A. A. (2008) Multimodal therapy. In R. J. Corsini and D. Wedding (eds), *Current Psychotherapies* (8th ed.). Belmont, CA: Thomson Brooks/Cole, pp. 368–401.

Lazarus, A. A. and Beutler, L. E. (1993) On technical eclecticism. *Journal of Counseling & Development, 71*, 381–5.

Lazarus, A. A., Beutler, L. E. and Norcross, J. C. (1992) The future of technical eclecticism. *Psychotherapy, 29*, 11–20.

Maslow, A. H. (1971) *The Farther Reaches of Human Nature*. Harmondsworth: Pelican.

McLeod, J. (2000) Research issues in counselling and psychotherapy. In S. Palmer (ed.), *Introduction to Counselling and Psychotherapy: The Essential Guide*. London: Sage, pp. 331–40.

Thompson, D. (ed.) (1995) *The Concise Oxford Dictionary of Current English*. Oxford: Clarendon Press.

Wedding, D. and Corsini, R. J (eds) (2014) *Current Psychotherapies* (10th ed.). Belmont, CA: Brooks/Cole.

GLOSSARY

ABBREVIATIONS

AT, Jung's analytical therapy; BT, behaviour therapy; CT, cognitive therapy; ET, existential therapy; GT, gestalt therapy; MIT, mindfulness in therapy; MMT, multimodal therapy; NT, narrative therapy; PA, Freud's psychoanalysis; PCT, person-centred therapy; PT, positive therapy; REBT, rational emotive behaviour therapy; RT, reality therapy; SFT, solution-focused therapy; and TA, transactional analysis.

ABCDE theory (REBT) A theoretical model for understanding psychological distress and change in which A = Adversities or activating events in a person's life, B = Beliefs, both rational and irrational, C = Consequences, both emotional and behavioural, D = Disputing irrational beliefs, and E = Effects and/or effective philosophy of life.

Acceptance (MIT) is to acknowedge the reality of a situation while not fighting against it or wanting it to be other than it is. A non-judgemental view that allows people to move forward toward self-directed goals.

Active imagination (AT) is a technique devised by Jung to help people get in touch with unconscious material. Clients begin by concentrating on a starting point. Then they allow their unconscious to produce a series of images, which may make a complete story.

Activity scheduling (CT) Activity scheduling involves planning and timetabling specific activities with clients. A principle of activity scheduling is to state what activity the client agrees to engage in rather than how much they will accomplish.

Actualizing tendency (PCT) is an active process representing the inherent tendency of the organism to develop its capacities in the direction of maintaining, enhancing and reproducing itself.

Adult (TA) An ego state oriented towards objective, autonomous data processing and probability estimating.

Anima and the animus (AT) The anima is the personification of the feminine nature in a man's unconscious, whereas the animus is the personification of the masculine nature in a woman's unconscious.

Archetypes (AT) are 'primordial images' and 'primordial thoughts' rather than the representations of the images or thoughts themselves. Archetypes provide instinctive patterns for mental activity.

Assertive training (BT) involves training clients in the appropriate verbal and non-verbal behaviours for expressing both negative and positive thoughts and feelings. Contemporary assertive training focuses on thinking assertively as well as on behaviour.

Auto-pilot (MIT) An unmindful habitual routine behaviour.

Automatic thoughts (CT) are less accessible to awareness than voluntary thoughts, but not so deeply buried as beliefs and schemas. Automatic thoughts are part of people's internal monologue – what and how they talk to themselves, can take the form of words, images, or both, occur very rapidly, and are usually at the fringe of awareness.

Autonomy (TA) refers to the capacity for non-script behaviour that is reversible, with no particular time schedule, developed later in life, and not under parental influence.

Awareness technique (GT) is a concentration technique in which clients are asked to become aware of their body language, their breathing, their voice quality and their emotions as much as of any pressing thoughts.

BASIC ID (MMT) Human personality can be divided into seven discrete, yet interacting, modalities or dimensions: behaviour, affect, sensation, imagery, cognition, interpersonal and drugs/biology.

Behavioural assessment (BT), sometimes known as a functional analysis, allows therapists to identify the context, antecedents and consequences of the responses they wish to treat. When conducted after initial sessions, behavioural assessment aims to assist both in evaluating treatment effectiveness and in deciding whether to continue, discontinue and alter treatment.

Being (ET) Being as a participle of a verb and implies that someone is in the process of becoming something. When used as a noun being can mean potential.

Break (SFT) The systematic tradition of family therapy emphasizes the need to step back emotionally and intellectually from the problem presented in order to clarify one's thinking. Many solution-focused therapists continue to use breaks in sessions.

Bridging (MMT) A rapport enhancement technique in which therapists deliberately tune into the clients' preferred modalities before gently helping them cross bridges into other modalities that may prove more productive.

Child (TA) The Child ego state is a set of feelings, thoughts, attitudes and behaviour patterns which are archaic relics of an individual's childhood. The Child ego state is exhibited in two major forms: the adapted Child, which follows parental directives, and the natural Child, which is autonomous.

Classical conditioning (BT), also known as respondent conditioning, is a form of learning whereby existing responses are attached to new stimuli by pairing these stimuli with those that naturally elicit the response.

Collective unconscious (AT) At its deepest levels the unconscious is a vast collective and universal historical storehouse whose contents belong to mankind in general. The contents of the collective unconscious have never been in consciousness, but owe their existence to heredity.

Complexes (AT) are an important feature of the personal unconscious and are accumulations of associations, sometimes of a traumatic nature, that possess strong emotional content – for example, the mother complex.

Conditions of worth (PCT) The internalization or introjection of others' evaluations, which do not truly reflect the person's actualizing tendency but may serve to impede it.

Cognitive behaviour therapy A term describing therapies that extend behaviour therapy to have a major focus on changing covert thoughts as well as overt behaviours: examples include cognitive therapy, rational emotive behaviour therapy, and multimodal therapy.

Cognitive distortions (CT) are information processing errors that both characterize and maintain psychological distress: for instance, arbitrary inference, selective abstraction, overgeneralization and dichotomous thinking.

Cognitive vulnerability (CT) refers to human's cognitive frailty. Because of their schemas, each person has a set of unique vulnerabilities and sensitivities that predispose them to psychological distress.

Collaborative empiricism (CT) Therapists and clients collaborate together in the scientific endeavour of examining the evidence to confirm or negate the client's cognitions, all of which are viewed as testable hypotheses.

Congruence (PCT) Consistency between the thoughts and feelings the therapist experiences and her or his professional demeanour; not putting on a professional façade.

Contact boundary (GT) is the boundary between organism and environment where all feelings, thoughts and actions take place. Contacting the environment represents forming a gestalt, whereas withdrawal is either closing a gestalt completely or mobilizing resources to make closure possible.

Counselling A relationship in which counsellors assist clients to understand themselves and their problems better. Then, where appropriate, counsellors use various interventions to assist clients to feel, think, communicate and act more effectively. The term counselling is often used interchangeably with psychotherapy. Since there are many different theoretical orientations, it may be more accurate to speak of counselling approaches than counselling.

Death anxiety (ET), the fear of ceasing to be, can be both conscious and unconscious. It is the fundamental source of anxiety, whether it be neurotic, normal or existential. Strong death anxiety is likely to be repressed.

Decision (TA) A childhood commitment to a certain form of behaviour, which later forms the basis of character.

Defence mechanisms (PA) are infantilisims that operate unconsciously to protect the ego and may impede realistic behaviour long after they have outlived their usefulness. Examples include repression, reaction formation, projection, fixation and regression.

Disputing (REBT) involves challenging and questioning unsubstantiated hypotheses that clients hold about themselves, others and the world.

Dominant story (NT) A client's pessimistic account of the problem, which excludes any hopeful or balancing elements.

Dream analysis (AT) Dreams are utterances or statements from the unconscious and are comparable to texts that appear unintelligible, but the therapist has to discover how to read them. An understanding of myths and symbols is fundamental for analysing dreams.

Dreamwork (GT) Dreams are existential messages, not just unfinished situations, current problems or symptoms. There are four stages to dreamwork: sharing the dream, retelling the dream in the present tense, talking to the different actors in the dream, and conducting a dialogue between different elements in the dream.

Eclecticism The practice of drawing from different counselling and therapy approaches in formulating client problems and implementing treatment interventions. A distinction can be made between theoretical eclecticism and practical or technical eclecticism.

Ego (PA) The ego or 'I' acts as an intermediary between the id and the external world and strives to bring the reality principle to bear upon the id in substitution for the pleasure principle.

Ego disturbance (REBT) arises from the demanding and irrational belief 'I *must* do well and win approval for all my performances' because it leads to people thinking and feeling that they are inadequate and undeserving persons when they do not do as well as they must.

Ego state (TA) A consistent pattern of feeling and experience directly related to a corresponding consistent pattern of behaviour.

Emotional intelligence (PT) A set of abilities that allows us to recognise and manage our own emotions and those of other people. Unlike cognitive intelligence ('IQ'), emotional intelligence can be increased substantially as a result of education and practice.

Empathy (PCT) The therapist's capacity to comprehend accurately the client's inner world or internal frame of reference and to sensitively communicate back this understanding.

Enquiry process (MIT) The willingness and ability to bring curiosity, enthusiasm, and an attitude of detailed exploration of experience to whatever is unfolding in the moment.

Exceptions (SFT) The absence of a problem is an exception, which can be used as the basis for a compliment and as evidence that the problem is not continuous or insurmountable.

Excitement (GT) The energy people create, which coincides with the physiological function of excitation.

Existential (ET) The word existence is derived from the Latin word *existere*, literally meaning 'to stand out, to emerge.' Existential approaches to therapy are concerned with the science and processes of being.

Existential defence mechanisms (ET) In addition to conventional defence mechanisms, there are specific defences for each of the four ultimate concerns – death, freedom, isolation and meaninglessness – to defend people against these fundamental fears.

Existential guilt (ET) Three forms of existential guilt are failure to live up to one's potential; distorting the reality of one's fellow humans; and 'separation guilt' in relation to nature as a whole.

Existential psychodynamics (ET) Existential conflicts and existential anxiety flow from people's inescapable confrontations with the givens of existence – death, freedom, isolation and meaninglessness.

Existential ultimate concerns (ET) Four existential ultimate concerns are death, freedom, isolation, and meaninglessness. Each concern begets a different existential conflict.

Experiments (CT) Beliefs are treated as testable hypotheses. Together therapists and clients set up cognitive and behavioural experiments that encourage clients to test the reality of their beliefs.

Experiments (GT) Therapists and clients develop experiments in which clients try out different ways of thinking and acting. Repeatedly clients are encouraged to 'Try this and see what you experience'.

Exposure (BT) In exposure, confrontation with the feared stimulus continues until the unwanted responses to the stimulus have been reduced.

Externalizing the problem (NT) Using terms which imply a separation between the problem and the identity of the client, such as 'depression invading your life' rather than 'your depression'.

Feedback (SFT) All sessions end with feedback to those attending and may emphasize skills, compliments and next steps.

Feminist therapy Approaches to counselling and therapy that address women's problems and issues in the context of constricting gender-role socialization and power imbalances in society. Feminist therapy emphasizes egalitarian therapist–client relationships, valuing women's experiences, liberating women from sex-role stereotypes, and working against oppression.

Fit (NT) A new idea's capacity to be absorbed into pre-existing ideas and concepts.

Flooding (BT) In contemporary flooding techniques, therapists arrange for clients to be exposed to relatively strong fear stimuli that, either real or imagined, are presented continuously.

Free association (PA) Clients must tell their analysts everything that occurs to them, even if it is disagreeable and even if it seems meaningless. The object of free association is to help lift repressions by making unconscious material conscious.

Frustration (GT) Providing situations in which clients experience being stuck in frustration and then frustrating their avoidances still further until they are willing to mobilize their own resources.

Future-oriented questions (SFT) These enquiries, such as the 'miracle question', aim to generate views of a positive future in which the problems have diminished. There are many examples of such questions that are to be adapted to the needs of each situation.

Game (TA) An ongoing series of complementary ulterior transactions progressing to a well-defined predictable outcome or payoff.

Gestalt (GT) means form or shape and among the meanings of the German verb *gestalten* are to shape, to form, to fashion, to organize and to structure. Other terms for gestalt are pattern, configuration or organized whole.

Goals (SFT) Goals are defined with the individual as clearly as possible since they are both a useful step and a guide to the progress of therapy.

Gratitude (PT) A feeling of thankfulness either for things that we recognize as 'gifts' or 'blessings' in our life ('gratitude for') or towards people who have favoured us in some way ('gratitude to').

Happiness (PT) A positive psychological state characterized by the experience of positive emotions and the sense that life is meaningful and worthwhile.

Homeostasis (GT) Homeostasis or organismic self-regulation is the process by which the organism satisfies its needs by restoring balance when faced with a demand or need that upsets its equilibrium.

Id (PA) The id or 'it' contains everything that is inherited and fixed in the constitution. Filled with energy from the instincts, the id strives to bring about the satisfaction of instinctual needs on the basis of the pleasure principle.

Identity (NT) A client's sense of who she/he is, derived from social interactions.

Impermanence (MIT) the stream of consciousness that makes up the subjective flow of human experience that all things rise and pass away. All conditional phenomena are unenduring.

Incongruence (PCT) A discrepancy between the self as perceived and the actual experience of the organism.

Individuation (AT) is the process by which the person becomes differentiated as a separate psychological individual, a separate whole as distinct from the collective psychology.

Inelegant and elegant change (REBT) Inelegant change largely consists of some kind of symptom removal. Elegant change goes further than developing an effective new philosophy that supports removal of specific symptoms to assisting clients to develop and implement an effective philosophy of life.

Instincts (PA) represent somatic or biological demands upon the mind, which are grouped into two basic instincts, *Eros* and the *destructive instinct.*

Integration Attempting to blend together theoretical concepts and/or practical interventions drawn from different therapeutic approaches into coherent and integrated wholes.

Interpretation (PA) involves offering constructions or explanations. Interpreting dreams represents an important – sometimes the most important – part of the analyst's work.

Intervention (SFT) This term is applied both to the feedback at the end of each session and to specific actions within the session designed to encourage change. Almost any question from the therapist can be regarded as an intervention, since it may lead to changes in thinking or perception.

Introjections (GT) are experiences that are swallowed as a whole rather than being properly digested and assimilated. The outcome of introjection is that undesirable as well as desirable thoughts, feelings and behaviours get retained.

Irrational beliefs (REBT) are rigid, dogmatic, unhealthy, maladaptive beliefs that mostly get in the way of people's efforts to achieve their goals. Such beliefs are characterized by demands, musts and shoulds.

Kindness/compassion (MIT) The development of an attitude of non-judgemental kindness that can be directed towards the experience of suffering.

Low frustration tolerance (REBT) or discomfort disturbance arises from the grandiose belief that people think they are so special that conditions must be easy and satisfying for them.

Meaning (PT) A person's life is meaningful if they have a direction that reflects their values and if they have the opportunities to employ their personal strengths and talents to significant purpose.

Men's therapy An underdeveloped area of counselling and therapy focusing on men's problems and issues. Many feminist therapy goals and principles are applicable to men's therapy, which is sometimes considered feminist therapy's missing half.

Mindfuness (MIT) is the practice of being fully aware in the present moment without judgement of the rising and passing away of phenomena in the field of direct experience.

Miracle question (SFT) The miracle question, in which people are asked to imagine their problem has been solved, is one example of a future-focused question often emphasized by trainers and therapists. It is not suitable for every situation, as intellectual ability or cultural values may affect its interpretation.

Modality Profile (MMT) A BASIC ID chart listing problems and interventions within each modality.

Modes (CT) are networks of cognitive, affective, motivational and behavioural schemas. Modes are fundamental to personality since they interpret and adapt to emerging and ongoing situations.

Multicultural therapy Approaches to counselling and therapy that take into account the cultures and worldviews of clients and therapists. Such approaches include making existing Euro-American therapies more culture-sensitive, developing multicultural counselling and therapy competencies, and using non-Western therapeutic approaches.

Multimodal Life History Inventory (MMT) A 15-page inventory that asks numerous questions about antecedent events and maintaining factors with the answers being divided into BASIC ID categories.

Negative explanation (NT) The consideration of external factors limiting or preventing a client's capacity to bring about change.

Non-being (ET) The opposite of being is non-being or nothingness. Death is the most obvious form of non-being. However, there are numerous other threats to being in the form of loss of potentiality through anxiety and conformity and through lack of clear self-awareness.

'Not-knowing' position (SFT) A solution-focused worker will assume that the other person is an expert on their own life and that the function of the sessions is for the person to develop their own ideas about next steps. The attitude is therefore one of respectful curiosity and not of expert knowledge.

Observational learning (BT) Learning behavioural and cognitive skills by observing models, including observing how the models' behaviours get reinforced.

Operant conditioning (BT) A way of learning in which the person or animal has to operate on the environment to produce a response. Responses are maintained, modified or extinguished by the likelihood of eliciting reinforcing consequences.

Optimism (PT) A style of judgement that focuses more on the positive than on the negative aspects of a present situation and regards the future with hope. Realistic optimism is associated with many benefits and can be increased through training and practice.

Outsider witnesses (NT) People other than the therapist who are invited to comment on how the client's developing story resonates with their lives.

Openness to experience (PCT) Allowing all significant sensory and visceral experiences to be perceived, the capacity for realistic perception without defensiveness.

Organismic valuing process (PCT) refers to a person's continuous weighing of experience and the placing of values on that experience in terms of its ability to satisfy the actualizing tendency.

Parent (TA) The Parent ego state is a set of feelings, thoughts, attitudes, and behaviours which resemble those of parental figures. The Parent ego state may be seen in one of two forms: the controlling Parent and the nurturing Parent.

Participant modelling (BT) involves therapists repeatedly modelling feared activities, for instance handling snakes or dogs. Then joint performance with therapists may enable clients to start engaging in activities that would be too threatening to engage in on their own. Ultimately clients perform the feared activities on their own.

Persona (AT) A concept derived from the mask worn by actors in antiquity. At one level, the persona is the individual's system of adaptation or way of coping with the world. At a different level, the persona is not just an individual mask, but a mask of the collective psyche.

Personal strengths (PT) Values-based attitudes and skills, including kindness, humility and hope. Exercising strenghts is seen as a way of achieving particular virtues. Thus the strengths of curiosity and love of learning pave the way to achieve the virtue of wisdom.

Personal unconscious (AT) The contents, which are definitely personal, fall into two main categories: material that lost its intensity either because it was forgotten or repressed; and material which never possessed sufficient intensity to reach consciousness but has somehow entered the psyche – for instance, some sense-impressions.

Positive emotions (PT) Emotions that lead to flourishing and wellbeing. The positive emotions, which include joy, empathy, love, curiosity, pride and serenity, have been shown to broaden awareness, providing opportunities for increased creativity and personal growth.

Positive mental health (PT) Not merely the absence of any mental disorder, but a positive state of mental fitness. Characteristics associated with this include compassion towards self and others, a realistic view of the world, the ability to manage emotions and psychological resources for dealing with adversity.

Positive psychology (PT) A relatively new approach within psychology that focuses on our understanding optimal human functioning and has the aim of improving the wellbeing of individuals and communities.

Post-structuralism (NT) A system of thought that questions or rejects the concept of universal, permanent structures of the mind independent of socio-cultural factors.

Preconscious (PA) The preconscious is latent and capable of becoming conscious, while the unconscious is repressed and is unlikely to become conscious without great difficulty.

Pre-session changes (SFT) Almost everyone will have made attempts to change their situation prior to seeking therapy. It is useful and respectful to enquire about these attempts as well as any deterioration in the situation.

Psychodynamics (PA) The concept of psychical or mental energy and its distribution among the id, ego and super-ego is central to psychoanalysis.

Psychotherapy Literally 'mind healing'. It is more accurate to speak of the psychotherapies since there are many different theoretical and practical approaches to psychotherapy.

Rational beliefs (REBT) Healthy, productive and adaptive beliefs that are consistent with social reality, and are stated as preferences, desires and wants.

Rational coping statements (REBT) range from articulating simple words of encouragement to generating longer statements containing preferential thinking. This step often, but not necessarily, follows vigorous disputing.

Rational emotive imagery (REBT) In rational emotive imagery (REI) clients (1) vividly imagine an adversity, (2) once feeling unhealthily upset, hold on to the image for a minute or two, and (3) then tell themselves strongly and repetitively sensible rational beliefs or coping statements.

Reattribution techniques (CT) test automatic thoughts and underlying beliefs by considering alternative ways of assigning responsibility and cause.

Re-authoring, re-storying (NT) Encouraging the client to extend the original problem-story into a narrative with more helpful elements.

Reciprocal inhibition (BT) encompasses all situations in which the elicitation of one response appears to bring about a decrement in the strength of evocation of a simultaneous response.

Reinforcement (BT) The presentation of a reward or the removal of an aversive stimulus following a response. Reinforcement always increases the future probability of the reinforced response. Schedules of reinforcement can be either intermittent or non-intermittent.

Relationships of choice (MMT) Not only matching the nature of therapeutic relationship to the client, but also to the clients' observed needs at different times in therapy.

Re-membering (NT) Calling on the client's memories of significant people from her/his past or present to give a sense of support and encouragement.

Resilience (PT) The capacity to withstand adversity and to 'bounce back' from disappointment, failure, loss or trauma.

Restraints (NT) Socio-culturally derived preconceptions that make it difficult to grasp unfamiliar ideas.

Scaling (SFT) A tool for simplifying discussion of complex situations and reducing goals to small manageable steps.

Schemas (CT) are structures that consist of people's fundamental beliefs and assumptions. They are relatively stable cognitive patterns that influence, through their beliefs, how people select and synthesize incoming information.

Script (TA) A life plan based on a decision made in childhood, reinforced by the parents, justified by subsequent events, and culminating in a chosen alternative. The purpose of script analysis is to get clients out of their script and thus to behave autonomously.

Second-order BASIC ID assessments (MMT) When impasses occur in treating clients, second-order BASIC ID assessments allow a more detailed review of behaviours, affective responses, sensory reactions, images, cognitions, interpersonal factions, and drugs/ biological factors in relation to the area in which change is proving difficult.

Self (AT) The self is the central archetype, the archetype of order. The self, that expresses the unity of personality as a whole, encompasses both conscious and unconscious components.

Self-actualizing (GT) is a process involving an effective balance of contact and withdrawal at the contact boundary and the ability to use energy or excitement to meet real rather than phony needs.

Self-actualizing (PCT) A process of living and of personal development, based on the an individual's organismic valuing process, that genuinely reflects their unique actualizing tendency.

Self-concept (PCT) is the self as perceived and the values attached to these perceptions, or what a person refers to as 'I' or 'me'.

Self-story (NT) A person's overall conceptualization of their life and problems, told to others and the self out of selective memory.

Shadow (AT) The shadow archetype reflects the realm of human's animal ancestors and, as such, comprises the whole historical aspect of the unconscious. For the most part, the shadow consists of inferior traits of personality that individuals refuse to acknowledge.

Socratic dialogue (CT) A Socratic style of questioning assists clients to expand and evaluate how they think. Typical questions are: 'Where is the evidence?', 'Where is the logic?', Are the other ways of perceiving the situation?', and 'What would be the worst thing that could happen?'.

Stimulus control (BT) entails either modifying in advance the stimuli or cues associated with maladaptive responses and/or establishing cues associated with adaptive responses.

Structural analysis (TA) consists of diagnosing and separating one feeling-thinking behaviour pattern or ego state from another.

Structural Profile (MMT) Clients rate themselves across each of the BASIC ID modalities on a 7-point scale with 1 being the lowest and 7 being the highest.

Suffering (MIT) refers to the awareness of the inevitability of physical illness, illness, aging and death. It also refers to the paychological distress that comes from the insatiability of desire, and the yearning for things to be different to the way they are.

Super-ego (PA) The super-ego is a residue formed within the ego in which parental influence is prolonged. Parental influence may be defined broadly to include cultural, racial and family influences.

Systematic desensitization (BT) involves three elements: (a) training in deep muscular relaxation; (b) the construction of hierarchies of anxiety-evoking stimuli; and (c) asking the client, when relaxed, to imagine items from the anxiety-evoking hierarchies.

Technical eclecticism (MMT) Technically eclectic therapists use procedures from different sources without necessarily subscribing to the theories or disciplines that spawned them.

Text analogy (NT) A comparison between a client's account of his/her experience, and the structure and content of works of fiction.

Therapist de-centring (NT) The therapist keeping the client's own skills and knowledge, and his/her significant personal relationships, at the heart of the therapeutic process.

Therapeutic document (NT) A permanent record of discoveries and progress, given to or created by the client.

Thresholds (MMT) People's differing capacities to tolerate negative stimuli such as pain, frustration, stress, cold, noise and pollution. Physiologically, people react to a variety of arousing stimuli with differing and distinctive patterns of autonomic nervous system activity.

Token economies (BT) Reinforcement programmes that use tokens as tangible conditioned reinforcers which may be exchanged for back-up reinforcers such as prizes, opportunities to engage in special activities, food or other purchases.

Tracking (MMT) refers to the careful assessment of the 'firing order', the ordering of the chain reaction of the different modalities to assist therapists in selecting and prioritizing treatment interventions.

Transaction (TA) In transactional analysis a stroke or unit of recognition is viewed as the fundamental unit of social interaction. An exchange of strokes constitutes a transaction. Transactions take place between ego states. Transactions between ego states may be complementary, crossed and/or ulterior.

Transference (PA) Clients perceive their analysts as reincarnations of important figures from their childhoods and transfer onto them moderate to intense feelings and emotions appropriate to these earlier models.

Unconditional positive regard (PCT) consists of two dimensions: first, prizing and feeling positively towards clients and, second, non-judgemental acceptance of clients' experiencing and disclosures as their subjective reality.

Unconditional self-acceptance (REBT) Clients can always choose to accept themselves just because they are alive and human, whether or not they perform well or are approved of by others.

Unconscious (PA) The unconscious, or unconscious proper, consists of material that is inadmissible to consciousness through repression. The censorship on unconscious material coming into awareness is very strong indeed.

Unique outcome (NT) An element in the client's problem-story that indicates an opening to an alternative and more helpful narrative.

Wellbeing (PT) A subjective state of being satisfied with the quality of one's life. Wellbeing is associated with the frequent experience of positive emotions, loving relationships, personal meaning and engagement in meaningful activities.

NAME INDEX

SUBJECT INDEX